T0376451

Biographical Dictionary of Chinese Women

ANTIQUITY THROUGH SUI
1600 B.C.E.–618 C.E.

中國婦女傳記詞典
上古至隋，公元前1600至公元618年

香港大學圖書館叢書之21

University of Hong Kong Libraries Publications, No. 21

Biographical Dictionary of Chinese Women

ANTIQUITY THROUGH SUI
1600 B.C.E.–618 C.E.

Editors-in-Chief
**Lily Xiao Hong Lee
and A. D. Stefanowska**

Assistant Editor-in-Chief
Sue Wiles

Coordinators
Shang: Elizabeth Childs-Johnson
Zhou: Constance A. Cook
Qin through Han: Yin Lee Wong
Three Kingdoms Through Sui: Lily Xiao Hong Lee

AN EAST GATE BOOK

LONDON AND NEW YORK

An East Gate Book

First published 2007 by M.E. Sharpe

Published 2015 by Routledge
2 Park Square, Milton Park, Abingdon, Oxon OX14 4RN
711 Third Avenue, New York, NY 10017, USA

Routledge is an imprint of the Taylor & Francis Group, an informa business

Copyright © 2007 Taylor & Francis. All rights reserved.

No part of this book may be reprinted or reproduced or utilised in any form or by any electronic, mechanical, or other means, now known or hereafter invented, including photocopying and recording, or in any information storage or retrieval system, without permission in writing from the publishers.

Notices
No responsibility is assumed by the publisher for any injury and/or damage to persons or property as a matter of products liability, negligence or otherwise, or from any use of operation of any methods, products, instructions or ideas contained in the material herein.

Practitioners and researchers must always rely on their own experience and knowledge in evaluating and using any information, methods, compounds, or experiments described herein. In using such information or methods they should be mindful of their own safety and the safety of others, including parties for whom they have a professional responsibility.

Product or corporate names may be trademarks or registered trademarks, and are used only for identification and explanation without intent to infringe.

Library of Congress Cataloging-in-Publication Data

Biographical dictionary of Chinese women / Lily Xiao Hong Lee and A.D. Stefanowska, editors
    p. cm.
   "An east gate book."
Includes bibliographical references (p.   ).

The Qing Period: ISBN: 0-7656-0043-9
The Twentieth Century: ISBN: 0-7656-0798-0
Antiquity Through Sui, 1600 B.C.E.–618 C.E.: ISBN: 978-0-7656-1750-7

    1. Women—China—Biography—Dictionaries. 2. China—Biography—Dictionaries.
I. Lee, Lily Xiao Hong. II. Stefanowska, A.D.

HQ1767.5.A3B56 1998
305.4′092′251—dc21   98-11262

ISBN 13: 9780765617507 (hbk)

Contents

Preface
vii

Editors' Note
x

Acknowledgments
xi

Guide to Chinese Words Used
xii

Contributors
xiii

Translators
xvi

Chronology of Dynasties and Major Rulers
xvii

Finding List by Background or Fields of Endeavor
xxiii

Biographies:
Antiquity Through Zhou • 3–97
Qin Through Han • 99–259
Three Kingdoms Through Sui • 261–395

Glossary of Chinese Names
397

Preface

This English-language edition of *Biographical Dictionary of Chinese Women: Antiquity Through Sui, 1600 B.C.E.–618 C.E.* is the third in a multivolume series. The first volume, *The Qing Period, 1644–1911,* was published in 1998, and the second, *The Twentieth Century, 1912–2000,* in 2003. The idea for this reference book originated within the then School of Asian Studies at the University of Sydney in Australia in the mid-1980s. Many English-language biographical dictionaries of eminent Chinese have been published over the years, covering many periods of Chinese history: *A Biographical Dictionary of the Qin, Former Han and Xin Periods, 221 B.C.–A.D. 24* (Michael Loewe [2000]); *Sung Biographies* (ed. Herbert Franke [1976]); *Dictionary of Ming Biography (1368–1644)* (ed. L. Carrington Goodrich and Chaoying Fang [1976]); *Eminent Chinese of the Ch'ing Period (1644–1912)* (ed. Arthur W. Hummel [1943]); *Biographical Dictionary of Republican China* (ed. Howard L. Boorman and Richard C. Howard [1967]); and the *Biographic Dictionary of Chinese Communism, 1921–1965* (ed. Donald W. Klein and Anne B. Clark [1971]). In these biographical works, however, the lives of women have been largely ignored. The only volume devoted to women is the recently published translation of the biographies of consorts and empresses of the Three Kingdoms period, *Empresses and Consorts: Selections from Chen Shou's Records of the Three States with Pei Songzhi's Commentary* (trans. Robert J. Cutter and William G. Crowell [1999]), but it is limited in both period and scope. The purpose of the present *Biographical Dictionary of Chinese Women* is thus to compile under one title biographies of Chinese women throughout history and furnish more complete biographical data on individual Chinese women than presently exists in the general dictionaries that have been published over the past three decades.

As with the previous volumes, the articles published here were not commissioned as original research but as a summary of existing knowledge and information. This modest aim has sometimes been very difficult to achieve, given the dearth of accurate and reliable information, especially for the early years of Chinese history. The articles for the Qin, Western Han, and Eastern Han were in the main contributed by mainland Chinese scholars, while those on China's earliest known women and most of those on women in the later periods were written by Western scholars. The translations contained in these biographies are generally the work of the authors of the articles. However, since several eminent scholars have already translated many of the Chinese classics into English, we have used their translations wherever possible, listing the relevant work under that scholar's name in the references that follow each biography. The sole exception to this is Burton Watson, who published his translations of selections from Ban Gu's *History of the Former Han* under the title *Courtier and Commoner in Ancient China*. In accordance with standard referencing practice, this work is listed in the references under Ban Gu, not under Watson.

In this volume, we have attempted to reach as far back into antiquity as possible. The period that, for lack of a more definite and accurate term, we call "antiquity" extends far into the legendary period of Chinese history, roughly from prehistory to

vii

viii PREFACE

the appearance of written records in the form of the oracle bones used in divination from around the thirteenth century B.C.E. While there can be no certainty as to the real historical existence of a number of women from this legendary or semi-legendary period, we have included them because of their cultural significance.

The earliest written records in China are to be found on the oracle bones of the Yin or Shang dynasty (sixteenth century–1066 B.C.E.), and our earliest historical woman, Fu Zi, is placed firmly in this period. She is included not only because she is the earliest woman who has left contemporary written records and archaeological objects to prove her existence, but also because of the rich details these records and objects provide.

The Zhou dynasty (1066–256 B.C.E.) lasted just under 800 years, although during a great part of this period its rule was nominal and China proper was divided into a varying number of large and small states vying for supremacy. While some historical works exist for this period, they are rarely concerned with women. Very little information would have filtered through from this long historical period had not the historian Liu Xiang (77–6 B.C.E.) conceived his *Biographies of Eminent Women* (Lienü zhuan) to educate women of his own time. This work has preserved for us the lives of some 120 women of the Zhou dynasty. However, the highly didactic nature of the text does compromise its value, and modern scholars suspect that exaggerations and perhaps even fabrications have crept into its biographies, thus detracting from its authenticity as a historical source. However, since Liu Xiang's is the only source in which a large amount of information about Zhou women can be found, apart from brief mentions in historical works such as the *Tradition of Zuo* (Zuo zhuan) and *Historical Records* (Shi ji), we have adopted most of his biographies, while trying to weed out what we consider the most suspicious elements, so that the stories of the women are at least told in some way.

The Han dynasty (206 B.C.E.–220 C.E.), which followed the Zhou dynasty, saw the beginning of the writing of official histories in China, and thereafter each dynasty had its own history, usually compiled by historians of the dynasty that replaced it. However, this did not ensure that information relating to women would be available. True, empresses and other consorts of emperors were written into these official histories, but little attention was given to women of lower social strata. Even noblewomen not belonging to that special group, such as princesses, have a place only in certain cases. This has led to a skewed vision of women in imperial China. However, since sources outside official histories are almost nonexistent or are deemed unreliable, we were faced with the choice of either following this skewed vision or not having any vision at all. We chose the former despite the unfortunate consequences. We take comfort, however, in knowing that many imperial women came from humble beginnings, so that their biographies in the official histories provide glimpses of their lives before entering the palace, thus shedding a little light on the lives of ordinary women in that period.

Information about women can be extracted from books other than the official histories, traditionally considered the most reliable sources. These other sources include literary and philosophical works, secondary histories or private histories compiled without imperial imprint, and geographical works. From the orthodox point of view, they are not reliable, yet one might say the same about the official histories, which often cover up certain faults, mistakes, and crimes of the ruling class while exaggerating their noble birth, intelligence, and humanity. In some cases, these unorthodox sources are the only ones available, making them an inevitable choice. When adopting such information, we always alert readers.

The decision to include certain legendary and semi-legendary women has been a difficult one. However, we feel that their cultural significance offsets the historical uncertainty surrounding them. Though not all scholars would agree, the importance of these women in the tradition of Chinese women and, indeed, in the culture and traditions of China as a whole, as well as their symbolic meaning, outweigh their less than perfect authenticity. For those who study Chinese women or even those who wish to know more about them, these cultural icons are indispensable in a reference work aiming at serving these needs.

The biographies in this volume cover a period of over 2,000 years. Rather than presenting them in one alphabetical list, we felt a better overview would be gained of the changing place and activities of women in various periods by dividing the volume into three sections: Antiquity through Warring States; Qin through the Han dynasties; Three Kingdoms and the Jin dynasties through the Northern and Southern Dynasties. This division is intended to provide some idea of the discrete periods in Chinese history and how these may have affected the lives of women. The social, economic, religious, and political environment of the early imperial period—the Qin, Western Han, and Eastern Han dynasties—was markedly different both from that of the preceding Zhou dynasty and the Warring States period and from the almost schizophrenic four centuries that followed it. While in historical works Sui is often linked with Tang, which it preceded, we have included it in this volume because in many ways it was more like the Northern Dynasties, which it followed, the imperial houses of the two being almost inseparable (*vide* Yang Lihua, Empress of Emperor Xuan of Northern Zhou).

We believe this arrangement provides the most effective backdrop against which the different influences upon women, and the different impacts women had upon society, can be assessed.

Lily Xiao Hong Lee
A.D. Stefanowska
Sue Wiles

Editors' Note

The style and format adopted in this volume of the *Biographical Dictionary of Chinese Women* conform to the biographical dictionaries of eminent Chinese mentioned in the Preface as well as to the two volumes already published.

As with the earlier volumes, *pinyin* Romanization has been used, and within each of the three sections the biographies are arranged alphabetically, word by word. Where possible, each woman is entered under her name; where her name is not known, she is entered under our English translation of her title or cognomen. Appropriate *see* references are provided from both *pinyin* and some alternate spellings of names and titles. It would have been impossible to document the biographies of Liu Xiang's *Biographies of Eminent Women* (Lienü zhuan) without referring to Albert R. O'Hara's classic translation, *The Position of Woman in Early China* (1971). While not always agreeing with O'Hara and sometimes offering updated information, we felt it also useful to provide *see* references from many of the titles he gave the women.

The Finding List by Background or Fields of Endeavor provides an alternative entry into the biographies in this volume. We encountered considerable difficulty in deciding upon some of the categories in this list because of the clear disjunction between traditional Chinese and modern Western values. Many traditional biographies praise widows for not remarrying, for example, describing them as "chaste" and "righteous," terms that have little meaning for modern Western readers in this context. We have therefore subdivided the category of "Moral Paradigms" fairly broadly, believing this to be the simplest solution to a complex cultural problem that is not within the purview of this publication, and have included the chaste and righteous under the heading "Loyalty."

As with the earlier volumes, we have followed Charles O. Hucker's *A Dictionary of Official Titles in Imperial China* in translating official titles. Thus, we have translated the Zhou-period title *gong* as Duke, but not without misgivings. Professor Constance A. Cook, who contributed the bulk of our Zhou biographies, presented us with this conundrum: "The translation [of *gong*] as 'Duke' derives from the days when everyone was convinced that Zhou was a 'feudal' state. I realize that 'Duke' is now conventional . . . but, alas, for the wrong reasons. It implies a common social structure with other 'feudal' states, now debunked. I generally use 'Sire' for *gong,* even though this is not perfect either." While we agree that Duke is not totally accurate we eventually decided to retain Duke as adequate for our present purposes.

Bibliographies given at the end of each biography are meant not to be exhaustive but to serve as suggestions for additional reading. As there are often several editions of modern publications of traditional works, we have standardized by citing *juan* and page numbers, for example, 4.13a–b is *juan* 4, pages 13a to 13b.

Lily Xiao Hong Lee
A.D. Stefanowska
Sue Wiles

Acknowledgments

The editors-in-chief wish to thank the University of Sydney for extending financial support over a number of years to this research project, and to acknowledge the financial assistance of the School of Languages and Cultures, which provided funds for research assistance with materials relating to the Southern and Northern Dynasties.

Our thanks also go to the contributors who donated time and expertise to researching and writing the articles in this volume, and to the translators who rendered into English the articles written in Chinese.

We are most appreciative of the work of the period coordinators, who arranged the writing and translation of the biographies in each section. This was time-consuming work that demanded selfless devotion, and we are greatly indebted to them.

Our special thanks go to Nancy Li and Sharon Tian of the University of Sydney's East Asian Collection held in Fisher Library for the help they have offered and given above and beyond the scope of their normal duties.

Guide to Chinese Words Used

Few Chinese words appear in this volume without explanation or translation. The following have been used, sparingly, because there are no simple and accurate English translations for them:

hao   A personal "style," usually revealing a person's tastes and aspirations.

juan   A bibliographic unit used in traditionally produced Chinese books; it means, approximately, "volume."

jun   A title of respect sometimes given to women; it is sometimes translated as Lady.

ming   Official personal name.

sui   The way the Chinese reckon age. A person is one *sui* at birth, and one *sui* is added after each lunar new year. In most cases people's age calculated the Chinese way is one year more than their age calculated the Western way.

zi   Courtesy name, used by friends.

Contributors

AU Chi Kin, Hong Kong Community College, the Hong Kong Polytechnic University, Hong Kong

AU YEUNG Ka Yi, Department of History, Chinese University of Hong Kong, Hong Kong

BAO Shanben, Nanjing, Jiangsu, PRC

CHAN Yuk Ping, Department of Chinese Studies, University of Sydney, Australia

CHAN, Hui Ying Sarah, Department of History, Chinese University of Hong Kong, Hong Kong

CHANG Sun Kang-i, Department of East Asian Languages and Literature, Yale University, USA

CHILDS-JOHNSON, Elizabeth, Old Dominion University, Departments of Art History and Asian Studies, Diehn Fine and Performing Arts Center, USA

CHING-CHUNG, Priscilla, Department of History, Chinese University of Hong Kong, Hong Kong

COOK, Constance A., Department of Modern Languages and Literature, Lehigh University, USA

DE CRESPIGNY, Rafe, Faculty of Arts, Australian National University, Canberra, Australia

EDWARDS, Louise, Institute for International Studies, University of Technology Sydney, Australia

FARMER, J. Michael, Department of History, Brigham Young University, USA

HE Tiancheng, Sichuan University, Chengdu, PRC

HENDRISCHKE, Barbara, Sydney, Australia

JAY, Jennifer W., Department of History and Classics, University of Alberta, Canada

KUCERA, Karil, Departments of Asian Studies and Art and Art History, St. Olaf College, USA

xiv CONTRIBUTORS

LAI Ming Chiu, Department of History, Chinese University of Hong Kong, Hong Kong

LAU Lai Ming, Department of History, Chinese University of Hong Kong, Hong Kong

LEE, Lily Xiao Hong, Department of Chinese Studies, University of Sydney, Australia

LI Yu-ning, Institute of Asian Studies, St. John's University, New York, USA

LONG, Laura, Wollongong, Australia

MU Meichun, College of Art, Nanjing Normal University, PRC

NG Kwok Leung, Department of History, Chinese University of Hong Kong, Hong Kong

NISHIMURA Fumiko, Faculty of Humanities and Social Sciences, Mie University, Japan

SHEN Jian, Department of Chinese, Dongnan University, Nanjing, Jiangsu, PRC

SHEN Lidong, Center for Educational Information, Nanjing Agricultural University, PRC

SU Zhecong, Department of Chinese Language and Literature, Wuhan University, PRC

SUN Kuo Tung, New Asia College, Chinese University of Hong Kong, Hong Kong

TAI Po Ying, Department of History, Chinese University of Hong Kong, Hong Kong

TAO, Chia-lin Pao, Department of East Asian Studies, University of Arizona, USA

TSAI, Kathryn A., San Jose, USA

WANG Bugao, Dongnan University, Nanjing, Jiangsu, PRC

WANG Lihua, Jiangsu Art & Literature Publishing House, PRC

WANG Shu-hwai, Institute of Modern History, Academia Sinica, Taiwan

WANG Xiaowen, Dean's Office, Jiangsu Lianyungang Economic School for Cadres, PRC

WILES, Sue, Department of Chinese Studies, University of Sydney, Australia

WONG Shiu-hin, Department of Chinese Language and Literature, Hong Kong Shue Yan College, Hong Kong

WONG Yin Lee, Department of History, Hong Kong Baptist University, Hong Kong

WU Jin, Nanjing Normal University, Jiangsu, PRC

The late WU Tiaogong, College of Art, Nanjing Normal University, PRC

XIA Chunhao, Department of Language & Literature, Huai Hai Institute of Technology, PRC

YANG Haiming, Faculty of Arts, Suzhou University, PRC

YAO Weidou, China Women Publishing House, Beijing, PRC

YEH Chia-ying, Department of Asian Studies, University of British Columbia, Canada

YIM Chi Hung, Institute of Chinese Literature & Philosophy, Academia Sinica, Nankang, Taiwan

ZANG Jian, Center for the Study of Ancient Chinese History, Peking University, PRC

ZHANG Qi, Sichuan University, Chengdu, PRC

ZHENG Bijun, Department of History/Center for Women's Studies, Peking University, PRC

ZHU Xiaofeng, Beijing, PRC

Translators

CHE Wai-lam, William, Department of English Language and Literature, Hong Kong Baptist University, Hong Kong

HE Tiancheng, Sichuan University, Chengdu, PRC

LEE, Lily Xiao Hong, Department of Chinese Studies, University of Sydney, Australia

LU Huici, Department of East Asian Studies, University of Arizona, USA

SHEN Jian, Department of Chinese, Dongnan University, Nanjing, Jiangsu, PRC

TAM Chui Han, June, Freelance Translator

WILES, Sue, Department of Chinese Studies, University of Sydney, Australia

WONG Tse Sheung, Freelance Translator

Chronology of Dynasties and Major Rulers

Antiquity Through Zhou

Xia 夏c. 2000–1500 B.C.E.
Yin 殷 (Shang) 1700–1027 B.C.E.

Western Zhou 西周1027–771 B.C.E.
Eastern Zhou 東周770–221 B.C.E.
  Spring and Autumn period
  春秋770–476 B.C.E.
  Warring States period 戰國
  475–221 B.C.E.

Lu 1108–250 魯 B.C.E.
Qi 齊 ?–264 B.C.E.
Jin 晉 c. 1000–376 B.C.E.
Qin 秦 ?–209 B.C.E.
Chu 楚 c. 1000–223 B.C.E.
Song 宋 c. 1000–286 B.C.E.
Wei 衛 ?–209 B.C.E.
Chen 陳 ?–479 B.C.E.
Cai 蔡c. 1000–447 B.C.E.
Cao 曹 c. 1000–488 B.C.E.
Yan 燕 ?–221 B.C.E.
Zheng 鄭 806–374 B.C.E.
Qi 杞 ?–444 B.C.E.
Wu 吳 585–473 B.C.E.
Zhao 趙 424–221 B.C.E.
Han 韓 424–229 B.C.E.
Wei 魏 424–224 B.C.E.

Personal Name	Lifetime	Temple Title	Period of Reign
		Qin Through Han	
	Qin Dynasty 秦221–206 B.C.E.		
Ying Zheng	259–210	Shihuangdi	221–210
Ying Huhai	230–207	Ershi	209–207
	Western Han Dynasty 西漢206 B.C.E.–8 C.E.		
Liu Bang	256–195	Gaozu	206–195
Liu Ying	210–188	Hui	194–188

Note: This is not a complete list of all rulers in any of the dynasties; minor rulers, nominal rulers, and those who ruled for very short periods are not included for the major dynasties, and only the dynastic names and dates are provided for all other dynasties.

xviii CHRONOLOGY

Personal Name	Lifetime	Temple Title	Period of Reign
Liu Hong	?192–184	Shao	187–184
Lü Zhi	241–180	Empress Lü	187–180
Liu Heng	202–157	Wen	179–157
Liu Qi	188–141	Jing	156–141
Liu Che	156–87	Wu	140–87
Liu Fuling	94–74	Zhao	86–74
Liu Xun / Bingyi	91–48	Xuan	73–48
Liu Shi	76–33	Yuan	48–33
Liu Ao	51–7	Cheng	32–7
Liu Xin	25–1	Ai	6–1
Liu Kan (Jizi)	8 B.C.E.–6 C.E.	Ping	1–6 C.E.
Liu Ying	4–25	Ruzi	6–9

Xin Dynasty 新 *9–23 C.E. (Interregnum)*

Wang Mang	45–23 C.E.	Xin	9–23

Eastern Han Dynasty 東漢 *25–220*

Liu Xiu	6 B.C.E.–57 C.E.	Guangwu	25–57
Liu Zhuang (Yang)	27–75	Ming	58–75
Liu Da	57–88	Zhang	76–88
Liu Zhao	78–106	He	89–106
Liu Long	105–106	Shang	106
Liu Hu/You	93–125	An	107–125
Liu Yi	c. 120–125	Shao	125
Liu Bao	115–144	Shun	126–144
Liu Zhi	132–168	Huan	147–168
Liu Hong	156–189	Ling	168–189
Liu Xie	181–234	Xian	189–220

Three Kingdoms Through Sui

Three Kingdoms 三國

Wei Dynasty 魏 *220–265*

Cao Cao	155–220	King of Wei	
Cao Pi	187–226	Wen	220–226
Cao Rui	205–239	Ming	226–239
Cao Fang (adopted)	231–274	Prince of Qi	239–254
Cao Mao	241–260	Duke of Gaoguixiang	254–260

CHRONOLOGY xix

Personal Name	Lifetime	Temple Title	Period of Reign
Cao Huan	245–302	Prince of Chen (Yuan)	260–265

Shu Dynasty 蜀 221–263

Liu Bei	161–223	Zhaolie	221–223
Liu Shan	207–271	Houzhu	223–263

Wu Dynasty 吳 222–280

Sun Quan	182–252	Dadi	222–252
Sun Liang	243–260	Guijiwang (King of Guiji)	252–258
Sun Xiu	236–264	Jing	258–264
Sun Hao	?242–284	Marquis of Wucheng (Mo)	264–280

Western Jin Dynasty 西晉 266–316

Sima Zhao	211–265	Wen (posthumous title)	
Sima Yan	236–290	Wu	265–290
Sima Zhong	259–306	Hui	290–306
Sima Zhi	284–313	Huai	307–312
Sima Ye	270–317	Min	313–316

Eastern Jin Dynasty 東晉 317–420

Sima Rui	276–322	Yuan	317–322
Sima Shao	299–325	Ming	323–325
Sima Yan	321–342	Cheng	325–342
Sima Yue	321–344	Kang	342–344
Sima Dan	343–361	Mu	344–361
Sima Pi	340–365	Ai	361–365
Sima Yi	342–386	Duke of Haixi (Fei)	365–371
Sima Yu	320–372	Jianwen	371–372
Sima Yao, *zi* Changming	362–396	Xiaowu An	372–396 396–419
Sima Dezong	382–419	Gong	419–420
Sima Dewen	385–421		

xx CHRONOLOGY

The Sixteen Kingdoms

Cheng-Han 成漢 303–347

Former Zhao 前趙 304–329

Former Liang 前涼 314–376

Later Zhao 後趙 328–350

Dai 代 338–376

Former Qin 前秦 351–394

Former Yan 前燕 352–370

Later Qin 後秦 394–417

Later Yan 後燕 384–409

Western Yan 西燕 384–394

Western Qin 西秦 385–431

Later Liang 後涼 386–403

Southern Liang 南涼 397–414

Northern Liang 北涼 397–460

Southern Yan 南燕 400–410

Western Liang 西涼 400–421

Xia 夏 407–431

Northern Yan 北燕 409–436

Personal Name	Lifetime	Temple Title	Period of Reign

Southern and Northern Dynasties 南北朝

Liu Song Dynasty 劉宋 420–479

Liu Yu	363–422	Wu	420–422
Liu Yifu	406–424	Shao	422–424
Liu Yilong	407–453	Wen	424–453

Personal Name	Lifetime	Temple Title	Period of Reign
Liu Jun	430–464	Xiaowu	454–464
Liu Ziye	449–?466	Qianfei	464–465
Liu Yu	439–472	Ming	465–472
Liu Yu	463–476	Houfei	472–477
Liu Zhun	469–479	Shun	477–479

Southern Qi Dynasty 南齊 *479–502*

Xiao Daocheng	427–482	Gao (Taizu)	479–482
Xiao Ze	440–493	Wu	483–493

Liang Dynasty 梁 *502–557*

Xiao Yan	464–549	Wu	502–549

Chen Dynasty 陳 *557–589*

Chen Baxian	503–559	Wu	557–559
Chen Shubao	553–604	Houzhu	582–589

Northern Wei Dynasty 北魏 *386–534*

Tuoba Gui	371–409	Daowu	386–409
Tuoba Si	393–423	Mingyuan	409–423
Tuoba Tao	408–453	Taiwu	423–451
Tuoba Jun	440–465	Wencheng	452–465
Tuoba Hong	454–476	Xianwen	465–471
Tuoba/Yuan Hong	467–499	Xiaowen	471–499
Yuan Ke	483–515	Xuanwu	499–515
Yuan Xu	510–528	Xiaoming	515–528
Yuan Ziyou	?506–530	Xiaozhuang	528–530

Eastern Wei Dynasty 東魏 *534–550*

Yuan Shanbei (Shanjian?)	?523–551	Xiaojing	534–550

Northern Qi Dynasty 北齊 *550–577*

Gao Huan	496–547	Shenwu (posthumous title)	
Gao Yang	529–559	Wenxuan	550–559
Gao Yin	544/545–560	Fei	559–560
Gao Yan	?534–561	Xiaozhao	560–561
Gao Zhan	537–569	Wucheng	561–565
Gao Wei	556–578	Houzhu	565–577

xxii CHRONOLOGY

Personal Name	Lifetime	Temple Title	Period of Reign
	Western Wei Dynasty 西魏 *535–556*		
Yuan Baoju	?506–551	Wen	535–551
	Northern Zhou Dynasty 北周 *557–581*		
Yuwen Yong	543–578	Wu	561–578
Yuwen Yun	558–580	Xuan	578–579
Yuwen Chan	573–581	Jing	579–581
	Sui Dynasty 隋 *581–618*		
Yang Jian	541–604	Wen	581–604
Yang Guang	569–618	Yang	605–617

Finding List by Background or Fields of Endeavor

AMBASSADORS/ MARRIAGE ALLIANCES

Antiquity
Ying, Wife of Duke Huai of Jin

Qin Through Han
Feng Liao
Liu Jieyou
Liu Xijun
Wang Zhaojun

Three Kingdoms Through Sui
Yuwen, Princess Qianjin of Northern Zhou

CONSORTS

Antiquity
Bao Si, Wife of King You of Zhou
Bo Ying, Wife of King Ping of Chu
Ehuang
Fan Ji, Wife of King Zhuang of Chu
Fu Zi, the Shang Woman Warrior
Goiter Girl of Qi, Wife of King Min
Jiandi
Jiang, Queen of King Xuan of Zhou
Jiang Yuan
Man-Clan Woman of Deng, Wife of King Wu
   of Chu
Nü Wa
Nüying
Pure Jiang, Wife of King Zhao of Chu
Tai Si, Wife of King Wen of Zhou
Tushan Woman
Yu Ji, Wife of King Wei of Qi
Yue Ji, Wife of King Zhao of Chu
Zhao, Wife of the King of Dai
Zheng Mao, Wife of King Cheng of Chu
Zhongli Chun of Qi, Wife of King Xuan
   of Qi
Zhuang Zhi, Wife of King Qingxiang of Chu

Qin Through Han
Hua Rong, Consort of Prince of Yanla
Tang, Consort of Prince Hongnong
Wang Wengxu
Yu, Consort of the Hegemon-King of Chu

DANCE

Three Kingdoms Through Sui
Lüzhu

EDUCATION

Antiquity
Instructress for the Daughter of Qi
Jing Jiang
Mencius's Mother
Mother Teacher of Lu
Tai Jiang
Tai Ren
Tai Si
Tushan Woman

Three Kingdoms Through Sui
Song, Lady Xuanwen

EMPRESSES

Qin Through Han
Bo, Empress of Emperor Jing
Cao Jie, Empress of Emperor Xian
Chen Jiao, Empress of Emperor Wu
Deng Mengnü, Empress of Emperor Huan
Deng Sui, Empress of Emperor He
Dou, Empress of Emperor Zhang
Dou Miao, Empress of Emperor Huan
Dou Yifang, Empress of Emperor Wen
Fu Shou, Empress of Emperor Xian
Guo Shengtong, Empress of Emperor
   Guangwu
Huo Chengjun, Empress of Emperor Xuan
Liang Na, Empress of Emperor Shun

xxiii

xxiv FINDING LIST BY BACKGROUND OR FIELDS OF ENDEAVOR

Liang Nüying, Empress of Emperor Huan
Lü Zhi, Empress of Emperor Gaozu
Ma, Empress of Emperor Ming
Shangguan, Empress of Emperor Zhao
Wang, Empress of Emperor Ping
Wang, Empress of Emperor Xuan
Wang, Empress of Wang Mang of Xin
Wang Zhengjun, Empress of Emperor Yuan
Wang Zhi, Empress of Emperor Jing
Wei Zifu, Empress of Emperor Wu
Xu, Empress of Emperor Cheng
Xu Pingjun, Empress of Emperor Xuan
Yin Lihua, Empress of Emperor Guangwu
Zhang Yan, Empress of Emperor Hui
Zhao Feiyan, Empress of Emperor Cheng

Three Kingdoms Through Sui
Dugu, Empress of Emperor Wen of Sui
Feng, Empress of Emperor Wencheng of Northern Wei
Feng, Empress of Emperor Xiaowen of Northern Wei
Gan, Empress of the Former Sovereign of Shu
Guo, Empress of Emperor Ming of Wei
Guo, Empress of Emperor Wen of Wei
Jia Nanfeng, Empress of Emperor Hui of Jin
Lou Zhaojun, Empress of Emperor Shenwu of Northern Qi
Mao, Empress of Emperor Ming of Wei
Wang Zhenfeng, Empress of Emperor Ming of Liu Song
Wu, Empress of the Former Sovereign of Shu
Xiao, Empress of Emperor Yang of Sui
Yang Lihua, Empress of Emperor Xuan of Northern Zhou
Yuan Qigui, Empress of Emperor Wen of Liu Song
Yang Yan, Empress of Emperor Wu of Jin
Yang Zhi, Empress of Emperor Wu of Jin
Zhen, Empress of Emperor Wen of Wei

ENTREPRENEURS

Qin Through Han
Qing, the Widow from Bashu

Three Kingdoms Through Sui
Guo of Western Jin

FINE ARTS

Antiquity
Qiu Hu's Wife

Three Kingdoms Through Sui
Wei Shuo

FINE ARTS; MUSIC

Antiquity
Han'e
Jiandi
Tushan Woman

Three Kingdoms Through Sui
Lüzhu

FINE ARTS; WEAVING

Three Kingdoms Through Sui
Su Hui

LEGENDARY FIGURES

Antiquity
Ehuang
Jiandi
Jiang Yuan
Meng Jiangnü
Nü Wa
Nüying
Queen Mother of the West
Tai Jiang
Tai Ren
Tai Si
Tushan Woman

Qin Through Han
Diao Chan
Liu Lanzhi

FINDING LIST BY BACKGROUND OR FIELDS OF ENDEAVOR xxv

LITERATURE; POETRY

Antiquity
Ding Jiang
Duke Mu of Xu's Wife
Instructress for the Daughter of Qi
Juan, Daughter of an Official of the Ford of Zhao
Shaonan Woman of Shen
Tao Ying
Widow of Wei

Qin Through Han
Ban Jieyu, Concubine of Emperor Cheng
Cai Yan
Liyu
Tangshan, Concubine of Emperor Gaozu
Xu Shu

Three Kingdoms Through Sui
Bao Linghui
Hu, Consort of Emperor Xuanwu of Northern Wei
Liu Lingxian
Su Boyu's Wife
Su Hui
Xie Daoyun
Zuo Fen

LITERATURE; PROSE

Antiquity
Liuxia Hui's Wife

Qin Through Han
Ban Jieyu, Concubine of Emperor Cheng
Ban Zhao
Xu Shu

Three Kingdoms Through Sui
Han Lanying
Liu Lingxian
Xie Daoyun
Zuo Fen

MARTIAL ARTS, MILITARY STRATEGY

Antiquity
Fu Zi
Man-Clan Woman of Deng
Yue Woman

Three Kingdoms Through Sui
Han of Eastern Jin
Mulan
Xian, Lady of Qiao State
Xun Guan

MEDICINE

Antiquity
Wei Huacun

Qin Through Han
Xu Deng

MORAL PARADIGMS; BENEVOLENCE

Antiquity
Tai Si
Zhong Zi

Qin Through Han
Mother Piao
Liu Yuan

MORAL PARADIGMS; CORRECTING UNACCEPTABLE BEHAVIOR

Antiquity
Bo Ying
Crone of Quwo of Wei
Dazi of Tao's Wife
Fan Ji
General of Gai's Wife
General Zhao Gua's Mother
Gongcheng of Lu's Elder Sister
Jiang, Queen of King Xuan of Zhou
Jiang-Clan Woman of Qi

xxvi FINDING LIST BY BACKGROUND OR FIELDS OF ENDEAVOR

Ji-Clan Woman
Jieyu's Wife
Jing Jiang
Lao Laizi's Wife
Official from Zhounan's Wife
Qiu Hu's Wife
Tian Ji of Qi's Mother
Wei Ji
Wife of the Chariot Driver for Yanzi, Minister of Qi
Wife of Yuling Zizhong of Chu
Zang Sun of Lu's Mother

MORAL PARADIGMS; FILIAL BEHAVIOR

Antiquity
Jing, Daughter of Shanghuai Yan of Qi
Qiu Hu's Wife

Qin Through Han
Chunyu Tiying
The Filial Widow from Chen
Woman of Integrity from the Capital
Zhao E
Zhou Qing, the Filial Woman of Donghai

MORAL PARADIGMS; LOYALTY

Antiquity
Abiding Wet Nurse of Wei
Bo Ji
Bo Ying
Bow Artisan of Jin's Wife
Ding Jiang
Duke Zhuang of Li's Wife
Ehuang
Gao Xing
Jing, Daughter of Shanghuai Yan of Qi
Loyal Maid of Zhu of Zhou
Man of Cai's Wife
Meng Jiangnü
Nüying
Official from Zhounan's Wife
Qiu Hu's Wife
Tao Ying
Righteous Nurse of Duke Xiao of Lu

Righteous Respected Female Elder of Lu
Righteous Stepmother of Qi
Widow of Wei
Yue Ji
Zhao, Wife of the King of Dai

Qin Through Han
Liu Yuan
Yu, Consort of the Hegemon-King of Chu

MORAL PARADIGMS; MORAL COURAGE

Antiquity
Bo Ying
Gao Xing
Righteous Nurse of Duke Xiao of Lu
Ying, Wife of Duke Huai of Yin

Qin Through Han
Chunyu Tiying
Youdi

Three Kingdoms Through Sui
Liu Yingyuan

MORAL PARADIGMS; NEGATIVE EXEMPLARS

Antiquity
Ai Jiang
Bao Si
Kong Bo Ji
Li Ji
Meixi
Mu Jiang
Nanzi
Wen Jiang
Xuan Jiang

Qin Through Han
Sun Shou
Zhu Maichen's Wife

Three Kingdoms Through Sui
Feng, Empress of Emperor Wencheng of Northern Wei

FINDING LIST BY BACKGROUND OR FIELDS OF ENDEAVOR *xxvii*

Feng, Empress of Emperor Xiaowu of
    Northern Wei
Guo Huai
Guo of Western Jin
Jia Nanfeng, Empress of Emperor Hui of Jin

MORAL PARADIGMS; OBEDIENCE

Antiquity
Bo Ji
Duke Zhuang of Li's Wife
Meng Ji
Pure Jiang

Qin Through Han
Two Obedient Women of the Wei Ancestral
    Temple

MORAL PARADIGMS; PATRIOTISM

Antiquity
Abiding Wet Nurse of Wei
Duke Mu of Xu's Wife
Loyal Maid of Zhu of Zhou
Righteous Nurse of Duke Xiao of Lu
Righteous Respected Female Elder of Lu
Wei Ji
Xi Shi
Ying, Wife of Duke Huai of Jin
Yu Ji, Wife of King Wei of Qi

MORAL PARADIGMS; SAGACITY

Antiquity
Crone of Quwo of Wei
Dazi of Tao's Wife
Duke Mu of Xu's Wife
Ehuang
General Zhao Gua's Mother
Gongcheng of Lu's Elder Sister
Instructress for the Daughter of Qi
Jiang, Queen of King Xuan of Zhou
Ji-Clan Woman
Jieyu's Wife
Jing, Concubine of Minister Guan Zhong of
    Qi

Jing Jiang
Kind Mother of the Mang Family of Wei
Lao Laizi's Wife
Liuxia Hui's Wife
Man-Clan Woman of Deng
Mencius' Mother
Mu Jiang
Nüying
Qian Lou of Lu's Wife
Qishi Woman of Lu
Shu Ji
Sunshu Ao's Mother
Wife of the Chariot Driver for Yanzi, Minister
    of Qi
Wife of Yuling Zizhong of Chu
Xi Clan Head's Wife
Zang Sun of Lu's Mother
Zheng Mao
Zhong Zi
Zhuang Zhi, Wife of King Qingxiang of
    Chu

Qin Through Han
Lü Xu
Sima, Yang Chang's Wife
Wang Ba's Wife
Wang Zhang's Wife
Yan Yannian's Mother

Three Kingdoms Through Sui
Yan Xian
Zhan, Tao Kan's Mother
Zhang, Concubine of Fu Jian

MORAL PARADIGMS; UPRIGHT BEHAVIOR

Antiquity
Bo Ji
Gao Xing
General of Gai's Wife
Goiter Girl of Qi
Liuxia Hui's Wife
Loyal Maid of Zhu of Zhou
Meng Ji
Meng Jiangnü

xxviii FINDING LIST BY BACKGROUND OR FIELDS OF ENDEAVOR

Mother Teacher of Lu
Nüzong
Pure Jiang
Qian Lou of Lu's Wife
Qiu Hu's Wife
Righteous Respected Female Elder of Lu
Righteous Stepmother of Qi
Ruji
Shaonan Woman of Shen
Tian Ji of Qi's Mother
Virgin of Egu
Widow of Wei
Yue Ji
Zhao, Wife of the King of Dai
Zheng Mao

Qin Through Han
Filial Widow from Chen
Huan, Liu Changqing's Wife
Huangfu Gui's Wife
Liu Yuan
Ma, Empress of Emperor Ming
Meng Guang
Two Honorable Women from Zhuya
Two Obedient Women of the Wei Ancestral
 Temple
Yue Yangzi's Wife

MOTHERS AND STEPMOTHERS

Antiquity
Foxi of Zhao's Mother
Jiandi
Jiang Yuan
Jing Jiang
Kind Mother of the Mang Family of Wei
Li Ji
Mencius's Mother
Mother Teacher of Lu
Nü Wa
Righteous Nurse of Duke Xiao of Lu
Righteous Respected Female Elder of Lu
Righteous Stepmother of Qi
Sunshu Ao's Mother
Tai Jiang
Tai Ren

Tai Si
Tian Ji of Qi's Mother
Tushan Woman
Zang Sun of Lu's Mother

Qin Through Han
Chen Ying's Mother
Li Mujiang
Lü's Mother
Wang Ling's Mother
Wen Jijiang
Yan Ming
Yan Yannian's Mother
Zhang Lu's Mother
Zhang Tang's Mother
Zhao Ji

Three Kingdoms Through Sui
Li Luoxiu
Wu, Wife of Caitiff-Smashing-General Sun
Zhan, Tao Kan's Mother

PALACE WOMEN

Qin Through Han
Ban Jieyu, Concubine of Emperor Cheng
Bo, Concubine of Emperor Gaozu
Feng, Concubine of Emperor Yuan
Fu, Concubine of Emperor Yuan
Li, Concubine of Emperor Wu
Qi, Concubine of Emperor Gaozu
Shen, Concubine of Emperor Wen
Tangshan, Concubine of Emperor Gaozu
Zhao Gouyi, Concubine of Emperor Wu
Zhao Hede, Concubine of Emperor Cheng

Three Kingdoms Through Sui
Bian, Wife of Cao Cao, King of Wei
Bu, Consort of Sun Quan
Ding, Consort of Cao Cao, King of Wei
Hu, Consort of Emperor Xuanwu of Northern
 Wei
Pan, Consort of Sun Quan
Wu, Wife of Caitiff-Smashing-General Sun

FINDING LIST BY BACKGROUND OR FIELDS OF ENDEAVOR xxix

POLITICS

Antiquity
Ding Jiang
Fan Ji
Fu Zi
Jiang-Clan Woman of Qi
Mu Jiang
Qishi Woman of Lu
Wen Jiang
Xi Shi
Xuan Jiang
Ying, Wife of Duke Huai of Jin
Yu Ji, Wife of King Wei of Qi
Zhongli Chun of Qi
Zhuang Zhi, Wife of King Qingxiang of Chu

Qin Through Han
Deng Sui, Empress of Emperor He
Dou Yifang, Empress of Emperor Wen
Fu Shou, Empress of Emperor Xian
Gongsun Shu's Wife
Liang Na, Empress of Emperor Shun
Lü Zhi, Empress of Emperor Gaozu

Three Kingdoms Through Sui
Bian, Wife of Cao Cao, King of Wei
Dugu, Empress of Emperor Wen of Sui
Feng, Empress of Emperor Wencheng of Northern Wei
Guo Huai
Guo of Western Jin
Hu, Consort of Emperor Xuanwu of Northern Wei
Jia Nanfeng, Empress of Emperor Hui of Jin
Lou Zhaojun, Empress of Emperor Shenwu of Northern Qi
Lu Lingxuan
Sun Luban
Sun Luyu
Xian, Lady of Qiao State
Yang Yan, Empress of Emperor Wu of Jin
Yang Zhi, Empress of Emperor Wu of Jin
Yuwen, Princess Qianjin of Northern Zhou

PRINCESSES

Qin Through Han
Liu Jieyou
Liu Piao, the Grand Princess
Liu Xijun
Liu Yuan

Three Kingdoms Through Sui
Liu Yingyuan
Yuwen, Princess Qianjin of Northern Zhou

REASONING SKILLS

Antiquity
Bow Artisan of Jin's Wife
Crone of Quwo of Wei
Discerning Woman of the Chu Wilds
Foxi of Zhao's Mother
Goiter Girl of Qi
Jiang Yi of Chu's Mother
Jing, Concubine of Minister Guan Zhong of Qi
Jing, Daughter of Shanghuai Yan of Qi
Juan, Daughter of an Official of the Ford of Zhao
Shu Ji
Virgin of Egu
Xu Wu of Qi
Yu Ji, Wife of King Wei of Qi
Zhongli Chun of Qi
Zhuang Zhi, Wife of King Qingxiang of Chu

Qin Through Han
Chen Siqian
Wang Ba's Wife

Three Kingdoms Through Sui
An Lingshou

REBEL LEADERS

Qin Through Han
Lü's Mother
Zheng Sisters

xxx *FINDING LIST BY BACKGROUND OR FIELDS OF ENDEAVOR*

REGENTS

Qin Through Han
Deng Sui, Empress to Emperor He
Dou, Empress of Emperor Zhang
Liang Na, Empress of Emperor Shun
Lü Zhi, Empress of Emperor Gaozu
Shangguan, Empress of Emperor Zhao

Three Kingdoms Through Sui
Feng, Empress of Emperor Xiaowen of Northern Wei
Hu, Consort of Emperor Xuanwu of Northern Wei
Lou Zhaojun, Empress of Emperor Shenwu of Northern Qi

RELIGIOUS

Qin Through Han
Zhang Lu's Mother

Three Kingdoms Through Sui
An Lingshou
Baoxian
Daoqiong
Fajing
Huiguo
Lingzong
Sengjing
Tanbei
Tanluo
Wei Huacun
Xu Baoguang
Zhi Miaoyin
Zhu Daoxin
Zhu Jingjian

ROMANTIC FIGURES

Antiquity
Ehuang
Nüying
Xi Shi

Qin Through Han
Yu, Consort of the Hegemon-King of Chu
Zhuo Wenjun

Three Kingdoms Through Sui
Lüzhu
Mulan

SCHOLARS

Qin Through Han
Ban Zhao
Fu Xi'e

Three Kingdoms Through Sui
Han Lanying
Song, Lady Xuanwen
Xie Daoyun

BIOGRAPHIES

Antiquity Through Zhou

Antiquity

Zhou (1027–221 B.C.E.)
Spring and Autumn Period (770–476 B.C.E.)
Warring States (475–221 B.C.E.)

A

The Abiding Wet Nurse of Wei
The Abiding Wet Nurse (Wei Jie Rumu) for the children of King Xia of Wei (Wei Wang Xia; one source gives his name as King Jia), fl. 661 B.C.E., was killed while protecting the last royal son of the state of Wei (in present-day Shanxi Province) after invaders from the state of Qin (present-day Shaanxi Province) had put the king and his other sons to death. Rather than accept a large monetary reward, she risked the punitive extermination of her own family to flee with the remaining prince. A turncoat Wei minister revealed her hiding place to the Qin, and although she covered the child with her own body in an attempt to protect him they were both killed, at least a dozen arrows piercing her body. Impressed with her loyalty and maternal instincts, the Qin king rewarded her brother with money and gave her a lavish burial. It was said that her kindness came from a good conscience, while she herself is quoted as saying that "all who nourish men's children have a duty to keep them alive and not to kill them" (O'Hara, 145). Her biography is included in "Biographies of the Chaste and Righteous" in *Biographies of Eminent Women* (Lienü zhuan).

Constance A. COOK

Liu Xiang. *Lienü zhuan.* Sibubeiyao ed., 5.8a–9a.
O'Hara, Albert R. *The Position of Woman in Early China According to the Lieh Nü Chuan, "The Biographies of Chinese Women."* Taipei: Mei Ya, 1971; 1978, 144–47.

Accomplished Woman of the Jiang Clan: *see* **Wen Jiang, Wife of Duke Huan of Lu**

Ah-liao: *see* **Yue Woman**

Ai Chiang of Duke Chuang of Lu: *see* **Ai Jiang, Wife of Duke Zhuang of Lu**

Ai Jiang, Wife of Duke Zhuang of Lu
Ai Jiang, or Mournful Woman of the Jiang Clan, d. 659 B.C.E., was a daughter of the royal house of Qi (in the north of present-day Shandong Province); she was also known as Furen Jiang Shi and as Minor Ruler (*xiao jun*). In 670, she was married to Duke Zhuang (Zhuang Gong, r. 692–661 B.C.E.), the ruler of Lu (in present-day Shandong Province) and son of Wen Jiang (*q.v.*). The marriage arrangements and exchange of gifts had begun three years earlier, the year of Wen Jiang's death, and one source says Ai Jiang frequently had "illicit relations" with her future husband before she went to Lu. Ai Jiang had no children, but her younger sister, Shu Jiang, who had accompanied her when she went as a bride to Duke Zhuang, had a son named Kai whom Ai Jiang wished to appoint heir apparent. Ai Jiang was forced to flee, however, when her sexual liaison with her brother-in-law, Qingfu, was dis-

6 AI JIANG

covered. Qingfu nevertheless fulfilled Ai Jiang's plan by killing the original heir apparent, which allowed her nephew, Kai, to inherit the title of Duke; he became known as Duke Min. Ai Jiang is said to have continued her affair with Qingfu, who was plotting with her to kill her nephew Duke Min and to usurp his position. When their plot was revealed they fled, Ai Jiang to Zhu and Qingfu to Qu. Duke Huan of Qi (Ai Jiang's home state) intervened at this point, installing Duke Xi as the ruler of Lu, and in 659 the men of Qi caught Ai Jiang, killed her, and took her body back to Qi. However, at the request of Duke Xi her body was returned to Lu, where it was buried. In 652, her ancestral tablet was placed in the Grand Temple during the *di* sacrifice, an act that later commentators claimed was improper due to the circumstances of her death and burial. The author of the *Zuo zhuan* commented that Qi had been "too severe" in killing Ai Jiang because she should have been dealt with by her husband's house of Lu, not her natal house of Qi.

In *Biographies of Eminent Women* (Lienü zhuan), where her biography is included in "Biographies of Pernicious and Depraved Women," Ai Jiang is described as proud, lustful, corrupt, evil, and perverse.

Constance A. COOK

Chunqiu and *Zuo zhuan*. Zhuang 22, 24, Min 2, Xi 1, 2, 8. Taipei: Fenghuang chubanshe, 1977. Vol. 1, 3.59, 70–71; 4.8, 14; 5.1, 4–5, 45.

Legge, James, trans. *The Chinese Classics, Vol. 5: The Ch'un ts'ew, with the Tso chuen.* Hong Kong: Hong Kong University Press, 1960; 1970, 101, 108, 126–36, 150–51.

Liu Xiang. *Lienü zhuan.* Sibubeiyao ed., 7.4a–b.

O'Hara, Albert R. *The Position of Woman in Early China According to the Lieh Nü Chuan, "The Biographies of Chinese Women."* Taipei: Mei Ya, 1971; 1978, 194–96.

Takikawa Kametarō. *Shiki kaichū kōshō [Shi ji].* Taipei: Hongshi, 1977, 33.31–34.

Aliao: *see* **Yue Woman**

B

Bao Si, Wife of King You of Zhou

Bao Si (the Woman of the Si Clan of Bao), fl. eighth century B.C.E., was the favored wife of King You (You Wang, r. 781–771 B.C.E.) of Zhou, in central China. She is blamed for the downfall of the Zhou house.

Legend has it that Bao Si was responsible for King You setting aside his Queen Shen, a daughter of the Marquis of Shen, and replacing the legitimate heir apparent with Bao Si's son, Bo Fu. Bao Si's evil nature was attributed to her natal house of Bao (in the southeast of present-day Shaanxi Province), which originated at the end of the Xia dynasty (c. 2100–1600 B.C.E.) when the spit of two dragons, named The Two Lords of Bao, was sealed in a vessel. It was not until the reign of King Li of Zhou (r. 878–841) that someone dared open the vessel, causing spit to flow out and fill the room. King Li had women undress and shout at it, believing this would stop its flow, but to no avail, for it changed into a dark tortoise (one source says a black snake), which entered the women's quarters and impregnated a virgin concubine of about seven years of age. She did not become pregnant immediately: *Biographies of Eminent Women* (Lienü zhuan) says she became pregnant when she was about fifteen ("when she fixed up her hair as marriageable"), but places this event at least fourteen years after her impregnation at seven. Nevertheless, she bore the child during the time of King Xuan (Xuan Wang, r. 827–781), but fearing it, she cast it out onto the road to die; this infant was Bao Si. Two fugitives saved the infant and took her with them to Bao, where she grew into a very beautiful young woman. Because of her beauty, a prince of Bao who had committed some crime gave her to King You to avoid punishment.

King You was warned against Bao Si but he nevertheless took her as his wife and was, in the words of later commentators, "led astray" by her. In an effort to make her laugh, he repeatedly lit beacon fires to summon the lords to come to protect Zhou from supposed invaders. When the Marquis of Shen joined forces with western barbarian tribes and finally did attack in revenge for the improper dismissal of his daughter, Queen Shen, the house of Zhou was defeated because the protecting lords did not believe King You's signals were genuine and were no longer prepared to respond. King You was killed in the attack, Bao Si was captured, and the nobles were reconciled with Zhou. Bao Si's name is forever associated with beautiful women and the fall of dynasties, and her biography is included in "Biographies of Pernicious and Depraved Women" in *Biographies of Eminent Women.*

Constance A. COOK

Guoyu. "Jinyu" 1. Sibubeiyao ed., 7.2b.
Liu Xiang. *Lienü zhuan.* Sibubeiyao ed., 7,2b–3a.
O'Hara, Albert R. *The Position of Woman in Early China According to the Lieh Nü Chuan, "The Biographies of Chinese Women."* Taipei: Mei Ya, 1971; 1978, 189–92.
Qu Wanli, ed. *Shi jing shiyi.* "Zheng yue," Mao no. 192. Taipei: Huagang, 1977, 152–55.
Takikawa Kametarō, *Shiki kaichū kōshō [Shi ji].* Taipei: Hongshi, 1977, 4.64–66.

Bo Ji, Wife of Duke Gong of Song

Bo Ji, the Older Woman of the Ji Clan (Song Gong Bo Ji), fl. early sixth century B.C.E., was the daughter of Duke Xuan (Xuan Gong, r. 608–591 B.C.E.) and Mu Jiang (*q.v.*) of the small state of Lu (in present-day Shandong Province) and a younger sister of Duke Cheng (Cheng Gong, r. 590–573). She is credited with unwavering obedience to the rules of propriety for women.

The first instance of her devotion to propriety related to her marriage in 582 to Duke Gong (Gong Gong, r. 588–575) of Song, a state that was slightly larger than and just to the south of Lu. Her intended husband did not come personally to welcome her when she arrived as a bride and, perceiving this to be a slight and a breach of protocol, she later refused to attend the ancestral temple for the completion of the marriage rites. Only after her widowed mother intervened did she comply. The second, fatal, instance took place in 543. The house in which she was staying caught fire one night, but she refused to leave until the matron and the governess arrived to

8 BO JI

accompany her out of the building, as required by the rules of righteousness. The matron arrived in time, but the governess did not and Bo Ji chose to remain and die in the fire, thereby attaining glory in the eyes of later Confucian scholars like Liu Xiang, author of *Biographies of Eminent Women* (Lienü zhuan). The fact that Liu Xiang praised this kind of extreme behavior on the part of women must surely have contributed to the appearance in late imperial China of the chastity cult. It is said that the state of Song was indemnified for Bo Ji's death while she herself was immortalized when her biography was included in "Biographies of the Chaste and Obedient" in *Biographies of Eminent Women.*

Bo Ji's death in the fire is also recorded in the *Zuo zhuan,* where the comment is made that in insisting on waiting for instructions at a time of crisis she had behaved more like a young girl than a married woman. In other words, she would have been justified in leaving the burning house alone: she had been a widow for nearly thirty years and must have been in her fifties at the time of her death.

Constance A. COOK

Chunqiu and *Zuo zhuan.* Cheng 9, Xiang 30. *Chunqiu jing zhuan yinde.* Shanghai: Guji shudian, 1983, 228, 330.
Legge, James, trans. *The Chinese Classics, Vol. 5: The Ch'un ts'ew, with the Tso chuen.* Hong Kong: Hong Kong University Press, 1960; 1970, 555, 556.
Liu Xiang. *Lienü zhuan.* Sibubeiyao ed., 4.1b–2a.
O'Hara, Albert R. *The Position of Woman in Early China According to the Lieh Nü Chuan, "The Biographies of Chinese Women."* Taipei: Mei Ya, 1971; 1978, 103–6.

Bo Ying, Wife of King Ping of Chu

Bo Ying (Chu Ping Bo Ying), fl. sixth century B.C.E., belonged to the Ying clan and was the daughter of a duke, possibly Duke Ai (Ai Gong, r. 538–501 B.C.E.), of Qin (present-day Shaanxi Province). She was married out to King Ping (Ping Wang, r. 528–516 B.C.E.) of Chu, a large state in what is now central China north of the Yangzi River, and her son became the ruler of Chu as King Zhao (Zhao Wang, r. 515–489 B.C.E.) upon the death of his father. When Wu (a state in the eastern region of present-day Jiangsu and Anhui provinces) captured the Chu capital of Ying (in present-day Hubei Province), King Zhao fled to his mother's homeland of Qin in the northwest. Upon entering the capital, the victorious king of Wu took for himself all of King Zhao's concubines and was about to take King Zhao's mother as well. With great courage, however, she took up a sword and threatened suicide: "All you desire to get from me is pleasure; if you draw near to me, I will die. What pleasure will you have, if you first kill me?" Admonishing the king of Wu for having cast aside his principles, she told him that for a woman to "have one husband is to be exalted, to have two husbands is to be disgraced" (O'Hara, 116), and that she would die if necessary to preserve her chastity. The shamed victor placed her under guard in the women's quarters for a month, by which time her son had returned with reinforcements. She is praised for being constant in her devotion to one husband and is certainly to be admired for her courageous refusal to submit meekly to what would now be considered rape. Her biography is included in "Biographies of the Chaste and Obedient" in *Biographies of Eminent Women* (Lienü zhuan).

Constance A. COOK

Liu Xiang. *Lienü zhuan.* Sibubeiyao ed., 4.5b–6a.
O'Hara, Albert R. *The Position of Woman in Early China According to the Lieh Nü Chuan, "The Biographies of Chinese Women."* Taipei: Mei Ya, 1971; 1978, 115–17.

The Bow Artisan of Jin's Wife
The Wife of the Bow Artisan of Jin (Jin Gonggong Qi), fl. sixth century B.C.E., was the daughter of an official in the state of Jin (in the north of the present-day provinces of Shanxi-Hebei). She saved her husband, who was the bow-maker for Duke Ping (Ping Gong, r. 557–532 B.C.E.), from execution by explaining to the duke that it was not because of the quality of the bow her husband had made that the Duke's arrows did not pierce the target but because of the duke's poor technique. She taught the duke proper technique, and so pleased was he with his subsequent success that he rewarded her with money and released her husband. Her biography is included in "Biographies of Those Able in Reasoning and Understanding" in *Biographies of Eminent Women* (Lienü zhuan).

Constance A. COOK

Liu Xiang. *Lienü zhuan.* Sibubeiyao ed., 6.2b–3b.
O'Hara, Albert R. *The Position of Woman in Early China According to the Lieh Nü Chuan, "The Biographies of Chinese Women."* Taipei: Mei Ya, 1971; 1978, 157–59.

Bow-Maker of Chin, The Wife of the: *see* **The Bow Artisan of Jin's Wife**

C

Cai Ren zhi Qi: *see* **Man of Cai's Wife**

Cao Xi zhi Qi: *see* **Xi Clan Head's Wife**

Chao She, The Wife of: *see* **General Zhao Gua's Mother**

Chao, Wife of the King of Tai, The Lady née: *see* **Zhao, Wife of the King of Dai**

Charioteer of the Minister of Ch'i, Wife of: *see* **Wife of the Chariot Driver for Yanzi, Minister of Qi**

10 CHI, NÉE FAN OF KING CHUANG OF CH'U

Chi, née Fan of King Chuang of Ch'u: *see* Fan Ji, Wife of King
Zhuang of Chu

Chi of Duke Mu of Ch'in: *see* Ji-Clan Woman, Wife of Duke Mu of Qin

Chi of Wei, Wife of Duke Huan of Ch'i: *see* Wei Ji, Wife of Duke
Huan of Qi

Ch'i Shih of Lu, The Woman of: *see* Qishi Woman of Lu

Chiang I of Ch'u, The Mother of: *see* Jiang Yi of Chu's Mother

Chiang of Ch'i, Wife of Duke Wen of Chin: *see* Jiang-Clan Woman of
Qi, Wife of Duke Wen of Jin

Chiang of Ch'u, the Chaste, of Chao: *see* Pure Jiang, Wife of King
Zhao of Chu

Chiang of Duke Hsuan of Wei: *see* Xuan Jiang, Wife of
Duke Xuan of Wei

Chiang, Queen of King Hsüan of the Chou Dynasty: *see* Jiang, Queen
of King Xuan of Zhou

Chiang Yuan: *see* Tai Jiang

Chieh Yü of the Kingdom of Ch'u, The Wife of: *see* Jieyu's Wife, and
The Wife of Yuling Zizhong of Chu

Ch'ien Lou of Lu, The Wife of: *see* Qian Lou of Lu's Wife

Chien Ti, the Mother of Hsieh: *see* Jiandi

Ching Chiang née Chi of the State of Lu: *see* Jing Jiang

Ching, the Concubine of Kuan Chung of Ch'i: *see* Jing, Concubine of
Minister Guan Zhong of Qi

Ch'iu of Lu, The Chaste Wife of: *see* Qiu Hu's Wife, the Pure Woman

Chong Er, Wife of: *see* Jiang-Clan Woman of Qi, Wife of Duke Wen of Jin

Chou Family, The Three Mothers of the: *see* Tai Jiang: Tai Ren; Tai
Si, Wife of King Wen of Zhou

Chou-nan, The Woman of: *see* The Official from Zhounan's Wife

CONCUBINE NÉE YU OF WEI OF CH'I 11

Chu Cheng Zheng Mao: *see* Zheng Mao, Wife of King Cheng of Chu

Chu Chu Zhuang Xing: *see* Zhuang Zhi, Wife of King Qingxiang of Chu

Chu Jiang Yi Mu: *see* Jiang Yi of Chu's Mother

Chu Jieyu Qi: *see* Jieyu's Wife, and The Wife of Yuling Zizhong of Chu

Chu Lao Lai Qi: *see* Lao Laizi's Wife

Chu of Chou, The Faithful Maid Servant of: *see* The Loyal Maid of Zhu of Zhou

Chu Ping Bo Ying: *see* Bo Ying, Wife of King Ping of Chu

Ch'ü Wu of Wei, The Old Woman of: *see* The Crone of Quwo of Wei

Chu Ye Bian Nü: *see* Discerning Woman of the Chu Wilds

Chu Yuling Qi: *see* Jieyu's Wife, and The Wife of Yuling Zizhong of Chu

Chu Zhao Yue Ji: *see* Yue Ji, Wife of King Zhao of Chu

Chu Zhao Zhen Jiang: *see* Pure Jiang, Wife of King Zhao of Chu

Chu Zhuang Fan Ji: *see* Fan Ji, Wife of King Zhuang of Chu

Chuan, the Woman of the Ferry in Chao: *see* Juan, Daughter of an Official of the Ford of Zhao

Chuang, a Woman of Ch'u, The Niece of: *see* Zhuang Zhi, Wife of King Qingxiang of Chu

Chuang Chiang: *see* Instructress for the Daughter of Qi

Chuang of Li, The Wife of Duke: *see* Duke Zhuang of Li's Wife

Chuang of Wei, Wife of Duke: *see* Instructress for the Daughter of Qi

Chung Tzu, Wife of Duke Ling of Ch'i: *see* Zhong Zi, Wife of Duke Ling of Qi

Chung-li Ch'un of Ch'i: *see* Zhongli Chun of Qi, Wife of King Xuan of Qi

Concubine née Yu of Wei of Ch'i, The: *see* Yu Ji, Wife of King Wei of Qi

The Crone of Quwo of Wei

The Crone of Quwo (Wei Quwo Fu), fl. late fourth century B.C.E., lived in Quwo in the state of Wei (in present-day Shaanxi Province) during the time of King Ai (Ai Wang, r. 318–296 B.C.E.). Her son, Ru'er, a minister in the government, did not dare censure King Ai when he took for himself the beautiful young woman sent in marriage to his son and heir apparent Zheng. The Crone described the king as "a mediocre man" who lacked discretion and righteousness and told her son Ru'er it was his duty as a loyal subject to admonish the ruler. Ru'er claimed he could not find the opportunity to broach the subject, however, and let it rest when he was sent as an envoy to the state of Qi (in present-day Shandong Province). Concerned that Wei was surrounded by powerful enemies, The Crone gained an audience with the king and explained the proper relations between the sexes. She told him he had "disrupted the basic principles of man, and . . . cast aside the duties of governmental principles" (O'Hara, 99). Without demurring, the king gave the concubine back to his son, rewarded The Crone with grain, and promoted Ru'er to the nobility. Thereafter, King Ai was said to have been "without hostile soldiers about him" (O'Hara, 100). While it is highly likely that the long-winded sermon attributed to The Crone of Quwo was composed later by highly educated Confucian scholars, The Crone herself appears to have been a historical character who may well have taken the courageous step of confronting her ruler about his unacceptable behavior. Her biography is included in "Biographies of the Benign and Wise" in *Biographies of Eminent Women* (Lienü zhuan).

Constance A. COOK

Liu Xiang. *Lienü zhuan*. Sibubeiyao ed., 3.9b–10b.
O'Hara, Albert R., *The Position of Woman in Early China According to the Lieh Nü Chuan, "The Biographies of Chinese Women."* Taipei: Mei Ya, 1971; 1978, 97–100.

D

Da Si: *see* **Tai Si, Wife of King Wen of Zhou**

Dai Zhao Furen: *see* **Zhao, Wife of the King of Dai**

Dazi, Conqueror of Tao, The Wife of: *see* **Dazi of Tao's Wife**

Dazi of Tao's Wife

The Wife of Dazi (Tao Dazi Qi), dates unknown, was married to a man named Dazi who had taken several years to subjugate Tao (in present-day Shanxi Province) before becoming a powerful official of the state. He did not, however, enjoy a good reputation, and his wife is remembered for admonishing him as being a man of little talent and merit who had become wealthy at the expense of the people: "My husband's ability is small and his position great; this is called 'stirring up trouble.' . . . At present, my husband is ruling Tao [as a high official]. His family is wealthy and the kingdom is poor" (O'Hara, 63–64). She predicted that ruin would come to one such as he, who was neither respected by his ruler nor loved by the people, and she fled with her son when her mother-in-law angrily threw her out. When Dazi and his family were eventually overthrown and killed, as she had foreseen, the wife returned to care for her mother-in-law, the only member of the family to have been spared and, ironically, the woman who had forced her to flee in the first place. This tale commends the Wife of Dazi for her foresight and outspokenness; more importantly, however, it commends her for returning to care for her elderly mother-in-law, thus fulfilling the duty of a woman toward the family into which she marries. Her story is included in "Biographies of the Virtuous and Wise" in *Biographies of Eminent Women* (Lienü zhuan).

Constance A. COOK

Liu Xiang. *Lienü zhuan.* Sibubeiyao ed., 2.6a–b.
O'Hara, Albert R. *The Position of Woman in Early China According to the Lieh Nü Chuan, "The Biographies of Chinese Women."* Taipei: Mei Ya, 1971; 1978, 63–65.

Deng Man: *see* **Man-Clan Woman of Deng, Wife of King Wu of Chu**

Ding Jiang, Wife of Duke Ding of Wei
Ding Jiang (Wei Gu Ding Jiang) was a woman of the Jiang clan and an Elder Female of Wei. She was the wife of Ding (r. 588–577 B.C.E.), the ruler of Wei, a state located in the region bounded by the present-day provinces of Henan, Shaanxi, Shanxi, and Hebei. Ding Jiang's son died very soon after he married and her daughter-in-law remained childless. Ding Jiang accompanied her daughter-in-law part of the way as the young woman set out to return to her natal home, and the poem she composed at their sad parting outside the city has been preserved in *The Book of Songs* (Shi jing):

> Swallow, swallow, on your flight,
> Now up, now down.
> Our lady that goes home,
> Far we go with her.
> Gaze after her, cannot see her,
> And stand here weeping. (Waley, 107)

Ding Jiang was intelligent, politically aware, and capable of advising her husband to agree when the powerful minister Sun Linfu wanted to return to Wei from exile in Jin. Despite her son having died young, she remained a powerful presence in Wei after her husband's death. The next ruler, the son of one of her husband's concubines, was a cruel and violent man who treated her poorly; Ding Jiang was able to have him exiled because of his violent behavior and to set up his younger brother as ruler. After Wei had successfully deflected an invasion by the state of Zheng in 563 B.C.E., Sun Linfu, the minister she had advised her husband to allow to return to Wei, consulted her about the proper interpreta-

14 DING JIANG

tion of divination results regarding military strategy. He, too, followed her advice and secured a victory. Nothing further is known of this woman, except that her literary works are described as elegant. Her biography is included in "Biographies Illustrating the Correct Deportment of Mothers" in *Biographies of Eminent Women* (Lienü zhuan).

Constance A. COOK

Liu Xiang. *Lienü zhuan*, Sibubeiyao ed., 1.5a–6a.
O'Hara, Albert R. *The Position of Woman in Early China According to the Lieh Nü Chuan, "The Biographies of Chinese Women."* Taipei: Mei Ya, 1971; 1978, 25–28.
Qu Wanli. *Shijing shiyi*. Mao no. 28. Taipei: Huagang, 1977, 110–11.
Waley, Arthur. *The Book of Songs*. London: George Allen & Unwin, 1937; 1969, 107.

The Discerning Woman of the Chu Wilds

The Discerning Woman of the Chu Wilds (Chu Ye Bian Nü), fl. sixth century B.C.E., is known by this epithet because she stood up for herself when an official from a neighboring state tried to bully her on a narrow road and she successfully argued her case against him. She had married into the Zhao family and was possibly the wife of Zhao Qujing, a member of the Chu aristocracy (Chu was a state in central China north of the Yangzi River).

The woman had been traveling alone, apparently driving her own carriage, and had pulled over to her side of the road to let another carriage pass. The two vehicles collided, however, causing the axle of the other carriage to break. The occupant of the other carriage—an emissary on official business for Duke Jian (Jian Gong, r. 564–530 B.C.E.) of the small state of Zheng (in present-day Henan Province)—became angry and was about to seize the woman and whip her. She argued, however, that it would hurt him more than it would hurt her if he punished her instead of his own driver, who, she said, was to blame for the accident because he had not made the slightest attempt to pull his carriage to one side. She thus extricated herself from a beating by shaming the official for his ungentlemanly behavior of becoming angry and shifting the blame for what had happened onto her. It is evident that the two people involved in this argument belonged to the same social, stratum, for while it was clearly ungentlemanly for the official to blame the woman, it was perfectly acceptable for her to "politely place the blame on the official's servant and not on the official himself." The woman went on to point out that by bullying her—a weak woman—the official was violating the teachings of old. So impressed was the official by this woman that he asked her to go with him to Zheng; she declined, saying she was already married. Her biography is included in "Biographies of Those Able in Reasoning and Understanding" in *Biographies of Eminent Women* (Lienü zhuan).

Constance A. COOK

Liu Xiang. *Lienü zhuan*. Sibubeiyao ed., 6.4b–5a.
O'Hara, Albert R. *The Position of Woman in Early China According to the Lieh Nü Chuan, "The Biographies of Chinese Women."* Taipei: Mei Ya, 1971; 1978, 161–63.

Discriminating Woman of the Wastelands of Ch'u, The: *see*
Discerning Woman of the Chu Wilds

Duke Mu of Xu's Wife

The Wife of Duke Mu (Xu Mu Furen), fl. c. 660 B.C.E., was the daughter of an illicit union between Xuan Jiang (*q.v.*) and Zhao Bo of Wei (in present-day Shanxi Province). In a later version of her tale, she is described as the daughter (or younger sister) of Duke Yi (Yi Gong, r. 668–660 B.C.E.) of Wei. She had originally advised her father to marry her to the ruler of Qi (present-day Shandong Province) in order to cement an alliance with that larger and more powerful state. Unfortunately, her father ignored her advice and married her out instead to Duke Mu (Mu Gong, r. 712–656 B.C.E.) of Xu (a small state to the southeast of Wei) around 671. Not long afterward, soldiers from the principality of Zhai to the west (or, in some sources, the Di tribe) wiped out almost the entire population of her home state of Wei. The Wife of Duke Mu is credited with composing the ode "Zai chi," which tells of her galloping home to comfort her father after this disastrous defeat and of her husband's neglect as well as her desire to return to Wei:

> I ride home, I gallop
> To lay my plaint before the lord of Wei,
> I gallop my horses on and on
> Till I come to Ts'ao.
> A great Minister, post-haste!
> How sad my heart.
> He [my husband in Xu] no longer delights in me;
> I cannot go back.
> And now, seeing how ill you use me,
> Surely my plan is not far-fetched! (Waley, 94)

She is commended for her "kind graciousness and her far-reaching knowledge" (O'Hara, 79), sadly proven by her prediction that Wei was vulnerable to attack without the backing of a powerful ally. Scholars in mainland China now interpret her poem as an expression of her strong love for her native land and hail her as a patriotic poet. Her biography is included in "Biographies of the Benign and Wise" in *Biographies of Eminent Women* (Lienü zhuan).

Constance A. COOK

Liu Shisheng. *Zhongguo gudai funüshi*. Qingdao: Qingdao chubanshe, 1991, 53–54.
Liu Xiang. *Lienü zhuan*. Sibubeiyao ed., 3.2a–b.
O'Hara, Albert R. *The Position of Woman in Early China According to the Lieh Nü Chuan, "The Biographies of Chinese Women."* Taipei: Mei Ya, 1971; 1978, 78–79.
Qu Wanli. *Shijing shiyi*. Mao no. 54. Taipei: Huagang, 1977, 40–41.
Waley, Arthur. *The Book of Songs*. Boston: Houghton Mifflin, 1937, 94.
Zuo zhuan. Min 2. Taipei: Fenghuang chubanshe, 1977, vol. 1, 83.

Duke Zhuang of Li's Wife

The Wife of Duke Zhuang of Li (Li Zhuang Furen), dates unknown, was the daughter of Archer-Lord of Wei (in the north of present-day Henan Province). She was sent in marriage to the neighboring state of Li (in present-day Shanxi Province), but her husband completely ignored her; he would not even receive her. He is said to have had "different desires," and since no mention is made of other wives or concubines it is quite probable that he kept her at a distance because he was homosexual and could not face the prospect of marriage to a woman. Despite the counsel of her governess that she should leave him, the wife upheld the vows of the Way of Woman (*fudao*) and stayed, awaiting her husband's command, which never came: "Although [he] has not treated me as his wife, how can I depart from the duty of the wife?" (O'Hara, 109). Her determination is associated with Ode no. 36, "Shi Wei," preserved in *The Book of Songs* (Shi jing):

> How few of us are left, how few!
> Why do we not go back?
> Were it not for our prince and his concerns,
> What should we be doing here in the dew? (Waley, 113)

Since she remained faithful to one husband rather than returning to her natal home, her biography is included in "Biographies of the Chaste and Obedient" in *Biographies of Eminent Women* (Lienü zhuan) and over the centuries was used as a didactic tool by those who wished women to remain loyal in a loveless marriage.

Constance A. COOK

Liu Xiang. *Lienü zhuan*. Sibubeiyao ed., 4.3a–b.
O'Hara, Albert R. *The Position of Woman in Early China According to the Lieh Nü Chuan, "The Biographies of Chinese Women."* Taipei: Mei Ya, 1971; 1978, 108–9.
Qu Wanli. *Shijing shiyi*. "Shi wei," Mao no. 36. Taipei: Huagang, 1977, 27.
Waley, Arthur. *The Book of Songs*. London: George Allen & Unwin, 1937; 1969, 113.

E

Egu Chunü: *see* The Virgin of Egu

Ehuang and Nüying

Ehuang and Nüying are legendary figures from China's prehistory. Sisters, they were daughters of the sage king Yao, who gave them as wives to his eventual successor, the sage king Shun (also known as Youyu), whom he recognized as a man of great virtue. These men are said to have ruled China in the third millennium B.C.E., before the Xia dynasty (which dates approximately 2100 to 1600 B.C.E.).

As daughters of the ruler, Ehuang and Nüying were considered to be of royal blood, yet they displayed neither arrogance nor willfulness when they became wives to Shun, who was then still a farmer. Instead, they managed his household frugally and with great diligence and were extremely loyal to him. Shun's father, stepmother, and two younger stepbrothers attempted several times to murder him, although no reasons are offered in traditional sources for their vicious behavior. Shun managed to escape a fiery death when the granary he had been sent to repair was deliberately set alight; by preparing an escape tunnel beforehand he avoided being buried alive after being sent to deepen a well; by drinking a potion that Ehuang and Nüying had prepared for him he foiled his father's plan to make him drunk and then kill him.

Yao eventually appointed Shun a prime minister yet still set many tests for him, each of which Shun discussed with Ehuang and Nüying before passing them. Upon Yao's death, Shun succeeded him and continued to consult his two wives on affairs of state. Ehuang, the elder sister, became his queen and Nüying became his concubine; in some sources Nüying is referred to as Royal Wife. Shun fell ill while on a tour of inspection and he died at Cangwu (in present-day Guangxi Province). Apparently not knowing what had happened to him, Ehuang and Nüying set out together to find him, but they died somewhere between the Yangzi River and the Xiang River, in what is now Hunan Province. In one version of their story, they threw themselves into the Xiang River and drowned when they discovered that Shun had died. This may be why they are sometimes referred to as the Queen of Xiang (Xiang Jun) and the Lady of Xiang (Xiang Furen). Some scholars, however, believe that Xiang Jun and Xiang Furen were two goddesses of the Xiang River completely unrelated to Shun's wives. Liu Xiang gave pride of place to the story of Ehuang and Nüying, which he titled The Two Consorts of Youyu (Youyu Er Fei), putting it first in "Biographies Illustrating the Correct Deportment of Mothers," the first chapter of his *Biographies of Eminent Women* (Lienü zhuan).

Legend has it that the reddish spots on the stalks of a bamboo called Xiang Consorts Bamboo (*xiangfeizhu*) that still grows in Hunan are Ehuang's and Nüying's tears of blood.

Laura LONG

Cihai. Zuixin zengding ed. Taipei: Taiwan Zhonghua shuju, 1980, 2.2744.
Liu Xiang. *Lienü zhuan*, Sibubeiyao ed., 1.1a–2a.
O'Hara, Albert R. *The Position of Woman in Early China According to the Lieh Nü Chuan, "The Biographies of Chinese Women."* Taipei: Mei Ya, 1971; 1978, 13–17.
"Zhongshan jing." in *Shanhai jing*. Sibucongkan ed., 5.32a–b.

Elder Female of Wei: *see* **Ding Jiang, Wife of Duke Ding of Wei**

F

Fan Ji, Wife of King Zhuang of Chu

Fan Ji, a woman of the Ji clan from Fan (Chu Zhuang Fan Ji), fl. late seventh century B.C.E., was the wife of King Zhuang (Zhuang Wang, r. 613–591 B.C.E.) of Chu, an ancient state located in the middle reaches of the Yangzi River. She is known for curbing

18 FAN JI

her husband's fondness for hunting by refusing to eat meat. We know from historical texts that the significance of this is that King Zhuang had made it clear that anyone who remonstrated with him did so on pain of death. Fan Ji's strategy was effective because she managed to remonstrate with him without angering him. She is also known for encouraging the selection of capable beauties as his concubines without herself becoming jealous that they might supplant her as his favorite. She is said to have drawn a contrast between her behavior in this matter and that of Yu Qiuzi, one of her husband's ministers, who appointed to office only members of his own clan. She told her husband that Yu Qiuzi's blatant nepotism had prevented the appointment of worthy men from other families. King Zhuang listened to what his wife had to say and changed this policy. He was thus able to enlist the aid of Sunshu Ao to oversee his officials and became the most powerful feudal lord of Chu. So influential was King Zhuang's wife that it is said his reign was "by the strength of Fan Ji." Her biography is included in "Biographies of the Virtuous and Wise" in *Biographies of Eminent Women* (Lienü zhuan).

Constance A. COOK

Guan Siping. *Houfei de mingyun*. Qingdao: Shandong chubanshe, 1991, 64–68.
Han shi waizhuan. Congshu jicheng ed. Taipei: Taiwan shangwu yinshuguan, 1965, 2.12f.
Kralle, Jianfei. "Fan Ji und Wei Ji." in *Die Frau im Alten China. Bild und Wirklichkeit*. Stuttgart: Steiner, 2001, 53–73.
Liu Shisheng. *Zhongguo gudai funüshi*. Qingdao: Qingdao chubanshe, 1991, 55.
Liu Xiang. Lienü zhuan. Sibubeiyao ed., 2.3b–4a.
O'Hara, Albert R. *The Position of Woman in Early China According to the Lieh Nü Chuan, "The Biographies of Chinese Women."* Taipei: Mei Ya, 1971; 1978, 56–58.
Shi ji. Beijing: Zhonghua shuju, 1973, 41.1700.

Female Ruler of the West: *see* **Queen Mother of the West**

Foxi of Zhao's Mother
The Mother of Foxi (Zhao Foxi Mu), fl. late fifth century B.C.E., is remembered for having saved herself from being killed as punishment for a rebellion led by her son. Her son, Foxi, was the steward and overseer of Zhongmou (the present-day city of Kaifeng in Henan Province) in Zhao (a small state in the south of the present-day provinces of Shandong and Shanxi), and he and his entire household were sentenced to death after the unsuccessful rebellion of Zhongmou against the state of Zhao. The Mother of Foxi protested, however, saying that she did not deserve to be put to death: "I ought not to die." The ruler of Zhao granted her an audience, during which she explained to him that the behavior of her son once he was an adult was the ruler's responsibility and no longer hers: "I raised my son, but you yourself chose him as your minister. . . . This minister of the king is not my son. I did not have a violent son; you have a violent minister." Besides, she pointed out, propriety obliged her as a widow to obey her son, not the other way round. The ruler was impressed and persuaded by her argument and released her without punishment. Her biography is included

in "Biographies of Those Able in Reasoning and Understanding" in *Biographies of Eminent Women* (Lienü zhuan).

Constance A. COOK

Liu Xiang. *Lienü zhuan*. Sibubeiyao ed., 6.7a–b.
Lunyu. "Yanghuo," 17. in Zhuzi jicheng. Shanghai: Shanghai shudian, 1986, vol. 1, 371.
O'Hara, Albert R. *The Position of Woman in Early China According to the Lieh Nü Chuan, "The Biographies of Chinese Women."* Taipei: Mei Ya, 1971; 1978, 167–69.

Fu Hao: *see* **Fu Zi, the Shang Woman Warrior**

Fu Zi, the Shang Woman Warrior
Fu Zi, or Noble Daughter Zi (Noble Daughter surnamed Child), is the most distinguished and powerful woman known in Shang history (ca. 1600–1100 B.C.E.); she is commonly referred to as Fu Hao in received literature. She lived a full life as a prominent queen mother and favorite consort (consort may be taken to be wife here, although Fu Zi's husband had more than one) as well as a heroic military leader, landowner, and administrator. Fu Zi was the most prominent of three queens betrothed to King Wu Ding of the Late Shang period. Wu Ding allegedly ruled for fifty-nine years during the thirteenth century B.C.E. from ancient Yinxu (present-day Anyang), located in what is now northern Henan Province. Fu Zi was posthumously revered as Queen Mother Xin (Hou Mu Xin), as Mother Xin (Mu Xin), and as Ancestress Xin (Bi Xin). She was awarded the status of queen after giving birth to her son and heir apparent Zu Ji, the first male offspring in line to succeed Wu Ding. Zu Ji died prematurely, before his father and mother, and before his father's second and third consorts, Queen Mother Gui (Hou Mu Gui) and Queen Mother Wu (Hou Mu Wu).

Archeological data and written sources in the form of oracle bone and bronze inscriptions provide a wealth of material to assess the historic significance of Fu Zi in Late Shang society. Her burial site was excavated in the fall of 1975 and 1976 at Xiaotun, south of the Late Shang royal cemetery at Xibeigang in modern Anyang or ancient Yin. Fu Zi's tomb was 5.6 m long, 4 m wide, and 5.7 m deep—considerably smaller than her husband's—and was undisturbed and intact before being excavated. Remains of a rectangular columned hall at ground level above her tomb indicate that a memorial structure was built and used by royal kin to honor her spirit. Of the 1,600-odd burial objects uncovered from her tomb, 460 were bronzes and 160 are inscribed Fu Zi, two graphs signifying her name and title, and her signature of ownership while alive. Other bronzes and artworks were inscribed with her posthumous title Queen Mother Xin. Still other bronzes were inscribed Queen Mother Qiao/Tu(?) Gui, the posthumous title and name of a former royal consort, possibly a wife of the thirteenth Shang king Zu Ding, and a queen on Fu Zi's maternal side.

As illustrated in bone and bronze inscriptions, Zi appears to have been a friendly (to the Shang) state and family name, located in today's Fen River valley in southwestern Shanxi Province.

20 FU ZI

The "frontier-style" bronze mirrors, socketed adzes, and ring-handled bronze knives found in Fu Zi's tomb are most likely to have been personal acquisitions or martial booty taken after or in honor of victorious battles rather than evidence that she was from a non-Shang background in the northwest of ancient China. Fu Zi was the most heroic of Shang female generals and spent much of her time defending the Shang's northwest frontier from the hostile Qiang and from other invasive and unfriendly tribal groups elsewhere along Shang's northeastern and southern borders. Her royal origins may be traceable to the earliest of Shang times.

Fu Zi was the first of the first-generation queens to receive ongoing royal ancestor cult sacrifices during the Late Shang period. The large pair of tetrapod *ding* meat vessels and the pair of tetrapod *gong* fermented beverage tureens inscribed Queen Mother Xin were most likely vessels commissioned and inscribed by her son Zu Ji, known to history as Filial Ji (Xiao Ji) and in King Wu Ding period inscriptions as Small King Ji (Xiao Wang Ji). Only kings and heirs apparent could own and use these large tetrapod *ding,* yet they were used in sacrificial rites addressed to both dead kings and queens.

Fu Zi's son and royal heir never succeeded to the throne, however. Filial Ji was a meritorious heir whose queen mother died prematurely, and for this reason, the histories state, he was banished: it is recorded in the *Bamboo Annals* (Zhushu jinian) that "During Wu Ding's twenty-fifth year, Royal Son Filial Ji died in the wild." His early death is corroborated in Shang inscriptions, as is the early death of his mother. That Filial Ji did not succeed to the throne may explain why Queen Fu Zi's tomb is modest in size compared to that of her queen generational sister, Queen Wu, the third consort of King Wu Ding. Although a famous and loved queen mother, her early death and her son's banishment must have precipitated a demotion that affected the mode of her burial.

Fu Zi's royal status is amplified by an ancestor queen's title, Queen Qiao/Tu(?) Gui, frequently abbreviated to Queen Qiao/Tu(?) in inscriptions on twenty-eight large ritual bronze fermented beverage vessels found in her tomb. Queen Qiao/Tu(?) Gui was the object of worship rather than the subject or maker of the vessels. Thus, Fu Zi must have commissioned these bronzes and used them in sacrifices addressing her maternal ancestress Queen Qiao/Tu(?) Gui, who in other bone inscriptions is called Ancestress Gui (Bi Gui):

> Crack-making on the *yimao* day, Bin divined: Should [I] summon Fu Zi to make a human sacrifice to Ancestress Gui?

The twenty-eight large and extremely refined bronzes are stylistically the earliest in date among the tomb's bronzes and are comparable with those vessels inscribed Fu Zi, suggesting that they were cast during Fu Zi's lifetime for use in worshipping her maternal relative. Vessels inscribed Fu Zi were also used by Fu Zi in rites but were not limited in worship to one royal spirit. Fu Zi was in charge of a variety of ritual sacrifices to royal kin. It is also noteworthy that there are no vessels in her tomb inscribed with male royal titles. Thus, on the basis of current data, Fu Zi had royal pedigree, tied to a former queen named Queen Qiao/Tu(?) Gui as well as to a clan and state, Zi, intimately allied with the Shang royal house.

In addition to her preeminent social status as first queen of King Wu Ding, Fu Zi had an illustrious military and administrative career. She ranked second in command to the king, as exemplified by a series of inscriptions recording battles against various unfriendly border states. She led successful campaigns against the unfriendly states of Ba in the southwest, Hu in the south, Tu and Gong in the north, Qiang in the northwest, and Yi in the northeast. This skill in military leadership is unequaled in Shang bone inscriptions by any other ranking military leader.

The following divination shows Fu Zi called upon to lead the well-known Shang general Zhi Fa and meet King Wu Ding in ambushing the southern Ba Fang:

> Crack-making on *xinwei* day, Zheng divined: If Fu Zi joins and leads Zhi Fa to attack the Ba Fang should the King from the East attack in trapping [the enemy] in sunken pits at the flank (position) of Fu Zi? [It was divined:] If Fu Zi joins and leads Zhi Fa to attack the Ba Fang should the King not from the East attack in trapping [the enemy] in sunken pits at the flank of Fu Zi?

Fu Zi was clearly a general of the first rank. Her outstanding responsibilities as a military leader are also attested to by the fact she was capable of raising enormous numbers of warriors, particularly in attacks against the troublesome Qiang of the northwest. King Wu Ding divined and queried whether Fu Zi should be summoned to attack the Qiang if she raised 13,000 soldiers at Xi, a record number of warriors for any military member of Shang society to assemble, and unmatched in Shang bone inscriptions. The bone inscriptions also reveal that the Shang frequently sacrificed large numbers of Qiang people to ancestor and other spirits by various methods, whether through cooking, beheading, or burning. Since the Qiang were one of the Shang's most feared enemies and a constant source of worry, Fu Zi played a pivotal role in heroically raising a huge number of men to defend the Shang domain against them.

Fu Zi's military heroics are also corroborated by her participation in royal hunts, as suggested by reference to an accident she had on the hunting fields. In another hunting-related inscription, King Wu Ding calls upon Diviner Wei to query if Fu Zi should make an offering. For the Shang king the royal hunt was a key demonstration of his singular power over the animal and spirit world. This religio-political power symbol evidently also extended to royal family participating in the hunt, particularly his queen, Fu Zi.

The large number of weapons buried with Fu Zi is testimony to her military prowess. Of the four *yue*-broad axes, two are small memorial gifts. The other two are heraldically inscribed with two female graphs framing the Zi graph just below another heraldic image in relief, a human face framed by open mouths of two profile tigers. The latter image is the well-honed royal Shang symbol of metamorphic power—human power to identify with and dominate the spirit realm of the hunted animal. These bronze *yue* are royal in size, suggesting that this pair of *yue* halberds distinguishes Fu Zi with the royal status of queen, as it characterizes her as woman warrior par excellence. The large number of

22 *FU ZI*

bronze *ge* dagger axes in her tomb, ninety-one in all, belong to four different types. Two of the types—the group of bronze *ge* with inlaid turquoise handles and decorated blades, and the second group with inlaid turquoise bronze handles and jade blades—are believed to have functioned as insignia, status symbols. The remaining three groups—thirty-six *ge* of the standard type with hooked handle, eight *ge* of another standard type with straight handle, and two *ge* with open socket handles—in most cases have clearly been used and have the remains of wooden handles. The use and ownership of so many *ge* daggers, forty-six in all, again underscores Fu Zi's military prowess in action.

In life, Fu Zi ranked second-in-command to King Wu Ding. Nonetheless, as with other royal house members, she paid tribute to the king in providing tortoise plastrons, cleaned and prepared for use in divination, and in providing harvest crops, theoretically from her estate of Zi but also from several tributary states.

Fu Zi received tribute and gifts from various Shang and distant state elites. As noted above, the uninscribed bronze knives, adzes, and mirrors of the type produced by or for northwest tribal groups in Fu Zi's tomb represent booty she collected on her northwestern campaigns, or perhaps keepsakes from her northwestern homeland. The calligraphically lyrical "phoenix"-shaped jade, the thick jade stick-pin of a bird with folded wings and tail feathers, and the jade disk fragment with notches derive from the Shandong and Shijiahe Longshan period, and thus represent imports or martial acquisitions from either northeast Shandong or south Hubei Province. A variety of small reworked late Neolithic period Hongshan jades, including a suspended ornament in an oval shape with two fangs, a comma-shaped handle, and a small horned animal mask, are in turn either trade items and heirlooms or booty from the far north in Liaoning or southeastern Inner Mongolia. In addition, a small black jade human head is similar in type to examples from the southwestern site of Shang-period Jinsha in Sichuan, suggesting acquisition at the time of her campaign against the southwestern Ba Fang.

In addition to these small artworks, illustrating contact with border cultures, are the numerous inscribed vessels that were either tribute or gifts proffered to Fu Zi. One piece of tribute is a large inscribed jade *ge* dagger blade, along with four other similar but uninscribed jade daggers in Fu Zi's tomb. The latter five daggers are jade insignia, probably delivered in recognition of Fu Zi's military leadership along the Shang's northwestern borders. Fu Zi also received tribute of a stone *sheng* chime from a high-ranking woman of the Zhu clan and state of northern Hebei. Two other bronzes, possibly also tribute but with inscriptions abbreviated to clan emblems on one vessel each, include the modest *jue* and the dragon-legged tripod *ding*. By far the most important gifts in Fu Zi's tomb derive from two elite royal house members (Ya Qi and Zi Shu Quan): twenty-two fermented beverage vessels, including a pair of round *zun,* a *jia,* and a set of ten *gu* and nine *jue,* and twenty-one fermented beverage vessels including a pair of large round *jia* and a set of ten *gu* and nine *jue.*

It is significant that the 111 vessels commissioned by Fu Zi are not limited to fermented beverage but include all sacrificial types—meat, grain, and water, in addition to fermented beverage—and those bronzes inscribed with Queen Mother Xin include the largest vessels, as represented by the pair of tetrapod *ding* meat-offering vessels, commissioned by her son Filial Ji.

Tribute gifts also come from another high-ranking male elite general (Ya Bi) who fought side by side with Fu Zi against the Qiang tribesmen. Vessels in Fu Zi's tomb inscribed with this general's name include a large-scale round tripod *ding* and a set of five *nao* bells and appear to have functioned as memorial gifts rather than as tribute, signifying Fu Zi's intimate connections with high-powered military personnel and royal family.

At present there is no intact excavated Shang tomb that can be used to compare with Fu Zi's to help in clarifying her special status as queen and military heroine. Nonetheless, on the basis of bone inscriptional evidence it is clear that she was revered as queen and militarily ranked second-in-command to Wu Ding. Her military power is also well illustrated by her burial goods, including tribute items from the highest-ranking members of the Shang elite and major clans within the Shang domain. It is evident that Fu Zi's influence was extensive in the northern Shang realm.

In addition to the enormous number of inscribed offerings in Fu Zi's tomb are sixteen sacrificial victims, mostly servants and guards, and five guardian dogs. These sacrificed victims are small in number by comparison to those hundreds sacrificed in Shang king burials. This enigmatic balance of rich ritual paraphernalia and tribute, yet modest burial pit and number of sacrificial humans, again is probably due to the fact that her son and heir did not occupy the Shang throne or survive to the time of his mother's burial.

Fu Zi also ranked second to the king as administrator. As with a few other generals and officials, she was commanded by King Wu Ding to send out royal emissaries, to hold royal audiences, and to supervise tributary harvests of border lands. Unlike others, however, she was also summoned to hold audience with the Many Royal Daughters (Duo Fu) and blind seers, but above all she was required to carry out sacrifices to dead ruling spirits. The most common places mentioned in connection with her administrative functions are sites located to the northwest of the Shang domain.

All of Fu Zi's sacrifices were carried out as a result of divinations by King Wu Ding and his retinue of diviners. Most of the extant divinations inscribed on oracle bones concerning sacrifices offered by Fu Zi are addressed to a limited number of royal spirits. The most frequent type of ceremony Fu Zi carried out was exorcism. It is wrong, however, to identify Fu Zi with the *shi fu,* the royal house female in charge of sacrifices referred to in ritual literature of the Warring States through Han eras, although her participatory role may have given rise to this position in later history. King Wu Ding was in charge of royal rites to ancestor spirits. Fu Zi responded to this charge by carrying out comparable sacrifices and rites, but always under the eye and command of King Wu Ding. As with the ancient Egyptians and Sumerians, the royal house was run by a group of powerful clans that operated under the authority of a king who was supreme religious and military head.

Finally, King Wu Ding's concern for every aspect of Fu Zi's life—health, childbirth, return from near and distant lands, military activities, harvests, royal audiences, death, and afterlife—testify to his overwhelming affection for his first queen. Fu Zi must have been involved in a life-threatening accident while hunting in Guo, a favorite hunting ground of King Wu Ding, after which she died. Her death and burial are both mentioned in early Wu Ding period inscriptions.

24 FU ZI

As revealed through the divinations of her husband, Wu Ding, and through the extensive collection of burial paraphernalia placed in her tomb, Fu Zi was a great woman warrior, second in command to her husband, and a great human being, unparalleled in Shang history.

Elizabeth CHILDS-JOHNSON

Cao Dingyun. *Yinxu Fu Hao Mu mingwen yanjiu.* Taipei: Wenjin chubanshe, 1993.

Chang Cheng-lang [Zhang Zhenglang]. "A Brief Discussion of Fu Tzu." In *Studies of Shang Archaeology*, ed. K.C. Chang [Zhang Guangzhi]. New Haven: Yale University Press, 1986, 103–19.

Chang Kwang-chih [Zhang Guangzhi]. "Yinxu Fuhao Mu yu Yinxu kaogu shang de Pan Geng, Xiao Xin, Xiao Yi shidai wenti." *Wenwu* 9 (1989) and Huaxia kaogu 2 (1989): 86–92.

Chen Zhida. "Fu Hao Mu ji qi xiangguan wenti." *Kaogu yu wenwu* 4 (1985): 53–56.

Childs-Johnson, Elizabeth. "Fu Zi: The Shang Woman Warrior." In *The Fourth International Conference on Chinese Paleography [ICCP] Proceedings.* The Chinese University of Hong Kong, October 15–17. Hong Kong: Chinese University of Hong Kong, 2003, 619–51.

———. "Identification of the Tomb Occupant and Periodization of M5," and "Excavation of Tomb No. 5 at Yinxu, Anyang." *Chinese Sociology and Anthropology* 15, no. 3 (1983): 1–131.

Chou, Hung-hsiang [Zhou Hongxiang]. "Fu-X Ladies of the Shang Dynasty." *Monumenta Serica* 19 (1970/71): 346–90.

Du Naisong. "Si Mu Wu Ding niandai wenti xintan." *Wenshizhe* 1 (1980): 63–64.

Hu Houxuan, Wang Yuxin, and Yang Shengnan. *Jiaguwen heji*, vols. 1–13. Beijing: Zhonghua shuju, 1978–1982.

Huang Tianshu. "Zi Zu buci yanjiu." *Zhongguo wenzi* 26 (1989) new series, 11–31.

Ikeda Suetoshi. *Inkyo shokei kōhen shakubun kō.* Hiroshima: Academic Institute of Hiroshima University, 1964.

Itō Michiharu. *Chūgoku kodai kokka no shihai kōzō.* Tokyo: Chūō Kōronsha, 1987.

Jao Tsung-i [Rao Zongyi]. "Fu: guanyu shifu wenti." *Guwenzi yanjiu* 12 (1985): 299–307.

Li Boqian. "Anyang Yinxu Fuhao Mu de niandai wenti." *Kaogu* 2 (1979): 165–70.

———. *Zhongguo qingtong wenhua jiegou tixi yanjiu.* Beijing: Kexue chubanshe, 1998.

Li Chi [Li Ji]. *Anyang.* Seattle: University of Washington Press, 1977.

Li Hsiao-ting [Li Xiaoding]. *Jiagu wenzi jishi.* 8 vols. Taipei: Zhongyang yanjiuyuan lishi yuyan yanjiusuo, 1965.

Li Xueqin. "Lun Fu Hao Mu de niandai ji youguan wenti." *Wenwu* 11 (1977): 32–37.

Linduff, Katheryn. "Art and Identity: The Chinese and Their 'Significant Others' in the Third and Second Millennium BC." In *Cultural Contact, History and Ethnicity in Inner Asia*, ed. Michael Gervers and Wayne Schlepp. Toronto: Joint Centre for Asia Pacific Studies, 1996, 12–48.

Shen Wu. "Fu Hao Mu yuqi cailiao tanyuan." *Zhongyuan wenwu* 1 (1991).

Shima Kunio. *Inkyo Bokuji Sōrui.* Rev. ed. Tokyo: Kyuuko, 1971.

———. *Yinxu buci yanjiu*, trans. Wen Tianhe and Li Shoulin. Taipei: Dingwen shuju, 1975.

Takashima, Ken-ichi. "Part Two: Language and Paleography." In *Studies in Early Chinese Civilization; Religion, Society, Language, and Palaeography.* 2 vols. Osaka: Kansai Gaidai University Press, 1996, 179–505.

Wang Yuxin. "Shilun Yinxu Wuhao Mu de niandai." *Zhengzhou daxue xuebao* 2 (1979).

Wang Yuxin, Zhang Yongshan, and Yang Shengnan. "Shilun Yinxu Wuhao Mu de Fu Hao." *Kaogu xuebao* 2 (1977): 1–22.

Yang Chia-luo [Yang Jialuo], ed. *Shi ji yinben ji shuzheng.* Taipei: Dingwen shuju, n.d.

Yang Hongxun. "Fu Hao Mu shang 'Mu Xin Zong' jianzhu fuyuan." *Wenwu* (1988): 62–66, 87.

Yao Xiaosui, ed. *Yinxu jiagu keci leizuan.* 3 vols. Beijing: Zhonghua shuju, 1989.

Yen Yi-p'ing [Yan Yiping]. "Fu Hao liezhuan." *Zhongguo wenzi* 3 (1981), new series, 1–104.
Zhang Peishan. "Anyang Yinxu Fu Hao Mu zhong yuqi baoshi de jianding." *Kaogu* 2 (1982): 204–61.
Zhang Yachu. "Dui Fu Hao zhi hao yu chengwei zhi hou de boxi." *Kaogu* 12 (1985): 1119–23.
Zheng Zhenxiang. "Fu Hao Mu bufen chengtao tongqi mingwen zhi tantao." *Kaogu* 10 (1985): 511–18.
———. "Fu Hao Mu chutu hou mian/tu mu mingwen tongqi de tantao." *Kaogu* 8 (1983): 940–47.
Zhongguo shehuikexueyuan kaogu yanjiusuo and Anyang gongzuo dui. "Anyang Yinxu Wuhao Mu zuotan jiyao." *Kaogu* 5 (1977): 341–50.
———. *Yinxu Fu Hao Mu.* Beijing: Wenwu chubanshe, 1980; and new volume, 1984.
Zhu Fenghan. "Lun buci yu Shang Zhou jinwen zhong de 'hou.'" *Zhongguo wenzi* 19 (1992): 422–43.

Fu-Hsi of Chao, Mother of: *see* **Foxi of Zhao's Mother**

Furen Jiang Shi: *see* **Ai Jiang, Wife of Duke Zhuang of Lu**

G

Gai General, Wife of the: *see* **The General of Gai's Wife**

Gai Jiang zhi Qi: *see* **The General of Gai's Wife**

Gao Xing, a Widow in Liang

Gao Xing (Liang Gua Gao Xing), dates unknown, was the title bestowed on a young widow who lived in the state of Liang (in present-day Shanxi Province). She was not interested in remarrying, determined to dedicate herself to raising her children and remaining faithful to her dead husband's memory. Her beauty attracted many suitors, however, including the king of Liang, who sent betrothal gifts to her. Eventually, she disfigured herself by cutting off her nose, and after this, as she had hoped, all talk of marriage ceased. It was at this point that the king bestowed on her the title Gao Xing (meaning "lofty behavior") as a mark of his esteem for her virtue. Her biography is included in "Biographies of the Chaste and Obedient" in *Biographies of Eminent Women* (Lienü zhuan) as an example for later generations of women of the "chaste, single-hearted, and pure" behavior expected of widows. Gao Xing's story is possibly the earliest example of self-mutilation, a practice that unfortunately gained something of a following in late imperial times.

Constance A. COOK

Liu Xiang. *Lienü zhuan.* Sibubeiyao ed., 4.8b–9a.
O'Hara, Albert R. *The Position of Woman in Early China According to the Lieh Nü Chuan, "The Biographies of Chinese Women."* Taipei: Mei Ya, 1971; 1978, 122–24.

The General of Gai's Wife

The Wife of the General of Gai (Gai Jiang zhi Qi), fl. eighth century B.C.E., is famous for using her own suicide both to teach her husband that suicide was proper behavior for a defeated general and to neutralize his fear of retribution against his family.

Gai was a small state within the larger state of Qi (present-day Shandong Province). After Rong armies from western China conquered it and killed the ruler they forbade the court officials of Gai to take their own lives, threatening to put to death the wives and children of any who disobeyed this order. The General of Gai nevertheless attempted suicide, only to be restrained by his companions. The response of the general's wife to this was to lecture him on the principles of being a filial and faithful general: "Now the army was defeated and the ruler died; how is it that you alone are alive? Fidelity and filial piety have perished in your person. How can you bear to come back here?" (O'Hara, 135). Brushing aside his excuse that he had wished to spare his wife and children, she told him that his public duty to serve his sovereign far outweighed his private love for his wife. "You have stolen your life and you are alive unjustly" (O'Hara, 136), she told him before she herself committed suicide. So impressed was the Rong ruler by her principled stand that he gave her a rich burial and employed her brothers in his new administration.

The sentiments expressed by the wife of the Gai General, that loyalty to the ruler and the state must always be placed above loyalty to wife and children, ensured that her biography was included in "Biographies of the Chaste and Righteous" in *Biographies of Eminent Women* (Lienü zhuan).

Constance A. COOK

Liu Xiang. *Lienü zhuan*. Sibubeiyao ed., 5.4a–b.
O'Hara, Albert R. *The Position of Woman in Early China According to the Lieh Nü Chuan, "The Biographies of Chinese Women."* Taipei: Mei Ya, 1971; 1978, 134–36.

General of Kai, The Wife of the: *see* The General of Gai's Wife

General Zhao Gua's Mother

The Mother of General Zhao Gua (Zhao Jiang Gua Mu), fl. third century B.C.E., lived in the state of Zhao (in present-day Shanxi Province). Her husband, Zhao She, was a general and lord of Mafu, a small fief in Zhao. When their son Zhao Gua, also a general, was ordered into battle she petitioned the king that he not be sent on the grounds that he was incompetent and greedy, unlike his father: "The father and the son are not alike; the grasp and the heart of each is different. I desire that you do not send him" (O'Hara, 100). The king insisted, however, so The Mother requested that when her son failed, as she was certain he would, she not be punished with death, as the family members of a defeated general would expect to be. Her son did indeed die in the battle against the Qin forces that took place in 246 B.C.E. and the Zhao army was wiped out. Thanks to The Mother's foresight, however, her family was not put to death for her son's failure. It is possible that The Mother of General Zhao Gua denigrated her son's abilities in an attempt to save him from certain defeat and death because she recognized the inevitability of the Zhao army's defeat by the all-conquering Qin armies. Whatever her motivation, at least she succeeded in saving her family, and her biography is included in "Biographies of the Benign and Wise" in *Biographies of Eminent Women* (Lienü zhuan).

Constance A. COOK

Liu Xiang. *Lienü zhuan*. Sibubeiyao ed., 3.10b–11a.
O'Hara, Albert R. *The Position of Woman in Early China According to the Lieh Nü Chuan, "The Biographies of Chinese Women."* Taipei: Mei Ya, 1971; 1978, 100–101.

The Goiter Girl of Qi, Wife of King Min

The Goiter Girl of Qi (Qi Suliu Nü), fl. early third century B.C.E., worked picking mulberry leaves by the east gate of the capital; she had always had a goiter, hence the name by which she was known. She is remembered because King Min (Min Wang, r. 323–284 B.C.E.) of Qi (in the north of the present-day province of Shandong) made her his queen after she convinced him that inner virtue was more important than outer beauty.

Whenever King Min passed through the streets on a pleasure trip with a large entourage of horses and carriages, the common people would all stop working and go to watch. As he passed on one occasion, the Goiter Girl was the only person who kept on working without even glancing at the king. When he noticed this he stopped and questioned her about it. "My parents told me to pick mulberry leaves," she replied. "They did not tell me to look [at the parade]." The king was impressed by her industriousness and obedience. When he expressed his regret that she had a goiter, the Goiter Girl replied that she saw no harm in having a goiter so long as she was faithful to her work. Now even more impressed by this talented young woman, King Min ordered her into one of his carriages. However, the Goiter Girl berated him for attempting to carry her off without her parents' permission, and the embarrassed monarch let her go on her way. He then sent an emissary to her parents with betrothal gifts and asked that she come to the palace. Her parents wanted her to bathe and dress in her best clothes, but again she refused, saying: "I was like this when I saw the king and if you change my appearance and my clothes, he will not recognize me" (O'Hara, 175).

The palace ladies dressed in all their finery when they heard from the king that a virtuous young woman who, he told them, "will replace all of you" was coming to the palace, but when they saw her they could not contain their mirth. King Min was mortified. "It is because she has not adorned herself; adornment can make a ten-fold difference or a one-hundred-fold difference." The Goiter Girl responded that adornment could in fact make a difference of tens of thousands, explaining that the sage kings Yao and Shun had not concerned themselves with outward adornment but had adorned themselves with righteousness and kindness. They had lived simple lives, and that was why their names were still remembered thousands of years later. However, the corrupt kings Jie and Zhou had built high terraces and adorned their women with pearls, jade, and silk. These men had caused their dynasties to fall and thousands of years later people were still criticiz-

28   THE GOITER GIRL OF QI, WIFE OF KING MIN

ing them. The palace ladies were greatly shamed by what the Goiter Girl said and King Min made her his queen. The state of Qi prospered while she was queen, but Yan (a principality centered on present-day Beijing) invaded it after her death. King Min fled but met his death at the hands of a general from the central Chinese state of Chu. The Goiter Girl's biography is included in "Biographies of Those Able in Reasoning and Understanding" in *Biographies of Eminent Women* (Lienü zhuan).

Constance A. COOK

Liu Xiang. *Lienü zhuan*. Sibubeiyao ed., 6.10a–11a.
O'Hara, Albert R. *The Position of Woman in Early China According to the Lieh Nü Chuan, "The Biographies of Chinese Women."* Taipei: Mei Ya, 1971; 1978, 174–77.

Golden Mother of the Jasper Pool: *see* **Queen Mother of the West**

Gong of Song, The Wife of Duke: *see* **Bo Ji, Wife of Duke Gong of Song**

Gongcheng of Lu's Elder Sister

Gongcheng's Elder Sister (Lu Gongcheng Si), dates unknown, was the sister of Gongcheng Zipi, a man of the state of Lu (in the present-day province of Shandong). She wept bitterly when the last of their clansmen died, but her brother said: "Don't carry on, I am about to arrange a marriage for you." That was the last she heard of it, however, and she remained unmarried. At that time a woman was not supposed to raise the subject of her marriage but was required to wait until a male relative spoke of it:

> Fallen leaves, fallen leaves,
> The wind, he blows you.
> O uncles, O elders,
> Set the tune and I will sing with you. (O'Hara, 95)

Gongcheng's sister is credited with warning her brother about his inability to be a good manager after he was invited by the ruler of Lu to take up a government post as a minister. She told him that his discussing marriage with her while they had been in mourning had revealed his lack of understanding of propriety. Further, the fact that he said nothing more about the proposed marriage even though she had passed the marriageable age indicated a greater incompetence on his part in managing affairs. Oblivious to good advice, Gongcheng accepted the government post but within a short time he was executed for some misdemeanor. His sister is praised for her intelligence, and her biography is included in "Biographies of the Benign and Wise" in *Biographies of Eminent Women* (Lienü zhuan).

Constance A. COOK

Liu Xiang. *Lienü zhuan*. Sibubeiyao ed., 3.8a–b.
O'Hara, Albert R. *The Position of Woman in Early China According to the Lieh Nü Chuan, "The Biographies of Chinese Women."* Taipei: Mei Ya, 1971; 1978, 94–95.

Gongcheng Zipi of Lu, Sister of: *see* **Gongcheng of Lu's Elder Sister**

Governess of the Lady of Ch'i, The: *see* **Instructress for the Daughter of Qi**

Grand Forbearance: *see* **Tai Ren**

Grand Jiang-Clan Woman: *see* **Tai Jiang**

H

Han'e

Han'e, who lived during the Warring States period, 475–221 B.C.E., in the state of Han (in present-day Hebei Province), is recorded in the third-century C.E. text known as the *Liezi* as China's first street singer. According to the *Liezi,* when she arrived at Linzi, the capital of the state of Qi (present-day Shandong Province), she stood at the Yongmen city gate, where merchants gathered to sell their goods, and sang for food. So beautiful was her voice that it was said to have lingered in the air for three days, and all who heard her were so deeply touched they did not even notice when she herself had gone.

On one occasion she was staying at an inn whose owner humiliated her in some way. Before leaving, she sang a slow, sad song that reduced everybody in the neighborhood to tears, and it is said that nobody could eat for three days. Someone was sent after her to bring her back, whereupon she sang a song that made everyone dance with happiness and forget their previous sorrow. This time the people who lived near Yongmen heaped gifts upon her before she went on her way and, thereafter, were known far and wide for their singing, which they had learned from Han'e.

Although little is known about her, as a talented singer whose singing had such a tremendous effect on her audience Han'e occupies an important place in the history of Chinese women. The phrase "reverberating around the beams for three days" (*rao liang san ri*), which is frequently used to praise someone's singing, is a direct reference to her.

Laura LONG

Liu Shisheng. *Zhongguo gudai funüshi.* Qingdao: Qingdao chubanshe, 1991, 68–69.
Ma Zhaozheng. *Zhongguo gudai funü mingren.* Beijing: Zhongguo funü chubanshe, 1988, 17–19.
"Tangwen." In *Liezi.* Sibubeiyao ed., 5.15a–16a.
Yin Wei. *Zhonghua wuqian nian yiyuan cainü.* Taipei: Guanya wenhua, 1991, 22–24.

Hsi Clan of Ts'ao, The Wife of the: *see* Xi Clan Head's Wife

Hsiao of Lu, The Righteous Nurse of Duke: *see* **Righteous Nurse of Duke Xiao of Lu**

Hsu-wu, the Woman of Ch'i: *see* **Xu Wu of Qi**

Huai-Ying of Yü of Chin: *see* **Ying, Wife of Duke Huai of Jin**

Huan, Ruler of Qi, Wife of Duke: *see* **Wei Ji, Wife of Duke Huan of Qi**

I

The Instructress for the Daughter of Qi

The Instructress for the Daughter of Qi (Qi Nü Fumu), fl. late eighth century B.C.E., is credited with correcting the behavior of her noble mistress. Her mistress, Zhuang Jiang (Woman of the Jiang Clan of Zhuang), a daughter of the royal house in the state of Qi (in the present-day province of Shandong), was also known as the Lady of Qi. A great beauty, Zhuang Jiang was married to Duke Zhuang (Zhuang Gong, r. 757–735 B.C.E.) of Wei (in the region bounded by the present-day provinces of Henan, Shaanxi, Shanxi, and Hebei). Her lineage and her appearance upon marriage are described in *The Book of Songs* (Shi jing) ode "Shuoren" (The Big One):

> Hands white as rush-down,
> Skin like lard,
> Neck long and white as the tree-grub,
> Teeth like melon seeds,
> Lovely head, beautiful brows.
> Oh, the sweet smile dimpling,
> The lovely eyes so black and white. (Waley, 80)

However, when Zhuang Jiang first entered the house of Wei, her conduct was considered lewd and, concerned as much for the honor of the ruler of Wei as for the disgrace to her mistress's ancestors, The Instructress counseled her to cultivate virtue and act in a proper manner. She composed an ode, which has been preserved in *The Book of Songs,* in which she called her mistress "a woman, splendid and upstanding" who should be a model for others and advised her to refine her "womanly heart" in order to raise her standards. Zhuang Jiang heeded her instructress's advice. Because she was childless, she adopted the son of a concubine; he was made heir apparent and subsequently became Duke Huan (Huan Gong), lord of Wei. While few women in China received an education of any kind in this period, The Instructress was clearly highly literate and knew the acceptable forms of ritual. The biography of The Instructress is included in "Biographies Illustrating the Correct Deportment of Mothers" in *Biographies of Eminent Women* (Lienü zhuan).

Constance A. COOK

Liu Xiang. *Lienü zhuan.* Sibubeiyao ed., 1.6a.
O'Hara, Albert R. *The Position of Woman in Early China According to the Lieh Nü Chuan, "The Biographies of Chinese Women."* Taipei: Mei Ya, 1971; 1978, 28–30.
Qu Wanli. *Shijing shiyi.* Mao no. 57. Taipei: Huagang, 1977, 43–45.
Waley, Arthur. *The Book of Songs.* London: George Allen & Unwin, 1937; 1969, 80.
Zuo zhuan. Yin 3, *Chunqiu jing zhuan yinde,* Shanghai: Guji shudian, 1983, 8.

J

Jiandi

Jiandi, a legendary figure who is said to have lived during the seventeenth century B.C.E., was the mother of Xie, the possibly legendary progenitor of the Shang dynasty (c. 1600–1100 B.C.E.). She was the elder of two daughters of a chieftain of the Yousong tribe, located in the region of present-day Shanxi Province, and became the second consort of god-king Di Ku (whose primary wife was Jiang Yuan, *vide* Tai Jiang). One source considers this marital relationship to be anachronistic, given that Di Ku and Jiandi were centuries apart in time. One day, Jiandi went to the river with two other young women to bathe and they saw a dark bird or a swallow drop two eggs. Jiandi swallowed one of the eggs, became pregnant, and gave birth to Xie. Thus Xie's was considered to have been a divine conception. This legend of the origin of the Shang dynasty is also referred to in a poem (Mao no. 303) preserved in *The Book of Songs* (Shi jing): "Heaven bade the dark bird / To come down and bear the Shang" (Waley, 275).

Jiandi is said to have been skilled at managing human affairs, to have taken pleasure in being kind to others, and to have had an understanding of astronomy. She passed on to her young son Xie her knowledge of managing affairs and maintaining order. On attaining manhood, Xie helped Yu the Great in his famous task of taming the waters, and was consequently appointed as *situ,* a post described in later dynasties as Minister of Education, by Shun, the legendary sage monarch of ancient China. Xie's skillful management of rulers' affairs, as well as many of his instructions and strategies, has traditionally been credited to the education he received as a child from Jiandi. The story of Jiandi is included in "Biographies Illustrating the Correct Deportment of Mothers" in *Biographies of Eminent Women* (Lienü zhuan), where it is said of Xie that his "becoming the Assistant of the ruler was probably a result of his mother's effort" (O'Hara, 20).

According to one source, Jiandi's father, chieftain of the Yousong, built a lofty terrace for Jiandi and her sister to live in. Jiandi enjoyed playing musical instruments at mealtimes and one day the King of Heaven sent two swallows to visit the sisters. They vied to catch the birds, covering them with a jade basket. When they eventually removed the basket, the swallows were gone and in their place were two eggs. The sisters sang the song "Swallows flew away," which is said to have been the beginning of the Northern school of music (*bei yin*). Thus, Jiandi is also credited with having founded this ancient Chinese school of music, the oldest of the four schools: the Northern, the Southern, the Eastern, and the Western.

Laura LONG

32 JIANDI

Legge, James, trans. *The Chinese Classics, Vol. 4: The She King.* Hong Kong: Hong Kong University Press, 1960, 636–38.

Liu Xiang. *Lienü zhuan.* Sibubeiyao ed., 1.2b.

Lüshi chunqiu, juan 6. In *Lüshi chunqiu jin zhu jin yi,* trans. Lin Pinshi. Taipei: Shijie shuju, 1985, vol. 1, 157–58.

O'Hara, Albert R. *The Position of Woman in Early China According to the Lieh Nü Chuan, "The Biographies of Chinese Women."* Taipei: Mei Ya, 1971; 1978, 19–20.

Shi ji. Beijing: Zhonghua shuju, 1973, vol. 1, 3.91; vol. 4, 49; 1967, 49; 1968, n. 5.

Waley, Arthur. *The Book of Songs.* London: George Allen & Unwin, 1937; 1969, 275.

Xie Wuliang. *Zhongguo funü wenxueshi.* Shanghai: Zhonghua shuju, 1916; Zhengzhou: Zhongzhou guji chubanshe, 1992, rpt, Section 1, 5.

Jiang, Queen of King Xuan of Zhou

This Jiang-Clan Woman (Zhou Xuan Jiang Hou), fl. c. 825 B.C.E., was a daughter of a ruler in the state of Qi (in the north of present-day Shandong Province) and queen of King Xuan (Xuan Wang, r. 827–781 B.C.E.) of Zhou (in what is now central China). Said to have been a woman of talent and virtue, she assumed the blame for her husband's improper behavior of coming late to court. This failure in propriety arose from his habit of going to bed early with his queen and rising late. The queen tactfully pointed out to him that the court could only gather from such behavior that he enjoyed her beauty and the satisfaction of his desires at the expense of virtue. This could only lead to disorder. "The source of the rise of disorder comes from me," she told him, "and I dare to acknowledge my fault." The king accepted her criticism but not her admission of guilt, saying that he himself had "given birth to these faults. It is not the crime of my wife" (O'Hara, 49). A rejuvenated man, King Xuan attended diligently to affairs of state from then on, retiring late and allowing his queen to depart his chambers at dawn.

This perceptive queen is praised in *The Book of Songs* (Shi jing) as "grave in deportment, of reputation consistent" (O'Hara, 50). She is a noteworthy departure from the many examples of women blamed throughout history for the lustful behavior of their mates. Her biography is included in "Biographies of the Virtuous and Wise" in *Biographies of Eminent Women* (Lienü zhuan).

Constance A. COOK

Liu Xiang. *Lienü zhuan.* Sibubeiyao ed., 2.1a–b.

O'Hara, Albert R. *The Position of Woman in Early China According to the Lieh Nü Chuan, "The Biographies of Chinese Women."* Taipei: Mei Ya, 1971; 1978, 49–50.

Jiang Shi, Daughter of the Royal House of Qi: *see* Wen Jiang, Wife of Duke Huan of Lu

Jiang Yi of Chu's Mother

The Mother of Jiang Yi (Chu Jiang Yi Mu), fl. c. 580–560 B.C.E., lived in the state of Chu (in what is now central China, north of the Yangzi River). She is remembered for arguing successfully that her son should be restored to office in the government of King Gong (Gong Wang, r. 590–560 B.C.E.) of Chu.

The palace was robbed when Jiang Yi was an official in the capital, Ying, and he was subsequently demoted after the governor blamed him for the robbery. Not long after this, Jiang Yi's Mother lost eight *xun* of cloth (a little under three meters). She immediately went to the governor and, in the presence of the king, accused him of stealing it, explaining that theft had been unknown when Sunshu Ao had been governor but that thieves and robbers operated openly under the present governor. Therefore, Jiang Yi's Mother said, the governor was to blame for her loss. The king pointed out that the governor, who held a high-ranking government position, could not have had anything to do with the thieves, who lived among the common people. Jiang Yi's Mother replied that her son had also been a government official but that he had been demoted because goods had been stolen from the palace. She reasoned that if her son was to be held responsible for stolen goods in the sphere of his responsibility, then the commanding minister (the governor, in this case) must bear responsibility for stolen property within the state at large. Her discussion of law and the responsibility of high officials for criminal behavior among the people revealed to the king his own responsibility in the matter. She refused to accept a reward for thus opening the king's eyes or to be reimbursed for the stolen cloth, but the king reemployed her son on the basis that the son of such a wise woman could not be unintelligent. Her biography is included in "Biographies of Those Able in Reasoning and Understanding" in *Biographies of Eminent Women* (Lienü zhuan).

Constance A. COOK

Liu Xiang. *Lienü zhuan.* Sibubeiyao ed., 6.1b–2b.
O'Hara, Albert R. *The Position of Woman in Early China According to the Lieh Nü Chuan, "The Biographies of Chinese Women."* Taipei: Mei Ya, 1971; 1978, 155–57.

Jiang Yuan: *see* **Tai Jiang**

The Jiang-Clan Woman of Qi, Wife of Duke Wen of Jin
The Woman of the Jiang Clan of Qi (Jin Wen Qi Jiang), fl. mid-seventh century B.C.E., was a daughter of Duke Huan (Huan Gong), ruler of Qi (in present-day Shandong Province). She was given in marriage to Chong Er (696–628 B.C.E.), a prince of the state of Jin (in the north of the present-day provinces of Shanxi-Hebei), during his nineteen-year exile in Qi, where he had fled to escape assassination. Chong Er was content to live out his life in peace and ease in Qi, but his wife discovered that his uncle and his followers were plotting to leave Qi and take him back to Jin. She killed the maidservant who had revealed the plot to her, then tried to persuade Chong Er to return to his homeland to restore order and regain his heritage. "It is not permitted to doubt [success], for if you doubt, you cannot accomplish your destiny," she told him. "If the one who is to possess the country of Jin is not you, who is it?" (O'Hara, 53). Unable to move him with her words, she conspired with his uncle to get him drunk, planning to kidnap him. This turned out not to be necessary, however. When he sobered up he agreed, albeit reluctantly, to return to Jin where, with the military

34 THE JIANG-CLAN WOMAN OF QI

assistance of Duke Mu (Mu Gong, r. 659–621) of Qin (present-day Gansu-Shaanxi provinces), he was installed as the ruler of Jin and assumed the title of Duke (Wen Gong, r. 636–627). Duke Wen brought peace to Jin, and under his leadership it became one of the five powerful states of the Spring and Autumn period. The Woman of the Jiang Clan was welcomed to Jin as his wife, as was the influential Huai Ying (*q.v.* Ying, Wife of Duke Huai of Jin), a daughter of Duke Mu. The biography of the Woman of the Jiang Clan is included in "Biographies of the Virtuous and Wise" in *Biographies of Eminent Women* (Lienü zhuan), where she is praised as being just and honest and as having urged her husband to action.

Constance A. COOK

Liu Xiang. *Lienü zhuan.* Sibubeiyao ed., 2.2a–b.
O'Hara, Albert R. *The Position of Woman in Early China According to the Lieh Nü Chuan, "The Biographies of Chinese Women."* Taipei: Mei Ya, 1971; 1978, 52–54.
Zuo zhuan. Zhuang 28, Xi 4. *Chunqiu jing zhuan yinde.* Shanghai: Guji shudian, 1983, 74, 93.

Jianzi, King of Zhao, Wife of: *see* **Juan, Daughter of an Official of the Ford of Zhao**

Ji-Clan Woman of Fan: *see* **Fan Ji, Wife of King Zhuang of Chu**

Ji-Clan Woman of the Yu Clan: *see* **Yu Ji, Wife of King Wei of Qi**

Ji-Clan Woman, Wife of Duke Mu of Qin
This Ji-Clan Woman (Qin Mu Ji), fl. mid-seventh century B.C.E., was the daughter of Duke Xian (Xian Gong) of Jin (in present-day Shaanxi Province) and Qi Jiang. In 655 B.C.E. she married Duke Mu (Mu Gong, r. 659–621) of the state of Qin (in the region of the present-day provinces of Shaanxi and Gansu). She became angry with her younger brother Yiwu when he persisted in forming illicit relationships with women, including their father's consort Jia Jun. Yiwu fled Jin after his father attempted to have him assassinated, but with the help of the state of Qin he returned after his father's death, to become known as Duke Hui (Hui Gong, r. 650–637), at which point the Ji-Clan Woman asked him to restore the status of their brothers who had been sent away by their father's wife Li Ji (*q.v.*). He ignored her request, however. Duke Hui further alienated his powerful ally Qin by refusing to provide grain when it experienced a famine, despite Qin's earlier generosity to Jin when it was in the grip of famine. His poor relations with Qin persisted until Qin attacked and captured him in 645. Although her brother, Duke Hui, had been intransigent on several occasions, the Ji-Clan Woman was not prepared to allow her husband, Duke Mu, to imprison and kill her brother. She expressed her sorrow about what was happening by taking her children (two boys and two girls) up into a tower with firewood spread over the steps, threatening to burn herself and her children to death if her husband confronted her brother. So shaken was Duke Mu by his wife's behavior that he allowed Duke Hui to return unharmed to Jin.

One version of the Ji-Clan Woman's story has her father (not her brother) captured by Qin. Another of her brothers—Chong Er—eventually returned to Jin after an exile of nineteen years to become its ruler, as Duke Wen (Wen Gong, r. 636–628), but she had apparently died by this time. Her biography is included in "Biographies of the Virtuous and Wise" in *Biographies of Eminent Women* (Lienü zhuan).

Constance A. COOK

Legge, James, trans. *The Chinese Classics, Vol. 5: The Ch'un ts'ew, with the Tso chuen.* Hong Kong: Hong Kong University Press, 1960; 1970, 144, 167–68.
Liu Xiang. *Lienü zhuan.* Sibubeiyao ed., 2.3a–b.
O'Hara, Albert R. *The Position of Woman in Early China According to the Lieh Nü Chuan, "The Biographies of Chinese Women."* Taipei: Mei Ya, 1971; 1978, 54–56.
Zuo zhuan. Xi 5, 15. *Chunqiu jing zhuan yinde.* Shanghai: Guji shudian, 1983, 96, 109–10.

Jieyu's Wife and The Wife of Yuling Zizhong of Chu

The Wife of Jieyu, a "crazy" wise man (Chu Jieyu Qi), dates unknown, lived in the state of Chu in what is now central China north of the Yangzi River. One day while she was away at the market and her husband was plowing, an envoy from the king arrived offering her husband a considerable sum of money, horses, and the post of governor of Huainan, a fertile area in the region between the present-day provinces of Henan and Anhui. Jieyu did not say yes, but he did not say no, and the envoy departed. On her return his wife asked who had visited and he explained what he had been offered, saying that he had accepted. His wife was not pleased, afraid that becoming rich in such an unrighteous manner could only compromise him. Her husband then told her he had *not* accepted the offer, which gave her a further fright: "If the King orders and you do not obey, that is disloyalty! If you obey him and then violate your principles, that is not righteousness" (O'Hara, 71). Realizing the danger they were in, the wife encouraged her husband to flee. They changed their names and moved away, preferring to live in peaceful poverty rather than become embroiled in the "cruel and disordered" politics of the day.

The Wife of Yuling Zizhong (Chu Yuling Qi), dates unknown, also lived in the state of Chu. Her husband wove sandals for a living, but such was his untapped talent that the Chu king sought him out, offering him a considerable sum of money if he would serve in government. Tempted by the prospect of teams of horses and other accoutrements of conspicuous consumption, he consulted his wife, who said: "You are surrounded by the lute and books and your happiness is in their midst. Whether you have a span of united horses, you have still just a small place to rest yourself on. If you eat off . . . a table ten feet square, you will have no more than the sweetness of one meat" (O'Hara, 74). She also warned him that his life might even be in danger if he served in the corrupt Chu government. Yuling Zizhong therefore declined the king's offer and fled with his wife, the couple supporting themselves by taking care of other people's gardens.

The biographies of both of these women are included in "Biographies of the Virtu-

36 *JIEYU'S WIFE*

ous and Wise" in *Biographies of Eminent Women* (Lienü zhuan) and are identical in theme—a wife warning her husband of the dangers of serving in government—to that of the wife of Lao Laizi (*q.v.* Lao Laizi's Wife).

Constance A. COOK

Han shi waizhuan. Congshu jicheng ed. Taipei: Taiwan shangwu yinshuguan, 1965, 2.19f, 9.121.
Liu Xiang. *Lienü zhuan.* Sibubeiyao ed., 2.9a–b, 2.10a–b.
O'Hara, Albert R. *The Position of Woman in Early China According to the Lieh Nü Chuan, "The Biographies of Chinese Women."* Taipei: Mei Ya, 1971; 1978, 70–71, 73–74.

Jin Gonggong Qi: *see* **The Bow Artisan of Jin's Wife**

Jin Mu: *see* **Queen Mother of the West**

Jin Wen Qi Jiang: *see* **Jiang-Clan Woman of Qi, Wife of Duke Wen of Jin**

Jin Yang Shu Ji: *see* **Shu Ji**

Jing, Concubine of Minister Guan Zhong of Qi
Jing (Qi Guan Qie Jing), fl. mid-seventh century B.C.E., was a concubine of Minister Guan Zhong (d. c. 643 B.C.E.) of the state of Qi (in the north of present-day Shandong Province). When she approached Guan Zhong in his room one day, asking what affairs of state depressed him so, she did not take offense at his arrogant rebuff: "It is nothing that you know of." Instead, she gently reprimanded him for his narrow-mindedness: "Do not treat the aged as aged; do not treat the ignoble as ignoble; do not treat the young as young; and do not treat the weak as weak" (O'Hara, 153). Drawing on her knowledge of historical precedent, she cited several examples of outstanding individuals who had done the unexpected. When the minister then sought her assistance she interpreted for him the apparently unintelligible poetic allusions made by a man from the state of Wei (in present-day Shanxi Province) who was offering his services to the state of Qi. The king of Qi accordingly employed the man, who served him well. Jing's biography is included in "Biographies of Those Able in Reasoning and Understanding" in *Biographies of Eminent Women* (Lienü zhuan).

Constance A. COOK

Liu Xiang. *Lienü zhuan.* Sibubeiyao ed., 6.1a–b.
O'Hara, Albert R. *The Position of Woman in Early China According to the Lieh Nü Chuan, "The Biographies of Chinese Women."* Taipei: Mei Ya, 1971; 1978, 153–55.

Jing, Daughter of Shanghuai Yan of Qi
Jing, the Daughter of Shanghuai (Qi Shanghuai Nü), fl. early fifth century B.C.E., was the daughter of a man named Yan who lived in the state of Qi (in the north of the

present-day province of Shandong). She is credited with saving the life of her father, who was under sentence of death for having harmed a favorite locust tree (*huai*) of Duke Jing (Jing Gong, r. 547–490 B.C.E.) of Qi; it was this that earned him the epithet Shanghuai (Harming the Locust Tree). Jing explained to the elderly minister Yanzi Ying that her father had been performing city-wall sacrifices proper to his office at the time of the offense and because he did not usually drink he had become drunk from the fermented grain used in the ceremony. She pointed out to the minister that, unlike the present Duke Jing, previous rulers had valued people over things and Yanzi understood the dangers of their ruler's behavior. Yanzi appealed to Duke Jing, who repealed the law that prescribed the death penalty for harming the tree and released Jing's father. Jing's biography is included in "Biographies of Those Able in Reasoning and Understanding" in *Biographies of Eminent Women* (Lienü zhuan).

Constance A. COOK

Liu Xiang. *Lienü zhuan.* Sibubeiyao ed., 6.3b–4a.
O'Hara, Albert R. *The Position of Woman in Early China According to the Lieh Nü Chuan. "The Biographies of Chinese Women."* Taipei: Mei Ya, 1971; 1978, 159–61.
Teschke, R. "Zwei Frauen im *Yan zi chun qiu* und im *Lie nü zhuan.*" In *Die Frau im alten China. Bild und Wirklichkeit,* ed. Dennis Schilling and Jianfei Kralle. Stuttgart: Steiner, 2001, 117–34.
Yan Ying. *Yanzi chunqiu.* In *Zhuzi jicheng,* ed. Jiang Lihong. Beijing: Zhonghua shuju, 1986, No. 2, 38–41.

Jing Jiang

Jing Jiang (meaning Respectful Jiang) was the title bestowed on a woman of the Jiang clan, fl. fifth century B.C.E., who was originally from Ju (in present-day Shandong Province) in the state of Lu. Her personal name was Dai Ji and her husband, Gongfu Mubo, was a Lu official. Jing Jiang was a knowledgeable woman well versed in propriety, and after her husband died she is said to have "preserved a righteous way of life," meaning that she did not remarry. Perceiving that her young son Wenbo was acting in an arrogant manner, expecting his friends to wait upon him, she admonished him with tales of able and wise Zhou rulers who had humbly listened to the advice of others and who would perform relatively menial tasks instead of delegating them to others. Because her son heeded her words, she is said to have been "perfect in transforming others." She continued to advise Wenbo after he was made the chief minister of Lu, instructing him on the qualities required of the various officials serving under him, such as generals, chief magistrates, and ministers. She also lectured him in detail on how virtuous kings had managed their realms. She herself continued to work at her spinning wheel, despite her son's exalted position, and when he asked her why she did this she reminded him of the duties incumbent on the wives of officials. So impressed was Confucius said to have been when told of her words that he exhorted his disciples to remember them.

After her son's death, she instructed his wives on proper mourning procedures and her nephew upon the distinctive operations of the inner and the outer courts. Confucius continued to be impressed by her understanding of ceremony, saying that she "dis-

38   JING JIANG

tinguished between the ceremonies for men and for women" and referring to her as Benevolent Mother or Kind Mother (*cimu*). Her biography is included in "Biographies Illustrating the Correct Deportment of Mothers" in *Biographies of Eminent Women* (Lienü zhuan).

Constance A. COOK

"Jiayu." In *Kongzi jiayu shuzheng,* ed. Chen Shike. Shanghai: Shanghai shudian, 1987, 10.266, 10.283.
Liu Xiang. *Lienü zhuan.* Sibubeiyao ed., 1.6b–9b.
O'Hara, Albert R. *The Position of Woman in Early China According to the Lieh Nü Chuan, "The Biographies of Chinese Women."* Taipei: Mei Ya, 1971; 1978, 30–37.

Jiu Tian Xuannü: *see* **Nü Wa**

Juan, Daughter of an Official of the Ford of Zhao
Juan, the Daughter of an Official of the Ford of Zhao (Zhaojin Nü Juan), fl. early fifth century B.C.E., became the wife of Jianzi (d. c. 476 B.C.E.), the ruler of Zhao (in the north of the present-day provinces of Shanxi-Hebei) after he recognized her talent. She is credited with having saved her father's life by taking up the oar when the king came to her father's ferry to cross the ford on his way to the South. Her father had passed out, she explained to the king, after drinking sacrificial wine; he had performed the full ceremonies to appease the water spirits of the Nine Rivers (*jiu jiang*) and the Three Huai Rivers in preparation for the king's crossing of the ford but had felt obliged to drink all of the wine in order to obtain safe passage for the king. After she pointed out that killing a drunken man was equivalent to the crime of killing an innocent man, since the drunken man would feel no pain nor would he realize he was being punished, the king decided not to put her father to death for being unfit to fulfill his duty of ferrying the king across the ford. Juan then proceeded to prove, by citing historical precedent, that it was not taboo for a woman to share a boat with men. Women, she claimed, had fought alongside the sage kings Tang of Xia and Wu of Zhou, and therefore it was quite proper for her to row the king of Zhao across the river. During the crossing she sang of the incident:

> He mounted the barge and his face beheld the pure stream.
> The waters were lashed up in waves. How dark and cloudy!
> His prayers asked blessings but he was drunk and did not awake.
> The death penalty was about to be added and I was alarmed at heart.
> The punishment was rescinded; the river became clear and I took up an oar and held the painter [of the ferry].
> The curled dragon assisted but the ruler was about to turn back.
> He called to her to come and row and they went ahead without suspicion. (Translated by O'Hara, 166–67, with slight changes)

So impressed was the king that he asked for her hand in marriage, which she refused until he sent gifts to her parents through a go-between. Her biography is included in "Biographies of Those Able in Reasoning and Understanding" in *Biographies of Eminent Women* (Lienü zhuan).

Constance A. COOK

Liu Xiang. *Lienü zhuan.* Sibubeiyao ed., 6.5b–6b.
O'Hara, Albert R. *The Position of Woman in Early China According to the Lieh Nü Chuan, "The Biographies of Chinese Women."* Taipei: Mei Ya, 1971; 1978, 165–67.

K

Kao-Hsing, the Widow of Liang: *see* Gao Xing, a Widow in Liang

The Kind Mother of the Mang Family of Wei

The Kind Mother of the Mang Family (Wei Mang Ci Mu), fl. third century B.C.E., lived in the state of Wei (in present-day Shanxi Province) and was a daughter of the Mengyang clan. She is known as a paragon among stepmothers. She was the second wife of Mang Mao, with whom she had three sons, but her husband's first wife had left him with five sons, none of whom liked their stepmother despite her insisting on treating them much better than she treated her own sons. After the middle of the five elder sons was condemned to death for some crime, she did everything in her power to redeem him, her righteous behavior finally reaching the ear of King Anli (Anli Wang, r. 267–243 B.C.E.), who pardoned the middle son and referred to her as a benevolent mother. Her unselfish love also moved her five stepsons to finally embrace her as their mother. The quality for which the kind mother was especially commended to later generations of women was her singleness of purpose in treating her five stepsons with as much care as if they were her own sons. Her biography is included in "Biographies Illustrating the Correct Deportment of Mothers" in *Biographies of Eminent Women* (Lienü zhuan).

Constance A. COOK

Liu Xiang. *Lienü zhuan.* Sibubeiyao ed., 1.12b–13a.
O'Hara, Albert R. *The Position of Woman in Early China According to the Lieh Nü Chuan, "The Biographies of Chinese Women."* Taipei: Mei Ya, 1971; 1978, 45–46.

Kong Bo Ji

The Mother of the Minister of the Ancestral Temple (Kong Bo Ji), d. 476 B.C.E., of Wei (in present-day Shanxi Province) was active during a period of great political instability. She was married to Kong Wenzi and their son, Kong Li, was a minister in the Wei government of Duke Chu (Chu Gong, r. 492–481 B.C.E.). Duke Chu was her nephew, the son of her younger brother Kuai Kui. After her husband died, Kong Bo Ji took as her lover a minor official named Hun Liangfu. Meanwhile, her brother Kuai Kui, who had been the heir apparent of Wei before his son Zhe (Duke Chu) ascended the throne, was plotting to regain what he saw as his rightful place as ruler. He tricked Kong Bo Ji

40 KONG BO JI

and Hun Liangfu into helping him. Disguised as women, he and Hun Liangfu managed to sneak into Kong Bo Ji's apartments. Then, at spear point, Kong Bo Ji forced her son, Kong Li, to agree to expel Duke Chu and set up Kuai Kui as Duke Zhuang (Zhuang Gong, r. 480–478 B.C.E.). One of Duke Zhuang's first acts as ruler was to have his sister's lover, Hun Liangfu, killed. Kong Bo Ji herself was killed four years later during another political coup when her nephew Duke Chu was welcomed back by the people of Wei. In *Biographies of Eminent Women* (Lienü zhuan), where her biography ("Two Disorderly Women of Wei") is included in "Biographies of Pernicious and Depraved Women," Kong Bo Ji is described as "a lustful concubine" who, along with Nanzi (*q.v.*), caused "the disorder of five generations" as well as her own destruction.

Constance A. COOK

Liu Xiang. *Lienü zhuan.* Sibubeiyao ed., 7.9a–b.
O'Hara, Albert R. *The Position of Woman in Early China According to the Lieh Nü Chuan. "The Biographies of Chinese Women."* Taipei: Mei Ya, 1971; 1978, 207–9.
Wen Shidan. "Chunqqiu bianqe shiqi funü congzheng huodong shuping." *Shixue yuekan,* no. 5 (1990): 8–9.

Kua of Chao, The Mother of General: *see* **General Zhao Gua's Mother**

Kung-ch'eng of Lu, The Elder Sister of: *see* **Gongcheng of Lu's Elder Sister**

L

Lao Lai of Ch'u, The Wife of: *see* **Lao Laizi's Wife**

Lao Laizi's Wife
The Wife of Lao Laizi (Chu Lao Lai Qi), fl. sixth century B.C.E., lived in the state of Chu in what is now central China, north of the Yangzi River. Lao Laizi was a hermit of the type not entirely approved of by Confucius: called a worthy and able man in this tale, he had fled the world and taken up farming rather than serve a corrupt government. When he was later approached by the Chu king with offers of jade and silk and a high position, he initially accepted. However, his wife warned him of the dangers he would face: "The one who can grow fat on wine and meat is also liable to be flogged; the one who can receive an official's salary is also liable to the headman's axe . . . will you be able to avoid falling into calamity?" (O'Hara, 72). Refusing to be controlled by others, the wife immediately threw down her basket of herbs and left. Her husband realized the soundness of her reasoning and fled with her to the east, eventually settling in Jiangnan (in the region of the present-day provinces of Jiangsu and Anhui),

where their civilizing sincerity and goodness attracted others and a community grew up around them. Her biography is identical in its theme—a wife warning her husband of the dangers of serving in government—to that of Jieyu's wife and Yuling Zizhong's wife (for both *v.* Jieyu's Wife and The Wife of Yuling Zizhong of Chu). Like theirs, it is included in "Biographies of the Virtuous and Wise" in *Biographies of Eminent Women* (Lienü zhuan).

Constance A. COOK

Liu Xiang. *Lienü zhuan.* Sibubeiyao ed., 2.9b–10a.
O'Hara, Albert R. *The Position of Woman in Early China According to the Lieh Nü Chuan, "The Biographies of Chinese Women."* Taipei: Mei Ya, 1971; 1978, 71–73.

Li Chi of Duke Hsien of Chin: *see* **Li Ji, Wife of Duke Xian of Jin**

Li Ji, Wife of Duke Xian of Jin
The Woman of the Ji Clan from Li (Li Ji,), fl. mid-seventh century B.C.E., was a daughter of a chief of the Li Rong, an ethnic group from western China. Despite a rather negative divination, Duke Xian (Xian Gong, r. 676–652 B.C.E.) of Jin (in the present-day provinces of Shanxi and Hebei) took her as a concubine after he had killed her father and defeated the Li Rong. Duke Xian already had several sons by various women and Li Ji bore him two more sons (some sources say one of these boys was her sister's child). She soon became his favorite, and he appointed her as his legal consort after the death of his wife, Qi Jiang, mother of the heir apparent, Shensheng. Because she wanted her son Xiqi to be appointed heir apparent, Li Ji persuaded Duke Xian to send his other three sons, including Shensheng, away from the court, ostensibly to keep control over the duke's ancestral city (Quwu) and the two frontiers. She then planted in the duke's mind a seed of suspicion about Shensheng, saying that the people loved him and that he could very well rebel against his father for the sake of the people. She then contrived a plan to capitalize on Duke Xian's suspicions about Shensheng. In 656, Shensheng returned to the capital to participate in a sacrifice to his dead mother, bringing with him meat and wine to offer to his father, Duke Xian. Li Ji poisoned Shensheng's sacrificial meat and wine, then made a very public display of feeding some of the meat to a dog and having a young servant taste the wine. Both the young servant and the dog died, and Li Ji immediately laid the blame on Shensheng, who, realizing the impossible situation this placed him in, promptly hanged himself. Duke Xian attempted to have his other two sons put to death but they managed to flee. Li Ji's son Xiqi was appointed heir apparent and upon the death of Duke Xian he ascended the throne. Three murders then took place in rapid succession: Xiqi was killed, his brother Zhuozi was placed on the throne and then killed, and Li Ji was "whipped and killed." Two further pretenders sat on the throne and died before Duke Xian's son Chong Er (Duke Wen, 696–628; r. 636–627) eventually returned to claim the throne in 636.

The biography of Li Ji in *Biographies of Eminent Women* (Lienü zhuan), which is under "Biographies of Pernicious and Depraved Women," says that she was a

42   LI JI

stepmother who plotted against the heir apparent, causing the death of princes and throwing the state into disorder for five successive reigns.

Constance A. COOK

Legge, James. *The Chinese Classics, Vol. V: The Ch'un ts'ew, with the Tso chuen.* Hong Kong: Hong Kong University Press, 1960; 1970, 114, 141–42.
Liu Xiang. *Lienü zhuan.* Sibubeiyao ed., 7.4b–6a.
O'Hara, Albert R. *The Position of Woman in Early China According to the Lieh Nü Chuan, "The Biographies of Chinese Women."* Taipei: Mei Ya, 1971; 1978, 52, 196–99.
Wen Shidan. "Chunqqiu biange shiqi funü congzheng huodong shuping." *Shixue yuekan,* no. 5 (1990): 10.
Zuo zhuan. Zhuang 28, Xi 4. *Chunqiu jing zhuan yinde.* Shanghai: Guji shudian, 1983, 74, 93.

Li Zhuang Furen: *see* **Duke Zhuang of Li's Wife**

Liang Gua Gao Xing: *see* **Gao Xing, a Widow in Liang**

Liang Jie Guzi: *see* **Righteous Respected Female Elder of Lu**

Ling, The Wife of King: *see* **Two Obedient Women of the Wei Ancestral Temple**

Ling of Qi, Wife of Duke: *see* **Zhong Zi, Wife of Duke Ling of Qi**

Liu-Hsia Hui, Wife of: *see* **Liuxia Hui's Wife**

Liuxia Hui Qi: *see* **Liuxia Hui's Wife**

Liuxia Hui's Wife
The Wife of Liuxia Hui (Liuxia Hui Qi), fl. seventh century B.C.E., was married to a minister of the state of Lu (in present-day Shandong Province) who, despite being demoted three times by the corrupt government, remained in office in order to help the people. She is remembered for her virtue, her intelligence, and her literary ability. When her husband died, his disciples were about to write his eulogy, but she insisted on writing it herself, saying: "None of you know his virtue as well as I." She wrote elegantly in praise of her husband's ability to accept injustice with equanimity and his willingness to serve in a humiliatingly low position in order to care for the people, and she expressed her deep sorrow that he had departed this world. She concluded her eulogy with the words "My husband's title after death is fittingly called 'Hui' [Gracious]" (O'Hara, 66). The disciples did not alter one word of the eulogy the wife wrote. Her biography is included in "Biographies of the Virtuous and Wise" in *Biographies of Eminent Women* (Lienü zhuan).

Constance A. COOK

Liu Xiang. *Lienü zhuan.* Sibubeiyao ed., 2.7a–b.

O'Hara, Albert R. *The Position of Woman in Early China According to the Lieh Nü Chuan, "The Biographies of Chinese Women."* Taipei: Mei Ya, 1971; 1978, 65–66.

The Loyal Maid of Zhu of Zhou

The Loyal Maid (Zhou Zhu Zhongqie), dates unknown, accompanied her mistress when she went in marriage as the primary wife to a grandee called Zhufu in the state of Zhou, in central China. Her mistress took a lover while Zhufu was away serving the Zhou administration and to forestall this affair being discovered the mistress prepared poisoned wine for Zhufu when he returned after an absence of two years. The mistress ordered The Loyal Maid to serve Zhufu the poisoned wine, but the maid deliberately dropped it rather than have Zhufu drink it. For this she was beaten by an angry master ignorant of the service she had done him. Fearing exposure, the furious mistress had the maid beaten even more harshly, in the hope that she would die. Still The Loyal Maid did not divulge her secret, preferring death to disgracing her mistress. The Loyal Maid's life was saved when Zhufu's younger brother intervened and exposed the wife's adultery and treachery, but this resulted in her mistress being beaten to death. The Loyal Maid then attempted suicide rather than accept Zhufu's offer of elevation to the status of his wife. Out of respect for her loyalty and integrity, Zhufu paid for her marriage to someone else. Her biography is included in "Biographies of the Chaste and Righteous" in *Biographies of Eminent Women* (Lienü zhuan).

Constance A. COOK

Liu Xiang. *Lienü zhuan.* Sibubeiyao ed., 5.7b–8a.

O'Hara, Albert R. *The Position of Woman in Early China According to the Lieh Nü Chuan, "The Biographies of Chinese Women."* Taipei: Mei Ya, 1971; 1978, 143–44.

Lu Gongcheng Si: *see* **Gongcheng of Lu's Elder Sister**

Lu Gua Tao Ying: *see* **Tao Ying, a Widow in Lu**

Lu Qian Lou Qi: *see* **Qian Lou of Lu's Wife**

Lu Qishi Nü: *see* **Qishi Woman of Lu**

Lu Qiu Jiefu: *see* **Qiu Hu's Wife, the Pure Woman**

Lu Xiao Yi Bao: *see* **The Righteous Nurse of Duke Xiao of Lu**

Lu Yi Guzi: *see* **Righteous Respected Female Elder of Lu**

Lu Zang Sun Mu: *see* **Zang Sun of Lu's Mother**

Lu zhi Mu Shi: *see* **Mother Teacher of Lu**

M

The Man of Cai's Wife

The Man of Cai's Wife (Cai Ren zhi Qi), dates unknown, was a daughter of a family from the state of Song (in what is now central China). She is credited with refusing to leave her husband on discovering that he had a disgusting and incurable illness, possibly leprosy, despite her mother's wish that she marry someone else. This tale is traditionally associated with Ode no. 8, "Fuyi" (Plantago Poem), preserved in *The Book of Songs* (Shi jing), on the analogy that foul-smelling plantain can be made into healing medicine:

> Thick grows the plantain;
> Here we go plucking it.
> . . .
> Thick grows the plantain;
> Here we are with handfuls of it. (Waley, 91)

The wife is described simply as "single of purpose and guileless" (O'Hara, 108) in her biography in "Biographies of the Chaste and Obedient" in *Biographies of Eminent Women* (Lienü zhuan). She became an example for later generations of a woman who observed chastity and remained devoted to one husband despite such unpleasant circumstances as a revolting disease.

Constance A. COOK

Liu Xiang. *Lienü zhuan*. Sibubeiyao ed., 4.2b–3a.
O'Hara, Albert R. *The Position of Woman in Early China According to the Lieh Nü Chuan, "The Biographies of Chinese Women."* Taipei: Mei Ya, 1971; 1978, 107–8.
Qu Wanli. *Shijing shiyi*. Mao no. 8. Taipei: Huagang, 1977, 6–7.
Waley, Arthur. *The Book of Songs*. London: George Allen & Unwin, 1937; 1969, 91.

Man of Teng, Queen of King Wu of Ch'u: *see* Man-Clan Woman of Deng, Wife of King Wu of Chu

Man of Ts'ai, The Wife of the: *see* The Man of Cai's Wife

The Man-Clan Woman of Deng, Wife of King Wu of Chu

The Woman of the Man Clan of Deng (Deng Man; Deng was a place in the south of the present-day province of Henan), fl. early seventh century B.C.E., was the wife of King Wu (Wu Wang, r. 740–690 B.C.E.) of Chu, a large state in what is now central China. King Wu frequently consulted his wife on matters of military and political strategy. She explained to him that his campaign against the small state of Luo (in present-day Hunan Province) would fail because the commander had underestimated his enemy. She also told King Wu he would die during his campaign against Sui (in present-day Hubei Province) because his time was over: "the sun after its meridian, must decline." As he was preparing to set out she told him: "The King's virtue is small and his income is great; you distribute but little and you obtain much. . . . If the troops remain unharmed, and your Majesty dies on the march, it will be a blessing for the State" (O'Hara, 77). King Wu did die on this campaign, and his wife is praised for understanding the way of Heaven that "after things reach their zenith, they must fail." Her biography is included in "Biographies of the Benign and Wise" in *Biographies of Eminent Women* (Lienü zhuan).

Constance A. COOK

Liu Xiang. *Lienü zhuan*. Sibubeiyao ed., 3.1a–b.
O'Hara, Albert R. *The Position of Woman in Early China According to the Lieh Nü Chuan, "The Biographies of Chinese Women."* Taipei: Mei Ya, 1971; 1978, 76–78.
Zuo zhuan. Zuo zhuan huijian. Huan 13, Zhuang 4. Taipei: Fenghuang chubanshe, 1977, vol. 1, 2.71–72; 3.7.

Mang [Family] of Wei, The Indulgent Mother of the: *see* The Kind Mother of the Mang Family of Wei

Mao, Ying-Clan Woman of Zheng: *see* Zheng Mao, Wife of King Cheng of Chu

Meixi

Meixi, fl. c. 1793–1760 B.C.E., also known as Moxi, was a favorite concubine of King Jie (r. 1818–1766 B.C.E.), the last ruler of the Xia dynasty (c. 2205–1766 B.C.E.), and is blamed for the downfall of the dynasty.

King Jie is traditionally described as "the tyrannical last ruler" of Xia and he acquired Meixi as a peace offering when he attacked the state of Youshi (in present-day Shandong Province). Meixi is described as "beautiful in appearance but poor in virtue . . . she threw the entire palace into confusion in an unvirtuous way. She acted like a woman but had the heart of a man by wearing a sword and a cap" (O'Hara, 186). King Jie was besotted with her and granted her every wish. Meixi loved the sound of tearing silk, for example, so the king ordered that silk be provided every day, just to please her. He had lavish palaces built where he would take his pleasure, feasting and drinking with Meixi and his palace ladies and slave girls day and night. Inevitably, however, King Jie tired of Meixi, and she fell out of favor when he acquired two new beautiful women—Wan and Yan—during an expedition against the state of Minshan.

Despite his military expeditions, the king is said to have paid no attention to affairs of state, preferring to live a dissipated life of pleasure and luxury. He ignored the growing signs of conflict within his state and aggression from without, including the threat posed by Tang, ruler of the new state of Shang to the east, who was intent on overthrowing King Jie. Tang sent a spy by the name of Yiyin to Xia, where the spy formed a relationship with Meixi. The pair lived together and became inseparable. Because Meixi is said to have "accepted Yiyin's ideas," presumably meaning the overthrow of King Jie, the early historians of China claimed that Meixi's union with Yiyin had helped destroy Xia. Tang eventually defeated and captured King Jie at Mingtiao (present-day Xia District in Shanxi Province) and exiled him. King Jie is said to have died in Nanchao on Lake Chaohu (the present-day city of Hefei in Anhui Province). His death brought an end to the Xia dynasty. There is no clear record of what happened to Meixi, although some sources claim she went with King Jie to Nanchao, where she died.

Meixi was blamed for the fall of the Xia dynasty, just as Daji (Danji) was blamed for the fall of the Shang dynasty, and Bao Si (*q.v.*) for the fall of Western Zhou. These women, who were traditionally invoked as negative role models, had very similar stories in that all three were taken by force from their families and their home states to serve conquering kings. Perhaps, as some historians suggest, that was the cause of the resentment that led them to seek revenge by working toward the destruction of their captors.

Laura LONG and Lily Xiao Hong LEE

Guoyu, "Jinyu." Sibubeiyao ed., 7.2b.
Liu Xiang. *Lienü zhuan*. Sibubeiyao ed., 7.1a–2b.
O'Hara, Albert R. *The Position of Woman in Early China According to the Lieh Nü Chuan, "The Biographies of Chinese Women."* Taipei: Mei Ya, 1971; 1978, 186–87.
Shi ji. Beijing: Zhonghua shuju, 1973, vol. 4, 49; 1967, 49; 1968, n. 4.
"Xia Jie Fei Moxi." Sohu.com. Wenhua pindao shouye, Lishi. April 4, 2005, http://cul.sohu.com/20050404/n225011347.shtml (accessed 13 April 2006).
Xunzi. "Jiebi." Sibubeiyao ed., 15.1b.

Mencius's Mother

The mother of Meng Ke (Zou Meng Ke Mu), also known as Meng Mu, or Mencius's Mother, fl. late fourth century B.C.E., lived in the principality of Zou (in present-day Shandong Province). Mencius (respectfully known as Mengzi, c. 372–289 B.C.E.) is the most famous transmitter of Confucius's teachings. Mencius added considerably to Confucius' teachings, notably the concept that people were by nature good, illustrating this by saying that anyone, without exception, who sees a child about to fall into a well will be alarmed and wish to save the child. Mencius's Mother is not described in her *Biographies of Eminent Women* (Lienü zhuan) biography as a widow, but apart from a footnote added to the English translation there is no mention of a husband, so she alone is credited with bringing up her son and instructing him so well in the importance of education and proper behavior that he became a famous scholar.

Stories about Mencius's Mother became staples of exemplary motherhood in traditional China. She is said to have moved twice before she was satisfied she had found a good environment for her son's education. Originally she lived with her young son near a graveyard, where Mencius played among the graves, imitating the building of graves and the burying of the dead. She moved from there to a place near a market, where Mencius played at selling goods, as if he were a merchant. Believing that this was not the right environment for her son, she moved to a dwelling beside a school, where Mencius imitated the sacrificial ceremonies and polite behavior when meeting people. She decided that that was where her son should live, saying, "Truly my son can dwell here."

The other well-known anecdote about Mencius's Mother related to her teaching her son the importance of persistence. Mencius came home one day and indicated that his studies were only half done. To his astonishment, his mother immediately cut the cloth she was weaving. When he asked her why, she explained that his being lax in his studies was like her cutting her half-finished cloth. Both signified discontinuing an endeavor before the final aim had been achieved.

Two other anecdotes are less well known. One tells of Mencius entering his room to find his wife in a state of undress. Displeased, he turned on his heel and would have nothing further to do with her. His wife bade farewell to her mother-in-law, saying that since Mencius was treating her as a mere guest instead of a wife, she wished to return to her parents. Mencius finally apologized and asked his wife to stay after his mother lectured him on proper manners. "According to propriety," she told him, "when you enter the front door, you should enquire who is at home in order to show respect. When you walk up the hall, you must raise your voice in order to warn others of your approach. When entering a room, you must lower your eyes for fear that you might see others' improprieties. Now since you yourself did not observe proper behavior [in walking in unannounced on your wife], how can you demand propriety of others?" The other anecdote is about Mencius's Mother noticing that he was worried when he was working as an adviser to the ruler of Qi. When asked, he finally told her that he wished to leave Qi because his ruler clearly did not intend to accept his advice, but that he was concerned this would mean his old mother would be forced to live in poverty. His mother assured him that as a mother her place was with her son and that she would always support him whatever he decided to do.

These tales were probably composed for didactic purposes well after the Confucian tradition had been established, during the Han dynasty. However, regardless of their provenance, they are part of the fabric of Chinese culture, having been an essential element of the Chinese tradition of motherhood for many centuries. The biography of Mencius's Mother is included in "Biographies Illustrating the Correct Deportment of Mothers" in *Biographies of Eminent Women*.

Constance A. COOK

Liu Xiang. *Lienü zhuan*. Sibubeiyao ed., 1.10a–11b.
O'Hara, Albert R. *The Position of Woman in Early China According to the Lieh Nü Chuan, "The Biographies of Chinese Women."* Taipei: Mei Ya, 1971; 1978, 39–42.

Meng Chi of Duke Hsiao of Ch'i: *see* Meng Ji, Wife of Duke Xiao of Qi

Meng Ji, Wife of Duke Xiao of Qi

Meng Ji, the Older Woman of the Ji Clan (Qi Xiao Meng Ji), fl. mid-seventh century B.C.E., was the eldest daughter of the Hua family of Qi and the wife of Duke Xiao (Xiao Gong, r. 642–633 B.C.E.) of Qi, in present-day Shandong Province.

48 MENG JI

She is credited with adhering so strictly to the rules of female propriety that she almost missed the age of marriage. On another occasion, she was at the point of suicide, believing she had been placed in the position of committing a breach of propriety.

Meng Ji had refused to marry until she found a man willing to perform the proper ceremonies; eventually she married Duke Xiao. As she was leaving with her prospective husband, her parents and other family members each bid her farewell with words of caution about remaining attentive to correct deportment at all times. Several years after they were married, she was accompanying Duke Xiao on an outing when there was a mishap that caused her to fall out of her cart. Her husband sent a men's cart to fetch her: this was a cart with no seats, which meant the passengers had to stand. Meng Ji refused to ride in this inappropriate chariot, however, saying: "when the royal wife passes over the threshold [of the gate], she must ride in a cart with seats and with curtains on four sides." There were apparently two reasons for these precautions. One was to help the woman remain chaste: "while in the wilderness, she takes a curtain of the cart to screen herself off, thus keeping her heart upright and her purpose single. She also regulates her own desires." The other was for safety: "As for a chariot without seats and without curtains, I dare not receive a command to ride in it, nor in the wilderness do I dare remain long without protection." Since her husband had neglected these requirements, she tried to commit suicide, saying: "This is the third time he has neglected many of the rules of propriety; it is better to die an early death than to live without the rules of propriety." A properly curtained cart was prepared in time and upon receiving this news her governess was able to revive her and she went home in it. She was praised for not displaying her beauty and her tale was later linked to Ode no. 225, "Du ren shi," about a well-dressed but inaccessible woman named Yin Ji, the daughter of a lord:

> That knight of the city
> In travelling hat and black headcloth;
> That lady his daughter,
> Thick and lovely her hair!
> Me, alas, she did not see!
> Sad is my heart within. (Waley, 52)

Her biography in "Biographies of the Chaste and Obedient" in *Biographies of Eminent Women* (Lienü zhuan) details in what appear to be her own words (here as translated by O'Hara, 111) the proper rules of propriety for women when they venture out of their homes.

Constance A. COOK

Liu Xiang. *Lienü zhuan*. Sibubeiyao ed., 4.3b–4a.
O'Hara, Albert R. *The Position of Woman in Early China According to the Lieh Nü Chuan, "The Biographies of Chinese Women."* Taipei: Mei Ya, 1971; 1978, 109–12.
Qu Wanli. *Shijing shiyi*. Mao no. 225. Taipei: Huagang, 1977, 196–97.
Waley, Arthur. *The Book of Songs*. London: George Allen & Unwin, 1937; 1969, 52.

Meng Jiangnü

Meng Jiangnü is a legendary figure, but she is based on a historical person who lived in the sixth century B.C.E. Her story has been elaborated over the centuries, and in later versions she is said to have lived in the third century B.C.E.

Meng Jiangnü first appears in the *Tradition of Zuo* (Zuo zhuan) as the wife of Qi Liang (d. 549 B.C.E.), a general of the state of Qi during the Spring and Autumn period. After Qi Liang was killed in battle, the Marquis of Qi offered his condolences upon meeting Qi Liang's widow in the suburbs. She, however, admonished the marquis for acting improperly in offering condolences in the roadway. Accordingly, the marquis went to Qi Liang's ancestral home to convey his condolences in the proper manner. The point of this story appears to be that Qi Liang's wife was possessed of propriety superior even to that of her ruler. Qi Liang's wife appears in other Confucian classics. In the *Book of Rites* (Li ji), she is also described as "knowing what is proper," with the additional detail that she is said to have cried sorrowfully at her husband's death. Her lament for her husband is highlighted in the *Mencius*, in which she is also said to have had the power to change the customs of the land.

In Han dynasty works, the lament of Qi Liang's wife for her husband became the focus of the story. Liu Xiang (late Western Han dynasty, 206 B.C.E.–8 C.E.) added a second part to her biography and included her in "Biographies of the Chaste and Obedient" in *Biographies of Eminent Women* (Lienü zhuan). His emphasis was on her moving lament for her husband and her widow-suicide. The first part of Liu Xiang's account corresponded to that of the *Tradition of Zuo;* in the second part, Liu Xiang added that, since she had no children or relatives to turn to, she remained crying beside her husband's body at the foot of the city wall until after ten days it crumbled. The sincerity of her emotions moved to tears those who heard her. After her husband was buried, she said: "A woman must have someone to rely on. She should rely on her father while he is alive, on her husband while he is alive, and on her son after the death of her husband. Now I do not have a father, a husband, or a son: I have no one to rely on to observe my sincerity at home, and I have no one to rely on to see that my chastity is maintained. How can I marry another? I can but die!" She then drowned herself in the Zi River.

The story of Qi Liang's wife underwent substantial changes in the Tang dynasty (618–907). In fragments, extant in Japan, of two lost works dating from the mid-eighth century C.E., the period in which she lived was moved from the sixth century to the third century B.C.E. This alteration in chronology became necessary when the storytellers changed the city wall beneath which she wept to the Great Wall, which was completed during the reign of the first emperor of Qin (Qin Shihuangdi, r. 221–210 B.C.E.). These two versions laid down, with slight variations, the basic story line that has been followed since. Qi Liang's wife is given her own name—Meng Zhongzi, or Meng Zi—at this time. Qi Liang is transformed from a general of the state of Qi to a native of the state of Yan, which is close to the Great Wall. One of the countless men conscripted to build the Great Wall but unable to bear this hardship any longer, he escaped and hid in the garden of Meng Chao, whose daughter Zhongzi was bathing in a pond. When she discovered him hiding in a tree, she asked him to marry her.

50 MENG JIANGNÜ

Qi Liang declined on the grounds of his lowly origin and his perilous situation, but relented when Zhongzi explained that she had to marry him now, since he had seen her body, and her body could not be seen by more than one man. Qi Liang went back to work on the Great Wall after their marriage but the overseer, angry at his having run away, beat Qi Liang to death and entombed him in the wall. On hearing this, Zhongzi went to the wall where she wailed until the wall crumbled, revealing vast quantities of bleached bones. Not knowing which were those of Qi Liang, Zhongzi pricked her finger and let her blood drip onto the bones, reasoning that Qi Liang's would be those into which her blood would seep. She finally discovered his bones and took them home for burial.

Among the texts found in the early twentieth century at Dunhuang on the Silk Road, one in the *bianwen* genre and two in the lyrics for songs (*quzici*) genre, all dating from the mid-tenth century, were related to Qi Liang's wife. It is in these that she is first known as Meng Jiangnü and is described delivering winter clothing to Qi Liang. This appears to be an echo of the many Tang dynasty poems on the theme of women who pined for their husbands serving at the border and who made winter clothes for them.

Many geographic locations have claimed Meng Jiangnü over the centuries and have erected memorials such as the temple near Shanhaiguan at the eastern end of the Great Wall. However, during the Cultural Revolution, Red Guards vilified this much-loved symbol and destroyed the images of Meng Jiangnü in the Shanhaiguan temple. Then, during the Chinese government's movement in the early 1970s to promote Legalism, which was closely linked with the Qin dynasty, Meng Jiangnü's anti-Qin Shihuangdi stance was perceived as a "reactionary Confucian" position. However, attitudes changed toward the end of the twentieth century, and Meng Jiangnü became once more an object of admiration and praise in mainland China.

The story of Meng Jiangnü appears in almost every major genre in Chinese popular literature and in every geographic region of China. It must indeed satisfy something deep in the psyche of the people. First, it portrays the helpless as being victorious over a despotic regime through a miraculous event that undid an unrightable wrong. Second, it reflects the trauma women suffered over the centuries when border wars and government conscription took their husbands from them. We should also note that the significance of Liu Xiang's inclusion of Meng Jiangnü as an example of a chaste and submissive woman seems to have been lost on the creators of popular folklore, who have always portrayed Meng Jiangnü as a strong and independent woman.

Lily Xiao Hong LEE

Gu Jiegang. "Meng Jiangnü gushi de zhuanbian." In *Meng Jiangnü gushi yanjiuji*. Shanghai: Shanghai guji chubanshe, 1984, 1–23.
———. "Meng Jiangnü gushi yanjiu." In *Meng Jiangnü gushi yanjiuji*. Shanghai: Shanghai guji chubanshe, 1984, 24–77.
Hatano Tarō. "Mōkyōjo koji sōsetsu." *Yokohama daigaku ronsō*, 24, no. 5 (April 1973): 146–82.
Iikura Shōhei; Wang Rulan, trans. "Mōkyōjo koji teki genkei." In *Meng Jiangnü gushi lun-*

wenji, ed. Gu Jiegang and Zhong Jingwei. Beijing: Zhongguo minjianwenyi chubanshe, 1984, 154–79. The article appeared in Japanese in *Tōkyō toritsu daigaku jimbun gakuhō*, 25 (1961): 133–62.

Liu Xiang. *Gu lienü zhuan*. Sibucongkan ed., 4.13a–b.

O'Hara, Albert R. *The Position of Woman in Early China According to the Lieh Nü Chuan, "The Biographies of Chinese Women."* Taipei: Mei Ya, 1971; 1978, 113–15.

"The Rehabilitation—and Appropriation—of Great Wall Mythology." *China Heritage Quarterly*, no. 7 (September 2006): www.chinaheritagequarterly.org/articles.php?searchterm=007_meng.inc&issue=007, accessed 4 October 2006.

Waley, Arthur. *Ballads and Stories from Tun-huang*. London: George Allen & Unwin, 1960, 145–49.

Wang, Ch'iu-Kuei [Wang, Qiugui]. "The Transformation of the Meng Chiang-nü Story in Chinese Popular Literature." Ph.D. dissertation, University of Cambridge, 1977–78.

Zuo zhuan. Xiang 23. Sibubeiyao ed., *Chunqiu zuoshi zhuan gu*, 5.12b–13a.

Meng K'o of Tsou, The Mother of: *see* **Mencius' Mother**

Meng Mu: *see* **Mencius's Mother**

Meng Zhongzi: *see* **Meng Jiangnü**

Meng Zi: *see* **Meng Jiangnü**

Miu Chiang of Duke Hsuan of Lu: *see* **Mu Jiang, Wife of Duke Xuan of Lu**

Miu Jiang: *see* **Mu Jiang, Wife of Duke Xuan of Lu**

Mo-hsi of Chieh of the Hsia Dynasty: *see* **Meixi**

Mother of Meng Ke of Zou: *see* **Mencius' Mother**

The Mother Teacher of Lu
The Mother Teacher (Lu zhi Mu Shi), fl. fifth century B.C.E., lived in the state of Lu (present-day Shandong Province); neither her given name nor her family name is known. She was a widow and she lived with her nine sons, all of whom were married. At the end of the year, when all the work had been done, she summoned her sons and formally requested permission to return to her natal home to supervise the annual sacrifices. Having received their permission, she summoned their wives and reminded them of a woman's duties: "A woman has the duty of the three followings [*sancong*]. In her youth she is bound to her parents, when she grows up she is bound to her husband, and when she is old she is bound to her sons." Then she asked her daughters-in-law to watch over the house until she returned in the evening. As it was still early when she got back, she waited at the city gate until evening before returning to her home. Questioned later by an official who had observed her unusual behavior, she said that she had been concerned that her arrival home before the appointed time

52 THE MOTHER TEACHER OF LU

might have inconvenienced her sons and their wives. When told of this incident, Duke Mu (Mu Gong) deduced that she was very knowledgeable about propriety and correct conduct for women, and he made her a teacher for his wives, giving her the title Mother Teacher. Her biography is included in "Biographies Illustrating the Correct Deportment of Mothers" in *Biographies of Eminent Women* (Lienü zhuan).

Constance A. COOK

Liu Xiang. *Lienü zhuan.* Sibubeiyao ed., 1.11b–12b.
O'Hara, Albert R. *The Position of Woman in Early China According to the Lieh Nü Chuan, "The Biographies of Chinese Women."* Taipei: Mei Ya, 1971; 1978, 43–44.

Mother Teacher of the State of Lu, The: *see* **The Mother Teacher of Lu**

Mou, Wife of King Ch'eng of Cheng of Ch'u: *see* **Zheng Mao, Wife of King Cheng of Chu**

Mournful Jiang-Clan Woman: *see* **Ai Jiang, Wife of Duke Zhuang of Lu**

Moxi: *see* **Meixi**

Mu Chiang: *see* **Mu Jiang, Wife of Duke Xuan of Lu**

Mu Jiang, Wife of Duke Xuan of Lu
Mu Jiang, c. 621–564 B.C.E., was the daughter of the Marquis of Qi (a powerful state in the north of present-day Shandong Province) and a woman of the Jiang clan. After she died, the descriptive Miu (The Misleading One) was placed before her name. It is by that name (Miu Jiang) that she is known in some sources, including *Biographies of Eminent Women* (Lienü zhuan).

Mu Jiang was married out to Duke Xuan (Xuan Gong, r. 608–591 B.C.E.) of Lu (in present-day Shandong Province) in 608, when she was about thirteen years old; this marriage was intended to highlight Lu's dependence on her home state of Qi. Her son succeeded his father, taking the title Duke Cheng (Cheng Gong, r. 590–573), while after him her grandson ruled Lu as Duke Xiang (Xiang Gong, r. 572–542). Both of these men were weak rulers, however, and Mu Jiang used her considerable influence as the daughter of the Marquis of Qi to shore up their position against certain powerful members of the Lu aristocracy, especially the Ji and the Meng clans, who had come to dominate the state. She appears to have been involved in negotiations with neighboring states and in decisions about war and peace; she also had a sexual relationship with a leading political figure and openly criticized her son's capacity to lead. In an attempt to neutralize her son's enemies, Mu Jiang urged him to expel the family heads of the Ji and Meng clans on the grounds of treason. Unfortunately, at the same time as she proposed this stratagem (in 575) war broke out between the two more southern states of Chu and Jin and her son led his armies out in support of Jin, promising Mu Jiang he would deal with the Ji and Meng clans when he returned. Rightly believing the matter to be too urgent to await her son's return, Mu Jiang dispatched her lover Shusun Qiao to Jin to try to garner support for expelling the troublesome family heads. Shusun Qiao failed in his bid to win the support of Jin, however, and was forced to flee Lu, while Mu Jiang was sent to the Eastern Hall to be kept under house arrest, presumably by members of the Ji and Meng clans.

Before going to the Eastern Hall, Mu Jiang consulted a diviner, who interpreted the divination as auspicious. The *Tradition of Zuo* (Zuo zhuan) records Mu Jiang as having disagreed with this interpretation, saying that she reflected on her actions and found herself a failure. Quoting her in the complex language of the *Book of Changes* (Yi jing) exegesis, this record documents Mu Jiang's great intellectual acumen, but it also became the source of her poor reputation throughout history.

Her biography in "Biographies of Pernicious and Depraved Women" in *Biographies of Eminent Women* says of her: "Alas, Miu Chiang! Although she had the makings of wisdom, in the end she did not succeed in hiding her licentiousness and disorder" (O'Hara, 201).

Constance A. COOK and Barbara HENDRISCHKE

Legge, James, trans. *The Chinese Classics, Vol. 5: The Ch'un ts'ew, with the Tso chuen.* Hong Kong: Hong Kong University Press, 1960; 1970, 371, 376, 398, 415, 437–40.

Liu Xiang. *Lienü zhuan.* Sibubeiyao ed., 7.6a–b.

O'Hara, Albert R. *The Position of Woman in Early China According to the Lieh Nü Chuan, "The Biographies of Chinese Women."* Taipei: Mei Ya, 1971; 1978, 199–201.

Schilling, Dennis. "Das Bekenntnis der Herzogin." In *Die Frau im alten China. Bild und Wirklichkeit,* ed. Dennis Schilling and Jianfei Kralle. Stuttgart: Steiner, 2001, 75–116.

Wen Shidan. "Chunqqiu biange shiqi funü congzheng huodong shuping." *Shixue yuekan* 5 (1990): 8.

Zuo zhuan. Cheng 9, 11, 16, Xiang 2, 9. *Chunqiu jing zhuan yinde.* Shanghai: Guji shudian, 1983, 228, 231, 243, 253–54, 267.

Mu of Hsü, The Wife of Duke: *see* **Duke Mu of Xu's Wife**

N

Nanzi, Wife of Duke Ling of Wei

Nanzi (Wei Ling Nanzi), d. c. 480 B.C.E., was from Song (in the east of the present-day province of Henan). She was a wife of Duke Ling (Ling Gong, r. 534–493 B.C.E.) of Wei (in present-day Shanxi Province). After her marriage, Nanzi had incestuous relations with her brother Zichao, an affair that distressed the Wei heir apparent Kuai Kui. The animosity between Nanzi and Kuai Kui then created a rift between father and son after Nanzi told her husband, Duke Ling, that his son wished to kill her. Fearing his father's anger, Kuai Kui fled Wei and sought refuge in the state of Song. Upon the death of Duke Ling, Kuai Kui's son Zhe inherited the title and became Duke Chu (Chu Gong, r. 492–481) but he was eventually unseated. Ushering in the final years

54 NANZI

of Wei, Kuai Kui ascended the throne as Duke Zhuang (Zhuang Gong, r. 480–478); during his brief reign, he had Nanzi executed.

Nanzi, who exerted a great deal of control through her husband, wished to see Confucius, who initially made excuses but eventually visited her. According to *The Analects* (Lunyu), as translated by James Legge, "The Master having visited Nantsze, Tsze-lu was displeased, on which the Master swore, saying, 'Wherein I have done improperly, may Heaven reject me! may Heaven reject me!'" Her biography is included, with that of Kong Bo Ji (*q.v.*), under the heading Two Disorderly Women of Wei in "Biographies of Pernicious and Depraved Women" in *Biographies of Eminent Women* (Lienü zhuan), where she is described as "deceitful and lustful." Nanzi and Kong Bo Ji are said to have "caused the disorder of five generations" as well as their own destruction.

Constance A. COOK

Legge, James, trans. *The Chinese Classics. Vol. 1 Confucian Analects. The Great Learning. The Doctrine of the Mean.* Hong Kong: Hong Kong University Press, 1960; 1970, 193.
Liu Xiang. *Lienü zhuan.* Sibubeiyao ed., 7.9a–b.
Lunyu. 7.6. In *Zhuzi jicheng*, ed. Jiang Lihong. Beijing: Zhonghua shuju, 1986, vol. 1, 131.
O'Hara, Albert R. *The Position of Woman in Early China According to the Lieh Nü Chuan, "The Biographies of Chinese Women."* Taipei: Mei Ya, 1971; 1978, 207–9.
Takikawa Kametarō. *Shiki kaichū kōshō [Shi ji].* Taipei: Hongshi, 1977, 47.39–40.

Niece of Zhuang of Chu: *see* **Zhuang Zhi, Wife of King Qingxiang of Chu**

Ninefold Numinous Grand and Realized Primal Ruler of the Purple Tenuity from the White Jade Tortoise Terrace: *see* **Queen Mother of the West**

Noble Daughter Surnamed Child: *see* **Fu Zi, the Shang Woman Warrior**

Noble Daughter Zi: *see* **Fu Zi, the Shang Woman Warrior**

Nü Kua: *see* **Nü Wa**

Nü Shin: *see* **Nü Wa**

Nü Tsung of Pao [Su] of Sung: *see* **Nüzong, the Wife of Baosu of Song**

Nü Wa

Nü Wa, also known as Nügua, Nü Kua, Nü Shin, and Jiu Tian Xuannü, is perhaps the oldest representative of Chinese women. She is often paired with Fu Xi (r. 2953–2838 B.C.E.), the first of the legendary Three Sovereigns. Nü Wa and Fu Xi are generally depicted paired, their snake-like lower bodies joined in a conjugal knot; the earliest known representation of them depicted in this way dates from the Han dynasty. As the sister/wife of Fu Xi, Nü Wa also has the dual status of goddess and ruler.

The earliest textual reference to Nü Wa can be found in the fourth century B.C.E. text "Questions of Heaven" (Tian wen) in *Songs of the South* (Chu ci): "Who shaped the body of Nü Wa?" This remark most likely referred to Nü Wa's unusual appearance as half woman/half snake. Some scholars argue that Nü Wa was a deification of shamaness rainmakers worshipped as early as the Shang dynasty (c. 1500–1050 B.C.E.), a surmise perhaps supported by the various etymological readings of her name, all of which point toward water as an important component of her persona. Stories related to Nü Wa were sometimes conflated with those of other female nature deities, the prime example being her later connection to the goddess of the Luo River.

The early tales of Nü Wa were amplified during the Han dynasty and eventually codified in both the *Huainanzi* (139 B.C.E.) and the *Liezi* (first recorded c. 370 C.E.). In these works, Nü Wa's role as rainmaker was extended to that of creator as well as savior of humankind. Some scholars have noted, however, that while Nü Wa's role was thus expanded, her power and independence were lessened, due to the Daoist leanings of the authors of the *Huainanzi*. She no longer functioned as an independent deity, but was required to submit to the will of the supreme male god, Taizu. Others attribute this change in tenor to the rise of Confucianism in Chinese society and the accompanying distaste for folk practices and animal-like deities. Scholars believe worship of Nü Wa and these types of deities was more popular among the ethnic minorities of southern China, although no research has so far been conducted to support this assertion.

The stories surrounding Nü Wa deserve consideration for what they can tell us about early popular practices in China, and for the way in which the Chinese explained biological and sociological phenomena through popular tales. These stories were not unique to China, but appear worldwide with different protagonists. The most commonly told story is that of Nü Wa's creation of humankind from the "yellow earth" of China. Therein lies an explanation not only for the genesis of human beings, but also for the separation of the nobility from the common people at birth, a reality explained by Nü Wa's inability to continue to hand-mold individuals from the earth. When fatigue set in, Nü Wa resorted to allowing the drips from her knotted cord to form into lesser people. Those created directly by her hand were clearly of higher rank and quality; those that were mere droplets of mud were apparently less worthy.

The image of Nü Wa is often found in conjunction with that other famous female life-giver, Queen Mother of the West (*q.v.*). Known for her elixirs of immortality, the Queen Mother of the West's connection to Nü Wa arguably expanded Nü Wa's role as creator and giver of life to that of one who promoted eternal life. Later folk beliefs would further and more explicitly expand Nü Wa's position as creator to become the giver of children; and some temples devoted to her and Fu Xi contained an opening referred to as an "offspring orifice," the touching of which would grant fertility and healthy babies.

56 NÜ WA

The second most commonly told story related to Nü Wa first appeared in the *Liezi*. This is the tale of Nü Wa fixing the firmament, bringing order to the cosmos, and ultimately saving the human beings she had created. The story has murky beginnings, with many variations on how the skies were rent asunder, thereby causing the world to be inundated. The most common version involved an attack on Mount Buzhou (Imperfect Mountain) by the demon Gonggong, whose fury, once unleashed, ripped the heavens open. Nü Wa restored order by cutting off the legs of a giant turtle to prop up the sky while she ground and smelted thousands of multicolored stones to fill up the firmament and prevent the rains from drowning the world below. These stones of many colors later became the rationale for the appearance of rainbows after heavy rains.

From this tale, Nü Wa came to be associated with both flood control and irrigation, the compass and square being used as the iconographic attributes of Nü Wa and Fu Xi. The terms for these two implements—*gui* for compass and *ju* for square—together create the compound *guiju*, meaning "order" or "proper conduct," and in fact Nü Wa's actions after the world was restored to order can be seen as reflecting Confucian ideals of feminine deportment. She did not boast of her actions, but remained modest and retiring.

Problematic within the Confucian mindset is Nü Wa's relationship to Fu Xi. After the deluge, Nü Wa and Fu Xi joined in marriage, their union creating offspring that helped to repopulate the earth. Although this may be viewed as a noble act, Nü Wa was in fact Fu Xi's younger sister, so their marriage was incestuous. This aspect of their relationship was rationalized by the importance Nü Wa placed on marriage: in time she came to be seen as the patron of matchmakers. According to some scholars, it was Nü Wa's extremely moral character that led her to insist that she and Fu Xi marry; some argue further that Nü Wa was responsible for the later practice forbidding people of the same clan name to marry. Some scholars have noted that the actions of Nü Wa and Fu Xi reflect similar, documented cases in which, in dire circumstances, incest was allowed, and can thereby be viewed as a rationalization of something that occasionally occurred in China during times of disease or famine.

Belief in Nü Wa continued into the medieval era and there is an image of her and Fu Xi on a piece of cloth found in a Tang dynasty (618–907) tomb. During Tang, Nü Wa came to be associated with numerous mountains and grottoes throughout China, often through references in poetic works. It was also at this time that she came to be associated with the beautiful goddess of the Luo River, a connection that reinforced Nü Wa's serpentine qualities. Throughout Tang, the general poetic approach toward Nü Wa largely highlighted her inhuman, "scaly" qualities, the one exception being the remarks of Li Bo (701–762) on her superior, creative powers: "Nü Wa played with the yellow earth, patting it into ignorant, inferior man."

Reference to Nü Wa is also found in the Tang dynastic histories. The disappearance and reemergence of her tomb under the waters of the Yellow River recorded in, respectively, 752 and 759 was interpreted as a harbinger of cataclysmic change to the dynasty. The restoration of the dynasty after the An Lushan Rebellion of

755–763, and the reappearance of Nü Wa's tomb from the river, were seen as further proof of divine approval for placing the future emperor Suzong (r. 756–762) on the throne.

The cult of Nü Wa continued in China until 1949, when it was halted with the rise of communism. News accounts out of China in the early twenty-first century hint at a resurrection of interest in Nü Wa, with a celebration in April 2003 in Wanrong District, Shanxi Province, to mark her mythological birthday. News accounts state that eight Chinese emperors have paid homage to Nü Wa at her ancestral temple over a period of 1,000 years, and clearly local residents there are hoping that trend will be revived.

Karil J. KUCERA

Birrell, Anne. *Chinese Mythology.* Baltimore, MD: Johns Hopkins University Press, 1993.
Guo Wei. *Zhongguo nüshen.* Nanning: Guangxi jiaoyu chubanshe, 2000, 88–169.
Liezi. *The Book of Lieh-tzu: A Classic of the Tao*, trans. A.C. Graham. London: Butler and Tanner, 1960, 96.
Liu An. *Huainanzi.* Sibubeiyao ed., 6.7b–8a.
Schafer, Edward H. *The Divine Woman.* Berkeley: University of California Press, 1973.

Nügua: *see* **Nü Wa**

Nüying: *see* **Ehuang and Nüying**

Nüzong, the Wife of Baosu of Song
Nüzong, the Wife of Baosu of Song (Song Bao Nüzong), dates unknown, lived in the state of Song (in the east of the present-day province of Henan) and has been made an exemplar for her adherence to the rules of proper conduct of the primary wife when a husband takes a mistress. Baosu was away from home for three years serving as an army official in the state of Wei (in present-day Shanxi Province) while his wife remained at home caring for his mother. When the family discovered that Baosu had taken a mistress in Wei, his sister told the wife she should leave their house: "When a husband has what he likes, then why should you stay?" The wife refused, however, saying that a wife has "not one righteous reason" to leave her husband, while a husband can divorce a wife for only seven reasons, none of which applied to her. The grounds for a husband divorcing his wife were given as jealousy, lewd behavior, theft, shrewishness, arrogance, barrenness, or gross illness such as leprosy. The wife therefore remained in Baosu's home, serving her mother-in-law with renewed zeal, and when the ruler of Song heard of her virtuous behavior he gave her the title Nüzong (meaning Female Ancestor) and honored her hometown. While it is possible that this is the tale of a historical individual, this biography may simply have been a vehicle for reinforcing the concept that wives must devote themselves to the service of their parents-in-law and the tradition, developed well after the Han dynasty, that widows should not remarry. Nevertheless, Nüzong is to be commended for her courage in resisting all efforts to oust her from her rightful

58 NÜZONG

position. Her biography is included in "Biographies of the Virtuous and Wise" in *Biographies of Eminent Women* (Lienü zhuan).

Constance A. COOK

Liu Xiang. *Lienü zhuan*. Sibubeiyao ed., 2.4b–5b.
O'Hara, Albert R. *The Position of Woman in Early China According to the Lieh Nü Chuan, "The Biographies of Chinese Women."* Taipei: Mei Ya, 1971; 1978, 60–61.

O

The Official from Zhounan's Wife

The Wife of the Official from Zhounan (Zhounan zhi Qi), dates unknown, is remembered for telling her neighbors how she had always encouraged her husband not to slacken off from his duty to the king during troubled times, always reminding him it was his duty to work hard in order to support his parents. This official from Zhounan (in central China, in the region of the present-day provinces of Hubei-Henan) had been sent to do flood-control work. When he did not return home on time his wife, fearing that he was neglecting his duty, spread abroad her opinions, citing the legendary hero Shun as one who had undertaken the most menial of tasks in order to fulfill his duty to his parents. The Wife recognized that it is natural to want to flee danger and hardship; however, one must put one's parents above all other considerations. She recited a poem on the theme of honoring one's parents regardless of the unfortunate situation in which one might find oneself:

> The bream has a red tail;
> The royal house is ablaze.
> But though it is ablaze,
> My father and mother are very dear. (Waley, 152)

Legge says that this poem (Mao no. 10) is about the affection of the wives of the Ru (the Ru River is in the southeast of present-day Henan Province) for their husbands and their concern for their husbands' honor. He further quotes commentators who say that the unnatural redness of the bream's tail must be produced by its tossing in shallow water. This represents the husbands' toil and suffering on service far from home. The verse is taken to be an exhortation to the husbands to do their duty to the Shang dynasty, and thus not disgrace their parents, despite the wickedness of Zhou, its last ruler.

This biography, which is included in "Biographies of the Virtuous and Wise" in *Biographies of Eminent Women* (Lienü zhuan), reinforces the concept of devotion and service to one's parents. It is possible that the wife of the official of Zhounan was not a historical personage. However, she probably represents women such as those from the Ru River region.

Constance A. COOK

Legge, James. *The Chinese Classics, Vol. IV. The She King, or the Book of Poetry*. Hong Kong: Hong Kong University Press, 1960; 1970, Part 1, 18.

Liu Xiang. *Lienü zhuan*. Sibubeiyao ed., 2.4a–b.

O'Hara, Albert R. *The Position of Woman in Early China According to the Lieh Nü Chuan, "The Biographies of Chinese Women."* Taipei: Mei Ya, 1971; 1978, 58–60.

Qu Wanli. *Shi jing shiyi*. Mao no. 10. Taipei: Huagang, 1977, 7–8.

Waley, Arthur. *The Book of Songs*. London: George Allen & Unwin, 1937; 1969, 152.

P

Pao Ssu of King Yu of Chou: *see* **Bao Si, Wife of King You of Zhou**

Po Chi: *see* **Kong Bo Ji**

Po Ying of King P'ing of Ch'u: *see* **Bo Ying, Wife of King Ping of Chu**

Po-chi of Kung of Sung: *see* **Bo Ji, Wife of Duke Gong of Song**

Public Spirited Aunt of Lu, The: *see* **Righteous Respected Female Elder of Lu**

Pure Jiang, Wife of King Zhao of Chu

Pure Jiang (Chu Zhao Zhen Jiang), fl. early fifth century B.C.E., is the epithet given to the Jiang-clan woman married to King Zhao (Zhao Wang, 515–489 B.C.E.) of Chu (in what is now central China, north of the Yangzi) who preferred to drown rather than flout an agreement and be accused of a lack of chastity. She was a daughter of the Marquis of Qi (in present-day Shandong Province).

King Zhao left his wife behind in the palace when he went on a pleasure trip, but when he heard that the river was rising and she was in danger he sent an official to fetch her. Despite the agreement previously made with his wife, he apparently forgot to remind the official to take the seal of commission that would reassure her that the order did indeed come from her husband. Pure Jiang therefore refused to go with the official, saying that she would rather stay where she was and die than break an agreement and violate righteousness; she also said "the brave person does not fear to die" (O'Hara, 117). She was swept away and drowned before the official had time to return with the proper seals. Her husband praised his wife for dying for "a rule of chastity" and she has since been eulogized as possessing "the rules of wifehood." Such an extreme act of self-sacrifice in the cause of female chastity appears unreasonable to the modern mind, but it ensured that her biography was included in "Biographies of the Chaste and Obedient" in *Biographies of Eminent Women* (Lienü zhuan).

Constance A. COOK

Liu Xiang. *Lienü zhuan*. Sibubeiyao ed., 4.6a–b.

O'Hara, Albert R. *The Position of Woman in Early China According to the Lieh Nü Chuan, "The Biographies of Chinese Women."* Taipei: Mei Ya, 1971; 1978, 117–18.

Q

Qi Guan Qie Jing: *see* **Jing, Concubine of Minister Guan Zhong of Qi**

Qi Huan Wei Ji: *see* **Wei Ji, Wife of Duke Huan of Qi**

Qi Liang Qi: *see* **Meng Jiangnü**

Qi Ling Zhong Zi: *see* **Zhong Zi, Wife of Duke Ling of Qi**

Qi Mu Tushan: *see* **The Tushan Woman**

Qi Nü Fumu: *see* **Instructress for the Daughter of Qi**

Qi Nü Xu Wu: *see* **Xu Wu of Qi**

Qi Shanghuai Nü: *see* **Jing, Daughter of Shanghuai Yan of Qi**

Qi Suliu Nü: *see* **The Goiter Girl of Qi, Wife of King Min**

Qi Tian Ji Mu: *see* **Tian Ji of Qi's Mother**

Qi Wei Yu Ji: *see* **Yu Ji, Wife of King Wei of Qi**

Qi Xiang Yanzi Puyu Qi: *see* **Wife of the Chariot Driver for Yanzi, Minister of Qi**

Qi Xiao Meng Ji: *see* **Meng Ji, Wife of Duke Xiao of Qi**

Qi Yi Jimu: *see* **The Righteous Stepmother of Qi**

Qi Zhongli Chun: *see* **Zhongli Chun of Qi, Wife of King Xuan of Qi**

Qian Lou of Lu's Wife
The Wife of Qian Lou (Lu Qian Lou Qi), fl. fifth century B.C.E., lived in the state of Lu (in present-day Shandong Province). Qian Lou was a teacher, a man of learning who refused all honors and offers of wealth, and when he died Zengzi (b. 506 B.C.E.) and his disciples went to pay their respects. Zengzi was a disciple of Confucius and he immediately noticed that the cotton quilt placed over Qian Lou's body was too short. He therefore suggested that the quilt be placed obliquely so that at least the head and feet would be covered. Qian Lou's Wife, who was directing the funeral, told Zengzi that since her husband had not liked crooked things during his lifetime it would be inappropriate to place the quilt awry simply because it was not long enough. Zengzi

then queried the posthumous name Qian Lou's Wife had given him: Kang, meaning "contentment" or "joy." He was soon satisfied, however, by her explanation that it reflected Qian Lou's genuine humility and contentment. Her husband, she told him, "was not sad in poverty and a humble position; he was not elated over wealth and honor. He sought benevolence and attained it; he sought righteousness and achieved it." Zengzi responded to her explanation with the comment: "Aye! Such a man and he had such a wife" (O'Hara, 68). Her biography is included in "Biographies of the Virtuous and Wise" in *Biographies of Eminent Women* (Lienü zhuan).

Constance A. COOK

Liu Xiang. *Lienü zhuan.* Sibubeiyao ed., 2.7b–8a.
O'Hara, Albert R. *The Position of Woman in Early China According to the Lieh Nü Chuan, "The Biographies of Chinese Women."* Taipei: Mei Ya, 1971; 1978, 66–68.

Qin Mu Ji: *see* Ji-Clan Woman, Wife of Duke Mu of Qin

Qi's Mother: *see* The Tushan Woman

The Qishi Woman of Lu

The Woman of Qishi (Lu Qishi Nü), fl. fifth century B.C.E., lived in the city of Qishi in the state of Lu (in present-day Shandong Province). Her neighbors mistakenly thought the woman, who had not yet wed, was despondent at having passed the time for marrying when in reality she was distressed over the state of the government. She explained to the local women that the ruler, Duke Mu (Mu Gong), was old and perverse while the heir apparent was young and foolish. This was a recipe for disaster. Such a state of affairs, she told them, was not solely the concern of men and ministers because the lives of all the common people were affected when soldiers' horses trampled crops and young men such as her brother lost their lives caring for others. So accurate was her reading of events that within three years the states of Qi, to the north, and Jin, to the west, invaded Lu and the people were pressed into service. It is said of the Woman of Qishi that her thoughts were far-reaching. Her biography is included in "Biographies of the Benign and Wise" in *Biographies of Eminent Women* (Lienü zhuan).

Constance A. COOK

Liu Xiang. *Lienü zhuan.* Sibubeiyao ed., 3.8a–9b.
O'Hara, Albert R. *The Position of Woman in Early China According to the Lieh Nü Chuan, "The Biographies of Chinese Women."* Taipei: Mei Ya, 1971; 1978, 95–97.

Qiu Hu's Wife, the Pure Woman

The Wife of Qiu Hu (Lu Qiu Jiefu), dates unknown, of the state of Lu (in present-day Shandong Province), was known as the Pure Woman. While she is not described as such, she may have been Qiu Hu's second wife since she spoke of raising "my husband's children" even though they had spent only five days together before he left to fulfill a

62 QIU HU'S WIFE

distant post in the west and did not return for another five years. As he neared his parents' house on his return home he attempted, unsuccessfully, to seduce a woman who was picking mulberry leaves (for silk worms) by the side of the road, only to later discover that the woman was in fact his wife. His wife accused him of being unfilial because he had tarried by the roadside instead of hurrying straight home to his mother after his five-year absence; further, if he could not be filial to a parent then he was also disloyal to his sovereign. She expressed her disapproval of his depraved conduct, saying that she could not live with him: "I cannot bear to see you take another wife; neither can I marry again." She then drowned herself in the river. She is described as "great in goodness," yet she committed suicide; her unrighteous husband is described as "unfilial nor had he a great love for his parents or for other people" (O'Hara, 142), yet he did not think it necessary to commit suicide on this account. Her biography is included in "Biographies of the Chaste and Righteous" in *Biographies of Eminent Women* (Lienü zhuan).

The Tang dynasty scholar of calligraphy Wei Xu claimed that Qiu Hu's wife created a special style of calligraphy that was called "worm script" (*chongshu*), but for some reason it fell into disuse.

Constance A. COOK

Liu Xiang. *Lienü zhuan*. Sibubeiyao ed., 5.6b–7b.
O'Hara, Albert R. *The Position of Woman in Early China According to the Lieh Nü Chuan, "The Biographies of Chinese Women."* Taipei: Mei Ya, 1971; 1978, 141–43.
Wei Xu. *Wushi liu zhong shufa: yi juan*. In "Mo shu." *Tangren shuxue lunzhu*. Taipei: Shijie shuju, 1971, 1–5.

Qiuzi, the Adjutant General of Gai, Wife of: *see* The General of Gai's Wife

Queen Mother of the West

Queen Mother of the West (Xiwangmu) is an ancient being who first appears in the *Zhuangzi*, a third-century B.C.E. Daoist text, as one of several personages who have attained the Dao, and thus immortality: it is said of her that no one knows her beginning and no one knows her end. She is identified in the *Xunzi*, a Confucian text of the third century B.C.E., as a teacher of the legendary sage Yu, while her description in the *Shanhai jing*, a geographical encyclopedia of possibly the same period, calls to mind a shamanistic deity:

> Another 350 *li* to the west is a mountain called Jade Mountain. This is the place where the Queen Mother of the West dwells. As for the Queen Mother of the West, her appearance is like that of a human, with a leopard's tail and tiger's teeth. Moreover she is skilled at whistling. In her disheveled hair she wears a *sheng* headdress. She is controller of the Grindstone and the Five Shards Constellations of the heavens. (Cahill, 15–16)

The earliest pictorial representation of Queen Mother of the West, on a tomb mural in Luoyang (Henan Province), dates from the first half of the first century B.C.E. Here, on wave-like clouds and attended by various animals, she is located midway between the goddess Nü Wa (*q.v.*) and the moon, representing the *yin* principle, and the male god Fu Xi and the sun, representing the *yang* principle. She appears to be wearing a *sheng* headdress, a pair of discs connected by a straight rod or bar.

Over the centuries Queen Mother of the West became associated with the magical Mount Kunlun in the far west, death and the search for immortality, communication between divine and mortal beings, autumn, and the forces of *yin*. Her meetings with legendary and historical rulers and her power to affect the rhythms of the cosmos have been linked to the annual meetings in the heavens of the Oxherd and the Weaving Maid (who in some traditions is her granddaughter) constellations. Finally, as a maternal deity of boundless compassion she is still worshipped today, by both Daoists and Buddhists.

Mount Kunlun has long been regarded as the locus of China's western paradise and home of the Queen Mother, yet the earliest texts, while they may mention Kunlun, do not specifically locate her in that magical place. The second-century B.C.E. *Huainanzi* says she dwelt at the "edge of the flowing sands" (now thought to be the Gobi Desert), while other early texts place her somewhere far to the west, well outside China's borders. In his *Daren fu*, composed between 130 and 120 B.C.E., Sima Xiangru (d. 117 B.C.E.) has her dwelling in a cave on the Yin Mountains:

> I went back and forth among the Yin Mountains and soared in great curves,
> So that I have moreover today looked upon the Queen Mother of the West.
> She is brilliant with her white head and high jade comb, yet she dwells in a cave.
> She also fortunately has her three green birds to be her messengers.
> If I were certain to live as long as she and not die,
> Although I were to traverse ten thousand ages, it would not be enough to make me glad. (Dubs, 232)

The first-century B.C.E. *Historical Records* (Shi ji) says that people living in the west had heard that the Queen Mother lived near the River of Weak Water and the Western Sea (possibly the Persian Gulf), but no one had ever seen her.

In the southern state of Chu (the present-day provinces of Henan and Hubei), Mount Kunlun was China's *axis mundi*, the primal link between the mortal world and Heaven, and this magical mountain was synonymous with immortality: the third-century B.C.E. poet Qu Yuan recounts in his *Li sao* his ecstatic shamanistic journey across the skies following the path of the sun to its resting place at Mount Kunlun, "the world's western end." While Emperor Wu (r. 140–87 B.C.E.) gave the name Kunlun to the mountains where the Yellow River has its source, it was not until the second century C.E. that the concept of immortality common to the Queen Mother and Mount Kunlun drew them sufficiently close in the Han mind for the Queen Mother to finally find her home in her western paradise on Mount Kunlun. There she resides in a palace whose delights include a scarlet courtyard, a rose-gem orchard, a turquoise (or jasper) pond, and a peach garden.

The quest for immortality preoccupied several ancient rulers, among them the first emperor of Qin (Qin Shihuangdi, r. 221–210 B.C.E.) and Emperor Wu. While female

64 QUEEN MOTHER OF THE WEST

wu had traditionally functioned as spirit mediums and shamans, channeling answers to mortal questioners while possessed by divinities, both of these emperors employed male magicians (*fangshi*) as technicians to assist them in their quest, but to no avail. In one famous episode a magician set up for Emperor Wu a doubtful viewing of his beloved deceased Consort Li (*q.v.* Li, Concubine of Emperor Wu). However, possibly even before this, a tale was circulating of a meeting between King Mu of Zhou (r. 1023–983 B.C.E.) and Queen Mother of the West: the king undertook a military expedition to the west, reached the Kunlun hill, and had an audience with the Queen Mother, who later returned his visit. This simple story, embroidered with notions of the king's search for immortality, from *The Songs of the South* (Chuci), and with magicians, magnificent steeds, an exchange of songs by the Turquoise Pond, and the king's reluctant departure without having attained immortality, from the *Liezi*, became a classic theme for poets during the Tang dynasty. The phrase "Turquoise Pond (or Jasper Lake) meeting" has entered the Chinese language, becoming the site of immortality, and is synonymous with the soul's journey to paradise after death.

Surprisingly, given the fanatical nature of his quest for immortality, the first emperor of Qin was never linked to the Queen Mother in literature or mythology. However, some 300 years after his death, Emperor Wu became the beneficiary of a dalliance with the Queen Mother on the seventh day of the seventh month, at his court, during which she offered him five "transcendent" peaches of immortality. The emperor kept the pits, intending to plant them, but the goddess laughed and said the peaches bore fruit only once every 3,000 years, implying he was not to attain immortality. The story of this meeting, which is first found in a third-century text (*Bamboo Annals* [Zhushu jinian]), was further developed in the sixth-century *Esoteric Transmissions Concerning the Martial Thearch of the Han* (Han Wudi neizhuan) and by poets of the Tang dynasty. In the following extract from *Esoteric Transmissions,* the Queen Mother has been transformed into a stunning young woman in fully human form who wears a crown instead of her former *sheng*:

> The Queen Mother rides an imperial carriage of purple clouds, harnessing nine-colored dappled *ch'i-lin*. Tied around her waist, she wears the whip of the Celestial Realized Ones; as a belt pendant, she has a diamond numinous seal. In her clothing of multicolored damask with a yellow background, the patterns and variegated colors are bright and fresh. The radiance of metal makes a shimmering gleam. At her waist is a double-bladed sword for dividing phosphors. Knotted flying clouds make a great cord. On top of her head is a great floriate topknot. She wears the crown of the Grand Realized Ones with hanging beaded strings of daybreak. She steps forth on shoes with squared, phoenix-patterned soles of rose-gem. Her age might be about twenty. Her celestial appearance eclipses and puts in the shade all others. She is a realized numinous being. (Cahill, 81)

This text presents the Queen Mother as she is immortalized in Highest Clarity Daoism, a school that flourished in southern China from the fourth century and derived its name from the Heavens of Highest Clarity (*shangqing*) from which divinities descended to dictate scriptures to a young male visionary (*vide* Wei Huacun). Highest

Clarity Daoists worshipped the Queen Mother as the highest female divinity, as one who controlled access to immortality, often through prescriptions for potent drugs, and as a transmitter of holy texts; she was also mother to several female deities.

It is in this manifestation that the Queen Mother was worshipped during the Tang dynasty. With the collapse of Tang, whose imperial family had supported Daoism, in the early tenth century the Daoist master and writer Du Guangting (850–933) set about preserving his scriptural heritage, one of his major works being *Records of the Assembled Transcendents of the Fortified Walled City* (Yongcheng jixian lu), a compendium of female deities and immortals. His biography of Queen Mother of the West, written as a traditional hagiography as of a real person, presents her as an "etherealized human being." The Queen Mother also exercised a fascination for Tang poets. In *Thoughts Arising in Autumn* (Qiu xing, no. 5), Du Fu (712–770) recalls his dream of her visit to Emperor Wu:

> P'eng-lai palace watchtowers face the Southern Mountains;
> Golden stalks for receiving dew from the Empyrean Han River are spaced like pillars.
> Gazing far westward to the Turquoise Pond, he causes the Queen Mother to descend;
> As she comes, a purple vapor fills the Envelope Pass.
> Clouds shift pheasant tail fans and open palace screens.
> Sun glints off dragon scales—I recognize the incomparable countenance.
> Once again I've fallen asleep by the Glaucous River—startled by the year's growing late;
> How many more times will I be on the dot for morning audience at the Blue Gemstone Gate? (Cahill, 168–69)

In her account of Tang dynasty conceptions and representations of the Queen Mother of the West, Suzanne Cahill describes this figure as the greatest Daoist goddess of that period, a goddess in whom people invested their "two greatest longings . . . : the wish to transcend death and the desire for perfect love." To women, she was "the ultimate abbess, the top authority in the religious family to which [women in Daoism] belong" and "the special patron of women outside the normal world of family"—the single, the widowed, nuns, hermits, prostitutes, artists and performers. To men, she was "the source of techniques for gaining entrance to paradise, guardian of the gates, and registrar of transcendents."

For most of her existence, Queen Mother of the West has been single. Initially she had been partnered in pictorial art in the first century C.E. by the Ji star, or the Master of the Wind, but Han cosmologists with a deep interest in the polar opposition of yin and yang soon provided her with a more appropriate partner: King Father of the East (Dongwanggong). An inscription on a bronze mirror cast in 106 C.E. wishes for "longevity like that of the King Father of the East and the Queen Mother of the West," and images of the pair appear on carvings from that time on. However, the King Father was never more than the pale shadow of a consort to his exotic and potent wife.

Popular worship of the Queen Mother crystallized in 3 B.C.E. in an outburst of what

66 QUEEN MOTHER OF THE WEST

might be seen as mass hysteria, described thus in the *History of the Han Dynasty* (Han shu):

> In the first month of [3 B.C.E.], there were people running around in a state of alarm, each holding a stalk of straw or hemp, carrying them on and passing them to one another, saying that they were transporting the wand of the goddess's edict. Large numbers of persons, amounting to thousands, met in this way on the roadsides, some with disheveled hair or going barefoot. . . .
>
> That summer the people came together in meetings in the capital city and in the commanderies and principalities. In the village settlements, in the lanes and paths across the fields, they held services and set up gaming boards; and they sang and danced in worship of the Queen Mother of the West. They also passed round a written message, saying: "The Mother tells the people that those who wear this talisman will not die." (Wu, 128)

This benign mass movement, with its elements of barefoot shamanism and the transmission of texts, which erupted at the close of the Western Han dynasty, prefigured the Daoist peasant uprisings of the Five Pecks of Rice and the Way of the Celestial Masters that swept China in the last decades of Eastern Han. The egalitarian Way of the Celestial Masters was in turn the forefather of Highest Clarity Daoism, which adopted the Queen Mother as its primary female deity, transmitter of texts.

Daoism never regained the high standing it had enjoyed during Tang, and the rise in popularity of Buddhism saw the two religions merge in many ways, the apparent similarity of many Buddhist concepts to those of Daoism—for example, reincarnation and immortality, Nirvana and nonactivity (*wuwei*), karma and natural allotment (*fen*)—making it inevitable that the two would coexist in the minds and lives of many people. This was already evident in the synthesis of Buddhist and Daoist concepts, rituals, and teachings in the Highest Clarity school of Daoism. Queen Mother of the West remained a revered divinity in folk religion, her great compassion (one of the most important attitudes of Buddhism) revealed through her ability to confer immortality. This compassion was easily extended to her becoming a merciful mother, and she became identified with the mother goddess known as the Eternal Mother or Unborn Venerable Mother (Wusheng Laomu) who longs for all beings to recover their true natures and return home to her paradise.

In the form of Golden Mother of the Jasper Pool (Yaochi Jinmu) or Queen Mother (Wangmu Niangniang), Queen Mother of the West has become the chief deity of the Compassion Society (Cihui tang, or Tz'u-hui t'ang), which was formed in Taiwan in 1949 and which Daniel L. Overmyer studied in detail in the late 1960s and early 1970s. Images of Guanyin, the Jade Emperor, the Earth Mother (Dimu), Nügua (Nü Wa), and the Mysterious Woman of the Nine Heavens (Jiutian Xuannü) appear alongside her on Compassion Society altars. Members of the society, most of whom are women, join to seek or give thanks for the healing of illness. This is effected by spirit mediums through whose mouths the Queen Mother reveals either advice or drug prescriptions. Through "worship, 'training,' and moral actions [members can] draw closer and closer to the Mother and enter her paradise after death, a realm of happiness, peace, and perpetual good health." This "training" (*xunlian*), or dancing, is described as a quest for and response to descent of a deity into one's body and is a clear echo of the spirit possession for which female *wu* were employed in pre-Han times. It underscores the eternal appeal of Queen Mother of the West as the conduit through which people have eternally sought divine guidance, comfort, and healing. She is the magnificent prototype of the *wu* who facilitated communication between mortal rulers and deities.

Sue WILES

Bodde, Derk. "Myths of Ancient China." In *Mythologies of the Ancient World*, ed. S. N. Kramer. Garden City, NY: Doubleday, 1961, 367–82.
Cahill, Suzanne E. *Transcendence & Divine Passion: The Queen Mother of the West in Medieval China*. Stanford, CA: Stanford University Press, 1993.
Dubs, H.H. "An Ancient Chinese Mystery Cult." *Harvard Theological Review* 35 (1942): 221–40.
Jordan, David K., and Daniel L. Overmyer. *The Flying Phoenix: Aspects of Chinese Sectarianism in Taiwan*. Princeton, NJ: Princeton University Press, 1986, xvii–xix, 16–35, 129–40.
Loewe, Michael. *Ways to Paradise: The Chinese Quest for Immortality*. London: George Allen & Unwin, 1979.
Wu, Hung. *The Wu Liang Shrine: The Ideology of Early Chinese Pictorial Art*. Stanford, CA: Stanford University Press, 1989, 108–41.

R

Righteous Mother, The: *see* **Righteous Stepmother of Qi**

The Righteous Nurse of Duke Xiao of Lu
The Righteous Nurse (Lu Xiao Yi Bao), fl. eighth century B.C.E., of Duke Xiao (Xiao Gong, 795–769 B.C.E.) of Lu (present-day Shandong Province), was a widow of the Zang clan. The Righteous Nurse had a son of her own when she was appointed as nurse for the youngest son of Duke Wu (Wu Gong); this boy, whose name was Cheng, later became Duke Xiao. After the death of Duke Wu, his oldest son became ruler of Lu but was murdered during a parricidal coup. With the heir apparent Cheng thus in mortal danger, the Righteous Nurse dressed her own son in Cheng's clothes and left him to be killed by the usurper while she escaped with Cheng, saving his life. This tale celebrates the self-sacrifice of the common people for the sake of the state. The nurse's trustworthiness in protecting the legitimate heir apparent at the enormous expense of her own son's life ensured that her biography was included in "Biographies of the Chaste and Righteous" in *Biographies of Eminent Women* (Lienü zhuan).

Constance A. COOK

Liu Xiang. *Lienü zhuan*. Sibubeiyao ed., 5.1a–b.
O'Hara, Albert R. *The Position of Woman in Early China According to the Lieh Nü Chuan, "The Biographies of Chinese Women."* Taipei: Mei Ya, 1971; 1978, 127–28.

Righteous Respected Female Elder of Lu

Righteous Respected Female Elder (Lu Yi Guzi), dates unknown, of Lu (present-day Shandong Province) is credited with saving her state from an invasion by armies from the neighboring state of Qi by her show of loyalty to the system of caring for one's older brother's children before one's own. This woman lived in the borderlands between the two states. She was carrying her own child, with her nephew following along behind, when the Qi armies reached the border. The commander saw her cast down the child in her arms and leave him behind, picking up the other child instead and hurrying on. When he questioned her, she explained her behavior thus: "To save my own son is a work of private love, but to save my brother's child is a public duty. Now, if I turn my back on a public duty, I turn to my private love; if I abandon my brother's child to die to save my own child, and by good fortune should I escape, . . . my sovereign will not tolerate me" (O'Hara, 137). She told him that she could not live in the state of Lu and be lacking in righteousness. So impressed with this living example of the righteousness of the Lu people was the army's commander that he dared not attack them. The (unnamed) ruler of Lu rewarded the woman with 100 bolts of silk. The extremely didactic nature of this tale, together with the lack of dates and names of rulers and military commanders, suggests that it may have been created purely to reinforce the message that individuals must not allow a private love to harm a public good. Her biography is included in "Biographies of the Chaste and Righteous" in *Biographies of Eminent Women* (Lienü zhuan).

The same chapter of *Biographies of Eminent Women* carries a similar tale in the biography of the Virtuous Aunt of Liang (Liang Jie Guzi). The Virtuous Aunt lived sometime before the seventh century B.C.E. in the state of Liang, in the north of the present-day province of Shaanxi. She fled her burning house with her own son, thinking it was her older brother's son. Realizing her mistake and that it was too late to save her nephew, she ran back into the house and burned to death rather than face the shame of being thought to have placed her private love of her son above her public duty of ensuring the continuation of her older brother's line. Whether this was a genuine mistake on her part or the only means she had to save her son's life can never be known.

Constance A. COOK

Liu Xiang. *Lienü zhuan*. Sibubeiyao ed., 5.4b–5b; 5.9a–b.
O'Hara, Albert R. *The Position of Woman in Early China According to the Lieh Nü Chuan, "The Biographies of Chinese Women."* Taipei: Mei Ya, 1971; 1978, 136–38, 147.

Righteous Stepmother of Ch'i, The: *see* The Righteous Stepmother of Qi

The Righteous Stepmother of Qi

The Righteous Stepmother (Qi Yi Jimu), fl. fourth century B.C.E., lived in the state of Qi (in the north of the present-day province of Shandong). She was a widow with two sons, the older her stepson, the younger her own son. One of them killed a man during a roadside fight but they both claimed responsibility separately, each attempting to protect the other. The magistrate could not decide which son was guilty, nor could the chief minister or King Xuan (Xuan Wang, r. 342–324 B.C.E.), so the widow was given the impossible task of deciding "which one she wants killed and which one [is] to live" (O'Hara, 140). The distraught woman said the younger son should be killed, and when questioned revealed that she had promised her husband on his deathbed that she would care for his first-born son. For her to let the older brother die so the younger could live would thus be to go back on her promise and to "cast aside a public duty for a private love." So impressed was King Xuan with the woman's righteousness that he let both sons go and honored her with the title The Righteous Mother. Her biography is included in "Biographies of the Chaste and Righteous" in *Biographies of Eminent Women* (Lienü zhuan).

Constance A. COOK

Liu Xiang. *Lienü zhuan.* Sibubeiyao ed., 5.6a–b.
O'Hara, Albert R. *The Position of Woman in Early China According to the Lieh Nü Chuan, "The Biographies of Chinese Women."* Taipei: Mei Ya, 1971; 1978, 139–41.

Ru'er's Mother: *see* **The Crone of Quwo of Wei**

Ruji

Ruji, fl. c. 258 B.C.E., is credited with using her special position as the favorite concubine of King Anli (r. 276–244 B.C.E.) of Wei to help prevent the fall of the capital of the state of Zhao to the invading Qin army.

By the mid-third century B.C.E., the state of Qin had become the most powerful of the seven states occupying what is now China proper and was gradually swallowing its neighbors: Wei, Han, Zhao, Chu, Qi, and Yan. Whenever Qin invaded one state, the others felt the pressure and would attempt to help one another in the face of the military superiority of their common foe. At that time, Zhao and Wei were joined in a marriage alliance: the Prince of Pingyuan, the younger brother of of the King of Zhao was married to the sister of King Anli of Wei. Therefore, when the Qin army invaded Zhao in 258 B.C.E., laying siege to its capital Handan (present-day Daming, Hebei Province), the prince's wife sent letters to her brother King Anli and to another brother, the Prince of Xinling, requesting help. King Anli responded by sending an army, under the leadership of a man named Jin Bi, to rescue Zhao. In the meantime, however, Qin attempted to forestall a Zhao–Wei alliance by threatening to invade Wei if it sent help to Zhao. Understandably apprehensive, King Anli ordered his general Jin Bi to station his troops at Ye (present-day Linzhang District, Hebei Province) and await further instructions.

As the situation in Handan grew more critical, the Prince of Pingyuan sent messengers to King Anli and his brother the Prince of Xinling, entreating and recriminating in turn. The Prince of Xinling also repeatedly requested King Anli to send his army; in addition, he dispatched his most eloquent advisers in a further attempt to persuade the king. All of these efforts proved to be in vain, however, and the Prince of Xinling

70 RUJI

finally decided to show his solidarity with Zhao by going to the besieged city of Handan to die with his sister and brother-in-law.

One of the prince's advisers devised a better plan, however. He reminded the Prince of Xinling that he had once avenged King Anli's favorite concubine, Ruji, by killing the man who had killed her father. Deeply indebted, Ruji had as yet found no opportunity to return the favor. The adviser suggested that the prince ask Ruji to steal from King Anli's bedroom the tiger talisman that would give him the authority to replace Jin Bi, thus enabling him to take charge of Jin Bi's army and lead it on to Zhao.

As anticipated, Ruji did not hesitate to steal the talisman for the Prince of Xinling, who went with it to demand Jin Bi hand his army over to him. When Jin Bi hesitated, a retainer of the prince bludgeoned him to death with a blunt instrument made of iron and the prince marched against the Qin army, which promptly lifted the siege of Handan. Feted by the people of Zhao and fearing retribution from his native Wei, the Prince of Xinling remained in Zhao for many years. Nothing, however, is known of what happened to Ruji. This is a fate shared by many women who played a crucial role at a critical time in Chinese history and who were never heard of again.

Lily Xiao Hong LEE

Liu Shisheng. *Zhongguo gudai funüshi.* Qingdao: Qingdao chubanshe, 1991, 69.
Shi ji. Beijing: Zhonghua shuju, 1959, vol. 5, 77.2377–82.
Sima Guang. "Xinjiao." *Zizhi tongjian.* Taipei: Shijie shuju, 1977, vol. 1, 5.179–83.

S

Shang Woman Warrior: *see* **Fu Zi, the Shang Woman Warrior**

Shang-huai of Ch'i, Daughter of: *see* **Jing, Daughter of Shanghuai Yan of Qi**

Shaonan Shen Nü: *see* **The Shaonan Woman of Shen**

The Shaonan Woman of Shen
The Shaonan Woman of Shen (Shaonan Shen Nü), dates unknown, is credited with refusing to go through with a marriage contract and with going to jail because the family of the man she was to marry did not fulfill their ceremonial obligations. Shen was a small state in the south of present-day Henan Province and it is thought that Shaonan refers to a place in the same area in which poems preserved in *The Book of Songs* (Shi jing) in a section with that title originated. Tradition associates this woman's tale with Ode no. 17, "Xing lu," in that section, suggesting that she wrote it:

The paths are drenched with dew.
True, I said 'Early in the night';
But I fear to walk in so much dew.
. . .
Who can say that you have no family?
How else could you bring this plaint?
But though you bring this plaint,
All the same I will not marry you. (Waley, 64–65)

Arthur Waley believed this ode to have been about a man who had "picked up with someone who . . . is trying to force him to marry her, by bringing a lawsuit, which shows that her account of herself was untrue." Other scholars, however, see the woman of Shen as an example of someone who understood the rituals; in other words, she observed the regulations and was steadfastly righteous. It appears that the woman of Shen died soon after writing her ode, whether by her own hand or in prison is not clear, as O'Hara's translation (103) shows: "then she, preferring to die rather than to go [to her husband's house], wrote a poem." Her biography is included in "Biographies of the Chaste and Obedient" in *Biographies of Eminent Women* (Lienü zhuan).

Constance A. COOK

Liu Xiang. *Lienü zhuan*. Sibubeiyao ed., 4.1a–b.
O'Hara, Albert R. *The Position of Woman in Early China According to the Lieh Nü Chuan, "The Biographies of Chinese Women."* Taipei: Mei Ya, 1971; 1978, 102–3.
Qu Wanli. *Shijing shiyi*. Mao no. 17. Taipei: Huagang, 1977, 12–13.
Waley, Arthur. *The Book of Songs*. London: George Allen & Unwin, 1937; 1969, 64–65.

Shen, Daughter of Marquis Shen, Queen: *see* Bao Si, Wife of King You of Zhou

Shen of Shao-nan, The Lady of: *see* The Shaonan Woman of Shen

Shi Yiguang: *see* Xi Shi

Shu Ji
Shu Ji, the Ji-Clan Woman of the Younger (Jin Yang Shu Ji), fl. sixth century B.C.E., was the wife of Yangshe Zi, a man of the Yangshe (Sheep's Tongue) clan in the state of Jin (in the north of the present-day provinces of Shanxi-Hebei). Her husband was an upright man whose probity often offended those around him. When he was presented with the gift of a poached sheep she gave him the following practical advice to save him from a tricky political situation. She persuaded him to accept the sheep, but when he wanted to give it to their two sons, Yang Shuxiang and Yang Shuyu, she suggested he bury the sheep whole in an earthenware jar. When the affair was discovered two years later he was able to show the magistrate the undisturbed skeleton of the sheep, thereby proving he had not consumed it and was therefore not guilty.

72   SHU JI

For this she is celebrated as being "able to forestall harm and keep suspicions at a distance" (O'Hara, 89).

She is also credited with perception and foresight in relation to her sons. She warned her older son, Yang Shuxiang, to choose a wife from her clan rather than going through with the marriage to a famous beauty that had been arranged by Duke Ping (Ping Gong, r. 557–532), the ruler of Jin, her reason being that any person upon whom Heaven bestows great beauty will certainly suffer great calamity. Reluctantly, and under pressure from Duke Ping, Yang Shuxiang married his beauty, who gave birth to a son who cried like a wolf. According to Shu Ji this was an omen of disaster for the Yang clan because such a child would have a wild, fierce heart. And indeed, this child when grown took part in a rebellion that led to the ruin of the clan. As for her younger son, Yang Shuyu, Shu Ji had predicted when she gave birth to him that greed and evil lay in store for him because of his animal-like features. This prediction was also fulfilled, for Yang Shuyu was accused of taking bribes and was killed by one of the parties to a quarrel over a field. Later, his body was exposed in the marketplace like that of a common criminal. Shu Ji is therefore credited with understanding human affections and being wise. Her biography is included in "Biographies of the Benign and Wise" in *Biographies of Eminent Women* (Lienü zhuan).

Constance A. COOK

Liu Xiang. *Lienü zhuan*. Sibubeiyao ed., 3.6a–7b.
Zuo zhuan. Zhao 28. *Chunqiu jing zhuan yinde*. Shanghai: Guji shudian, 1983, 426.
O'Hara, Albert R. *The Position of Woman in Early China According to the Lieh Nü Chuan, "The Biographies of Chinese Women."* Taipei: Mei Ya, 1971; 1978, 89–92.

Shu-chi of Yang of Chin: *see* **Shu Ji**

Si-Clan Woman of Bao: *see* **Bao Si, Wife of King You of Zhou**

Song Bao Nüzong: *see* **Nüzong, the Wife of Baosu of Song**

Song Gong Bo Ji: *see* **Bo Ji, Wife of Duke Gong of Song**

Su Woman with the Goitre of Ch'i, The: *see* **The Goiter Girl of Qi, Wife of King Min**

Suliu Nü: *see* **The Goiter Girl of Qi, Wife of King Min**

Sunshu Ao Mu: *see* **Sunshu Ao's Mother**

Sunshu Ao's Mother
Sunshu Ao Mu, was the mother of Sunshu Ao, fl. sixth century B.C.E., who became the Commanding Minister of the state of Chu, a state in what is now central China.

Some commentators state that his surname was Wei, his given name was Ao, and his courtesy name was Sunshu. Sunshu Ao's Mother is credited with correctly reading an omen involving her son's killing and burial of a two-headed snake.

While playing outside as a child, Sunshu Ao saw a two-headed snake, which he killed and buried so that others would not see it because it was believed that seeing such a snake was a bad omen. Upon returning home he began crying and in response to his mother's inquiry told her that he thought seeing such an omen foretold a bad fate. His mother, however, realized that since he had killed and buried the snake his virtue would lead him instead to greatness and she believed that Heaven would reward his kindness with blessings. His mother is thus said to have known "the order of virtue," and her biography is included in "Biographies of the Benign and Wise" in *Biographies of Eminent Women* (Lienü zhuan).

Constance A. COOK

Liu Xiang. *Lienü zhuan*. Sibubeiyao ed., 3.3a–b.
O'Hara, Albert R. *The Position of Woman in Early China According to the Lieh Nü Chuan, "The Biographies of Chinese Women."* Taipei: Mei Ya, 1971; 1978, 81–82.

T

Ta Tzu of T'ao, The Wife of: *see* **Dazi of Tao's Wife**

T'ai Chiang: *see* **Tai Jiang**

T'ai Jen: *see* **Tai Ren**

Tai Jiang
Grand Jiang-Clan Woman (Tai Jiang), late twelfth–early eleventh century B.C.E., is also known as Jiang Yuan (meaning "Source"), an ancestress of the Zhou people. She is described variously as a daughter of Tai Shi (clan head of the Tai, who lived in present-day Shaanxi Province), a daughter of the Marquis of Tai (Tai Hou), and a daughter of the Youlü clan. In some tales, she is known as a consort to Gu Gong Danfu (a pre–Zhou dynasty Zhou-clan head) and as the mother of Gu Gong's third son, Li Li. In other tales, she is known as the mother of Tai Bo (Grand Elder, the founder deity and ancestor of the Zhou nation), Da Bo Zhong Yong, and Wang Ji. By Han times, she had been deified as one of the Three Mothers of the Zhou House (*qq.v.* Tai Ren; Tai Si) who were consulted by the Zhou kings.

In the form of Jiang Yuan, she was the primary wife of god-king Di Ku and mother of Hou Ji, the god of agriculture and genitor of the Zhou people and their Ji clan. Her pregnancy occurred after she stepped on a giant footprint in the wilds. Her initial attempts to abandon Hou Ji, this seemingly inauspicious baby (nicknamed Qi, meaning "Castaway"), are recounted in the ode *Giving Birth to the People* (Sheng min), preserved in *The Book of Songs* (Shi jing):

74 TAI JIANG

> So blessed were her sacrifice and prayer
> That easily she bore her child.
> Indeed, they put it in a narrow lane;
> But oxen and sheep tenderly cherished it.
> Indeed, they put it in a far-off wood;
> But it chanced that woodcutters came to this wood.
> Indeed, they put it on the cold ice;
> But the birds covered it with their wings.
> The birds at last went away,
> And Hou Chi began to wail. (Waley, 241)

Noticing the extraordinary behavior of the animals and birds toward the child, she finally took it home.

Later versions of this tale credit Tai Jiang with teaching her son Hou Ji, later revered as the god of agriculture, his skills: "She liked to sow, cultivate, and harvest. When her son grew up, she taught him to plant trees—the mulberry and hemp." She is invariably described as being of a mild and tranquil disposition, a docile woman who taught her son(s) well and "was without faults." Her biography is included in "Biographies Illustrating the Correct Deportment of Mothers" in *Biographies of Eminent Women* (Lienü zhuan).

Constance A. COOK

Liu Xiang. *Lienü zhuan*. Sibubeiyao ed., 1.2b; 1.4a.
O'Hara, Albert R. *The Position of Woman in Early China According to the Lieh Nü Chuan, "The Biographies of Chinese Women."* Taipei: Mei Ya, 1971; 1978, 17–19, 22–25.
Qu Wanli. *Shijing shiyi.* "Xing wei." Mao no. 246. Taipei: Huagang, 1977, 224–26.
Takikawa Kametarō. *Shiki kaichū kōshō* [*Shi ji*]. Taipei: Hongshi, 1977, 4.2, 4.8.
Waley, Arthur. *The Book of Songs.* London: George Allen & Unwin, 1937; 1969, 241.

Tai Ren

Tai Ren (Grand Forbearance), early eleventh century B.C.E., was the middle daughter of Ren Shi (Clan Head of the Ren; this clan name is given in one source as Zhi Ren) and consort of Li Li, the son of Tai Jiang (*q.v.*). However, it is because she was the mother of King Wen (Wen Wang), the posthumous title of Chang, the first king of Zhou, that she is honored as a virtuous woman. King Wen's sagehood is credited to her *in utero* education of him through such virtuous acts as not gazing on evil things, not listening to lewd sounds, and not speaking insolent words. She is thus said to have understood the principle of "prenatal instruction" whereby a woman who is affected by good things will give birth to a good child. In Han times, she was deified along with Tai Jiang and Tai Si (*q.v.*) as one of the Three Mothers of the Zhou House and described as "upright, sincere, decorous, and engaged solely in virtuous conduct." Her biography is included in "Biographies Illustrating the Correct Deportment of Mothers" in *Biographies of Eminent Women* (Lienü zhuan).

Constance A. COOK

Liu Xiang. *Lienü zhuan.* Sibubeiyao ed., 1.4a–b.

O'Hara, Albert R. *The Position of Woman in Early China According to the Lieh Nü Chuan, "The Biographies of Chinese Women."* Taipei: Mei Ya, 1971; 1978, 22–25.

Qu Wanli, ed. *Shijing shiyi.* "Xing wei." Mao no. 246. Taipei: Huagang, 1977, 224–26.

Takikawa Kametarō. *Shiki kaichū kōshō [Shi ji].* Taipei: Hongshi, 1977, 4.8.

Waley, Arthur, trans. *The Book of Songs.* London: George Allen & Unwin, 1937; 1969, 207–8.

Tai Si, Wife of King Wen of Zhou

Tai Si (Great Si-Clan Woman), early eleventh century B.C.E., was a daughter of the Si clan of Xin (in present-day Shaanxi Province), who were descendants of the hero-founder Yu the Great. She was the wife of King Wen (Wen Wang) of Zhou and is credited with the virtuous upbringing of their ten sons, the most famous of whom are King Wu (Wu Wang) and the Duke of Zhou (Zhou Gong). The marriage of this "coy and comely" young woman to King Wen is eulogized in an ode that describes her crossing the Wei River on a bridge of boats.

> King Wen was blessed.
> A great country had a child,
> A great country had a child
> Fair as a sister of Heaven.
> King Wen fixed on a lucky day
> And went himself to meet her at the Wei;
> He joined boats and made of them a bridge;
> Dazzling with radiance! (Waley, 262)

In Han times, she was deified as one of the Three Mothers of the Zhou House and was considered to have been the most virtuous of these three most virtuous women (*qq.v.* Tai Jiang; Tai Ren). She was "compassionate and understood what was right"; she was also "benevolent, intelligent, and possessed virtues." Posthumously, she was referred to as Wen Mu (The Accomplished Mother) because she toiled diligently from morning to night, ruled within the palace, and diligently instructed all of her sons. In this, she was the first true exemplar of the model wife for countless generations of Chinese women. Her biography is included in "Biographies Illustrating the Correct Deportment of Mothers" in *Biographies of Eminent Women* (Lienü zhuan).

Constance A. COOK

Liu Xiang. *Lienü zhuan.* Sibubeiyao ed., 1.4b.

O'Hara, Albert R. *The Position of Woman in Early China According to the Lieh Nü Chuan, "The Biographies of Chinese Women."* Taipei: Mei Ya, 1971; 1978, 22–25.

Qu Wanli. *Shijing shiyi.* Mao no. 236. Taipei: Huagang, 1977, 205–7.

Waley, Arthur. *The Book of Songs.* London: George Allen & Unwin, 1937; 1969, 262.

T'ai Ssu: *see* Tai Si, Wife of King Wen of Zhou

Taisi: *see* Tai Si, Wife of King Wen of Zhou

76 TAO DAZI QI

Tao Dazi Qi: *see* **Dazi of Tao's Wife**

Tao Ying, a Widow in Lu

Tao Ying (Lu Gua Tao Ying), dates unknown, lived in the state of Lu (in the present-day province of Shandong). Widowed young, she turned to spinning to support herself and her orphaned children and is credited with refusing a second marriage despite being left to bring up her young children without support. The song she sang to discourage suitors expressed her deep sadness at losing her mate:

> The yellow snow-goose was early widowed and for seven years it did not mate.
> It hid its head alone in passing the night and did not go about with the rest of its kind.
> During half of the night it called forth sadly as it thought of its former mate.
> Since it was Heaven's will that I should become a widow quite early, what harm is it for me to pass the night alone?
> The widowed wife thinks of the husband and her tears fall as she recalls his actions.
> Alas, alas! the dead cannot be forgotten.
> If the bird is estimable, how much more so a chaste and good person.
> Although one may find a worthy mate, to the end one does not marry a second time.
> (O'Hara, 122)

Tao Ying's poignant song acknowledges the loneliness to which women such as she were condemned, yet men would remarry almost immediately if their wives died. Her biography is included in "Biographies of the Chaste and Obedient" in *Biographies of Eminent Women* (Lienü zhuan) as an example for later generations of women of the behavior expected of widows.

Constance A. COOK

Liu Xiang. *Lienü zhuan*. Sibubeiyao ed., 4.8a–b.
O'Hara, Albert R. *The Position of Woman in Early China According to the Lieh Nü Chuan, "The Biographies of Chinese Women."* Taipei: Mei Ya, 1971; 1978, 121–22.

T'ao Ying, the Widow of Lu: *see* **Tao Ying, a Widow in Lu**

Three Mothers of the Zhou House: *see* **Tai Jiang** *and* **Tai Ren** *and* **Tai Si, Wife of King Wen of Zhou**

Tian Ji of Qi's Mother

The Mother of Tian Ji (Qi Tian Ji Mu), fl. fourth century B.C.E., lived in the state of Qi (in the north of present-day Shandong Province). Her son was a minister in the government of King Xuan (Xuan Wang, r. 342–324 B.C.E.) of Qi and had made a considerable profit from his subordinates, who paid him "interest on loans" in silver. He appears to have been engaged in an activity tantamount to usury. When he tried to give this money to his mother as a gift she refused it, saying it was money unfairly gained, and she threatened to disown him: "I have learned that an official acts ethically, is chaste in conduct, and does not act for unfair gain . . . on the contrary, you appear to be far removed from loyalty. One who, as a minister, is disloyal is also disobedient as a son. I will not possess wealth that is unjust; I will not have a son who is not filial" (O'Hara, 47). The mother's words shamed her son, who returned the money and approached the king asking to be punished. King Xuan, impressed with the mother's integrity, rewarded her financially, and pardoned and reinstated her son. Her biography is included in "Biographies Illustrating the Correct Deportment of Mothers" in *Biographies of Eminent Women* (Lienü zhuan) as an example of how sons will benefit if their mothers instruct them on the evils of corruption and the need to be loyal to their rulers.

Constance A. COOK

Liu Xiang. *Lienü zhuan.* Sibubeiyao ed., 1.13a–b.
O'Hara, Albert R. *The Position of Woman in Early China According to the Lieh Nü Chuan, "The Biographies of Chinese Women."* Taipei: Mei Ya, 1971; 1978, 46–48.

T'ien Chi Tzu of Ch'i, The Mother of: *see* **Tian Ji of Qi's Mother**

Ting Chiang, a Maiden of Wei: *see* **Ding Jiang, Wife of Duke Ding of Wei**

Tsang Sun of Lu, The Mother of: *see* **Zang Sun of Lu's Mother**

T'u Shan, the Mother of Ch'i: *see* **The Tushan Woman**

Tushan Nü: *see* **The Tushan Woman**

The Tushan Woman
The Tushan Woman (Tushan Nü) is a legendary figure said to have lived in the twenty-first century B.C.E. She was given this name because she was from Tushan, which is generally thought to have been in the vicinity of the present-day city of Chongqing in Sichuan Province, although one source locates it in Dangtu, present-day Huailing District in Anhui Province. In some sources she is also known as Nüjiao or Nüqiao.

The Tushan Woman was taken as a wife by Yu the Great, the legendary hero who tamed the waters, when he passed through Tushan on his vast flood-control project. Yu was thirty years old at the time. In due course, the Tushan Woman gave birth to a son, Qi, who is celebrated for consolidating the Xia dynasty (c. 2100–1600 B.C.E.). Some sources say that Yu left Tushan to continue his flood-control work just four days after he took the woman to wife; other sources say he left four days after she gave birth to their son. All sources agree that it was many years before Yu returned to his family and that while he passed close by their home three times during that time, he did not visit them. The Tushan Woman was therefore entirely responsible for naming, raising, and educating her son and for this she is given credit, for when he grew to manhood Qi is

78 THE TUSHAN WOMAN

said to have followed his mother's guidance and gained a good reputation. Eventually, he took over from Yu the Xia dynasty, which lasted another four centuries. The Tushan Woman is included in "Biographies Illustrating the Correct Deportment of Mothers" in *Biographies of Eminent Women* (Lienü zhuan).

She is also credited with having founded the Southern school of ancient music (*nan yin*). According to one source, when Yu had not returned home for several years the Tushan Woman sang the song "Waiting for That Man" (Hou ren xi yi), which marks the beginning of the Southern school.

Laura LONG

Liu Xiang. *Lienü zhuan*. Sibubeiyao ed., 1.3a–b.
Lüshi chunqiu, juan 6. In *Lüshi chunqiu jin zhu jin yi*, trans. Lin Pinshi. Taipei: Shijie shuju, 1985, vol. 1, 156.
O'Hara, Albert R. *The Position of Woman in Early China According to the Lieh Nü Chuan, "The Biographies of Chinese Women."* Taipei: Mei Ya, 1971; 1978, 20–21.
Shi ji. Beijing: Zhonghua shuju, 1973, vol. 1, 2.80–81; vol. 4, 49; 1967, 49; 1968, n. 3.
Xie Wuliang. *Zhongguo funü wenxueshi*. Shanghai: Zhonghua shuju, 1916; Zhengzhou: Zhongzhou guji chubanshe, 1992, rpt, I, 5.

Two Disorderly Women of Wei: *see* **Kong Bo Ji** *and* **Nanzi, Wife of Duke Ling of Wei**

Two Royal Wives of Yu, The: *see* **Ehuang and Nüying**

Tzu-mao: *see* **Zheng Mao, Wife of King Cheng of Chu**

V

The Virgin of Egu
The Virgin of Egu (Egu Chunü), fl. c. early fifth century B.C.E., attracted the attention of Confucius while he was traveling south with his disciples. She was wearing a hanging jade ornament and washing clothes by the roadside when they came upon her. Through his disciple Zigong, whom he asked to approach the young woman three times asking three different things of her, Confucius intended to test her knowledge of propriety. She passed his test, as he had anticipated she would.

First, Confucius gave Zigong a cup and instructed him to speak with the young woman in order to observe what her aspirations were. When Zigong asked her for a cup of water she told him the stream was sometimes clear and sometimes muddy. She first took the cup and filled it with water against the current of the stream and threw it out, then she filled the cup following the current of the stream until it overflowed. Finally she set the cup down on the sand and said: "According to propriety, I should not give the cup to you directly." Confucius next gave Zigong a zither from which he had removed the tuning peg and told Zigong to ask the young woman to tune it. She declined, saying: "I am from the countryside, ignorant and guileless, how can I tune a zither?" Lastly, Confucius pulled out a piece of fine linen and handed it to Zigong, who said to the young woman: "I have a piece of fine linen. Not that I am so bold as to presume that it is equal to your worth, I simply wish to leave it by the water." She replied: "You may wish to share your property and leave it in the wilderness but I am afraid to accept it because I am very young. Perhaps you are not yet spoken for, but I might have already been spoken for by some unrefined country lad."

Each time Zigong reported what had happened, Confucius said: "I knew it." Confucius said of the Virgin of Egu: "She knows human affairs well, she understands propriety, and she is not licentious." Her biography in *Biographies of Eminent Women* (Lienü zhuan) is included under "Biographies of Those Able in Reasoning and Understanding."

This tale as recorded in Liu Xiang's *Biographies of Eminent Women* is almost identical with that in Han Ying's *Hanshi waizhuan*. Since Han Ying (fl. 150 B.C.E.) lived almost a century before Liu Xiang (?77–?6 B.C.E.), it would appear that his version provided the material for Liu Xiang's.

Constance A. COOK

Han Ying. *Hanshi waizhuan*. Sibucongkan ed., 1.1b–3b.
———. *Han shih wai chuan: Han Ying's Illustrations of the Didactic Application of the Classic of Songs; An Annotated Translation by James Robert Hightower*. Harvard-Yenching Institute Monograph Series, no. 11. Cambridge, MA: Harvard University Press, 1952, 13–15.
Hong Mai. *Rongzhai suibi wuji*, Sibucongkan ed., II, 8.4b.
Liu Xiang. *Lienü zhuan*. Sibubeiyao ed., 6.5a–b.
O'Hara, Albert R. *The Position of Woman in Early China According to the Lieh Nü Chuan, "The Biographies of Chinese Women."* Taipei: Mei Ya, 1971; 1978, 163–65.

Virtuous Aunt of Liang, The: *see* **Righteous Respected Female Elder of Lu**

W

Wangmu Niangniang: *see* **Queen Mother of the West**

Wei, Mother of the Minister of the Ancestral Temple in: *see* **Kong Bo Ji**

Wei, The Virtuous Nurse of: *see* **The Abiding Wet Nurse of Wei**

Wei, The Widowed Wife of: *see* **The Widow of Wei**

Wei Gu Ding Jiang: *see* **Ding Jiang, Wife of Duke Ding of Wei**

Wei Guafuren: *see* **The Widow of Wei**

Wei Hsüan Chiang: *see* **Xuan Jiang, Wife of Duke Xuan of Wei**

80 WEI JI

Wei Ji, Wife of Duke Huan of Qi

Wei Ji (Qi Huan Wei Ji), fl. mid-seventh century B.C.E., was the wife of Duke Huan (Huan Gong, r. 684–642 B.C.E.), ruler of Qi (in the north of the present-day province of Shandong). Duke Huan was attempting to form an alliance between several states, with his own state of Qi at its head. Since only Wei remained aloof, refusing to attend his court, he developed a plan to attack Wei. However, Wei Ji was a daughter of the Marquis of Wei, and when she realized what her husband was planning to do she approached him in an attitude of submission, begging forgiveness for any offense the state of Wei might have committed. Her husband denied he had any quarrel with Wei, but she explained that she could tell from his demeanor what he was about to do. She could see that he was angry, she told him, because his mood was one of "attack and punishment. Today, I looked at my Lord raising his footsteps high, his aspect severe, and his voice raised; his intent was to attack Wei" (O'Hara, 51). Duke Huan so admired her loyalty that he gave his word he would not attack Wei and raised her to the rank of first wife, giving her authority to rule the inner apartments.

Wei Ji is also credited with having healed her husband from what is described as "his excessive love of music"; it must be presumed that his love of music was seen as excessive because it interfered with his political duties. The Han writer Cui Bi immortalized her benign influence on the ruler in his "Precepts for Distaff Families" (Waiqi zhen). Indeed, so respected was Wei Ji that it was her conduct that is said to have enabled her husband to become one of ancient China's most successful rulers. Her biography is included in "Biographies of the Virtuous and Wise" in *Biographies of Eminent Women* (Lienü zhuan).

Constance A. COOK

Cui Bi. "Waiqi zhen." In *Hou Han shu*. Beijing: Zhonghua shuju, 1973, 80.2619.
Kralle, Jianfei. "Fan Ji und Wei Ji." In *Die Frau im Alten China. Bild und Wirklichkeit*, ed. Dennis Schilling and Jianfei Kralle. Stuttgart: Steiner, 2001, 53–73.
Liu Xiang. *Lienü zhuan*. Sibubeiyao ed., 2.1b–2a.
"Lüshi chunqiu," 18. In *Lüshi chunqiu jiaoshi*, ed. Chen Qiyu. Shanghai: Xuelin chubanshe, 1984, 1168.
O'Hara, Albert R. *The Position of Woman in Early China According to the Lieh Nü Chuan, "The Biographies of Chinese Women."* Taipei: Mei Ya, 1971; 1978, 50–52.

Wei Jie Rumu: *see* The Abiding Wet Nurse of Wei

Wei Ling Nanzi: *see* Nanzi, Wife of Duke Ling of Wei

Wei Mang Ci Mu: *see* The Kind Mother of the Mang Family of Wei

Wei of Qi, Wife of King: *see* Yu Ji, Wife of King Wei of Qi

Wei Quwo Fu: *see* The Crone of Quwo of Wei

Wen Chiang of Duke Huan of Lu: *see* **Wen Jiang, Wife of Duke Huan of Lu**

Wen Jiang, Wife of Duke Huan of Lu

Wen Jiang, or Accomplished Woman of the Jiang Clan, d. 673 B.C.E., was a daughter of the royal house of Qi (in the north of present-day Shandong Province); she is also known as Jiang Shi. After Qi was attacked by Northern Rong peoples, her father tried several times to marry her to the heir apparent of the state of Zheng (in present-day Henan Province), which had provided military aid to Qi. These offers of marriage were rejected and finally, in 709 B.C.E., Wen Jiang was sent in marriage to Duke Huan (Huan Gong, r. 719–697 B.C.E.) of Lu (in present-day Shandong Province) where, three years later, she gave birth to a son. Twelve years after the birth of her son, she accompanied her husband back to her homeland of Qi, where she was seduced by her brother, Duke Xiang (Xiang Gong). After this became known, Duke Xiang took his father's advice and attempted to appease his brother-in-law by throwing a feast for him. Duke Xiang's son (in one version it is his half-brother) then killed Duke Huan, who had been lulled into a state of drunkenness during the feast. Upon the death of Wen Jiang's husband, her son was enthroned in Lu as Duke Zhuang (Zhuang Gong, r. 692–661 B.C.E.). In some accounts, Wen Jiang remained in Qi while in others she returned to Lu with her husband's body. One source says that she stopped at the Qi–Lu border on her way back to Lu, sending a message to her son that she wished to remain at the border. Her son had a residence built for her and she lived there until her death.

In *Biographies of Eminent Women* (Lienü zhuan), where her biography is included in "Biographies of Pernicious and Depraved Women," it is said that she and her brother Duke Xiang had indulged in an incestuous relationship even before she married Duke Huan and that they resumed this relationship when she returned to Qi with her husband. Her travels to other states, including Qi, before and after the death of Duke Xiang in 685, suggest that she was a politically powerful figure, as the Lu archivist referred to her as "our Minor Ruler" (*wo xiao jun*).

Constance A. COOK

Chunqiu and *Zuo zhuan*. Huan 3, 6, 18; Zhuang 1–2, 4–7, 15, 21–22. Taipei: Fenghuang chubanshe, 1977, vol. 1, 28, 32–33, 45, 46–48, 51–53, 62, 67–68.
Guan Siping. *Houfei de mingyun*. Jinan: Shandong wenyi chubanshe, 1991, 190–95.
Liu Xiang. *Lienü zhuan*. Sibubeiyao ed., 7.5b–6a.
O'Hara, Albert R. *The Position of Woman in Early China According to the Lieh Nü Chuan, "The Biographies of Chinese Women."* Taipei: Mei Ya, 1971; 1978, 193–94.
Takikawa Kametarō. *Shiki kaichū kōshō [Shi ji]*. Taipei: Hongshi, 1977, 33.28, 42.10.

Wen Mu: *see* **Tai Si, Wife of King Wen of Zhou**

Wen of Jin, The Wife of Duke: *see* **Jiang-Clan Woman of Qi, Wife of Duke Wen of Jin**

The Widow of Wei

The Widow of Wei (Wei Guafuren), dates unknown, was a daughter of the ruler of the state of Qi (in present-day Shandong Province). She was given in marriage to the ruler of Wei, in the north of the present-day province of Henan, but he died just as she was about to enter the city. Instead of returning home as she was advised to do, she took up her station and performed three years' mourning. After this period of mourning, she received a proposal of marriage from her brother-in-law, the younger brother of her dead husband and now ruler of Wei. She refused his proposal, preferring to remain faithful to the husband she never knew. Her brother-in-law asked her brothers in Qi to pressure her but she remained steadfast in her refusal. Ode no. 26, "Bo zhou," preserved in *The Book of Songs* (Shi jing), is credited to her:

> My heart is not a stone;
> It cannot be rolled.
> My heart is not a mat;
> It cannot be folded away.
> . . .
> My sad heart is consumed, I am harassed
> By a host of small men.
> . . .
> Sorrow clings to me
> Like an unwashed dress.
> In the still of night I brood upon it,
> Long to take wing and fly away. (Waley, 71)

She is praised for not violating her widowhood, and her biography is therefore included in "Biographies of the Chaste and Obedient" in *Biographies of Eminent Women* (Lienü zhuan).

Constance A. COOK

Liu Xiang. *Lienü zhuan*. Sibubeiyao ed., 4.2a–b.
O'Hara, Albert R. *The Position of Woman in Early China According to the Lieh Nü Chuan, "The Biographies of Chinese Women."* Taipei: Mei Ya, 1971; 1978, 106–7.
Qu Wanli, ed. *Shijing shiyi.* "Bo zhou." Mao no. 26. Taipei: Huagang, 1977, 18–19.
Waley, Arthur. *The Book of Songs.* London: George Allen & Unwin, 1937; 1969, 71.

The Wife of the Chariot Driver for Yanzi, Minister of Qi

The Wife of the Chariot Driver for Minister Yanzi (589–500 B.C.E.) (Qi Xiang Yanzi Puyu Qi), fl. c. 550–530 B.C.E., lived in the state of Qi (in the north of the present-day province of Shandong). She is remembered for pointing out to her husband that, while he was very tall, his grandiose and self-satisfied behavior as a chariot driver was in striking contrast to the thoughtful and respectful demeanor of Minister Yanzi, a man of small stature. Her husband heeded her rebuke and altered his behavior accordingly. Minister Yanzi noticed the change, inquired the reason for it, and subsequently promoted the chariot driver. He also named the wife Mingfu (Woman of the

Mandate) in recognition of her intelligence and goodness. Her biography is included in "Biographies of the Virtuous and Wise" in *Biographies of Eminent Women* (Lienü zhuan) as an example of how wives must always strive to teach their husbands to become better people.

Constance A. COOK

Liu Xiang. *Lienü zhuan*. Sibubeiyao ed., 2.8a–b.
O'Hara, Albert R. *The Position of Woman in Early China According to the Lieh Nü Chuan, "The Biographies of Chinese Women."* Taipei: Mei Ya, 1971; 1978, 68–70.
Teschke, R. "Zwei Frauen im *Yan zi chun qiu* und im *Lie nü zhuan*." In *Die Frau im alten China. Bild und Wirklichkeit*, ed. Dennis Schilling and Jianfei Kralle. Stuttgart: Steiner, 2001, 117–34.
Yan Ying. *Yanzi chunqiu*. In *Zhuzi jicheng*, ed. Jiang Lihong. Beijing: Zhonghua shuju, 1986, No. 25, 5.146.

Wife of Yuling Zizhong of Chu, The: *see* **Jieyu's Wife, and The Wife of Yuling Zizhong of Chu**

Wo Xiao Jun: *see* **Wen Jiang, Wife of Duke Huan of Lu**

Wu of Chu, The Wife of King: *see* **Man-Clan Woman of Deng, Wife of King Wu of Chu**

X

The Xi Clan Head's Wife
The Wife of the Head of the Xi Clan (Cao Xi zhi Qi), fl. mid-seventh century B.C.E., is credited with saving her husband's village in Cao (a small state in the southwest of present-day Shandong Province) from the wrath of Duke Wen (Wen Gong, 696–628 B.C.E.; r. 636–628 B.C.E.), the ruler of the northern state of Jin (in the present-day provinces of Shanxi and Hebei). This came about because of an earlier incident when Duke Wen, then known by his personal name of Chong Er, had passed through Cao during a period of exile. The ruler of Cao, Duke Gong, had insulted him at that time: having heard that Chong Er had sides of solid bone instead of ribs, Duke Gong had spied on him as he was about to bathe. However, the wife of clan head Xi Fuji had recognized the leadership qualities of Chong Er and his men and realized that any perceived disrespect toward them was certain to have disastrous repercussions. She had therefore encouraged her husband to treat Chong Er with respect. Chong Er did not forget this and when he later invaded Cao he ordered his soldiers not to enter Xi Fuji's village. The inhabitants of this village therefore owed their lives entirely to the foresight and political nous of the clan head's wife. Her biography is included in "Biographies of the Benign and Wise" in *Biographies of Eminent Women* (Lienü zhuan).

Constance A. COOK

84 THE XI CLAN HEAD'S WIFE

Liu Xiang. *Lienü zhuan.* Sibubeiyao ed., 3.2b–3.
O'Hara, Albert R. *The Position of Woman in Early China According to the Lieh Nü Chuan, "The Biographies of Chinese Women."* Taipei: Mei Ya, 1971; 1978, 79–81.
Zuo zhuan. Zuo zhuan huijian. Xi 23. Taipei: Fenghuang chubanshe, 1977, vol. 1, 6, 34–35.

Xi Shi

Xi Shi, c. 503–c. 473 B.C.E., is traditionally considered the most beautiful of the four most beautiful women of ancient China, the other three being Wang Zhaojun (*q.v.*), Diao Chan (*q.v.*), and Yang Guifei (719–756; see *Biographical Dictionary of Chinese Women,* Tang to Ming volume). Born Shi Yiguang and also known as Xi Zi and Xian Shi, Xi Shi was a native of Ningluo (south of present-day Zhuji, Zhejiang Province) in the southern state of Yue. Most of the inhabitants of the two villages nestled at the foot of Ningluo Mountain went by the surname Shi, and since she lived with her poor parents in the western (*xi*) village she was called Xi Shi. Her father sold firewood for a living, her mother was a weaver, and Xi Shi is said to have been a silk washer (*wansha nü*). From childhood she was renowned for her natural beauty and, living during the late Spring and Autumn period, her life reflected the vicissitudes of the states of Yue (present-day Zhejiang Province) and Wu (the present-day provinces of Jiangsu and Anhui).

These two states became bitter rivals following the death of the Five Hegemons, the five most powerful princes, and in 494 Wu defeated Yue. The vanquished King of Yue, Goujian, retreated to Kuaiji (present-day Shaoxing, Zhejiang Province) and offered himself to Fuchai, the King of Wu, in exchange for a guarantee that Yue would not be destroyed. He then traveled to Wu with his wife and a minister named Fan Li and for three years served Fuchai in the lowly job of keeper of the horses. In 491, he was released and allowed to return to Yue. Desperate for revenge, Goujian sought the advice of his loyal ministers Fan Li and Wen Zhong, who proposed, among other measures, that Goujian send a number of beautiful women to Fuchai as tribute. The purpose of this tactic was to distract Fuchai from his proper duties as ruler, thus diverting his attention from Yue. This would allow Yue to rebuild in relative peace, training soldiers, reviving the economy, and restoring law and order.

Goujian approved this suggestion and a search was undertaken for suitable candidates. Xi Shi and her friend Zheng Dan were selected and underwent three years of training in proper etiquette, dancing, and singing before being escorted to Wu in 487 by Fan Li. It is said that Xi Shi and Fan Li fell in love during that journey but that they chose love for their country above love for one another and continued their journey to Wu. As hoped, Fuchai was totally enchanted by Xi Shi's beauty. Bewitched, he spared no effort to please her and show his love. Among his extravagant projects were the Palace of Beautiful Women (Guanwa gong), which he had built on the slope of Yanshi Hill (present-day Lingyan Hill) south of the capital city Gusu (present-day Suzhou, Jiangsu Province), and the entrancing Promenade of Musical Shoes (Xiangxie lang), beneath which stood thousands of earthenware jars that chimed when Xi Shi and the other women walked or danced on it. Zheng Dan died in 486, but Xi Shi continued to fascinate Fuchai, who neglected his official duties while bestowing favors on the state of Yue, presumably out of gratitude for its gift of Xi Shi. So besotted was he that in 484 he put to death his loyal minister Wu Zixu who had been warning him against Xi Shi. From that time on, Wu grew weaker while Yue grew stronger.

It is said that Xi Shi urged Fuchai to build a canal linking Lake Tai, a freshwater lake in present-day southern Jiangsu Province, with Gusu in order to more easily make pleasure trips there. Once the canal was completed, she made a detailed map of the topography and military facilities of Gusu, folded the map into the shape of a white flower, and slipped it to a fellow countryman, instructing him to pass it on to Fan Li. This information enabled Goujian to decide upon his strategy and in 473 he attacked and comprehensively defeated Fuchai, who had no alternative but to take his own life.

Fan Li voluntarily retired from office and became a recluse in the five-lakes area of the Lake Tai basin, but the fate of Xi Shi remains uncertain. Some sources, believing that Xi Shi and Fan Li had been lovers, say she joined him in his retirement, a fairy-tale ending to the story of a patriotic couple. Others say she was thrown into a river and drowned, suggesting that she was no longer of any use, politically or otherwise; Fan Li, Goujian, and his wife have all been suggested as possible culprits. This second theory testifies to the harsh reality of "casting the bow aside when the birds have been killed" (*niao jin gong cang*). A third theory, put forward by her fellow villagers, is that she returned to Ningluo Village where she died after falling into the river while washing silk. One source says she died in 473 B.C.E., the year Yue vanquished Wu.

Xi Shi is unique among legendary Chinese beauties in that, quite rightly, she has not been condemned for bringing down a state. Both the eighteenth-century *Historical Novel of Various Kingdoms of Eastern Zhou* (Dong Zhou lieguozhi) and the modern commentator Lu Xun (1881–1936) describe her as a heroine of ancient China, likening her to a Trojan Horse. This view contrasts strongly with the longstanding belief that beauty is always evil (*hong yan huo shui*).

Yet, for all this, history has focused solely on her looks. She has gone down in history as the symbol of peerless beauty. The Chinese equivalent of "beauty is in the eye of the beholder" employs her name as a synonym for beautiful women: "a lover sees a Xi Shi in his beloved" (*qingren yanli chu Xi Shi*). Many poems, drawings, stories, and plays have been written about her. Such famous poets as Wang Wei, Li Bo, and Su Dongpo have all written about her in their poetry. Su Dongpo compared her to the West Lake in Hangzhou, one of the best-known scenic spots in China, calling the lake Xi [Shi] hu or Xi Zi hu. She has been described as a perfect natural beauty who never failed to appeal, whether she was frowning or smiling, and her well-proportioned figure has been hailed as the ultimate in female perfection.

Many tourist attractions, food items, cosmetics, and so on in China are named after her, mostly for publicity and commercial reasons. Her statue now stands with those of the other three famous beauties in a Zhuji park in front of a bus terminus about 250 km south of Shanghai. Zhuji also houses the magnificent Xi Shi Temple.

The story of Xi Shi, partly fact and partly fiction, reflects the traditional mentality of the Chinese people. For a woman to win admiration she must be beautiful; if she is to command respect she must possess the qualities of chastity and wisdom, and demonstrate that she has the courage and the ability to serve a cause imposed upon her by men. Xi Shi bewitched the King of Wu and ultimately brought him down. By so doing, she helped consolidate the strength of her home state, Yue, and wiped away the humiliation of her ruler, Goujian. In her case, the end seems to have justified the means. It is apparent from her story that for Chinese historians patriotism overrode the usual demands that a woman be chaste, truthful, and self-effacing and refrain from meddling in politics. Xi Shi is portrayed as a wonder woman blessed with shrewd judgment, the willingness to sacrifice herself, and single-mindedness in attaining her goal. However, the variant endings to her story reveal a divided psyche: should a patriotic and respectable woman be deservedly rewarded by finally being with the man she loves and disappearing gracefully into obscurity, or should political reality and human weakness be brought to the fore?

The earliest and most authentic source materials on Xi Shi are the Eastern Han texts *Wu Yue chun qiu* and *Yue jue shu,* written centuries after her time. While they do not always agree on details, these texts are undoubtedly enriched with (or tainted by) folk tales, legends, and hearsay. Perhaps, therefore, rather than attempting to sort fact from fiction, it may be more fruitful to seek an insight into Chinese values through what we have been told about this beauty.

CHAN Yuk Ping

Chen Weijun. *Xi Shi.* Hangzhou: Zhejiang wenyi chubanshe, 1995, 4–5, 876–77.
Feng Menglong and Cai Yuanfang, eds, *Dong Zhou lieguozhi.* Hong Kong: Mingliang shuju, n.d., vol. 3, 797–843.
Liu Shisheng. *Zhongguo gudai funüshi.* Qingdao: Qingdao chubanshe, 1991, 57–60.
Ma Zhaozheng and Zhou Fuchang. "Meinü aiguo hua Xi Shi." In *Zhongguo gudai funü mingren,* ed. Ma Zhaozheng and Zhou Feitang. Beijing: Zhongguo funü chubanshe, 1988, 27–30.
Xu Tianxiao. *Shenzhou nüzi xinshi.* Taipei: Daoxiang chubanshe, 1993, Part 1, 18–19.
Yu Jidong. *Yue jue shu quan yi.* Guiyang: Guizhou renmin chubanshe, 1996, 170, 231–32, 310.
Zhang Jue. *Wu Yue chun qiu quan yi.* Guiyang: Guizhou renmin chubanshe, 1993, 1, 6, 217, 356, 420.

Xi Wang Mu: *see* **Queen Mother of the West**

Xi Zi: *see* **Xi Shi**

Xian Shi: *see* **Xi Shi**

Xiang Furen: *see* **Ehuang and Nüying**

Xiang Jun: *see* **Ehuang and Nüying**

Xiangzi, Elder Sister of: *see* **Zhao, Wife of the King of Dai**

Xiao Jun: *see* **Ai Jiang, Wife of Duke Zhuang of Lu**

Xiao of Qi, Wife of Duke: *see* **Meng Ji, Wife of Duke Xiao of Qi**

Xie Mu: *see* **Jiandi**

Xie's Mother: *see* **Jiandi**

Xiwangmu: *see* **Queen Mother of the West**

Xu Mu Furen: *see* **Duke Mu of Xu's Wife**

Xu Wu of Qi
Xu Wu (Qi Nü Xu Wu), dates unknown, was a poor woman who lived in the Dong-hai region in the state of Qi (in the north of present-day Shandong Province). The women of her neighborhood would pool their candles at night, sharing their heat and light while they did their weaving. However, they tried to exclude Xu Wu from their evening gatherings because she had fewer candles than they did. She is remembered for her eloquence in explaining to these women that poverty should not have been a reason for leaving her out because one additional person in a lighted room did not make it any darker for the other occupants. Xu Wu argued that it cost them no extra to share their light with a poorer woman and that doing so could be regarded as a gracious deed on their part. Her biography is deservedly included in "Biographies of Those Able in Reasoning and Understanding" in *Biographies of Eminent Women* (Lienü zhuan).

Constance A. COOK

Liu Xiang. *Lienü zhuan.* Sibubeiyao ed., 6.13a–b.
O'Hara, Albert R. *The Position of Woman in Early China According to the Lieh Nü Chuan, "The Biographies of Chinese Women."* Taipei: Mei Ya, 1971; 1978, 182–83.

Xuan Jiang, Wife of Duke Xuan of Wei
Xuan Jiang, c. 730–c. 690 B.C.E., was a woman of the Jiang clan. She was a daughter of the Marquis of Qi (in the north of the present-day province of Shandong) and a wife of Duke Xuan (Xuan Gong, r. 718–700 B.C.E.) of Wei (in the north of the present-day province of Henan). Having produced two sons, she wanted the older one to become the heir apparent, but she was not Duke Xuan's first wife and an heir apparent had already been appointed. This heir apparent—Jizi—was the son of a woman named Yi Jiang, and Xuan Jiang was originally to have married him. She was so beautiful, however, that his father, Duke Xuan, had taken her for himself. After Jizi's mother hanged herself (the reason for her suicide is not given in the records), Xuan Jiang set in train a disastrous series of events. She plotted with her younger son to have the heir apparent Jizi murdered by soldiers disguised as robbers on his way to her home state of Qi. Her older son, Shou, learned of this, however, and warned Jizi, to whom he was clearly very close. When Jizi would

88 XUAN JIANG

not change his itinerary to avoid the ambush, Shou got him drunk and took his place. Jizi chased after his half-brother but was too late to save him and he asked the soldier-robbers to kill him as well. Xuan Jiang's younger son, Shuo, thus became heir apparent by default, eventually ascending the throne of Wei as Duke Hui (Hui Gong, r. 699–697, 686–669).

According to the *Tradition of Zuo* (Zuo zhuan), Duke Hui was very young when he first succeeded to the throne of Wei, possibly too young to sire offspring, and Xuan Jiang's father coerced her into a sexual alliance with her stepson, Zhao Bo of Wei, in what appears to have been a bid to expand his sphere of influence through his daughter. The strategy appears to have been successful, since this union produced five children who either became rulers or who married rulers of a number of small states around Qi.

The biography of Xuan Jiang, included in "Biographies of Pernicious and Depraved Women" in *Biographies of Eminent Women* (Lienü zhuan), claims: "Ultimately Wei went to ruin and for five generations there was no peace. This disaster started from [Xuan Jiang]" (O'Hara, 193).

Constance A. COOK

Legge, James, trans. *The Chinese Classics, Vol. 5, The Ch'un Ts'ew, with the Tso Chuen.* Hong Kong: Hong Kong University Press, 1960; 1970, 66, 137.

Liu Xiang. *Lienü zhuan.* Sibubeiyao ed., 7.3a–4a.

O'Hara, Albert R. *The Position of Woman in Early China According to the Lieh Nü Chuan, "The Biographies of Chinese Women."* Taipei: Mei Ya, 1971; 1978, 192–93.

Wen Shidan. "Chunqqiu biange shiqi funü congzheng huodong shuping." *Shixue yuekan* 5 (1990): 6–7, 9.

Zuo zhuan. Huan 16, Min 2, Zhao 20. *Chunqiu jing zhuan yinde.* Shanghai: Guji shudian, 1983, 43, 83–84, 401.

Xuan of Qi, Queen of King: *see* **Zhongli Chun of Qi, Wife of King Xuan of Qi**

Y

Yang She-tzu, The Wife of: *see* **Shu Ji**

Yangshe Zi of Jin, The Wife of: *see* **Shu Ji**

Ying, Wife of Duke Huai of Jin

The Woman née Ying (Ying Shi), fl. c. 650–620 B.C.E. was a head of the Ying clan and a daughter of Duke Mu (Mu Gong, r. 659–621 B.C.E.) of Qin (present-day Shaanxi Province). She is also known as Huai Ying (literally [Duke] Huai's [Wife née] Ying) because her father gave her in marriage to Yu, the heir apparent of the rival state of Jin (in the present-day provinces of Shanxi and Hebei), who had been taken hostage by Qin in 643 and who later became Duke Huai (Huai Gong). When Yu was preparing to escape back to his homeland of Jin several years later, in 638, he asked The Woman née Ying if she would go with him. She refused, explaining the difficult position this placed her in. Her father had given her in marriage to Yu to make sure he remained in Qin, but since this had clearly not had the desired effect she would be abandoning her father if she went to Jin with her husband. On the other hand, she would be violating "the righteousness of wifehood" if she were to divulge her husband's plan to her father. She had no option, she told him, but to let him escape, alone, and not breathe a word of his plan. It is also possible that The Woman née Ying did not accompany Yu because she believed he intended to use her as a form of security against the repercussions of his escape from Qin.

Some time later, Yu's uncle, Duke Wen (Wen Gong, c. 696–628; r. 636–627, often referred to by his personal name, Chong Er), visited Qin before returning to Jin, where he was to replace his nephew as ruler. On that occasion, The Woman née Ying was sent, along with four others, to serve him. She reprimanded Duke Wen when he hesitated to accept her because of her loyalty to her father in Qin, reminding him of her rank and of his dependence on Qin for support. She then accompanied him to Jin, where she continued to intervene in political decisions in the interest of her home country of Qin. We may conclude that The Woman née Ying had been assigned the task of establishing good relations between Qin and Jin and that she succeeded in this task. Sources praise her for being impartial and for "controlling her heart very evenly" (O'Hara, 131); her biography is included in "Biographies of the Chaste and Righteous" in *Biographies of Eminent Women* (Lienü zhuan).

Constance A. COOK and Barbara HENDRISCHKE

Liu Xiang. *Lienü zhuan.* Sibubeiyao ed., 5.2b–3a.
O'Hara, Albert R. *The Position of Woman in Early China According to the Lieh Nü Chuan, "The Biographies of Chinese Women."* Taipei: Mei Ya, 1971; 1978, 131.
Ptak, R. "Huai Ying." In *Die Frau im alten China. Bild und Wirklichkeit,* ed. Dennis Schilling and Jianfei Kralle. Stuttgart: Steiner, 2001, 25–52.
Takikawa Kametarō. *Shiki kaichū kōshō [Shi ji].* Taipei: Hongshi, 1977, 39.66.
Zuo zhuan. Xi 17, 23, 24. 33. Taipei: Fenghuang chubanshe, 1977, vol. 1, 113, 122, 123, 142.

Ying Shi: *see* **Ying, Wife of Duke Huai of Jin**

Ying-Clan Head: *see* **Ying, Wife of Duke Huai of Jin**

Young Lady at A-ku, The: *see* **The Virgin of Egu**

Youyu Er Fei: *see* **Ehuang and Nüying**

Yu Ji, Wife of King Wei of Qi
Yu Ji (Qi Wei Yu Ji), fl. fourth century B.C.E., was a woman of the Ji clan from the state of Yu (in the present-day province of Shanxi). Her personal name was Juan

90 YU JI

and she was a wife of King Wei (Wei Wang, r. 378–343 B.C.E.) of Qi, in present-day Shandong Province. Concerned at King Wei's neglect of his government, Yu Ji tried to convince him that he should appoint a worthy minister to replace his current prime minister, a deceitful flatterer who had controlled the government for nine years. Fearful for his position, this corrupt prime minister retaliated by slandering Yu Ji, saying that she had once been a woman of ill repute who had formed a relationship with the worthy minister she was now recommending. The king had her incarcerated in a nine-storied tower while the matter was being investigated, but the prime minister bribed the official in charge to bring in a guilty finding. Fortunately for Yu Ji, the king then questioned her personally, and ultimately her ability to clearly discuss the issue citing historical precedent protected her against the powerful slanderers bent on destroying her. Yu Ji, who "loved goodness," is credited with awakening King Wei to his responsibilities such that Qi was well ruled from then on. Her biography is included in "Biographies of Those Able in Reasoning" in *Biographies of Eminent Women* (Lienü zhuan).

Constance A. COOK

Liu Xiang. *Lienü zhuan.* Sibubeiyao ed., 6.7b–8b.
O'Hara, Albert R. *The Position of Woman in Early China According to the Lieh Nü Chuan, "The Biographies of Chinese Women."* Taipei: Mei Ya, 1971; 1978, 169–71.

Yu Juan: *see* **Yu Ji, Wife of King Wei of Qi**

Yü Ling of the Kingdom of Ch'u, The Wife of: *see* **Jieyu's Wife, and The Wife of Yuling Zizhong of Chu**

Yue Ji, Wife of King Zhao of Chu
Yue Ji (Chu Zhao Yue Ji), fl. early fifth century B.C.E., was a woman of the Ji clan and a daughter of King Goujian of Yue (present-day Zhejiang Province). She was one of the two wives of King Zhao (Zhao Wang, r. 515–488 B.C.E.) of Chu, a large state in what is now central China, north of the Yangzi River. While traveling early in their marriage, King Zhao asked his wives if they would die with him since they had shared such pleasure together. His other wife, Cai Ji, swore she would die with him but Yue Ji refused to so swear, saying he had not proved himself virtuous in government. Twenty-five years later, however, when King Zhao fell mortally ill during a military campaign, he refused to allow his ministers and generals to sacrifice themselves in his place. So impressed was Yue Ji at the virtue he thus exhibited that she committed suicide in an attempt to dispel the evil red cloud around the sun that signaled his death and to clear his path to the underworld of foxes. Before she took her life she told him that while she had not been prepared to die for the pleasure of the king she would gladly die for the righteousness of the king. Cai Ji, on the other hand, did not fulfill the promise she had made years earlier to follow her husband in death. Because of Yue Ji's loyalty, her son was chosen as the next ruler of Chu. Her

biography is included in "Biographies of the Chaste and Righteous" in *Biographies of Eminent Women* (Lienü zhuan).

Constance A. COOK

Liu Xiang. *Lienü zhuan.* Sibubeiyao ed., 5.4b–5a.
O'Hara, Albert R. *The Position of Woman in Early China According to the Lieh Nü Chuan, "The Biographies of Chinese Women."* Taipei: Mei Ya, 1971; 1978, 131–34.

The Yue Woman

The Yue Woman (Yuenü), also known as Aliao, was a skilled swordswoman who is said to have lived in the southern state of Yue (in the region of present-day Zhejiang Province) during the Spring and Autumn period. Her father was a hunter and she went hunting with him from a very young age, which may explain why she became such a skilled swordswoman and archer. Her prowess was such that her reputation reached the King of Yue, who, having set his mind on avenging himself on the neighboring state of Wu, was searching for the means to achieve this. He therefore invited The Yue Woman to court and asked her to demonstrate her skill. When asked about her technique with the sword, she replied: "The art of the sword is profound and hard to understand despite appearing insignificant and easy. It is similar to a door, in that it can be opened or closed; it can be divided into yin and yang. The way of fighting, in general, is to strengthen one's inner spirit while remaining outwardly calm and well mannered. She may look like an elegant lady, but she fights like a fierce tiger. With this imposing manner, you can pit a single fighter against one hundred, and pit one hundred against one thousand." The king then granted her the title "The Yue Woman" and decreed that her skills be adopted in training his army.

The Yue Woman's exposition on the art of the sword is the earliest recorded theory on this topic, and it informed Chinese martial arts theory for countless generations.

Lily Xiao Hong LEE

Ma Zhaozheng and Zhou Feitang. *Zhongguo gudai funü mingren.* Beijing: Zhongguo funü chubanshe, 1988, 31–32.
Mou Yangzhu and Yang Mingtai. *Zhonghua nü jie zhi zui.* Shanghai: Shanghai renmin chubanshe, 1993, 215.
Zhao Ye. *Wu Yue chunqiu quan yi,* annot. and trans. Zhang Jue. Guiyang: Guizhou renmin chubanshe, 1993, 9.366–70.

Yueh Chi of King Chao of Ch'u: *see* Yue Ji, Wife of King Zhao of Chu

Yuenü: *see* The Yue Woman

Yuling Zizhong of Chu, The Wife of: *see* Jieyu's Wife, and The Wife of Yuling Zizhong of Chu

92 ZANG SUN OF LU'S MOTHER

Z

Zang Sun of Lu's Mother

The Mother of Zang Sun (Lu Zang Sun Mu), fl. seventh century B.C.E., lived in the state of Lu (in the present-day province of Shandong). Her son, who was also known as Zang Wenzhong (d. 617 B.C.E.), was a minister in the government of Lu but he had made many enemies through his intolerable behavior: even his mother told him he was "insulting and unmerciful." She predicted that he would come to harm when he was sent as an envoy from Lu to the neighboring state of Qi. At that time, Qi was planning to invade Lu with the collusion of certain ministers of Lu, and the arrest of Zang Sun would have served the dual purpose of revenge for his harshness and of provoking trouble between the two states. She did what she could to help him, encouraging him to change his behavior and befriend certain powerful people. Later, Zang Sun was indeed arrested by Qi, as his mother had feared. He nevertheless managed to send a letter to Lu, written in a code that only his mother could decipher, revealing Qi's plan to invade Lu. His mother thus saved Lu from invasion and gained his release and return home from Qi. Zang Sun's mother is credited with being far-sighted, and her biography is included in "Biographies of the Benign and Wise" in *Biographies of Eminent Women* (Lienü zhuan).

Constance A. COOK

Liu Xiang. *Lienü zhuan*. Sibubeiyao ed., 3.5a–6a.
O'Hara, Albert R. *The Position of Woman in Early China According to the Lieh Nü Chuan, "The Biographies of Chinese Women."* Taipei: Mei Ya, 1971; 1978, 86–88.

Zang Wenzhong of Lu, Mother of Minister: *see* Zang Sun of Lu's Mother

Zhao Foxi Mu: *see* Foxi of Zhao's Mother

Zhao Gua, The Mother of General: *see* General Zhao Gua's Mother

Zhao Jian, Daughter of: *see* Zhao, Wife of the King of Dai

Zhao Jiang Gua Mu: *see* General Zhao Gua's Mother

Zhao, Wife of the King of Dai

Lady Zhao, the Wife of the King of Dai (Dai Zhao Furen), b. c. 490 B.C.E., was commended for refusing to marry her younger brother, Zhao Xiangzi (c. 480–425 B.C.E.), after he conquered Dai, before the proper mourning rituals for their father had been completed. Lady Zhao had married the king of Dai (a small state in the north of the present-day province of Zhejiang) ten years previously, but not long after the death of her father, Zhao Jianzi (c. 517–458; one source says he died c. 476), her younger brother killed her husband, raised an army, and invaded Dai. It appears that her younger brother wanted to take her back home as his wife, for in refusing she said: "Now Dai has been extinguished, but how can I return home? I have heard that a wife's righteousness comes from not having two husbands. How could I have two husbands then?! It is not right for me to either insult my husband with my younger brother or insult my younger brother with my husband. I dare not cause resentment and hence can not return." In tears, she called up to Heaven and committed suicide with her hairpin.

While her brother is not criticized for wanting to commit incest with his sister, Lady Zhao is praised for "stating clearly the rules of chastity and propriety" and for not showing hatred toward him before committing suicide. Her biography is included in "Biographies of the Chaste and Righteous" in *Biographies of Eminent Women* (Lienü zhuan).

Constance A. COOK

Liu Xiang. *Lienü zhuan*. Sibubeiyao ed., 5.5b–6a.
O'Hara, Albert R. *The Position of Woman in Early China According to the Lieh Nü Chuan, "The Biographies of Chinese Women."* Taipei: Mei Ya, 1971; 1978, 138–39.

Zhaojin Nü Juan: *see* Juan, Daughter of an Official of the Ford of Zhao

Zhen Jiang of the Jiang Clan: *see* Pure Jiang, Wife of King Zhao of Chu

Zheng Mao, Wife of King Cheng of Chu
Zheng Mao (Chu Cheng Zheng Mao), also known as Zi Mao, fl. seventh century B.C.E., was a woman of the Ying clan from the small state of Zheng (in present-day Henan Province). Sent with the primary wife in marriage to King Cheng (Cheng Wang, r. 671–626 B.C.E.) of Chu, she was elevated to the position of wife for her steadfastness to principle.

One day soon after she went to Chu (a large state in what is now central China, north of the Yangzi River), King Cheng was looking down into the rear palace (the women's quarters) from a terrace and all of the palace women except Zi Mao looked up at him. Intrigued, he tested her by offering to make her the primary wife if she looked up. When she would not, he offered to give her 1,000 pieces of gold and to enfeoff her father and brothers. She still refused to look up at him, explaining when he came down to speak to her that had she accepted his offers of becoming his primary wife and of money and nobility for her family she would have been guilty of covetousness. This would have meant she had forgotten her principles. Delighted at her integrity, the king made her his primary wife.

94 *ZHENG MAO*

About a year later, King Cheng sought the advice of his chief minister, the governor of the capital territory, on whether he should appoint his son Shangchen as the heir apparent. The governor advised him not to do it, saying that he feared Shangchen was capable of anything: "[he] has the eyes of a wasp and the voice of a wolf; he is a severe man and may not be given the position" (O'Hara, 129). The king then consulted Zi Mao, who agreed with the governor. Choosing to ignore their advice, King Cheng nevertheless went ahead and appointed Shangchen heir apparent; Shangchen later slandered the governor, wrongly blaming him for a military failure, and had him killed.

Some time later, the king decided he would replace Shangchen as heir apparent, appointing in his stead Zhi, one of his younger sons by a concubine. Fearing that this would lead to a disastrous rebellion, Zi Mao again advised King Cheng against this course of action but he refused to answer her. She then told her governess that she believed the king thought she had spoken ill of the heir apparent because she was not the boy's mother and that to continue living under suspicion was equivalent to living without righteousness. Knowing that these last words would reach King Cheng after her death, she committed suicide. Zi Mao had obviously understood the political situation very well: soon after she died the heir apparent rose in rebellion and King Cheng was himself driven to suicide. Her biography is included in "Biographies of the Chaste and Righteous" in *Biographies of Eminent Women* (Lienü zhuan).

Constance A. COOK

Liu Xiang. *Lienü zhuan.* Sibubeiyao ed., 5.1b–2b.
O'Hara, Albert R. *The Position of Woman in Early China According to the Lieh Nü Chuan, "The Biographies of Chinese Women."* Taipei: Mei Ya, 1971; 1978, 128–30.

Zhong Zi, Wife of Duke Ling of Qi

Zhong Zi, or Middle Zi-Clan Woman (Qi Ling Zhong Zi), fl. mid-sixth century B.C.E., was a secondary wife of Duke Ling (Ling Gong, r. 581–554 B.C.E.) of Qi, a powerful state in the north of present-day Shandong Province. She was a daughter of the Song house (in present-day Shanxi Province).

She and her sister Rong Zi were said to be maidservants of Duke Ling. They were in fact concubines and when Zhong Zi gave birth to a son named Ya, the child was handed into the care of her sister, Rong Zi, who was their master's favorite. Rong Zi pleaded that Ya be appointed heir in place of Duke Ling's eldest son, born to his primary wife, Sheng Ji. (An earlier account claims that the eldest son, Guang, was in fact the son of the primary wife's niece, who probably accompanied her mistress from Lu when she was given in marriage.) Rong Zi's wish was granted but the child's biological mother, Zhong Zi, refused to accept Duke Ling's decision, claiming it would be an ill-fated move: "I will not allow it. I recognize the sprouting seeds of calamity that shall become a fight to the death" (O'Hara, 86). Her prescient advice was ignored, however, and the death of Duke

Ling sparked a bloody struggle over the succession. Once the rightful heir, Guang, came to power, Rong Zi was put to death. Zhong Zi, however, is remembered for her kindness and wisdom and for having understood the principle of things. Her biography is included in "Biographies of the Benign and Wise" in *Biographies of Eminent Women* (Lienü zhuan).

Constance A. COOK

Liu Xiang. *Lienü zhuan.* Sibubeiyao ed., 3.4b–5.
O'Hara, Albert R. *The Position of Woman in Early China According to the Lieh Nü Chuan, "The Biographies of Chinese Women."* Taipei: Mei Ya, 1971; 1978, 85–86.
Zuo zhuan. Xiang 19. Taipei: Fenghuang chubanshe, 1977, vol. 2, 16, 27–28.

Zhongli Chun of Qi, Wife of King Xuan of Qi

Zhongli Chun (Qi Zhongli Chun), fl. fourth century B.C.E., was from Wuyan Village in the state of Qi (in present-day Shandong Province). Despite her age (she was approaching forty), her unprepossessing appearance (she is said to have been "an ugly person without equal"), and the fact that she could not be given away, let alone sold, Zhongli Chun approached her ruler, King Xuan (Xuan Wang, r. 342–324 B.C.E.), and volunteered to be his wife. Apparently aware of the king's interest in the occult, she gained his attention by revealing to him her special powers of invisibility. First she startled him by disappearing before his eyes, thus proving that she understood the occult art of invisibility. When the king summoned her again, wishing to learn more about this skill, she warned him about the four dangers threatening the safety of his state. The first was strong neighboring states and a corrupt internal administration; the second was his conspicuous consumption, at the people's expense; the third was a court filled with flatterers and tricksters; the fourth was his own licentious behavior. The king was deeply impressed with Zhongli Chun's analysis and immediately instituted reforms within the palace, put the economy in order, strengthened the army, and repaired the city gates. He also appointed an heir apparent and honored Zhongli Chun as his queen. By these means, the state of Qi became secure. The biography of Zhongli Chun is included in "Biographies of Those Able in Reasoning and Understanding" in *Biographies of Eminent Women* (Lienü zhuan), and her story has been handed down through the ages in literature and drama. Her tale has also been found on a painted brick dating from the Han dynasty.

Constance A. COOK

Guan Siping. *Houfei de mingyun.* Jinan: Shandong wenyi chubanshe, 1991, 68–71.
Liu Shisheng. *Zhongguo gudai funü shi.* Qingdao: Qingdao chubanshe, 1991, 66–67.
Liu Xiang. *Lienü zhuan.* Sibubeiyao ed., 6.8b–10a.
O'Hara, Albert R. *The Position of Woman in Early China According to the Lieh Nü Chuan, "The Biographies of Chinese Women."* Taipei: Mei Ya, 1971; 1978, 171–74.

96 ZHOU XUAN JIANG HOU

Zhou Xuan Jiang Hou: *see* **Jiang, Queen of King Xuan of Zhou**

Zhou Zhu Zhongqie: *see* **The Loyal Maid of Zhu of Zhou**

Zhounan zhi Qi: *see* **The Official from Zhounan's Wife**

Zhuang Jiang: *see* **The Instructress for the Daughter of Qi**

Zhuang of Chu, The Niece of: *see* **Zhuang Zhi, Wife of King Qingxiang of Chu**

Zhuang of Chu, The Wife of King: *see* **Fan Ji, Wife of King Zhuang of Chu**

Zhuang Xing: *see* **Zhuang Zhi, Wife of King Qingxiang of Chu**

Zhuang Zhi, Wife of King Qingxiang of Chu
Zhuang Zhi (Chu Chu Zhuang Zhi), fl. c. 260 B.C.E., was a village girl who became the wife of a king. One source indicates that the character *zhi* may be a misreading of the character *xing*. There is further disagreement as to whether *zhi* is a name or means "niece"; in some sources she is known as the niece (*zhi*) of a person called Zhuang. Zhuang Zhi lived in the district capital of Chu (a large state in what is now central China north of the Yangzi River) at a time when the ruler, King Qingxiang (Qingxiang Wang, r. 298–263 B.C.E.), was surrounded by ministers who were being bribed by the rival state of Qin (in the region of the present-day provinces of Shaanxi and Gansu). Consequently, none of his upright ministers, including Qu Yuan, a man famous through the ages for his integrity, were able to get close to King Qingxiang to warn him of Qin's plan to overthrow him. When his corrupt ministers urged the king to go on a pleasure trip to Tang, some 500 *li* (270 km) south of his capital, Zhuang Zhi realized they were planning to stage a coup in his absence. Even though she was only twelve years old, she saw the danger her country was in and wanted to approach the king and suggest he mend his lax ways. Her mother forbade her to go, but she disobeyed and ran away to sit by the side of the road with a red flag to catch the attention of the king as he was passing by.

King Qingxiang duly noticed her and asked that she be brought to him, whereupon she explained to him the danger he was in. She also warned him of the danger to his government of focusing on luxuries at the expense of the people. Despite the vast difference in their ages (she was twelve while he was in his forties) and status, the king heeded her words and turned back to the capital. As Zhuang Zhi had anticipated, the rebels had already closed the gates to the capital. King Qingxiang was nevertheless able to raise an army from provinces loyal to him and managed to quell the rebellion, whereupon he made Zhuang Zhi his queen. Her biography is included in "Biographies of Those Able in Reasoning and Understanding" in *Biographies of Eminent Women* (Lienü zhuan).

Constance A. COOK

Liu Xiang. *Lienü zhuan.* Sibubeiyao ed., 6.12a–13b.
O'Hara, Albert R. *The Position of Woman in Early China According to the Lieh Nü Chuan, "The Biographies of Chinese Women."* Taipei: Mei Ya, 1971; 1978, 179–82.

Zi Mao: *see* **Zheng Mao, Wife of King Cheng of Chu**

Zou Meng Ke Mu: *see* **Mencius' Mother**

Qin Through Han

Qin (221–206 B.C.E.)
Western Han (206 B.C.E.–8 C.E.)
Xin Interregnum (9–23)
Eastern Han (25–220)

B

Ban Huiji: *see* **Ban Zhao**

Ban Jieyu, Concubine of Emperor Cheng

Ban Jieyu, or Lady of Handsome Fairness Ban (Xiao Cheng Ban Jieyu), fl. late first century B.C.E., of Anling District, Fufeng Commandery (in the vicinity of present-day Xianyang and Xingping in Shaanxi Province), was a concubine of Emperor Cheng (Liu Ao, 51–7 B.C.E.; r. 32–7 B.C.E.). Her personal name is not recorded. Her father, Ban Kuang, was a Commandant of Cavalry (*yue qi jiaowei*) under Emperor Cheng, and she was a paternal great-aunt of Ban Gu (?32/34–?92/94 C.E.) and his sister Ban Zhao (*q.v.*), who completed the *History of the Han Dynasty* (Han shu).

Ban Jieyu was beautiful and possessed of literary talent, the sole woman of letters of Western Han. Her *Elegy for Myself* (Zidao fu) is the only extant work by a woman in the rhapsody (*fu*) genre, for which Western Han is famous. According to biographical material contained in the *History of the Han Dynasty,* which was edited by her grandniece and grandnephew, Ban Jieyu was clever, her conduct above reproach, and her scholarship unequaled. In Emperor Cheng's time the daughters of ministers entered the imperial women's quarters and thus it was that she was selected for the palace at the start of Emperor Cheng's reign, initially appointed as a Young Attendant (*shaoshi*). She quickly rose to the rank of Lady of Handsome Fairness (*jieyu*), the highest grade of concubine at that time, and became a favorite of the emperor. She bore the emperor two sons, but both died a few months after birth.

The *History of the Han Dynasty* emphasized the virtues valued by Confucianism in praising Ban Jieyu, describing her as highly respectful and having taken to heart the sentiments expressed in the *Book of Poetry* (Shi jing), especially those concerning women. She did not grow arrogant or wanton, but rather felt humbled by the love Emperor Cheng bestowed upon her. In *Elegy for Myself* she recalled her feelings:

> Already receiving blessings beyond what I deserved,
> I yet ventured to hope for more happy times,
> Sighing repeatedly, waking or asleep,
> Undoing my girdle strings with thoughts of the past. (Watson, 263)

It may not have been only the beauty of the poetry that ensured the preservation of Ban Jieyu's famous elegy, for she clearly upheld Confucian values, citing imperial consorts of previous rulers as guiding her behavior. Determined not to allow incautious actions on her part to affect Emperor Cheng in any way, she abided by the accepted womanly virtues, taking as positive exemplars Ehuang and Nüying (*q.v.*), the virtuous and loyal concubines of the legendary Emperor Shun; Tai Ren (*q.v.*), the mother of King Wen of Zhou; and Tai Si (*q.v.*), the mother of King Wu of Zhou. She saw the story of King You of Zhou, who was besotted by his consort Bao Si (*q.v.*) and responsible for the downfall of Zhou, as a warning. On one occasion when Emperor Cheng invited Ban Jieyu to ride in his carriage during a visit to the women's quarters, she refused, saying: "Ancient

102 *BAN JIEYU*

paintings of the sage rulers of old always show them accompanied by distinguished officials. It wasn't until the last years of Zhou that rulers appear accompanied by their female favorites. If you invite me to accompany you in the imperial carriage, will you not appear to resemble the more recent examples?" Emperor Cheng acknowledged that she was right. When the empress dowager (*q.v.* Wang Zhengjun, Empress of Emperor Yuan) heard of this she was delighted, describing Ban Jieyu as a modern-day Lady Fan (*q.v.* Fan Ji, who refused to eat meat as a protest against the King of Chu's excessive love of hunting). From about 20 B.C.E., however, Emperor Cheng became increasingly obsessed with women. First he promoted Ban Jieyu's maid Li Ping (whose surname he ordered changed to Wei) to the rank of Lady of Handsome Fairness, equivalent to her mistress. Then he summoned the singer and dancer Zhao Feiyan (*q.v.* Zhao Feiyan, Empress of Emperor Cheng) and her sister Zhao Hede (*q.v.* Zhao Hede, Concubine of Emperor Cheng) to the palace and appointed them as Ladies of Handsome Fairness. Ban Jieyu and Empress Xu (*q.v.* Xu, Empress of Emperor Cheng) both fell from favor and had very little contact with the emperor from then on.

Until then the family of Emperor Cheng's mother, Empress Dowager Wang, had held the reins of power. However, once the Zhao sisters became favorites there was turmoil in the court, as the *History of the Han Dynasty* records in the biography of Emperor Cheng: "The Zhaos were the cause of promiscuity in the inner quarters; the distaff clan usurped political power." After Empress Xu fell out of imperial favor, Zhao Feiyan made her move, intent on becoming empress. In 18 B.C.E., she claimed that Empress Xu had colluded with her elder sister Xu Ye, consort of Marquis Gang of Ping'an, and with Ban Jieyu. They had practiced witchcraft, Zhao Feiyan said, to bring harm to Beauty (*meiren*) Wang, who was then carrying the emperor's child, and to General-in-Chief (*da jiangjun*)/Commander-in-Chief (*da sima*) Wang Feng, an older brother of Empress Dowager Wang. In a fury, Empress Dowager Wang ordered an inquisition. Empress Xu was deposed because of these charges and Xu Ye was among those executed. Ban Jieyu remained fearless under questioning, saying: "I have heard that life and death are decreed by Fate, and wealth and eminence are decided by Heaven. Even when one follows correct behavior he cannot be certain of good fortune, so what could he hope for by committing evil? If the gods have understanding, then they will not listen to the pleas of a disloyal subject; and if they have no understanding, what good would it do to offer pleas to them? Therefore I would never resort to such actions!" (Watson, 262–63). Recognizing the justice of her words, Emperor Cheng withheld punishment and rewarded her instead with a large quantity of gold.

It was clear to Ban Jieyu that with the palace in crisis she was in danger, so she asked to be sent to serve Empress Dowager Wang in Changxin Palace (Palace of Lasting Trust). She wrote in *Elegy for Myself:*

> I serve the empress dowager in her eastern palace,
> Take my place among lesser maids in the Palace of Lasting Trust;
> I help to sprinkle and sweep among the curtains,
> And shall do so till death brings my term to a close.
> Then may my bones find rest at the foot of the hill,
> A little shade of pine and cypress left over for my grave. (Watson, 264)

Despairing when that deathly loneliness became a reality, she was overwhelmed by sadness. It was in these circumstances that she wrote *Elegy for Myself.* In one part she tells of how, deep within the deserted palace, the rooms were closed up all day long and the magnificent halls were covered in dust. Moss grew over the white marble stairs and the courtyards were overgrown; the curtains were drawn and her light silk gown flapped in the cold wind that blew through the halls. A woman forsaken, she was out of sight and out of mind in this silent and deserted place. Finally, Ban Jieyu came to this deeply felt conclusion:

> I reflect that man, born into this world,
> Passes as swiftly as though floating on a stream.
> Already I've known fame and eminence,
> The finest gifts the living can enjoy.
> I will strive to please my spirit, taste every delight,
> Since true happiness cannot be counted on.
> "Green Robe"—"White Flower"—in ancient times as now. (Watson, 264)

Ban Jieyu believed that Emperor Cheng's abandonment of her reached far beyond the individual destiny of one person, citing the similar example in antiquity of King You of Zhou (d. 771 B.C.E.) dismissing Queen Shen (*vide* Bao Si). Green Robe in her elegy refers to a wife whose place has been usurped by concubines, while White Flower refers to the deposed Queen Shen. Yet, abandoned by Emperor Cheng, Ban Jieyu served at the imperial tomb after he died. When her tragic life ended, she was buried in the funerary park.

ZHENG Bijun
(Translated by Lily Xiao Hong LEE and Sue WILES)

Ban Gu. *Courtier and Commoner in Ancient China. Selections from the "History of the Former Han" by Pan Ku.* trans. Burton Watson. New York: Columbia University Press, 1974, 261–65.
Han shu. Beijing: Zhonghua shuju, 1983, vol. 12, 97*xia.*3983–88.
Liu Xiang. *Lienü zhuan.* Sibubeiyao ed., 8.6b–7b.
Loewe, Michael. *Crisis and Conflict in Han China: 104 BC to AD 9.* London: George Allen & Unwin, 1974, 87, 156–57.
O'Hara, Albert R. *The Position of Woman in Early China According to the Lieh Nü Chuan, "The Biographies of Chinese Women."* Taipei: Mei Ya, 1971; 1978, 230–35.

Ban Zhao

Ban Zhao, c. 40–c. 120, also known as Ban Huiji and Cao Dagu, of Fufeng (in the vicinity of present-day Xianyang and Xingping in Shaanxi Province), is best known for her ultra-Confucian work *Precepts for Women* (Nüjie) and for her part in completing the *History of the Han Dynasty* (Han shu). She was the youngest child of Ban Biao (3–54), a literary man and historian, and a sister of Ban Gu (32–92) and Ban Chao (33–103). Ban Gu was the author of the *History of the Han Dynasty* and of the famous *Liang du fu,* while Ban Chao was an eminent

104 BAN ZHAO

ambassador to China's western regions. Her husband's name was Cao Wei (also known as Shishu).

Although Ban Zhao was married by the time she was fourteen years of age and gave birth to several children, she was extremely well educated in Confucian classics and in the histories. She composed sixteen literary works classified as rhapsodies (*fu*), eulogies (*song*), inscriptions (*ming*), dirges (*lei*), questions (*wen*), annotations (*zhu*), laments (*aici*), letters (*shu*), treatises (*lun*), memorials (*shangshu*), and exhortations (*yiling*). These works, gathered in the three-volume *Collected Works of Ban Zhao* (Ban Zhao ji) by her daughter-in-law née Ding, were recorded in the bibliographic chapter of the *History of the Sui Dynasty* (Sui shu jingji zhi) but most are now lost. Her *Rhapsody on the Eastern Campaign* (Dongzheng fu), *Rhapsody on Needle and Thread* (Zhenlü fu), *Rhapsody on the Great Bird* (Daque fu; this is incomplete), *Rhapsody on the Cicada* (Chan fu; this is incomplete), *Memorial Seeking a Replacement for My Elder Brother Chao* (Wei xiong Chao qiu dai shu), *Memorial to Empress Dowager Deng* (Shang Deng taihou shu), and *Ode on a Leaning Vessel* (Qiqi song; this is a fragment) were collected in the Qing dynasty by Yan Kejun in his *Quan Hou Han wen*. Her *Rhapsody on the Eastern Campaign* is a refined, short piece that exerted some influence on the development of the short rhapsody genre in later Han. It tells of her journey from Luoyang eastward to the place where her son was stationed; interspersed with allusions, it describes the route she took and the scenery along the way. *Rhapsody on Needle and Thread* is notable for its apt allusions, while *Rhapsody on the Great Bird* and *Rhapsody on the Cicada* are written in a fresh and elegant style.

Ban Zhao was a woman of very wide learning. Apart from Confucian classics, history, and literature, she was also proficient in annotations, two examples being her *Annotations to Liu Xiang's* Biographies of Eminent Women (Liu Xiang Lienü zhuan zhu) and *Annotations to Ban Gu's* Youtong fu (Ban Gu Youtong fu zhu). Remnants of the former work are in Wang Zhaoyuan's *Lienü zhuan buzhu,* while the latter is quoted in other works of annotation. The sixteen-passage supplement to *Biographies of Eminent Women* (Lienü zhuan) traditionally attributed to Ban Zhao is now thought not to be hers.

Ban Zhao was in her late forties or early fifties when her brother Ban Gu died, leaving unfinished his monumental *History of the Han Dynasty*, the "Astronomical Records" and eight tables of notable persons remaining incomplete. Emperor He (Liu Zhao, 78–104; r. 89–104) ordered that Ban Zhao, "erudite and competent in writing prose," and the eminent scholar Ma Xu finish the *History,* and it is in the completion of this work that Ban Zhao's historical insight and learning are most evident. Ma Xu wrote the "Astronomical Records" alone, then worked with Ban Zhao to compile the eight tables of princes, meritorious subjects, and other ancient and contemporary personages. The *History of the Han Dynasty* was considered a difficult work when it was first published, and the breadth of Ban Zhao's extraordinary learning is demonstrated in the fact that Ma Rong (79–165), a brother of her colleague Ma Xu, studied it under her tutelage. The circumstances of this tutelage, as described in the *History of the Later Han Dynasty* (Hou Han shu) give the impression that Ban Zhao was in a highly esteemed position while Ma Rong took a lowly position in front of her.

The *History of the Later Han Dynasty* records that Ban Zhao was frequently summoned to the palace where, by imperial decree and with the title of Great Lady (*dagu*), a form of address reserved for women held in high esteem, she tutored Empress Deng (*q.v.* Deng Sui, Empress of Emperor He) and the palace women. "When Empress Dowager Deng acted as regent, Ban Zhao participated in government affairs. When Ban Zhao died, the empress dowager dressed in somber clothes as a sign of mourning, and officials were sent to supervise the funeral arrangements."

Ban Zhao had considerable influence at court and was prepared to wield it when she thought it warranted. Her brother Ban Chao was Protector General of the Western Regions (*xiyu*) and had been granted the title of Marquis for Pacifying Faraway Lands (*dingyuan hou*) for his achievements. Having spent almost thirty years in the western regions, however, he wished to return home as he grew older, but his official request was denied. Ban Zhao submitted a memorial to the throne on Ban Chao's behalf, explaining his position and warning of the danger to the court should he fall ill in his old age; Ban Chao was immediately recalled. Ban Zhao performed a similar service for General-in-Chief Deng Zhi (d. 121), an elder brother of Empress Dowager Deng, when his resignation upon the death of his mother was refused. At least one of her sons was honored by the court, being granted the title of Marquis of Guannei and promoted to Minister of Qi.

Ban Zhao was probably in her early fifties when she wrote *Precepts for Women*. Having lived a life of literary endeavor and political influence, tutored an empress dowager, and completed an official history by order of the emperor, she claimed that she wrote *Precepts for Women* for her "girls." It is not difficult to see, however, that her intention was to set moral standards for women. In the preface she wrote: "I grieve for my 'girls,' who are now of marriageable age but have not yet assimilated our teachings and manners for women. I am often distressed that they will forget their manners before their in-laws and disgrace our family. So I have written this seven-chapter work." The seven chapters are "Humility," "Husband and Wife," "Respect and Caution," "Womanly Qualifications," "Devotion," "Acquiescence," and "Harmonious Relations with Brothers- and Sisters-in-Law." Ban Zhao spelled out in *Precepts for Women* the severe social constraints she believed women should accept in their daily lives. In stark contrast to her own experience of a life of scholarship, knowledge, and politics, she did not encourage women to excel in anything, counseling them instead to be mediocre in all things. Women, she said, did not need to be brilliant, outstanding, or unique, and there was no need for a woman's work to be cleverer than that of anyone else.

The guiding principle laid down in *Precepts for Women*—that "men are valued for their strength while women are praised for their weakness"—did not originate with Ban Zhao but can be found in the wide variety of Confucian classics she had studied since childhood. However, *Precepts for Women* received a mixed reception from Ban Zhao's contemporaries and did not immediately enjoy universal recognition. Her student Ma Rong praised it, demanding that his wife and daughters study it, but according to Ban Zhao's biography, her sister-in-law Cao Fengsheng wrote her a letter "querying it." However, since this letter is no longer extant, we do not know what issues Cao Fengsheng raised with her. The fact that *Precepts for Women* was praised by a man and queried by a woman may be indicative of a gendered response to Ban Zhao's work during her lifetime, but in late imperial times, when women were under harsher constraints, her work enjoyed wider recognition, even among women. *Precepts for Women* also spawned scores of similar works over the centuries, such as *Nü xun* (Jin dynasty, third century), *Nü lunyu* (Tang dynasty or Song dynasty), and *Nei xun* (Ming dynasty). Emperor Shen (1563–1620) ordered that this latter work, written by Empress Ma (1333–1382), be printed with *Precepts for Women* in a single volume, that women of all ages throughout the nation might take it as their standard of behavior. This volume, with a preface by Emperor Shen, was extremely influential in spreading Ban Zhao's conservative concepts as Song neo-Confucianism subsequently became entrenched in the Ming–Qing period.

Today Ban Zhao is still widely recognized as China's foremost female scholar and there is no doubt that she was extremely erudite, her learning extending to literature, history, ethics, and philology. In this respect, she has been a role model for Chinese women through the ages. In the area of gender relations, however, Ban Zhao remains a figure of contention. While her *Precepts for Women* was regarded in pre-modern China as a seminal work in the genre of women's texts and she was credited with justifying the right of women to be educated, in modern times this text is regarded as having placed too many constraints on women. Worse, Ban Zhao espoused the view that women should not be encouraged to excel in any area, even in work traditionally carried out only by women, such as needlework and cooking. This may very well have served to restrict women's personal development for many centuries.

WONG Shiu-hin
Addended by Lily Xiao Hong LEE
(Translated by CHE Wai-lam William)

Chen Dongyuan. *Zhongguo funü shenghuo shi.* Shanghai: Shangwu yinshuguan, 1937.

Dull, Jack. "Marriage and Divorce in Han China: A Glimpse at 'Pre-Confucian' Society." In *Chinese Family Law and Social Change in Historical and Comparative Perspective,* ed. David C. Buxbaum. Seattle: University of Washington Press, 1978, 23–74.

Han shu. Beijing: Zhonghua shuju, 1983.

Hou Han shu. Beijing: Zhonghua shuju, 1973, vol. 10, 84.2784–92.

Lee, Lily Xiao Hong. *The Virtue of Yin: Studies on Chinese Women.* Sydney: Wild Peony, 1994, 11–24.

Liu Xiang. *Lienü zhuan.* Sibubeiyao ed.

Swann, Nancy Lee. *Pan Chao: Foremost Woman Scholar of China, First Century* A.D. New York: Century, 1932.

Wong Yin Lee. *Handai funü wenxue wujia jinjiu.* Hong Kong: Asia Pacific International Press, 1990.

Xiao Tong. *Wenxuan, or, Selections of Refined Literature,* trans. David R. Knechtges. Princeton, NJ: Princeton University Press, 1982–1966.

———. *Zhaoming wenxuan.* Taipei: Guangwen shuju, 1964.

Yan Kejun. *Quan shanggu sandai Qin Han Sanguo Liuchao wen. Quan Hou Han wen.* Taipei: Shijie shuju, 1963, chapter 96.

Bashu Guafu Qing: *see* Qing, The Widow from Bashu

Bo, Concubine of Emperor Gaozu

Lady Bo (Gaozu Bo Ji), d. 155 B.C.E., from Wu District in present-day Jiangsu Province, was a palace woman of Emperor Gaozu (Liu Bang, 256–195 B.C.E.; r. 202–195 B.C.E.) and mother of Emperor Wen (Liu Heng, 202–157 B.C.E.; r. 179–157 B.C.E.); her given name is not known.

Lady Bo's mother, The Woman Wei, was a member of the imperial clan of Wei, one of the kingdoms of the Warring States period, and gave birth to her daughter after an illicit liaison with a man named Bo. She kept the child and brought her up in the palace, and when the king, Wei Bao, overheard a fortune-teller predicting that the girl was destined to give birth to an emperor he took the girl as a concubine. During the war between Chu and Han for sovereignty over China, Wei Bao changed sides several times before being taken prisoner by Liu Bang, then King of Han. Considered a traitor to his own land, he was eventually killed by one of his ministers.

Taken as a slave, Lady Bo was set to work in the weaving room in the rear palace but was later promoted as a palace woman after Liu Bang caught sight of her and admired her beauty, even though she was still very young. In the rear palace she had become friendly with Consort Guan and Consort Zhao Zi'er, and the three young women swore never to betray their friendship should they ever be favored by the king. However, not long after Consort Guan and Consort Zhao Zi'er received Liu Bang's favor, he heard them mocking the pact they had made with the palace woman Bo. He asked them about it and about palace woman Bo and was so touched that he called her to his bed that very day. When she told him that the previous night she had dreamed of a green dragon on her belly, he was very pleased. The child she conceived that day was Liu Heng, the future Emperor Wen, and upon his birth she was promoted to Lady Bo. She remained in this inferior position and saw little of Liu Bang, not being granted any titles even after he became emperor.

Upon the death of the emperor, Empress Lü (*q.v.* Lü Zhi, Empress of Emperor Gaozu) confined to the palace all the concubines the emperor had ever favored, except for Lady Bo, who had been so rarely favored. Lady Bo was among those who received titles at this time. She was made Dowager Princess of Dai when her son was enfeoffed the Prince of Dai, and she went to the state of Dai to live with her son.

Empress Lü reigned as de facto ruler until her death in 180 B.C.E., at which time her natal Lü clan fell from power. It was then decided that Liu Heng should be enthroned as emperor, an important consideration being the kind and virtuous nature of his mother, Lady Bo. The ministers of state responsible for this decision clearly believed her to be incapable of the political machinations that had kept Empress Lü in power for many years. When her son became emperor, Lady Bo was granted the title Empress Dowager Bo.

The rites of Han prescribed that Empress Dowager Bo, who was considered a descendant of the imperial family of Wei, grant offerings and titles to her family according to degrees of kinship. She was also responsible for the conferring of other titles. Her younger brother Bo Zhao was made Marquis of Zhi to help restore the glory of the Wei clan. When her grandson Liu Qi (Emperor Jing, r. 156–141 B.C.E.) was appointed heir apparent, Empress Dowager Bo recommended that his mother be appointed Empress Dou (*q.v.* Dou Yifang, Empress of Emperor Wen), since a mother must be honored if her son is.

Empress Dowager Bo was a cautious woman, careful not to interfere in dangerous situations. The Prince of Huainan, Liu Chang, was one of the younger sons of Emperor Gaozu, by the concubine née Zhao, but had been raised by Empress Lü. Believing himself to be Emperor Wen's closest relative, he began to behave disobediently and arrogantly. The emperor was generous to his younger relative, however, and treated him with kindness. Liu Chang harbored a deep hatred for Shen Yiji (d. 177 B.C.E.), who had been the lover of Empress Lü and who had caused the early death from sadness of Liu Chang's biological mother, Concubine Zhao. Liu Chang was immensely strong and he battered Shen Yiji to death with an iron mallet. He then presented himself to the emperor, apologizing for his crime and expecting to be punished. The emperor, however, pardoned him, knowing that he had murdered Shen Yiji only out of revenge for his dead mother. The only effect this had was to make Liu Chang even more arrogant, yet Empress Dowager Bo said nothing about this.

On another occasion, however, Empress Dowager Bo did castigate her son for the behavior of members of the younger imperial generation. Liu Qi, the heir apparent, and his brother Liu Wu came to court in a carriage one day to pay a ritual visit to their father. Ignoring court etiquette, they drove straight through the Sima Gate instead of descending from their carriage. The Gate Traffic Control Officer (*gongcheling*) Zhang Shizhi stopped them and reported their disrespectful action to the emperor. Not until Emperor Wen admitted to Empress Dowager Bo that he had been remiss in teaching his sons did she give the order that the heir apparent and Liu Wu be pardoned and be allowed into the palace. For his part in this incident, Zhang Shizhi was promoted to Ordinary Grand Master (*zhongdafu*).

Empress Dowager Bo was made Grand Empress Dowager when her grandson Liu Qi (the future Emperor Jing) succeeded to the throne in 157 B.C.E. She died two years later and was buried in the South Tomb.

In contrast to her predecessor the feisty Empress Lü, Lady Bo was considered a kind, obedient, and virtuous woman, and it has been said that it was because of this consideration that her son became emperor. Good she may have been, but her virtue clearly lay in abiding by court ritual and tradition, and both the imperial family and ministers of state would undoubtedly have found this a most attractive and useful quality in an emperor's mother.

BAO Shanben

Chen Quanli and Hou Xinyi, eds. *Hou fei cidian.* Xi'an: Shaanxi renmin jiaoyu chubanshe, 1991, 12.
Han shu. Beijing: Zhonghua shuju, 1983, vol. 12, 97.3941–42.
Shi ji. Beijing: Zhonghua shuju, 1989, vol. 4, 49.1970–72.
Sima Guang. *Zizhi tongjian.* Beijing: Zhonghua shuju, 1976, vol. 1, 14.456–59.

Bo, Empress of Emperor Jing

Empress Bo (Xiao Jing Bo Huanghou), d. 147 B.C.E., whose given name is not recorded in the histories, was a grandniece of Empress Dowager Bo (*q.v.* Bo, Concubine of Emperor Gaozu) and the first empress of Emperor Jing (Liu Qi, 188–141 B.C.E.; r. 156–141 B.C.E.).

Empress Bo married the then heir apparent Liu Qi in 179, a marriage arranged by her great-aunt Empress Dowager Bo, who was also the paternal grandmother of Liu Qi. Empress Bo did not produce any children, however, and the heir apparent transferred his affections to two other palace women, Concubine Li (Li Ji), who bore his eldest son, Liu Rong, and Consort Wang (*q.v.* Wang Zhi, Empress of Emperor Jing), who bore him three daughters and a son, Liu Che. Although appointed empress when Liu Qi ascended the throne, as a childless wife Empress Bo was in an unenviable position. Her situation worsened after the death in 155 of her great-aunt and mentor, Empress Dowager Bo. Within two years Liu Rong, the son of Concubine Li, had been appointed heir apparent and two years after that, in 151, Empress Bo was deposed. She died of melancholy and despair four years later and was buried in 147 south of Pingwang Pavilion in the eastern section of the capital, Chang'an.

Although Empress Dowager Bo was Emperor Jing's grandmother, the Bo family was not politically powerful. Empress Bo was a classic example of a woman who, even though she had the strong backing of her family, lost status and position because she did not produce any children, especially sons.

BAO Shanben

Chen Quanli and Hou Xinyi, eds. *Hou fei cidian.* Xi'an: Shaanxi renmin jiaoyu chubanshe, 1991, 13.
Han shu. Beijing: Zhonghua shuju, 1983, vol. 12, 97.3945.
Shi ji. Beijing: Zhonghua shuju, 1962, vol. 4, 49.1976.
Sima Guang. *Zizhi tongjian.* Beijing: Zhonghua shuju, 1956, vol. 1, 16.532.

Bo Ji: *see* Bo, Concubine of Emperor Gaozu

C

Cai Wenji: *see* Cai Yan

Cai Yan

Cai Yan, fl. late second century, of Chenliu (present-day Qi District, Henan Province), *zi* Wenji (Lady of Literary Refinement), was also known as Cai Zhaoji. The years 174, 177, and 178 have all been suggested as the year of her birth but conclusive evidence is still lacking. She has been described as the most hapless poet of the Han dynasty but her two poems both titled *Beifen shi* (this title has been translated as *Indignant Grief* and as *Poem of Affliction*) and her long poem *Eighteen Songs of a Nomad Flute* (Hujia shiba pai) are literary masterpieces.

110 *CAI YAN*

Cai Yan was the daughter of Cai Yong (133–192; *zi* Bojie), a famous scholar of late Eastern Han who died in prison, and she was learned, versatile, eloquent, and musically gifted. She married at least three times, not always of her own volition. She was childless when her first husband, Wei Zhongdao of Hedong, died, so she returned to her native place. However, in the chaotic last decade of the second century Cai Yan was captured by soldiers of the southern Xiongnu people (often referred to in English as the Huns) and taken as a concubine by the Xiongnu nobleman Zuo Xianwang. She lived in an alien land with these non-Han people for twelve years, during which time she gave birth to two sons; one source says she was given in marriage to a second Xiongnu husband when her first husband died. The powerful Han warlord Cao Cao (155–220) had been a good friend of Cai Yan's father and, regretting that his friend had died with no Han grandchildren, Cao Cao sent an emissary to the southern Xiongnu in about 206 to redeem Cai Yan with gold and jade. She returned to her own people but was required to leave her sons behind.

Cao Cao acted out of self-interest and brought Cai Yan immeasurable heartache by redeeming her, as the scholar Dore Levy indicates: "Cai Yan found herself ostracized at court because of both her family connections and her degrading multiple marriages."

It is as the wife of Dong Si, an army officer in the service of Cao Cao, that Cai Yan is recorded in the official history of the Eastern Han dynasty, the *History of the Later Han Dynasty* (Hou Han shu). Cai Yan's knowledge, versatility, and eloquence were brought into play in this marriage. Her husband held the position of State Farms Defender (*tuntian duwei*), but he was accused of a breach of the law and was sentenced to death. Cai Yan went to Cao Cao to plead for her husband's life, arriving to find the place packed with noblemen, literary celebrities, and foreign envoys and translators. Just as Cao Cao was telling his guests that Cai Bojie's daughter was about to call on him, she entered,

> her hair unkempt and her feet bare. She kowtowed and apologized and then, facing Cao Cao, spoke for her husband with the full force of justice behind her. So clear and eloquent was her speech and so poignant what she said that all present were moved. Cao Cao said: "I really sympathize with you but the indictment document has already been sent. There is nothing I can do now." Cai Yan replied: "Your Honor has thousands of horses in his stable and gallant soldiers by the hundreds to do his bidding. Would you not spare one man and a fast horse to save a person from imminent death?"

With this, Cao Cao relented and Cai Yan won a reprieve for Dong Si. In an apparent reference to visits he had made to Cai Yan's father when she was a child, Cao Cao asked her if she was still able to recite from memory the classics her family home had been filled with. Cai Yan replied: "My late father bestowed on me some 4,000 volumes of books but none survived those chaotic years. I can remember only some 400 articles now." She is said to have written down for him in fine calligraphy the articles she could recite by heart.

The bibliographical chapter of the *History of the Sui Dynasty* (Sui shu), the official history of the Sui dynasty (581–618), notes that there had been a *Collected Works of Cai Wenji* in one volume but it was then no longer extant. Only three of Cai Yan's works have survived. Her two works titled *Indignant Grief* are recorded in the *History of the Later Han Dynasty,* but controversy remains over whether she wrote both poems. The first is a narrative poem (*xushi shi*) with 108 lines of five characters each, totaling 540 characters; it is generally agreed that Cai Yan wrote this poem. The second is a lyric-style poem (*shuqing shi*) in the style of the pre-Han *Songs of the South* (Chu ci) with thirty-eight lines of seven characters each, totaling 266 characters; this poem is generally thought to be a forgery. The first scholar to raise doubts about the authenticity of the poems was the Song dynasty poet Su Shi (*zi* Dongpo, 1036–1101), who claimed that the candid and sorrowful diction of the poems was similar to the style of *Ballad of Mulan,* a style that had not existed in Luoyang during Cai Yan's lifetime. He added that the tale narrated in the poems of Cai Yan having been driven out by the usurping general Dong Zhuo (d. 192) and captured by the Xiongnu raised further doubts as to their authenticity, since her father had still been alive then and would have protected her. Later scholars have challenged this view. Notwithstanding this controversy, the poems won high praise from the Qing (1644–1911) critic Shen Deqian for being "well paragraphed without marks of transition, discrete yet coherent, neither fragmented nor confusing. Shaoling's [Du Fu] *[Five Hundred Words] to Express My Feelings [When I Went from the Capital to] Fengxian* (Fengxian yonghuai) and *Journey North* (Beizheng) are similar to them in many respects." Currently, the dominant view is that the five-character poem is by Cai Yan, while the work in the style of *Songs of the South* was written by a later hand. The following excerpt from *Poem of Affliction (Indignant Grief),* translated by Dore Levy (128), reveals a woman whose heart aches for the two beloved sons she has been forced to leave behind when she is brought back to China, where she no longer has any family:

> Desolate, I faced my orphan shadow;
> Grief and anger swelled in my entrails.
> I climbed a hill to look off into the distance,
> And my spirit seemed suddenly to fly from me;
> But just when I seemed to be at my last breath,
> Some people near me acted with great kindness.
> So again I forced myself to go on living,
> But though I lived, what had I to depend on?
> I entrusted my life to yet another husband,
> I did my utmost to force myself to go on.
> My homeless life completes my suffering;
> My constant fear is to be cast off again.
> How long can one person's life endure?
> I shall harbor my grief to the very end of my days!

Eighteen Songs of a Nomad Flute is a long lyric-style poem made up of eighteen songs, or sections, totaling 1,297 characters. It was first recorded under "Cai Yan of Eastern Han" in the eleventh-century Song dynasty *Yuefu shiji.* Zhu Xi (1130–1200) included it as a poem by Cai Yan in his *Chu ci jizhu houyu,* commending it even more

112   CAI YAN

highly than the two *Indignant Grief* works. However, authorship of this work remains even more contentious than that of *Indignant Grief*. The famous playwright Guo Moruo (1892–1978) asserted that Cai Yan was indeed its author, while the scholar Wang Dajin claimed it was a forgery. The American scholar Dore Levy writes: "While it may never be possible to prove Cai Yan's authorship, the sequence is unique in early poetry for the direct, passionately expressed identity of the woman's voice. . . . [*Eighteen Songs of a Nomad Flute*] stress the particularity of the speaker's voice with repeated personal pronouns and raw emotion. They ring with unassuaged grief—a style impossible for the formulaic voice of female narrators after the fifth century" (Levy, 23). In Song 13 of the *Eighteen Songs,* Cai Yan weeps for her lost sons:

> I had never dreamed I would ever go home again;
> I caress, I embrace my nomad sons, the flowing tears soak our clothes.
> To escort me the envoy from China has a team of horses,
> My nomad children wail till they lose their voices—alas! who could have known
> That while we still lived there would come a time that would separate us like death?
> . . .
> In my thirteenth song the strings are passionate, the tones melancholy,
> My bowels feel cut to pieces, and no one knows what I have known. (Levy, 27)

Eighteen Songs of a Nomad Flute exerted an especially strong influence on northern literature during the Wei, Jin, and Six Dynasties periods (i.e., from the third to the sixth centuries). Shen Deqian said of *Indignant Grief:* "Impassioned and full of grief, they are so forceful they startle tumbleweed and arouse gravel to flight. They are the most powerful poems of the Eastern Han dynasty." Despite their stylistic differences, *Indignant Grief* and *Eighteen Songs of a Nomad Flute* tell movingly of the tragedy of Cai Yan. Hers was a miserable and difficult life, but her tragedy surely lies in her being simply an "unfortunate victim of war and politics." Yet Cai Yan's tenacity and indomitable spirit as much as her deep grief reach out to us across the centuries.

NISHIMURA Fumiko
(Translated by CHE Wai-lam William)

Chen Zumei. "Cai Yan shengnian kaozheng buyi jianshu qi zuopin de zhenwei ji pingjia zhong de wenti." *Zhonghua wenshi luncong* (1983): 2, 219–30.
Guo Maoqian. *Yuefu shiji.* Beijing: Zhonghua shuju, 1979, vol. 3, 59.860–65.
Guo Moruo. *Cai wenji.* Beijing: Wenwu chubanshe, 1959.
Hou Han shu. Beijing: Zhonghua shuju, 1965, 1973, vol. 5, 84.2800–3.
Hu Guorui. *Wei Jin Nanbeichao wenxue shi.* Shanghai: Shanghai wenyi chubanshe, 1980, 28–32.
Hu Zi. *Tiao xi yuyin conghua.* Beijing: Renmin wenxue chubanshe, 1981, vol. 1, 1.1–6.
Levy, Dore J. "Cai Yan." In *Women Writers of Traditional China: An Anthology of Poetry and Criticism,* ed. Kang-i Sun Chang and Haun Saussy. Stanford, CA: Stanford University Press, 1999, 22–30.
———. *Chinese Narrative Poetry: The Late Han Through T'ang Dynasties.* Durham, NC: Duke University Press, 1988, 82–102, 125–28.

Liang Yizhen. *Zhongguo funü wenxue shigang.* Shanghai: Shanghai shudian, 1990 reprint, 78–94.

Liu Kaiyang. "Guanyu Cai Yan de shengnian." In *"Hujia shiba pai" taolun ji,* ed. Wenxue yichan bianjibu. Beijing: Zhonghua shuju, 1959, 171–77.

Luo Genze. *Yuefu wenxue shi.* Taipei: Wenshizhe chubanshe, 1974, 75–77.

Shen Deqian. *Gushi yuan.* Beijing: Zhonghua shuju, 1973, 3, 63–65.

Wang Dajin. "'Hujia shiba pai' fei Cai Yan zuo buzheng." In *"Hujia shibapai" taolun ji,* ed. Wenxue yichan bianjibu. Beijing: Zhonghua shuju, 1959, 184–86.

Zheng Zhenduo. *Chatuben Zhongguo wenxue shi.* Beijing: Wenxue gujishe, 1959, vol. 1, 110–12.

Zhu Xi. *Chu ci jizhu houyu.* Taipei: Taiwan shangwu yinshuguan, 1985, 3.428–31.

Cai Zhaoji: *see* **Cai Yan**

Cao Dagu: *see* **Ban Zhao**

Cao Jie, Empress of Emperor Xian

Empress Cao (Xiandi Cao Huanghou), c. 196–260, was empress to Emperor Xian (Liu Xie, 181–234; r. 189–220) of Eastern Han. She was the second daughter of Cao Cao (155–220), the posthumous Emperor Wu of Wei, and her name was Cao Jie.

During the chaotic last years of Eastern Han, rebellious peasants joined the Yellow Turban Uprising and local governors annexed territory. As Counselor-in-Chief (*chengxiang*) of Han, Cao Cao monopolized the court, wielding almost absolute power in the Yellow River and Huai River region of north China. He defeated the governors who had declared their independence and in the fifth month of 213 declared himself Duke of Wei. In the traditional preliminary to usurping the throne, he granted himself the "nine presents" (*jiu xi*) and two months later presented his three daughters—Cao Xian, Cao Jie, and Cao Hua—to the court as concubines. All three were given the title Worthy Lady (*guiren*) but because Cao Hua was still a child she remained at home for a further year. As a show of strength, Cao Cao had Wang Yi, who was Chamberlain of the National Treasury (*taichang dasi*) and Marquis Ting of Anyang, come to his home with betrothal gifts of jade and thousands of bolts of silk. Among the party were five armed officials who had been given the civil title Court Gentlemen for Consultation (*yilang*) and another who was called their deputy.

Empress Fu (*q.v.* Fu Shou, Empress of Emperor Xian) had long been deeply concerned at Cao Cao's growing power and had written to her father asking help in containing him. When this plot was revealed, in 214, Cao Cao had Empress Fu confined in the Drying House, where she died. The following year, Worthy Lady Cao Jie was promoted to empress, a position she held until the Han dynasty finally collapsed in 220.

After Cao Cao died in 220, his son—and Empress Cao's brother—Cao Pi (187–226) forced Emperor Xian to abdicate, demoting him to Duke of Shanyang. Cao Pi declared a new dynasty—the Wei dynasty—and installed himself as emperor (Emperor Wen, r. 220–226). Not long after this, he sent emissaries to his sister, the former Empress Cao, requesting her to return the emperor's imperial seal and ribbon. Several times she refused to see the emissaries but finally she called them in and proceeded to

114 *CAO JIE*

reprimand them one by one for the crime of usurpation. She then flung the seal and ribbon at them and, in such a rage that none dared look up at her, cried: "You will not be blessed by heaven!"

Empress Cao was demoted to Duchess of Shanyang and lived in retirement with the former emperor until his death in 234. She lived on as a widow for another twenty-six years, dying in 260, and was buried alongside her husband in Shan Tomb, her funeral ceremonies following the tradition of the Han dynasty. It is notable that Empress Cao remained loyal not to her father or to her brother, but to her husband, in the Confucian tradition of the "three followings" (*sancong*), whereby a woman's husband is her heaven and she is obliged to belong to him; this is known as "double heaven."

WANG Bugao

Chen Quanli and Hou Xinyi, eds. *Hou fei cidian.* Xi'an: Shaanxi renmin jiaoyu chubanshe, 1991, 29.
Hou Han shu. Beijing: Zhonghua shuju, 1965, vol. 2, 9.388–91; vol. 2, 10xia.455–58.
Sanguo zhi. Beijing: Zhonghua shuju, 1989, vol. 1, 1.1–55.

Chang T'ang, The Mother of: *see* Zhang Tang's Mother

Chen Gua Xiaofu: *see* The Filial Widow from Chen

Chen Jiao, Empress of Emperor Wu

Chen Jiao (Xiao Wu Chen Huanghou), b. c. 160 B.C.E., also known as Ajiao, was the first empress of Emperor Wu (Liu Che, 156–87 B.C.E.; r. 140–87 B.C.E.). She herself was of imperial descent: her maternal grandfather was Emperor Wen (Liu Heng, 202–157 B.C.E.; r. 179–157 B.C.E.), her grandmother was Empress Dou (*q.v.* Dou Yifang, Empress of Emperor Wen), and her mother was the Grand Princess Liu Piao (*q.v.*). Chen Jiao's father, Chen Wu, had been the Marquis of Tangyi, a title he inherited from his father, Chen Ying. Chen Ying had risen in rebellion against Qin with Xiang Yu (*vide* Yu, Consort of the Hegemon-King of Chu) but had switched his loyalty to Liu Bang, the future founding emperor of Han, for which he had been rewarded with the title of Marquis.

Liu Che, the future Emperor Wu, had been made Prince of Jiaodong when he was an infant. When he was still very young, Chen Jiao's mother (i.e., his aunt Liu Piao) took him on her lap and asked him if he wanted a wife. Pointing to Chen Jiao, she asked him if she was not indeed beautiful, to which the child replied: "If I could have Ajiao as my wife, I would build a house of gold for her." Liu Piao later arranged a marriage between her daughter and Liu Che, and was instrumental in Liu Che's being appointed heir apparent.

Liu Che was sixteen years old when he ascended the throne, and he appointed his wife Chen Jiao as empress. However, after ten years of marriage during which the emperor favored her, Empress Chen had not borne him a son. She was also said to have become overbearing and jealous, and she gradually lost the emperor's favor. After Emperor Wu took a new favorite, Wei Zifu (*q.v.* Wei Zifu, Empress of Emperor Wu), who had been brought into the palace on the recommendation of his eldest sister, Princess of Pingyang, Empress Chen tried to bring pressure on him by attempting suicide. The emperor became increasingly irritated with her and when it was discovered that she had turned to witchcraft and sorcery, her daughter and a witch named Chu Fu being involved in performing sorcery and incantations, the emperor ordered that all those involved, some 300 people, be put to death. This was in 130 B.C.E. Empress Chen was spared, but an edict was issued saying that she had broken the law by engaging in sorcery with witches, which made her unworthy of being empress.

Empress Chen was relieved of the imperial seal and ribbon, deposed, and sent to live in Changmen Palace. Chen Jiao paid the famous poet Sima Xiangru (179–117 B.C.E.) one hundred *jin* of gold to write her a rhapsody (*fu*) expressing her grief and sorrow. This was the well-known *Changmen fu,* which did indeed move the emperor when he read it. He visited her briefly but did not reinstate her as empress. Poets and writers of later generations have retold this in poetry and prose as a charming story.

Chen Jiao lived out her lonely life in Changmen Palace and was buried after her death east of Langguanting in Baling (the eastern outskirts of present-day Xi'an in Shaanxi Province).

WANG Lihua

An Zuozhang, ed. *Hou fei zhuan.* Zhengzhou: Henan renmin chubanshe, 1990, 45–56.
Chen Quanli and Hou Xinyi, eds. *Hou fei cidian.* Xi'an: Shaanxi renmin jiaoyu chubanshe, 1991, 13.
Han shu. Beijing: Zhonghua shuju, 1983, vol. 9, 59.2638; vol. 12, 97.3948–49.
Loewe, Michael. *Crisis and Conflict in Han China.* London: George Allen & Unwin, 1974.
Shi ji. Beijing: Zhonghua shuju, 1959, vol. 4, 49; 1967–86.

Chen Siqian

Chen Siqian, the wife of Zhang Liangze (Zhang Liangze Qi Chen Siqian), of the Eastern Han dynasty, was from Chenggu (in present-day Shaanxi Province).

Chen Siqian's husband was from Nanzheng (also in present-day Shaanxi Province) and he had been appointed to a position in Fufeng, in the same area. When his subordinates suggested devising a harsh prohibition system to prevent disorder and wrongdoing , he sought the advice of his wife. Chen Siqian told him that she believed in restoring moral teachings and appealing to people's sense of honor and shame. "There are five major punishments. Add the supplementary punishments to this and that gives a total of 3,000 penalties. There are already too many; why would you consider creating more?" Zhang Liangze saw the reason in what she said and decided against his subordinates' suggestion. He was later promoted and transferred to Zangke (to the west of present-day Dejiang County, Guizhou Province) as governor (*taishou*). He put conciliatory policies in place that won him great respect and fame in the south, where he was given the sobriquet Slumbering Tiger. His next position was Regional Inspector of Liangzhou and after that he was made Commandery Governor of Wei; in each post he brought order and security to the community.

116 CHEN SIQIAN

Chen Siqian's brother Chen Bosi was obsessed with a Daoist regimen for becoming a transcendent (*xian*) but she dissuaded him from this path, saying: "What a gentleman is concerned with is not a short life but being unable to excel or to win fame and honor during his lifetime. Becoming immortal is as foolish as trying to tie down the wind and catch shadows. It is not worth doing." Another brother, Chen Botai, greatly admired her, calling her "a descendant of a female imperial secretary." So learned and rational was Chen Siqian that few men could equal her, and that is the reason her name has been deservedly preserved in the historical records.

SHEN Lidong

"Guiyuan dian: Guishu bu." In *Gujin tushu jicheng*, ed. Chen Menglei. Shanghai: Zhonghua shuju, 1934, Book 420, 15a.

Chen Ying Mu: *see* Chen Ying's Mother

Chen Ying's Mother

Chen Ying's Mother (Chen Ying Mu), fl. c. 208 B.C.E., lived in Dongyang (northeast of present-day Tianchang District, Anhui Province) during the reign of the second emperor of the Qin dynasty (221–206 B.C.E.). Her given and family names were not recorded, and she is known to history only as the mother of Chen Ying, who held the post of clerk (*lingshi*) of Dongyang.

The last years of the short-lived Qin dynasty were chaotic, with rebellions breaking out throughout the empire. Chen Sheng (d. 208) led the first of such local uprisings and, after he was defeated, the young men of Dongyang killed the county magistrate and gathered together several thousand men. Unable to decide upon a leader, they eventually chose Chen Ying who, as the clerk of Dongyang, lived in the district seat. He had always been discreet and trustworthy, and had gained the respect of the people as a wise elder. Chen Ying, however, declined to lead them, excusing himself on the grounds that he lacked insight and ability. The youths, by now numbering nearly 20,000, nevertheless forced him to assume the post of leader and began to talk of making him their king.

Concerned that her son was being swept out of his depth, Chen Ying's Mother counseled him thus: "In all the years since I entered the Chen family as a daughter-in-law, I have never heard of any of your ancestors being noble or distinguished. It is not an auspicious sign for you to have won such a high title [as king] overnight. It would be far better if you were to attach yourself to someone else, so that if they succeed you can expect to be granted a title. If they fail, however, you will not be held responsible and will escape blame for the consequences." Chen Ying heeded her advice and refused the mob's demands that he be declared king. Instead, he told his military attendants to join the cause of the rebel leader Xiang Liang (d. 208 B.C.E.) of the state of Chu. The Xiang clan, he told them, had produced generations of generals, and in their attempt to overthrow the Qin dynasty the people could do no better than to rely on a famous noble family such as this who were accustomed to victory. The people of Dongyang did as Chen Ying said, but eventually Liu Bang, the King of Han and founding emperor of the Han dynasty (*vide* Gaozu Lü Huanghou), defeated the Xiang Liang–Xiang Yu faction. As his mother had predicted, Chen Ying was able to then pledge his allegiance to the new emperor, who granted him the title of Marquis of Tangyi.

The *Biographies of Eminent Women* (Lienü zhuan) said of Chen Ying's Mother that she was praiseworthy because "she knew the mandate of heaven and was able to preserve the way of Chen Ying's ancestors, thus bringing benefit to his descendants." She has been described as astute and resourceful, a sagacious mother who devised a good stratagem to protect her son and help him achieve success.

SHEN Jian

Liu Xiang. *Lienü zhuan.* Sibubeiyao ed., 8.2.
O'Hara, Albert R.*The Position of Woman in Early China According to the Lieh Nü Chuan, "The Biographies of Chinese Women."* Taipei: Mei Ya, 1971; 1978, 218–19.
Shi ji. Beijing: Zhonghua shuju, 1985, vol. 1, 7.298.

Cheng Wenju Qi: *see* **Li Mujiang**

Cheng Wenju's Wife: *see* **Li Mujiang**

Chi Zhaopeng: *see* **Lü's Mother**

Ch'in Chia's Wife: *see* **Xu Shu**

Chunyu Tiying
Chunyu Tiying, fl. mid-second century B.C.E., of Taicang, in Qi (the present-day city of Zibo, Shandong Province), was the fifth daughter of Chunyu Yi, district magistrate of Taicang.

During the reign of Emperor Wen (Liu Heng, 202–157 B.C.E.; r. 179–157 B.C.E.) of Western Han, Chunyu Yi committed a crime for which the sentence was physical mutilation; this punishment took such forms as branding on the forehead, cutting off the nose, or castration. Before being sent to Chang'an to receive his punishment, Chunyu Yi bemoaned the fact that he had no sons, because "daughters are useless during an emergency." Upon hearing this, his youngest daughter, Chunyu Tiying, was so distressed that she went with him to Chang'an, where she presented the following memorial to Emperor Wen:

> My father is an official who is well known in Qi for his honesty and integrity. He has come to receive punishment for a crime. I am saddened, however, that the dead cannot be brought back to life and that criminals who have been punished cannot be made whole again, because, once mutilated, those who want to start afresh are unable to do so. I offer myself as a government slave to atone for my father's crime so that he may have the chance to start afresh.

118 CHUNYU TIYING

Moved by the young woman's eloquence, Emperor Wen issued the following edict:

> I have heard that in the time of Youyu [Shun], criminals were required to wear certain clothes or had their clothes painted and that this acted as a deterrent. How wonderful! Today there are five different kinds of punishments but crimes are still committed. Is this because my virtue is insufficient to teach the people? I am ashamed because if we don't teach properly then the people will suffer. *The Book of Songs* calls benevolent gentlemen the father and mother of the people. I am saddened that instead of being educated those who do wrong now are punished, so that there is no way for them to change. Physical mutilation is horrible because it leaves no way for people ever to recover. How can we do this and still call ourselves the father and mother of the people? Let us do away with physical punishment.

Thenceforth, physical punishment of that kind was no longer practiced and Chunyu Tiying's father was exonerated of his crime. Her contemporaries claimed that, because she was right, Chunyu Tiying inspired a holy emperor with a single word.

Chunyu Tiying was an exemplar of benevolence, filial piety, and courage. Her words brought about the abolition of physical mutilation as punishment for crimes, a deed of unlimited merit. Her story has been handed down through the centuries and Ban Gu, who compiled the *History of the Han Dynasty* (Han shu), composed the poem *On Historical Events* (Yongshi) to commemorate the event, praising Chunyu Tiying highly.

YAO Weidou

Han shu. Beijing: Zhonghua shuju, 1983, vol. 4, 23.1097–98.
Liu Shisheng. *Zhongguo gudai funüshi.* Qingdao: Qingdao chubanshe, 1991, 114–15.
Liu Xiang. *Lienü zhuan.* Sibubeiyao ed., 6.13–14.
Liu Ziqing. *Zhongguo lidai xianneng funü pingzhuan.* Taipei: Liming wenhua, 1978, 85–89.
O'Hara, Albert R. *The Position of Woman in Early China According to the Lieh Nü Chuan, "The Biographies of Chinese Women."* Taipei: Mei Ya, 1971; 1978, 183–85.

Chu-Yai, The Two Righteous Ones of: *see* **Two Honorable Women from Zhuya**

D

Deng Chen Qi Xinye Gongzhu: *see* **Liu Yuan**

Deng Chen's Wife: *see* **Liu Yuan**

Deng Mengnü, Empress of Emperor Huan
Deng Mengnü (Huandi Deng Huanghou), c. 140–165, was empress to Emperor Huan (Liu Zhi, 132–167; r. 147–167) of Eastern Han. She was the daughter of Deng Xiang and his wife, who was known as Xuan. Deng Mengnü's father was a great-nephew of Empress Dowager Deng (*q.v.* Deng Sui, Empress of Emperor He). The family had

been respected and powerful in Nanyang Commandery (the southwest of present-day Henan Province) for many generations, and one member of the clan had been a leading supporter of the founding Emperor Guangwu (r. 25–57) of Eastern Han. After the death of Empress Dowager Deng in 121, however, the power of her family had been broken by Emperor An (r. 107–125), and Deng Xiang was no longer regarded as a man of noble descent. He first held low-ranking probationary appointment as a Gentleman of the Interior (*langzhong*) and never rose higher than the position of a junior official in the office of the Lateral Courts (*yeting*), the bureau that supervised the affairs of the harem. He died comparatively young, a few years after the birth of his daughter, and his widow Xuan soon married again. Xuan's second husband, Deng Mengnü's stepfather, was Liang Ki (the variant transcription Ki is used here to distinguish him from Liang Ji, as their names have the same transliteration), maternal uncle to Sun Shou (*q.v.*), wife of the General-in-Chief Liang Ji. Though Liang Ki was not directly related to the general-in-chief, Deng Xiang's widow and children shared in the prosperity of the imperial relatives by marriage, and Deng Mengnü took her stepfather's surname of Liang.

It was under the influence of Sun Shou, moreover, that Deng Mengnü entered the harem in 153 or 154; she was at that time probably thirteen *sui,* the most common age for such entry. First appointed a Lady of Elegance (*cainü*), lowest of the three ranks of imperial concubines, she was extremely beautiful and attracted the attention and favors of Emperor Huan, so that she was swiftly promoted to Worthy Lady (*guiren*), highest rank below the empress. Recognizing the girl's physical attractions, Sun Shou evidently hoped she would act as an agent or support for her adopted relatives. At first the plan appears to have been successful: Worthy Lady Deng contrived to avoid any quarrel with the reigning empress, Liang Nüying (*q.v.* Liang Nüying, Empress of Emperor Huan), sister of Liang Ji, and she also obtained special favors for her own family. A year after she entered the harem, presumably at the time she was promoted to Worthy Lady, her elder brother Deng Yan (d. c. 156) was enfeoffed as a county marquis in Nanyang with the high rank of Specially Advanced (*tejin*) and precedence next only to the highest ministers of state.

On the other hand, Worthy Lady Deng's stepfather, Liang Ki, died soon after her entry into the harem, so the connection with Sun Shou and Liang Ji was weakened, and in the autumn of 159 the situation was dramatically changed by the unexpected death of Empress Liang. The late empress's brother, General-in-Chief Liang Ji, had no longer any direct connection to the imperial harem; in order to regain his influence there, he now proposed to adopt Worthy Lady Deng as his daughter and have her established as empress.

Emperor Huan had no objection to this arrangement on personal grounds—he still preferred Worthy Lady Deng to any other woman available—but there were growing signs that he resented Liang Ji's dominance at court. Now twenty-seven, he had been kept from all practical influence in government and was resentful about many individual cases of Liang Ji's harsh measures against protest and dissent. So long as Liang Ji had the support and approval of Worthy Lady Deng's own family, notably her mother, Xuan, there was no room for political maneuver, but at this point Xuan

120 DENG MENGNÜ

and her immediate relatives came to realize that they would lose much of their influence if Worthy Lady Deng came under Liang Ji's control, while Xuan herself saw the golden opportunity of official rank as mother-in-law to the emperor. She refused to approve the adoption.

An elder sister of Worthy Lady Deng had married a certain Bing Zun, who held the low-ranking post of consultant (*yilang*) at the court. He could also see the opportunities presented by the good fortune of his sister-in-law, and he took the lead in urging Xuan to oppose Liang Ji's plans. Within a few days Liang Ji had sent a group of his retainers to kill him, but Xuan still refused to change her mind, and Liang Ji sent his men against her, too.

Xuan's mansion in the capital was directly next door to the house of the eunuch Regular Attendant Yuan She. Like other great houses of the time, it was surrounded by a high wall and Liang Ji's men broke into Yuan She's compound in order to gain entry to Xuan's. Upon discovering them, Yuan She beat on a drum to summon his own servants and called out to warn Xuan. She ran to the palace, reached the emperor, and told him the story.

If Liang Ji could act so directly, Emperor Huan himself was now clearly in danger of his life. He had little time to act before Liang Ji reestablished control within the harem, but he drew up the necessary orders and sent a mixed force of eunuchs and palace gentlemen to surround the residences of Liang Ji and Sun Shou, taking back their insignia of rank and office and ordering them to exile in the far south of Vietnam. As both husband and wife committed suicide, the power of the Liang family was ended.

Five days later, on 14 September 159, Worthy Lady Deng became empress. She and her relatives had renounced their connection with the Liang family, and the emperor insisted that his new consort should adopt the surname Bo. There is some speculation, largely unsubstantiated, that Bo was Xuan's surname before her marriage to Deng Xiang and it is possible that was the reason this surname was chosen, but more likely it was a reminder of the good example of the modest Lady Bo (*q.v.* Bo, Concubine of Emperor Gaozu) of Western Han, mother of Emperor Wen (Liu Heng, 202–157; r. 179–157). In 161, however, senior court officials memorialized that it was inappropriate for the empress to avoid the name of her true father, and an edict restored her surname to Deng. Deng Xiang was granted the posthumous title Marquis and accorded further honors, while Xuan was enfeoffed as Lady of Kunyang, a prosperous county in Nanyang. Various other members of the Deng family had both honors and money bestowed upon them, but although her relatives commanded various units in the palace guards and the Northern army was stationed at the capital, only one member of the empress's family was appointed to significant office besides being appointed to a marquisate; his favor may have been due less to the influence of the empress than to the fact that he had been a friend of the emperor before he was brought to the throne.

Though their perquisites were modest compared to the extravagance and power once enjoyed by the Liang family, the Deng family were not popular with the regular officials of the court, and Emperor Huan received many complaints and protests against them and against the honors he had granted. In particular, and very strangely—though the Deng had long been a leading family, and there appears to have been no direct question raised about the empress's legitimacy—she was often described as a woman of low birth. The emperor paid small attention to these criticisms, and Empress Deng continued to receive his favors.

Sadly, however, she bore her consort no sons, and though two imperial daughters appeared about this time, it is not likely that either of them was hers. By this time, indeed, the emperor had gathered a vast harem, alleged to number five or six thousand women, with servants and slaves, and ministers were protesting that the cost was becoming a major strain on the finances of the empire. The numbers may be exaggerated, though Emperor Huan is known as a builder and constructed at least one additional palace and a pleasure park. For her own part, Empress Deng, now in her late twenties and faced with constant competition from new, ambitious rivals, was in an increasingly weak position. It is recorded that she had a furious quarrel with Worthy Lady Guo, and each told tales about the other, while there is also reference to Empress Deng's drunkenness. Her biography says that she was arrogant and overbearing and the emperor became tired of her presumptions and importunities.

On 27 March 165, Empress Deng was dismissed and imprisoned in the Drying House, the harem hospital that was also used for the seclusion of high-ranking ladies when they were out of favor. A short time later she was dead, officially through an excess of grief. One account says that she was disgraced for misbehavior and then compelled to commit suicide, while two other passages claim that she was found guilty of "heretical doctrines" (*zuodao*), that is, non-Confucian teachings and superstition. Apart from her erratic behavior under the pressure of harem rivalries, it may well be that the unfortunate empress had been in search of some fertility charm or drug that might enable her to bear the emperor a son. Innocent and well intentioned though this may have been, the implications at one level, of supernatural interference with the sacred person of the emperor, and at another, of the possibility of poison, were dangerous and potentially devastating. The accusation of witchcraft was a cliché of harem politics, but it may nonetheless have been true, while "death through grief" may indeed conceal forced suicide or even murder.

With the fall of the empress, her relatives were removed from their positions at court; stripped of their honors and their property, some died in prison while others were sent back to their home county in Nanyang.

About this time, moreover, two of Emperor Huan's eunuch favorites were dismissed and one—Zuo Guan—was obliged to commit suicide. Zuo Guan had been heavily involved in the development of the imperial worship of the divinity Huang–Lao, a combination of the legendary Yellow Emperor and the sage Laozi. The Huang–Lao cult was well established in the Han period, but Emperor Huan was the first ruler to grant it his personal patronage. In the first month of 165, Zuo Guan had been sent to make sacrifice at the shrine constructed at the reputed birthplace of Laozi in Chen kingdom (present-day eastern Henan Province), and it may be that this ritual reflected an enterprise of Empress Deng, seeking mystical support for herself, her husband, and his dynasty. The imperial interest continued even after the empress's death and that of Zuo Guan, and it culminated in a ceremony of worship to Huang–Lao and the new,

DENG MENGNÜ

alien divinity of the Buddha, held at the imperial palace in Luoyang in the summer of 166. It has been suggested that Emperor Huan's third empress, Empress Dou (*q.v.* Dou Miao, Empress of Emperor Huan), was responsible for this development, but it is more probable that the worship of Huang–Lao by Emperor Huan reflected the involvement of Empress Deng in unorthodox religions and her unsuccessful quest for a son and heir who might preserve her husband's affections and her own imperial status.

Rafe de CRESPIGNY

Crespigny, Rafe de. *Emperor Huan and Emperor Ling.* Canberra: Australian National University, Faculty of Asian Studies, 1989, vol. 1, 8–14; 58.
———. "The Harem of Emperor Huan; A Study of Court Politics in Later Han." *Papers on Far Eastern History* 12 (1975): 11, 34.
———. "Politics and Philosophy Under the Government of Emperor Huan." *T'oung Pao* 66 (1980): 41–83.
Hou Han shu. Beijing: Zhonghua shuju, 1965, vol. 2, 10*xia.*444–45.
Seidel, Anna K. *La Divinisation de Lao Tseu dans le taoisme des Han.* Paris: Publications de l'École Française d'Extrême-Orient, 1969, vol. 71.
———. "The Image of the Perfect Ruler in Early Taoist Messianism: Lao-tzu and Li Hung." *History of Religions* 9, no. 2–3 (1969–70): 216–47.

Deng Sui, Empress of Emperor He

Deng Sui (Hedi Deng Huanghou), 81–121, was empress to Emperor He (Liu Zhao, 78–104; r. 89–104) of Eastern Han. She was a granddaughter of Grand Mentor (*taifu*) Deng Yu (2–58), who had contributed greatly to the establishment of Eastern Han. Deng Sui's father, Deng Xun (d. 92), was Commandant for the Protection of the Territory (*hujiang xiaowei*) and her mother, née Yin, was a grandniece of Emperor Guangwu's Empress Yin (*q.v.* Yin Lihua, Empress of Emperor Guangwu).

The biography of Empress Deng contained in the *History of the Later Han Dynasty* (Hou Han shu; compiled in the first half of the fifth century), upon which this article is based, criticizes her for clinging to power through her regency, while praising her ability and the achievements of her reign. As was usual for such official biographies, it also tends to the hagiographic, especially in relating her early years. Deng Sui was five when her paternal grandmother accidentally cut her forehead while cutting her hair. The child said nothing and when asked about it replied: "Grandmother cut my hair because she loves me. I did not want to upset her, so I bore the pain." By the age of six she could read the fifteen-chapter Zhou dynasty work by the Grand Astrologer Zhou (*taishi* Zhou), which was written in the antiquated and difficult great-seal characters, and by the age of twelve she was familiar with the classics *The Book of Songs* (Shi jing) and *The Analects* (Lunyu). Her mother would say to her: "You don't learn needlework but absorb yourself in studying. Are you planning to become a court academician?" Deng Sui did eventually learn needlework and worked at it in the daytime, but at night she continued to study the classics. Her family nicknamed her The Confucian Student (*zhusheng*) and her father, aware of her unusual talents, enjoyed discussing all manner of things with her. Deng Sui was selected to enter the imperial palace in 92, when she was eleven years old, but her father died that year so she did not go. She missed her father so much that she wept day and night, and for three years refused to take any salted dishes, growing pale and thin. Once, she dreamed of touching the sky and glimpsing something like a stalactite, from which she drank. A fortune-teller to whom this dream was told said it was a sign of very good fortune, and when he saw Deng Sui in the flesh he was astonished to see that she had the countenance of the enlightened monarchs Cheng and Tang. Deng Sui's uncle Deng Gai said: "It is said that the descendants of those who have saved the lives of 1,000 people will receive titles. As a receptionist (*yezhe*), my brother Deng Xun built up the banks of the Shijiu River, saving thousands of lives. His family should thus be blessed." Deng Sui's grandfather Deng Yu had previously said: "I have led millions of soldiers but have never killed anyone without cause. My descendants will surely rise."

In 95, Deng Sui was again selected to enter the palace of Emperor He, where her distinctive beauty charmed everybody. The following year, at the age of sixteen, she was promoted to Worthy Lady (*guiren*) and was moved into the imperial concubines' quarters. She behaved properly and with great composure, serving her maternal cousin Empress Yin attentively, and those who were her equal in rank, as well as palace women and servants, graciously. When she fell ill, Emperor He ordered her mother and her brothers to take care of her in the palace, which outsiders were normally forbidden to enter, but Worthy Lady Deng thought this was inappropriate. The emperor was extremely impressed, saying: "You are truly unrivaled. Everyone treasures the opportunity to be visited, but you simply worry about it." While all the other imperial concubines would dress up for banquets, Worthy Lady Deng would dress plainly. Should her dress happen to be the same color as that of Empress Yin, she would immediately change. Whenever the emperor summoned her and Empress Yin at the same time, Worthy Lady Deng would not sit fully on her chair or stand level with the empress and would walk bent over, to give the appearance of humility. When the two were asked a question, Worthy Lady Deng would not answer before the empress did.

Gradually, Emperor He's love for Empress Yin faded, but when he called to see Worthy Lady Deng she would use illness as an excuse to avoid seeing him. Several of the emperor's sons had died as infants, so Worthy Lady Deng, concerned that there were so few heirs, would send suitable concubines to the emperor in her place. As Worthy Lady Deng rose in the emperor's esteem, it is said that jealousy led Empress Yin to practice witchcraft for the purpose of harming her rival. At one stage the emperor fell seriously ill and was close to death. It was reported to Worthy Lady Deng that Empress Yin had said that if she gained power she would not allow any members of the Deng clan to live. Worthy Lady Deng burst into tears and, determined to die in place of the emperor but also out of fear that she might suffer the same tragic fate as Consort Qi (*q.v.* Qi, Concubine of Emperor Gaozu), she swore to commit suicide. As she was about to swallow a draft of poison, however, a loyal servant falsely told her that the emperor had recovered and Worthy Lady Deng cast the draft aside. As it turned out, the emperor recovered the following day.

After Empress Yin was found to have been practicing witchcraft, she was deposed in 102. Worthy Lady Deng was appointed empress in the winter of that year. She immediately instituted a policy of frugality, bringing an end to the tradition of vassal

124   DENG SUI

states having to present precious gifts to the empress and ordering instead that they contribute only paper and ink. She also resisted the emperor's attempts to bestow titles on members of her family: her elder brother Deng Zhi (d. 121), for example, rose only to Inner Gentleman Brave as a Tiger (*huben zhonglang*) during the emperor's reign.

More than ten of Emperor He's sons had died as infants. His eldest son was a sickly boy, and the sons who had not died had been spirited away soon after birth to be brought up in safety outside the palace. When Emperor He died in 104, Empress Deng placed on the throne his three-month-old infant son Liu Long (Emperor Shang; r. 105–106). Now Empress Dowager Deng, she assumed control of the court as regent, a practice that by this time was assuming the status of a dynastic institution. An empress dowager could become regent for a very young emperor (as in this case), when the emperor was very ill, upon the sudden death of an emperor, or according to his posthumous edict. In later times an empress dowager would be required to rule from behind a screen, but this practice did not exist in Eastern Han.

To consolidate her power, Empress Dowager Deng ennobled Deng Zhi as Marquis of Cai and promoted him to Chariot and Horse General (*cheqi jiangjun*) in charge of government affairs. She also bestowed on her younger brothers Deng Kui, Deng Hong, and Deng Chang the title of Marquis. Empress Dowager Deng delegated a great deal of power to the eunuchs Zheng Zhong (d. 144) and Cai Lun (d. 121), an arrangement that was regarded by later commentators as "inevitable when a woman reigns." However, although she allowed members of her natal family to become involved in politics in order to consolidate her power, Empress Dowager Deng kept a tight rein on the family's power so that the Deng family remained loyal to the imperial court. Among the reforms Empress Dowager Deng instituted were an amnesty for those imprisoned during Eastern Han and restitution of their civil rights, curtailment of imperial expenses on clothes and food within the palaces, and a halving of state and commandery contributions to the court. She also ordered that all female servants and slaves in attendance in the palace and on the royal family who were too old to serve be given the option of staying or being sent back to their native places.

The infant Emperor Shang died of illness eight months after being placed on the throne. Behind closed doors, Empress Dowager Deng and her brother Deng Zhi decided to appoint as his successor Liu Hu (Emperor An, 93–125; r. 106–125), a twelve-year-old nephew of Emperor He. The boy was enthroned in 106 and Empress Dowager Deng continued to wield power as regent. The following year an official named Du Gen memorialized her on behalf of several of his colleagues, requesting her to cede rule to the young Emperor An. Infuriated, she ordered that Du Gen and his colleagues be placed in heavy silk bags and beaten to death. It appears that those in charge of this punishment instructed the executioner to be lenient, however, and Du Gen survived. He fled "to an obscure place where he served incognito as a waiter in a wine shop." When the empress dowager died fifteen years later, Du Gen returned to court and was honored for his loyalty to the imperial family.

As regent for Emperor An, Empress Dowager Deng was careful in appointing members of her natal family. A letter she wrote has been preserved in the *History of the Later Han Dynasty:*

Looking back, I find that the distaff family and guests of previous emperors tended to abuse their power, to behave imprudently, and even to interfere in government administration, harming the interests of the people. This happened because the law was not enforced effectively and appropriately. Today, distaff family members such as Deng Zhi serve the imperial government respectfully. However, it is very important to strictly enforce the law because of the sheer size of distaff families and their many sly sycophants; there have been many cases where they have tried to interfere in government. Conniving and covering up crime are prohibited.

Correctly interpreting this as a warning, the Deng family dared not abuse their power. During Deng Sui's sixteen-year reign, her relatives never threatened the rule of the imperial family, a testament to her skill and talent. She ruled the country cautiously and attentively. She so loved the people that she could not sleep when there was a famine, and she cut the palace budget as a means of providing relief. She was enlightened in her appointment of officials, emphasizing that outspoken, able, and virtuous men who had a good understanding of politics and history should be recruited. The Du Gen affair may be seen as a rare deviation from this course, presumably because it directly threatened her right to rule. Her brother Deng Zhi recommended talented and virtuous men such as He Xi, Yang Qin, Li He, and Tao Dun to the court and recruited as advisers to the empress dowager Yang Zhen, Zhu Chong, and Chen Chan. The empress dowager placed a high value on education for the imperial family, establishing a school for all members, male and female, over the age of five. She was personally involved in the school, acting as invigilator during examinations. The empress dowager in her turn had received lessons on the Confucian classics, astronomy, and mathematics from the female scholar Ban Zhao (*q.v.*) from the time she entered the palace. She selected over fifty Confucian scholars and Erudites to proofread books in the Eastern Library, and ordered eunuchs to study the Confucian classics in the library so that they would be able to teach the palace women. She was herself productive; eighteen pieces of her works were gathered together in a collection after her death.

Empress Dowager Deng died of illness in the third month of 121 at the relatively young age of forty-one and was buried alongside Emperor He in Shen Tomb. Empress Dowager Deng was clever in the way she gained power and fortunate that in the absence of an obvious successor to Emperor He, she could manipulate the succession and assume the role of regent, thus becoming the de facto ruler. Had she been a man she would not have been able to do this; any man appointed as regent would have had to remain an official. She performed well as ruler, abiding by Confucian ideals and not allowing her family to step beyond its proper role. She has been criticized for not ceding rule to the rightful ruler sooner, but scholars have also recognized that, because Emperor An did not rule well after her death, Empress Dowager Deng had the interests of the nation, not personal aggrandizement, at heart in retaining the regency.

WONG Yin Lee
(Translated by CHE Wai-lam William)

126 *DENG SUI*

Hou Han shu. Beijing: Zhonghua shuju, 1973, vol. 2, 10*shang*.418–30; vol. 7, 57.1839.
Li Anyu. *Zhongguo lidai huanghou quanshu.* Beijing: Zhongguo youyi chubanshe, 1990, vol. 1, 137–47.
Swann, Nancy Lee. "Biography of the Empress Teng." *Journal of the American Oriental Society* 51 (1931): 138–59.
Wu Puzhao. "Hedi Liu Zhao huanghou Deng Sui." In *Zhongguo huanghou quanzhuan,* ed. Che Jixing, Jinan: Shandong jiaoyu chubanshe, 1993, 75–82.
Yan Kejun. *Quan shanggu sandai Qin Han Sanguo Liuchao wen. Quan Han wen.* Taipei: Shijie shuju, 1963, vol. 1, 9.518.
Yang, Lien-sheng. "Female Rulers in Imperial China." *Harvard Journal of Asian Studies* 23 (1960/61): 47–61.

Diao Chan

Diao Chan, fl. late second century, appeared in the Chinese folklore and historical fiction *The Romance of the Three Kingdoms* (Sanguo yanyi) as the adopted daughter of Wang Yun (137–192) and wife of Lü Bu (d. 198), a general active in the last years of the Eastern Han dynasty. She is credited in this novel with helping her father kill her husband's commander and adoptive father, the warlord Dong Zhuo (d. 198), an evil figure who was wreaking havoc on the country. Dong Zhuo harbored ambitions to usurp the Han throne and wielded immense influence at court because of his strong army. Wang Yun was one of several courtiers who plotted to kill him, but since Dong Zhuo would not let any armed person except his trusted adopted son Lü Bu near him they were unable to find a way to do this. Diao Chan was at that time Wang Yun's maid, but she came up with a plan to kill Dong Zhuo, using herself as bait. Diao Chan is said to have used her beauty to entrap both Lü Bu and Dong Zhuo, and she successfully set Lü Bu against Dong Zhuo in this love triangle, thereby manipulating Lü Bu into killing Dong Zhuo. In gratitude, Wang Yun made her his adopted daughter.

No such person as Diao Chan exists in historical records, however. The closest model for her may have been a maid called Fupi, who was Dong Zhuo's housemaid. Lü Bu is said to have been involved with this maid when he visited Dong Zhuo, but she has never been implicated in the killing of Dong Zhuo. Therefore, it seems that the beautiful Diao Chan of folklore and literature was merely a creation of later generations.

Despite her uncertain origin, Diao Chan lives in the hearts of the Chinese people as one of the Four Great Beauties (*si da meiren*) of Chinese history, the other three being Xi Shi (*q.v.*), Wang Zhaojun (*q.v.*), and Yang Guifei (719–756; see *Biographical Dictionary of Chinese Women,* Tang to Ming volume). Diao Chan is remembered as the clever woman who, through her maneuvering, rid the state of an evil minister and saved the Han empire.

Laura LONG

Luo Guanzhong. *Sanguo yanyi.* Beijing: Zuojia chubanshe, 1953, vol. 1, 9–10, 61–75.
Ma Zhaozheng and Zhou Feitang. *Zhongguo gudai funü mingren.* Beijing: Zhongguo funü chubanshe, 1988, 78–80.
Roberts, Moss, trans. *Three Kingdoms: A Historical Novel, Complete and Unabridged.* Beijing: Foreign Languages Press, 1994, 93–117.

DOU, EMPRESS OF EMPEROR ZHANG 127

Ding of Dingtao, Lady: *see* **Fu, Concubine of Emperor Yuan**

Ding'an Duke, Empress Dowager of the: *see* **Wang, Empress of Emperor Ping**

Dingtao, Empress Dowager: *see* **Fu, Concubine of Emperor Yuan**

Dingtao Ding Ji: *see* **Fu, Concubine of Emperor Yuan**

Dong Si's Wife: *see* **Cai Yan**

Donghai Xiaofu Zhou Qing: *see* **Zhou Qing, the Filial Woman of Donghai**

Dou, Empress of Emperor Zhang
Empress Dou (Zhangdi Dou Huanghou), d. 97, was empress to Emperor Zhang (Liu Da, 57–88; r. 76–88) of Eastern Han. Her personal name is not recorded in the histories. She was from Pingling in Fufeng (in the vicinity of present-day Xianyang and Xingping in Shaanxi Province) and was a great-granddaughter of Dou Rong (16 B.C.E.–62 C.E.), who had been Grand Minister of Works (*da sikong*) in the early years of Eastern Han. Her mother, Princess Biyang, was a daughter of Liu Qiang, Prince Gong of Donghai. Her father, Dou Xun, committed a crime for which he was sentenced to death and thereafter the family's fortunes declined. They frequently brought fortune-tellers and sorcerers into their home to consult them about illnesses or their future prospects, and each one of them predicted that the eldest daughter, the future Empress Dou, would become very distinguished. She was very bright as a child, able to read at the age of six, and her whole clan marveled at her intelligence.

Dou and her younger sister were selected to enter Changle Palace in 77, the year after Liu Da (Emperor Zhang) succeeded to the throne. The young emperor was already aware of Dou's reputed intelligence and beauty and from time to time had asked the governesses in the palace about her. When she finally entered the palace he saw that she was surprisingly well mannered, acting with proper decorum and possessed of a graceful beauty. Empress Dowager Ma (*q.v.* Ma, Empress of Emperor Ming) was also very impressed with her and had her moved into the imperial concubines' quarters. Dou was loving and intelligent and her wholehearted devotion to attending the emperor won her praise and prestige. The following year (78), she was appointed empress. Her sister was promoted to the highest rank of Worthy Lady (*guiren*) and their father received the posthumous title Marquis Si of Ancheng.

Empress Dou received special favor and came to monopolize the rear palace. She remained childless, however, and became jealous of the other palace women. She tried to drive a wedge between the emperor and Worthy Lady Song when the latter gave birth to a son (Liu Qing); her allegations of sorcery eventually forced Worthy Lady Song to commit suicide. When Worthy Lady Liang gave birth to a son (Liu Zhao) in 78, Empress Dou wrote an anonymous letter accusing the lady's father, Liang Song, the Marquis Min of Baoqin, of a crime for which he was then imprisoned and executed. Worthy Lady Liang's entire family was exiled to Jiuzhen (in present-day Vietnam), where she and her sister are said to have soon died of sadness and resentment. Empress Dou then adopted Worthy Lady Liang's son, Liu Zhao (Emperor He, 78–104; r. 89–104), who succeeded to the throne at the age of eleven upon the death of his father. Empress Dowager Dou acted as regent for the boy emperor. She appointed her mother, Princess Biyang, as Grand Princess and granted her the territory and income of 3,000 households; she ennobled her brothers Dou Xian (d. 92), Dou Du, and Dou Jing and gave them complete power over the court.

In 92, however, her three brothers were executed when it was revealed that they had been part of a criminal conspiracy. Empress Dowager Dou died five years later, but even before she had been buried a memorial was submitted to Emperor He claiming that his biological mother, Worthy Lady Liang, and her sister had been wronged and put to death within the palace. The author of this memorial was Liang Yi, a sister of Worthy Lady Liang who had earlier been exiled with her family. At the same time, several high officials requested that Empress Dowager Dou be stripped of her imperial title and not be buried alongside the late emperor. Emperor He could not bring himself to act on their request, however, and instead issued the following edict:

> Although [Empress Dowager Dou] has broken the law, she was often modest in her demands. After serving her for ten years, I am deeply aware of her kindness to me. In *Book of Rites,* there is no record of a son downgrading someone of an older generation. Because of my love for her, as a grateful man and a filial son I cannot part from her and her kindness; on principle, I cannot treat her badly. There is also the case of Empress Dowager Shangguang [*q.v.* Shangguan, Empress of Emperor Zhao], who was not dethroned. Therefore, I will not consider this request.

Empress Dowager Dou was buried in the Jing Tomb alongside Emperor Zhang; she had been empress for eighteen years. Despite the good example of her immediate predecessor Empress Dowager Ma, Empress Dowager Dou appears to have been following in the footsteps of Empress Lü (*q.v.* Lü Zhi, Empress of Emperor Gaozu) of Western Han in seeking power. She acted capably as regent for Emperor He for six years but is depicted in the histories as an evil empress saved only by the kind nature of her adopted son.

YANG Haiming

Chen Quanli and Hou Xinyi, eds. *Hou fei cidian.* Xi'an: Shaanxi renmin jiaoyu chubanshe, 1991, 22.
Hou Han shu. Beijing: Zhonghua shuju, 1965, vol. 2, 10*shang*.415–17.
Liu Xiang. *Lienü zhuan.* Sibubeiyao ed., 8.12a–13a.
O'Hara, Albert R. *The Position of Woman in Early China According to the Lieh Nü Chuan.* "*The Biographies of Chinese Women.*" Taipei: Mei Ya, 1971; 1978, 249–51.

Dou Miao, Empress of Emperor Huan

Dou Miao (Huandi Dou Huanghou), c. 151–172, was empress to Emperor Huan (Liu Zhi, 132–167; r. 147–167); she had her registered place of origin west of Chang'an, present-day Xi'an in Shaanxi Province. She joined the imperial harem early in 165, the year Empress Deng (*q.v.* Deng Mengnü, Empress of Emperor Huan), consort of Emperor Huan, was dismissed, imprisoned, and died. Probably selected at the time of the regular autumn recruitment, in which case she would have been some thirteen to fifteen years old, she was promptly appointed as a Worthy Lady (*guiren*), the highest rank of concubine, and at the end of 165 she was proclaimed empress.

Dou Miao was the eldest daughter of Dou Wu, a descendant of the northwestern warlord Dou Rong (16 B.C.E.–62 C.E.), who had been the rival and later an ally of the founding Emperor Guangwu (r. 25–57) of Eastern Han. Dou Rong's great-granddaughter (*q.v.* Dou, Empress of Emperor Zhang) became the empress of Emperor Zhang (r. 76–88) and after the emperor's death in 88 she and her family controlled the government of the young Emperor He (r. 89–104) until their overthrow in 92. Although the Dou had not recovered their political importance at the capital, members of the family still had personal influence in their home country and considerable wealth. Dou Wu's father had been administrator of a northern frontier commandery, and Dou Wu himself had established his reputation as a scholar of the classics who ran a private academy near his home. When Dou Miao was appointed Worthy Lady, Dou Wu was granted a probationary appointment as a Gentleman of the Palace (*langzhong*). When she became empress he was appointed colonel of a regiment in the Northern Army, central strategic reserve of the empire, and was enfeoffed as a marquis with revenue from 5,000 households.

The selection of Worthy Lady Dou as empress was not so straightforward as a summary of Chinese records might indicate. First, it is clear that Emperor Huan was under considerable pressure from senior ministers at court to appoint her, and his own position was evidently not strong enough to withstand their arguments. His personal favorite was Tian Sheng, a Lady of Elegance (*cainü*), the lowest rank of concubine, who regularly shared his bed with eight unnamed companions. He had no interest in Worthy Lady Dou, and attended her very rarely, if at all.

The argument of his ministers was that it was essential for the good of the dynasty that the emperor take a woman of good family as his consort, and the Dou were presented as a most appropriate alliance. There seems no doubt that Tian Sheng was of humble origin and, surprisingly, the former Empress Deng had also been criticized on these grounds. From the point of view of the dynasty, however, and particularly in terms of the succession, the arguments for a woman of good family are very strange. The Liang family of Emperor Huan's first empress, Liang Nüying (*q.v.* Liang Nüying, Empress of Emperor Huan), had dominated the government since the days of his predecessor Emperor Shun (*vide* Liang Na, Empress of Emperor Huan), while Empress Liang herself had been responsible for the abortion of any children he conceived with other women of the harem. It was not until 159 that the emperor had been able to rid himself of that overbearing family, and one might expect that the last thing he would wish to inflict upon his dynasty was another generation of aristocratic relatives by marriage. It seems very likely, moreover, that Tian Sheng and her eight companions were engaged not only for their qualities as sexual partners, but also in the hope that one of the magical number nine might conceive a son.

130 *DOU MIAO*

It appears that Emperor Huan's position was weak. There had been increasing complaints about the size and cost of his harem, while a number of his eunuch allies and favorites had lately been disgraced for corruption. The fall of Empress Deng and her family gave the reform party at court the opportunity to press for a new influence within the palace. They evidently regarded the scholarly Dou Wu as a supporter of their cause, and the emperor was obliged to accept their wishes.

Dou Wu was later promoted to the post of colonel of the city gates (*chengmen xiaowei*), an independent command responsible for the outer defenses of the capital. He gave particular attention to students and junior clerks, recommending many of them for promotion and distributing rewards and subsidies, while keeping his own style of life simple and plain. With a fine reputation and many recipients of his patronage and bounty, he confirmed his alliance with leading officials and established a substantial position at court. Emperor Huan, however, disliked Dou Wu and continued to reject the empress. Still more importantly, though two daughters were born about this time, he sired no son and heir.

It has been suggested that Empress Dou had some influence on the emperor's patronage of the cult of Huang–Lao, a combination of the legendary Yellow Emperor and the sage Laozi, which culminated in a great ceremony of sacrifice at the capital in the summer of 166. It is more probable that the ruler's interest in Huang–Lao had first been inspired by his late Empress Deng and a number of the eunuch officials, and that it was developed further, not in combination with the Dou, but rather in opposition to the Confucianism represented by Dou Wu and his allies. It may even be that the emperor was seeking an alternative source of spiritual legitimacy for his personal regime, independent of traditional ideology.

At the end of 167 the emperor became seriously ill and he died on 25 January 168, still only in his mid-thirties. Upon his deathbed he promoted Tian Sheng and her colleagues to be Worthy Ladies, but after he was dead, and while his body yet lay in state in the palace, Empress Dou, now Empress Dowager Dou, killed Tian Sheng. Through the intervention of two senior eunuchs she was obliged to spare the lives of the other eight favorites, but she and her father now controlled the government.

As the emperor had died without an heir, the customs of Han allowed Empress Dowager Dou a free choice among the cadets of the imperial house. Probably still aged no more than twenty, she consulted her father. Despite his association with members of the outer court and the bureaucracy, Dou Wu made no attempt to involve any senior ministers in the decision. He did ask an imperial clerk for a recommendation and when the twelve-*sui*-old Village Marquis of Jiedu Liu Hong (156–189) was suggested, an escort was sent to bring the boy to the capital. On 17 February 167, Liu Hong was proclaimed emperor; he is commonly known by his posthumous title Emperor Ling (r. 168–189). Though we are told the imperial clerk had been asked to nominate members of the imperial clan who were noted for their moral qualities, it is difficult to see how these criteria should have led necessarily to Liu Hong, and it would seem from this that the Dou were more interested in their own power than in the good of the dynasty. The new emperor was little more than ten years old at the time he was chosen and almost twelve when he was placed upon the throne.

His great-grandfather Liu Kai, Prince of Hejian, had been a son of Emperor Zhang, and Liu Hong was thus a member of the same lineage as his predecessor Emperor Huan. However, while old enough to avoid the risks of infant mortality, he was young enough to require the guidance of a regent, thus ensuring the hegemony of the dowager's clan for some years to come.

With his family's power thus established, Dou Wu and his daughter arranged fiefs and rewards for their relatives and clients and, like the Liang family before them, members of the Dou family held significant military and police appointments about the capital. Dou Wu became General-in-Chief (*dajiangjun*), the same position as had been held by Liang Ji, brother of the empresses Liang Na and Liang Nüying, which formally gave command over the whole Northern army, the major professional force at the capital. Dou Wu also established a close partnership with Chen Fan, named as Grand Mentor (*taifu*), and the two men shared control over the Imperial Secretariat, center of government authority.

In accordance with the wishes of their popular constituency, young men about the capital who wished to see a revival of reform on idealistic Confucian lines, Dou Wu and Chen Fan planned to destroy the power of the harem eunuchs. The empress dowager, however, unable to make the decision herself and influenced by leaders of the eunuchs, rejected her father's proposals and continued to protect the attendants in the harem. As months passed, the frustration of the reformers became more obvious, and in the autumn of 168 matters came to a head. Chen Fan and Dou Wu ordered the arrest of Empress Dowager Dou's two leading eunuchs, but others joined together in self-defense and persuaded the boy emperor to support them. As his men deserted him, Dou Wu committed suicide. Other members of the family were killed, and remnant relatives and clients were exiled to the far south of the empire in present-day Vietnam. Chen Fan and many of his supporters among the officials were also killed, and there was a general proscription against all the Confucian reformists throughout the empire.

Empress Dowager Dou herself was placed under house arrest in the Cloud Terrace of the Southern Palace at Luoyang. She was not treated well by her eunuch jailers, and despite high-level protests and orders from the emperor himself her situation did not greatly improve. In the winter of 171, as Emperor Ling made a special visit and held court to pay his respects to Empress Dowager Dou for having brought him to the throne, the matter of her ill treatment was raised once more. The emperor was concerned, and gave her increasing quantities of supplies and provisions, but charges of impiety were fabricated against the eunuch who had spoken for her, and he was executed.

In 172 the mother of Empress Dowager Dou died in exile in the south, and it is said that the empress dowager became ill from grief. She died on 18 July, and one must suspect that she was assisted to her end. The eunuchs argued that her funerary rites should be no more than those of a Worthy Lady, but Emperor Ling determined that she should be buried with full imperial honors, and on 8 August she was placed in the same tomb as her late consort Emperor Huan.

Rafe de CRESPIGNY

132 DOU MIAO

Bielenstein, Hans. "Lo-yang in Later Han Times." *Bulletin of the Museum of Far Eastern Antiquities* 48 (1976).

Ch'ü T'ung-tsu. *Han Social Structure,* ed. Jack L. Dull. Seattle: University of Washington Press, 1972, 484–90.

Crespigny, Rafe de. *Emperor Huan and Emperor Ling.* Canberra: Australian National University, Faculty of Asian Studies, 1989, vol. 1, 64, 88–102, 121–26.

———. "The Harem of Emperor Huan: A Study of Court Politics in Later Han." *Papers on Far Eastern History* 12 (1975): 25–42.

———. "Politics and Philosophy Under the Government of Emperor Huan." *T'oung Pao* 66 (1980): 41–83.

Hou Han shu. Beijing: Zhonghua shuju, 1965, vol. 2, 10*xia*.445–46; vol. 8, 69.2239–44.

Seidel, Anna K. *La Divinisation de Lao Tseu dans le taoisme des Han.* Paris: Publications de l'École Française d'Extrême-Orient, 1969, vol. 71.

———. "The Image of the Perfect Ruler in Early Taoist Messianism: Lao-tzu and Li Hung." *History of Religions* 9, no. 2–3 (1969–70): 216–47.

Dou Yifang, Empress of Emperor Wen

Dou Yifang (Xiao Wen Dou Huanghou), c. 206–135 B.C.E., from Guanjin in Qinghe (in the southeast of present-day Wuyi District, Hebei Province), was empress of Emperor Wen (Liu Heng, 202–157 B.C.E.; r. 179–157 B.C.E.). Born on the eve of the establishment of the Han dynasty, she lived through the reigns of Emperor Gaozu, Empress Lü (*q.v.* Lü Zhi, Empress of Emperor Gaozu), Emperor Wen, and Emperor Jing and into the reign of her grandson Emperor Wu. It has been suggested that such was Empress Dou's strength of will and her devotion to Daoism that Emperor Wu was obliged to wait until she died before he could implement Confucianism as the official court philosophy.

Dou Yifang was born into a poor family in the state of Zhao, and she and her two brothers were orphaned when she was very young. The three siblings supported themselves by farming and weaving until as a "daughter of an honest family" Dou Yifang was selected to enter the palace and wait upon Empress Dowager Lü. Not long afterward she and four other young women were assigned as a gift to Liu Heng, the Prince of Dai, in the remote north (present-day Yanmen Pass in Shanxi Province). She set out on the journey reluctantly, her request to be sent to her home state of Zhao having been overlooked. Liu Heng's consort had already borne him four sons, and although Liu Heng favored Dou Yifang she remained a concubine with the title Lady Dou. Lady Dou bore Liu Heng a daughter, Liu Piao (*q.v.*), and two sons, Liu Qi (Emperor Jing, 188–141 B.C.E.; r. 156–141 B.C.E.) and her favorite child, Liu Wu (d. 144 B.C.E.).

After considerable political maneuvering between the Lü and the Liu clans upon the death of Empress Dowager Lü in 180, and much discussion, the powerful court officials selected Liu Heng (the future Emperor Wen) to ascend the throne. Liu Heng's consort had died before he became emperor and their four sons all died of illness after he became emperor. In the first year of his reign, Emperor Wen therefore appointed Lady Dou's elder son Liu Qi heir apparent. Han tradition required that once a male achieved distinction his mother must also be elevated in status, and Lady Dou thus became Empress Dou, enjoying the highest honor and favor.

Empress Dou's family also benefited from her elevation in status. Her long-dead parents were granted the titles of Marquis and Marquise of Ancheng and her elder brother (*zi* Zhangjun) was allowed to move to the capital, Chang'an. However, her younger brother Dou Shaojun had been sold as a slave several times over and had recently fled to Chang'an after surviving the collapse of the charcoal kiln in the mountains in Yiyang (present-day Henan Province). Learning that the newly appointed empress bore the surname Dou and came from Guanjin, he submitted a statement to the court in the hope that she might be his sister. The emperor questioned him closely, but Shaojun could recall nothing but falling out of a tree while picking mulberry leaves, and revealed the scar this had left. However, he also recounted how his sister had washed his hair and fed him in an inn before she left for the west. On hearing this, the empress realized he was indeed her younger brother and all present wept as she went to him and grasped his hands. Emperor Wen thereupon made a generous grant of money as well as land and houses to Shaojun so that he could live in Chang'an. The emperor also gave permission for all of Empress Dou's paternal male cousins to settle in the capital. Mindful of the way Empress Lü's relatives had monopolized the court, generals Zhou Bo (d. 169 B.C.E.) and Guan Ying (d. 176 B.C.E.) chose virtuous and respectable people for the newcomers to associate with. Empress Dou's brothers proved to be of noble character and conducted themselves well, remaining respectful and modest despite their distinguished status.

Not long after this, Empress Dou lost her sight as a result of illness. Emperor Wen no longer favored her, transferring his attentions instead to Consort Shen (*q.v.* Shen, Concubine of Emperor Wen) of Handan and Lady Yin, but neither of these two women posed a threat to the empress because they did not produce any children. On the death of Emperor Wen in 157, his eldest son by Empress Dou, the thirty-two-year-old Liu Qi, was installed as emperor; Empress Dou was made Empress Dowager Dou.

Despite the handicap of her blindness, Empress Dowager Dou continued her deep involvement in court affairs. After Emperor Jing suppressed a rebellion of several states instigated in 154 by Liu Pi (213–154 B.C.E.), the Prince of Wu, he issued an edict that all the officials and commoners who had been implicated with the prince be set free. He also intended to enfeoff Liu Guang, the younger brother of the prince, as the new Prince of Wu and install Liu Li, son of the former Prince of Chu (one of the rebellious states), as the new Prince of Chu. Empress Dowager Dou saw the dangers of this and dissuaded her son, saying that he should not let the descendants of the rebel Liu Pi become princes. The emperor partially heeded her: he did not appoint Liu Guang as Prince of Wu, but did appoint Liu Li as Prince of Chu.

The empress dowager's younger son, Liu Wu, had been appointed Prince of Liang during the reign of his father. While visiting the capital in 154 he attended a feast with his brother, Emperor Jing. After they had drunk a little, the emperor said in an off-hand manner: "The Prince of Liang will succeed me when I die." Secretly pleased at his brother's comment, as was their mother, Liu Wu nevertheless gracefully declined the honor. However, Dou Ying (d. 131), Supervisor of the Household and the trusted son of the empress dowager's cousin, drank to Emperor Jing with the words: "Since Emperor Gaozu established the Han dynasty the throne has been handed down from father to son. How can it be that the emperor could offer the throne to [his brother] the Prince of Liang simply because he wants to?" Empress Dowager Dou grew annoyed at Dou Ying's

134 DOU YIFANG

remark and, on the pretext of his ill health, dismissed him from his post, expunged his name from the clan records, and forbade him to pay his respects at court.

As Liu Wu grew more arrogant after this episode, Emperor Jing decided to appoint Liu Rong, his son by Concubine Li (Li Ji), as heir apparent in 153. At the same time, he appointed Liu Che, his son by Consort Wang (*q.v.* Wang Zhi, Empress of Emperor Jing), as Prince of Jiaodong. Empress Dowager Dou's daughter, Liu Piao, now Princess of Guantao, very much hoped her daughter Chen Jiao would marry the heir apparent (the girl's maternal cousin). Concubine Li rejected this proposal, much to the chagrin of Liu Piao, who immediately approached Consort Wang; Consort Wang accepted the proposal on behalf of her son Liu Che. The ill feeling this affair created between Concubine Li and Liu Piao deepened the conflicts within the imperial clan, and when the heir apparent was deposed and downgraded to the Prince of Linjiang, Concubine Li died, it is said, from a broken heart. Consort Wang was appointed empress when her son was made heir apparent.

With the dismissal of Liu Rong, Empress Dowager Dou demanded during a feast that the emperor appoint his brother Liu Wu as heir apparent. The emperor agreed immediately, but changed his mind in favor of Liu Che after discussing it with his ministers. One minister in particular, Yuan Ang (d. 148 B.C.E.), insisted that the tradition of the throne passing from father to son was an inalienable principle that must be respected, thus earning the deep hatred of Liu Wu. Liu Wu therefore had Yuan Ang and some ten other senior ministers assassinated, and Emperor Jing rightly laid the blame for these murders at the feet of Liu Wu. Fearing the emperor's retribution, Liu Wu ordered the two men who had carried out the murders (Yang Sheng and Gongsun Gui) to commit suicide and he presented their bodies to the emperor; he also approached Wang Xin, a brother of Empress Wang, asking for help. This pacified Emperor Jing, but Empress Dowager Dou remained tearful and refused to eat, worried that Liu Wu had broken the law by his murderous actions. Her fears proved groundless, however, after the official sent to deal with the case reported to the emperor: "Sparing the Prince of Liang [Liu Wu] would break the law of Han; killing him would deeply distress the empress dowager, and upset the emperor even more. I believe it would be best to let this matter rest and not pursue it further." Once the official had reported to her that Liu Wu was officially innocent and that the assassination had been carried out by his two favorite officials, who had been punished according to the law, Empress Dowager Dou became calm.

Soon after this, the empress dowager again became distressed when she thought that the emperor had killed his wayward brother. Once the brothers were reconciled, however, she expressed her deep gratitude to Wang Xin (Empress Wang's brother) for his handling of the affair, asking that he be appointed a marquis. The emperor did not accede to her request, citing Counselor-in Chief (*xiangguo*) Zhou Yafu that some form of achievement was a prerequisite to anyone being granted a title. However, as soon as Zhou Yafu retired due to illness, Wang Xin was made Marquis of Gai.

Empress Dowager Dou preferred to reward and punish officials on the basis of services they performed or errors they made. One such was Zhi Du. During an imperial hunting party, a wild boar ran at Lady Jia, one of the emperor's concubines, as she was relieving herself. The emperor moved to protect her but Zhi Du, then Leader of Court Gentlemen (*zhonglang jiang*), stopped him with the words: "If Your Majesty is so careless of his own life, how can he be worthy of his ancestors and of the hope and love of the empress dowager?" The emperor desisted just as the boar decided to walk away, and no harm was done. Empress Dowager Dou rewarded Zhi Du for his loyalty with 100 *jin* of gold. However, later, as Chamberlain for the Imperial Insignia (*zhongwei*), Zhi Du refused the request of Liu Rong, the deposed and imprisoned heir apparent, for a knife to carve on bamboo tablets a memorial to present to the emperor. Someone else sent Liu Rong a knife, which he apparently used to kill himself after inscribing the memorial. Upon hearing this story, Empress Dowager Dou had Zhi Du put to death for what she called the crime of "endangering the law."

The empress dowager continued to spoil her younger son, Liu Wu, showering him with material rewards. His palace in the state of Liang was the ultimate in luxury, and he is said to have had one million *jin* of gold and more jewels than the imperial court. Although Liu Wu had not received any legal punishment for the murder of Yuan Ang, he was kept at a distance by the emperor. In 144, however, Liu Wu went to the capital to pay his respects and submitted a memorial asking to be permitted to stay a little longer. His older brother refused his request and Liu Wu returned to Liang, fell into a depression, became ill, and finally died of a high fever. Empress Dowager Dou was distraught, blaming the emperor for his younger brother's death. Emperor Jing was more afraid than mournful, and at a loss as to what to do. In consultation with his sister, he divided the state of Liang into five territories, appointing each of Liu Wu's five sons as a prince of one of the new states and granting his five daughters land. This greatly gratified the empress dowager.

In her later years Empress Dowager Dou was devoted to Daoism. Because she was blind, she had her attendants, as well as Emperor Jing and the heir apparent, read to her from the Yellow Emperor's *Neijing* and Laozi's *Daodejing*. The emperor, however, invited Confucian scholars to the court in the capacity of erudites (*boshi*) to revise the Confucian books. When in her presence the famous scholar Yuan Gu contemptuously dismissed Laozi's writings as "domestic chatter," the empress dowager, herself of peasant origin, was enraged and retorted: "Should we then read books about law and punishment?" By this, she was denouncing the Confucian concept of achieving the best result most quickly and with the least effort, which she was equating with Legalist works. She punished Yuan Gu by sending him to the piggery, where there was a wild boar, but the emperor slipped him a knife behind his blind mother's back, thus enabling him to kill the wild boar. To avoid further conflict, the emperor had Yuan Gu sent to Qinghe as the prince's grand mentor (*taifu*).

On the death of the emperor, his son Liu Che (Emperor Wu, 156–87 B.C.E.; r. 140–87 B.C.E.) ascended the throne and the empress dowager became Grand Empress Dowager Dou. By now quite old, she nevertheless retained her involvement in court affairs and wielded considerable authority. The new emperor's imperial tutor Wang Zang and Censor (*yushi dafu*) Zhao Wan soon memorialized him, requesting that the upper chamber and imperial university be established and Confucianism be promoted, recommending that Shen Gong, the famous eighty-year-old scholar from Lu, be placed in charge. Emperor Wu sent emissaries offering gifts of silk and jade and a four-horse court carriage

136 DOU YIFANG

to bring Shen Gong to the court. Zhao Wan suggested that because of her involvement with Daoism, Grand Empress Dowager Dou should not be fully informed. Angry at this attempted deception, Grand Empress Dowager Dou made thinly veiled threats, in the meantime secretly gathering information on the wrongdoings of Zhao Wan and Wang Zang to present to the emperor. She had the two men stripped of their posts and imprisoned, and they both committed suicide. Shen Gong was also dismissed and sent home to Lu, while two other high officials were also dismissed. Although she had thus prevented the establishment of the imperial university, Grand Empress Dowager Dou remained unappeased, believing Confucian scholars to be all words and no substance. Instead, because he and his family had been of great service but of few words, she appointed the two sons of the late Emperor Jing's imperial tutor Shi Fen as Chamberlain for Attendants (*langzhong ling*) and Chamberlain for the Capital (*neishi*).

Grand Empress Dowager Dou was over seventy when she died in 135; she was buried beside Emperor Wen in Baling. She willed all her possessions to her daughter Liu Piao. Although as imperial mother and grandmother she wielded considerable power in her later years, Grand Empress Dowager Dou did not, on the whole, abuse it. She let the people be, not burdening them with heavy taxes or conscription, and she did not attempt to usurp power, as Empress Lü had. She seemed intent on using her maternal power, often in the form of tantrums, to influence succession and continue her family line. Her son Emperor Jing appeased her, and her grandson Emperor Wu was obliged to wait until she died before he could complete the establishment of Confucianism as a state doctrine. Grand Empress Dowager Dou deserves to be known as the last of the Daoist *grandes dames* of Western Han.

BAO Shanben

An Zuozhang, ed. *Hou fei zhuan.* Zhengzhou: Henan renmin chubanshe, 1990, 36–44.
Chen Quanli and Hou Xinyi, eds. *Hou fei cidian,* Xi'an: Shaanxi renmin jiao yu chubanshe, 1991, 12.
Shi ji. Beijing: Zhonghua shuju, 1989, vol. 4, 49.1970–75, 2084–86, 2091–91; vol. 6, 121.2123.
Sima Guang. *Zizhi tongjian.* Beijing: Zhonghua shuju, 1956, vol. 1, 16.518–48; 17.549–78.

Dou'e: *see* **Zhou Qing, the Filial Woman of Donghai**

E

Eqin: *see* **Zhao E**

F

Fan Kuai Qi: *see* **Lü Xu**

Fan Kuai's Wife: *see* **Lü Xu**

Feng, Lady: *see* **Feng Liao**

Feng, Concubine of Emperor Yuan

Lady of Bright Deportment Feng (Xiao Yuan Feng Zhaoyi), c. 60–6 B.C.E., was a concubine of Emperor Yuan (Liu Shi, 76–33 B.C.E.; r. 48–33 B.C.E.) and grandmother of Emperor Ping (Liu Kan, 8 B.C.E.–5 C.E.; r. 1–5 C.E.).

Her father, Feng Fengshi (c. 110–35 B.C.E.), had served with distinction as a military man in the western regions, and by the time he was in his sixties he had risen to the position of chamberlain for the imperial insignia (*zhi jinwu*). In 47 B.C.E., the year after Liu Shi (Emperor Yuan) ascended the throne, Lady Feng was selected to enter the palace as a junior palace woman (*changshi*). Within a few months she had been granted the title Beauty (*meiren*), and in the year 42 B.C.E. she was promoted to Lady of Handsome Fairness (*jieyu*) after she gave birth to a son (Liu Xing, d. 7 B.C.E.). This son was later enfeoffed as Prince Xiao of Zhongshan. It was believed that her father's promotion to Right General (*you jiangjun*) and Chamberlain for Attendants (*guangluqing*) and the appointment of her elder brother to the post of guardian of the left (*zou pingyi*) came about because of the men's extraordinary ability, not because of the emperor's special fondness for Lady of Handsome Fairness Feng.

A now-famous incident that took place sometime between 38 and 34 B.C.E. increased the emperor's respect for Lady Feng. Attended by all his concubines, the emperor was watching beasts fighting in the tiger fold when a bear broke free and began to climb the railing, headed toward the emperor. All of the concubines fled except for Lady Feng, who confronted the bear, standing squarely between it and the emperor as guards struggled to subdue and kill it. The emperor was astonished at her courage, but Lady Feng explained that she had been thinking only of keeping the emperor from being attacked by the bear, "therefore I put myself in its way." This left the other concubines, including the emperor's favorite Lady Fu (*q.v.* Fu, Concubine of Emperor Yuan), feeling deeply ashamed of their cowardly behavior. The following year Lady Feng's young son was granted the title Prince of Xindu and she herself was promoted to Lady of Bright Deportment (*zhaoyi*).

After Emperor Yuan died in 33 B.C.E. and Liu Ao (Emperor Cheng, 51–7 B.C.E.; r. 32–7 B.C.E.) succeeded to the throne, Lady Feng was given the title Princess Dowager of Xindu and moved with her son to live in Chuyuan Palace. Three or four years later she accompanied her son when he took his family to live in his fief, the state of Xindu (in the region of the present-day provinces of Shandong and Hebei). Her son was granted the title Prince Xiao of Zhongshan (in present-day Hebei Province) in 7 B.C.E. and her title was accordingly changed to Princess Dowager of Zhongshan. When her son died that same year, his infant son, Liu Kan—Lady Feng's grandson—inherited the princeship. By the time the infant was one year old he was already suffering from a liver disease, which at that time was taken as a sign of his having been bewitched. His grandmother cared for him and visited the temple on several occasions to pray for his recovery.

In the early years of the reign of Emperor Ai (Liu Xin, 25–1 B.C.E.; r. 6–1 B.C.E.), a physician named Zhang You presented himself at the palace in Zhongshan offering to cure the infant Liu Kan. Zhang You was apparently psychotic, however, and at one point he flew into a rage and took himself off to Chang'an. Fearing retribution for his flighty behavior if he returned to Zhongshan, he laid a false accusation that Lady Feng

138 FENG, CONCUBINE OF EMPEROR YUAN

had wished ill to Emperor Ai and his grandmother, the former Lady Fu, who now held the title Empress Dowager Fu. There had long been antagonism between these two women, once both favorites of Emperor Yuan, so Empress Dowager Fu seized this opportunity to initiate an investigation, which escalated into persecution and an interrogation of the accused. The investigating censor arrested over 100 people, including Lady Feng's brothers, who were in Zhongshan, and the servants and officials of Lady Feng's grandson. These people were divided into groups and interrogated separately in the city of Luoyang and the commanderies of Wei and Julu for a month or so, but nothing came of it. Undeterred, Empress Dowager Fu instructed Director of Palace Receptionists Shi Li to interrogate everyone together with the counselor-in-chief's aide and the assistant to chamberlain for dependencies, neither official possessing significant prestige or position. In addition to the original charge, Shi Li accused Lady Feng of conspiring against the emperor. When she refused to plead guilty, Shi Li goaded her, saying she no longer had the same courage to admit her guilt as when she had confronted the bear to protect Emperor Yuan so many years before. Realizing the hopelessness of her situation, Lady Feng committed suicide by drinking poison.

Before Lady Feng died, a memorial was sent to Emperor Ai requesting that she be executed rather than being allowed to commit suicide, but he could not bring himself to do this. Instead, he ordered that she be demoted to commoner status and moved to Yunyang Palace. The emperor was later informed that Lady Feng had died before being demoted to a commoner, so she was buried according to the rites befitting a dowager to a prince or a marquis. Some of her kin followed her lead and committed suicide while others pleaded guilty; those who survived were demoted to commoner status and sent back to their native places. The physician Zhang You and Director of Palace Receptionists Shi Li were promoted and rewarded for their efforts.

Six years later, however, when Lady Feng's nine-year-old grandson Liu Kan (Emperor Ping) ascended the throne, Grand Minister of Education (*da situ*) Kong Guang revealed that Zhang You's original accusation had been false and that Shi Li had built a false case, resulting in a miscarriage of justice. Both men were deprived of their posts and official titles, demoted to commoner status, and exiled to Hepu (in present-day Guangdong Province). Finally, the unjust verdict against Lady Feng was overturned. Although history has rightly seen fit to exonerate her, this is but one of several recorded cases during this period in which an innocent woman lost her life while the men who were guilty of hounding her to death were merely demoted and exiled.

SHEN Lidong

Ban Gu. *Courtier and Commoner in Ancient China. Selections from the "History of the Former Han" by Pan Ku,* trans. Burton Watson. New York: Columbia University Press, 1974, 277–78.

Han shu. Beijing: Zhonghua shuju, 1983, vol. 12, 97*xia*.4005–7.

Loewe, Michael. *Crisis and Conflict in Han China: 104 BC to AD 9.* London: George Allen & Unwin, 1974, 232–36.

O'Hara, Albert R. *The Position of Woman in Early China According to the Lieh Nü Chuan, "The Biographies of Chinese Women."* Taipei: Mei Ya, 1971; 1978, 227–28.

Feng Furen: *see* Feng Liao

Feng Liao

Feng Liao, fl. 122–49 B.C.E., whose native place is not recorded, was an official Han emissary and an attendant of Princess Jieyou (*q.v.* Liu Jieyou), who was sent to the western region of China in 101 B.C.E. to fulfill a Han dynasty marriage alliance. Princess Jieyou was married out initially to Cenzou (Junxumi; d. c. 99 B.C.E.), King of Wusun, the most powerful state in what is now Xinjiang Autonomous Region. When Cenzou died, the princess married his nephew Wengguimi (d. 65 B.C.E.), and when Wengguimi died she married her first husband's son Nimi (d. ?53 B.C.E.).

Nothing is known of Feng Liao's antecedents, but she is said to have been a learned woman, well read, and experienced in human affairs. She accompanied Princess Jieyou on her journey to Wusun as an emissary with government credentials, and in the name of the Han dynasty offered gifts to all the kingdoms in the region, winning their respect and trust in the process. She thus strengthened the diplomatic ties of the Han dynasty with other small states in the region as well as with the Wusun. She was given the title Lady Feng (Feng *furen*) and contracted a Wusun marriage with a right grand general (*you dajiangjun*) who had connections with Wusun aristocracy. This relationship enabled her to play a key role mediating, on behalf of Han, during struggles for Wusun leadership between Princess Jieyou's son Yangguimi and stepson Wujiutu.

After the death of her second husband, Princess Jieyou married his successor, Mad King Nimi, who was a son of her first husband and therefore her stepson. She attempted to have him assassinated, but in the end it was another of her stepsons—Wujiutu, a son of her second husband—who killed Nimi. Wujiutu then assumed the title of King of Wusun. At this point, Feng Liao was instructed to approach Wujiutu and suggest that he would be wise to abandon his pretensions to Wusun leadership, lest Han send armies to overthrow him. Wujiutu saw the sense of Feng Liao's argument and agreed to step down on condition that he be appointed Lesser King of Wusun. Feng Liao was then appointed official Han ambassador to Wusun, and two male vice-ambassadors were assigned to escort her to Chigu, the capital of Wusun. She traveled to Chigu in a carriage trimmed with brocade, and there in 53 B.C.E. granted the Imperial Seal and Ribbon of the Greater King to Yuanguimi, the eldest son of Wengguimi and Princess Jieyou. She also granted the Imperial Seal and Ribbon of the Lesser King to Wujiutu, in accordance with their earlier agreement. Feng Liao is thus credited with avoiding a war by mediating a peace accord with Wusun that was more favorable to the Han.

SHEN Lidong

Han shu. Beijing: Zhonghua shuju, 1983, vol. 12, 96*xia*.3907–8.
Liu Shisheng. *Zhongguo gudai funü shi.* Qingdao: Qingdao chubanshe, 1991, 106–7.
Ma Zhaozheng and Zhou Feitang. *Zhongguo gudai funü mingren.* Beijing: Zhongguo funü chubanshe, 1988, 48–52.
Yingwen Zhongguo funü, ed. *Gujin zhuming funü renwu.* Vol. 1. Shijiazhuang: Hebei renmin chubanshe, 1986, 39–44.

140 FENG YISHENG

Feng Yisheng: *see* Zhao Feiyan, Empress of Emperor Cheng

The Filial Widow from Chen

The Filial Widow (Chen Gua Xiaofu), fl. 179–157 B.C.E., was from Chen (present-day Xiangcheng District, Henan Province) and lived during the time of Emperor Wen of the Western Han dynasty. O'Hara's translation of her story from *Biographies of Eminent Women* (Lienü zhuan) says that Chen was "a state of Chou times . . . absorbed by Ch'u in about B.C. 479" and places The Filial Widow in the time of an earlier Emperor Hsiao-wen "of pre-Han times."

The Filial Widow had married at the age of sixteen, but had not had any children by the time her husband was sent with the army to defend the borders. As he departed, her husband enjoined her to care for his aging mother if he was killed, since he had no brothers. The young woman promised she would do this, and after her husband was indeed killed while serving at the frontier she devoted herself to caring for her mother-in-law. She gave no thought to remarrying but was content to support herself by spinning and weaving. When the traditional three-year mourning period for her husband was over, however, her parents suggested that she return home and get married, since she was still young. Their daughter's response was that "it is a basic moral principle to keep one's promise, and righteous people should act in a principled manner. From a very young age I was taught that I should serve my husband well. Now that he has entrusted his aging mother to me, it would be immoral to break my promise to him. I couldn't do that." When her mother protested that she was too young to live out her life as a widow, the Filial Widow insisted that she would rather die than live immorally. "As a wife," she said, "I must take care of my husband's parents. My husband was unable to fulfill his duty as a son because he died young. If I then abandoned the elderly it would reflect badly on him as well as on me. How could I go on living if I were not filial, trustworthy, and righteous?" By this time The Filial Widow was on the point of suicide so her parents let the matter rest and never again raised the topic of her remarrying. The Filial Widow cared for her mother-in-law for twenty-eight years, until the latter's death, and after that she faithfully observed the appropriate sacrifices for the rest of her life.

The commandery governor (*taishou*) of Huaiyang reported her filial deed to the emperor, who praised highly her lofty morality, faithfulness, and fine deeds. In addition, he granted her forty catties of gold and the official title of Filial Woman (*xiaofu*). Clearly, the respect for morality so treasured by the governor and the emperor was very much in the Confucian tradition of filial piety, because The Filial Widow's reason for refusing to remarry was not to preserve her chastity but rather to keep her promise that she would care for her husband's mother, just as he would have had he lived.

SHEN Jian

Liu Xiang. *Lienü zhuan*. Sibubeiyao ed., 4.9.
Liu Ziqing. *Zhongguo lidai xianneng funü pingzhuan*. Taipei: Liming wenhua, 1978, 82–84.
O'Hara, Albert R. *The Position of Woman in Early China According to the Lieh Nü Chuan, "The Biographies of Chinese Women."* Taipei: Mei Ya, 1971; 1978, 124–26.

Filial Wife, the Widow of the Country of Ch'en, The: *see* The Filial Widow from Chen

Fu, Concubine of Emperor Yuan

Lady of Bright Deportment Fu (Xiao Yuan Fu Zhaoyi), c. 73–2 B.C.E., was a concubine of Emperor Yuan (Liu Shi, 76–33 B.C.E.; r. 48–33 B.C.E.) and paternal grandmother of Emperor Ai (Liu Xin, 25–1 B.C.E.; r. 6–1 B.C.E.). Her posthumous title was Empress Fu of Emperor Yuan (Xiao Yuan Fu Huanghou).

Lady Fu entered the palace when she was young, becoming a lady of talents (*cairen*) under Grand Empress Dowager Shangguan (*q.v.* Shangguan, Empress of Emperor Zhao). At some point after he was appointed heir apparent in 65 B.C.E., Lady Fu became a concubine of Liu Shi, whose mother, Empress Xu (*q.v.* Xu Pingjun, Empress of Emperor Xuan), had been poisoned when he was about six years old. Lady Fu is said to have been resourceful, but she was also amenable and would often perform libations at feasts to wish the guests health and good luck. After Liu Shi (Emperor Yuan) ascended the throne, in 48 B.C.E., Lady Fu was promoted to the rank of lady of handsome fairness (*jieyu*) and continued to enjoy his favors. She gave birth to a son—Liu Kang (d. 22 B.C.E.), the future Prince Gong of Dingtao—and a daughter—the Princess of Pingdu. The emperor's other favorite at that time was Lady of Handsome Fairness Feng (*q.v.* Feng, Concubine of Emperor Yuan), who had also borne him a son—Liu Xing (d. 7 B.C.E.), the future Prince Xiao of Zhongshan. Emperor Yuan rewarded both women for their excellent demeanor and signified their superiority and nobility by promoting them to the rank of lady of bright deportment (*zhaoyi*). Perhaps this was intended as some form of consolation for these two ladies, for the son of neither one was appointed heir apparent. Liu Ao (Emperor Cheng, 51–7 B.C.E.; r. 32–7 B.C.E.), the son of Empress Wang (*q.v.* Wang Zhengjun, Empress of Emperor Yuan), was finally appointed heir apparent.

In accordance with tradition, after Emperor Yuan died Lady Fu was given a title. She was appointed Princess Dowager Dingtao and moved with her son to his fief, the state of Dingtao (in the southwest of present-day Shandong Province). Her son, Liu Kang, was probably in his late teens at this time and he took Lady Ding (c. 45–5 B.C.E.) of Xiaqiu in Shanyang (present-day Jinxiang County in Shandong Province) as a concubine (*ji*). Lady Ding gave birth to Liu Xin in 25 B.C.E. and when Liu Kang died three years later, his title—Prince of Dingtao—passed to Liu Xin, the future Emperor Ai. Having been disappointed when her son was passed over for the position of heir apparent, Princess Dowager Dingtao appears to have decided to place her imperial hopes in her grandson, Liu Xin, for she chose to raise him herself rather than leaving him in the care of his mother, now Lady Ding of Dingtao. In 9 B.C.E., Liu Xin and his half-brother Prince Xiao of Zhongshan visited Emperor Cheng, who remained without an heir. Empress Dowager Dingtao took advantage of their visit to send gifts to several powerful people in the emperor's inner circle. She sent gifts to the emperor's favorite, Zhao Feiyan (*q.v.* Zhao Feiyan, Empress of Emperor Cheng), and her sister the Lady of Bright Deportment Zhao (*q.v.* Zhao Hede, Concubine of Emperor Cheng), and to Cavalry General Wang Gen, the emperor's uncle, who recommended Liu Xin to the

142 *FU, CONCUBINE OF EMPEROR YUAN*

emperor. Emperor Cheng was impressed by the young man and the following year appointed him heir apparent. Liu Xin was then seventeen years old.

Emperor Cheng decreed that neither Liu Xin's grandmother (Empress Dowager Dingtao) nor his mother (Lady Ding) were to call on Liu Xin, now that he had been appointed heir apparent. Emperor Cheng's mother, the former Empress Wang and now Empress Dowager Wang, decided to overrule her son, however, and granted permission for them to visit every ten days. Emperor Cheng in turn protested, saying that Liu Xin should devote himself to Empress Dowager Wang rather than to his own relatives. It was finally decided that Empress Dowager Dingtao would be permitted to visit her grandson because she had demonstrated kindness in raising him, but that Lady Ding would be denied access to her son because she had not raised him. After the death of Emperor Cheng in 7 B.C.E., Liu Xin (Emperor Ai) ascended the throne and Empress Dowager Wang then decreed that both his mother and his grandmother would be permitted to visit him in Weiyang palace every ten days. The two women were also awarded titles of honor. The *History of the Han Dynasty* (Han shu) said of their families that they "rose to sudden prominence for the space of a year or two and enjoyed extraordinary success. But the authority and power which [Emperor Ai] entrusted to them was not excessive and it was not comparable with that which the Wang family had possessed in the days of [Emperor Cheng]." Lady Ding became Empress Gong and a year later was entitled Emperor's Dowager (*di taihou*) Ding. She died two months later, and five years after that was posthumously demoted to Lady Ding. In 5 C.E. Commander-in-Chief Wang Mang declared that her funeral had surpassed the rites due to her; he had her remains reburied in the style suited for a commoner and her tomb was razed.

Empress Dowager Dingtao became Empress Dowager Fu, then Grand Empress Dowager (*di taitaihou*) Fu, and finally August Empress Dowager (*huang taitaihou*) Fu. She resided in Yongxin Palace and grew increasingly arrogant; she referred contemptuously to Empress Dowager Wang as "that old woman," for example. More sinister, however, was the deep hatred she had long harbored for Lady of Bright Deportment Feng, whom she now charged with having placed curses on Emperor Ai and forced to commit suicide by drinking poison.

The August Empress Dowager Fu, once the humble Lady of Talents Fu, died in 2 B.C.E. and was buried alongside Emperor Yuan in Weiling.

WU Jin

Chen Quanli and Hou Xinyi. eds. *Hou fei cidian.* Xi'an: Shaanxi renmin jiaoyu chubanshe, 1991, 19.
Han shu. Beijing: Zhonghua shuju, 1983, vol. 12, 97*xia.*3999–4004.
Loewe, Michael. *Crisis and Conflict in Han China: 104 BC to AD 9.* London: George Allen & Unwin, 1974, 156, 160–61, 270–75.

Fu Shou, Empress of Emperor Xian

Fu Shou (Xiandi Fu Huanghou), d. 214, was empress to Emperor Xian (Liu Xie, 181–234; r. 189–220) of Eastern Han. She was from Dongwu in Langye (present-day Zhucheng District, Shandong Province) and was the daughter of Fu Wan, Marquis of

Buqi, and Liu Ying, who had been Princess of Yang'an during the reign of Emperor Huan (Liu Zhi, 132–167; r. 147–167). Fu Shou was selected to enter the palace in 190, the year after General-in-Chief (*da jiangjun*) Dong Zhuo (d. 192) overthrew Emperor Shao, installed eight-year-old Liu Xie (Emperor Xian) in his place, and moved the capital to Chang'an. She was initially appointed as a Worthy Lady (*guiren*) but in 195 she was appointed empress.

After the death of Dong Zhuo, the remnants of his army staged a revolt against the government. Emperor Xian fled across the Yellow River under cover of night and Empress Fu led the concubines and palace women out on foot, taking with her several bolts of silk. During their journey, the emperor's maternal uncle Dong Cheng tried to take the silk from Empress Fu; several attendants were killed in the melee and the empress's clothes were spattered with blood, but she clung doggedly to the silk. By the time they reached Anyi (northwest of present-day Xia District in Shanxi Province), their clothes were thin and worn and they were subsisting on the fruit and nuts they could find on trees along the way. At that time, Cao Cao (155–220) was in charge of local forces resisting the rebellious armies and he escorted Emperor Xian and the women into Xuchang for protection. A further motive for bringing the imperial refugees to Xuchang, however, was so that he could keep an eye on them. As a reward for rescuing them, Cao Cao was appointed Grand Minister of Works (*da sikong*) and Chariot and Horse General (*cheqi jiangjun*). The court returned to Luoyang in 196, but there was so little food and the city was so dilapidated that later in the year the capital was moved to Xuchang.

As his power at court increased, Cao Cao began to put to death those who opposed him. The emperor's maternal uncle Dong Cheng concocted a plot to kill Cao Cao but was himself put to death in 200 when the conspiracy was revealed. Despite the emperor's entreaties, Cao Cao also killed Dong Cheng's daughter, Worthy Lady Dong, then pregnant with Emperor Xian's child. Held virtual hostage and in great fear, Empress Fu eventually sent a letter to her father, Fu Wan, informing him of Cao Cao's brutality and asking him to have Cao Cao assassinated. Fearful of Cao Cao's power, Fu Wan dared not countenance such a course of action and when the plot was discovered, in 214, Cao Cao was indeed enraged. He forced Emperor Xian to demote Empress Fu and, usurping the emperor's authority, issued an edict stating that, having been empress for twenty-four years, she no longer had the virtue to teach the people. The edict claimed that Empress Fu was a jealous and spiteful person and had planned murder, and therefore she was not qualified to remain empress. She was ordered to return her imperial seal and ribbon and vacate the central palace. The edict concluded: "It is a great pity, but she has brought this upon herself. We are not handing her over to the court for trial because we are treating her leniently." Soldiers were sent to arrest Empress Fu, who had hidden in a wall cavity. As she was led, barefoot and with disheveled hair, past Emperor Xian in the outer palace, her last words to him were: "Can't you save my life?" The emperor replied: "I don't know when my turn will come." Empress Fu was sent to the Drying House, where palace women were sent when they were ill or had committed some crime, and there she died. One record states that Cao Cao "killed" her in the eleventh month. Her

144 FU SHOU

two sons were poisoned, and over 100 members of her family were put to death. Her mother, however, was exiled with nineteen others to Zhu Commandery (the present-day city of Zhuzhou, Hebei Province).

Empress Fu was a politically active woman who attempted to salvage the ailing Han dynasty, but whose actions instead led to virtually her entire family being exterminated. Cao Cao had little compunction in having her and other imperial women killed, but he needed Emperor Xian alive as a puppet through whom he could control the other lords. This tactic has been immortalized in the saying "Command the lords by controlling the emperor."

YANG Haiming

Chen Quanli and Hou Xinyi. eds. *Hou fei cidian.* Xi'an: Shaanxi renmin jiaoyu chubanshe, 1991, 29.
Hou Han shu. Beijing: Zhonghua shuju, 1973, vol. 1, 10*xia*.452–54.

Fu Xi'e: *see* **Song, Lady Xuanwen**

G

Gaozu Bo Ji: *see* **Bo, Concubine of Emperor Gaozu**

Gaozu Lü Huanghou: *see* **Lü Zhi, Empress of Emperor Gaozu**

Gaozu Qi Furen: *see* **Qi, Concubine of Emperor Gaozu**

Gaozu Tangshan Furen: *see* **Tangshan, Concubine of Emperor Gaozu**

Gong'ai, Empress: *see* **Xu Pingjun, Empress of Emperor Xuan**

Gongsun Shu Qi: *see* **Gongsun Shu's Wife**

Gongsun Shu's Wife
Gongsun Shu's Wife (Gongsun Shu Qi), d. 36, was the wife of Gongsun Shu (d. 36) of Maoling in Fufeng (in the vicinity of present-day Xianyang and Xingping in Shaanxi Province); her given names, her surname, and her birthplace are not recorded.

The Western Han dynasty came to an end in 8 C.E., when Wang Mang (d. 23) usurped the authority of the ruling Liu clan, declaring himself emperor of the Xin (also called the Xin Mang) dynasty. Within a few years, military opposition to Wang Mang grew, with many peasant-based groups also threatening the stability of the nation. The death of Wang Mang saw the end of his Xin interregnum, and the following year Liu Xuan, a member of the ruling Liu clan, established the Gengshi regime. This regime was overthrown a year later, when Liu Xiu (Emperor Guangwu, 6 B.C.E.–57 C.E.; r. 25–57) assumed the throne and reestablished the Han dynasty. This has come to be known as the Eastern (or Later) Han dynasty.

In the period immediately after the death of Wang Mang, Gongsun Shu defeated the troops of Liu Xuan, which were stationed in the region of Yizhou (the eastern part of present-day Sichuan Province). This placed him in a powerful position, since Sichuan was a strategically placed land of rich natural resources and fertile lands. On the advice of one of his officials, a man named Li Xiong who worked in his Labor Section (*gongcao*), Gongsun Shu decided to establish an independent regime in Yizhou, making the city of Chengdu his capital. His venture succeeded and attracted many men from distant places.

Li Xiong soon suggested to Gongsun Shu that he declare himself emperor, but Gongsun Shu was hesitant to take this step, believing in the divine right of emperors and doubting his own nobility. One night, however, he was told in a dream "Ba Si Sun will be emperor for twelve years." (The *gong* part of his surname is a composite of the characters *ba* and *si*, and "Ba Si Sun" are therefore the three components of Gongsun.) Upon waking, he told his wife of his dream, adding: "Noble and distinguished as it is to be emperor, twelve years is much too short a period." His wife responded: "If you attained wisdom in the morning, it would be worth dying that very evening. Twelve years would be a great boon!" It is said that about that time a dragon appeared above his palace, glowing in the night, and Gongsun Shu took this as an auspicious sign. Thus in 25 Gongsun Shu declared himself Emperor of Chengjia (the House of Cheng), deriving the name from his capital, Chengdu.

Gongsun Shu was overthrown twelve years later, in 36, when he was killed in battle by the Han general Wu Han (d. 44). Gongsun Shu's Wife was also killed at that time. This story suggests that Gongsun Shu's Wife was politically more decisive than her husband and was much more willing to accept whatever challenges life presented.

SHEN Lidong

Hou Han shu. Beijing: Zhonghua shuju, 1965, vol. 2, 13.533–44.

Gongxian Jun: *see* **Wang, Empress of Wang Mang of Xin**

Gouyi: *see* **Zhao Gouyi, Concubine of Emperor Wu**

Guanglie, Empress: *see* **Yin Lihua, Empress of Emperor Guangwu**

Guangwudi Guo Huanghou: *see* **Guo Shengtong, Empress of Emperor Guangwu**

Guangwudi Yin Huanghou: *see* **Yin Lihua, Empress of Emperor Guangwu**

Guantao, Princess of: *see* **Liu Piao**

Guo Shengtong, Empress of Emperor Guangwu

Guo Shengtong (Guangwudi Guo Huanghou), d. 52, was empress to Emperor Guangwu (Liu Xiu, 6 B.C.E.–57 C.E.; r. 25–57 C.E.), the first emperor of Eastern Han. She was born in Gao District, Zhending Commandery (southwest of present-day Gaocheng District, Hebei Province). Her father, Guo Chang, was from a prominent clan and worked in the commandery Labor Section. He had won praise for his generosity in giving a considerable portion of his property in the form of houses and land to a younger half brother. Her mother, Princess Guo (d. 50), is said to have been a courteous and thrifty woman who embodied the motherly virtues. Princess Guo belonged to the Han imperial family: her father, Liu Pu, Prince Gong of Zhending, was a seventh-generation descendant of Emperor Jing (156–141 B.C.E.) of Western Han.

The death in 23 of Wang Mang saw the end of his brief Xin dynasty interregnum (9–23) and an intensification of the struggle for military and political supremacy in China. The following year, the future inaugural emperor of Eastern Han, Liu Xiu, won over to his cause his fellow clansman Liu Yang, Prince of Zhending and a maternal uncle of Guo Shengtong. Liu Xiu then made his base in Zhending and in 25 took Guo Shengtong as a wife. In the sixth month of 25, Liu Xiu ascended the throne at Hao (in present-day Hebei Province), soon shifting the capital to Luoyang. He took with him Guo Shengtong, who held the rank of Worthy Lady (*guiren*), at the same time dispatching an envoy to escort another of his wives—Worthy Lady Yin (*q.v.* Yin Lihua, Empress of Emperor Guangwu)—to Luoyang. He had married Worthy Lady Yin in 23 in Yuan (present-day Nanyang, Henan Province), and the year after he ascended the throne he indicated that he wanted to make her his empress. She declined, however, on the grounds that Worthy Lady Guo had already given birth to a son (Liu Qiang, 25–58). Worthy Lady Guo was thus elevated to empress in 26 and her son Liu Qiang was made heir apparent. During the seventeen years of her marriage to the emperor, Empress Guo gave birth to five sons: Liu Qiang (Prince Gong of Donghai), Liu Fu (Prince Xian of Pei), Liu Kang (Prince An of Jinan), Liu Yan (Prince Zhi of Fuling), and Liu Yan (Prince Jian of Zhongshan).

However, while Empress Guo may have been empress and borne sons, it was Worthy Lady Yin the emperor loved. This uncomfortable situation so distressed Empress Guo that she is said to have harbored "recurrent resentment," which was given as the cause of her eventual demotion in 41. The imperial edict announcing the removal of Empress Guo gave two reasons for Emperor Guangwu's decision. First, Empress Guo had apparently voiced complaints against him and "disregarded his teachings" and, second, she was unable to live in harmony with her husband's concubines. She had behaved as imperiously as Empress Lü (*q.v.* Lü Zhi, Empress of Emperor Gaozu) and Empress Huo (*q.v.* Huo Chengjun, Empress of Emperor Xuan), the edict said, "bullying the concubines like a hawk preying on small birds." His mother's demotion placed the heir apparent Liu Qiang in an untenable position. His *Book of Songs According to Han* (Han shi) tutor reminded him: "the honor of the mother comes from the son. Your Highness, it is now best for you, as your attendants and other princes have advised, to assume blame and resign to wait upon your mother in order to demonstrate the principles of the Confucian teachings and be worthy of your mother's devotion." Liu Qiang therefore advised his father that he was prepared to stand aside and simply "be one of the princes." Accordingly, he was appointed Prince of Donghai. That same year (41), Worthy Lady Yin was made empress and, two years later her son Liu Yang (i.e., Liu Zhuang, Emperor Ming, 27–75; r. 58–75) was elevated to the position of heir apparent.

Despite the criticism that had accompanied Empress Guo's demotion, Emperor Guangwu continued to take meticulous care of her. It appears that Empress Guo had no political ambitions and was therefore not a danger either to the throne or to Empress Yin. Also, her family had helped Emperor Guangwu gain power, which placed on him an obligation to ensure her safety and comfort. Not long after Empress Guo was demoted, her second son, Liu Fu (d. 84), was promoted from Duke Youyi to Prince of Zhongshan and was allocated the taxes of Changshan Commandery; the ex-empress was accordingly designated Princess Dowager of Zhongshan. In the year 44, Liu Fu was made Prince of Pei and she became Princess Dowager of Pei.

The emperor also dealt favorably with other members of her family. Her younger brother Guo Kuang (9–58) had been appointed Gentleman Attendant at the Palace Gate (*huangmen shilang*) in 25, when he was just sixteen. In 26 he was granted the title Marquis Mianman and in 38 he was promoted to the post of commandant of the capital gates (*chengmen xiaowei*). In 41 he was granted the title Marquis of Anyang and at some later stage was promoted to the position of chamberlain for dependencies (*da honglu*). Although he was some fifteen years younger than the emperor, Guo Kuang appears to have become quite close to his brother-in-law, who "often visited him at his residence, where they had feasts with dukes, ministers, marquises, and members of the Guo clan. [The emperor] awarded him money and large amounts of fine silk, so that people in the capital, Luoyang, referred to Guo Kuang's house as 'The Golden Cave.'" Even after the death of Emperor Guangwu, Guo Kuang continued to "receive awards repeatedly" from Emperor Ming. Emperor Guangwu's bounty extended to his ex-empress's cousin Guo Jing, who was granted the title Marquis of Xinqi for his military exploits and later promoted to Minister of Donghai. And when her mother, Princess Guo, died of illness in 50, the emperor himself joined the funeral procession. He also dispatched an envoy to fetch the coffin of the princess's husband, Guo Chang, so that they might be buried in the one grave, with the seal and the silk ribbon of the Marquis of Yang'an; Guo Chang was posthumously granted the title Marquis Si of Yang'an.

Empress Guo died in 52, from illness, and was buried in Beimang (north of the city of Luoyang). After her death, the emperor reaffirmed the relationship between the Guo and the Liu clans by marrying his fourth daughter, Princess Yuyang, to Guo Huang, a son of Guo Kuang.

The *History of the Later Han Dynasty* (Hou Han shu) commented thus on the way Emperor Guangwu dealt with Empress Guo:

> The rise and fall of things follow inexorable laws. . . . The emperor was estranged when Empress Guo lost her youth, and her complaints brought about a divorce yet the emperor ensconced her in a villa and treated her relatives extremely well. Her

148 GUO SHENGTONG

son the Prince of Donghai showed propriety in the manner he resigned from his position as heir apparent, which protected the emperor from the taint of partiality. In its way, this added a glorious page to history.

The demotion of an empress in traditional China occurred as a result of love, power, and propriety; such a momentous affair was not simply a matter of an emperor loving one woman more than another. This led to a precarious and unpredictable existence and placed empresses in an extremely vulnerable position. Empress Guo, however, may well have been the luckiest demoted empress in imperial China, able to live on for a further eleven years and enjoy a comfortable life thanks to the benevolence of her husband, Emperor Guangwu.

WONG Yin Lee and NG Kwok-leung
(Translated by CHE Wai-lam William)

An Zuozhang, ed. *Hou fei zhuan.* Zhengzhou: Henan renmin chubanshe, 1990, vol. 1, 134–43.
Hou Han shu. Beijing: Zhonghua shuju, 1973, vol. 1, 1.1–94; vol. 2, 10*shang*.402–5; vol. 3, 21.760–61; vol. 4, 29.1023–32; vol. 5, 42.1423–56.
Sima Guang. *Zizhi tongjian.* Beijing: Zhonghua shuju, 1956, vol. 2, 40, passim.
Yuan Hong. *Hou Han ji.* Shanghai: Shangwu yinshuguan, n.d., 7.54–63.

H

Hedi Deng Huanghou: *see* **Deng Sui, Empress of Emperor He**

Hongnong Wang Tang Ji: *see* **Tang, Consort of Prince Hongnong**

Ho-Yang, The Loving Younger Sister of: *see* **Youdi**

Hsü Shu: *see* **Xu Shu**

Hsü Teng: *see* **Xu Deng**

Hua Rong, Consort of Prince of Yanla

Consort Hua Rong (Yanla Wang Hua Rong Furen), ?116–80 B.C.E., was the wife of Liu Dan (c. 120–80 B.C.E.), Prince of Yanla and the third son of Emperor Wu (Liu Che, 156–87 B.C.E.; r. 141–87 B.C.E.).

Emperor Wu had appointed his eldest son, Liu Ju (128–91 B.C.E.), heir apparent in 122 B.C.E. but Liu Ju committed suicide in 91 B.C.E. (*vide* Wei Zifu, Empress of Emperor Wu) and the emperor's second son died of illness not long after. Believing that by seniority he was the rightful successor to the throne, Liu Dan memorialized Emperor Wu asking to be made a member of the palace guard. This angered the emperor, and later his dislike of his son was compounded when Liu Dan's grant of land was reduced for the crime of harboring an escaped prisoner. Emperor Wu therefore appointed his youngest son Liu Fuling (Emperor Zhao, 94–74 B.C.E. r. 87–74 B.C.E.) heir apparent.

After Emperor Wu's death and the enthronement of Liu Fuling, Liu Dan started to plot unrest with the aim of unseating the new young emperor. This plot was foiled but although everyone else implicated was executed on the emperor's orders, Liu Dan was not charged with any crime. Some time later, Liu Dan began plotting with his sister (the Grand Princess of Gai), Left General Shangguan Jie (d. 80 B.C.E.), and Censor-in-Chief (*yushi dafu*) Sang Hongyang (152–80 B.C.E.) to bring about the downfall of General-in-Chief (*da jiangjun*) Huo Guang (d. 68 B.C.E.) and eventually to depose Emperor Zhao. This conspiracy was also exposed, however, and Shangguan Jie was among the many put to death. Knowing he was doomed, Liu Dan gave a feast in Wanzai Palace to which he invited guests, his courtiers, Consort Hua Rong, and his concubines. At the feast, Liu Dan composed a song:

> In the end an empty city,
> No dogs barking,
> No chickens crowing.
> Angling streets broad and bare—
> How well I know there's no one left alive in my land! (Watson, 63)

Consort Hua Rong rose to dance and sang in response a song that later commentators have dubbed *Dancing Song* or *Continued Song:*

> Hair knotted and tangled, clotting the moat,
> Bones heaped about, nowhere to lay them—
> The mother seeks her dead son,
> The wife seeks her dead husband,
> Wandering back and forth between the two moats.
> Can you alone, my lord, find a place to rest? (Watson, 63)

Initially, Emperor Zhao sent a letter of pardon, but this was followed by a letter in which he accused his older brother, saying: "you join with men of different surnames and other clans to plot injury to the altars of the soil and grain. You draw close to those who are most distant, and behave distantly to those who should be most close. You have a heart filled with treachery and betrayal, one in which there is no thought of loyalty or love" (Watson, 64). Full of shame and indignation, Liu Dan hanged himself. Consort Hua Rong and over twenty of his concubines also committed suicide. Poignant testimony to innocent lives destroyed by imperial power struggles, Consort Hua Rong's poem remains evocative to this day.

SHEN Lidong

Ban Gu. *Courtier and Commoner in Ancient China: Selections from the "History of the Former Han" by Pan Ku,* trans. Burton Watson. New York: Columbia University Press, 1974, 54–65.

150 HUA RONG

Han shu. Beijing: Zhonghua shuju, 1983, vol. 9, 63.2750–59.

Shen Lidong. *Lidai houfei shici jizhu.* Beijing: Zhongguo funü chubanshe, 1990, 83–85.

Zhang Xiurong. *Han–Tang guizu yu cainü shige yanjiu.* Taipei: Wenshizhe chubanshe, 1985, 22–23.

Huan, Liu Changqing's Wife

Liu Changqing's Wife (Liu Changqing Qi Huan Shi), fl. 168–189, was known only by her family name of Huan. She was from Longkang in Pei Commandery (present-day Jixi in Anhui Province) and was admired in her own time for her virtuous and moral deeds.

Liu Changqing's Wife was a daughter of the famous Confucian scholar Huan Luan (108–184) and had therefore been raised in an intellectual environment. Her great-great-grandfather Huan Rong, her great-grandfather Huan Yu, her granduncle Huan Yan (d. 143), her uncle Huan Lin, and her cousins Huan Dian and Huan Bin (133–178) were all Confucian scholars. The family was held in high esteem in the community for their moral teachings. Members of her family had instructed each of the Eastern Han emperors in the Confucian classics, and most of the men of the family had held official position or been appointed ministers.

Liu Changqing was from the same commandery and after their marriage she bore him a son. Even though this highly respected woman née Huan is known to posterity only as Liu Changqing's Wife, all that is known of him is that he died when their son was five years old. Having been well schooled in Confucian ideals, Liu Changqing's Wife knew that she must safeguard her family's reputation by remaining a chaste widow. This involved not only refusing to remarry but also displaying complete devotion to her husband's family. She refused to go back to see her parents for fear people might think she intended to return there permanently. And when her son died at the age of fifteen she forbore showing her grief, preferring instead to cut off both her ears to demonstrate her loyalty to the Liu family and her determination to remain a chaste widow to the end of her life.

Many of the women in the Liu family felt sorry for this young widow and assured her they knew she was sincere in her determination not to remarry. They told her there was no need for her to place such importance on righteousness that she felt she had to mutilate herself to prove her moral rectitude. To this Liu Changqing's widow replied: "For five generations my ancestors have been teachers to whom other scholars have looked for guidance. They have also been the emperors' tutors. The sons of the Huan family are known far and wide for their loyalty and the daughters of the family are praised and admired for their chastity and filial piety to their parents-in-law." She also quoted from *The Book of Songs* (Shi jing): "Do not be always talking about your ancestors; simply cultivate your own morality." She had mutilated herself, she said, to show her true feelings.

By the end of Eastern Han, Confucian teachings had become state orthodoxy and deeds such as those of Liu Changqing's widow were considered chaste and honorable, so that those in power would praise them and make them known to the people as fine examples. The counselor-delegate (*guoxiang*) of Pei Commandery therefore memorialized Emperor Shao (r. 189), informing him of Liu Changqing's widow's chaste deeds. Her neighborhood was granted the inscription Righteous Widow Huan, and it was decreed that she would get a share of the meat offerings at every commandery sacrificial ceremony.

In these early years of Confucian orthodoxy many women would have had their own reasons for performing similar "chaste deeds." Liu Changqing's Wife had clearly felt an enormous responsibility to uphold the Confucian teachings her noble family respected. As the centuries rolled on, however, such partly voluntary acts of self-sacrifice came to be expected of all widows, and these early women were transformed into greatly respected exemplars.

BAO Shanben

Hou Han shu. Beijing: Zhonghua shuju, 1965, vol. 10, 84.2797.

Huandi Deng Huanghou: *see* **Deng Mengnü, Empress of Emperor Huan**

Huandi Dou Huanghou: *see* **Dou Miao, Empress of Emperor Huan**

Huandi Liang Huanghou: *see* **Liang Nüying, Empress of Emperor Huan**

Huang Huangshi Zhu: *see* **Wang, Empress of Emperor Ping**

Huangfu Gui Qi: *see* **Huangfu Gui's Wife**

Huangfu Gui's Wife
Huangfu Gui's Wife (Huangfu Gui Qi), d. 190, was the second wife of Huangfu Gui (104–174); nothing is recorded in the histories of her name or her place of origin.

Huangfu Gui was from Anding (present-day Nanzheng District in Shaanxi Province) and was something of a strategist. Very resourceful, he was once recommended for the official post known as worthy and excellent, straightforward and upright (*xianliang fangzheng*), but he was not appointed because he satirized General-in-Chief Liang Ji. After Liang Ji was executed in 159, however, Huangfu Gui was appointed to the position of governor of Taishan. Between 158 and 167, during the last years of the reign of Emperor Huan (r. 147–167), Huangfu Gui pacified the Qiang minority people in the north of China and was rewarded by appointment as Duliao General. He was stationed on the northern border for several years and won the love and respect of the Qiang people. In 167, he was promoted to imperial secretary (*shangshu*) and died in office as Commandant Protector of the Qiang (*hu Qiang xiaowei*).

Huangfu Gui had remarried when his first wife died, the year unrecorded. His second wife was widely admired as a good, beautiful, versatile, and educated woman. Her cursive calligraphy was excellent and, skilled at composition, she often helped

152 *HUANGFU GUI'S WIFE*

her husband draft documents. She was still young and beautiful when her husband died of illness.

In the increasing unrest toward the end of the Eastern Han dynasty, General-in-Chief (*da jiangjun*) Dong Zhuo (d. 192) took advantage of a riot started by ten attendants-in-ordinary to enter the capital and appoint himself counselor-in-chief (*chengxiang*). Once in power, he became overbearing. Having heard of the ability and beauty of Huangfu Gui's widow, Dong Zhuo decided to take her as a concubine. He sent an entourage with betrothal gifts that included one hundred carriages, twenty horses, and maids, and cash and had her brought to his residence. Dressed in simple clothes, Huangfu Gui's widow knelt before Dong Zhuo and in a poignant speech begged him not to force her into marriage but to allow her to remain loyal to her dead husband. Enraged, Dong Zhuo ordered his servants to draw their swords and form a circle around her. He declared that he could "bend everyone within the four seas to my will. How could I not have what I want of a woman?" Knowing that she was doomed, Huangfu Gui's widow stood her ground, cursing him: "You are a descendant of the barbarian Qiang. You have brought calamity to the whole country! My ancestors were exemplars of morality and my husband's Huangfu family excelled in civil and martial arts. He was a loyal official in the service of the Han sovereign. Were not your parents servants of the Huangfu family? How dare you violate the wife of a superior!" Dong Zhuo had a carriage brought into the courtyard and had Huangfu Gui's widow yoked to it by the head, ordering his men to whip her. She died under the carriage, challenging those whipping her to kill her quickly.

Huangfu Gui's Wife was esteemed for her loyalty and righteousness. In one portrait she is called "The one who achieved the ultimate in propriety." Her integrity lay not so much in loyalty to her dead husband as in her courage in the face of brute force. It was exceptional, and deemed worthy of note, that such a frail young woman would sacrifice her life for righteousness and moral integrity. Chinese records rightly say of her that she "put to shame those lowly and mean people who bow and scrape to despotic power." However, her unflinching courage was also a useful reminder to those who came after that she died defending the morality of the house of Han against barbarians in revolt.

WU Tiaogong

Hou Han shu. Beijing: Zhonghua shuju, 1965, vol. 10, 84.2798.

Huo Chengjun, Empress of Emperor Xuan

Huo Chengjun (Xiao Xuan Huo Huanghou), d. 54 B.C.E., of Pingyang in Hedong (southeast of present-day Lingfen District, Shanxi Province), was the second empress of Emperor Xuan (Liu Xun or Liu Bingyi, 91–49 B.C.E.; r. 74–49 B.C.E.).

Huo Chengjun was the daughter of General-in-Chief (*da jiangjun*) Huo Guang (d. 68 B.C.E.) and his wife née Xian, who had long cherished the hope that her daughter would one day become empress. Even as she was preparing the bridal gown for her daughter, Xian bribed a female doctor to poison Empress Xu (*q.v.* Xu Pingjun,

Empress of Emperor Xuan) immediately after the empress gave birth to her second child, a son. Xian then asked her husband to submit a memorial asking that their daughter be admitted into the palace. In tacit acknowledgment that Huo Chengjun had been the court's original choice of empress before his appointment of Empress Xu, Emperor Xuan agreed to this request. He appointed Huo Chengjun empress in April 70 B.C.E., granting her his special favor. Empress Huo followed the example of her predecessor and visited Changle Palace every five days to call on Grand Empress Dowager Shangguan (*q.v.* Shangguan, Empress of Emperor Zhao) and to wait upon her. However, while Empress Xu and her attendants had practiced economy in all matters, Empress Huo was more extravagant, giving her subordinates gifts of up to 10,000 cash.

Empress Huo's father died almost three years after she became empress and not long afterward Emperor Xuan appointed Liu Shi (Emperor Yuan, 76–33 B.C.E.; r. 48–33 B.C.E.), his son by Empress Xu, as heir apparent. This so angered Empress Huo's mother that she refused to eat and eventually vomited blood. Xian said of Liu Shi that "born of a commoner, he was not entitled to the position of heir apparent," and complained that any son that Empress Huo might give birth to in the future could hope for nothing more than appointment as a prince. She therefore ordered her daughter to murder the heir apparent. Empress Huo accordingly invited Liu Shi to dine with her on several occasions, but because his attendants pre-tasted his food the plan failed. It was also later revealed that Empress Xu had been poisoned.

Xian, her sons-in-law, and her male relatives then plotted rebellion, their plan being to depose Emperor Xuan. The plot was disclosed, however, and all involved were sentenced to death. Emperor Xuan issued an edict accusing Empress Huo of being evil and immoral in attempting to poison the heir apparent: "She is not worthy of being a mother of the people and an empress. She is not fit to serve the imperial temple as an empress. She must leave the palace and must relinquish her imperial seal and ribbon."

Empress Huo was thus deposed in 66 and sent to Zhaotai Palace (in Shaoling yuan, west of the present-day city of Xi'an). She had been empress for five years. Twelve years later she was moved to Yunling Residence. She finally killed herself and was buried in Kunwu Pavilion (in present-day Lantian District, Shaanxi Province).

WANG Xiaowen

Ban Gu. *Courtier and Commoner in Ancient China: Selections from the "History of the Former Han" by Pan Ku,* trans. Burton Watson. New York: Columbia University Press, 1974, 143, 259.

Chen Quanli and Hou Xinyi, eds. *Hou fei cidian.* Xi'an: Shaanxi renmin jiaoyu chubanshe, 1991, 15.

Han shu. Beijing: Zhonghua shuju, 1983, vol. 12, 97*shang.*3968–69.

Loewe, Michael. *Crisis and Conflict in Han China: 104 BC to AD 9.* London: George Allen & Unwin, 1974, 113, 129–30.

Huoli Zigao Qi: *see* **Liyu**

I

Imperial Grandson, by Shi, Consort of the: *see* **Wang Wengxu**

J

Jiangdu, Princess of: *see* **Liu Xijun**

Jiao Zhongqing Qi: *see* **Liu Lanzhi**

Jiao Zhongqing's Wife: *see* **Liu Lanzhi**

Jieyou, Princess: *see* **Liu Jieyou**

Jieyou Gongzhu: *see* **Liu Jieyou**

Jijiang: *see* **Wen Jijiang**

Jingshi Jienü: *see* **Woman of Integrity from the Capital**

L

Li, Concubine of Emperor Wu

Consort Li (Xiao Wu Li Furen), after 140–?104 B.C.E., of Zhongshan (present-day Ding District, Hebei Province), was a beloved concubine of Emperor Wu (Liu Che, 156–87 B.C.E.; r. 140–87 B.C.E.). Her given name is not known, nor are the years of her birth and death.

Consort Li was a beautiful young woman who excelled at singing and dancing. Her father and her brother Li Yannian (c. 140–c. 87 B.C.E.) were both skilled musicians. Her brother was an entertainer but he specialized in music theory; the new poems he set to music were highly admired. At some stage he had been castrated "after some involvement with the law" and had become a palace musician to Emperor Wu, who was quite fond of him. Li Yannian once sang to the emperor:

> Beautiful lady in a northern land,
> standing alone, none in the world like her,
> a single glance and she upsets a city,
> a second glance, she upsets the state!
> Not that I don't know she upsets states and cities,
> but one so lovely you'll never find again! (Watson, 247)

The emperor asked if there was such a beauty and his elder sister, the Princess of Pingyang, confirmed that Li Yannian's younger sister was indeed as beautiful as the song suggested. Emperor Wu had the girl called to the court and he favored her, granting her the rank of Consort (*furen*) Li. She gave birth to a son, Liu Bo (d. 88 or 86 B.C.E.), who was later appointed Prince of Changyi.

However, Consort Li fell ill soon after giving birth and was bedridden. The emperor visited her when it became clear that she would not recover, but by then she had lost her beauty and she hid under the covers, refusing to let him see her face despite his entreaties. When she entrusted their son and her brothers to the emperor, he promised riches and high office for them if she would let him look at her. She replied: "It is up to Your Majesty to assign offices as you please—it does not depend on one glimpse of me" (Watson, 248). Then she turned to the wall, weeping, refusing to let him see her. Displeased, the emperor left. To the protests of her sisters that she had angered the emperor, Consort Li responded that those such as she who win grace and favor because of their beauty will just as quickly lose that grace and favor when their beauty has faded. If the emperor saw her as she now was, she said, he would be filled with loathing and disgust and would dismiss her from his thoughts. "Then what hope would there be that he would ever think kindly of me again and remember to take pity on my brothers?" (Watson, 249). Consort Li then died. Emperor Wu had her buried with the honors appropriate to an empress. He appointed her brother Li Guangli (d. 90 B.C.E.) Ershi General and Marquis of Haixi, and her brother Li Yannian Director of Imperial Music (*xielü duwei;* this title has also been translated as Harmonizer of the Tones).

Emperor Wu never ceased grieving over the death of Consort Li. He ordered her portrait painted and hung in Ganquan Palace. He also employed a magician (*fangshi*) named Shao Weng, from the state of Qi, who claimed to be able to summon the spirits of the dead. In a now famous episode, Shao Weng erected a tent in which he placed a table laid with offerings of food and drink. The tent was well lit with torches from within and the emperor was positioned behind a curtain at a distance while Shao Weng performed his rituals. A beauty with a likeness to Consort Li was seen to circle within the tent, sit down and then rise and walk again. Unfortunately, the emperor was unable to get a close look at this apparition, but from then on is said to have missed her even more. Emperor Wu wrote a poem about the summoning:

> Is it she?
> is it not?
> I stand gazing from afar:
> timid steps, soft and slow,
> how long she is in coming! (Watson, 249)

He had the court musicians in the Music Bureau set his poem to music and to further mourn her he wrote a long rhapsody (*fu*) expressing his deep love and affection.

Emperor Wu died in 87, four years after Empress Wei (*q.v.* Wei Zifu, Empress of Emperor Wu) was deposed and died. In accordance with his wishes, a memorial was presented to the court asking that Consort Li be posthumously appointed Empress Xiaowu (Empress of the Pious Wu). Remarkable in Consort Li was her awareness of the fickle nature of people's love, based as it so often is on physical beauty that is so evanescent.

SHEN Lidong

156   LI, CONCUBINE OF EMPEROR WU

An Zuozhang, ed. *Hou fei zhuan*. Zhengzhou: Henan renmin chubanshe, 1990, 45–56.
Ban Gu. *Courtier and Commoner in Ancient China: Selections from the "History of the Former Han"
   by Pan Ku,* trans. Burton Watson. New York: Columbia University Press, 1974, 247–51.
Chen Quanli and Hou Xinyi, eds. *Hou fei cidian*. Xi'an: Shaanxi renmin jiaoyu chubanshe,
   1991, 14.
Han shu. Beijing: Zhonghua shuju, 1983, vol. 12, 97*shang*.3951–56.
Loewe, Michael. *Crisis and Conflict in Han China*. London: George Allen & Unwin, 1974.
Zhang Xiurong. *Han–Tang guizu yu cainü shige yanjiu*. Taipei: Wenshizhe chubanshe, 1985, 6–7.

Li Mujiang

Li Mujiang, the wife of Cheng Wenju (Cheng Wenju Qi Li Mujiang), fl. 89–105,
was from Nanzheng (in present-day Shaanxi Province); Mujiang was her *zi,* but her
personal name has not been recorded.

Li Mujiang was the second wife of Cheng Wenju of Hanzhong (the present-day city
of Hanzhong in Shaanxi Province), who was Magistrate of Anzhong District (present-day Nanyang in Henan Province). She was also an elder sister of Li Fa, Palace
Attendant and Grand Master for Splendid Happiness (*shizhong guanglu dafu*) and
Governor of Runan during the reign of Emperor He (Liu Zhao, 78–104; r. 89–104). Li
Fa was an upright and morally respectable man, but he had offended the emperor by
submitting an admonitory memorial and had been downgraded to commoner status.
He remained outspoken after he was reinstated as an official and did not hesitate to
remonstrate with the court in a direct and impassioned manner. Li Mujiang, an amiable
and kind woman, also understood moral principles and was unfailingly benevolent
and dutiful.

Cheng Wenju died in office, of illness, leaving Li Mujiang to care for her two sons
as well as his four sons from his first marriage. Her four stepsons disliked Li Mujiang
intensely for the simple reason that she was not their mother and they incessantly spoke
badly of her. Li Mujiang was not provoked by this, however, and took even greater
care of them than she did of her biological sons. She gave them better food, dressed
them in finer clothes, and provided other material comforts. So badly did her stepsons
behave, however, that people advised Li Mujiang to divide up the family property and
live apart from them. She insisted that it was more profitable for her stepsons that she
stay and teach them by virtue of her own kind deeds, so as to bring them back to the
path of goodness.

The turning point in this relationship came when Cheng Xin, her eldest stepson,
fell seriously ill. Li Mujiang cared for him lovingly through his long illness as if he
were her own son; she nursed him, brewed medicine, and prepared his meals herself.
When he finally recovered, Cheng Xin was so grateful for Li Mujiang's innate kindness and forgiving nature that he called his brothers together and went with them
to the prison officer in Nanzheng. There they told of their virtuous stepmother and
asked to be punished for not only having failed to be grateful to her but for having
repaid her with enmity. The local magistrate reported the case to the governor of the
commandery, who praised Li Mujiang's deeds and ordered that her family be exempt
from corvee. He then set her four stepsons free, offering them a chance to start anew,
and they did indeed become good men.

Li Mujiang enjoyed her later years and lived to over eighty. On her deathbed she reminded her sons that her brother Li Fa had been a wise and sensible man who left a will insisting on the least expensive burial. "That was the ultimate in righteousness and the deed of a saint," she told them. "I hope you will all follow his example and not go along with worldly customs to disgrace me." When she died, her wishes were respected and she was buried with the simplest ceremony.

Throughout her life, Li Mujiang had been generous and open-minded, able to live with a clear conscience. She was also able to maintain a very strong sense of self, even when faced with the enmity of her stepsons, an admirable trait in any stepmother.

SHEN Lidong

Hou Han shu. Beijing: Zhonghua shuju, 1965, vol. 10, 84.2793–94.
Liu Ziqing. *Zhongguo lidai xianneng funü pingzhuan.* Taipei: Liming wenhua, 1978, 134–35.

Liang Hong's Wife: *see* **Meng Guang**

Liang Ji's Wife: *see* **Sun Shou**

Liang Na, Empress of Emperor Shun
Liang Na (Shundi Liang Huanghou), 116–150, was empress to Emperor Shun (Liu Bao, 115–144; r. 126–144) and a member of the powerful Liang family that provided several empresses and concubines for Eastern Han emperors. She was a great-niece of Worthy Lady Liang, who was the natural mother of Emperor He (Liu Zhao, 78–104; r. 89–104) but had been murdered in 83 by Empress Dou (*q.v.* Dou, Empress of Emperor Zhang). The Liang family had suffered political eclipse for a time, but had been fully restored to political status at the capital in 97, and three brothers of the late Worthy Lady Liang were enfeoffed as marquises. Liang Na's father, Liang Shang, succeeded to his own father's fief in 126.

Liang Na's biography claims that a splendid light accompanied her birth, that she was skilled in women's work of spinning and needlework while she was still young, and that she could recite *The Analects* (Lunyu) and had studied *The Book of Songs* (Shi jing) by the age of nine. It is said, moreover, that she kept portraits of the worthy women celebrated in *Biographies of Eminent Women* (Lienü zhuan) always beside her to compare her conduct with theirs and remind herself of the moral standards she must seek to attain, while her father spoke admiringly of her as the means by which the Liang house would greatly prosper. Some of this may be true, but these are also the clichés by which Chinese history and legend may enhance the facts about any person of future consequence.

Liang Na was formally selected for the harem in 128, but her family connections were surely of major importance in gaining her entry and securing the emperor's attention. She was thirteen years old at the time by Chinese reckoning, and Emperor Shun was just one year older. Liang Na was accompanied by one of her paternal aunts: this second woman of the Liang family may have been young enough to attract the ruler's

158   LIANG NA

interest, but it is more probable that she served as an escort and guardian to her niece in the dangerous political milieu of the palace; she is in any case not heard of again.

The physiognomist who took part in the selection exclaimed at Liang Na's exceptional and most noble appearance, and when her fortune was tested by the techniques of oracle bones and *Book of Changes* (Yi jing), the signs were remarkably good. She was appointed Worthy Lady (*guiren*), the highest rank of concubine, and was especially favored by the emperor. With erudite quotations from the *Book of Changes* and *The Book of Songs,* however, she urged her consort not to devote all his attention to her lest she suffer the jealousy and calumny of others; we are told that the emperor was all the more impressed with her good sense.

Emperor Shun took the cap of manhood in 129, and by 132 the senior ministers were pressing for the appointment of an empress. Worthy Lady Liang was only one of four concubines to have attracted the young ruler, and the choice between favorites was uncertain. At one stage there was a proposal to decide the matter by casting lots, so that the spirits might decide, but senior officials of the Imperial Secretariat argued that there was a well-established hierarchy of criteria for such a significant decision. First came the question of family background, then the comparison of virtue; if virtue was equal, there was the consideration of age; and finally one should think of physical attraction. Upon this basis, Worthy Lady Liang was chosen as a woman of excellent family, and on 2 March 132 she was named empress.

The new empress's father, Liang Shang, was immediately made a palace attendant, a supernumerary post with right of regular access to the ruler, and his marquisate was increased in size and value. He also became colonel of a regiment in the Northern army, the central strategic reserve of the empire, and soon afterward was promoted again to be chief of the police at the capital, comparable in rank to a senior ministry. In 135, moreover, after refusing a previous offer, he accepted appointment as General-in-Chief (*dajiangjun*), formally a military post with command over the Northern army but, more significantly, providing authority over government at the highest level. On previous occasions under the Han, generals-in-chief had exercised the functions of a regent, and though Emperor Shun was of age, he was effectively sharing his rule with Liang Shang.

In the system and traditions of Han there was nothing unusual or inappropriate about the possession of such power by an imperial relative through marriage. As had been argued earlier, the empress should be a woman of good family, and one reason for this was the general recognition that she and her male relatives would hold power and influence at court. Liang Shang died in 141, but he was immediately succeeded as general-in-chief by his eldest son Liang Ji, and with the aid of his sister the empress in the inner palace, the Liang group continued to dominate the court.

We are told that Empress Liang continued to behave with intelligence and good will, that she took no false pride in the advancement her virtues had gained her, that she studied the lessons of the past with utmost care, and that whenever there was an eclipse she would make particular confession of her faults and failings. She did not, however, bear her husband any children, and when Emperor Shun died in 144, his only son was the infant Liu Bing (Emperor Chong, 143–145; r. 145), born the previous year to Beauty (*meiren*) Yu and proclaimed heir just a few months before his father's death.

According to the traditional constitution of Han, when an emperor died leaving a recognized heir who was under age, his empress, now entitled Empress Dowager, became regent for the infant successor. She took part in formal gatherings of the court, and the relationship was symbolized by the physical arrangements: while an emperor of full age and authority sat in the throne room facing south, if the ruler was a child his place was on the east of the dais, facing west, and the regent dowager was opposite him, in matching position but behind a screen. Beauty Yu, though she came of respectable family and had given Emperor Shun a daughter as well as a son, had not been awarded any special status before he died and she was now granted only the empty style of Great Lady (*dagu*).

Early in 145, after only a few months of nominal rule, the infant Emperor Chong was dead, and there was now no named heir to the throne. In these circumstances an empress dowager of Han acquired even greater power, for she had undisputed authority to choose the next emperor from any of the male members of the imperial family. In doing so, she could take such advice as she wished, but the matter was not open to public debate, nor was any minister of state, no matter how high his rank, entitled to effective intervention. The precedent for this dated back to Western Han but had been decisively confirmed by Empress Dowager Deng (*q.v.* Deng Sui, Empress of Emperor He) in 105 and 106.

So in 145 Empress Dowager Liang took counsel with her brother within the private quarters of the harem and after three weeks the choice fell upon Liu Zuan (Emperor Zhi, 138–146; r. 146), a great-great-grandson of Emperor Zhang. Eight years old by Chinese reckoning, Liu Zuan was the son of Liu Hong, Prince of Le'an, by the Lady Chen, a former singing girl who had been taken by the king but had not even been granted the position of concubine in his royal harem. Apart from the fact that he was old enough to avoid the risks of infant mortality and young enough to require the guidance of a regent, Liu Zuan was in no way superior to any other cadet of the imperial house, while his mother's ancestry left much to be desired. Another candidate for the throne appeared well qualified and had considerable support within the court; at twenty years of age, however, he would have had no need of the guidance of a regent and was therefore unacceptable to the Liang party.

One year later, Emperor Zhi was dead. Despite his youth, he had perceived the tight limits to his notional authority, but he was unfortunately not perceptive enough to appreciate the need to keep silent, and on one occasion he referred publicly to Liang Ji as "an overbearing general." A short time later the emperor was eating dumplings when he was seized by stomach cramps and died. It was traditionally argued that Liang Ji had poisoned the boy, but it may indeed have been bad cooking and the young emperor was perhaps naturally weak and sickly. What is most suspicious about the affair, however, is that even before Emperor Zhi's death the future Emperor Huan, Liu Zhi, then fifteen *sui,* had been called to the capital and was betrothed to Liang Nüying (*q.v.* Liang Nüying, Empress of Emperor Huan), younger sister of Empress Dowager Liang. Had Emperor Zhi been expected to reign for a normal lifetime, this young woman would

160   LIANG NA

surely have been committed to him in order to maintain the influence of her family. As it is, one may suspect that Liang Ji and his elder sister had early knowledge of his fate. The physicians were impeached and the death was investigated, but nothing came of it, and Liang Ji and his family were free to maintain their power.

For the next few years, Empress Dowager Liang held formal control of the government in association with her brother Liang Ji. The historians of Han have accused Liang Ji and his wife Sun Shou (*q.v.*) of inordinate greed, luxury, and extravagance. They may indeed have extorted great wealth from rival families, but Empress Dowager Liang herself is praised for her devotion to duty in difficult times, after the second great rebellion of the Qiang people in the northwest and a series of disturbances with the Xiongnu on the northern frontier. Inside China, reflecting these troubles, there were frequent small-scale rebellions, increased feuding among local gentry, and a gradual alienation from the imperial regime.

The government had been in serious financial straits since the first great Qiang rebellion of 107–118, and its general weakness was symbolized by the plundering of the tomb of Emperor Shun outside Luoyang within a year of his burial. The biography of Empress Dowager Liang in the *History of the Later Han Dynasty* (Hou Han shu) says that she was restrained and frugal, that she appointed good officials, sent out troops to deal with disorder, and that all the empire was settled by her efforts. One may observe a literary contrast between the worthy sister and the wicked brother, and both are no doubt exaggerated, but the empress dowager does well from the comparison.

Emperor Huan took the cap of manhood at the beginning of 148, but Empress Dowager Liang maintained her regency, on the grounds of the disturbances in the empire, for another two years. She formally relinquished her office in the first month of 150, and she died a few weeks later, on 6 April, at the age of thirty-four.

Rafe de CRESPIGNY

Hou Han shu. Beijing: Zhonghua shuju, 1965, vol. 2, 10*xia*438–40; vol. 5, 34 [*liezhuan* 24], 1178–87.

Liang Nüying, Empress of Emperor Huan

Liang Nüying (Huandi Liang Huanghou), c. 125–159, was empress to Emperor Huan (Liu Zhi, 132–167; r. 147–167). She was a younger sister of Liang Na (*q.v.* Liang Na, Empress of Emperor Shun). Her father was the General-in-Chief (*dajiangjun*) Liang Shang and her brother Liang Ji succeeded him in that position.

In 146, Liang Nüying's elder sister, now empress dowager and regent, arranged her betrothal to Liu Zhi, the Marquis of Liwu, then aged fifteen *sui,* whom the empress dowager had summoned to the capital. The throne was at that time occupied by the empress dowager's previous selection, the nine-year-old Emperor Zhi (Liu Zuan, 138–146; r, 146), but the boy had shown disapproval of Liang Ji's dominance over the court, and he died suddenly soon afterward. His death was investigated but nothing was found, though the betrothal of Liu Zhi and Liang Nüying throws considerable suspicion upon the affair: had the young emperor been expected to reign for a normal lifetime, Liang Nüying would surely have been betrothed to him. As it is, one must assume that Liang Ji and his elder sister had early knowledge of the boy's fate.

Liu Zhi (Emperor Huan) was immediately placed upon the throne, and Empress Dowager Liang maintained her regency. In the summer of the following year (147), Liang Nüying entered the imperial harem and in the autumn she was made empress. The marriage ceremony was modeled on precedents of 191 B.C.E., when the young Emperor Hui (r. 194–188 B.C.E.) had been under the authority of his biological mother, Empress Dowager Lü (*q.v.* Lü Zhi, Empress of Emperor Gaozu), and, perhaps more significantly, those of the year 4, when the young Emperor Ping (r. 1–5), last ruler of Western Han, was married to a daughter of Wang Mang. The betrothal money was 20,000 pounds of gold, while imperial presents to the bride's family included wild geese (because they follow the natural relationship of yin and yang), jade *bi*-rings, a team of four horses, and a quantity of bolts of silk. Inside the palace, it appears that the empress shared the extravagant tastes of her brother Liang Ji rather than the frugality of her sister the empress dowager. Her apartments and pavilions were expensively carved and ornamented, and her clothing and jewelry, trinkets, and brightly painted carriages were more ostentatious than those of any of her predecessors.

It is not possible to make a firm estimate of the age of Empress Liang. Her elder sister was born in 116, and her father died in 141. Many women came to the harem at the age of thirteen *sui,* but the age for general selection could be as high as twenty, and it is likely that in this special case the empress was in her early twenties, born in about 125 and some ten years younger than her sister. With support from her family to deal with eunuchs and other attendants within the harem, and with her own physical attractions to influence her young husband, it is not surprising that, as her biography says, she monopolized Emperor Huan's attentions and favors. During these first years, at least, no other women were permitted to approach him.

Emperor Huan took the cap of manhood at the beginning of 148, aged sixteen *sui,* but there was no real change to the political system of control: the empress dowager justified her continued exercise of power by emergencies at the frontier and internal rebellion, while Liang Ji controlled the troops and officials at the capital. Early in 150, however, Empress Dowager Liang formally ended the regency and a few weeks later she was dead.

In practical terms this made little difference, for Liang Ji's authority over the court as general-in-chief was unimpaired and Empress Liang was well placed to supervise the inner palace. On the other hand, Emperor Huan now possessed a little more freedom, which he expressed in the first instance by inviting his mother, Worthy Lady Yan Ming (*q.v.*), to come to Luoyang and take up residence in the Northern Palace. At the same time, his personal relationship with the empress was naturally weakened. The fact that she was expected to maintain some surveillance over him on behalf of her family caused inevitable tension; also, she had not borne an imperial son and heir, and we may assume that the charms of an older woman were less fascinating to a young man of eighteen than they had been to an *ingénu* three years earlier.

From this time, therefore, Emperor Huan embarked upon the sexual career that was to make him celebrated in Chinese history. With little opportunity for political

162 *LIANG NÜYING*

involvement outside the palace, the emperor gave his attention to a vast number of concubines, one after another, and sometimes several at once. His fluctuating favors encouraged intrigue among the women of the harem, and gave frequent opportunity for patronage and self-advancement to the senior eunuchs who arranged to satisfy his wishes.

In some respects it served the interests of the Liang family that the emperor should distract himself in this way, and though the empress may have been jealous and frustrated, she had no means to affect her husband's choice of partners. What she could do, however, was control the results, and in a telling passage the histories remark, "if a woman of the palace became pregnant, she seldom reached full term." How many concubines suffered miscarriage or induced abortion, we do not know, nor do we know how many children were stillborn or killed at birth. It appears that only one child, the Princess Hua, was born at this time and survived to maturity.

In the autumn of 159 Empress Liang died. She was probably in her mid-thirties, about the same age as her elder sister the empress dowager had been at the time of her death nine years earlier. There is no reason to believe the empress did not die of natural causes, but her demise was evidently unexpected and brought an immediate crisis in the central government of the empire. Within a few weeks Liang Ji and his clan had been destroyed by a coup of the emperor supported by his eunuchs and, with the installation of Empress Deng (*q.v.* Deng Mengnü, Empress of Emperor Huan), the former empress was posthumously demoted to the senior concubine's rank of worthy lady (*guiren*).

Rafe de CRESPIGNY

Crespigny, Rafe de. *Emperor Huan and Emperor Ling.* Canberra: Australian National University, Faculty of Asian Studies, 1989, vol. 1, 8–14.
———. "The Harem of Emperor Huan: A Study of Court Politics in Later Han." *Papers on Far Eastern History* 12 (1975): 4–11.
Hou Han shu. Beijing: Zhonghua shuju, 1965, vol. 2, 10*xia*.443–44; vol, 5, 34 [*liezhuan* 24], 1178–87.

Liu Bian's Wife; *see* **Tang, Consort of Prince Hongnong**

Liu Changqing Qi Huan Shi: *see* **Huan, Liu Changqing's Wife**

Liu Dan's Wife: *see* **Hua Rong, Consort of Prince of Yanla**

Liu Jieyou
Liu Jieyou, 121–49 B.C.E., also known as Princess Jieyou (Jieyou Gongzhu) and Princess of Wusun, was not as closely related by blood to the reigning Han imperial family as was Liu Xijun (*q.v.*), but, like her, she was from a disgraced branch of the family. She may be one of the very few princess brides whose natal name is known to us. Her grandfather, the Prince of Chu (present-day Anhui Province), had an incestuous relationship and in 154 B.C.E. committed suicide after participating in the

failed rebellion of the seven princes. Liu Jieyou was born thirty-three years after her grandfather's crime, and had she remained in Han territory she would have been labeled the descendant of a political criminal and lived out her days as a palace servant. But designation as a princess bride in 101 launched her on a half-century of excitement and considerable influence in the western region of China. She became wife to three Wusun kings; mother, grandmother, and great-grandmother to three other Wusun kings; mother to the King of Suoju; and mother-in-law and grandmother to Kucha kings. Wusun, Suoju, and Kucha were states in the western region, Wusun being the most powerful at that time.

In order to isolate the Xiongnu tribes to the north of China, the Western Han dynasty, under Emperor Wu (r. 140–87 B.C.E.), did not want to terminate the marriage alliance with the Wusun that he had initiated with Liu Xijun. Therefore, after the princess Liu Xijun died in 101, Liu Jieyou was immediately sent out as her replacement. She thus married Cenzou (Junxumi), the King of Wusun and Liu Xijun's second husband. Unlike Liu Xijun, Liu Jieyou did not protest having to comply with the Wusun's custom of the levirate, or a widow marrying her husband's male relative, and when Cenzou died she remarried a second and a third time. Her second marriage to Wengguimi (Fat King), the new Wusun king and Cenzou's nephew, lasted over three decades (from about 99 to 65 B.C.E.) and produced three sons and two daughters.

Although Wengguimi had a Xiongnu wife whose position as Lady of the Left was senior to Liu Jieyou's as Lady of the Right, Liu Jieyou played an active role in Wusun politics and relations with the western region of China. From 87 to 71 B.C.E. she helped to transform the western region from Xiongnu domination to Chinese influence. In fact, it could be said that before the protectorate of the western region was established in 60 B.C.E., Liu Jieyou was the unofficial liaison representative between Han China and the western region. In the next decade she and Wengguimi repeatedly wrote to the Han emperor asking for help against the Xiongnu, who had demanded that Wengguimi surrender Liu Jieyou. China sent 150,000 soldiers from five directions to the region and in 71 B.C.E. the Xiongnu and Jushi were defeated, thus strengthening Han's relations with Wusun. Liu Jieyou's maid Feng Liao (*q.v.*), who was knowledgeable in history and classics as well as practical matters, was married to a Wusun general whose connections with the aristocracy of the Wusun and the western region facilitated her mediation work as Liu Jieyou's envoy in the western region states. In particular, Feng Liao was instrumental in securing the succession of Liu Jieyou's son in 53 and strengthening the reign of her grandson Xingmi in 51.

In 65 B.C.E., Liu Jieyou had probably persuaded Wengguimi to write to the Han court seeking a Han princess for their eldest son, Yuanguimi, whom they intended to be Wengguimi's successor. The Han designated Liu Xiangfu, the daughter of Liu Jieyou's younger brother, as the bride, but when her entourage arrived at Dunhuang it was turned back because Wengguimi had just died and Yuanguimi did not immediately succeed as the new Wusun king.

Instead, Nimi (Mad King), who was the son of Liu Jieyou's first husband by his Xiongnu wife, obtained the throne in 64 and married Liu Jieyou. The *History of the Han Dynasty* (Han shu) and other historical sources indicate that Liu Jieyou had a son, Chimi, with Nimi, but this seems unlikely, given that she would have been fifty-seven years old when he was born; this is a notable point that appears to have been ignored, or not noticed, by primary and secondary sources. Nimi was a brutal king and theirs was a tumultuous marriage. Liu Jieyou plotted to have him assassinated, but he escaped, only to be killed by Wujiutu, the son of Wengguimi and his Xiongnu wife. In 53, Wujiutu set himself up as the King of Wusun but was persuaded by Feng Liao to agree to the division of Wusun territory and take the title of Lesser King, while Yuanguimi, Liu Jieyou's son and Wujiutu's stepbrother, became the Greater King. Yuanguimi died of illness in 51, and Chimi, whom the histories claim, probably erroneously, to have been Liu Jieyou's youngest son, died at the same time. Half a century after her departure from Han China, Liu Jieyou, now seventy *sui,* wrote that year to the Han emperor requesting permission to return to Han territory because she was old and homesick and wanted her bones to be buried in native soil. In the capital Chang'an she was treated with the respect and luxury due to an imperial princess, and when she died two years later, her three grandchildren, who had accompanied her on the journey, remained to tend her grave.

During the time spent in Wusun, Liu Jieyou and her descendants were deeply involved in the politics and cultural exchange between the western region and Han China. Her second son, Wannian, became king of the state of Suoju around 70 B.C.E. when its king, who was without an heir, appointed Wannian, whom he loved, as his successor. Wannian was in Han territory at the time of the king's death and he hastened back to Suoju to accept the kingship. But Wannian turned out to be a bad king, and he was killed in 65 by the previous king's brother, who then set himself up as king.

Liu Jieyou's elder daughter had a longer and greater impact on Kucha (Qiuzi), another state in the western region. In 71 B.C.E., Han China attacked Kucha with 50,000 men. Jiangbin, Kucha's king, sued for peace with the Han dynasty and sent a mission to Wusun requesting permission to marry a daughter of Liu Jieyou. Liu Jieyou's elder daughter, Dishi, happened to be passing through Kucha at that time on her return home from Chang'an, where she had been receiving a musical education. The Kucha king detained her and, with her mother's permission, married her. The marriage was a happy one, and the couple went to Chang'an in 65, stayed for a year, and returned to Kucha with generous gifts. They visited Chang'an several more times, and liked Han culture so much that they adopted Han architecture and rituals such as gongs and symbols for announcing the arrival of guests. Their son Chengde (a Chinese name), who succeeded to the Kucha throne, considered himself a maternal grandson of the Han dynasty; he had frequent communication and close relations with Han China between 32 and 1 B.C.E.

There is more information on Liu Jieyou than on Liu Xijun because the former resided for such a long period in Wusun and the western region. The sources are either vague or contradictory on the dates of Liu Jieyou's marriages and the deaths of her second and third husbands. This biography follows the *History of the Han Dynasty,* the most contemporaneous material, rather than *Zizhi tongjian,* whose dates and sequences are problematic.

Jennifer W. JAY

Han shu. Beijing: Zhonghua shuju, 1962, vol. 7, 36.1923–24; vol. 12, 96*xia.*3904.

Hulsewé, A.F.P. *China in Central Asia. The Early Stage: 125 B.C.–A.D. 23.* Leiden: Brill, 1979.

Jagchid, Sechin, and Van Jay Symons. *Peace, War, and Trade Along the Great Wall. Nomadic-Chinese Interaction Through Two Millennia.* Bloomington: Indiana University Press, 1989, 12–43.

Loewe, Michael. *A Biographical Dictionary of the Qin, Former Han and Xin Periods.* Leiden: Brill, 2000, 320; 366–67.

Pan Yihong. "Marriage Alliances and Chinese Princesses in International Politics from Han Through T'ang." *Asia Major* 10, no. 1–2 (1997): 99–100.

Shi ji. Beijing: Zhonghua shuju, 1959, vol. 10, 123.3174.

Sima Guang. *Zizhi tongjian.* Beijing: Zhonghua shuju, 1956, vol. 2, *juan* 25–27.

Liu Lanzhi

Liu Lanzhi is said to have lived in the Ji'an period (196–220) and to have been the wife of Jiao Zhongqing of late Eastern Han. There is, however, no evidence that she was a real person. Made famous in the ballad *The Peacock Flies Southeast* (Kongque dongnan fei), she typifies the daughter-in-law who suffered under the tyrannical hold of her mother-in-law. Her story resonated through the ages because this situation was so common in traditional China; it was eventually inscribed on the psyche of Chinese women, each generation producing its own Liu Lanzhi.

The ballad tells of Jiao Zhongqing, a petty official from Lujiang (in present-day Anhui Province), who married a young woman named Liu Lanzhi. The couple loved one another but Jiao Zhongzing's mother accused Liu Lanzhi of being disobedient and self-willed and told her son to rid himself of his young wife. Jiao Zhongqing initially resisted but eventually decided to appease his mother. Required to be absent from home for a time on account of his work, he bid Liu Lanzhi return to her natal home, promising to fetch her when he returned.

However, in the meantime a matchmaker made Liu Lanzhi's family a good offer of marriage for her. She was able to persuade her mother to decline this offer, but when a second, even better, offer was made her brother was keen to accept it. Liu Lanzhi understood that her brother was the real master of the house and that she had little choice but to comply with his wishes. Jiao Zhongqing, hearing of this proposed marriage, took leave from his office. When he reached Liu Lanzhi's home she heard his horse and went out to meet him. He congratulated her on an excellent match, but she answered that neither of them was free to do what they wanted. In parting, they swore to see each other in the nether world and that evening Liu Lanzhi drowned herself in a pond. When Jiao Zhongqing was told this news, he hanged himself on the southeastern branch of a tree. The families of the lovers agreed to bury them together and planted beautiful trees around their grave. A pair of birds appeared in these trees and sang to each other every night, a sad reminder of this unfortunate couple.

An English translation of this ballad, under the title *A Peacock Southeast Flew,* can be found in *New Songs from a Jade Terrace,* Anne Birrell's translation of the anthology *Yutai xinyong.* As with Mulan (*q.v.*), whose life is also celebrated in a famous ballad, Liu Lanzhi may never have existed. Her lasting legacy, however, is that she represented many women who had similar experiences.

Lily Xiao Hong LEE

166   *LIU LANZHI*

Birrell, Anne, trans. *New Songs from a Jade Terrace: An Anthology of Early Chinese Love Poetry*. London: Allen & Unwin, 1982, 53–62.

Ding Fubao, ed. *Quan Han Sanguo Jin Nanbeichao shi*. Taipei: Shijie shuju, 1978, vol. 1, 4.81–84.

Xu Ling, comp. *Yutai xinyong,* Sibubeiyao ed., 1.19b–25b.

Liu Piao, the Grand Princess

Liu Piao, the Grand Princess (Zhang Gongzhu Piao), c. 190–?130/120 B.C.E., was born in what is now Yanmen Pass in Shanxi Province. She was the eldest daughter of Liu Heng (202–157 B.C.E., then Prince of Dai, but later to become Emperor Wen, r. 179–157 B.C.E.) and his concubine Lady Dou (later to become Empress Dou, *q.v.* Dou Yifang, Empress of Emperor Wen). She was also the older sister of Liu Qi (Emperor Jing, 188–141 B.C.E.; r. 156–141 B.C.E.). She was granted the title Princess of Guantao when her father became emperor, and after marrying Chen Wu, a grandson of Chen Ying, Marquis of Tangyi, she gave birth to a daughter whom they named Chen Jiao (*q.v.* Chen Jiao, Empress of Emperor Wu).

During the reign of her brother, Liu Piao was free to come and go in the court. Her beloved daughter Chen Jiao (whose nickname was Ajiao) therefore grew up in the rear palaces with her maternal cousin Liu Che (Emperor Wu, 156–87 B.C.E.; r. 140–87 B.C.E.). Liu Piao paid a great deal of attention to Liu Che, who was granted the title Prince of Jiaodong when he was four years old. One day in his residence she sat him on her lap and, pointing to his maids, asked him if he wanted a beautiful wife. None of the maids pleased the boy, but when Liu Piao pointed to Chen Jiao and asked the same question he replied with delight: "If I could have Ajiao as my wife I would build a house of gold for her!" However, Liu Piao was ambitious and when another of the emperor's sons, Liu Rong, was appointed heir apparent she approached his mother, Concubine Li (Xiao Jing Li Ji), proposing a marriage between their children. To Liu Piao's great surprise, Concubine Li rejected her proposal, leading her to put the marriage proposal to Consort Wang (*q.v.* Wang Zhi, Empress of Emperor Jing), the mother of Liu Che, who accepted immediately on her son's behalf.

This incident saw a worsening of relations between Liu Piao and Concubine Li. Liu Piao felt a deep hatred for Concubine Li, whose refusal had foiled her ambitions for her daughter to be consort of the heir apparent. For her part, Concubine Li had already fallen out of favor with the emperor, and she blamed Liu Piao, who had introduced beauties to the emperor whom he favored over her, for this reversal in her fortunes. Liu Piao therefore spoke ill of Concubine Li in the presence of the emperor, while praising Liu Che, the son of Consort Wang. Emperor Jing began to dislike Concubine Li and, because he had always been fond of his son Liu Che, he considered removing Concubine Li's son from the position as heir apparent and appointing Liu Che instead. Ostensibly to formalize the existing situation, Consort Wang persuaded officials to suggest to the emperor that he elevate Concubine Li (as mother of the heir apparent) to the position of empress. Enraged at this suggestion, Emperor Jing dismissed Liu Rong as heir apparent, appointed seven-year-old Liu Che in his place, and made Consort Wang his empress. Liu Piao was extremely satisfied with this outcome, since her daughter was now to be consort to the heir apparent.

Liu Che ascended the throne when he was sixteen years old and appointed Chen Jiao his empress. After ten years of marriage, however, she had not borne him any children; she was also overbearing and jealous, while her mother, Liu Piao, had become exceedingly greedy. The emperor grew disgusted with both of them and transferred his affections to Wei Zifu (*q.v.* Wei Zifu, Empress of Emperor Wu), who had been brought into the palace on the recommendation of his eldest sister, the Princess of Pingyang. Empress Chen attempted suicide to regain the emperor's favor and resorted to sorcery and incantations, performed by a witch named Chu Fu. When these activities were brought to light Chu Fu and some 300 others were put to death, while Empress Chen was deposed and sent to live in Changmen Palace. Undaunted, Liu Piao complained to the Princess of Pingyang about the emperor's ungratefulness in abandoning his empress, claiming that he would not have become emperor without Liu Piao's help. While the princess explained that Empress Chen had been deposed simply because she had not produced any children, the emperor argued that he had been unable to do otherwise, since "the empress engaged in unlawful activities." Though Empress Chen had been deposed, he told Liu Piao, she was living in great comfort in Changmen Palace. This effectively silenced Liu Piao, who could do no more for her daughter.

Liu Piao had long been a widow when, in her early fifties (c. 138), she took as her lover a handsome young servant named Dong Yan. Dong Yan visited Liu Piao's house with his mother, who made her living selling jewelry, and Liu Piao was so taken with him that she retained him as a servant. She gave him gifts and ensured he received an education. Dong Yan was an amiable young man; he acted as Liu Piao's groom as well as her servant and her lover. However, Dong Yan's close friend Yuan Shu suggested to him that he might be committing a crime of some sort by having a secret liaison with Liu Piao, a princess of the imperial house. Yuan Shu also suggested that, as a precaution, Liu Piao be persuaded to offer to Emperor Wu the Changmen Gardens, which he had long desired. All went according to plan and the emperor transformed the gardens into the Changmen Palace, using it as a place of recreation.

Some time later, Yuan Shu hatched a further plot involving Dong Yan and Liu Piao, his aim this time being to have Dong Yan received by the emperor. Liu Piao therefore pretended to be ill and, as expected, Emperor Wu (her nephew and son-in-law) called on her to show his concern for her well-being. They exchanged the usual pleasantries, Liu Piao assuring the emperor that she was well satisfied with the rank and income that had been assigned to her. All she wished, she told him, was that he visit her from time to time so that she would have the opportunity to entertain him. On recovering from her feigned illness Liu Piao asked to again see the emperor, who prepared a feast for her costing some ten million cash. Several days later, the emperor again called at her residence. Dressed as a commoner, Liu Piao went to greet him, but the emperor immediately asked to meet "the lord of the house," meaning Dong Yan. This so frightened Liu Piao that she removed her jewelry, her hair ornaments, and her shoes and apologized with lowered head for her crime of disgracing the imperial family by having illicit relations with a servant. As soon as Emperor Wu pardoned her, however, she put her jewelry, her hair ornaments, and her shoes back on and went to the east wing to fetch Dong Yan. Also dressed as a commoner, Dong Yan knelt while Liu Piao addressed the emperor: "Dong

Yan, the cook of Princess of Guantao [Liu Piao], risks death to pay his humble respects to Your Majesty." When, however, the emperor ordered official garb for Dong Yan, so relieved and pleased was Liu Piao that she immediately served her best wine and herbal tonics. She then proposed that all the generals and marquis present be rewarded with gifts of money, hoping that Dong Yan would win their support. It was in this way that Dong Yan received the emperor's favor. In the emperor's company he frequently enjoyed such amusements as hunting, horseback riding, watching cockfights, shuttlecock, and horse and dog races. Emperor Wu was delighted and ordered a special feast in honor of Liu Piao, requesting that Dong Yan attend.

As the emperor was about to enter Xuanshi Palace, however, he was stopped by the Superior Grand Master of the Palace (*taizhong dafu*) Dongfang Shuo. Lance in hand, Dongfang Shuo dissuaded Emperor Wu from bringing Dong Yan into the palace on the grounds that the young man had committed three crimes serious enough to deserve capital punishment. He enumerated the crimes as corrupting moral values by having a secret liaison with a princess, disrupting matrimonial etiquette and the relations between men and women, and causing harm to imperial institutions by his debauchery. Dongfang Shuo said that the emperor was young and still accumulating knowledge about the six classics and court affairs, but it was clear that Dong Yan did not respect the classics, nor was he concerned with encouraging the emperor in learning. Instead, Dong Yan was urging the emperor to a decadent debauched life of taking pleasure in dogs, horses, dancing, and music. "Such a man," Dongfang Shuo said, "could not be admitted to the stately palace [of Xuangshi]." Emperor Wu was therefore obliged to hold his feast in the North Palace and make Dong Yan enter through the Outer Palace Gates (Sima men).

After that the emperor lost interest in Dong Yan, who died not long afterward at the age of thirty. Liu Piao, who had by then been appointed Grand Princess, died a few years after Dong Yan and was buried by his side in Baling. As an imperial princess, Liu Piao was allowed considerable freedom in her personal life and was able to manipulate her relationships with her brother and her nephew, both emperors of Han.

BAO Shanben

Han shu. Beijing: Zhonghua shuju, 1983, vol. 9, 64*xia*.2853–56; vol. 12, 97*shang*.3946–48.
Loewe, Michael. *Crisis and Conflict in Han China: 104 BC to AD 9.* London: George Allen & Unwin, 1974, 49–51, 88.
Shi ji. Beijing: Zhonghua shuju, 1982, vol. 4, 49.1976–77.
Sima Guang. *Zizhi tongjian.* Beijing: Zhonghua shuju, 1956, vol. 1, 17–18 passim.

Liu Xijun

Liu Xijun, ?123–101 B.C.E., also known as Princess Xijun (Xijun Gongzhu), Princess of Wusun, and Princess of Jiangdu, came from a disgraced branch of the Han imperial family. She may be one of the very few princess brides whose natal name is known to us. Her grandfather Liu Fei, a brother of Emperor Wu (r. 140–87 B.C.E.), had won merit by quelling the revolt of the seven princes in 154 B.C.E. and become the Prince of Jiangdu (present-day Jiangsu and Zhejiang provinces). Her father, Liu Jian, who inherited the title and territory in 127, was described as brutal, incestuous, and depraved. Six years later, when Liu Xijun was an infant, he was implicated in a rebellion and forced to commit suicide; in the same year, her mother was publicly executed for practicing witchcraft. As minor children in a criminal family, the orphaned Liu Xijun and her siblings were probably brought up in palaces as slaves or servants.

Sixteen years after the death of her parents, Liu Xijun was elevated in 105 to the status of princess when Emperor Wu married her off to Wusun, the most powerful state in the western region. The purpose of this marriage was to conclude a diplomatic alliance intended to break the menacing Xiongnu confederacy (the Xiongnu were a tribal people on China's northern border; they are generally known as the Huns in Western works). After the Han court received the betrothal gift of 1,000 horses, Liu Xijun's new staff of several hundred officials, servants, and eunuchs accompanied her on the journey of nearly 3,000 miles (5,000 km) from Chang'an (present-day Xi'an) to Wusun. Located in the Ili valley between Lake Balkash and Issykkul, Wusun had a population of 630,000, or just over 1 percent of Han China's population of 58 million. On arrival Liu Xijun became the Lady of the Right to Lieqiaomi, the aging *kunmo* or King of Wusun, whose Lady of the Left, a Xiongnu princess, enjoyed higher status. Liu Xijun experienced great difficulty with the language and communicating with the *kunmo,* whom she saw only once or twice a year. When the *kunmo* used the pretext of his old age to divorce her and give her up to his grandson Cenzou (Junxumi), Xijun protested to Emperor Wu. She wrote to him that such a marriage, which would require her to marry her step-grandson, violated Chinese propriety. Emperor Wu was unsympathetic and instructed her to comply with the customs of Wusun, so as to reinforce his overall strategy of uniting with Wusun to isolate the Xiongnu. Liu Xijun's marriage to Cenzou, who became King of Wusun upon the death of her first husband, produced a daughter, Shaofu. Liu Xijun died in 101 B.C.E., having adjusted poorly to nomadic food, clothing, residence, and customs in the four or five years she spent in Wusun as wife to two successive kings. Given this short time in Wusun in relative isolation from Wusun society and without producing a male heir, her influence on Han foreign relations was limited.

The *History of the Han Dynasty* (Han shu) monograph on the western region ascribes a poem to Liu Xijun describing her homesickness:

> My family married me off—other side of heaven,
> Entrusting my welfare to a foreign country—the King of Wusun.
> The yurt my residence—the felt my wall,
> Meat my food—fermented milk my drink.
> Living here, constantly longing for my native soil—a broken heart.
> Would that I change into a yellow heron—homeward bound!

Her words moved Emperor Wu, who sought in vain to console her with envoys and gifts every other year. More importantly, the poem has preserved the memory of her brief and sorrowful life as a princess bride in the history of Chinese-nomadic relations.

Jennifer W. JAY

170 LIU XIJUN

Han shu. Beijing: Zhonghua shuju, 1962, vol. 8, 53.2414; 2416–17; vol. 12, 96*xia*.3901–3.

Hulsewé, A.F.P. *China in Central Asia. The Early Stage: 125 B.C.–A.D. 23.* Leiden: Brill, 1979.

Jagchid, Sechin, and Van Jay Symons. *Peace, War, and Trade Along the Great Wall. Nomadic-Chinese Interaction Through Two Millennia.* Bloomington: Indiana University Press, 1989, 142–43.

Loewe, Michael. *A Biographical Dictionary of the Qin, Former Han and Xin Periods.* Leiden: Brill, 2000, 316–17, 377.

Pan Yihong. "Marriage Alliances and Chinese Princesses in International Politics from Han Through T'ang." *Asia Major* 10, no. 1–2 (1997): 98–99.

Sima Guang. *Zizhi tongjian.* Beijing: Zhonghua shuju, 1956, vol. 2, *juan* 21.

Yu Ying-shih. "Han Foreign Relations." In *The Cambridge History of China. The Ch'in and Han Empires, 221 B.C.–A.D. 220,* ed. Denis Twitchett and Michael Loewe. Cambridge, U.K.: Cambridge University Press, 1986, 405–21.

Liu Yuan

Liu Yuan, Princess of Xinye (Deng Chen Qi Xinye Gongzhu Liu Yuan), d. 22, was the wife of Deng Chen (d. 49) of Xinye, Nanyang Commandery (present-day Xinye District, Henan Province); she bore him a son and three daughters. Orphaned as a child, Liu Yuan was a descendant of Emperor Gaozu (Liu Bang, 256–195 B.C.E.; r. 206–195 B.C.E.), founder of the Western Han dynasty, and a sister of Emperor Guangwu (Liu Xiu, 6 B.C.E.–57 C.E.; r. 25–57 C.E.), founder of the Eastern Han dynasty.

In the tenth month of 22, during the interregnum of Wang Mang's Xin dynasty, two of Liu Yuan's brothers—Liu Yan and Liu Xiu—took part in a rebellion in Yuan District (the present-day city of Nanyang, Henan Province). This was by no means a well-organized rebellion of precision troops. Liu Yan began his uprising by recruiting peasants from Xingshi and Pinglin to attack Wang Mang's forces in the west and rode an ox as he led his untrained troops. It was not until he killed the district defender of Xingye that he had a horse of his own.

After taking Tutangzi Village, Liu Xiu killed the district defender of Huyang, then traveled to Jiyang, where he and his fellow rebel Deng Chen joined forces. In the ensuing battle of Little Chang'an, Liu Xiu was defeated. A heavy fog rolled in and the families of his generals dispersed. Liu Xiu galloped off on horseback to find his missing family and on the way to his home he came upon his youngest sister, Liu Boji. He took her up onto his horse and continued on his way. Not long after, he met Liu Yuan and her three daughters on the road. Liu Xiu told his sister to mount the horse with him and Liu Boji but Liu Yuan refused, saying: "You go on and leave me here, Wenshu [Liu Xiu's *zi*]. It is important that you be victorious. The enemy is not far behind. You cannot save me and it will avail nothing if we are both killed." Liu Xiu kept calling out to her but Liu Yuan remained steadfast: "Go, go! You want to rescue me but I have my three daughters with me. They will be killed and then what point will there be for me to go on living?" With the enemy drawing ever closer, Liu Xiu had no choice but to ride away and leave her. Liu Yuan and her daughters were killed soon after.

Once installed as emperor, Liu Xiu promoted Liu Yuan's husband, Deng Chen, to Marquis of Fangzi and posthumously appointed Liu Yuan as Righteous and Martyred

Grand Princess of Xinye (Xinye Yijie Zhang Gongzhu). He had a temple built in the west of the district to mourn her death and he appointed Deng Fan (the eldest son of Deng Chen) Marquis of Wufang, with the responsibility of looking after the sacrifices at Liu Yuan's tomb. When Deng Chen died in 49, the emperor sent emissaries from the palace to prepare rituals for a princess to call Liu Yuan's spirit back home and then had her reburied in Beimang alongside Deng Chen. Emperor Guangwu and Empress Yin (*q.v.* Yin Lihua, Empress of Emperor Guangwu) attended the funeral.

Liu Yuan is an example of perception and decisive action. In a life-and-death crisis, she swiftly assessed the situation and made a decision, first of all, not to be a burden to her brother and sister who were already mounted on the horse, and, second, not to abandon her daughters in order to save her own life. However, her brother, the future emperor, remembered her as a righteous martyr. She is also remembered for her devotion to her daughters, refusing to leave them in the face of certain death. She was indeed a woman of great courage, devotion, and determination.

WANG Bugao

Hou Han shu. Beijing: Zhonghua shuju, 196, vol. 1, 1.2–3; vol. 3, 15.582–84.
Li Fang. *Taiping yulan.* Beijing: Zhonghua shuju, 1960, 441.9.

Liyu

Liyu is believed to have lived during the Han dynasty, but nothing is known of her origins. She was the wife of Huoli Zigao, who was in charge of a Korean ferry pier.

One morning Huoli Zigao rose early and as he poled his boat along the river he saw an old man, his white hair disheveled and with a crazy look about him, walking upstream along the bank. He was holding a pot in one hand and following him was a woman who must have been his wife, as she was trying to catch him. Suddenly, the old man fell into the river and he drowned. The old man's wife extemporized a song to express her grief, accompanying herself on a *konghou* (an ancient musical instrument like a harp). "I asked you not to cross the river, my dear, but you crossed it anyway. You fell in and now you are dead. What more could I have done?" Her song was full of sadness, and when she had sung her song she, too, plunged into the river and drowned. Huoli Zigao told his wife, Liyu, of this tragic affair when he returned home and so moved was she that she played the song to a tune on the *konghou*. Whenever she played it her listeners wept, and eventually Liyu taught the song to a local girl named Lirong.

Liyu's tune, which was titled *Konghou Prelude* (Konghou yin), was in the form of an ancient folksong and told in simple language the tragic story of two ordinary people. It was melodious and gentle, sighs interspersed with the singing. Indeed, it was a heartbreakingly sad song. Given that Liyu lived on the Chinese-Korean border and clearly had neither status nor connections with literati, it is remarkable that her song, and her authorship of it, gained prominence and was passed down through the ages. It is very possible, however, that hers was one of the innumerable folksongs collected from all over China after Emperor Wu (r. 140–87 B.C.E.) created the Music Bureau

172 *LIYU*

(Yuefu) during the Western Han dynasty. Nevertheless, Liyu must have been a skilled musician, and her fame may have spread quite far from her home on the border.

Konghou Prelude became the model for poems of later times based on this theme. Liu Xiaowei (Liang dynasty, 502–557), Zheng Zhengjian (Chen dynasty, 557–589), and the Tang dynasty poets Li Bai, Wang Jian, and Wen Tingyun all wrote *yuefu* (ballad-style) poetry with the title *Do Not Cross the River, My Dear.* The Tang poet Li He also composed a piece called *Konghou Yin.*

SHEN Lidong

Guo Maoqian, ed. *Yuefu shiji.* Beijing: Zhonghua shuju, 1979, vol. 2, 26.377–78.

Lü Exu: *see* Lü Zhi, Empress of Emperor Gaozu

Lü Mu: *see* Lü's Mother

Lü Xu

Lü Xu, d. 180 B.C.E., of Shanfu in Dang Commandery (present-day Shan District, Shandong Province), was a younger sister of Lü Zhi (*q.v.* Lü Zhi, Empress of Emperor Gaozu) and the wife of Fan Kuai (d. 189 B.C.E.).

Because the father of the Lü sisters was on good terms with District Magistrate Shan of Pei District, he decided to move there with his family to escape troubles in his native place. He was skilled at physiognomy and as soon as he laid eyes on Liu Bang (256–195 B.C.E.), then head of a local neighborhood but later to become Emperor Gaozu (r. 202–195), he decided this man had a powerful destiny. He therefore offered his older daughter Lü Zhi (the future Empress Lü) to Liu Bang in marriage. He also matched his younger daughter Lü Xu to a dog-meat vendor named Fan Kuai, who in time allied himself with Liu Bang in the struggle for control of China in the dying years of the Qin dynasty. As brothers-in-law as well as brothers-in-arms, the men were close, and Fan Kuai became a distinguished general in Liu Bang's army, appointed Marquis of Wuyang in gratitude for his loyalty in establishing the Han dynasty.

As Emperor Gaozu lay dying, word reached him that Fan Kuai was plotting with the Lü clan to murder the entire family of Liu Ruyi (d. 194 B.C.E.), the emperor's favorite son. Liu Ruyi was his child by the tragic Lady Qi (*q.v.* Qi, Concubine of Emperor Gaozu), who was soon to be murdered on the orders of Empress Lü. Outraged at the news of Fan Kuai's treachery, false though it turned out to be, the emperor ordered that Chen Ping (d. 178 B.C.E.), who was then Protector Commandant of the Center (*hujun zhongwei*), seek out Fan Kuai and behead him. Chen Ping was to be accompanied on this mission by Zhou Bo (Marquis of Jiang, d. 169 B.C.E.), who was commissioned to take over Fan Kuai's military post. On their way to find Fan Kuai, the two men decided that the emperor's orders had been issued in a moment of anger, since Fan Kuai had always been loyal and was related by marriage to the emperor. Fearing that Emperor Gaozu would later regret his decision, they decided to take Fan Kuai prisoner and bring him before the emperor. Chen Ping therefore summoned Fan Kuai, showed him

LÜ XU 173

his credentials, and had him transported back to Chang'an in a prisoners' carriage. On their way back, however, they received news that Emperor Gaozu had died.

With Fan Kuai imprisoned and in his charge, Chen Ping immediately worried that Lü Xu, Fan Kuai's wife, might speak ill of him to her sister, the bereaved Empress Lü (now Empress Dowager Lü). He therefore tried to forestall any misunderstanding by tearfully explaining the full story to the empress dowager, who responded by promoting him to Chamberlain for Attendants (*langzhongling*) and Mentor (*shifu*) to her son, the young Emperor Hui. As soon as Fan Kuai arrived in the capital, the empress dowager pardoned him, restoring his title and land. When Fan Kuai died a few years later, his son Fan Kang succeeded to the title of Marquis of Wuyang.

Emperor Hui was a kind and gentle young man who was so shocked at his mother's barbarous treatment of Lady Qi that he withdrew entirely from court life, thus allowing his mother to assume de facto rule of the empire. The empress dowager consolidated her power by appointing many of her relatives to positions of authority. After the death of her son in 188 she placed an infant on the throne, and when he died three years later she assumed full imperial power in her own name until her death in 180. It was during this latter period that Empress Dowager Lü appointed her sister Lü Xu Marquise of Linguang, the only time in Chinese history a woman was appointed marquise in her own right, not as the wife of a marquis. Although the Liu clan remained very powerful and many men of the family had been appointed as princes, marquis, ministers, or generals, Empress Dowager Lü continued to appoint members of her own clan to important posts. In addition, by proposing in 187 that all males of her clan be appointed princes she flouted the Oath of Baima—the White Horse Oath—whereby the people were to attack anyone not of the Liu clan (Emperor Gaozu's family) who was granted the title of Prince.

Chen Ping remained cautious as Empress Dowager Lü's power grew, and he was rewarded for his apparent support by promotion to Right Counselor-in-Chief (*you chengxiang*). When Lü Xu spoke ill of him in the presence of her sister, saying that he habitually drank and disported himself with women, Chen Ping was happy to play along with this false image in order to allay any doubts Empress Dowager Lü may have had about his loyalty, his dissolute behavior indicating he was unconcerned about the transference of power from the Liu clan to the Lü clan. His ploy was so successful that, in the presence of her sister, Empress Dowager Lü told Chen Ping not to "take seriously the gossiping of children and women. . . . Don't pay too much attention to what Lü Xu says about you."

Lü Xu, however, understood more than the empress dowager gave her credit for. During her final illness, in early 180, Empress Dowager Lü warned the men of her clan that they should delay the announcement of her death in order to gain time to consolidate military control over the imperial Liu clan. However, by the time she died in July, Lü Lu (a nephew of the empress dowager and of Lü Xu) and Lü Chan had only just begun preparing their attack. Chen Ping, Zhou Bo (now Defender-in-Chief), and Liu Zhang (Marquis of Zhu Xu) managed to force a distant Lü relative by the name of Li Ji to trick Lü Lu into handing military power over to Zhou Bo. Lü Lu so trusted Li Ji, in fact, that he would leave him in charge of his entire army while he himself went

174 LÜ XU

hunting. On one such occasion Lü Lu called on his aunt, Lü Xu, as he returned from hunting. In a fury, she accused him of having abandoned his army, without which the Lü clan was lost. Emptying her jewels and treasures on the floor, she said: "I don't want to keep these for others to enjoy."

A month after the death of Empress Dowager Lü, Zhou Bo and Liu Zhang had killed Lü Chan, seized control of the Northern and the Southern armies, and virtually exterminated the Lü clan, including Lü Xu's son Fan Kang, just as Lü Xu had predicted. They eventually caught Lü Lu and decapitated him, had Lü Xu flogged to death, and exposed their bodies in the marketplace. As a younger sister of Empress Dowager Lü, Lü Xu was a relatively minor player in the early years of the Han dynasty, and her clear perception of who should and should not be trusted could not, in the end, save her from the tragedy that engulfed her clan.

BAO Shanben

An Zuozhang, ed. *Hou fei zhuan*. Zhengzhou: Henan renmin chubanshe, 1990, 11–36.
Shi ji. Beijing: Zhonghua shuju, 1982, vol. 1, 9.406–10; vol. 4, 56.2058–61.
Sima Guang. *Zizhi tongjian*. Beijing: Zhonghua shuju, 1976, vol. 1, 12–13 passim.
Yang Youting. *Houfei waiqi zhuan zhengshi*. Xiamen: Xiamen daxue chubanshe, 1994, 17–35.

Lü Zhi, Empress of Emperor Gaozu

Lü Zhi (Gaozu Lü Huanghou), 241–180 B.C.E., also known as Lü Exu, from Shanfu in present-day Shandong Province, was empress of Emperor Gaozu (Liu Bang, 256–195 B.C.E.; r. 202–195 B.C.E.), founder of the Western Han dynasty, and after his death she ruled as regent for many years. She is usually cited as an exemplar of cruelty and ambition, a "hen crowing in the morning," but she brought a period of peace during which the country was able to recover from long years of civil war.

Her father had enemies but was on good terms with the magistrate of Pei District, so he moved there for reasons of safety. The magistrate gave a banquet in his honor that all the local gentry attended. Chief Administrator Xiao He (d. 193 B.C.E.) stipulated that those who offered cash gifts of less than ten coppers would not be admitted. The then neighborhood head, Liu Bang, despite being penniless, said he would give a cash gift of 10,000 coppers, thus securing for himself the seat of honor. Lü Zhi's father was interested in physiognomy and found Liu Bang's face so powerful that he betrothed his daughter to him. She later bore Liu Bang two children: a son (Liu Ying) who became Emperor Hui (210–188 B.C.E.) and a daughter who was later known as Princess Yuan of Lu.

During the chaotic last years of the Qin dynasty, Liu Bang was one of many who rose in rebellion. He suffered defeat in the year 205 B.C.E., however, and Lü Zhi and her father were taken hostage by Xiang Yu of Chu (*vide* Yu, Consort of the Hegemon-King of Chu). Lü Zhi was released two years later, after Chu and Han negotiated a peace, and in 202 Liu Bang ascended the throne; Lü Zhi became Empress Lü.

The official *History of the Han Dynasty* (Han shu) describes Empress Lü as a "resolute and steadfast" woman who helped the emperor establish his sovereignty over the whole country. It also says that she "played an important role in putting chief officials to death." An early example of this took place during a revolt in 197 B.C.E. led by Chen Xi. When Emperor Gaozu went to quell the revolt, Han Xin (d. 196 B.C.E.), the Marquis of Huaiyin, claiming to be ill, did not join forces with the emperor; instead he sent an envoy to conspire with Chen Xi to attack Empress Lü and the heir apparent. Learning of this conspiracy, Empress Lü consulted with Xiao He, now Counselor-in-Chief (*xiangguo*), and they spread the rumor that Chen Xi had died. This news required officials to go to court to offer their congratulations, thus deceiving Han Xin into appearing at court. Empress Lü ordered Han Xin captured and bound, and had him executed in the Changle Palace. During this same revolt, Empress Lü was also responsible for the death of Peng Yue (d. 196 B.C.E.), the Prince of Liang, who had been imprisoned in Luoyang on a probably false charge of conspiracy against Emperor Gaozu. The empress warned her husband of "a legacy of trouble" if he merely exiled Peng Yue, whom she described as a brave man, and advised the emperor to have Peng Yue killed. This he did.

Nor was the empress slow to heed advice herself. When Qing Bu, the Prince of Huainan, rebelled in 196 B.C.E., Emperor Gaozu was ill and suggested that the young heir apparent (Liu Ying) go in his stead to suppress the rebellion. The Four Old Men (*sihao;* four worthy men who refused to serve the Han emperor and became recluses) told the empress that her son should not go, whereupon she was able to convince the emperor not to send Liu Ying.

Liu Ying, known to history as Emperor Hui, ascended the throne in 195 B.C.E. upon the death of Emperor Gaozu, and Empress Lü was made Empress Dowager Lü. Previously, while still King of Han, Emperor Gaozu had fallen in love with a woman called Qi (*q.v.* Qi, Concubine of Emperor Gaozu) from Dingyao, whom he married and who bore him a son, Ruyi (d. 194 B.C.E.), the Prince of Zhao. The emperor had desired to appoint Ruyi heir apparent in place of Liu Ying, who was a weak but kindly youth. However, with the assistance of the Four Old Men and chief officials such as Zhang Liang (d. 189 B.C.E.) and Shusun Tong, Empress Lü had managed to thwart the push to advance Ruyi. Nevertheless, she harbored a deep hatred for Ruyi's mother, Lady Qi, and soon after Emperor Gaozu died, Empress Dowager Lü had Lady Qi imprisoned. She ordered her to be dressed in prison garb and to be put to work pounding rice; she then summoned Ruyi to court, where he was clearly in danger of his life, but the chief minister of Zhao, Zhou Chang, refused to let him go. She then summoned first the chief minister, then Ruyi. Knowing of his mother's hatred, the young Emperor Hui welcomed Ruyi into the palace as his guest in an attempt to protect him. Empress Dowager Lü eventually succeeded in having Ruyi killed when she found the opportunity to send someone to him with poisoned wine. She then had Lady Qi put to a barbarous death, ordering that her hands and feet be cut off, her eyes be gouged out, her ears be burned to deafen her, and that poison be poured into her mouth to destroy her vocal cords. She had Lady Qi confined to the sewage pit, calling her a "human pig," and summoned Emperor Hui to look upon her. The emperor was horrified at such barbarity and sent the following message to his mother: "This is utterly inhuman, and I am your son. Therefore, I am not fit to

176 *LÜ ZHI*

rule the country." From then on the emperor refrained from handling affairs of state, and Empress Dowager Lü became the de facto ruler.

Two aspects of Empress Dowager Lü's rule are noteworthy. The first is that she established good relations with neighboring countries, abandoned harsh policies, and created an environment that enabled the country and the people to gather strength. Her policy of benevolence included exempting those over seventy and under ten from physical punishment if they were found guilty of a crime, and reducing the crop tax to one-fifteenth of the harvest. The second is that she attempted to secure her power by granting titles to members of her natal Lü clan.

By 192 B.C.E. the Xiongnu to the north of China had grown strong enough for their *shanyu* (leader), a man named Maodun, to send an envoy to Empress Dowager Lü conveying a disrespectful message. Infuriated, Empress Dowager Lü nevertheless followed the advice of the official Ji Bu and, instead of attacking the Xiongnu, sent a return letter accompanied by gifts of chariots and horses. Relations improved and the empress finally sent a daughter of the imperial family to marry into the Xiongnu. In her later years, however, the empress neglected diplomacy, and the Southern Yue forces eventually attacked Changsha and several other cities.

Before his death, Emperor Gaozu had nominated Cao Can (d. 190 B.C.E.) as the next counselor-in-chief to succeed Xiao He. His second choice for the post had been Wang Ling (d. 181 B.C.E.), assisted by Chen Ping (d. 178 B.C.E.), with Zhou Bo (d. 169 B.C.E.) as defender-in-chief (*taiwei*). Cao Can assumed the post of counselor-in-chief in 193, and immediately adopted a policy of noninterference. Within three years, he had won over the people's hearts and minds.

Empress Dowager Lü exempted all men recommended as filial sons, loving brothers, or diligent farmers from corvee in 191 B.C.E. so that they might act as examples for the people. She declared a nationwide amnesty when her son, Emperor Hui, came of age, reviewed laws and decrees that interfered with officials and the common people, and annulled the statute forbidding people to carry or store books. After Cao Can died in 190, Wang Ling, Chen Ping, and Zhou Bo were appointed in accordance with Emperor Gaozu's deathbed wish. After Emperor Hui died in 188, another nationwide amnesty was declared and his three-year-old son Liu Gong was chosen as emperor. Empress Dowager Lü thus became sole ruler and the histories record this period under the name "Empress Lü." She was referred to as Female Ruler (*nüzhu*); she issued imperial decrees; and her reign was recorded in the "Annals" of the first-century B.C.E. *Historical Records* (Shi ji).

The empress acted benevolently toward the people, in 187 B.C.E. rescinding the decree that made heresy a crime and abolishing the punishment imposed on offenders' relatives who had not been involved in the crime. She reformed the currency and in 186 issued a *bashu* coin. In 183 she ordered that garrison soldiers be replaced annually instead of being left at their posts for an indefinite period.

As a means of securing her power, on the death of Emperor Hui the empress had it suggested to Counselor-in-Chief Wang Ling that Lü Tai, Lü Chan, and Lü Lu be appointed as generals to lead the Northern army and the Southern army and that other members of the Lü clan be summoned to court to fill important posts. When she proposed, the following year, that the title of Prince be granted to all male members of the Lü clan, Wang

Ling objected, claiming that this would contravene the Oath of Baima (that anyone not of the Liu clan, i.e., Emperor Gaozu's family, who is granted the title of Prince will be attacked by the people). She therefore demoted Wang Ling to Grand Mentor, causing him to resign, and promoted his former assistant Chen Ping to Right Counselor-in-Chief. As Left Counselor-in-Chief she appointed her favorite Hou Shiqi (d. 177 B.C.E.), whom the chief officials had to consult before making decisions; his responsibilities, however, were restricted to court affairs, like a chamberlain for attendants.

Before granting titles to her own Lü clan, the empress made some preparatory moves. She had women of the Lü clan marry men of the Liu clan, and made her granddaughter Zhang Yan (*q.v.* Zhang Yan, Empress of Emperor Hui) empress by marrying her to Emperor Hui. She granted her father and elder brother the posthumous titles of Prince of Xuan and Prince of Daowu in 187, and the same year granted to Zhang Yan (the son of her daughter, Princess Yuan of Lu) the title of Prince of Lu. Then she granted the title of Prince to male members of her husband's Liu family, making Liu Qiang Prince of Huaiyang and Liu Buyi Prince of Changshan. However, she continued to bestow honors on the Lü clan. Her nephew Lü Tai became Prince of Lü, and Lü Chan, Lü Lu, and Lü Tong were also made princes, while Lü Zhong, Lü Ping, Lü Xu, Lü Tuo, Lü Fen, and Lü Gengshi were all appointed to the rank of marquis.

Emperor Gaozu had sired eight sons, but only one (Emperor Hui) with Empress Dowager Lü. The empress had at least three of these eight sons killed—Ruyi, Liu You, and Liu Hui—and persecuted others. At least four died unnatural deaths. Only one of Emperor Hui's sons, all born to concubines, died at Empress Dowager Lü's order, however. This was Liu Gong, the heir apparent, whom Emperor Hui's empress Zhang Yan had taken from a concubine to be her own child before having the concubine killed. When Liu Gong discovered the truth of his heritage and his mother's death he swore to avenge her. Fearful of a potential revolt, Empress Dowager Lü had him secretly put to death.

Upon the death of Empress Dowager Lü in 180 B.C.E., Chen Ping and Zhou Bo had all members of the Lü clan put to death and supported the ascension of Emperor Wen (202–157 B.C.E.), thus marking the end of the power of the Lü clan.

Empress Dowager Lü's failure is attributed to her suspicious nature and the appointment of members of her natal family to important positions, thereby revealing that self-interest was her sole aim. However, this political struggle was limited to the Liu and the Lü clans and did not implicate the people. The historian Sima Qian commented that when Emperor Hui withdrew from affairs of state, Emperor Gaozu's empress conducted government affairs from within the court, but that the country was peaceful. Punishment was seldom administered and there were few criminals, he wrote; the people working hard at farming had plenty of food and clothing. Even though as a sign of disapproval Emperor Guangwu (r. 25–57) later had her tablet removed from Emperor Gaozu's temple, Empress Dowager Lü Zhi does indeed deserve to be known as a great stateswoman.

WANG Shu-hwai
(Translated by CHE Wai-lam William)

178 LÜ ZHI

An Zuozhang. *Hou fei zhuan.* Zhengzhou: Henan renmin chubanshe, 1990, vol. 1, 11–35.
Ge Hong. *Xijing zaji.* Taipei: Taiwan shangwu yinshuguan, 1967.
Goodrich, Chauncey S. "Two Chapters in the Life of an Empress of the Later Han." *Harvard Journal of Asian Studies* 25 (1964/5): 165–77.
Han shu. Beijing: Zhonghua shuju, 1983, vol. 12, 97.3933–4012.
Liu Ziqing. *Zhongguo lidai xianneng funü pingzhuan.* Taipei: Liming wenhua gongsi, 1978, 60–78.
Shi ji. Beijing: Zhonghua shuju, 1959, vol. 1, 9.395–412.
Sima Guang. *Zizhi tongjian.* Beijing: Zhonghua shuju, 1976, vol. 1, 9–13 passim.
Yang, Lien-sheng. "Female Rulers in Imperial China." *Harvard Journal of Asian Studies* 23 (1960/1): 47–61.

Lü's Mother

Lü's Mother (Lü Mu), fl. c. 14 C.E., was from Haiqu in Langye (east of present-day Ju County, Shandong Province); her given names and surname are not recorded. Her son, who had been a district official (*xianli*), had been executed after being charged by the district magistrate with a misdemeanor. Naturally, Lü's Mother harbored a deep hatred for the magistrate, and as part of her plan for revenge she covertly set about gathering people together. The Lü family was quite wealthy, with property amounting to several million cash and, being in the business of making and selling wine, Lü's Mother prepared a considerable quantity of fine wine and got in a good store of clothing as well as an armory of knives and swords. If young men came to her for drink, she would give them credit; if the poor came to her, she would lend them clothes. She made contact with a large number of people in this way, and over a period of several years she exhausted almost all of her money and possessions. Whenever the young people promised they would one day repay her, tears would come to her eyes and she would reply: "I am not doing this because I want you to repay me, but because I want you to take revenge on that magistrate who had my son killed for a trivial crime. Will you gentlemen take up my cause?" Moved by her courage and, perhaps more importantly, by her kindness, they all promised they would help her.

Several hundred young men banded together, calling themselves "The Fierce Tigers," and went with Lü's Mother to an island where fugitives had sought refuge, to enroll them in her cause. By the time she was in her sixties, she was able to declare herself commander-in-chief of several thousand people and at that time she led her army to Haiqu. With the islands in the Yellow Sea as her base, she secured the district and captured the magistrate responsible for her son's death. When the district officials kowtowed to her, pleading for the magistrate's life, she told them: "My son should not have been put to death for such a minor crime. A murderer should pay with his life. What do you have to say to that?" She then killed the magistrate and took his head to her son's grave as a sacrifice. Afterward, she and her army retreated to the islands, where they lived as fugitives. Some years later, Fan Chong from Langye, also in Shandong Province, raised troops from among the people. They were known as the Red Eyebrows, and they were largely responsible for defeating Wang Mang in 23 C.E. After this victory the Red Eyebrows retreated to the Haiqu area. Lü's Mother had died of illness by this time, so her followers joined various peasant armies, including the Red Eyebrows, the Bronze Horse, and the Green Horn. Another contemporary of

Lü's Mother was a woman named Chi Zhaopeng, who also gathered several thousand men in Pingyuan (present-day Pingyuan District, Shandong Province) and took part in the peasant uprisings of that period.

Lü's Mother was undoubtedly seen as an outlaw, but her story reveals a remarkable talent for planning and strategy as well as considerable strength of character and leadership ability sufficient to muster and control such a large troop of young men.

SHEN Jian

Hou Han shu. Beijing: Zhonghua shuju, 1965, vol. 2, 11.477–78.
Liu Shisheng. *Zhongguo gudai funüshi.* Qingdao: Qingdao chubanshe, 1991, 117–19.
Ma Zhaozheng and Zhou Feitang. *Zhongguo gudai funü mingren.* Beijing: Zhongguo funü chubanshe, 1988, 67–68.
Yingwen Zhongguo funü, ed. *Gujin zhuming funü renwu.* Shijiazhuang: Hebei renmin chubanshe, 1986, 56–61.

M

Ma, Empress of Emperor Ming

Empress Ma (Mingdi Ma Huanghou), 39–79, was empress to Emperor Ming (Liu Zhuang, 27–75; r. 58–75) of Eastern Han. Her given names are not recorded in the histories.

Ma was the youngest daughter of General Ma Yuan (14 B.C.E.–48 C.E.), who died at the age of sixty-two while leading a military expedition against the minority Xi people in Wuxi. He had importuned Emperor Guangwu to allow him to lead imperial forces against the revolt of the Xi but had encountered strong resistance; this setback, together with the steaming summer heat, had weakened the aging general and led to his death. The late general's posts and titles were rescinded after an influential relative of the emperor defamed Ma Yuan for his ignominious defeat and death. This was the first in a series of tragedies for the Ma clan. Ma Yuan's son Ma Keqing died of illness, and Ma Yuan's wife became so depressed that she developed a mental disorder. The future Empress Ma was only ten years old at this time, but she assumed responsibility for managing the household, impressing even her older siblings with her skill for organizing the family's affairs.

The constant bullying from the rich and powerful to which the Ma clan was subjected led Ma Yan (17–98) to memorialize the emperor suggesting that the young women of the clan be selected into the palace. Ma thus became one of the virgins assigned to the heir apparent, Liu Zhuang. She was thirteen when she entered the palace of the twenty-four-year-old heir apparent, and she earned the admiration of all for her elegance, modesty, and courtesy as well as for the sincerity and devotion with which she served Empress Yin (*q.v.* Yin Lihua, Empress of Emperor Guangwu) and her peers. The heir apparent also favored her. She was slender, of a graceful bearing, and had beautiful hair, which she liked to comb up from the hairline into a big knot around which she coiled the rest of her hair three times.

180 MA, EMPRESS OF EMPEROR MING

Upon the death of Emperor Guangwu (Liu Xiu, 6 B.C.E.–57 C.E.; r. 25–57), the heir apparent ascended the throne but did not appoint an empress immediately. Ma had not produced any children, so when he promoted her to the highest rank of Worthy Lady (*guiren*) he ordered her to adopt as her son Liu Da (Emperor Zhang, 57–88; r. 76–88), the infant son of Worthy Lady Jia. Worthy Lady Ma bestowed great love and care on the child. In the year 60, Emperor Ming was urged to appoint an empress, and when he hesitated Empress Dowager Yin advised him to select Worthy Lady Ma, as she was "the most virtuous among the imperial concubines." Worthy Lady Ma may have been humble, but once appointed as Empress Ma she became even more so. She led a simple life and, to the astonishment of the palace women, wore coarse clothes with no ornamentation on her skirts.

Empress Ma was a learned young woman who enjoyed reading, especially classical texts such as *Book of Changes* (Yi jing), *Spring and Autumn Annals* (Chunqiu), *Songs of the South* (Chu ci), *Rites of Zhou* (Zhou li), and Dong Zhongshu's *Luxuriant Gems of the Spring and Autumn* (Chunqiu fanlu). Emperor Ming admired her learning, and when he tested her with memorials to the throne and controversial issues she was always able to analyze them and make judgments. For example, in the year 70 Liu Ying, the Prince of Chu, was accused of plotting an uprising and suspects were jailed awaiting a judgment. As the case dragged on year after year, more and more people became implicated. Empress Ma felt pity for the growing number of prisoners and eventually explained her understanding of the case to the emperor with great earnestness; he was so touched that he granted amnesty to many of the prisoners. However, while the emperor often discussed political affairs with Empress Ma and gained a good deal of insight from her views, she is said to have never meddled in politics, thus winning his love and respect. After Emperor Ming died in 75, her adopted son Liu Da (Emperor Zhang) succeeded to the throne, and Empress Ma became Empress Dowager Ma.

In her book *Annotations on the Daily Life of Emperor Ming* (Xianzong [Mingdi] qiju zhu), Empress Dowager Ma omitted the account of her older brother Ma Fang, the medical practitioner who served Emperor Ming with such great care, saying: "I do not want later generations to think that the emperor was close to his in-laws." The empress dowager had three older brothers—Ma Liao, Ma Fang, and Ma Guang—but they had not been promoted during the reign of Emperor Ming because she did not want her relatives to take up senior posts. Early in his reign, Emperor Zhang promoted these three maternal uncles, intending to grant them titles of nobility. Empress Dowager Ma, however, would not allow this. The following year there was a drought over most of China. Memorials were submitted urging the emperor to grant titles and bounties to his adoptive uncles according to the ancient rites, believing the failure to do so was the cause of the natural disaster. Empress Dowager Ma issued an edict in which she wrote:

> Those who submitted memorials to urge the emperor to grant bounties to my relatives simply want to flatter me. During the reign of Emperor Cheng, Empress Dowager Wang's five brothers were given titles on the same day, and on that day the sky

was covered with yellow smog and there was no sign of rain. This demonstrates that we should not believe portents about the will of Heaven. During the reign of Emperor Wu, his distaff relatives Tian Fen and Dou Ying took advantage of this close relationship and their arrogant behavior led to the downfall of the dynasty. As the mother of the nation, I wear coarse clothes and eat plain food in the hope that this will set a good example to the people. However, the other day when I passed the Zhuolong Gate I saw members of my natal family riding in luxurious carriages and wearing extravagant clothes, showing no concern for the nation. How could we grant noble title to these people? To do so would be a violation of the will of the late emperor, bringing harm to the virtue of the ancestors, and falling into the ways of the previous [Western Han] dynasty, which collapsed because of the distaff families' intervention in politics.

Despite the pleas of Emperor Zhang, the empress dowager would not be swayed but silenced him with these words:

Emperor Gaozu decreed that only members of the imperial family and those families who had made a military contribution could be granted the title of Marquis. My natal family has made no such contribution, so why should they be granted titles? I have thought deeply about this and have resolved any doubts I had. Filial piety demands that making our parents comfortable is our first duty. I have been worrying day and night that the price of grain is rising because of the unstable weather, but you are concerned only about granting titles to a distaff family and acting against my will. When the weather improves and the nation is at peace I will no longer have anything to do with political affairs but shall concentrate on raising my grandchildren. Then you can do whatever you wish.

Empress Dowager Ma promoted a frugal way of living. When members of her natal family were found to be leading luxurious lives or abusing the law, their posts were seized, they were sent back to their native place, and their names were removed from the clan register. Those who led humble lives and performed righteous acts, however, were rewarded. Her pleasures were simple. She ordered the construction of a weaving room and she enjoyed going there to watch the silkworms; she discussed political affairs with Emperor Zhang; and she taught the princes the Confucian classics. She was extremely content that everyone in the palace lived peacefully.

Four years into the reign of Emperor Zhang, farmers finally enjoyed good harvests and the nation was at peace. The emperor therefore decreed in 79 that the three brothers of his adoptive mother be granted the title Marquis. However, fearing the anger of their sister, the three men accepted only the title Marquis of Guannei, which did not carry with it feudal manors and territory. They immediately returned their titles when they heard what Empress Dowager Ma had to say about them:

When I was young I wished for nothing but to leave a good name in history. Even now, in the twilight of my life, I still observe the teaching of Confucius: refrain from taking. So closely did I follow this teaching in order not to disappoint the late emperor that I never enjoyed a comfortable house nor ate to the full. I wanted my brothers to observe this teaching as well so that I would have no deathbed regrets but that is not to be. This makes me very sad.

MA, EMPRESS OF EMPEROR MING

Empress Dowager Ma fell ill that year. She had no faith in witches and refused to be prayed over and blessed by them; she died in the sixth month of 79, at the age of just over forty, twenty-three years after assuming the title of empress.

Distaff relatives had caused enormous political strife in late Western Han, having been implicated in the collapse of the dynasty and Wang Mang's seizure of the throne. Empress Ma is recognized as having exerted a positive influence in early Eastern Han by controlling the power of her natal family and she has been greatly admired throughout history for contributing to political stability during the reigns of Emperor Ming and Emperor Zhang. She clearly knew her place in the Confucian scheme of things, and it is not surprising that her words and deeds have been preserved in such detail in the histories, since they so precisely mirror Confucian ideals. Highly lauded by Confucian scholars, Empress Ma was the perfect exemplar for imperial women: learned, humble, frugal, and entirely lacking in political ambition.

SUN Kuo Tung
(Translated by CHE Wai-lam William)

Ban Gu. *Dong guan Han ji*. Beijing: Zhonghua shuju, 1985, vol. 1, 6.45–46.
Gujin tushu jicheng, juan 32. Shanghai, Zhonghua shuju, 1934, 248.1b–2a.
Hou Han shu. Beijing: Zhonghua shuju, 1965, vol. 2, 10*shang*.407–14.
O'Hara, Albert R. *The Position of Woman in Early China According to the Lieh Nü Chuan, "The Biographies of Chinese Women."* Taipei: Mei Ya, 1971; 1978, 243–48.
Sima Guang. *Zizhi tongjian*. Beijing: Zhonghua shuju, 1976, vol. 1, 45–46 passim.

Meng Guang

Meng Guang, *zi* Deyao, fl. 58–75, of Pingling District, Fufeng, Shaanxi Province, is famous for her virtue. She is also said to have been ugly, of a dark complexion, and so strong she could lift a dipper-shaped grain grinder made of stone.

When her parents asked her why, having reached the age of thirty, she remained unmarried, she replied that she was seeking a man as virtuous and learned as Liang Boluan. Boluan was the *zi* of Liang Hong, a native of the same district as Meng Guang and a son of Liang Rang, Commandant of the Capital Gates (*chengmen xiaowei*) and Earl of Xiuyuan. He had grown up in the tumultuous times at the end of the Western Han dynasty and the interregnum of Wang Mang and had studied at the National University. Although poor, he was a man of integrity, widely read, and not content to limit himself to analyzing the syntax of the Confucian classics. After graduating, he decided to rear pigs in the Imperial Forest Park. On one occasion, through carelessness he caused a fire in the park that damaged a neighboring house, so he gave all his pigs to the owner of the house by way of compensation. When this did not satisfy the owner, Liang worked for him day and night. His other neighbors so admired Liang Hong for this that they negotiated a release with the owner of the damaged house and a return of Liang's pigs. Liang Hong was thus able to stop working for that family, but he refused to take the pigs back. Word of his honorable behavior preceded him to his native place, where many rich families wanted him as a son-in-law. Having rejected all proposals of marriage, Liang Hong finally proposed to Meng Guang after he heard what she had told her parents, and she accepted his proposal.

Dressed in full wedding attire, Meng Guang went to Liang Hong, who appeared piqued and did not speak to her for several days. Finally she knelt by his bed and asked him why, having chosen to marry a woman who had turned down many marriage proposals, he was treating her in this way. She asked if she had done anything wrong. Liang Hong replied that he had been seeking a wife who "used a thorn as a hairpin and wore a cloth skirt and would accompany me in retreat to a remote area. How can I be happy when you dress yourself in a beautiful silk skirt and wear make-up?" Meng Guang replied that she had been testing him and had already prepared simple clothes for their retreat. The pair went to live in a mountainous area in Shuangling and supported themselves by farming and weaving.

Some time later, Liang Hong visited the capital. Distressed at the extravagance of the imperial palace while the people suffered, he composed *Song of Five Laments* (Wu yi ge). Emperor Ming (r. 58–75) was enraged at this insult and ordered the arrest of Liang Hong, who changed his name and managed to make his escape. He and Meng Guang went to live between the states of Qi and Lu (in the region of present-day Shandong Province) and later moved to the state of Wu (present-day Jiangsu Province). There they lived on the verandah of a rich man by the name of Gao Botong, who employed Liang Hong to grind grain. When Liang returned from his labors Meng Guang would prepare a meal for him. She "dared not look straight at Hong [her husband] but raised the bowl level with her eyebrows." This expression has been handed down through the centuries as a synonym for an ideal couple who treat one another with respect. Seeing how the couple treated each other, their patron, Gao Botong, realized that Liang Hong must have "some extraordinary qualities" and released him from manual labor. Liang submerged himself in writing and produced over ten works before he died of illness. As requested in Liang Hong's will, Gao had him buried beside the tomb of a hero named Yaoli instead of having his body returned to his native place. People said: "Yaoli was a hero; Boluan [Liang Hong] was virtuous. It is fitting that they be buried side by side." Meng Guang returned with her children to Fufeng; it is not known when she died.

Meng Guang did not write anything, nor did she engage in any remarkable social events or make any political contribution. Yet she is well known to later generations as a woman of outstanding morality.

WONG Yin Lee
(Translated by TAM Chui-han June)

Hou Han shu. Beijing: Zhonghua shuju, 1965, vol. 10, 83.2765–68.

Huangfu Mi. *Gaoshi zhuan.* Beijing: Zhonghua shuju, 1985, vol. 2, 92–94.

Liu Xiang. *Xu Lienü zhuan.* In *Lienü zhuan,* Sibubeiyao ed. Taipei: Zhonghua shuju, 1966, vol. 2, 8.10a–b.

O'Hara, Albert R. *The Position of Woman in Early China According to the Lieh Nü Chuan, "The Biographies of Chinese Women."* Taipei: Mei Ya, 1971; 1978, 242–43.

184 MINGDI MA HUANGHOU

Mingdi Ma Huanghou: *see* **Ma, Empress of Emperor Ming**

Mingfei: *see* **Wang Zhaojun**

Mingjun: *see* **Wang Zhaojun**

Mother Piao

Mother Piao (Piao Mu) or the Bleaching Woman, fl. c. 220 B.C.E., was from Huaiyin (the present-day city of Huai'an, Jiangsu Province). Her given name and surname are not recorded; she was called Mother Piao because she supported herself by bleaching (*piao*) silk yarn.

The story of Mother Piao has been handed down because of her association with a man named Han Xin (d. 196 B.C.E.), Marquis of Huaiyin, who was ennobled during the reign of Emperor Gaozu (r. 206–195 B.C.E.) of Western Han (*vide* Lü Zhi, Empress of Emperor Gaozu). In his youth, Han Xin lacked the talent and virtue to be appointed to an official position and he did not possess the skill to be a trader, so he had no means of earning a living. Reduced to begging, he became a despised outcast. Han Xin several times sought refuge with the head of the neighborhood of Nanchang, in Xiaxiang, but, considering him nothing but a nuisance and a burden, the head's wife did everything she could to discourage him. At lunchtime, for example, knowing Han Xin would come looking for something to eat, the head's wife would prepare lunch early and eat it in bed. She would then refuse to prepare anything for Han Xin when he arrived. Once Han Xin realized this, he was so enraged he swore never to go there again. Not long after this he was fishing in the moat under the city wall. Nearby, a group of women were bleaching silk yarn, among them Mother Piao. She was an older woman and, realizing that he was hungry, she shared her meal with Han Xin. This continued for over ten days, until the work of bleaching was done. Han Xin was moved by Mother Piao's kindness and promised that he would one day repay her. Affronted, Mother Piao replied: "It is a shame a dignified man like you cannot support himself. I shared my food with you because I took pity on you. Did you think I did it because I hoped for some repayment?"

During the struggle for supremacy between Han and Chu in the last years of the Qin dynasty, Han Xin was appointed commander-in-chief of the armies of Liu Bang (256–195 B.C.E.), King of Han, and the future founding emperor of the Han dynasty. Such was Liu Bang's gratitude when Chu was defeated that he granted Han Xin the state of Qi and made him Prince of Qi. In 202, Liu Bang (by then emperor) made Han Xin the Prince of Chu, moving the capital of Chu to Xiapi (the present-day city of Pizhou, Jiangsu Province). As soon as he arrived in Xiapi, Han Xin summoned Mother Piao and gave her 1,000 *tael* of gold as a token of his gratitude for her earlier kindness.

The story of Mother Piao's kindness and Han Xin's gratitude made its way into Chinese literature when the great Tang dynasty poet Li Bai (701–762) included these lines in his poem *Night on Five-Pine Mountain at Old Lady Xun's:* "Ashamed to face Mother Piao / I declined thrice unable to eat." Both the fishing terrace where Han Xin met Mother Piao and Mother Piao's temple have been preserved in Huaian City and have become popular tourist sites.

SHEN Jian

Shi ji. Beijing: Zhonghua shuju, 1985, vol. 8, 92.2609–10, 2626.
Sima Guang. *Zizhi tongjian.* Beijing: Zhonghua shuju, 1956, vol. 1, 9.309–10.

P

Pan Chao: *see* **Ban Zhao**

Pang Yu Mu: *see* **Zhao E**

Pang Yu's Mother: *see* **Zhao E**

Piao Mu: *see* **Mother Piao**

Q

Qi, Concubine of Emperor Gaozu
Lady Qi (Gaozu Qi Furen), d. 194 B.C.E., of Dingtao (northwest of Dingtao District in present-day Shandong Province) was a concubine of Liu Bang (256–195 B.C.E.), who later became Emperor Gaozu (r. 202–195 B.C.E.).

Lady Qi gave birth to a son named Ruyi (d. 194 B.C.E.) who was later enfeoffed as Prince of Zhao. Emperor Gaozu's eldest son, Liu Ying, had been appointed heir apparent, but he was a mild youth, unlike his father, and the emperor wanted to replace him with Ruyi as his heir apparent. Little love was lost between Lady Qi, the mother of Ruyi, and Empress Lü (*q.v.* Lü Zhi, Empress of Emperor Gaozu), the mother of the official heir apparent Liu Ying. The younger woman, Lady Qi, who frequently accompanied the emperor when he was away from the capital and stationed in the east of Hangu Pass, would tearfully entreat him to appoint their son Ruyi heir apparent. In the meantime, Empress Lü remained in the capital and seldom saw her husband, so that she gradually lost his favor. However, with the aid of senior ministers, Empress Lü was able to secure her son's position as heir apparent, and when Emperor Gaozu died of illness in 195, Liu Ying (Emperor Hui, 210–188 B.C.E., r. 195–188 B.C.E.) ascended the throne. Empress Lü thereupon assumed the title of Empress Dowager Lü.

Empress Dowager Lü immediately had Lady Qi imprisoned in Yongxiang Palace. Lady Qi's head was shaved, an iron ring was placed around her neck, she was dressed in prison clothes and was put to work pounding rice and herbs with a pestle. Filled with sadness and indignation, she composed a lament: "My son is a prince but I am a prisoner pounding rice all day long and often in the company of death. We live a thousand *li* apart. Who should I send to tell you of this?" This song enraged Empress

186 QI, CONCUBINE OF EMPEROR GAOZU

Dowager Lü. Knowing that Lady Qi wanted to be close to her son, Empress Dowager Lü summoned Ruyi to the capital and murdered him with poisoned wine. She then put Lady Qi to an horrific death: she had her hands and feet cut off and her eyes gouged out; she had her deafened and made dumb by scouring her throat with poisoned wine. Before having her killed, she confined her to a tiny room (some sources call it a toilet), calling her a "human pig" (*renzhi*).

This atrocious death transformed Lady Qi into a figure deserving sympathy who had suffered at the hands of a gravely jealous Empress Dowager Lü. The later folk custom of sacrificing to the "toilet goddess" may have originated with Lady Qi's confinement and death. It is also said that names similar in sound to "Qi" have over the years been given to the toilet goddess: the Qi (seven) Woman (Qigu), the Zi (purple; son) Woman (Zigu), and the Ce (toilet) Woman (Cegu). That common folk have recompensed Lady Qi for her tragic death by worshipping her as the "toilet goddess" is indeed a touching memorial.

WANG Lihua

Chen Quanli and Hou Xinyi, eds. *Hou fei cidian.* Xi'an: Shaanxi renmin jiaoyu chubanshe, 1991, 12.
Han shu. Beijing: Zhonghua shuju, 1983, vol. 22, 97.3933–4012.
Liu Shisheng. *Zhongguo gudai funü shi.* Qingdao: Qingdao chubanshe, 1991, 87–90.

Qin Jia's Wife: *see* **Xu Shu**

Qin Shihuangdi's Mother: *see* **Zhao Ji**

Qing, the Widow from Bashu
Widow Qing (Bashu Guafu Qing), fl. 259–210 B.C.E., of Fuling, Bashu (present-day city of Fuling, Sichuan Province), was famous as a successful mine owner during the reign of the first emperor of Qin (Qin Shihuangdi, r. 221–210 B.C.E.). She is recorded in the *History of the Han Dynasty* (Han shu) as Qing, the Widow from Ba, while in *Historical Records* (Shi ji), whose author lived only a century after she did, she is referred to as Qing, the Widow from Bashu. She was widowed young and never remarried, Qing being her given name; neither her surname nor her husband's was recorded for posterity. Her ancestors had become exceedingly wealthy from mining cinnabar, and Widow Qing had developed this family business into an even more prosperous concern. The extent of her involvement in the technical side of the family's mining enterprise is not touched upon in the official histories. She lived by herself in a remote village, and her great wealth enabled her to live free from harassment. Qin Shihuangdi is said to have treated her with courtesy as a virtuous woman and he built a terraced tower (*nü huai qing tai*) in her memory.

Sima Qian wrote admiringly of her in *Historical Records,* saying that she was treated as an equal by an emperor and that her name was known throughout the empire.

SHEN Lidong

Han shu. Beijing: Zhonghua shuju, 1983, vol. 11, 91.3679–95.
Shi ji. Beijing: Zhonghua shuju, 1985, vol. 10, 129.3253–83.

R

Ren Yanshou Qi: *see* **Youdi**

S

Shangguan, Empress of Emperor Zhao

Empress Shangguan (Xiao Zhao Shangguan Huanghou), ?89–37 B.C.E., of Shanggui (south of present-day Tianshui, Gansu Province) became empress to the twelve-year-old Emperor Zhao (Liu Fuling, 94–74 B.C.E.; r. 87–74 B.C.E.) when she was six years old. Her personal name is not known.

Empress Shangguan was a granddaughter of Shangguan Jie (d. 80 B.C.E.), a gate guardsman of the palace guard (*yulin qimenlang*) who rose to the influential court position of general of the left (*zuojiangjun*) during the last days of Emperor Wu (Liu Che, 156–87 B.C.E.; r. 141–87 B.C.E.). On his deathbed, Emperor Wu directed that Shangguan Jie and General-in-Chief (*da jiangjun*) Huo Guang (d. 68 B.C.E.) act as regents when his youngest son, Liu Fuling, then seven years old, succeeded to the throne. From then on Shangguan Jie and Huo Guang shared the duty of making court decisions, and the tie between them was strengthened by the marriage of Shangguan Jie's son Shangguan An to Huo Guang's eldest daughter (her name has not been recorded in the histories). Empress Shangguan was born of this union and, after her father offered an appropriate bribe, she was accepted into the palace, where the young emperor lived in the care of his elder sister Princess of Gai, who had been granted the rank of Lady of Handsome Fairness. At this time, Shangguan An was promoted to Commandant of Cavalry (*ji duwei*) and in 83 B.C.E., when his daughter was appointed empress, he was granted the title of Marquis of Sangle and further promoted to Chariot and Horse General (*cheji jiangjun*). Shangguan An took easily to the luxury these posts afforded him and is said to have led a debauched life.

Empress Shangguan's maternal grandfather, however, remained committed to his responsibility of assisting the young emperor and did not seek personal gain. This honorable stance of Huo Guang engendered considerable jealousy and antagonism on the part of Shangguan Jie and Shangguan An, who were no longer able to abuse their position and influence the fourteen-year-old emperor after Huo Guang gained complete control over the court. Further tensions arose when Huo Guang refused the request of the Princess of Gai for an official post for her lover Ding Wairen, and refused that of the Censor-in-Chief (*yushi dafu*) Sang Hongyang (152–80 B.C.E.) for official positions for his sons. The emperor's older brother Liu Dan, the Prince of Yanla, had long resented being passed over for the succession, and he joined the Princess of Gai, Shangguan Jie, and Shangguan An in an attempt to unseat Huo Guang. The young emperor was not deceived, however, when Shangguan Jie pre-

188 SHANGGUAN, EMPRESS OF EMPEROR ZHAO

sented a memorial accusing Huo Guang of abusing his power and position, and he declared that anyone who dared speak ill of Huo Guang would be imprisoned and prosecuted. Undeterred, Huo Guang's enemies devised a plot to murder him, remove Emperor Zhao from the throne, appoint Liu Dan emperor, and elevate Shangguan Jie to the rank of prince. Shangguan An went further, conspiring to murder Liu Dan, depose Emperor Zhao, and place Shangguan Jie on the throne as emperor. These conspiracies were exposed, and Emperor Zhao ordered that Shangguan Jie, Shangguan An, Sang Hongyang, and Ding Wairen be put to death along with their families. The Princess of Gai committed suicide, and Liu Dan was granted permission to hang himself, while his wife and some twenty concubines took their own lives. Empress Shangguan, granddaughter of the upright Huo Guang, was deemed not to have been involved in these conspiracies; she was pardoned and allowed to retain her position as empress.

Emperor Zhao died in 74 B.C.E. at the age of twenty-one, leaving Empress Shangguan, then fourteen or fifteen years old, a widow and childless. Since the emperor had died without producing an heir, Empress Shangguan (now Empress Dowager Shangguan) became titular head of state, although Huo Guang retained de facto control of affairs of state. Huo Guang eventually decided to appoint as emperor Liu He, a son of the Prince of Changyi Liu Bo and a grandson of Emperor Wu and Consort Li (*q.v.* Li, Concubine of Emperor Wu). Within a short time, however, it became clear from his licentious and arrogant behavior that Liu He was unworthy of this honor. Once Huo Guang and the other senior ministers had decided that Liu He should be deposed, they explained their decision to the empress dowager. By virtue of her position as head of state, Empress Dowager Shangguan had Liu He summoned into her presence in the Hall of Inherited Brilliance (Chengming Gong) in the Eternal Palace. At one point during this audience, while the ministers' accusatory memorial was being read aloud, the empress dowager became incensed and called out: "Stop! Could any subject or son behave in such a shameful and disorderly fashion?" (Watson, 134). Liu He kowtowed in fright but the reading continued, and after the memorial had been read out in its entirety the empress dowager commanded that he be deposed. Liu He had occupied the throne for a mere twenty-seven days. Instead of banishment he was ordered to return to Changyi, where he was granted land and permitted to retain the property he possessed, while some 200 of his officials and retainers were executed.

Since the empress dowager was nominally in charge of state affairs until a new emperor was appointed, Huo Guang arranged for her to be tutored in the Confucian classics, the scholar Xiahou Sheng teaching her *The Book of Documents* (Shang shu). The search for the next emperor continued until Bing Ji (d. 55 B.C.E.), who had held the post of inspector of law enforcement during the reign of Emperor Wu, submitted a memorial to Huo Guang suggesting the eighteen- or nineteen-year-old great-grandson of Emperor Wu as an appropriate choice. This young man, Liu Bingyi (or Liu Xun: Emperor Xuan, 91–49 B.C.E.; r. 74–49 B.C.E.), had been the sole survivor when his grandfather Liu Ju's entire household died or were put to death during the witchcraft scare of 91 B.C.E. (*vide* Wei Zifu, Empress of Emperor Wu). Rescued and initially supported by Bing Ji, this infant son of Liu Jin was sent to his deceased grandmother's home when a general amnesty was declared and was looked after by his great-grandmother Zhenjun. Later, by imperial order, he was taken to the rear palace to be raised and was entered into the register of the imperial house. In 77 B.C.E., when he was only fourteen or fifteen, Liu Bingyi married Xu Pingjun (*q.v.* Xu Pingjun, Empress of Emperor Xuan), a marriage arranged by the Director of Palace Discipline Zhang He (d. 70 B.C.E.). Liu Bingyi had been schooled in literature and history and was said to have been aware of the vicissitudes of government and the suffering of the people during the reign of Emperor Zhao.

Bing Ji's nomination was well received, and Huo Guang and other ministers memorialized Empress Dowager Shangguan, requesting permission for Liu Bingyi to succeed to the throne. They wrote that Liu Bingyi had "received instruction in the *Odes,* the *Analects,* and the *Classic of Filial Piety.* His conduct is temperate and restrained and he is kind and benevolent to others. He is suited to become the heir of Emperor [Zhao], to carry on the service of the ancestral temples (Watson, 137). Once the empress dowager had approved the ministers' decision, the young man was brought into her presence in the Eternal Palace so that she could enfeoff him as Marquis of Yangwu. Having thus been elevated from commoner status, Liu Bingyi was installed as emperor (Emperor Xuan), and Empress Dowager Shangguan retired to Changle Palace as Grand Empress Dowager Shangguan.

Upon the death of Emperor Xuan in 49 B.C.E., the heir apparent Liu Shi (Emperor Yuan, 76–33 B.C.E.; r. 49–33 B.C.E.) ascended the throne and the forty-year-old grand empress dowager became Great Grand Empress Dowager Shangguan. She died in 37 B.C.E. and was buried in Pingling alongside Emperor Zhao. Bound in a political marriage at the age of six, Empress Shangguan was widowed at fifteen and lived alone for the remaining thirty-two years of her life. Historical sources present her in a positive light, saying that she behaved with such propriety during the short period she was in charge of state affairs (under the tutelage of Huo Guang) that "she put men to shame."

Empress Shangguan is possibly the earliest example of an imperial woman being required to issue decrees of abdication or surrender; in her case it became her duty to depose an unsuitable emperor. Empress Dowager Cixi fulfilled much the same function when she presided over the last years of the Qing dynasty (*q.v.* Empress Xiao Qin Xian, *Biographical Dictionary of Chinese Women, The Qing Period, 1644–1911*).

BAO Shanben

Ban Gu. *Courtier and Commoner in Ancient China: Selections from the "History of the Former Han" by Pan Ku,* trans. Burton Watson. New York: Columbia University Press, 1974, 47, 125–38.
Chen Quanli and Hou Xinyi, eds. *Hou fei cidian.* Xi'an: Shaanxi renmin jiaoyu chubanshe, 1991, 14.
Han shu. Beijing: Zhonghua shuju, 1983, vol. 12, 97*shang*.3957–64.
Loewe, Michael. *Crisis and Conflict in Han China.* London: George Allen & Unwin, 1974.
Sima Guang. *Zizhi tongjian.* Beijing: Zhonghua shuju, 1956, vol. 1, 23.749–74, 24.775–807.

Shen, Concubine of Emperor Wen

Consort Shen (Xiao Wen Shen Furen), fl. 180–157 B.C.E., of Handan (present-day Shanxi Province) was a favorite concubine of Emperor Wen (Liu Heng, 202–157 B.C.E.; r. 180–157 B.C.E.). Little is recorded of Consort Shen in the official histories, including the *Historical Records* (Shi ji) and the *History of the Han Dynasty* (Han shu), except that she was an "elegant" imperial concubine of significant status, that she was in the good graces of Emperor Wen, and that she was often in his company.

Her place of origin, Handan, was situated between the Zhang River and the Yellow River and had been the capital of the prosperous state of Zhao before China was unified by the Qin dynasty. In early Western Han the city enjoyed an economic boom and became famous as a place of commerce, situated conveniently as it was between Zhuolu (in the northwest of present-day Hebei Province, near Beijing) to the north and the states of Zheng and Wei to the south. Known for the luxurious way of life of its inhabitants, the state of Zhao was also known for its beautiful women, "as pretty as jade." Their lives were described as lavish and they were said to be skilled at playing the *qin* (a seven-stringed instrument that was plucked) and the *se* (a twenty-five-stringed instrument, also plucked), and to be able to sing and dance as well. They dressed in fashionable slippers and dancing dresses with long sleeves, displaying themselves for all to admire. Many of the women in the imperial palace of the first emperor of Qin (Qin Shihuangdi, 259–210 B.C.E.; r. 221–210 B.C.E.) were from Zhao and Wei, as was his mother, Zhao Ji, and many of those who waited on him were gentle and graceful women of Zhao.

Emperor Wen of Han, however, was a frugal monarch and he did not amass palaces, parks or pets, clothes or carriages during his reign; he is said to have "sacrificed his own comfort for the interest of the people." He himself often wore coarse black clothes, and he requested Consort Shen to demonstrate her frugality by not wearing long dresses that dragged on the ground and not having patterned and embroidered bed curtains. She heeded the emperor and turned her back on her extravagant upbringing, discarding her dancing dresses and embroidered fabrics and leading an exemplary life of simplicity and frugality.

On one occasion Consort Shen accompanied the emperor to Baling. He was in a good mood and, pointing to the Xinfeng road that led to Handan, asked her to play the *se* while he joined in the chorus. Suddenly, however, he became depressed, saying to his officials: "Oh! If my coffin were to be made of Beishan stone and padded with silk wool and sealed with lacquer, no-one would be able to open it!" The only official to disagree with him was Leader of Court Gentlemen (*zhonglang jiang*) Zhang Shizhi, who replied: "With valuables inside the tomb, people would find ways to break into it even if it were as strong as the southern mountains. But if it contained no valuables, Your Majesty would have no need to worry about burglars even if the coffin were not made of stone." Emperor Wen was impressed with Zhang Shizhi's wisdom and later promoted him; Consort Shen made no comment at the time on Zhang's words, which may indicate that she agreed with them.

Consort Shen did not bear Emperor Wen a son, but she appears to have been held in the same high esteem as Empress Dou (*q.v.* Dou Yifang, Empress of Emperor Wen), the two women sharing the emperor's table in the imperial palace. Once, however, on a trip to Shanglin Park the three were seated together as usual when Leader of Court Gentlemen Yuan Ang led Consort Shen to another table, located beneath the platform on which the emperor and empress were seated. Affronted, Consort Shen refused to sit down. The emperor also became angry and returned immediately to the imperial palace. Yuan Ang counseled Emperor Wen against allowing a concubine to sit at the same table as him and the rightfully appointed empress. This, he said, violated the hierarchical order of seniority and could only cause disharmony. Further, he warned that even though the emperor loved her, by treating Consort Shen in this way he was placing her life in jeopardy, reminding him of the story of the "human pig" (*renzhi*), a reference to the cruel death of Emperor Gaozu's concubine Consort Qi (*q.v.* Qi, Concubine of Emperor Gaozu). Emperor Wen approved this advice and explained to Consort Shen the reason for Yuan Ang's action. Consort Shen then presented Yuan Ang with fifty *jin* of gold as a token of her gratitude.

These brief episodes indicate that Consort Shen was an intelligent woman, capable of observing and making judgments as well as heeding sound advice.

ZHANG Qi
(Translated by HE Tiancheng and TAM Chui-han June)

Han shu. Beijing: Zhonghua shuju, 1983, vol. 8, 50.2307–12.
Shen Deqian. *Gushi yuan.* Beijing: Zhonghua shuju, 1978, 4.90–91.
Shi ji. Beijing: Zhonghua shuju, 1989, vol. 1, 9.395–412; vol. 1, 10.413–38; vol. 4, 49.1967–86; vol. 8, 87.2539–63; vol. 8, 101.2737–45; vol. 10, 129.3253–83.

Shi Huangsun Wang Furen: *see* **Wang Wengxu**

Shundi Liang Huanghou: *see* **Liang Na, Empress of Emperor Shun**

Shun-yü T'i-jung: *see* **Chunyu Tiying**

Shun-yu Tirong: *see* **Chunyu Tiying**

Sima Shi Yang Chang Qi: *see* **Sima, Yang Chang's Wife**

Sima Xiangru Qi: *see* **Zhuo Wenjun**

Sima Xiangru's Wife: *see* **Zhuo Wenjun**

Sima, Yang Chang's Wife
Yang Chang's Wife née Sima (Sima Shi Yang Chang Qi), fl. c. 73 B.C.E., was from Yangxia (in the south of present-day Hancheng District, Shaanxi Province). She was a daughter of the great historian and man of letters Sima Qian (145–?86 B.C.E.) and wife of the military man Yang Chang of Huayin (in present-day Shaanxi Province).

Yang Chang was initially a division commander (*jun sima*) in the army of General-

192 SIMA, YANG CHANG'S WIFE

in-Chief (*dajiangjun*) Huo Guang (d. 66 B.C.E.), who thought a great deal of him. He was eventually promoted to censor-in-chief (*yushi dafu*). After the death at the age of twenty-one of Emperor Zhao (r. 86–74 B.C.E.), the fifteen-year-old empress (*q.v.* Shangguan, Empress of Emperor Zhao) became titular ruler of the empire. However, Huo Guang was by then de facto ruler and he appointed Liu He, a grandson of Emperor Wu, as emperor. Within days, it became clear that Huo Guang had made an error of judgment, and he immediately began to plot with Chariot and Horse General (*cheji jiangjun*) Zhang Anshi for the removal of the licentious and arrogant young emperor. Their plan was to replace him with Liu Bingyi (Liu Xun), a great-grandson of Emperor Wu. Having made this decision, Huo Guang and Zhang Anshi sent the Chamberlain for the National Treasury (*da sinong*) to notify Yang Chang. So shocked was Yang Chang at this clearly unexpected news that he broke into a sweat and was rendered almost speechless, barely managing to mumble his assent. When the chamberlain left the room to relieve himself, Sima hurriedly emerged from the east wing and said to her husband: "This is a very important matter. The general-in-chief has made this decision and has sent the chamberlain to inform you of it, yet instead of indicating your ready support you behaved hesitantly and appeared to be at a loss what to do. You are really asking for trouble." When the chamberlain returned, therefore, husband and wife together conferred with him and gave their firm support, asking Huo Guang to go ahead with the plan. Within twenty-seven days the young emperor had been removed from the throne and in due course Liu Bingyi was installed as emperor (Emperor Xuan, r. 73–49 B.C.E.).

The active involvement in the politics of the day of Yang Chang's Wife, whereby she participated openly in this discussion with the chamberlain and her husband, seems not to have been unusual; several imperial women in the later years of Western Han did much more than simply give advice. What this incident is praising is her decisiveness and political acuity. However, the fact that she was the daughter of the historian Sima Qian cannot be discounted as another reason why the incident was recorded in the first place.

SHEN Jian

Han shu. Beijing: Zhonghua shuju, 1983, vol. 9, 66.2888–89.
Liu Ziqing. *Zhongguo lidai xianneng funü pingzhuan.* Taipei: Liming wenhua, 1978, 90–91.

Sun Shou

Sun Shou, d. 159, was the wife of the General-in-Chief (*dajiangjun*) Liang Ji, brother of Empress Liang Na (*q.v.* Liang Na, Empress of Emperor Shun) and of Empress Liang Nüying (*q.v.* Liang Nüying, Empress of Emperor Huan).

Liang Ji succeeded his father, Liang Shang, as general-in-chief in 141. In combination with his sister he dominated the court, and when his brother-in-law Emperor Shun (Liu Bao, 115–144; r. 126–144) died, Liang Ji shared in his sister's regent government for the infant Emperor Chong (Liu Bing, 143–145; r. 145). After the death of this child emperor a few months later, they placed the eight-year-old Liu Zuan (Emperor Zhi,

138–146; r. 146) upon the throne, and the following year, after he too died in somewhat suspicious circumstances, they chose Liu Zhi (Emperor Huan, 132–167; r. 147–167) to succeed him. To confirm the position of the family, moreover, Liang Ji and Empress Dowager Liang married their younger sister Liang Nüying to the young ruler.

Liang Ji's wife Sun Shou is first mentioned by the histories about the time of the death of Empress Dowager Liang, in 150, when she was enfeoffed as Lady of Xiangcheng in Yingchuan (present-day central Henan Province). With additional revenues from a neighboring county, her annual income amounted to fifty million cash, while her seal and insignia were equal to those of a senior princess.

The historians acknowledge that Sun Shou was extremely beautiful, but in all other respects she is described in most unflattering terms. Sensual and seductive in appearance and manner, she had her eyebrows shaped and her cheeks painted to give a mournful, languorous look and wore her hair on one side in a style described as "falling from a horse." Her smiles appeared forced and painful, "as if she suffered from toothache," and she walked with delicate, mincing steps as though her feet could barely support her. For his part, and influenced by her pretensions, Liang Ji acquired strange mannerisms, wearing robes of inordinate length and a narrow headdress that drooped to one side, carrying a great fan, and riding in an unusual, flat-topped carriage.

Liang Ji also acquired a mistress, You Tongji, who had formerly been a member of the harem of Emperor Shun. He kept her in a house west of the capital, but Sun Shou sent slaves to follow him, found her hiding place, seized her, beat her, cut off her hair, and slashed her face. Sun Shou then intended to report the matter to the court, which would have raised a considerable scandal, but Liang Ji managed to get her mother to dissuade her. He continued to visit his mistress and had a son by her, and though Sun Shou eventually had her own son, Liang Yin, kill You Tongji, Liang Ji managed to hide their infant son from his wife.

Later, also in the west of the city and probably in the same area, Liang Ji established a separate complex of pavilions to house the multitude of women who became his concubines. Some came from respectable families but all became his slaves and they were known as "women who have sold themselves."

We are also told that Liang Ji had a homosexual affair with the slave Qin Gong, whom Sun Shou took to her bed as well. Qin Gong acquired inordinate influence in the court and the government, and became one of the couple's most ruthless agents.

Despite these tensions and jealousies, Liang Ji was apparently besotted with Sun Shou and totally under her influence. In particular, he allowed her to persuade him to replace many of his own kinsmen with members of her family. Some ten of the Liang were dismissed from their posts in government, ostensibly as a sign of modesty and restraint, but their places were taken by relatives of Sun Shou, who acquired senior rank in both the capital and the provinces, while many of them adopted the Liang surname. All were greedy and cruel, and they sent out private retainers and clients to arrest wealthy men on false charges, then beat them until they paid ransom. Liang Ji behaved in the same way and was notorious for his seizure of private property and his exploitation of government officers, but Sun Shou's family shared in these opportunities. When Liang Ji constructed a great town house, Sun Shou built a mansion

194 SUN SHOU

to match it across the street, and both had great pleasure grounds; husband and wife were wheeled about their gardens in carriages decorated with gold and silver, covered by a canopy of feathers.

About 153 or 154 Sun Shou arranged for the entry of the young Deng Mengnü (*q.v.* Deng Mengnü, Empress of Emperor Huan) into the harem of Emperor Huan. Deng Mengnü was a stepdaughter of Sun Shou's maternal uncle Liang Ki (the variant transcription Ki is used to distinguish him from the general-in-chief because their names have the same transcription; he was not directly related to the general-in-chief). She was extremely beautiful, the emperor was delighted with her, and she was swiftly promoted to be a Worthy Lady (*guiren*), ranking next only to the empress. Sun Shou evidently planned that Worthy Lady Deng would act as support for her family within the harem.

At first this plan worked well, but Liang Ki died soon afterward, and as Empress Liang died in 159 and Emperor Huan planned to replace her with Worthy Lady Deng, there was a desperate struggle for influence. Liang Ji sought to have Worthy Lady Deng adopted into his own clan as a means of maintaining connection, but her natural mother, the Lady Xuan, encouraged by her son-in-law Bing Zun, wanted to keep the advantages of imperial favor for herself and her own close relatives. She thus rejected the proposal.

Liang Ji sent his favorite Qin Gong with a band of retainers to kill the Lady Xuan's son-in-law Bing Zun, and a few days later they attempted to break into Xuan's mansion and murder her, too. She fled to tell Emperor Huan, who called on a small group of trusted eunuchs for a coup against Liang Ji. Aided by the fact that, with the death of the empress, Liang Ji and his associates had lost much of their contact with the harem and the inner palace, the emperor sent a mixed force of eunuchs and palace gentlemen to surround the residences of Liang Ji and Sun Shou. Their insignia of rank and office were withdrawn and they were ordered into exile in the far south of Vietnam. Sun Shou and her husband committed suicide, while their relatives and clients were dismissed from office; many of them were arrested, executed, or exiled.

In later generations, the name of Sun Shou became proverbial for beauty and willful extravagance.

Rafe DE CRESPIGNY

Hou Han shu. Beijing: Zhonghua shuju, 1965, vol. 5, 34.1179–81.

T

T'ai Ts'ang of Ch'i, The Woman of: *see* **Chunyu Tiying**

Tang, Consort of Prince Hongnong
Lady Tang, Consort of Prince Hongnong (Hongnong Wang Tang Ji), fl. late second century, was from Yingchuan (near the present-day city of Xuchang in Henan Province); her personal name is not recorded in the histories. She was a daughter of Tang Mao, Governor of Guiji, and at some stage had been taken into the impe-

rial palace and given as a wife to Emperor Shao (Liu Bian, 171–190 C.E.; r. 189 C.E.) of Eastern Han.

Lady Tang was unfortunate in that she lived in the chaotic times of the declining Eastern Han dynasty. Upon the death of Emperor Ling (Liu Hong, 156–189; r. 168–189), Liu Bian succeeded to the throne. The court was in complete disarray, however, since Liu Bian's maternal uncle General-in-Chief (*da jiangjun*) He Jin (d. 189) had been killed by the eunuchs, whom he had planned to do away with. The Regional Governor of Bingzhou, Dong Zhuo (d. 192), was summoned to Luoyang to quell the disturbance but instead seized power. He removed eighteen-year-old Liu Bian from the throne and demoted him to Prince of Hongnong. He then installed eight-year-old Liu Xie (Emperor Xian, 181–234; r. 189–220) as emperor.

Not content with demoting Liu Bian, the following year Dong Zhuo ordered him to commit suicide by drinking poisoned wine served by Chamberlain for Attendants Li Ru. Realizing that he could not escape death, Liu Bian gave a feast so that he might take leave of Lady Tang and his concubines. During the feast, Liu Bian sang in great sorrow: "The world has changed, how hard is my life. Deprived of my throne, I have withdrawn to my fiefdom. Persecuted by a treacherous minister, death is at hand. I leave you to go to the nether regions." He then asked Lady Tang to dance, and as she danced, her sleeves flying, she sang: "The heavens have crashed down, the earth is collapsing. My emperor, you are forced to die young. We are going separate ways, you to your death while I go on living. How lonely and sad I will be without you!" Lady Tang sobbed with grief and all present were moved to tears. Liu Bian bid her farewell with these words: "You are an imperial concubine. Never degrade yourself by becoming the wife of an ordinary man. Do not lose your self-respect. Now, I am going forever." He drank the poisoned wine and died.

Still a very young woman, Lady Tang returned to her native village but resisted her father's attempts to make her remarry. Dong Zhuo died soon afterward, in 192, and the remnants of his army, under the command of Li Jue, rose in rebellion against the government, taking the city of Chang'an. After occupying Guandong, Li Jue's soldiers captured Lady Tang, who concealed her true identity. Li Jue wanted to take her as his wife, but she resolutely refused to marry him. When the imperial secretary heard of this many years later, he sent a memorial to Emperor Xian telling him what had happened. Emperor Xian took pity on Lady Tang and issued an edict that she be escorted back to the court. He granted her the title Princess of Hongnong and she lived out her life in the gardens of his palace. Lady Tang was a courageous young woman who remained loyal to the imperial family in difficult times. Her young husband did not ask her to die with him and she chose to live on, but her words and her deeds reveal the depth of her affection for him.

SHEN Lidong

Hou Han shu. Beijing: Zhonghua shuju, 1973, vol. 1, 10*xia*.450–51.
Shen Lidong. *Lidai houfei shici jizhu.* Beijing: Zhongguo funü chubanshe, 1990, 82–83.

196 TANG JI

Tang Ji: *see* **Tang, Consort of Prince Hongnong**

Tangshan, Concubine of Emperor Gaozu

Consort Tangshan (Gaozu Tangshan Furen), fl. 200–195 B.C.E., was a concubine of
Han Emperor Gaozu (Liu Bang, 256–195 B.C.E.; r. 202–195 B.C.E.). Tangshan was her
family name but nothing is known of her family background since histories such as
the *Historical Records* (Shi ji) and the *History of the Han Dynasty* (Han shu) do not
give an account of her life. According to "Treatise on Ritual and Music" (Li yue zhi)
contained in the *History of the Han Dynasty,* Consort Tangshan composed *Sacrificial
Ode: Inside the Chamber* (Fangzhong ciyue), also called *Ode [to Pacify the World]:
Inside the Chamber* ([Anshi] Fangzhong ge).

"Treatise on Ritual and Music" records that a song called *Sacrificial Ode: Inside
the Chamber* had been known earlier, in the Zhou dynasty, and had been renamed
Longevity (Shou ren) in Qin. Since Emperor Gaozu enjoyed the music of the southern
state of Chu, *Sacrificial Ode: Inside the Chamber* was sung to a Chu melody and
played on Chu instruments. Consort Tangshan composed seventeen verses of *Ode:
Inside the Chamber,* and it is clear from her choice of words that she was well versed
in the classics and folk songs. Most of the verses were adapted from folk songs, which
indicates that she may have been a commoner who had been selected for or nominated
into the imperial palace. Her familiarity with classical literature, particularly *The Book
of Songs* (Shi jing) and *Songs of the South* (Chu ci), reflected in the verses and in the
form of her song, makes it likely that she was not an entertainer or a singing girl. Even
if she was a commoner, Consort Tangshan had probably been born into a prominent
family that gave her the opportunity to cultivate her literary knowledge.

Ode: Inside the Chamber was famous during Han as a temple song, and was classified under "Temple Songs" in Guo Maoqian's *Yuefu shiji,* published in the Song
dynasty (960–1279). It was also one of three major ballads (*yuefu*) composed in early
Han by members of the ruling class. Most of the titles of the seventeen verses are now
missing, and the number of verses and their divisions vary in different editions.

The song itself is mainly about worshipping ancestors and divinities, and blessings and didacticism, with a special emphasis on filial piety. It was composed in the
early years of Han, when the turmoil associated with the founding of the dynasty was
still fresh in people's minds. Holding to the ancient belief in the "union of human
and heavenly affairs" (*tian ren he yi*), the song emphasized that the dynasty had been
founded with the assistance of divinities. Consort Tangshan stressed the importance
of morality and laying down systems for being gracious to all those on the borders,
which earned the approval of Emperor Gaozu. Her song was therefore used in ancestral
worship ceremonies.

In later times, *Ode: Inside the Chamber* was considered obscure, its verses elegant but so abstruse as to have little literary value. However, the late Ming scholar
Zhong Xing (1574–1624) wrote: "Women's poems are usually somewhat seductive.
Tangshan's work is so profound and classic that it overshadows first-class writers. It
is admirable to find a woman who can compose a grand temple song." The famous
ballad critic Shen Deqian (1673–1769) commented that *Ode: Inside the Chamber*

was a profound and great literary work of harmony and peace, neither superficial nor vulgar, with classical allusions and a distinctive pattern.

The song contributed greatly to the development of Chinese literature, its unique literary features including rich diction and musical rhyme reminiscent of folk songs:

> All waters flow to the sea, the people admire the wise. The grand mountain nurtures many species of flowers. Whom do the people respect? They respect the virtuous. (*Ode: Inside the Chamber,* Verse six)

When folk songs became more popular during Han, many works were written that were similar to *Ode: Inside the Chamber* in their use of rhetoric and rhyme, so that Consort Tangshan in turn influenced the folk songs of a later age. One such was *Han Bonan yao,* written in the year 67:

> The virtue of Han is so vast that it opens up regions that have not submitted, reaching to Bonan Mountain, across Lanjin River, and to Lancang River to benefit others.

In terms of syntax and style, Consort Tangshan's song foreshadowed the development of poems with three characters and seven characters in each line. Verses seven and eight both consist of three-character lines:

> All creatures are set peacefully in their own positions, content with what they produce and carry forward for ever and ever. The flying dragon in autumn flies into the sky. The virtuous worthy has a grace that pleases the people. (Verse seven)
> Plants prosper and lichen grows everywhere. Isn't that good! Who can interfere with this? Teaching the people with morality is the most important thing of all and its achievement has no end. (Verse eight)

Three-character lines did not originate with Consort Tangshan, who adapted this syntax from songs in "Nine Songs" (Jiu ge) in *Songs of the South,* simply omitting the rest character *xi* from each line. But it was this omission of the character *xi* that created the new form that so greatly influenced poetry in Han. The best example of this is *Song of the Heavenly Horse* (Tianma ge) of Emperor Wu (156–87 B.C.E.). First found in "Treatise of Music" (Yue shu) in the first-century B.C.E. *Historical Records,* each line of this song contained the character *xi,* which had dropped out less than two hundred years later in the *History of the Han Dynasty* version, which records the verses of this song as simple three-character lines. Many famous folk songs of Han featured three-character lines and they must have been influenced by *Ode: Inside the Chamber.* Something the upper classes enjoyed would certainly have been taken up with greater enthusiasm by the lower classes.

Ode: Inside the Chamber's seven-character lines were also adapted from *Songs of the South,* as, for example, in Verse six: "All waters flow to the sea, the people admire the wise." Each line has a caesura after the first four characters, and the end-words are rhymed. Consort Tangshan has deleted from the older tradition extraneous words in the middle or at the end of lines. Again, she did not originate this rhythm and rhyme, but she deeply influenced the poetry of Han. Many works of Emperor Wu and of Emperor Huan (132–167), for example, used the seven-character lines.

198 TANGSHAN, CONSORT OF EMPEROR GAOZU

Literary historians of Ming and Qing compared *Ode: Inside the Chamber* to the hymns (*song*) and the odes (*ya*) recorded in *The Book of Songs*. While her song is perhaps slightly inferior, Consort Tangshan must be credited with having created a vigorous and refined temple song of rich diction and elegant rhetoric that influenced aristocratic literature and temple songs as well as the form and style of ballads of the entire Han dynasty. Building on *The Book of Songs* and *Songs of the South,* she evolved a new form and style that paved the way for the development of poetry with three-character and seven-character lines as well as of temple songs and folk songs.

WONG Yin Lee and NG Kwok-leung
(Translated by CHE Wai-lam William)

Guo Maoqian, ed. *Yuefu shiji,* Beijing: Zhonghua shuju, 1979, vol. 1, 8.109–22.
Han shu. Beijing: Zhonghua shuju, 1983, vol. 4, 22.1043–52.
Hu Yinglin. *Shisou.* Shanghai: Shanghai guji chubanshe, 1979, 125–42.
Shen Deqian. *Gushi yuan.* Beijing: Zhonghua shuju, 1973, 35.
Wong Yin-lee. *Handai funü wenxue wujia yanjiu.* Hong Kong: API Press, 1990, 11–40.
Xiao Difei. *Han–Wei–Liuchao yuefu wenxue shi.* Beijing: Renmin wenxue chubanshe, 1984, 33–42.
Yang Shen. *Fengya yipian, gujin fengyao, gujin yaoyan.* Shanghai: Gudian wenxue chubanshe, 1958, 102.
Zhong Xing. *Ming–Yuan shigui.* Shanghai: Youzheng shuju, 1918.

Two Honorable Women from Zhuya

The Two Honorable Women from Zhuya (Zhuya Er Yi) are said to have lived during the Western Han dynasty. One, whose given name was Chu, was the thirteen-year-old daughter of the district magistrate of Zhuya (the present-day city of Haikou, Hainan Province). The other, whose name is not recorded, was the magistrate's second wife.

According to *Biographies of Eminent Women* (Lienü zhuan), the magistrate's first wife died, leaving him with an infant daughter, Chu. The magistrate remarried and his second wife bore a son who was four years younger than Chu. When the magistrate died of illness in Zhuya, Chu was thirteen and her stepbrother was nine and the bereaved family began preparing to accompany the magistrate's coffin back to his native place on the mainland for burial. At that time there was an abundance of pearls in Zhuya but it was against the law for individuals to traffic in pearls or to smuggle them onto the mainland, the penalty for such crimes being death. The magistrate's widow was accustomed to wearing a pearl bracelet but, knowing the law, she took it off and put it aside, intending to leave it behind in Zhuya. Her son, however, picked it up out of curiosity and put it in her jewel box; neither she nor Chu knew the boy had done this. When the family passed through customs with the coffin, the customs officer found ten pearls in the widow's jewel box and asked who was responsible.

At this, thirteen-year-old Chu stepped forward and declared that she was to blame, explaining that when her stepmother had cast the pearl bracelet aside after the magistrate's death she had thought it a pity. "I like pearls, too, so I picked it up and put it in her jewel box without her knowing." The widow anxiously asked Chu if she was telling the truth

TWO OBEDIENT WOMEN OF THE WEI ANCESTRAL TEMPLE 199

and believed the girl when she said that she had indeed done this and that she was the one who should be punished. However, the widow was deeply attached to her stepdaughter and, not wanting the girl to be executed, she told the customs official that it was she, and not the girl, who had committed the crime. "After my husband died," she said, "I took the bracelet off and put it in my jewel box and I completely forgot about it in my haste to prepare to accompany the coffin. I am the guilty one." Chu immediately protested that she had done it, but the widow insisted it was she who had done it and that Chu was trying to protect her by taking the blame. The widow then burst into tears. Chu in her turn insisted that her stepmother did not know the real story and was taking the blame merely to save Chu from losing her young life. Then Chu burst into tears.

The mourners accompanying the coffin started sobbing and even the onlookers were moved to tears, while the customs officer was at a loss to know what he should write down. The magistrate in charge wept over the case and could not bring himself to bring down a sentence. Finally, he declared: "I would rather take the blame myself than condemn either of these honorable women, each of whom is determined to claim responsibility. How could I make a judgment?" Thereupon he threw the pearls away and set both the widow and her stepdaughter free. It was later discovered that neither of them had in fact been guilty but that the nine-year-old boy had unintentionally brought the whole situation about.

To this story in *Biographies of Eminent Women* is appended the comment that the deeds of these two—the loving stepmother and the filial stepdaughter—set a good example because each of them had little regard for her own life and was willing to sacrifice herself to save the other. The tale is indeed a celebration of Confucian family values, where members of the older generation demonstrate loving kindness to the younger generation, even if they are not related by blood, while members of the younger generation are forever filial to their elders.

SHEN Lidong

Liu Xiang. *Lienü zhuan.* Sibubeiyao ed., 5.9–10.
O'Hara, Albert R. *The Position of Woman in Early China According to the Lieh Nü Chuan, "The Biographies of Chinese Women."* Taipei: Mei Ya, 1971; 1978, 147–49.

Two Obedient Women of the Wei Ancestral Temple

The Two Obedient Women of the Wei Ancestral Temple (Wei Zong Ershun), fl. c. 225–210 B.C.E., lived in the state of Wei (in present-day Shanxi Province). After Wei was defeated by the neighboring state of Qin, to the west, the husband of the older of the two women was granted Wei as a fiefdom. This woman was childless but the other woman, her protective servant (in one source she is referred to as the chief concubine), had a son by her mistress's husband. The servant had cared for her mistress for eight years when her mistress's husband died. Despite the protests of her servant, the older woman, childless and now a widow, decided that it would be proper for her to leave the household, arguing that, according to propriety, she should be dismissed because she was childless. The servant in her turn did not wish to become the head of the household since she was distressed at the thought of the roles of servant and mistress being confounded. Only when she threatened suicide did the widow relent. The servant continued to care for her mistress as before, thereby preserving the principle of propriety. Their biography is included in the "Biographies of the Chaste and Obedient" in *Biographies of Eminent Women* (Lienü zhuan).

Constance A. COOK

Liu Xiang. *Lienü zhuan*. Sibubeiyao ed., 4.7a–8a.
O'Hara, Albert R. *The Position of Woman in Early China According to the Lieh Nü Chuan, "The Biographies of Chinese Women."* Taipei: Mei Ya, 1971; 1978, 119–21.

V

Virtuous Woman of the Capital, The: *see* **The Woman of Integrity from the Capital**

W

Wang, Empress Dowager: *see* **Wang Zhengjun, Empress of Emperor Yuan**

Wang, Empress Dowager (Qiongcheng): *see* **Wang, Empress of Emperor Xuan**

Wang Ba Qi: *see* **Wang Ba's Wife**

Wang Ba's Wife
Wang Ba's Wife (Wang Ba Qi), c. 10 B.C.E.–57 C.E., of Guangwu in Taiyuan, in present-day Shanxi Province, was the wife of the hermit Wang Ba, *zi* Ruzhong, of Taiyuan; her names are not recorded in the histories. It should be noted that her husband was not the Wang Ba (*zi* Yuanbo) Marquis of Huailing who had helped Emperor Guangwu (Liu Xiu, 6 B.C.E.–57 C.E.; r. 25–57 C.E.) in his movement to restore the Han dynasty.

Wang Ba became known as the "incorrupt young official" after he resigned from his high-ranking post and broke off relations with government officials during the interregnum of Wang Mang (45 B.C.E.–23 C.E.; r. 9–23 C.E.) at the end of the Western Han dynasty. When he first retired from public life, Wang Ba was not really content to live in the countryside as a recluse. At one point his friend Linghu Zibo, commandery governor of Chu, sent his son to deliver a letter to Wang Ba. This poised young man, who arrived in a magnificent carriage with an impressive entourage, made Wang Ba's son look shabby and distressed, and after his guests had departed Wang Ba retreated to his bed for several days. When his wife sought to find out what was troubling him, he told her that he was depressed to see his son so shabbily dressed and shy and behaving so clumsily in the presence of such a healthy, well-mannered young visitor. He said that he felt he had not fulfilled his paternal duties.

His wife, however, had a different view. She reminded him that he had always believed in living simply and had looked down upon riches and fame. "Do you think [Linghu] Zibo's rich life is superior to your simple but honorable life?" she asked him. "How can you betray your principles and feel ashamed of your own child?" Wang Ba admitted that what she said was true.

Wang Ba was recruited from among the common people for possible appointment to an official post during the reign of Emperor Guangwu. However, since there was a lack of agreement among those in power he did not receive an appointment, and it is believed that this was a heavy blow for him. Giving illness as his reason, he returned to his native place and refused to respond to the government's subsequent requests that he come out of retirement to fill an official post. Wang Ba led the life of a hermit but he was not as comfortable in the role as his very perceptive wife was.

XIA Chunhao

Hou Han shu. Beijing: Zhonghua shuju, 1965, vol. 10, 83.2762; vol. 10, 84.2782–83.

Wang Chang, The Wife and Daughter of: *see* **Wang Zhang's Wife**

Wang, Empress of Emperor Ping
Empress Wang (Xiao Ping Wang Huanghou), 9 B.C.E.–23 C.E., was empress to Emperor Ping (Liu Kan, 8 B.C.E.–5 C.E.; r. 1–5 C.E.). She was a daughter of Wang Mang (45 B.C.E.–23 C.E.), who usurped the Han throne in 9 C.E. and established the Xin dynasty, and his wife (*q.v.* Wang, Empress of Wang Mang of Xin).

She was also a grandniece of Empress Dowager Wang (*q.v.* Wang Zhengjun, Empress of Emperor Yuan), who appointed Wang Mang Commander-in-Chief (*da sima*) upon the ascension of Liu Kan to assist the nine-year-old emperor with affairs of state. However, it was against the wishes of his powerful aunt that Wang Mang betrothed his daughter to Emperor Ping in 4 C.E., when she was thirteen years old. Once his daughter became empress, Wang Mang was ennobled as the Duke Anhan and granted a large tract of land; three months later he was granted the title of Steward-Regulator of State (*zaiheng*), which outranked marquis and prince. Finally, when Emperor Ping died in 5 C.E., Wang Mang appointed as emperor a one-year-old infant (Liu Ying, the great-great-grandson of Emperor Xuan and son of Liu Xian the Marquis of Guangji) for whom he acted as regent. Three years later, Wang Mang usurped the throne, declaring himself emperor of the Xin dynasty (9–23 C.E.). He granted the deposed Liu Ying the title of the Duke Ding'an and made his widowed daughter Dowager Wang of the Ding'an Duke (Ding'an Gong Taihou).

Empress Wang was eighteen years old when her father deposed the Liu clan. She was a quiet and obedient young woman of great integrity and often excused herself on the grounds of illness from having to attend court meetings. Her father, however, wanted her to remarry. He changed her title to Illustrious Princess of the Imperial Clan (Huang Huangshi Zhu) and had the son of Sun Jian, the Duke of Chengxing and Dynasty-Founding General (*liguo jiangjun*), call on her, dressed in his finery, as a suitor but accompanied by doctors, who were to appear to ask after her health. In high dudgeon, Empress Wang had his bodyguards whipped. Then she retired to her bed, ill, and refused to get up, whereupon Wang Mang abandoned his plan to force her to remarry.

Wang Mang was eventually overthrown, defeated by Han dynasty armies in 23 C.E. Before hurling herself onto the flames as the Weiyang Palace burned, Empress Wang is reported to have said, "How can I face the people of the Han imperial family with a clear conscience?" Throughout her short life, this young woman was a pawn for her father's ambition. The tragedy of her situation is that she appears to have been fully aware of this and had no recourse other than to feign illness. Her heart-wrenching last words reveal the extent of her awareness.

MU Meichun

Chen Quanli and Hou Xinyi, eds. *Hou fei cidian.* Xi'an: Shaanxi renmin jiaoyu chubanshe, 1991, 20.
Han shu. Beijing: Zhonghua shuju, 1983, vol. 12, 97*xia.*4009–11.
Liu Xiang. *Lienü zhuan.* Sibubeiyao ed., 8.9.
O'Hara, Albert R. *The Position of Woman in Early China According to the Lieh Nü Chuan, "The Biographies of Chinese Women."* Taipei: Mei Ya, 1971; 1978, 238–40.

Wang, Empress of Emperor Xuan

Empress Wang (Xiao Xuan Wang Huanghou), ?90–16 B.C.E., whose given names are not recorded, was a native of Pei District (present-day Pei District, Jiangsu Province). Empress to Emperor Xuan (Liu Xun or Liu Bingyi, 91–49 B.C.E.; r. 74–49 B.C.E.), she later became in turn Empress Dowager Wang and Grand Empress Dowager Qiongcheng.

By the time she reached her teens, the future Empress Wang had been engaged more than once; each time, however, her husband-to-be had died before the marriage. Her ancestors had served Emperor Gaozu (Liu Bang, 256–195 B.C.E.; r. 202–195 B.C.E.) with merit and had been granted the title Marquis of Guannei, which her father, Wang Fengguang, inherited. Wang Fengguang had become acquainted with Liu Xun through their common love of cockfighting, so when Liu Xun ascended the throne in 74 B.C.E. the young woman was selected into the palace, quickly rising to the rank of Lady of Handsome Fairness (*jieyu*). She was appointed empress in 65 B.C.E., after Empress Huo (*q.v.* Huo Chengjun, Empress of Emperor Xuan) was deposed for attempting to kill the heir apparent, Liu Shi (Emperor Yuan, 76–33 B.C.E.; r. 48–33 B.C.E.), the emperor's son by Empress Xu (*q.v.* Xu Pingjun, Empress of Emperor Xuan). Although not a favorite, Empress Wang was chosen over three other Ladies of Handsome Fairness who were at that time receiving the emperor's favor: Lady Hua (mother of the Prince of Guantao), Lady Zhang (mother of the Prince of Huaiyang), and Lady Wei (mother of Prince Xiao of Chu). It is said that the reason Empress Wang was appointed was that she was childless and of a kind disposition and was therefore the most suitable imperial woman to raise the motherless heir apparent Liu Shi.

Empress Wang's appointment was clearly political: during the sixteen years she held this position the emperor rarely favored her and she remained childless. Upon

Emperor Xuan's death and the succession of Liu Shi, she was elevated to the position of Empress Dowager Wang. Because the mother of Emperor Cheng (*q.v.* Wang Zhengjun, Empress of Emperor Yuan) also bore the surname Wang, Empress Dowager Wang was known as Empress Dowager Qiongcheng; her father had received the title of Marquis of Qiongcheng when she first became empress.

Empress Wang was over seventy when she died, having lived through the reigns of four emperors: over a period of forty-nine years she had been empress, empress dowager, or grand empress dowager to three emperors. She was a rarity among imperial women in that not having a son worked to her advantage. When she died in 16 B.C.E. she was buried alongside Emperor Xuan in the Duling, also known as the Eastern Mausoleum (Dongyuan), on Shaoling Plain in present-day Chang'an District, Shaanxi Province.

WANG Xiaowen

Chen Quanli and Hou Xinyi, eds. *Hou fei cidian.* Xi'an: Shaanxi renmin jiaoyu chubanshe, 1991, 16.
Han shu. Beijing: Zhonghua shuju, 1983, vol. 12, 97*shang*.3969–70.

Wang, Empress of Wang Mang of Xin

Empress Wang (Xin Mang Wang Huanghou), d. 21 C.E., was a daughter of Wang Xian, Marquis of Yichun, and the wife of Wang Mang (45 B.C.E.–23 C.E.), who usurped the Han throne in 9 C.E. Wang Mang's fourteen-year reign has traditionally been regarded as simply an interregnum between the Western and Eastern Han dynasties, but in recent years scholars have begun to acknowledge Wang Mang's as a new dynasty, the Xin, which he ruled in his own right, and distinct from the Han.

During the reign of Emperor Ping (r. 1–5 C.E.), who was nine years old when he was installed, Wang Mang gained increasing power and was awarded many titles through his aunt, Empress Dowager Wang (*q.v.* Wang Zhengjun, Empress of Emperor Yuan). She made him Commander-in-Chief (*da sima*) so that he could assist the young emperor in court affairs, and gave him the title of Marquis of Xindu. This was the first step in his ascension. He was next ennobled as the Duke Anhan, his wife becoming the Duchess Anhan; in 4 C.E. he married his daughter to the boy emperor and was granted the title Steward-Regulator of State (*zaiheng*), which ranked above that of duke, his wife becoming Lady of Evident Merit (*gongxian jun*). Finally, Wang Mang became regent (6–8 C.E.) when an infant was installed as emperor after the death of Emperor Ping.

Although Wang Mang has generally been reviled throughout Chinese history for having usurped the Han throne, he was diligent and modest, inviting good and wise men to fill important positions in his new regime. His wife, now Empress Wang, also continued to be a cautious housekeeper and remained humble. For example, when Wang Mang's mother was ill, the dukes and marquis sent their wives to call on her (she was apparently living with Wang Mang and his wife). Empress Wang came out to welcome the wives of the nobility and they took her for a housemaid or a servant, for

204 WANG, EMPRESS OF WANG MANG OF XIN

she was dressed in a skirt that did not reach the ground, her knees covered only with a cotton cloth. The visitors were astonished when they discovered who she was.

In addition to the daughter who married Emperor Ping, Empress Wang bore four sons: Wang Yu, Wang Huo, Wang An, and Wang Lin. Two of her sons—Wang Yu and Wang Huo—were executed when they opposed their father during the reign of Emperor Ping, and Empress Wang wept so bitterly over their deaths that she is said to have gone blind. Once installed as emperor, Wang Mang appointed their son Wang Lin heir apparent, enjoining him to care for his mother. Wang Mang had by then transferred his affections to her maid, Yuan Bi.

Empress Wang died in 21 C.E. She was granted the posthumous title Empress Xiaomu and was buried in Yinian Tomb in Changshou Garden in Weiling (present-day Xanyang in Shaanxi Province).

YANG Haiming

Chen Quanli and Hou Xinyi, eds. *Hou fei cidian.* Xi'an: Shaanxi renmin jiaoyu chubanshe, 1991, 20.
Han shu. Beijing: Zhonghua shuju, 1983, vol. 12, 99 passim.

Wang Jingbo's Wife: *see* **Wen Jijiang**

Wang Ling, The Mother of: *see* **Wang Ling's Mother**

Wang Ling Mu: *see* **Wang Ling's Mother**

Wang Ling's Mother
Wang Ling's Mother (Wang Ling Mu), fl. mid-third century B.C.E., is known only by this name, her given name and surname not being recorded. Her son Wang Ling (233–202 B.C.E.) rose to the position of right counselor-in-chief (*you chengxiang*) during the reign of Emperor Gaozu (Liu Bang, 256–195 B.C.E.; r. 206–195 B.C.E.), the founder of Western Han.

Before Liu Bang came to power as emperor, he and Wang Ling had been as close as brothers. A man of honor and courage, Wang Ling lent his full support to Liu Bang when he was King of Han during the chaotic final years of the Qin dynasty. When Liu Bang rose in rebellion, Wang Ling gathered together several thousand followers and occupied Nanyang (in the southwest of present-day Henan Province). At that time, Liu Bang was locked in a struggle for supremacy with the rival rebel leader Xiang Yu (232–202 B.C.E.) of the state of Chu (*vide* Yu, Consort of the Hegemon-King of Chu). Xiang Yu held the upper hand after defeating Liu Bang in 205, and among those he captured and held hostage to Han was Wang Ling's Mother; another was Liu Bang's wife, Lü Zhi (*q.v.* Lü Zhi, Empress of Emperor Gaozu), who was taken hostage in 205 along with her father. When a messenger from Wang Ling arrived at the Chu camp, Xiang Yu placed Wang Ling's Mother in the place of honor facing the east, in the hope of persuading him to change sides. However, as she was seeing the messenger off, Wang Ling's Mother spoke to him in private, telling him that her real message to her son was that he must remain loyal to the King of Han, Liu Bang. "Tell my son never to betray the King of Han for my sake," she instructed the messenger. "Take these back as my final words." She then fell upon a sword and died. This so enraged Xiang Yu that he had her body boiled. This barbarous act in turn firmed Wang Ling's resolve to remain loyal to Liu Bang, who eventually pacified the empire, rewarding Wang Ling with the title Marquis of Anguo, which remained in his family for five generations, and promoting him to Right Counselor-in-Chief.

Wang Ling's Mother has been praised throughout Chinese history for sacrificing her life for her son's just cause—the establishment of the Han dynasty. In commemorating her, *Biographies of Eminent Women* (Lienü zhuan) describes her suicide as "kindness" (*ren*) and cites *The Book of Songs* (Shi jing): "Though for my person you have no regard, at least pity my brood" (Waley, 100). As an exemplar of female behavior, the story of Wang Ling's Mother emphasizes the nobility of self-sacrifice.

SHEN Lidong

Han shu. Beijing: Zhonghua shuju, 1983, vol. 7, 40.2046–47.
Liu Xiang. *Lienü zhuan.* Sibubeiyao ed., 8.2–3.
O'Hara, Albert R. *The Position of Woman in Early China According to the Lieh Nü Chuan, "The Biographies of Chinese Women."* Taipei: Mei Ya, 1971; 1978, 220.
Waley, Arthur. *The Book of Songs.* Boston: Houghton Mifflin, 1937, 100.

Wang Qiang: *see* Wang Zhaojun

Wang Wengxu

Wang Wengxu, c. 109–91 B.C.E., of Zhu Commandery (the present-day city of Zhuzhou, Hebei Province), was the mother of Emperor Xuan (Liu Xun or Liu Bingyi, 91–49 B.C.E.; r. 74–49 B.C.E.). During her lifetime, Wang Wengxu had no official title; she and the other wives and concubines of Liu Jin (Emperor Wu's grandson) were all referred to as "daughters of commoners." However, because her son eventually became emperor, Wang Wengxu is recorded in the official histories as Consort of the Imperial Grandson, by Shi (Shi Huangsun Wang Furen). This is because her husband was the son of Liu Ju and Related Lady of Excellence Shi (Wei Taizi Shi Liangdi).

Wang Wengxu's mother, later known simply as Old Lady Wang or Dame Wang, was from Zhu Commandery and had married twice. Her first husband, Wang Gengde, whom she married when she was fourteen, died of illness. Her second husband, Wang Naishi, was from Guangwang District and she bore him two sons and a daughter (Wang Wengxu). When Wang Wengxu was eight or nine, she was sent as a foster child to the house of Liu Zhongqing, a younger son of Marquis Jie of Guangwang, and there she learned to sing and dance. Four or five years later, a merchant from Handan came seeking singers and dancers. When it became apparent that Liu Zhongqing was going to give her to the merchant Jia Chang'er, Wang Wengxu fled with her mother to the mother's native village. They were followed, however, and brought back to Guangwang, where Liu Zhongqing falsely assured them he would not give the girl to Jia Chang'er. Only a few days later, Wang Wengxu was driven past her mother's house

206 WANG WENGXU

in Jia Chang'er's carriage: Wang Wengxu called out to her mother that they were on their way to Liusu. Her mother followed the carriage there but finally had to bid her daughter a tearful farewell. She did not find out until more than twenty years later what happened to her daughter.

Upon their arrival at the capital Chang'an, Wang Wengxu was sent to the house of Liu Ju, the heir apparent. She became a concubine of Liu Ju's son, Liu Jin, sometime between 96 and 93 B.C.E. and in 91 gave birth to a son. This child was named Liu Bingyi (he is also called Liu Xun), but he was known as "the imperial great-grandson" (of Emperor Wu). Just a few months after the birth of her son, Wang Wengxu was among the hundreds of people put to death when the heir apparent and Empress Wei (*q.v.* Wei Zifu, Empress of Emperor Wu) were implicated in a witchcraft scare. The sole surviving member of his family, Liu Bingyi owed his life to an official named Bing Ji (d. 55 B.C.E.), who protected and nurtured him out of human kindness. After Liu Bingyi was enthroned in 74, he honored his mother posthumously as Mournful Empress and had her reburied in a new grave set in a funerary park with a village and officials to maintain her tomb. Emperor Xuan searched for and eventually found Wang Wengxu's mother (his maternal grandmother), bestowing upon her the title of Lady Boping (Boping Jun) and assigning to her the income of two districts. He later gave her the posthumous title of Lady Sicheng (Sicheng Furen).

WANG Xiaowen

Ban Gu. *Courtier and Commoner in Ancient China: Selections from the "History of the Former Han" by Pan Ku,* trans. B. Watson. New York: Columbia University Press, 1974, 47, 253–57.
Chen Quanli and Hou Xinyi, eds. *Hou fei cidian.* Xi'an: Shaanxi renmin jiaoyu chubanshe, 1991, 15.
Han shu. Beijing: Zhonghua shuju, 1983, vol. 12, 97*shang*.3961–64.

Wang Zhang Nü: *see* **Wang Zhang's Wife**

Wang Zhang Qi: *see* **Wang Zhang's Wife**

Wang Zhang's Wife
Wang Zhang's Wife (Wang Zhang Qi), fl. c. 33–20 B.C.E., is remembered as a woman of insight; her given names and surname are not recorded. Her husband came from Juping in Taishan (near present-day Dawenkou, southeast of the city of Tai'an, Shandong Province) and had been appointed as an official when he was still quite young. He had considerable literary ability and was upright and straightforward. O'Hara states in a footnote that Wang Zhang was a maternal uncle of Emperor Cheng (r. 32–7 B.C.E.) and that he died in 26 B.C.E.

When Wang Zhang went to study in Chang'an, his wife accompanied him. He fell ill, however, and without a quilt was unable to keep warm, so he slept under a hemp blanket of the type used to keep cattle warm. He was so sick and depressed that he became tearful, telling his wife that he was going to die, but his wife merely scolded him for his lack of spirit. Wang Zhang survived this illness and was eventually recommended—by the powerful General-in-Chief (*da jiangjun*) Wang Feng (d. 22 B.C.E.), also a maternal uncle of Emperor Cheng—to the position of metropolitan governor (*jing zhaoyin*). Despite having been recommended by Wang Feng, Wang Zhang later composed a memorial to Emperor Cheng requesting the demotion of Wang Feng because he wielded too much power at court. Wang Zhang's Wife, however, tried to dissuade him from submitting the memorial, saying: "We should be content with what we now have. Surely you recall the time when you were weeping as you huddled under the cattle blanket?" Wang Zhang retorted that she was merely a woman who understood nothing about politics and he proceeded to hand in the memorial. While the emperor took no heed of the request, Wang Feng concocted a charge against Wang Zhang and had him, his wife, and his children arrested. One night, Wang Zhang's twelve-year-old daughter woke in the middle of the night crying. "I have been hearing the prisoners call out their numbers, from one to nine, but just now only eight called out. My father has always been upright and resolute; it must have been he who was executed first!" Wang Zhang's wife asked the following day and was told that the girl had been correct and that Wang Zhang was dead.

Wang Zhang's Wife and her children were then exiled to Hepu (present-day Hepu District, Guangdong Province). There, the family worked in the pearl industry and accumulated considerable wealth, their property worth several million cash. After the death of Wang Feng, his brother Wang Shang was appointed to the position of general-in-chief. Knowing that Wang Zhang had been innocent of any crime, Wang Shang requested that Wang Zhang's family be allowed to return to their home in Taishan. When they returned, the commandery governor of Taishan told them they could buy back their old house.

Wang Zhang's Wife appears to have been a strong woman of acute political perception and knowledge of human nature. She was clearly not prepared to take any nonsense, least of all from her husband, a characteristic that would have stood her in good stead as she went about making a fortune while in exile in Guangdong.

SHEN Jian

Han shu. Beijing: Zhonghua shuju, 1983, vol. 10, 76.3238–42.
Liu Xiang. *Lienü zhuan.* Sibubeiyao ed., 8.6.
O'Hara, Albert R. *The Position of Woman in Early China According to the Lieh Nü Chuan, "The Biographies of Chinese Women."* Taipei: Mei Ya, 1971; 1978, 229–30.

Wang Zhaojun

Wang Qiang (three variant characters), fl. 33–20 B.C.E., *zi* Zhaojun, is also known as Mingjun and Mingfei. However, she is most commonly known as Wang Zhaojun. Given in marriage to the khan (*shanyu,* or chief) of the nomadic Xiongnu people and sent to live with them beyond the northern border of China, she was undoubtedly a historical personage, but over the centuries historians, poets, playwrights, novelists, painters, and musicians have elaborated on her simple yet tragic story, creating the legendary Wang Zhaojun, a woman of great and enduring charm who for 2,000 years has been pitied, admired, and praised.

The earliest mention of Wang Zhaojun is in historical sources. In the "Annals of Emperor Yuan" and "Xiongnu" chapters of the *History of the Han Dynasty* (Han shu; compiled in the first century C.E.), she is described as being from "a good family," which usually meant those not belonging to the medical, shaman, merchant, or laboring classes. She had an older brother: the *History of the Han Dynasty* records his son Wang Xi as Marquis of Peace Marriages (*heqin hou*) and another, by the name of Wang Sa, as Marquis of Manifest Kindness (*zhande hou*). Wang Zhaojun was taken into the palace (*yeting*) to "await the imperial order" of Emperor Yuan (r. 48–33 B.C.E.). She was never summoned into his presence, however, and remained a woman of the household (*jiarenzi*), meaning that she was not a concubine nor was she honored with any of the titles given to women in the fourteen ranks of imperial concubines.

In 33 B.C.E., Wang Zhaojun was given in marriage to Huhanye, a khan of the nomadic Turkish-speaking Xiongnu tribes who roamed the northern grasslands of what is now Outer Mongolia and are known in the West as the Huns. The Xiongnu had raided China's northern border regions for almost a millennium and by the early years of Western Han had established a large empire on the steppes. The founder of the Han dynasty, Emperor Gaozu (r. 206–195 B.C.E.), initiated a policy of marriage alliances—"peace marriages" (*heqin*)—to resolve this northern-border problem by diplomatic rather than military means. The purpose of these peace marriages was to form a "brother-states" relationship between the Han and the Xiongnu: it was initially suggested that the eldest Han princess be offered in marriage to the Xiongnu but the daughter of a clansman was chosen instead. This policy of peace marriages was continued throughout Western Han (*vide* Liu Xijun and Liu Jieyou) and opened the way for the economic and cultural exchanges necessary for the two nations to coexist peacefully. By the mid-first century B.C.E., however, a series of natural disasters and internal problems had reduced the Xiongnu to tributary status. When Huhanye made his third visit to the Chinese capital of Chang'an (the present-day city of Xi'an) to renew the rituals of tribute in 33 B.C.E., a peace marriage was proposed with Wang Zhaojun as the bride; it may well have been the reduced tributary status of the Xiongnu that led Emperor Yuan to choose her, a young woman of good family, rather than a member of the imperial family. Nevertheless, the political and military importance Emperor Yuan attached to Wang Zhaojun's crossing of the border is evident from the unprecedented act of declaring a new reign title—*jingning* (peace at the border)—in honor of this peace marriage. Emperor Yuan died four months after Wang Zhaojun was given in marriage.

Wang Zhaojun was merely one of Huhanye's many consorts, of equal rank with several Xiongnu wives who had between them given birth to at least ten sons. By the time Huhanye died, two years later, after reigning for twenty-eight years, she too had borne him a son. This child, Yitu Zhiyashi, was initially enfeoffed as King of Youluli, possibly because Huhanye placed in this child of his old age the hope that he might consolidate the Xiongnu–Han alliance, and he eventually assumed the title of King of Zuoxian, ranking second only to the khan in importance.

When Huhanye died, the oldest son (his name was Diaotaomogao) of his senior consort assumed leadership of the Xiongnu as Khan Fuzhulei Ruoti (d. 20 B.C.E.). It was the custom of the Xiongnu for a man to marry his stepmothers when his father died and to marry his brother's widows, so Fuzhulei Ruoti took Wang Zhaojun as his wife. She bore him two daughters during the ten years of his reign. The older daughter, Yun, was known as Princess Xubu after she married the Xiongnu nobleman Xubu Dang. Princess Xubu and her husband belonged to the pro-Han faction of the Xiongnu court and during Emperor Ping's short reign (r. 1–5 C.E.) Commander-in-Chief Wang Mang (45 B.C.E.–23 C.E.) invited them to serve the empress dowager (*q.v.* Wang Zhengjun, Empress of Emperor Yuan) in the capital, Chang'an, where they were presented with many gifts. Together with their son Xubu She, they visited Chang'an again in 18 C.E., during Wang Mang's short-lived Xin dynasty. After the death from illness of Xubu Dang, Wang Mang arranged for Princess Xubu's son to marry his daughter Princess Lulu (Wang Jie), giving him the title Duke of Hou'an and intending to provide military aid that would allow him to become the Xiongnu khan. Princess Xubu and her son were killed, however, during the uprising that overthrew Wang Mang in 23 C.E. Wang Zhaojun's second daughter, whose name is unrecorded, became known after her marriage as Princess Dangyu and had at least one son, King Xidu.

As a result of Wang Zhaojun's marrying out to the Xiongnu, members of her natal family were appointed to court as diplomats. Her two nephews paid many visits to the Xiongnu on behalf of the court. Wang Sa may also have been honored by having the Han imperial surname, Liu, bestowed upon him, as there is a record of an emissary by the name of Liu Sa in 30 C.E. The *History of the Han Dynasty* says no more of Wang Zhaojun after recording her second marriage and gives no indication of when or where she died. However, the hope of peace between the Han and the Xiongnu that was the reason for her marriage lasted less than half a century.

This sad story of a young woman condemned to exile in a far-off land and given in marriage to at least two "barbarian" men is the historical basis of the Wang Zhaojun legend.

Within 200 years, the first legends had already grown up around Wang Zhaojun, with similar anecdotal additions to her story appearing in the second-century *Qin cao* (Tunes for the *qin*) by Cai Yong (132–192) and in the official history of Eastern Han, *History of the Later Han Dynasty* (Hou Han shu; compiled in the fifth century). In these texts she is given both a father—Wang Xiang (or Rang) of Qi (in the north of the present-day province of Shandong)—and a native place. The *History of the Later Han Dynasty* records her native place as Zigui in Nan Commandery (the western part of present-day Hubei Province bordering on Sichuan Province). North of Zigui there is indeed a Zhaojun Village, where in recent years faux-ancient buildings and a white statue have been constructed, presumably to attract tourists. Unfortunately, this area of Zigui will be submerged when the massive Three Gorges Dam is completed. However, there is also a Zhaojun Village on Mount Wu in Sichuan, leading some to claim Wang Zhaojun for that province. The famous Tang poet Du Fu (712–770) wrote: "If you say the women of Wushan are rough and ugly, how is it possible for Zhaojun Village to be there?" One source says Wang Zhaojun was from Shandong, and in Song times she was said to have come from Xingshan District, an administrative unit that did not exist when she was alive.

Wang Zhaojun did enter the palace as a potential concubine of Emperor Yuan

210 WANG ZHAOJUN

but *Qin cao* and the *History of the Later Han Dynasty* elaborate further, saying she had grown sad and resentful after spending several years in the women's quarters without even meeting the emperor, let alone being chosen to "serve" him sexually. She therefore volunteered to be sent to the Xiongnu in a peace marriage, and when the emperor finally laid eyes on her at her farewell banquet he was so stunned by her beauty that he regretted having to let her go. Honor, however, demanded that he keep his word to the Xiongnu khan Huhanye, and she left the palace with four other palace women (names unrecorded) who were assigned as concubines; no explanation has been offered as to why Wang Zhaojun alone of the five women became a consort. The early-twentieth-century scholar Zhang Changgong proposed that she may have seen this as an opportunity to raise her status, thus ensuring that her family would receive more favorable treatment from the Han court.

The few historical facts given in the *History of the Han Dynasty* have provided fertile ground for later legend. The *History* adds a second son to her marriage to Huhanye. It also says that her son Yitu Zhiyashi was killed by one of his half-brothers in the early first century C.E., by which time she may have already died.

As already mentioned, when Huhanye died, his oldest son became the Khan Fu-zhulei Ruoti (d. 20 B.C.E.) and, according to custom, he took Wang Zhaojun as his wife. Naturally, no indication is given in the *History of the Han Dynasty* of how Wang Zhaojun reacted to this custom of marrying her husband's son, but Han Chinese people traditionally considered such unions as incest. Understandably perhaps, the *History of the Later Han Dynasty* and *Qin cao* go into considerable detail on this point. Horrified at the prospect of marrying her stepson, Wang Zhaojun is said to have sought permission from the Han court to return to China instead of going through with this second marriage. Her plea was rejected, with Emperor Cheng (r. 32–7 B.C.E.) ordering her to abide by the custom of the Xiongnu. *Qin cao* goes further, claiming improbably that it was her own son (Shiwei, who could have been no more than fifteen months old at the time) who succeeded Huhanye and insisted on taking her as a wife. She preferred suicide to marrying her son and took poison.

Wang Zhaojun's story and the legends associated with her have been celebrated by poets through the ages. *Mingjun ci,* written by Shi Chong (249–300) of the Western Jin dynasty, was a very popular lyric said to have been adapted into a dance performed by his concubine Lüzhu (*q.v.*). Shi Chong's poem established a genre in which Wang Zhaojun was "a tragic figure, a woman who could not gain the favor of the emperor and died in a foreign land, a victim of greed and treachery." The famous Tang poets Li Bai, Du Fu, and Bai Juyi all wrote poems on this theme. Both Qi Jiguang (1528–1587) of Ming and Wang Anshi (1021–1086) of Song wrote songs entitled *Mingfei qu,* Wang Anshi's presenting "a woman overwhelmed by sorrow . . . the most extraordinary beauty in the history of Chinese literature":

> When the Luminous Lady married a Xiongnu man,
> Her carriages were tended by Xiongnu maids.
> Her heart was full but to whom could she speak?
> Her *pipa* gave voice to her deepest feelings.

A plectrum of gold, hands evoking spring breeze
Sang of migrating geese as her cup filled with Xiongnu wine.
Maid servants from the Han court hid their tears;
Travellers over the sands looked back as they passed.

Few are the favours of Han, strong the Xiongnu's love—
In mutual regard lies the true joy of life.
Her green grave is now lost to rampant grass,
But the music of her sad strings lingers in our ears. (Translated by Eva Hung)

Music, and especially the *pipa,* similar to a Western lute, has long been associated with Wang Zhaojun. *Qin cao* added this musical element when it quoted the *Song Lamenting Banishment,* which she is said to have composed before leaving Han, and she is often portrayed in Chinese art holding a *pipa.* The earliest known painting of Wang Zhaojun is by Han Gan (fl. 742–755).

In his *Autumn in the Han Palace* (Hangong qiu), the Yuan dynasty playwright Ma Zhiyuan (c. 1260–1335) took as his theme the love between Emperor Yuan and Wang Zhaojun. Entranced by Wang Zhaojun's *pipa* playing and, when he finally sees her, by her beauty, the emperor falls in love with her and takes her as his concubine, only to have to give her up when the Xiongnu khan, captivated by a portrait of her, threatens to invade China. Realizing it is the only way to avert war, Wang Zhaojun volunteers to sacrifice herself by going to the Xiongnu, but at the border she throws herself in the Heilong (Amur) River and drowns. Ma Zhiyuan's was the first of many plays that dramatized this touching love affair and Wang Zhaojun's consequent suicide by drowning at the border. In more recent times, the idea that Wang Zhaojun volunteered to go to the Xiongnu was taken up by Cao Yu (1910–1996) in his play *Wang Zhaojun,* written in the 1960s but not produced until 1979. Wang Zhaojun had inspired many writers during the 1960s campaign of national unification at a time when "the authorities insisted that Wang Zhaojun be presented as a happy and smiling woman who had gone of her own volition to live with the Xiongnu, as an ambassadress charged with erasing the chauvinism and xenophobia of the Han people." In a 1978 interview, Cao Yu spoke openly of how Premier Zhou Enlai had advised him to "write a new work on Wang Zhaojun highlighting the national union of the Chinese people," and indeed Cao Yu's play presents a totally different Wang Zhaojun from the traditional image of her.

The legend that the grass on Wang Zhaojun's grave remains green in that land "where the grass was dry and white," appears to have originated in *Qin cao,* while the name by which her grave is now known—the Green Grave or Green Tumulus—was already current during the Tang dynasty, as can be seen from these famous lines from a Du Fu poem:

Once she had left the purple towers, she was swallowed by the northern deserts;
Only her Green Grave remains in the dusk.

Archeological evidence may one day pinpoint this Green Grave, but in the meantime there are several theories as to its location. The contemporary scholar Liang Rongruo

212   WANG ZHAOJUN

wrote: "All three of the possible graves of Wang Zhaojun are in Suiyuan Province. There are no relics at the one in Liangchen. There is one on the south bank of the Yellow River seventy *li* west of Baotou, and the third is on the south bank of the Hei River thirty *li* southeast of Guisui city. . . . I paid a visit to this one in 1946 and found a place an acre in size (four or five *mu*) and thirty meters high (ten *zhang*) surrounded by healthy green willows some of whose trunks were as thick as my embrace." The playwright Cao Yu later wrote: "I examined two of Wang Zhaojun's possible graves during visits to Inner Mongolia: one in Baotou and a very large one in Hohhot that was bigger than Yuefei's tomb. Hohhot used to be called Guisui, which would therefore make that the grave Liang Rongruo visited, because Zhang Changgong's research also located her grave in Guisui."

Thus, the scant reliable information available on Wang Zhaojun allows us only a glimpse of her. Too distant to be seen clearly, she may be smiling or she may be weeping. The mists surrounding her and the many forms in which her story has been told across the centuries have recently become the focus of research in various disciplines, literature and gender and cultural studies among them. Never in any of her guises does Wang Zhaojun appear to have harbored political ambitions. She seems to have sacrificed her personal happiness out of obedience to the Han court, and therein lies both the tragedy and the greatness of Wang Zhaojun.

LI Yu-ning
(Translated and expanded by Lily Xiao Hong LEE and Sue WILES)

Cao Yu. *Wang Zhaojun.* Chengdu: Sichuan renmin chubanshe, 1979.
Han shu. Beijing: Zhonghua shuju, 1975, vol. 8, 94*xia*.3803–7.
Hou Han shu. Beijing: Zhonghua shuju, 1973, vol. 5, 89.2941.
Hung, Eva. "Wang Zhaojun: From History to Legend." *Renditions* 59 & 60 (2003): 7–26, 62.
Jian Bozan. *Lishi wenti luncong.* Beijing: Renmin chubanshe, 1962.
Kwong, Hing Foon. *Wang Zhaojun. Une héroïne chinoise de l'histoire à la légende.* Mémoires de l'Institut des Hautes Études Chinoises, vol. 27. Paris: Collège de France, 1986.
Lei, Daphne Pi-Wei. "Wang Zhaojun on the Border: Gender and Intercultural Conflicts in Premodern Chinese Drama." *Asian Theatre Journal* 13, no. 2 (1996): 229–37.
Liang Rongruo. *Wenshi luncong.* Taizhong: Donghai daxue, 1961.
Liu Shisheng. *Zhongguo gudai funüshi.* Qingdao: Qingdao chubanshe, 1991, 107–9.
Zhang Changgong. "Wang Zhaojun." *Lingnan xuebao* 2, no. 2 (July 1931): 114–36.

Wang Zhengjun, Empress of Emperor Yuan

Wang Zhengjun (Xiao Yuan Wang Huanghou), 71 B.C.E.–13 C.E., was empress to Emperor Yuan (Liu Shi, 76–33 B.C.E.; r. 48–33 B.C.E.). She was the mother of Emperor Cheng (Liu Ao, 51–7 B.C.E.; r. 32–7 B.C.E.) and an aunt of Wang Mang (45 B.C.E.–23 C.E.; r. 9–23 C.E.), whose usurpation of the Han crown in 9 C.E. presaged the breakdown of the Western Han dynasty. Her family originally came from Dongpingling (southeast of present-day Licheng District, Shandong Province) but later moved to Yuancheng in Wei Prefecture (east of present-day Daming District, Hebei Province).

Wang Zhengjun's father, Wang Jin, held the post of clerk for the chamberlain of law enforcement (*tingwei shi*), and he and his wife, whose name is not recorded, had four daughters. It is said that when Wang Zhengjun's mother became pregnant with her, their second daughter, she dreamt of the moon entering her lap, clearly an auspicious omen. Wang Zhengjun grew to be a mild and virtuous young woman and received several offers of marriage. However, each of her husbands-to-be died before the wedding could be held. Even more strangely, the Prince of Dongping also died as he was about to take her as his concubine. So puzzled was Wang Jin that he approached a fortune-teller, who told him that his daughter would become very distinguished. Wang Jin decided to prepare her for this by teaching her to read and instructing her in music, and in 53 B.C.E., when she was eighteen, Wang Zhengjun entered the palace as one of the unranked palace women with the title of Woman of the Household (*jiarenzi*).

Two years later, by a bizarre turn of events, Wang Zhengjun was chosen as a concubine for the heir apparent, Liu Shi (the future Emperor Yuan), and she bore him his first son, Liu Ao. This is how it came about. The heir apparent's favorite concubine, Related Lady of Excellence (*liangdi*) Sima, died in 51 B.C.E. and on her deathbed she told Liu Shi that his other concubines were to blame for her death since they had placed curses on her. Liu Shi became ill with grief and fell into a deep depression, refusing to see any of his concubines. When his father, Emperor Xuan (Liu Xun or Liu Bingyi, 91–49 B.C.E.; r. 74–49 B.C.E.), was eventually told of this, he instructed his Empress Wang (*q.v.* Wang, Empress of Emperor Xuan) to select five women of the household to serve the heir apparent, with the intention of enticing him out of his depression. Empress Wang then instructed a palace attendant (*shizhong*) to ask the heir apparent discreetly which of the five he preferred. Not taken by any of the young women but unwilling to disappoint the empress, the grief-stricken heir apparent managed to reply, "I like only one of them." The palace attendant took this remark to be directed at Wang Zhengjun, who was sitting closest and who wore an attractive loose gown hemmed with red ribbon, and reported accordingly to the empress. The heir apparent did not protest when Wang Zhengjun was brought to him; she immediately became pregnant and gave birth to a son (Liu Ao). After the birth of her son, Wang Zhengjun was promoted to the rank of Lady of Handsome Fairness (*jieyu*), but Liu Shi rarely favored her from then on and she had no more children.

The birth of his grandson Liu Ao delighted Emperor Xuan, who gave him the title Taisun (Grandson Successor). Upon the death of Emperor Xuan in 49 B.C.E., Liu Shi (Emperor Yuan) was enthroned, Wang Zhengjun became Empress Wang, and their son Liu Ao became the heir apparent. On many occasions, however, Emperor Yuan wished to depose Liu Ao and appoint in his place another of his sons—Prince Gong of Dingtao—who was the son of a later favorite, Lady of Bright Deportment Fu (*q.v.* Fu, Concubine of Emperor Yuan). Liu Ao managed to retain his position as heir apparent until his father's death largely because of the affection that his grandfather Emperor Xuan had shown to him, together with the innate cautiousness of his mother, Empress Wang, and the support of Palace Attendant Shi Dan.

Upon the ascension of Liu Ao (Emperor Cheng) to the throne, his mother was granted the title Empress Dowager Wang and her paternal relatives gradually gained in influence. Her father had been appointed Marquis of Yangping when she gave birth to Liu Ao and now her elder brother Wang Feng was appointed General-in-Chief (*da jiangjun*), Commander-in-Chief (*da sima*), and Concurrent Imperial Secretary (*ling shangshu shi*). After the death of Emperor Cheng, the throne passed briefly to his nephew Liu Xin (Emperor Ai, 25–1 B.C.E.; r. 6–1 B.C.E.), then to another of his nephews, the nine-year-old Liu Kan (Emperor Ping, 8 B.C.E.–5 C.E.; r. 1–5 C.E.). Empress Dowager Wang, now Grand Empress Dowager Wang, decreed that her nephew Wang Mang be appointed Commander-in-Chief to assist Emperor Ping, who was a sickly boy, with affairs of state when he became emperor. In this position of great power, Wang Mang grew autocratic, but nevertheless did his best to please his aunt. Early in the year the boy emperor died (5 C.E.). Grand Empress Dowager Wang showed special favor to Wang Mang, granting him the imperial reward known as the Nine Gifts (*jiuxi*). However, after the emperor's death—it is said that Wang Mang had the boy poisoned—she was unable to prevent Wang Mang from seizing more power by appointing Liu Ying (r. 6–8 C.E.), a great-great-grandson of Emperor Xuan, as heir apparent and making himself his regent. Although not in favor of these political machinations, Grand Empress Dowager Wang blocked moves by members of the imperial Liu clan to topple Wang Mang, apparently believing that he would soon realize the error of his ways.

When Wang Mang declared himself emperor on January 9, 9 C.E., however, and asked her for the imperial seal and ribbon, Grand Empress Dowager Wang was so enraged that she threw them to the ground, crying and cursing him. Upon becoming emperor, Wang Mang changed the name of the dynasty from Han to Xin (New); he also changed Grand Empress Dowager Wang's title to Grand Empress Dowager Mother Wen. He had previously given Emperor Yuan (Grand Empress Dowager Wang's husband) the posthumous temple name of Gaozong; now he had the temple destroyed. Grand Empress Dowager Wang was distraught at the unfolding tragedy in which she had unwittingly had a hand and resisted Wang Mang's every effort to please and flatter her. She took her meals and refreshments only with her personal attendants and repeatedly refused to obey his edicts. When, for example, Wang Mang altered the dress for court officials from black to yellow marten coats and changed the calendar, Grand Empress Dowager Wang ordered her officials to wear black marten coats and to continue using the Han calendar.

Grand Empress Dowager Wang died in 16 C.E. at the age of eighty-four and was buried in Wei Tomb (in the present-day city of Xianyang) alongside Emperor Yuan.

The *History of the Han Dynasty* (Han shu) cites Ban Biao (3–54 C.E.) in commenting on Wang Zhengjun in "Yuanhou zhuan." Empress Wang of Emperor Yuan, it says, was the mother of the state for sixty years, through four reigns. With power already having been transferred to the Wang clan through her brothers and cousins receiving imperial titles, five of them as generals and ten as marquis, the tragedy of Wang Mang's usurpation was inevitable. What was pitiful, the *History of the Han Dynasty* continues, was that in finally withholding the imperial seal, in itself a futile act, she acted "as only a woman would." However, while it is clear that Grand Empress Dowager Wang made a grave mistake in making so many concessions to Wang Mang in her last years, it may be too simplistic to hold her alone accountable for the overweening ambitions of the male members of her paternal clan that brought about the demise of Western Han.

SHEN Lidong

Anderson, Greg. "To Change China: A Tale of Three Reformers." *Asia Pacific: Perspectives* 1, no. 1 (2001): 1–18. www.pacificrim.usfca.edu/research/perspectives/app_v1n1.html.

Chen Quanli and Hou Xinyi, eds. *Hou fei cidian.* Xi'an: Shaanxi renmin jiaoyu chubanshe, 1991, 16.

Han shu. Beijing: Zhonghua shuju, 1983, vol. 12, 98.4013–37.

Loewe, Michael. "The Cosmological Context of Sovereignty in Han Times." *Bulletin of the School of Oriental and African Studies* 65 (2002): 342–49.

Wang Zhi, Empress of Emperor Jing

Wang Zhi (Xiao Jing Wang Huanghou), d. 126 B.C.E., of Huaili in Fufeng (in the southeast of present-day Xingping District, Shaanxi Province), was the second empress of Emperor Jing (Liu Qi, 188–141 B.C.E.; r. 156–141 B.C.E.) and mother of the famed Emperor Wu (Liu Che, 156–87 B.C.E.; r. 140–87 B.C.E.).

Wang Zhi was the daughter of Wang Zhong and of Zang Er, who was a granddaughter of Zang Tu, the late king of the state of Yan, and who was later given the title Lady of Pingyuan (Pingyuan Jun). The eldest of three children, Wang Zhi had a brother, Wang Xing, and a sister, Wang Xu. Her mother remarried after Wang Zhong died, this second marriage to a man named Tian from Changling (in the northeast of the present-day city of Xianyang, Shaanxi Province) producing two more sons (Tian Fen, d. 131 B.C.E., and Tian Sheng). Wang Zhi was herself married off to a local man, Jin Wangsun, to whom she bore a daughter named Jin Su. Wang Zhi's mother, however, had never become reconciled to the decline in her family's fortunes. Therefore, when a fortune-teller predicted that both of her daughters were destined for riches and honor, Zang Er went to Jin Wangsun demanding that the marriage be annulled and that her daughter be allowed to return to her natal home. Not surprisingly, Jin Wangsun refused, so Zang Er smuggled her daughter into the palace of the heir apparent, Liu Qi.

Wang Zhi was a charming young woman and she immediately won the heart of Liu Qi, who conferred on her the title Consort Wang. She bore him three daughters and, according to the official histories, the night she conceived her son she claimed to have dreamt of the sun falling into her lap. This delighted Liu Qi, who saw this as a sign of the child's nobility. The year Liu Qi ascended the throne, Consort Wang gave birth to a son, Liu Che.

This did not change her status, however, because the emperor's official wife had been appointed empress upon his enthronement. Emperor Jing was not fond of his wife, Empress Bo (*q.v.* Bo, Empress of Emperor Jing), whom he had married at the behest of his grandmother and her great-aunt Empress Dowager Bo (*q.v.* Bo, Concubine of Emperor Gaozu). Therefore, after Empress Dowager Bo died (155 B.C.E.) the emperor deposed Empress Bo on the pretext of her not having produced any children and not being favored by him.

Emperor Jing appointed Liu Rong, his eldest son by Concubine Li (Li Ji), heir apparent in 153 B.C.E. but did not elevate Concubine Li in status. When, soon afterward, the emperor repeatedly fell ill and became depressed, he asked Concubine Li to take care of his sons, who had all been appointed princes, after he died. Concubine Li angrily refused, her rudeness annoying the emperor, who nevertheless hid his irritation. At about the same time, Concubine Li also refused a match between her son and the

216 WANG ZHI

daughter of Liu Piao (*q.v.*), the emperor's older sister. Consort Wang, however, willingly agreed to a match between her son, Liu Che, and Liu Piao's daughter, Chen Jiao (*q.v.* Chen Jiao, Empress of Emperor Wu), who was his maternal cousin. Thenceforth, Liu Piao sang the praises of Consort Wang, and the emperor became so fond of his youngest son Liu Che that he considered deposing his eldest son and appointing Liu Che. Aware that the emperor was still angry with Concubine Li and that a final decision on the heir apparent had not yet been made, Consort Wang secretly sent someone to urge the ministers responsible to persuade the emperor to appoint Concubine Li as empress. When the Minister for Rites accordingly requested Emperor Jing's approval for Concubine Li's appointment as empress, on the grounds that her son held the position of heir apparent, the emperor flew into a rage. He declared the proposal "not appropriate," sentenced the Minister for Rites to death, and deposed Liu Rong, demoting him to Prince of Linjiang. Not long afterward, Concubine Li died, the cause of her death said to be "sadness and hatred." Consort Wang was made Empress Wang in 150, Liu Che was appointed heir apparent, and the empress's three daughters were appointed princesses of Yangxin, Nangong, and Longlü.

On the death of Emperor Jing, Liu Che (Emperor Wu) succeeded to the throne, his wife Chen Jiao becoming Empress Chen. Empress Wang became Empress Dowager Wang; her mother Zang Er became Lady of Pingyuan (Pingyuan Jun); her deceased father Wang Zhong was granted the posthumous title of Marquis of Gong; and her half-brothers Tian Fen and Tian Sheng were appointed Marquis of Wu'an and Zhouyang, respectively. Emperor Wu had been unaware that he had a half-sister, Empress Dowager Wang's daughter Jin Su, and complained when she informed him of her existence that he should have been told earlier. He immediately went to Changling, sought her out, and treated her with the utmost courtesy. He took her back to Changle Palace, where Jin Su and her mother were reunited in a poignant meeting. Emperor Wu granted Jin Su the title Lady of Xiucheng (Xiucheng Jun) and showered her with gifts.

The interaction between three generations of imperial maternal relations in the palace was extremely complex, but Empress Dowager Wang managed this admirably. At the beginning of Emperor Wu's reign, Grand Empress Dowager Dou was displeased at his attempt to elevate Confucian scholars, while the emperor was displeased with the greedy behavior of his aunt, Liu Piao, now mother of his empress. Empress Chen was beautiful, extremely jealous, and overbearing. Yet despite the emperor's devotion to her and despite vast amounts of gold being spent on medicines to help her become pregnant, she did not produce any children and gradually lost the emperor's favor. Empress Dowager Wang therefore counseled Emperor Wu to be more careful in dealing with the two women, and accordingly he offered them gifts and was more courteous than before. He was nevertheless quite dissolute and soon found new favorites.

Empress Dowager Wang also had her say in affairs of state. Her half-brother Tian Fen, who from time to time served as counselor-in-chief, lived extravagantly and became quite arrogant because of his imperial connections. He bore a grudge against Guan Fu (d. 131 B.C.E.), a former minister of Yan (the state of which his great-grandfather had been king). Although no longer powerful and influential, Guan Fu was an upright and outspoken man and he had offended Tian Fen several times at various feasts. Tian Fen memorialized the emperor that Guan Fu's family was running wild in Yingchuan and causing suffering to the people there. Guan Fu and his clan were therefore sentenced to death. Guan Fu's friend Dou Ying (d. 131 B.C.E.) memorialized the emperor defending his friend, so Emperor Wu ordered Dou Ying and Tian Fen to debate the matter in Changle Palace. Dou Ying was related to the emperor through his paternal grandmother; Tian Fen was a maternal uncle. To settle the case, Emperor Wu asked his ministers who they thought was in the right, but they were unable to come to a firm decision; enraged, the emperor declared he would kill the lot of them. This brought the debate to a close and the emperor went to dine with Empress Dowager Wang, but she was so furious that she would not eat. "You trample on my brother while I'm still alive. When I am dead you will kill my relatives like fish!" she told him in her rage. Emperor Wu thus felt that he had no choice but to have Guan Fu and his entire clan put to death, and he told his high officials to settle the case of Dou Ying by sentencing him to death as well. This has been described by historians down through the ages as an "obvious example of calamities caused by imperial in-laws."

Empress Dowager Wang died in 126 B.C.E. and was buried beside Emperor Jing in Yangling tomb. She is sometimes cited as an example of how empresses and the distaff side of imperial families interfered in court affairs, but a more modern analysis might speak of her political acumen and her understanding of human nature and relationships.

BAO Shanben

Chen Quanli and Hou Xinyi, eds. *Hou fei cidian.* Xi'an: Shaanxi renmin jiaoyu chubanshe, 1991, 13.
Han shu. Beijing: Zhonghua shuju, 1983, vol. 12, 97.3945–48.
Shi ji. Beijing: Zhonghua shuju, 1982, vol. 4, 49.1975–78.
Sima Guang. *Zizhi tongjian.* Beijing: Zhonghua shuju, 1956, vol. 1, 17.559–85.

Wanshi Yan Yu: *see* **Yan Yannian's Mother**

Wei Clan, The Two Obedient Ones of the: *see* **Two Obedient Women of the Wei Ancestral Temple**

Wei Zifu, Empress of Emperor Wu
Empress Wei (Xiao Wu Wei Huanghou), c. 153–91 B.C.E., of Pingyang, Hedong (present-day Linfen District, Shanxi Province), was the second empress of Emperor Wu (Liu Che, 156–87 B.C.E.; r. 140–87 B.C.E.) of Western Han. Her personal name is not known, but her courtesy name was Zifu.

Wei Zifu's father, Zhen Ji, served in the house of Cao Shou, Marquis of Pingyang and grandson of Cao Can (d. 190 B.C.E.). Zhen Ji's liaison with a housemaid known simply as The Woman Wei produced seven children, including Wei Zifu, all of whom went by their mother's surname, Wei. The marquis married an elder sister of Emperor Wu, the Princess of Yangxin, whose title was later changed to the Princess of Ping-

218 WEI ZIFU

yang. Growing up in the household of the marquis, Wei Zifu was trained in singing and dancing and served the Princess of Pingyang as a singer.

Because her brother Emperor Wu, still in his teens, had not produced a son, the Princess of Pingyang selected some ten beauties from decent families and kept them on hand, dressed in all their finery, in case he might call upon her. In the third lunar month of 139 B.C.E. the emperor performed a cleansing ritual in the river at Bashang and the princess prepared a feast to be held in his honor on his return from the ritual. She introduced the beauties, none of whom appealed to the emperor, then ordered her singers to entertain him. Emperor Wu was very taken by Wei Zifu and arranged that she wait on him when he went to relieve himself during the feast, so that he could have sex with her. When, happy and satisfied, he returned to the feast, he granted the princess 1,000 *jin* of gold and she asked him to take Wei Zifu into the palace. As they left, the princess said to Wei Zifu: "Don't forget me when you have become important." Wei Zifu remained the emperor's favorite for a time, but he was promiscuous and after about a year lost interest in her. The rear palace became full, most of the women being under thirty years old, so the emperor reviewed them one by one in order to cull those who no longer appealed to him and send them back to their native places. When Wei Zifu's turn came she dissolved into tears and asked to be sent home. Moved, Emperor Wu became enamored of her again and over the next few years she gave birth to three daughters and a son.

Empress Chen (*q.v.* Chen Jiao, Empress of Emperor Wu), who in ten years of marriage had not borne a son, grew fearful of her position with the success of Wei Zifu. She attempted suicide before turning to sorcery but was unsuccessful in both endeavors and was eventually deposed in 130 B.C.E. The empress's mother, the Grand Princess Liu Piao (*q.v.*), was also jealous of the growing power of the Wei clan and imprisoned one of Wei Zifu's brothers, Wei Qing (d. 106 B.C.E.), intending to have him put to death, but Wei Qing's friends managed to have him released. Emperor Wu was displeased with the behavior of Liu Piao, who was his aunt as well as his mother-in-law, and immediately appointed Wei Qing Director of Jianzhang Palace and Palace Attendant (*jianzhanggong jian, shizhong*), giving him 1,000 *jin* of gold as well. Soon after, he elevated Wei Zifu to the rank of consort and made Wei Qing Superior Grand Master of the Palace (*taizhong dafu*). Wei Qing was further rewarded after proving himself during the victorious northern expedition against the Xiongnu by being appointed Chariot and Horse General (*cheji jiangjun*) and Marquis of Changping. He later married the Princess of Pingyang, widow of his former employer the Marquis of Pingyang and sister of the emperor.

In the spring of 128, Consort Wei gave birth to a son, Liu Ju (128–91 B.C.E.), and was appointed empress of the twenty-eight-year-old Emperor Wu; six years later (122 B.C.E.) her son was appointed heir apparent. The emperor also continued to honor Empress Wei's kin. In recognition of his military achievements Emperor Wu granted her nephew Huo Qubing (145–117 B.C.E.), the son of her sister Wei Shao'er and of Huo Zhongru, the rank of Cavalry General (*piaoji jiangjun*) and then the title of Marquis of Guanjun. He ennobled Wei Shao'er's new husband, Chen Zhang, who held the post of Supervisor of the Household (*zhanshi*), even though Chen Zhang had not performed any service of merit. He promoted Wei Zhangjun, an elder brother of Empress Wei, to the position of palace attendant (*shizhong*). The bounty that Emperor Wu bestowed on the Wei clan gave rise to a popular song: "Don't be delighted at the birth of a son; don't be disappointed at the birth of a daughter. Can't you see, Wei Zifu is becoming an overlord!"

In time, however, Empress Wei's beauty began to fade and she lost her hold on the emperor. Because of this and because the emperor was not impressed by the mild character of the heir apparent, she and her son Liu Ju began to feel insecure. In an effort to reassure them, Emperor Wu told her brother Wei Qing that they were not to be concerned, because he trusted the heir apparent, believing him to be sincere and quiet, and capable of ruling. On hearing this, Empress Wei removed her hair clasp to confess that she had transgressed by having been suspicious and to request punishment from the emperor. From then on, Emperor Wu entrusted the affairs of state to Liu Ju, the heir apparent, and entrusted palace matters to Empress Wei.

Liu Ju would report his most important decisions to his father but on the whole the aging emperor, by then in his early fifties, was content to let him do as he pleased. However, while Emperor Wu adhered strictly to the law and appointed officials who would execute the law to the letter, the kinder and more forgiving Liu Ju would more often than not reverse decisions condemning people to punishment. While his kindness won him the love and respect of the people, his style of government aroused the disapproval of many officials and he was subjected to more criticism than praise, especially after the death of his uncle Wei Qing in 106 B.C.E.

Some years later, an official named Jiang Chong (d. 91 B.C.E.) impressed Emperor Wu with his impartial investigation of a case of immorality and incest; earlier, however, this same official had alienated Empress Wei by dealing equally impartially with an erring servant of Liu Ju. In 91, Jiang Chong was made responsible for investigating crimes of sorcery. Two of Empress Wei's daughters were implicated and put to death for practicing witchcraft. Realizing that the emperor, already sixty-six years old, was ill and fearing retribution at the hands of the heir apparent Liu Ju, Jiang Chong manipulated the evidence to implicate Liu Ju and Empress Wei in sorcery. Liu Ju took the initiative, however, and had Jiang Chong arrested and put to death. Unfortunately, the affair appeared to Emperor Wu to be an attempt on the part of Liu Ju to rebel and he sent soldiers to put an end to it. The defeated heir apparent hanged himself, while his wife, his concubines, his sons, and his daughter were all put to death; only one grandson, a babe in arms, survived. All those who had lived under Liu Ju's patronage and their families were also put to death. Empress Wei was stripped of the imperial seal and ribbon and she took her own life.

Emperor Wu was enraged at this catastrophe and his ministers were at a loss as to what to do. However, one elderly man, Linghu Mao, boldly spoke out for justice when he memorialized the emperor to redress the wrong done to the heir apparent. Emperor Wu did not pardon his wife and son publicly, but investigated the matter and realized that Liu Ju had put Jiang Chong to death out of fear, not out of treachery. Another official, Tian Qianqiu, also sent a memorial defending the heir apparent, and Emperor Wu finally acted, ordering Jiang Chong's entire family be put to death. Out of pity for

220 WEI ZIFU

his innocent son, Emperor Wu had a palace and a terrace built in his memory in Lake District (present-day Wenxiang District, Henan Province), where Liu Ju had died.

When his grandson (Emperor Xuan) succeeded to the throne almost twenty years later, Liu Ju was granted the posthumous title of Perverse Heir Apparent; his wife, Related Lady of Excellence Shi (Wei Taizi Shi Liangdi), was granted the title of Perverse Consort. At that time Empress Wei was also reburied in a solemn ceremony and granted the posthumous title Memorable Empress.

BAO Shanben

An Zuozhang, ed. *Hou fei zhuan*. Zhengzhou: Henan renmin chubanshe, 1990, 45–56.
Chen Quanli and Hou Xinyi, eds. *Hou fei cidian*. Xi'an: Shaanxi renmin jiaoyu chubanshe, 1991, 13.
Han shu. Beijing: Zhonghua shuju, 1983, vol. 6, 63.2742–48; vol. 8, 97*shang*.3949–50.
Liu Shisheng. *Zhongguo gudai funü shi*. Qingdao: Qingdao chubanshe, 1991, 91–92.
Loewe, Michael. *Crisis and Conflict in Han China*. London: George Allen & Unwin, 1974.
Shi ji. Beijing: Zhonghua shuju, 1982, vol. 4, 49, 1978–83; vol. 9, 111.2922–28.
Sima Guang. *Zizhi tongjian*. Beijing: Zhonghua shuju, 1956, vol. 1, 17 passim; vol. 1, 22 passim; vol. 1, 24 passim.

Wei Zong Ershun: *see* **Two Obedient Women of the Wei Ancestral Temple**

Wen, Grand Empress Dowager Mother: *see* **Wang Zhengjun, Empress of Emperor Yuan**

Wen Jijiang
Wen Jijiang, fl. late second century, of Zitong (the present-day city of Mianyang in Sichuan Province) was the second wife of Wang Jingbo, a chamberlain for the palace buildings (*jiangzuo dajiang*), of Guanghan (in the northwest of present-day Suining District in Sichuan Province). She was a charismatic and benevolent woman who is remembered for her filial behavior and for instilling respect in her children through her good example.

She must have been born into a literati family, for as a child she is said to have read many of the Confucian classics, especially *The Book of Songs* (Shi jing) and *Book of Rites* (Li ji). Wang Jingbo's first wife had given birth to a son (Wang Bo) and a daughter (Wang Jiliu), while Wen Jijiang bore him three sons and three daughters. Wen Jijiang treated all eight children with equal love. She was also extremely filial to her elders. When she first married Wang Jingbo, his grandmother was still alive. She was a very harsh old woman who flogged her sons and grandsons even though they were high-ranking officials and who would punish the women of the family by ordering them to kneel on the hall floor. Perhaps very sensibly, Wen Jijiang did not neglect this violent and perverse old woman but took great care of her. She took her with the family to each of the five prefectures her husband was appointed to and when the grandmother was too old to travel Wen Jijiang would often remain behind and wait upon her.

When her stepdaughter, Wang Jiliu, was preparing to get married, Wen Jijiang sent her own maid to wait on her. Her stepson, Wang Bo, was fond of calligraphy and Wen Jijiang would go to the trouble of fashioning for him with her own hands the accoutrements of writing. Her good manners and consideration for others influenced the entire family, who were self-effacing in all things. Wang Bo's wife, Yang Jin, and his daughter-in-law Zhang Shuji heeded Wen Jijiang's teachings and were highly regarded for their benevolence and wisdom; the three women were known collectively and with great affection as the "Three Mothers' Family." The wives of Wen Jijiang's three sons also respected Yang Jin and deferred to her as to an elder, setting a virtuous example for all.

Wen Jijiang lived to the age of eighty-one, and when she died her four daughters mourned her, as did her four sons, who retired from office for the prescribed period. Over 100 government officials came to offer condolences at her funeral, which was conducted with great honor and grandeur. The increasing prosperity of the Wang family has traditionally been attributed to the effort Wen Jijiang put into caring for the family.

WANG Bugao

Chang Qu. "Zitong shinü zhi." In *Shuofu,* ed. Tao Zongyi. Taipei: Taiwan shangwu yinshuguan, 1985, vol. 58.
"Guiyuan dian: Guishu bu." In *Gujin tushu jicheng,* ed. Chen Menglei. Shanghai: Zhonghua shuju, 1934, Book 396, 57b.

The Woman of Integrity from the Capital

The Woman of Integrity from the Capital (Jingshi Jienü), lived during the Western Han dynasty. She was married to a man from Dachangli in the capital Chang'an (the present-day city of Xi'an), but neither her name nor her husband's name is recorded.

The woman's husband had an enemy who had been unable to find a way of avenging some unspecified wrong. Eventually, having heard that the woman was kindhearted and filial and that she valued integrity, the enemy kidnapped her father, forcing the old man to tell his daughter to do as she was told. The woman thought deeply about the situation, knowing that her father would surely be killed if she refused to obey and that her husband would be killed if she did obey. Her dilemma was that it would be unfilial to jeopardize her father's safety, yet it would be immoral and disloyal to be responsible for her husband's death. Unable to live with the shame of being either unfilial or disloyal, the woman concluded that the only thing she could do was to sacrifice her own life.

She therefore told her husband's enemy: "Tomorrow, the person who will wash their hair and then sleep in the east room upstairs will be the one. I'll leave the door open for you." When she returned home she told her husband that she had met with his enemy; she then asked him to sleep somewhere other than where they normally slept. Then she washed her hair, went upstairs, and went to bed in the east room. At midnight, as anticipated, her husband's enemy came, cut off the head of the person sleeping in

222 THE WOMAN OF INTEGRITY FROM THE CAPITAL

the east room, wrapped it up, and took it home. When it was light, he unwrapped the parcel and found the head of his enemy's wife. So moved was he by her morality and loyalty that he deeply repented and forswore his revenge on her husband.

This is one of many similar tales handed down from this period by Liu Xiang in his *Biographies of Eminent Women* (Lienü zhuan) that were clearly intended to shape the behavior of women. In these stories, the noble and moral heroine is placed in a dilemma, often created by the behavior of her male relatives, that requires her to sacrifice herself for her father, her husband, or her son. Most of these tales emphasize the superior moral understanding of the heroine and her readiness to sacrifice herself.

SHEN Lidong

Liu Xiang. *Lienü zhuan.* Sibubeiyao ed., 5.11.
Liu Ziqing. *Zhongguo lidai xianneng funü pingzhuan.* Taipei: Liming wenhua, 1978, 79–84.
O'Hara, Albert R. *The Position of Woman in Early China According to the Lieh Nü Chuan, "The Biographies of Chinese Women."* Taipei: Mei Ya, 1971; 1978, 151–52.

Wusun, Princess of: *see* **Liu Jieyou; Liu Xijun**

X

Xi Chu Bawang Fei Yu Ji: *see* **Yu, Consort of the Hegemon-King of Chu**

Xiandi Cao Huanghou: *see* **Cao Jie, Empress of Emperor Xian**

Xiandi Fu Huanghou: *see* **Fu Shou, Empress of Emperor Xian**

Xiangcheng, Lady of: *see* **Sun Shou**

Xiao Cheng Ban Jieyu : *see* **Ban Jieyu, Concubine of Emperor Cheng**

Xiao Cheng Xu Huanghou: *see* **Xu, Empress of Emperor Cheng**

Xiao Cheng Zhao Huanghou: *see* **Zhao Feiyan, Empress of Emperor Cheng**

Xiao Cheng Zhao Zhaoyi: *see* **Zhao Hede, Concubine of Emperor Cheng**

Xiao Hui Zhang Huanghou: *see* **Zhang Yan, Empress of Emperor Hui**

Xiao Jing Bo Huanghou: *see* **Bo, Empress of Emperor Jing**

Xiao Jing Wang Huanghou: *see* Wang Zhi, Empress of Emperor Jing

Xiao Ping Wang Huanghou: *see* Wang, Empress of Emperor Ping

Xiao Wen Dou Huanghou: *see* Dou Yifang, Empress of Emperor Wen

Xiao Wen Shen Furen: *see* Shen, Concubine of Emperor Wen

Xiao Wu Chen Huanghou: *see* Chen Jiao, Empress of Emperor Wu

Xiao Wu Gouyi Zhao Jieyu: *see* Zhao Gouyi, Concubine of Emperor Wu

Xiao Wu Li Furen: *see* Li, Concubine of Emperor Wu

Xiao Wu Wei Huanghou: *see* Wei Zifu, Empress of Emperor Wu

Xiao Xuan Huo Huanghou: *see* Huo Chengjun, Empress of Emperor Xuan

Xiao Xuan Wang Huanghou: *see* Wang, Empress of Emperor Xuan

Xiao Xuan Xu Huanghou: *see* Xu Pingjun, Empress of Emperor Xuan

Xiao Yuan Feng Zhaoyi: *see* Feng, Concubine of Emperor Yuan

Xiao Yuan Fu Huanghou: *see* Fu, Concubine of Emperor Yuan

Xiao Yuan Fu Zhaoyi: *see* Fu, Concubine of Emperor Yuan

Xiao Yuan Wang Huanghou: *see* Wang Zhengjun, Empress of Emperor Yuan

Xiao Zhao Shangguan Huanghou: *see* Shangguan, Empress of Emperor Zhao

Xijun, Princess: *see* Liu Xijun

Xijun Gongzhu: *see* Liu Xijun

Xin Mang Wang Huanghou: *see* Wang, Empress of Wang Mang of Xin

Xindu, Empress Dowager of: *see* Feng, Concubine of Emperor Yuan

224 XINYE, PRINCESS OF

Xinye, Princess of: *see* **Liu Yuan**

Xinye Gongzhu: *see* **Liu Yuan**

Xinye Yijie Zhang Gongzhu: *see* **Liu Yuan**

Xu Deng

Xu Deng, fl. c. 200, of Minzhong (the present-day city of Quanzhou, Fujian Province), was born female but is said to have eventually "become a male."

Xu Deng, who lived in the chaotic period at the end of Eastern Han when plagues were ravaging the country, excelled at casting spells (*jinzhou wushu*). One day by a creek in Wushang (in present-day Yiwu District in Zhejiang Province), Xu Deng came across a magician (*shushi*) named Zhao Bing. Having sworn to use their magic to cure the sick, they agreed to demonstrate their skills for each other "since we have sworn to share one aim in life." Thereupon Xu Deng made incantations and brought the water in the creek to a standstill, while with his magic (*jinzhou shifa*) Zhao Bing brought a dead tree to life, with a growth of thick, green leaves. They burst into delighted laughter at what they were able to do.

From then on they practiced medicine together. Xu Deng was the older of the two and assumed the role of Zhao Bing's teacher. They lived simply and frugally. For example, they used pure water instead of wine, and mulberry bark instead of sacrificial offerings in performing their ceremonies. Everyone they treated was cured. After Xu Deng died, Zhao Bing moved to Zhang'an (present-day Taizhou District in Zhejiang Province). He is said to have performed several sensational acts of magic, which led the magistrate there to arrest him and have him executed for misleading the people. Xu Deng and Zhao Bing lived at the time of the Yellow Turban uprising, when superstition was rife and the authorities distrusted magic, and this may have been the immediate reason for Zhao Bing's execution.

No explanation is offered in the histories for Xu Deng's transformation from a female to a male, nor is any indication given of at what point in her life this transformation occurred. She may have been a transvestite, or she may have even been a woman who discovered, as many women in many cultures have done, that it was much easier to move about freely and practice her craft in male guise. Whatever the reason for Xu Deng's change of gender, it is clear that Xu Deng and Zhao Bing enjoyed a lifelong relationship, marked by genuine affection for one another and for the afflicted who sought their help.

SHEN Lidong

Hou Han shu. Beijing: Zhonghua shuju, 1965, vol. 10, 82*xia*.2741–43.

Xu, Empress of Emperor Cheng

Empress Xu (Xiao Cheng Xu Huanghou), d. 10 B.C.E., from Shanyang (in present-day Shandong Province), was empress to Emperor Cheng (Liu Ao, 51–7 B.C.E.; r. 32–7

B.C.E.). Her father, Xu Jia, was Marquis of Ping'en and had served as Commander-in-Chief in the administration of Emperor Cheng's father, Emperor Yuan (Liu Shi, 76–33 B.C.E.; r. 48–33 B.C.E.). Xu Jia was also a cousin of Emperor Yuan's mother, Empress Xu (*q.v.* Xu Pingjun, Empress of Emperor Xuan). This earlier Empress Xu had been poisoned in 70 B.C.E.

It is said that Emperor Yuan had chosen Xu Jia's daughter for his son Liu Ao as some recompense to the Xu family for his mother's poisoning and had been delighted to hear that Liu Ao was fond of the girl. She soon gave birth to a boy, but he died at birth. Upon Liu Ao's ascension to the throne in 32 B.C.E. he made her his empress; she gave birth to a daughter, but this baby also died.

Empress Xu was intelligent, acted with propriety, and was well versed in literature and history. Emperor Cheng initially respected these traits and accorded her considerable favor. However, his mother, Empress Dowager Wang (*q.v.* Wang Zhengjun, Empress of Emperor Yuan), and his uncles were concerned at the lack of an heir, an unfortunate circumstance compounded by frequent natural calamities and unexpected incidents. Several high officials began to blame these calamities on the empress, so Emperor Cheng ordered that Empress Xu's palace expenses be cut. The empress submitted a memorial protesting the cuts but it was rejected.

At that time Empress Dowager Wang's older brother General-in-Chief (*da jiang-jun*)/Commander-in-Chief (*da sima*) Wang Feng (d. 22 B.C.E.) wielded absolute power at court. Some time later, public opinion turned against him when he was blamed for an eclipse of the sun; however, his supporters managed to shift the blame for the eclipse onto Empress Xu. Wang Feng's enmity toward the empress stemmed from his earlier antagonism toward her father, Xu Jia, an antagonism that was symptomatic of the relationship between the Wang and Xu clans. Given these court machinations, Emperor Cheng gradually lost interest in his empress and found new favorites among the palace women. The campaign against Empress Xu eventually came to a head when she was implicated in a case of witchcraft.

In 18 B.C.E., one of the emperor's new favorites—Zhao Feiyan (*q.v.* Zhao Feiyan, Empress of Emperor Cheng)—accused Empress Xu and Ban Jieyu (*q.v.* Ban Jieyu, Concubine of Emperor Cheng) of engaging in illicit activities. The empress's sister Xu Ye was charged with practicing sorcery (*wugu*) with the intention of bringing harm to Wang Feng and to Beauty (*meiren*) Wang, who was then carrying the emperor's child. Empress Dowager Wang flew into a rage when this was brought to her attention and ordered an investigation. Empress Xu was implicated and deposed and sent to Zhaotai Palace, while her relatives were sent back to Shanyang. Her sister Xu Ye was among those sentenced to death. Her nephew, the Marquis of Ping'en, was told to return to his fief.

Some years later, in 10 B.C.E., Emperor Cheng relented and proclaimed that the Marquis of Ping'en and the deposed empress's relatives in Shanyang could return to the capital. Another of the deposed empress's sisters, Xu Mi, a widow, was among those who returned, and she soon embarked on an affair with Chunyu Chang, a nephew of Empress Dowager Wang. Chunyu Chang had acted as a messenger during the earlier negotiations to gain the empress dowager's consent to Zhao Feiyan being installed

226 XU, EMPRESS OF EMPEROR CHENG

as empress, and now he boasted that he could ask his aunt to reappoint the deposed empress Xu as Left Empress. The deposed empress Xu therefore offered him a bribe and they exchanged letters. It was then revealed that Chunyu Chang had been disrespectful in one of his letters, and the deposed empress was again implicated. Emperor Cheng dispatched an official to order her to take her own life by drinking poison. She did so and was buried in Yanling, southwest of Xianyang city in present-day Shaanxi Province. Empress Xu was the second woman carrying that title to die by poison as a direct consequence of court politics: her predecessor was murdered to make way for a daughter of the Huo family to become empress, while the later empress was forced to commit suicide to remove her as a threat to the Wang clan's hold on imperial power.

WU Jin

Ban Gu. *Courtier and Commoner in Ancient China. Selections from the "History of the Former Han" by Pan Ku,* trans. Burton Watson. New York: Columbia University Press, 1974, 262, 265, 273.
Han shu. Beijing: Zhonghua shuju, 1983, vol. 12, 97*xia*.3973–83.
Loewe, Michael. *Crisis and Conflict in Han China: 104 BC to AD 9.* London: George Allen & Unwin, 1974, 156–57.

Xu Pingjun, Empress of Emperor Xuan

Xu Pingjun (Xiao Xuan Xu Huanghou), d. 71 or 70 B.C.E., of Changyi (in present-day Shandong Province), was empress to Emperor Xuan (Liu Xun or Liu Bingyi, 91–49 B.C.E.; r. 74–49 B.C.E.). She was the mother of Emperor Yuan (Liu Shi, 76–33 B.C.E.; r. 48–33 B.C.E.).

Xu Pingjun's father, Xu Guanghan, had been found guilty of a serious crime on two separate occasions during the reign of Emperor Wu (r. 141–87 B.C.E.). As punishment he had been castrated and was later demoted to the position of bailiff in the palace isolation building (one source describes this position as orderly in charge of the women's sickroom in the women's quarters). When Xu Pingjun was fourteen or fifteen years old she was promised in marriage to the son of Ouhou, the Director of Palace Servants (*neizhe ling*), but the young man died just before the wedding was to take place. Xu Pingjun's mother (whose name is not recorded in the histories) then asked a fortune-teller to divine her daughter's fate and was told that the girl would gain great distinction. About this time, the Director of the Palace Discipline Service (*yeting ling*) entertained Xu Pingjun's father at a feast with the intention of proposing a marriage between Xu Pingjun and Liu Xun, the "imperial great-grandson" (*vide* Shangguan, Empress of Emperor Zhao). Xu Guanghan accepted the marriage proposal on behalf of his daughter, but her mother was very unhappy with this arrangement because she wanted greater things for her daughter: for although he belonged to the imperial clan (he was a great-grandson of Emperor Wu), Liu Xun was a commoner. More to the point, he was under a political cloud as he had been the sole survivor when his grandfather Liu Ju's entire household died or were put to death during the witchcraft scare of 91 B.C.E.

The marriage was nevertheless made and a year later Xu Pingjun gave birth to a son, Liu Shi. Several months after that, the case against Liu Xun was resolved and he ascended the throne. Xu Pingjun was elevated to the rank of Lady of Handsome Fairness (*jieyu*), then the highest grade of concubine. Despite tacit agreement among the ministers and high officials that another young woman should be appointed empress, Emperor Xuan recommended that his "old sword" (Xu Pingjun), who had been by his side before he became emperor, be made empress. His recommendation was adopted and in December 74 B.C.E. Lady of Handsome Fairness Xu Pingjun became Empress Xu. Because Xu Guanghan had a criminal record, he was not immediately ennobled, as was customary for the father of an empress. Instead, he was enfeoffed about a year later as Lord of Changcheng, quite a lowly rank.

One of the officials who had objected to the investment of Xu Guanghan as a lord was the powerful General-in-Chief (*da jiangjun*) Huo Guang (d. 68 B.C.E.), and it was his youngest daughter, Huo Chengjun (*q.v.* Huo Chengjun, Empress of Emperor Xuan), whom the ministers and high officials had originally favored as empress over Xu Pingjun. Huo Guang's wife née Xian had not given up hope of their daughter becoming empress, however, so she bribed the female doctor (Chunyu Yan) who was attending Empress Xu. Xian told the doctor: "Hardly one woman out of ten survives [childbirth] . . . It would be quite possible to put poison in her medicine and do away with her, and then [my daughter Chengjun] could be made empress in her place" (Watson, 260). As soon as Empress Xu had given birth, Chunyu Yan administered the poison in the form of ground aconite mixed with the pill prepared by the chief doctor. Not long after, the empress complained of a severe headache and asked if the medicine had been poisoned. Chunyu Yan denied this but the empress's headache worsened and she died in agony. After her death, in early March 71 B.C.E., a memorial was submitted charging the imperial doctors with neglecting their duty of care for Empress Xu. The doctors, including Chunyu Yan, were imprisoned and questioned but the case was never settled because Huo Guang used his position to prevent further prosecution.

Empress Xu had been empress for only three years. She was buried in the South Duling Gardens tomb in Dunan (in the south of Shaoling yuan in present-day eastern Chang'an District) with the posthumous title Empress Gong'ai (Reverent and Pitiable Empress).

WANG Xiaowen

Ban Gu. *Courtier and Commoner in Ancient China. Selections from the "History of the Former Han" by Pan Ku,* trans. Burton Watson. New York: Columbia University Press, 1974, 257–61.
Chen Quanli and Hou Xinyi, eds. *Hou fei cidian.* Xi'an: Shaanxi renmin jiaoyu chubanshe, 1991, 15.
Han shu. Beijing: Zhonghua shuju, 1983, vol. 12, 97*shang*.3964–68.
Loewe, Michael. *Crisis and Conflict in Han China: 104 BC to AD 9.* London: George Allen & Unwin, 1974, 128–30.

Xu Shu

Xu Shu, b. c. 135, was from either Longxi (south of present-day Lintao, Gansu Province) or Pingxiang (present-day Tongwei District, Gansu Province). She was the wife of Qin Jia of Longxi and is said to have been a "fine match" for him because she was a gifted writer.

228 XU SHU

Qin Jia was an accounts clerk (*shangji li*) and after their marriage he was promoted to a position in Luoyang. Xu Shu fell ill, however, and returned to her parents' home to recuperate. As he was about to leave to take up his post, Qin Jia sent a carriage to her parents' house with a letter expressing his hope that she would come to bid him farewell. Xu Shu wrote in reply that she was too ill to go out ("Reply to My Husband Qin Jia" [Zhi qu gui zhang]). As a gesture of his love, Qin Jia then sent her his "Reply to My Wife" (Ju huan kong fan) and *Poem to My Wife* (Zeng fu shi) together with a mirror, a jeweled hairpin, some perfume, and a *qin* (a stringed instrument). In response, Xu Shu sent him her "A Further Reply to Qin Jia" (Ji hui lingyin) and the famous *Poem in Reply to My Husband* (Qieshen xi buling; this title has also been translated as *Response to My Husband, Ch'in Chia*) together with a gold-plated bowl and a glass bowl. After serving for several years in Luoyang, where he rose to the position of Gentleman of the Palace Gate (*huangmen lang*), Qin Jia fell ill and died.

Thus widowed in her youth, Xu Shu was pressured by her brothers to remarry. After writing to tell them of her determination to remain true to the memory of her husband, she mutilated her face and went into mourning for the rest of her life. Not having any children of her own, Xu Shu adopted a boy and raised him as her son. When she died, the boy was sent back to his birth parents but an official changed his place of origin and recorded him as a descendant of the Qin family.

Xu Shu was elegant and refined and wrote with a natural grace. She was described by a Tang dynasty (618–907) scholar as "among the wise and able women of the Eastern Han. . . . A refined poet, she distinguished herself with her talent and her virtue. Conforming with propriety, her words were a model for others." This scholar singled out for special mention her act of mutilating her face so that she would not be forced to remarry and her lifelong mourning for her husband. In the late Ming dynasty (1368–1644), the literary achievements of Qin Jia and Xu Shu, as a couple, were bracketed with those of Sima Xiangru and Zhuo Wenjun (*q.v.*) and Emperor Wen of Wei and Empress Zhen (*q.v.* Zhen, Empress of Emperor Wen of Wei). However, of these three women only Xu Shu was considered refined in manners and deeds; in contrast, "Zhuo Wenjun remarried and Empress Zhen was unfaithful; their lives and deeds were unremarkable." Xu Shu is one of five women considered to have been sophisticated poets, unmatched by male literati. The other four are Ban Jieyu (*q.v.* Ban Jieyu, Concubine of Emperor Cheng), Zhuo Wenjun, Su Boyu's Wife (*q.v.*), and Wang Zhaojun (*q.v.*).

Xu Shu's poems are well balanced in terms of rationality and emotion and are "accented by elegant diction." In her *Poem in Reply to My Husband,* she reveals a natural flow of real affection through the use of plain words, fusing her depression and longing with the sorrowful setting of the poem. Critics have said that the "tortuous communication back and forth between husband and wife reflected in the poem depicts a story and affections so true that the poem will last forever, outstripping any created from the imagination." What marks the unique style of this poem is the Chinese word *xi,* an empty word used to indicate a pause or emotion; it is usually left untranslated in English. The following translation is by Anne Birrell (*Response to My Husband, Ch'in Chia*).

My poor body felt so unwell,
Weighed down with illness I came home.
I lie limp indoors,
Seasons pass, I don't improve.
I am remiss not being at your side,
Neglectful in love and respect.

You have now received your commission,
Gone far away to the capital.
A vast gulf divides us,
There is no way to tell you my feelings.
Hoping to see you I dance for joy,
Then stand still, perplexed.
I long for you, my feelings tangle,
I dream I see your radiant face.

You set out on your journey
From me more remote each day.
I hate not having feather wings
To fly up high in pursuit of you.
I moan for ever, sigh long sighs,
Tears fall and soak my blouse.

This poem, with its four-character lines in the pattern of two characters–*xi*–two characters, is seen as marking the transition between the pre-Han *Songs of the South* (Chu ci) and the mature development of poems with five-character lines. It is always cited in discussions of five-character poetry of Eastern Han, even though one of the five characters is the particle *xi*, which, strictly speaking, is not a word. However, the addition of the particle *xi* began to change the meter of the poems and in the opinion of some scholars heralded five-character poems.

Xu Shu's prose has also been much admired. Her three letters collected in *Quan Shanggu Sandai Qin Han Sanguo Liuchao wen* are of great literary value and in terms of rhetoric outstrip her famous poem. In "Reply to My Husband Qin Jia," her use of plain words heightens the effect of the letter, with its subtle narration and rich metaphors. In "A Further Reply to Qin Jia," Xu Shu expresses her affection for her husband in the manner of an ancient Chinese lady with such sentences as "I need you to be here when I play the *qin*." In her "Letter to My Brothers Swearing Not to Remarry" (Wei shishu yu xiongdi), she demonstrates her faithfulness in love by the use of strong words, as in "Men of integrity have an unchanging mind and faithful women are constant in love."

It would be surprising if Xu Shu had written nothing else after she penned the poems addressed to her husband and her letter to her brothers vowing to remain a chaste widow; nevertheless, it appears that these works, which reflected the interests of the literati, are the only ones that have been recorded in the literature. The complete works of Xu Shu are listed in the *History of the Sui Dynasty* (Sui shu) but are now mostly lost. Some are found in *Yutai xinyong, Yiwen leiju, Taiping yulan,*

230 *XU SHU*

and *Quan Han Sanguo Jin Nanbeichao shi*. Yan Kejun included a "Biography of Xu Shu" in *Tieqiao mangao*.

YEH Chia-ying and ZHU Xiaofeng

Birrell, Anne, trans. *New Songs from a Jade Terrace: An Anthology of Early Chinese Love Poetry*. London: Allen & Unwin, 1982, 47.
———. "Response to My Husband, Ch'in Chia." In her *Popular Songs and Ballads of Han China*. Honolulu: University of Hawaii Press, 1993, 47.
Ding Fubao. *Quan Han Sanguo Jin Nanbeichao shi*. Beijing: Zhonghua shuju, 1959, vol. 1, 3.55.
He Wenhuan. *Lidai shihua*. Beijing: Zhonghua shuju, 1981.
Hu Yinglin. *Shisou*. Shanghai: Shanghai guji chubanshe, 1979, 1, 125–42.
Li Fang. *Taiping yulan*. Beijing: Zhonghua shuju, 1960.
Liang Yizhen. *Zhongguo funü wenxue shigang*. Shanghai: Shanghai shudian, 1990, 73–78.
Liu Zhiji. *Shitong*. Shanghai: Shanghai guji chubanshe, 1978, 8.
Ouyang Xun. *Yiwen leiju*. Shanghai: Shanghai guji chubanshe, 1982, vol. 3, 73.1261–63.
Xie Wuliang. *Zhongguo funü wenxue shi*. Shanghai: Shanghai shudian, 1990, 28–30.
Xu Ling. *Yutai xinyong*. Wu Zhaoyi annotated ed. Beijing: Zhonghua shuju, 1985, vol. 1, 1.32.
Yan Kejun. *Quan Shanggu Sandai Qin Han Sanguo Liuchao wen*. Beijing: Zhonghua shuju, 1958, vol. 1, 66.833–34.

Y

Yan Ming

Yan Ming, c. 110–152, of Hejian (in the southeast of present-day Hebei Province), was the mother of Emperor Huan (Liu Zhi, 132–167; r. 147–167) of Eastern Han.

Yan Ming became a concubine (*yingqie*) of Liu Yi, Marquis of Liwu, in about 130. Liu Yi already had a principal wife, a woman of the Ma surname, but they do not appear to have had any children, and certainly no sons. Liu Yi was a grandson of Emperor Zhang (Liu Da, 57–88; r. 76–88), and at one time the regent Empress Dowager Deng (*q.v.* Deng Mengnü, Empress of Emperor Huan) had considered him for the imperial succession. Named King of Pingyuan on the North China plain, he had been kept at the capital, but after the death of Empress Dowager Deng in 121 he was reduced to a petty marquis and sent back to live in seclusion in Hejian. In 130, on petition from his father, the county of Liwu was taken from Hejian state and granted him as a fief.

Liu Zhi, eldest son of Liu Yi by Yan Ming, was born in 132, and Liu Yi is known to have fathered at least two other sons and two daughters, probably also by Yan Ming. Liu Yi died about 140, Liu Zhi succeeded to the fief, and Yan Ming would no doubt have lived out her days in obscurity but for the politics of succession at the imperial capital.

In 146 the nine-year-old Emperor Zhi (Liu Zuan, 138–146; r. 146) died at Luoyang. This boy had been chosen for the throne by Empress Dowager Liang (*q.v.* Liang Na, Empress of Emperor Shun), who, in alliance with her brother the General-in-Chief (*dajiangjun*) Liang Ji, controlled the government after the death of Emperor Shun (Liu Bao, 115–144; r. 126–144). In the absence of an appointed heir apparent, an empress dowager had the right to choose the successor to the throne, and after the death in 145 of the late emperor's only son, the infant Emperor Chong, Empress Dowager Liang had selected the boy Liu Zuan. Even before his death, however, she had summoned Liu Zhi to the capital and betrothed him to her younger sister Liang Nüying (*q.v.* Liang Nüying, Empress of Emperor Huan). As soon as Liu Zuan was dead, Liu Zhi (Emperor Huan) was placed upon the throne and in the following year, 147, he was married to Liang Nüying.

The new emperor's father, the late Liu Yi, was now honored as Emperor Xiao Chong (*xiao,* meaning "filial," was a common part of posthumous titles for all rulers of Han other than the two founders), and the name of his tomb in Hejian was changed to Boling. The emperor's mother, Yan Ming, was named Worthy Lady (*guiren*) of the Funerary Park at Boling. Worthy Lady was the highest rank of concubine, immediately below the empress, but the appointment to attend her husband's tomb meant that Worthy Lady Yan could not live at the capital with her son. The Liang group had no wish to provide an alternative center of power for any faction that might turn the young emperor against them.

The full widow of Liu Yi was likewise appointed as Worthy Lady of Boling and she was also appointed as guardian for the emperor's younger brother, Liu Shi (also known as Liu Gu). Liu Shi had been granted the restored title of Prince of Pingyuan but he was frequently drunk and incapable of carrying out his duties.

When Empress Dowager Liang died in 150, Emperor Huan, now eighteen years old, was able to arrange for his mother to be brought to the capital. One of the highest ministers of state was sent with authority to grant Worthy Lady Yan an imperial seal and ribbon, and she was escorted to her new residence in the Northern Palace at Luoyang. Her apartments were known as the Palace of Perpetual Joy and her household, headed by a Grand Coachman and a Privy Treasurer, was protected by guardsmen of the Feathered Forest and Rapid Tiger troops. She also received a pension from the tax revenues of nine counties of Julu Commandery (in the southern part of present-day Hebei). This was the first time in Eastern Han that the mother of an emperor had not been the wife or concubine of a previous ruler, and the honors paid her were based upon those recorded from Western Han. However, Worthy Lady Yan played no part in the politics of the court.

In 152, the honorary empress dowager née Yan died. Her son Liu Shi was named chief mourner, accompanied by another son (Liu Kui, Prince of Bohai) and two daughters who were now princesses. A decorated coffin, jade shroud, and other grave goods were provided by the special workshops of the Eastern Garden at Luoyang, and an extravagant funerary cortege back to Hejian was led by one of the highest ministers of state. Neighboring princes and marquises, and all imperial officials for over 100 miles around, were ordered to attend the final ceremony at the Boling tomb, where Lady Yan was laid to rest beside her husband.

Rafe de CRESPIGNY

Hou Han shu. Beijing: Zhonghua shuju, 1965, vol. 2, 10*xia.*441–42.

Yan Yannian Mu: *see* **Yan Yannian's Mother**

Yan Yannian's Mother

Yan Yannian's Mother (Yan Yannian Mu), fl. 116–49 B.C.E., was from Xiapi in Donghai (in the region of the present-day provinces of Jiangsu and Shandong); her given names and surname are not recorded. Since all five of her sons became high-ranking officials, with each son on an annual salary of 2,000 bushels of grain, people used to call her Old Woman Yan Worth 10,000 Bushels of Grain (Wanshi Yan Yu).

Her son Yan Yannian (d. 58 B.C.E.) was initially appointed governor of Zhuo Commandery and he proved to be a strict and cruel official. According to the official *History of the Han Dynasty* (Han shu), he used his authority to execute members of rich and powerful families without mercy, but this caused trouble and led to revolts, which in turn so unsettled the people that no one dared even to pick up articles they found on the thoroughfares for fear of being accused of theft. He was later appointed governor of Henan, where he continued his harsh treatment of the powerful and rich while at the same time helping the poor and weak. When the poor broke the law he would do everything possible to pardon them; when the rich and powerful harmed the ordinary people in any way, Yan Yannian would find some sound excuse to punish them. His judgments became unpredictable: he pardoned those who people believed should die and by means of crafty arguments he executed those who deserved to live. Thus the people of Henan lived in fear of committing an offense. Yan Yannian's records were all in order and his arguments were watertight, so there was no possibility that his judgments could be overturned. Prisoners were executed in the winter months and blood ran deep in the streets. People in Henan called him The Butcher.

One year, Yan Yannian's Mother traveled from Xiapi to spend the winter sacrifice (the *la* festival) with him. Just as she arrived in Luoyang, however, she witnessed her son reading out the names of those he had sentenced to death. She was so shocked that she stopped at the government inn instead of going to her son's residence. When Yan Yannian went to greet her there she remained in the attic, refusing to see him. Eventually, after Yan Yannian had doffed his hat and kowtowed, she agreed to see him, but then she scolded him: "You have had the good fortune to be made a governor of this nation and wield authority over a vast area. I have not heard that you have taught the people with love and kindness, making them feel secure, I have heard only that you have been killing people through abuse of the law in order to appear more dignified and awe-inspiring. Surely this is not being the father of the people!" Yan Yannian did not reject his mother's criticism but kowtowed to her twice before escorting her to his residence. His mother celebrated the winter sacrifice and the New Year in the governor's residence, but before she left to return home she warned her son: "There are deities and there is a divine order of things. We must never kill at will. I will not remain here to see you put to death in the prime of your life [because of your sacrilegious behavior]. I must return home to prepare a tomb for you."

After Yan Yannian's Mother returned home she often spoke with relatives of how disappointed she was in her son. Just over a year later, Yan Yannian was found guilty of several matters and sentenced to death, as his mother had predicted. Yan Yannian's Mother has been praised through the ages for her wisdom.

XIA Chunhao

Han shu. Beijing: Zhonghua shuju, 1983, vol. 11, 90.3667–72.
Liu Xiang. *Lienü zhuan.* Sibubeiyao ed., 8.5.
O'Hara, Albert R. *The Position of Woman in Early China According to the Lieh Nü Chuan. "The Biographies of Chinese Women."* Taipei: Mei Ya, 1971; 1978, 226–27.

Yang Chang Qi: *see* **Sima, Yang Chang's Wife**

Yanla Wang Hua Rong Furen: *see* **Hua Rong, Consort of Prince of Yanla**

Yen Yen-nien, The Mother of: *see* **Yan Yannian's Mother**

Yen-shou's Wife: *see* **Youdi**

Yin Lihua, Empress of Emperor Guangwu
Yin Lihua (Guangwudi Yin Huanghou), 5–64, was empress to Emperor Guangwu (Liu Xiu, 6 B.C.E.–57 C.E.; r. 25–57 C.E.), the first emperor of Eastern Han. She was born in Xinye, Nanyang Commandery (present-day Xinye District in Henan Province). Her father, Yin Lu, was wealthy, and the youthful Liu Xiu, a member of the Han-dynasty ruling Liu clan, became enamored of her after he heard people talking of her beauty. Later, when he was in the capital Chang'an, Liu Xiu was impressed by the power and grandeur of an army of vehicles and horses belonging to a chamberlain for the imperial insignia (*zhijinwu*). This is what inspired his well-known comment: "One should aim at chamberlain for the imperial insignia as one's official career and at having Yin Lihua as one's wife."

Liu Xiu and his elder brother Liu Yan (d. 23) rose against the usurper Wang Mang (45 B.C.E.–23 C.E.) at Nanyang in 22, declaring their purpose to be the "resumption of the [Han] throne handed down from Emperor Gaozu." In the middle of the following year he took nineteen-year-old Yin Lihua as his wife at Dangchengli in Yuan District (the present-day city of Nanyang in Henan Province). As Metropolitan Commandant (*sili xiaowei*), Liu Xiu traveled to Luoyang in the west, taking his new wife with him. They returned to her family in Xinye, but Yin Lihua then went to stay with her elder brother Yin Shi before going to stay for a time with relatives of her mother, née Deng. At the end of that year, Liu Xiu was ordered to lead his fighting men to Hebei.

The following year (24), Liu Xiu took another woman to wife; this was Guo Shengtong (*q.v.* Guo Shengtong, Empress of Emperor Guangwu), a niece of his fellow clansman Liu Yang. This was a marriage of convenience, contracted for political ends. In 25, Liu Xiu ascended the throne at Hao (present-day Baixiang District in Hebei Province), soon moving his capital to Luoyang. He immediately dispatched a palace attendant (*shizhong*) to fetch his first wife, Yin Lihua, and granted her the title Worthy

234 YIN LIHUA

Lady (*guiren*). Worthy Lady Yin was of an elegant and generous disposition, and the emperor thought so highly of her that he decided to appoint her empress. She declined this honor, however, explaining that because she had not produced a son she was not suited for the position of empress. Since Guo Shengtong had by this time borne a son, she was made empress; her son, Liu Qiang, was appointed heir apparent. A few years later, in 28, Worthy Lady Yin bore a son—Liu Zhuang, Prince of Donghai—while accompanying the emperor on a military expedition to Pengchong. The emperor continued to favor Worthy Lady Yin, and he was deeply grieved when her mother and her younger brother Yin Xin died at the hands of bandits in 33. After this distressing incident the emperor issued an imperial edict to the Grand Minister of Works:

> I married Yin in my lowliness but then my task of commanding the army separated me from her. Fortunately we both managed to survive the perils. Considering her motherly virtues, I deemed her suitable for the position of empress but she steadfastly declined, remaining a concubine. In reward for her modesty, I promised to confer territories upon her younger brothers. It is heartbreaking that tragedy befell her brother Xin, together with her mother, before his conferment. The "Lesser Odes" (Xiao ya) in *The Book of Songs* (Shi jing) says: "In days of peril, in days of dread / It was always 'I and you.' / Now in the time of peace, of happiness, / You have cast me aside" [Waley, 102]. May not one take this warning to heart? I will posthumously confer upon Yin's father [Yin] Lu the title of Marquis Ai of Xuan'en and upon [Yin] Xin the title of Marquis Gong of Xuanyi; her younger brother [Yin] Jiu will inherit the title Marquis Ai.

Empress Guo increasingly resented the emperor's favoritism of Worthy Lady Yin and her son and did not hesitate to voice her complaints, which caused further alienation. Finally, in late 41, Emperor Guangwu issued an edict declaring that he was demoting Guo Shengtong and appointing Yin Lihua empress: "Worthy Lady Yin comes from a good family and married me in my lowliness . . . Therefore it is appropriate for her to succeed to the ancestral temple and be the mother of the nation." Accordingly, Liu Qiang was demoted and appointed Prince of Donghai while Empress Yin's son, Liu Zhuang (Emperor Ming, 27–75; r. 58–75), was made heir apparent in his place.

Empress Yin was modest, uncontentious, demure, and serious. She was by nature kind and filial; although her father had died when she was very young, she unfailingly broke into tears at the mention of his name, and even the emperor was moved by this, time and again. Her brothers were also modest and did not cause strife. They did not presume upon the emperor's favor and become boastful, as many previous imperial in-laws had done. Her older brother Yin Shi, for example, declined the emperor's offer of additional territory in 26 in recognition of his military exploits. Similarly, in 33 her younger brother Yin Xin also declined an additional title. Empress Yin ceased requesting official positions for her relatives after receiving this reply from Yin Xin as to why he had declined the additional title:

> Has Your Majesty not read the classics? *The Book of Changes* [Yi jing] says: "The dragon that goes too high has regrets." This speaks of excess. I would not have an easy conscience if as relatives of Your Majesty we should be so immodest as to desire

notables for sons-in-law and princesses for daughters-in-law. Riches and honor should be kept within the bounds of propriety; extravagance simply makes others sneer.

Empress Yin outlived Emperor Guangwu by seven years. When she died in 64, at the age of fifty-nine, she had been empress for twenty-three years and she was given the posthumous title Empress Guanglie (Guanglie Huanghou) and buried alongside Emperor Guangwu. Empress Yin had been in a position to assume considerable power during her years in the palace but she showed admirable restraint in not insisting on honors and riches for her family. She has been known throughout history as being kind, and she clearly went to great pains to avoid conflict with Empress Guo throughout their time together in the palace. Whether through kindness or intelligent restraint, she behaved with great propriety at a time when the calamitous mistakes of previous generations of imperial women and distaff clans were very fresh in people's minds.

Chia-lin PAO-TAO
(Translated by LU Huici)

An Zuozhang, ed. *Hou fei zhuan*. Zhengzhou: Henan renmin chubanshe, 1990, vol. 1, 134–43.
Ban Gu. *Dongguan Hanji*. Beijing: Zhonghua shuju, 1985, vol. 1, 1.47.
Gujin tushu jicheng, 248. Shanghai, Zhonghua shuju, 1934, 3.1a–b.
Hou Han shu. Beijing: Zhonghua shuju, 1965, vol. 2, 10*shang*.405–6.
Liu Ziqing. *Zhongguo lidai xianneng funü pingzhuan*. Taipei: Liming wenhua, 1978, 108–9.
Sima Guang. *Zizhi tongjian*. Beijing: Zhonghua shuju, 1976, vol. 2, 40 passim.
Waley, Arthur, *The Book of Songs*. London: Houghton Mifflin, 1937, 102.
Yuan Hong. *Hou Han ji*. Shanghai: Shangwu yinshuguan, n.d., 7.54–63.

Ying Zheng Mu: *see* Zhao Ji

Youdi

Youdi (*zi* Ji'er), who lived during the Western Han dynasty (206 B.C.E.–8 C.E.), was from Taiyang (present-day Dali District, Shaanxi Province). She was married to Ren Yanshou, also of Taiyang, with whom she had one daughter and two sons. O'Hara says that Ren Yanshou was a city official of Heyang.

After Youdi's father died, her older brother Jizong quarreled with Ren Yanshou over the matter of the burial. Ren Yanshou and his friend Tian Jian then killed Jizong but the murder was discovered and Tian Jian was executed. For some reason, Ren Yanshou was exempted from any penalty and set free in a court amnesty. On his return home, he told his wife of his arrest and his involvement in her brother's death. "*Now* you tell me!" Youdi retorted indignantly. She stormed from the room as if to leave him, saying, "And who was your accomplice?" Ren Yanshou explained that his friend Tian Jian had already been executed for complicity in the murder; then he said: "I must take responsibility and pay for the murder with my own life. Please take my life." Youdi protested that it would be as immoral for her to kill her husband as it would be for her to live with and serve her brother's murderer. Ren

236 YOUDI

Yanshou was clearly sympathetic and offered to give her everything he owned so that she could go wherever she wanted to, with or without him. Youdi, however, saw no such easy way out of the dreadful dilemma her husband had placed her in. "How would that ease my conscience and allow me to live in such a difficult situation? My brother's murderer has got off scot-free and I cannot be united with my family and my children but must live under the same roof and share the same bed as my brother's enemy." So ashamed was Ren Yanshou that he left Youdi and their children, not telling them where he was going.

Before hanging herself, Youdi explained the tragic situation to her daughter, the eldest of her three children. "Your father killed my brother, so morally I cannot remain at home with him. However, while your father is still alive I cannot remarry. I have no option but to abandon you three children and kill myself. I leave my sons in your care." The Prince of Fengyi (Liu Rang) was so moved at the moral integrity of Youdi when he heard what had happened that he ordered the district magistrate to exempt her three children from the corvee and labor. Youdi was buried in a specially constructed tomb and a stone tablet was erected praising her fine deed.

Caught as she was in a dilemma created by her male relatives, she could not fulfill her moral obligations to either her natal family or the family she had married into. In stark contrast to her husband, Youdi did not shirk what she saw as her moral responsibility. While modern sensibilities would perhaps prevent us from describing her act as a "fine deed," we cannot but admire the moral courage she exhibited in resolving the problem with great dignity, at the cost of her own life.

SHEN Jian

Liu Xiang. *Lienü zhuan*. Sibubeiyao ed., 5.10–11.
O'Hara, Albert R. *The Position of Woman in Early China According to the Lieh Nü Chuan, "The Biographies of Chinese Women."* Taipei: Mei Ya, 1971; 1978, 150–51.

Yu, Consort of the Hegemon-King of Chu

Lady Yu (Xi Chu Bawang Fei Yu Ji), d. 202 B.C.E., was consort of Xiang Yu (232–202 B.C.E.), the Hegemon-King of Chu. One source suggests that Yu was her surname, but it is generally accepted that it was her given name; the nearly contemporaneous *Historical Records* (Shi ji) records her simply as Beauty Yu.

In the strife that marked the last years of the Qin dynasty, Xiang Yu of Chu (located in the lower reaches of the Yangzi River) rose in rebellion. *Historical Records* tells of Beauty Yu accompanying Xiang Yu in battle as he fought Qin and, after the fall of Qin, struggled with Liu Bang (256–195 B.C.E.) of the state of Han for sovereignty over China. By 202 B.C.E., however, Xiang Yu was all but defeated, besieged by Liu Bang's armies at Gaixia (southeast of present-day Lingbi District, Anhui Province). Deep into the night, on all sides, Xiang Yu heard the songs of Chu, leading him to believe the men of Chu had defected to Liu Bang and that Chu had fallen to his enemy. Heartbroken, Xiang Yu rose in his tent to drink with Lady Yu, his constant companion throughout his campaigns, and composed the *Gaixia Song:*

My strength uprooted mountains,
My spirit overshadowed the world;
But the times are against me
And my horse can gallop no more.
My horse can gallop no more,
What can I do?
Yu, Yu,
What is to become of you?

After he had sung this song of grief several times, Lady Yu composed her *Response to Gaixia Song:*

Han soldiers stepped onto Chu land.
The songs of Chu echoed everywhere.
Your Majesty in despair,
How can I hope to live on?

Her poignant song brought tears to Xiang Yu's eyes, and all the soldiers present were moved to tears. When she finished singing, Lady Yu drew a sword and took her own life. Xiang Yu is said to have cut his throat to escape capture. According to legend, this took place in Dingyuan District, Haozhou (present-day Fengyang District, Anhui Province), and Lady Yu's grave is said to lie sixty *li* (twenty miles) west of Dingyuan. Her story was later carved on a stele that stands in Lingbi District, where over the centuries people came to pay their respects.

It was remarkable for a woman to accompany her lover through all his military campaigns. However, it is for having killed herself without hesitation at the fall of Xiang Yu, thereby avoiding humiliation and preserving her integrity, that Lady Yu has been praised throughout history. Her story and her song were made into the opera *Farewell, My Concubine* (Bawang bieji), which in turn inspired the award-winning 1993 film of the same name starring Gong Li (*vide Biographical Dictionary of Chinese Women, The Twentieth Century*).

SU Zhecong and SHEN Lidong

Chen Quanli and Hou Xinyi, eds. *Hou fei cidian.* Xi'an: Shaanxi renmin jiaoyu chubanshe, 1991, 11.
Liu Shisheng. *Zhongguo gudai funü shi.* Qingdao: Qingdao chubanshe, 1991, 82–84.
Ma Zhaozheng and Zhou Feichang. *Zhongguo gudai funü mingren.* Beijing: Zhongguo funü chubanshe, 1988, 35–37.
Shi ji. Beijing: Zhonghua shuju, 1985, vol. 1, 7.295–339.

Yue Yangzi Qi: *see* **Yue Yangzi's Wife**

Yue Yangzi's Wife
Yue Yangzi's Wife (Yue Yangzi Qi), of the Eastern Han dynasty (25–220), was from present-day Henan Province. Her name is not recorded in the histories.

238 YUE YANGZI'S WIFE

Yue Yangzi found a piece of gold on his travels and gave it to his wife when he returned home. She told him: "I hear that an upright and ambitious man will not drink from a bandit's spring and an honest man will not accept food and drink offered discourteously, let alone dishonor his reputation by picking up lost gold." Shamed, Yue Yangzi discarded the gold and set out on a long journey to pursue his studies. A year later, however, he called a halt to his studies and returned home. When his wife asked him why, he answered: "No reason. It's simply that I've been away too long. I was homesick and missed my family." His wife fetched a knife and, standing beside her loom, told him that the fabric on the loom was made from silk from silkworms that was spun into thread and then woven into cloth. "It is done by adding one line of thread after another so that inch by inch and foot by foot it grows until it is a complete bolt. If I cut the cloth now I will destroy it and everything I have done will have been a waste of time and effort. It is exactly the same with your studies. You should keep learning every day so as to enrich your knowledge and refine your character. Your stopping half way is no different from my cutting the unfinished cloth on the loom." Moved by his wife's words, Yue Yangzi returned to his studies and did not go home once in the seven years it took him to complete them. His hard-working and thrifty wife took care of the household and supported his mother. She even sent him money to support him through his studies.

On one occasion, a neighbor's chicken found its way into her yard and her mother-in-law caught it, killed it, and secretly cooked it. Yue Yangzi's Wife wept when she saw the cooked chicken and refused to eat it. Her bewildered mother-in-law asked the reason for her tears. "It is poverty that has driven us to eat a stolen chicken," she replied. Deeply shamed, her mother-in-law threw the chicken away.

Some time later a bandit attacked the two women, intending to rape Yue Yangzi's Wife by threatening her mother-in-law. Yue Yangzi's Wife seized a knife and ran out to attack the bandit, who told her to put the knife down and do as he said or he would kill her mother-in-law. Yue Yangzi's Wife looked heavenward and with a deep sigh killed herself with her knife. The terrified bandit released his hostage and fled but was tracked down and imprisoned. The commandery governor sent several bolts of silk to show the high esteem in which he held Yue Yangzi's Wife and had her buried with proper ritual, commending her as "one who upheld her chastity and righteousness."

WANG Lihua

Hou Han shu. Beijing: Zhonghua shuju, 1965, vol. 10, 84.2792–93.
Liu Shisheng. *Zhongguo gudai funü shi.* Qingdao: Qingdao chubanshe, 1991, 138.
Liu Ziqing. *Zhongguo lidai xianneng funü pingzhuan.* Taipei: Liming wenhua, 1978, 131–33.

Z

Zhang Gongzhu Piao: *see* **Liu Piao**

Zhang Liangze Qi: *see* **Chen Siqian**

Zhang Lu Mu: *see* **Zhang Lu's Mother**

Zhang Lu's Mother

Zhang Lu's Mother (Zhang Lu Mu), fl. late second century, was active in the region of today's Chengdu in Sichuan Province and played an important role in the creation of the Daoist Way of the Celestial Masters, although she is rarely granted the status of Master on her own behalf. In his discussion of Daoist celibacy, Michel Strickmann cites a fourth-century text edited by Tao Hongjing (*vide* Xu Baoguang) in which "the Three Masters are enumerated as the Celestial Master, the Lady-Master (*nü-shih*), and the Inheriting Master (*hsi-shih:* the usual designation of Chang Lu . . .). A female figure, though mysterious, is still prominent. She may well have been Chang Lu's mother, whose liaison with the governor of the province was noted by the historians." Zhang Lu's Mother is generally assumed to have been the wife of the son of Zhang Daoling (fl. 140), the legendary founder of religious Daoism, thus making her son Zhang Daoling's grandson. However, the only son of Zhang Daoling that sources ever refer to is Zhang Heng, and his name has never been linked with Zhang Lu's Mother. It therefore seems possible that Zhang Lu's Mother was a practitioner of early Daoism in the Way of the Celestial Masters tradition and that historians have preferred to grant her son kinship with Zhang Daoling than credit her with independently passing her tradition on to her son.

Zhang Lu's Mother is described in the *History of the Later Han Dynasty* (Hou Han shu) as a licentious woman, not unprepossessing in appearance, who practiced sorcery, or the Way of Demons (*guidao*). Her son, Zhang Lu (fl. 188–220), created a state-like Daoist community in northwestern China that was administered according to the principles of Celestial Master Daoism, involving faith healing and welfare measures. The priesthood was hereditary and women were expected to participate in religious and administrative tasks and in particular in the conversion of new adepts.

Zhang Lu's Mother played an important role in establishing this community due to her personal contacts with Liu Yan (d. 194), provincial governor of Yi and a member of the Han imperial clan. The *History of the Later Han Dynasty* tells us that she was a frequent visitor to Liu Yan's home by virtue of her beauty and knowledge of the magic arts. Through her influence her son obtained official rank and the Daoist community developed for some thirty years, largely without interference from the Han dynasty state apparatus. When Liu Yan died, however, his son Liu Zhang attempted to rein in Zhang Lu, using Zhang Lu's Mother and other relatives as hostages, and eventually having them put to death. Zhang Lu continued to increase the independence of his Daoist community in the Hanzhong area (present-day Shaanxi Province), thus strengthening its historical relevance as the point of origin for China's only indigenous religion. The Celestial Master tradition is still practiced today, with the sixty-fourth Celestial Master ensconced in Taiwan and his nephew practicing in mainland China, where official tolerance of Daoism has allowed a comparatively recent resurgence of interest in this religion.

Barbara HENDRISCHKE and Sue WILES

Bumbacher, Stephan P. *The Fragments of the Daoxue zhuan: Critical Edition, Translation, and Analysis of a Medieval Collection of Daoist Biographies.* Frankfurt/Main: Peter Lang, 2000, 513–17.

240 *ZHANG LU'S MOTHER*

Hou Han shu. Beijing: Zhonghua shuju, 1963, vol. 9, 75.2432f, 2435f.
Sanguo zhi. Beijing: Zhonghua shuju, 1982, vol. 1, 8.263f; vol. 4, 31.867.
Schipper, Kristofer. "The Taoist Body." *History of Religions* 17 (1978): 375.
Stein, Rolf A. "Religious Taoism and Popular Religion from the Second to Seventh Centuries."
   In *Facets of Taoism: Essays in Chinese Religion,* ed. Holmes Welch and Anna Seidel. New
   Haven, CT: Yale University Press, 1979, 60–62.
Strickmann, Michel. "A Taoist Confirmation of Liang Wu Ti's Suppression of Taoism." *Journal
   of the American Oriental Society* 98, no. 4 (1978): 469–70.

Zhang Tang Mu: *see* Zhang Tang's Mother

Zhang Tang's Mother

Zhang Tang's Mother (Zhang Tang Mu), c. 165–110 B.C.E., was a native of Duling, in Chang'an (the present-day city of Xi'an); her given names and surname are not known. Her husband was an aide to the governor of Chang'an; their son, Zhang Tang (d. 115 B.C.E.), rose to the position of censor-in-chief (*yushi dafu*) during the reign of Emperor Wu (r. 140–87 B.C.E.). Zhang Tang was a strict official and in executing the law he could be cruel, but he excelled at implementing economic reforms.

For some ten years, between 129 and 119 B.C.E., Emperor Wu sent expensive military expeditions against the Xiongnu people who roamed China's northern frontier. Also during this period, however, Shandong in the northeast was devastated by floods and then a drought that eventually forced the poor to leave their homes and seek help from local magistrates, who were in turn unable to sustain such a drain on their resources. Fearing a financial disaster, the emperor saw the necessity of implementing economic reforms. He therefore entrusted Censor-in-Chief Zhang Tang with the tasks of minting silver and *wuzhu*-denomination coins, collecting the salt and iron revenues, preventing rich merchants from making excessive profits, issuing money in small denominations, and stopping powerful families from acquiring land from the poor. Zhang Tang became so influential that all matters of importance were brought to him for decision instead of being submitted to the Counselor-in-Chief (*chengxiang*) Qing Zhai. Not surprisingly, while Emperor Wu approved of Zhang Tang's handling of the economy, those who stood to lose by these reforms did all they could to hamper him. District magistrates, for instance, did not benefit from the emperor's reforms and this led some court officials to resort to robbing the poor by forcing them to borrow. Zhang Tang was not to be diverted from his task, however, and he punished offenders according to the letter of the law, thereby leaving himself open to public criticism.

After seven years in the post of censor-in-chief, Zhang Tang was finally brought down by the slander of the counselor-in-chief's three trusted aides, Zhu Maichen (*vide* Zhu Maichen's Wife), Wang Chao, and Bian Tong, whose words eroded Emperor Wu's trust in Zhang Tang. Apparently believing his cause to be lost, Zhang Tang committed suicide in 115. The three aides had accused Zhang Tang of offering privileged information to a colleague who had thus been able to corner certain markets and share the profits with Zhang Tang. After Zhang Tang's death, however, it was discovered that he had not profited in any such way, his total assets being some 500 cash, all of which he had derived from his salary and perfectly proper gifts from the emperor.

With Zhang Tang cleared of all impropriety, his male relatives wanted to give him an extravagant funeral. His mother opposed this, however, saying: "He was a minister of the state working for the emperor and slanderous rumors forced him to take his own life. What good is it now to bury him with grand ceremony?" Thus Zhang Tang was buried simply, in a single coffin, not in a coffin within an outer coffin in the customary way. Emperor Wu is reported to have said, upon hearing of this, "Like mother, like son," indicating his admiration for their integrity. Some time later, the three aides who had slandered Zhang Tang were executed and the counselor-in-chief committed suicide. Zhang Tang's Mother, who had been upright, discreet, and strict in raising her children, is credited with the stern and righteous behavior of Zhang Tang when he was censor-in-chief. These same virtues were seen in Zhang Tang's son Zhang Anshi (d. 62 B.C.E.), whose wife continued to weave at home and whose young servants all pursued a trade even when Zhang Anshi had become Marquis of Fuping, a fief town of 10,000 households.

XIA Chunhao

Han shu. Beijing: Zhonghua shuju, 1983, vol. 9, 59.2637–46.
Liu Xiang. *Lienü zhuan.* Sibubeiyao ed., 8.3.
O'Hara, Albert R. *The Position of Woman in Early China According to the Lieh Nü Chuan, "The Biographies of Chinese Women."* Taipei: Mei Ya, 1971; 1978, 221.

Zhang Yan, Empress of Emperor Hui

Zhang Yan (Xiao Hui Zhang Huanghou), d. 163 B.C.E., was the imperial consort of her maternal uncle Emperor Hui (Liu Ying, 210–188 B.C.E., r. 194–188 B.C.E.). The year of her birth is not recorded and she is little known in history; hers was a difficult life, yet she lived through the reigns of the first four rulers of the Han dynasty.

Zhang Yan's father, Zhang Ao, was Prince of Zhao and her mother, Princess Yuan of Lu, was the eldest daughter of Emperor Gaozu and Empress Lü (*q.v.* Lü Zhi, Empress of Emperor Gaozu). Her royal heritage, however, did not protect her as her family suffered changes and upheaval from the time she was a small child. Emperor Gaozu passed through the state of Zhao at the end of 200 B.C.E. while on a military expedition against the northern Xiongnu. As a dutiful son-in-law, Zhang Ao humbly received the emperor according to the traditional rites, but the emperor's arrogant behavior so angered the two counselors-in-chief (*chengxiang*) of Zhao that they plotted rebellion. Although Zhang Ao had steadfastly refused to be part of their plan, when the plot was uncovered in 198 B.C.E. he was among those arrested. Empress Lü pressed for the release of her son-in-law, to no avail, but an official investigation finally confirmed Zhang Ao's innocence and he was set free. Despite this, Emperor Gaozu rescinded the title of Prince of Zhao and demoted Zhang Ao to Marquis of Xuanping. Her parents' caution and display of deep respect to her grandfather appear to have been the source of Empress Zhang's timidity and the submissiveness she exhibited throughout her life.

Three years after Zhang Ao's downfall, Empress Lü's son Liu Ying (Emperor

Hui) ascended the throne. Emperor Hui was a kind and gentle young man and his mother's barbaric murder of Consort Qi (*q.v.* Qi, Concubine of Emperor Gaozu) and the consort's son Ruyi in the pursuit of palace politics so shocked him that he fell ill. From that time on he abstained from affairs of state, indulging instead in alcohol and sex, and allowed his mother, now Empress Dowager Lü, to hold the reins of power. To consolidate her son's reign, Empress Dowager Lü attempted to unseat the feudal princes belonging to her husband's Liu clan who might be pretenders to the throne. At the same time, she sought a suitable empress for her son, finally deciding to marry her granddaughter Zhang Yan to her son in order to create an intricate network of kin to strengthen her political power.

Thus, in late 191 B.C.E., the adolescent Zhang Yan became empress to her uncle Emperor Hui, who was then twenty-one years old. Although the traditional rites did not forbid marriage between a man and his maternal niece, this was indeed verging on incest. Nobody dared raise this objection to Empress Dowager Lü.

The histories give no insight into this imperial marriage that lasted only three years. According to her biography in the *History of the Han Dynasty* (Han shu), however, Empress Zhang "did not produce a son, after trying every means, and therefore adopted the son of a palace woman [*meiren*]." The Song dynasty *Zizhi tongjian* is more explicit: "Empress Dowager Lü ordered Empress Zhang to adopt a boy and to kill the boy's mother; the boy was made heir to the throne." When Emperor Hui died, the infant heir apparent, Liu Hong (Emperor Shao, d. 184 B.C.E.), ascended the throne and Empress Dowager Lü remained de facto ruler, taking complete charge of affairs of state. Empress Zhang continued to live in the imperial palace but remained aloof from court politics.

Empress Dowager Lü retained control of the court for eight years. When the young emperor became discontented upon discovering the truth of his mother's execution, the empress dowager had her grandson secretly assassinated. Another son of Emperor Hui, Prince Yi, was placed upon the throne but the real power remained in the hands of Empress Dowager Lü, who proceeded to grant the title of prince to male members of her natal Lü clan. While this aroused the ire of many senior officials, it had little effect on Empress Zhang, who had no political power and had never been involved in politics.

In the internecine strife that followed the death of Empress Dowager Lü, the Liu clan princes joined forces to kill her Lü kin. Emperor Gaozu's son Liu Heng (Emperor Wen) was chosen for the throne and was installed as emperor. Empress Zhang's relationship to Empress Dowager Lü placed her in a dangerous position. She was not executed, however, but was sent instead to a palace in the north, where she spent her remaining sixteen years. No record exists of her later life, but she died in the spring of 163 B.C.E., bringing to a close the life of an unremarkable empress of Han.

ZANG Jian
(Translated by TAM Chui-han June)

Chen Quanli and Hou Xinyi, eds. *Hou fei cidian.* Xi'an: Shaanxi renmin jiaoyu chubanshe, 1991, 12.
Han shu. Beijing: Zhonghua shuju, 1983, vol. 1, 2.90; vol. 12, 97*shang*.3940.

Shi ji. Beijing: Zhonghua shuju, 1959, vol. 2, 8.386; vol. 2, 9.395–412; vol. 4, 49.1969; vol. 8, 89.2583–85.

Sima Guang. *Zizhi tongjian.* Beijing: Zhonghua shuju, 1956, vol. 1, 12.418.

Zhangdi Dou Huanghou: *see* **Dou, Empress of Emperor Zhang**

Zhao E

Zhao E, the mother of Pang Yu (Pang Yu Mu Zhao E), fl. 179, also known as Eqin, was the daughter of Zhao An (or Jun An) of Fulu District (present-day Jiuchuan in Gansu Province). She is known by her *zi,* E, her given name being unknown. Her son, Pang Yu, was appointed Marquis of Guannei (*guannei hou*) during the reign of Emperor Wen (Cao Pi, 187–226; r. 220–226) of the Wei dynasty.

According to the biography of Pang Yu in the *History of the Wei Dynasty* (Wei shu), the *Record of the Three Kingdoms* (Sanguo zhi), and Huangfu Mi's *Biographies of Eminent Women* (Lienü zhuan), Zhao E's father was killed by a man named Li Shou of the same district. Li Shou was so well protected, however, that none of Zhao E's three younger brothers was able to avenge their father's death before they themselves died in a plague. Overjoyed at the news of their deaths, Li Shou invited his clansmen to a celebration where he announced: "All the strong ones of the Zhao clan are now dead and only a weak daughter remains. I need worry no longer." He therefore began to let his guard down. Zhao E was enraged when she heard from her son what Li Shou had said and tearfully she vowed: "Li Shou, don't you be happy. I will not let you live, for that would bring shame on the three sons of our family. How can you be so sure that Eqin cannot kill you with her own hands? You are not as lucky as you think."

Harboring vengeance for her father's death, she secretly bought a famous sword and sharpened it day and night, even as she honed her hatred for Li Shou. Hearing of this, Li Shou resumed his old habit of vigilance, wearing his sword at his belt when he rode out on his horse. He was a vicious man of whom the villagers were terrified. A neighbor of Zhao E, a Madame Xu, tried to dissuade her from her mission, saying: "Li Shou is a man accustomed to violence. He is also on his guard. No matter how great your determination, you are no match for him and catastrophe will befall you when you find yourself unable to kill him. He will wipe out your entire household, causing untold pain and humiliation. For the sake of your family, I ask you to reconsider your plan." To this Zhao E replied: "It is wrong to share the same heaven and earth, sun and moon with the murderer of one's parent; if Li Shou lives, I cannot. Now that all my male siblings are dead, I must seek revenge. If I did as you say, no one would kill Li Shou, and I would not be able to live with myself." Her family and neighbors scoffed at these words, but Zhao E continued: "Well may you laugh at me, a mere woman, vowing to kill Li Shou, but you will see when I stain this blade with the blood of Li Shou's neck."

Zhao E became obsessed with Li Shou, abandoning all else to stalk him from a small cart in which she rode. On a fine day early in the second month of 179, she finally confronted him at the metropolitan post-house in Jiuquan. Descending from her cart, she grabbed the bridle of his horse and began to abuse him. When Li Shou

244 *ZHAO E*

tried to yank his horse away, Zhao E lashed out with her sword, wounding both him and the horse. Li Shou was thrown from his horse and landed in the gutter, where Zhao E fell on him, stabbing him repeatedly with her sword. She did not manage to kill him, however, and in her wild haste she broke her sword on a tree. She tried to grab Li Shou's sword, but he continued to resist, all the while calling loudly for help. He attempted to get up but Zhao E held him down with her left hand, hitting him repeatedly across the throat with her right fist. When he finally stopped struggling she chopped off his head with his sword.

Having killed Li Shou, Zhao E went straight to the district office to give herself up and then started walking toward the jail. The magistrate, however, could not bring himself to sentence her and was ready to hang up his seal and resign from his position, allowing Zhao E to abscond. One version of the story has Zhao E and the magistrate running away together at this point.

But Zhao E was determined to pay for her deed. "Having killed my enemy, I should die. Clearly, this is my lot. As a magistrate, you are responsible for administering the laws and meting out punishment; I dare not treasure my life at the expense of the law." News of Zhao E's integrity attracted a crowd of awed onlookers and even her guards were moved, to the extent that they intimated to her that they would look the other way were she to run away. An emotional Zhao E told them: "It is not my wish to escape death at the cost of contravening the law. Now that I have wrought vengeance it is right that I die. I beg you to let me bear the full force of the law so that good government will not be jeopardized. I would rather give my life ten thousand times than destabilize the law." When the guards still would not listen, she said: "I may be just a humble woman, but I do understand the law, and I know that the crime of murder is not pardonable. I do not want to run away, I want to receive the punishment due for my crime and be executed in the marketplace in order to uphold the emperor's law." She showed no sign of fear but grew increasingly fervent, so the guards stopped arguing and simply bundled her into a carriage and took her home. Another version is that she did go to jail but was granted amnesty and was able to go home.

Several people, including Zhou Hong, the regional inspector of Liangzhou, and Liu Ban, the governor of Jiuquan, memorialized the emperor about Zhao E's integrity, and her story was inscribed on a stone stele so that her family might be glorified. Zhang Huan, who held the position of chamberlain for ceremonies (*taichang*), presented her with twenty bolts of silk out of admiration for her actions. Zhao E's act of revenge was recorded in official histories and spread far and wide by word of mouth, while men of letters of later ages immortalized her in biographies and poetry. Liang Kuan of late Eastern Han, for instance, wrote her biography, and Zuo Yannian of the Three Kingdoms period praised her integrity in his ballad *Qinnü xiu xing*. *Qinnü xiu xing* is also the title of a poem written by Fu Xuan of Western Jin telling of a woman who braved the powerful to avenge her father, and then gave herself up. In this latter poem the woman is called Pang's wife and one line runs, "One good daughter is worth one hundred sons."

Huangfu Mi (215–282) had this to say of Zhao E in his *Lienü zhuan*: "It is expected of a man that he not share heaven and earth with his parents' murderer, yet Eqin, a mere woman, also experienced the hurt and humiliation of the murder of her father. Paying no mind to the danger she placed herself in, in an unprecedented deed she killed both her enemy and his horse with her own hands, thus pacifying the wronged spirit of her father and wiping away the regret of her three younger brothers. Those words found in *The Book of Songs* [Shi jing], 'Prepare my lance and my spear, I will fight with you,' apply to Eqin."

The Tang poet Li Bai (702–762) also praised Zhao E's chivalrous deed in a poem also titled *Qinnü xiu xing*.

SHEN Lidong
(Translated by Lily Xiao Hong LEE and Sue WILES)

Guo Maoqian. *Yuefu shiji*. Beijing: Zhonghua shuju, 1979, 3.887.
Hou Han shu. Beijing: Zhonghua shuju, 1965, vol. 5, 84.2796–97.
Huangfu Mi. *Lienü zhuan*, quoted in *Sanguo zhi*. Beijing: Zhonghua shuju, 1959, 18.548–50, Pei Songzhi's commentary.
Sanguo zhi. Beijing: Zhonghua shuju, 1975, vol. 2, 18.548.

Zhao Feiyan, Empress of Emperor Cheng

Zhao Feiyan (Xiao Cheng Zhao Huanghou), 43–1 B.C.E., said to have come from Jiangdu (present-day Yangzhou in Jiangsu Province), was originally named Feng Yisheng. She first became famous as a dancer and a singer, and then as empress to Emperor Cheng (Liu Ao, 51–7 B.C.E.; r. 32–7 B.C.E.). Her younger sister Zhao Hede (*q.v.* Zhao Hede, Concubine of Emperor Cheng) also became a favorite of Emperor Cheng and, according to some sources, she too excelled as a singer and dancer.

Left to die at birth, Feng Yisheng was fortunate that she survived long enough for her impoverished parents to relent and decide to raise her. Her father, Feng Wanli, was a musician and he died when she was still quite young, leaving her and her sister stranded in the city of Chang'an. There they were adopted by Zhao Lin, housekeeper for a rich family, who gave them a good education. The girls took their benefactor's surname and initially made their living at embroidery. However, through Zhao Lin they had the opportunity to serve as maidservants in the house of the Princess of Yang'e, where they learned singing and dancing. Lithe and slim, Zhao Yisheng was as agile as a swallow when she danced and people began calling her *feiyan*, "flying swallow," so that eventually she came to be known as Zhao Feiyan. She came to the notice of Emperor Cheng when she danced at a feast given by the Princess of Yang'e. Captivated by her graceful figure, he summoned her to the imperial palace, where she became his favorite concubine, and he promoted her to the rank of Lady of Handsome fairness (*jieyu*).

The imperial distaff clans had become increasingly influential during the reigns of Emperor Yuan and Emperor Cheng, with the Huo, the Xu, and the Wang clans each gaining power in turn. Of lowly birth and with no powerful family behind her, Zhao Feiyan maintained her position by recommending her younger sister to the emperor, who was entranced by Hede's beauty and charm. By 20 B.C.E., Empress Xu (*q.v.* Xu, Empress of Emperor Cheng) had become a victim of the volatile political climate and

246 *ZHAO FEIYAN*

had fallen into disfavor, being held responsible for the emperor not having sired a son and heir. Disasters such as serious floods in the capital and unusual phenomena around 30 B.C.E. were also cited as inauspicious omens. The Zhao sisters became involved in court intrigues and in 18 B.C.E., with the support of the Wang family, including Empress Dowager Wang (*q.v.* Wang Zhengjun, Empress of Emperor Yuan), they laid accusations that Empress Xu and Ban Jieyu (*q.v.* Ban Jieyu, Concubine of Emperor Cheng) had practiced witchcraft (*wugu*) to invoke curses on the women's quarters and on the emperor himself. Empress Xu was deposed, while Ban Jieyu wisely requested to be allowed to serve the empress dowager, effectively retiring from court life. Empress Dowager Wang hesitated to consent to the installation of Zhao Feiyan, a woman of extremely humble origins, but gave her approval after her nephew Chunyu Chang interceded. Zhao Feiyan was made empress in 16 B.C.E. and her benefactor, Zhao Lin, was honored with the title of Marquis of Chengyang.

After she became empress, Zhao Feiyan was largely replaced in the emperor's affections by her sister Zhao Hede, with whom she resided in the opulent Zhaoyang Palace. Zhao Hede remained loyal to her sister, however, speaking well of her to the emperor so that Zhao Feiyan's position was unaffected. Nevertheless, Zhao Feiyan did her best to retain the emperor's favor, a famous example being that, on learning of the emperor's voyeuristic tendencies—he apparently liked peeping at Zhao Hede when she was bathing—Zhao Feiyan invited him to watch her sister bathe. In another attempt to regain Emperor Cheng's favor she told him, untruthfully, that she was pregnant. Although they monopolized the emperor for over ten years, neither of the Zhao sisters became pregnant. They were both well aware that unless they could bear a son for the emperor, who was approaching middle age, their position at court would become increasingly perilous. It is said that Zhao Feiyan tried to become pregnant by having relationships with men other than the emperor, and that Zhao Hede bribed the eunuchs to keep a close watch on the other concubines. In 12 B.C.E. a palace woman named Cao Gong bore the emperor a son. Although of as humble origin as the Zhao sisters, Cao Gong had learned to read and had at one stage instructed Zhao Feiyan in the classics. Now Zhao Hede compelled Emperor Cheng to have this infant put to death. A year later, Beauty (*meiren*) Xu bore the emperor a son, but this child too was murdered. A children's song thought to satirize the behavior of the Zhao sisters had long circulated among the people:

> Wooden gates
> gray-green fixtures
> Swallow comes flying
> pecks imperial grandsons
> Imperial grandsons die
> swallow pecks turds. (Watson, 277)

Emperor Cheng died suddenly one morning in 7 B.C.E. He had not been ill and suspicion immediately fell on Zhao Hede, with some saying his death was caused by sexual indulgence. As soon as Empress Dowager Wang announced there would be an investigation, Zhao Hede committed suicide.

Emperor Ai (Liu Xin, 25–1 B.C.E.; r. 6–1 B.C.E.) promoted Zhao Feiyan to empress dowager in 6 B.C.E., and enfeoffed her adopted brother Zhao Qin as Marquis of Xincheng. A few months later, however, the emperor relieved the male members of the Zhao family of their titles and demoted them to the rank of commoner when the results of the investigation into Emperor Cheng's death implicated Zhao Hede. He protected Zhao Feiyan, however, because she had helped him become heir apparent. Zhao Feiyan also found allies in Emperor Ai's grandmother Empress Dowager Fu (*q.v.* Fu, Concubine of Emperor Yuan) and his mother, Lady Ding, but the ultimate winner in this grand power struggle was Empress Dowager Wang.

Upon the death of Emperor Ai, the nine-year-old Liu Kan (Emperor Ping, 8 B.C.E.–5 C.E.; r. 1–5 C.E.) was placed on the throne. Commander-in-Chief Wang Mang immediately approached Empress Dowager Wang (his aunt) about Empress Dowager Zhao (Zhao Feiyan) and within a short time Zhao Feiyan had been demoted to Empress of Emperor Cheng and moved to the Northern Palace. A month later an imperial edict was issued describing Zhao Feiyan as "lacking in the proper ways of a woman, failing to wait on her superiors according to ritual, she possesses the malice of a wolf or a tiger" and demoting her to the rank of commoner. She committed suicide the same day, after having been empress for sixteen years.

AU Chi-kin
(Translated by CHE Wai-lam William)

Ban Gu. *Courtier and Commoner in Ancient China. Selections from the "History of the Former Han" by Pan Ku*, trans. Burton Watson. New York: Columbia University Press, 1974, 266–77.

Ge Hong. *Xijing zaji.* Beijing: Zhonghua shuju, 1985, 1.5–8.

Han shu. Beijing: Zhonghua shuju, 1983, vol. 12, 97*xia*.3988–99.

Li Anyu. *Zhongguo lidai huanghou zhizui.* Beijing: Zhongguo youyi chubanshe, 1990, vol. 1, 85–97.

Ling Xuan. "Zhao Feiyan wai zhuan." In *Biji xiaoshuo daguan.* Taipei: Xinxing shuju, 1974, 5493–97.

Liu Xiang. *Lienü zhuan.* Sibubeiyao ed., 8.8a–b.

Loewe, Michael. *Crisis and Conflict in Han China: 104 BC to AD 9.* London: George Allen & Unwin, 1974, 87, 157.

Ma Xiaoguang. "Gongzhong sheidiyi, Feiyan zai Zhaoyang: Handai huanghou Zhao Feiyan de yisheng." *Wenshi zhishi* 1 (1988): 82–86.

Meng Xinbo and Liu Sha. *Ershisan ge houfei.* Changchun: Jilin wenshi chubanshe, 1986, 56–63.

O'Hara, Albert R. *The Position of Woman in Early China According to the Lieh Nü Chuan, "The Biographies of Chinese Women."* Taipei: Mei Ya, 1971; 1978, 235–38.

Sima Guang. *Zizhi tongjian.* Beijing: Zhonghua shuju, 1976, vol. 31, 999–1002.

Wang Fanting. *Zhonghua lidai funü.* Taipei: Shangwu yinshuguan, 1966, 26–29.

Yin Wei. *Zhonghua wuqian nian yiyuan cainü.* Zhengzhou: Zhongzhou guji chubanshe, 1992, 31–35.

Zhao Gouyi, Concubine of Emperor Wu

Lady of Handsome Fairness Zhao Gouyi (Xiao Wu Gou Yi Zhao Jieyu), 113–88 B.C.E., was born in Hejian (in the east of present-day Xian District, Hebei Province);

248 *ZHAO GOUYI*

her surname was Zhao but her given name is not recorded. Her father was castrated at some stage as punishment for an offense and served in the capital, Chang'an, in the minor eunuch position of palace attendant (*zhong huangmen*).

Emperor Wu (Liu Che, 156–87 B.C.E.; r. 141–87 B.C.E.) was on a hunting expedition in Hejian when an astrologer told him that there was "a person of significance" in the northeast, describing this person as a young woman of the Zhao family. When the emperor had her summoned, Zhao came into his presence with both fists clenched. As soon as Emperor Wu caressed her hands, however, her fingers relaxed and unfolded. The emperor took her as his favorite, naming her Consort Gouyi (Consort of the Fists). She was quickly promoted to the rank of Lady of Handsome Fairness (*jieyu*) and installed in Gouyi Palace within Ganquan Palace outside the city. After a pregnancy said to have lasted fourteen months, she gave birth to a son, Liu Fuling (Emperor Zhao, 94–74 B.C.E.; r. 87–74 B.C.E.). Because the legendary monarch Yao was also said to have been born after fourteen months in the womb, Emperor Wu named the gate where Liu Fuling was born the Gate of the Mother of Yao.

Soon after the birth of Liu Fuling, the court was thrown into a state of crisis that saw hundreds of people executed on what may well have been false accusations of witchcraft and necromancy. Court politics saw the heir apparent, Liu Ju, and his mother, Empress Wei (*q.v.* Wei Zifu, Empress of Emperor Wu), both implicated, and although they were innocent of either treachery or witchcraft they were both driven to suicide in late 91. With the death of the heir apparent, Consort Gouyi's son became a contender for the throne. Two of Emperor Wu's sons—Liu Hong (d. 109 B.C.E.), the son of Lady Wang, and Liu Bo (d. 88 or 86 B.C.E.), the son of Consort Li (*q.v.* Li, Concubine of Emperor Wu)—had already died. Two other sons—Liu Dan and Liu Xu—born to a Lady Li were excluded from consideration because of their dissolute behavior and misdeeds. Liu Fuling, however, was already sturdy and knowledgeable by the age of six. Emperor Wu believed the boy to be much like him and loved the child because of his unusually long gestation period.

However, Emperor Wu hesitated to appoint Liu Fuling heir apparent because Consort Gouyi was still young and he feared she might seize power through her son. Desiring instead that Huo Guang (d. 66 B.C.E.) should assist the boy once he ascended the throne, Emperor Wu commissioned a painting of the legendary Zhou Gong carrying his nephew King Cheng on his back and receiving the other feudal lords; he then gave the painting to Huo Guang. The officials and Consort Gouyi understood from this that the emperor intended that Liu Fuling be his successor. A few days later the emperor fell ill and, still concerned about the power he might be releasing into the hands of Consort Gouyi, he summoned her and berated her. Bewildered, Consort Gouyi removed her hairpins and earrings and kowtowed to the enraged emperor, begging forgiveness. Emperor Wu, however, ordered that she be taken to the prison in the women's quarters. As Consort Gouyi turned to look at the emperor he said: "Out, quickly! You cannot be saved!" In her biography, the almost contemporaneous *History of the Han Dynasty* (Han shu) records that she died of anxiety, while in his *Zizhi tongjian,* Sima Guang reports that she was "ordered to die" (*ci si*).

After the death of Consort Gouyi, Emperor Wu asked his retinue what people were saying about it. His attendants replied that people could not understand why the emperor had killed the boy's mother, since he had already decided to appoint Liu Fuling as his successor. The emperor explained that his actions may well have been misunderstood by "children and fools," but that a young emperor with a young mother had always led to political unrest. It was inevitable, he said, that, wielding power as empress dowager, the mother would "behave in a willful, unlicensed, and wanton way, and nothing [would] check her" (Watson, 253, n. 3). He cited as evidence for his view the example of Empress Lü (*q.v.* Lü Zhi, Empress of Emperor Gaozu). People have never ceased taking sides about the death of Consort Gouyi, either accusing Emperor Wu of cruelty or admiring him for his foresight. No one, however, ever charged him, as they should have, with hypocrisy, given that he himself had behaved as wantonly and willfully as any empress dowager.

Many stories have been told over the centuries about the death of Consort Gouyi. One is that her corpse gave off a fragrance that wafted more than ten *li* and that persisted for a month, from the time of her death until her burial. Another, recorded in the Song dynasty *Taiping yulan,* is that Consort Gouyi told Emperor Wu that she was destined to bear him a son and to die when the son was seven. "I will die this year," she said. "The palace is full of evil humors that are harmful." And then she died. It is also said that her coffin in Yunyang was empty after she died. The *Yunyang ji* records that to communicate with Consort Gouyi's spirit, Emperor Wu built in Ganquan Palace a rostrum on which a blue bird would often perch. After Liu Xun (Emperor Xuan, 91–49 B.C.E.; r. 73–49 B.C.E.) succeeded to the throne, however, the bird was never seen again.

In the seventh month of the year he succeeded to the throne, Consort Gouyi's son conferred on her the posthumous title of empress dowager. He then mobilized 20,000 soldiers to build a grave mound for her at Yunling and established a township of 3,000 households to tend the grave. Emperor Zhao bestowed upon his maternal grandfather the title of Marquis of Shuncheng, and presented his maternal great-aunt with gifts of money, slaves, and several houses. The emperor rewarded other male relatives of his mother's clan with gifts but, apart from Consort Gouyi's father, did not confer any office or title on any member of the family.

WONG Yin Lee
(Translated by Che Wai-lam William)

Ban Gu. *Courtier and Commoner in Ancient China: Selections from the "History of the Former Han" by Pan Ku,* trans. Burton Watson. New York: Columbia University Press, 1974, 251–53.
Bi Yuan, ed. *Sanfu huangtu.* Beijing: Zhonghua shuju, 1985, 3.23–27.
Han shu. Beijing: Zhonghua shuju, 1983, vol. 6, 68.2932; vol. 12, 97*shang*.3956–57.
Li Fang. *Taiping yulan.* Beijing: Zhonghua shuju, 1960, vol. 1, 136, 661.
Loewe, Michael. *Crisis and Conflict in Han China.* London: George Allen and Unwin, 1974.
Shi ji. Beijing: Zhonghua shuju, 1959, vol. 4, 49.1967–86.
Sima Guang. *Zizhi tongjian.* Beijing: Zhonghua shuju, 1976, vol. 1, 22 passim.
Zhang Hua. *Bowu zhi.* Beijing: Zhonghua shuju, 1985, vol. 1, 2. 7–15.

Zhao Hede, Concubine of Emperor Cheng

Lady of Bright Deportment Zhao Hede (Xiao Cheng Zhao Zhaoyi), d. 7 B.C.E., said to have come from Jiangdu (present-day Yangzhou in Jiangsu Province), became notorious as a favorite concubine of Emperor Cheng (Liu Ao, 51–7 B.C.E.; r. 32–7 B.C.E.). She was the younger sister of Zhao Feiyan (*q.v.* Zhao Feiyan, Empress of Emperor Cheng) and, according to some sources, excelled as a singer and dancer.

Zhao Hede was born into an extremely poor family—her father, Feng Wanli, was a musician—and her original name was Feng Hede. However, after her father died, she and her sister were adopted in Chang'an by Zhao Lin, housekeeper for a rich family, who gave them a good education. The girls took their benefactor's surname and initially made their living at embroidery. Through Zhao Lin they had the opportunity to serve as maidservants in the house of the Princess of Yang'e, where they learned singing and dancing. While Zhao Feiyan, the older sister, was lithe and slim, Zhao Hede was fair-skinned and plump.

Zhao Feiyan was the first to enter the palace, summoned by Emperor Cheng after he saw her dance at a feast given by the Princess of Yang'e. She became his favorite concubine, and he promoted her to the rank of Lady of Handsome Fairness (*jieyu*). Not long afterward, she recommended her younger sister Zhao Hede to the emperor who, entranced at Hede's beauty, promoted her to the rank of Lady of Handsome Fairness as well. So besotted was the emperor by Zhao Hede that he chose to ignore the warning of the Court Tutor Nao Fangcheng (Lady Nao) when she predicted: "This is a source of trouble. She will certainly destroy Han." In 18 B.C.E., the Zhao sisters accused Empress Xu (*q.v.* Xu, Empress of Emperor Cheng) and Ban Jieyu (*q.v.* Ban Jieyu, Concubine of Emperor Cheng) of practicing witchcraft (*wugu*) to invoke curses on the women's quarters. Empress Xu was deposed, while Ban Jieyu requested to be allowed to serve the empress dowager, effectively retiring from court life. After some hesitation, Empress Dowager Wang (*q.v.* Wang Zhengjun, Empress of Emperor Yuan) approved Emperor Cheng's request that Zhao Feiyan be made empress (16 B.C.E.), but from this time on Zhao Hede was the emperor's favorite. He appointed Zhao Hede as a lady of bright deportment (*zhaoyi*) and installed her in Zhaoyang Palace, a residence of unprecedented opulence whose "courtyards were painted vermilion and its halls lacquered, with sills of bronze coated with a layer of gilt. It had steps of white jade, and where the laths of the walls were exposed to view they were studded at intervals with golden rings inlaid with decorations of Lan-t'ien jadeite, shining pearls, or pieces of kingfisher feather" (Watson, 266).

For over ten years the Zhao sisters, and Zhao Hede in particular, monopolized the emperor's affections, even though neither of them bore him a child or even became pregnant. This inability to bear a son placed them in a perilous situation, and Zhao Hede became extremely jealous of any concubine who bore Emperor Cheng a son. She is believed to have orchestrated the deaths of concubines and of at least two infant boys, one born in 12 B.C.E. to a palace woman named Cao Gong and one born a year later to Beauty (*meiren*) Xu. The official *History of the Han Dynasty* (Han shu) contains an unusually detailed account of an investigation that incriminated Zhao Hede in the murders of these babies and their mothers. Emperor Cheng died suddenly one morning in the spring of 7 B.C.E. He had not been ill and suspicion immediately fell on Zhao Hede, with some saying his death was caused by sexual indulgence. As soon as Empress Dowager Wang announced there would be an investigation, Zhao Hede committed suicide.

Not long after Liu Xin (Emperor Ai, 25–1 B.C.E.; r. 6–1 B.C.E.) succeeded to the throne, a report was submitted detailing the results of the investigation into Emperor Cheng's untimely death. Of Zhao Hede it said that she had "brought danger and chaos to our sacred dynasty and is personally responsible for wiping out the line of succession—her family and associates deserve to suffer the punishment of Heaven!" (Watson, 273). The male members of Zhao Hede's adoptive family were accordingly reduced to the rank of commoner, but because Zhao Feiyan had helped Emperor Ai become heir apparent, he did not allow her to become implicated. However, almost immediately after the nine-year-old Liu Kan (Emperor Ping, 8 B.C.E.–5 C.E.; r. 1–5 C.E.) ascended the throne, Empress Dowager Wang issued an edict downgrading Zhao Feiyan to mere Empress of Emperor Cheng. The Zhao sisters, the edict proclaimed, had "replaced all the other palace ladies in the ruler's affections [and monopolized his bedchamber]. But they turned to schemes of violence and disorder, destroying and wiping out the line of succession and thereby betraying their duty to the ancestral temples. A profaner of Heaven and offender against the former rulers, [Zhao Feiyan] is not fit to act as mother of the empire" (Watson, 276). When, a month later, Zhao Feiyan was demoted to the rank of commoner, she committed suicide like her younger sister before her.

SHEN Jian
(Translated by SHEN Jian and CHE Wai-lam William)

An Zuozhang, ed. *Hou fei zhuan.* Zhengzhou: Henan Renmin chubanshe, 1990, 130–31.

Ban Gu. *Courtier and Commoner in Ancient China. Selections from the "History of the Former Han" by Pan Ku,* trans. Burton Watson. New York: Columbia University Press, 1974, 266–77.

Chen Quanli and Hou Xinyi, eds. *Hou fei cidian.* Xi'an: Shaanxi renmin jiaoyu chubanshe, 1991, 18.

Han shu. Beijing: Zhonghua shuju, 1983, vol. 12, 97*xia*.3988–99.

Ling Xuan. *Zhao Feiyan wai zhuan.* Taipei: Xinxing shuju, 1960, 273.

Liu Xiang. *Lienü zhuan.* Sibubeiyao ed., 8.8.

O'Hara, Albert R. *The Position of Woman in Early China According to the Lieh Nü Chuan, "The Biographies of Chinese Women."* Taipei: Mei Ya, 1971; 1978, 235–38.

Zhao Ji

Zhao Ji (The Woman from Zhao), c. 280–228 B.C.E., whose name is not recorded, was the mother of Ying Zheng (259–210 B.C.E.), the man who unified China and became its first emperor (Qin Shihuangdi, r. 221–210 B.C.E.). She was also instrumental in putting her son on the throne.

By the mid-third century B.C.E., during the Warring States period, the powerful state of Qin was on the point of swallowing up the other six states occupying what is now China proper. According to the second-century B.C.E. *Historical Records* (Shi ji), the first comprehensive history of China, Zhao Ji was a singer and dancer from the

252 *ZHAO JI*

state of Zhao and she became the mistress of a wealthy merchant named Lü Buwei (d. 239 B.C.E.). At that time, a grandson of the Qin ruler (Zhao Wang, 324–251 B.C.E.; r. 306–251 B.C.E.) was living as a hostage in Zhao and, not one to let an opportunity slip, Lü Buwei approached this man—Prince Zichu (Zhuangxiang Wang, r. 249–247 B.C.E.)—with a plan designed to assure him his place in the line of Qin succession. Lü Buwei told the prince he was willing to invest his wealth in this project, whereby he would provide sufficient funds for the prince to return to Qin while the prince was to show deference to the childless but official wife of his father (the heir apparent). For his part, Lü Buwei was to ply the official wife with gifts in an effort to persuade her to adopt the prince.

Lü Buwei then introduced his mistress Zhao Ji to the prince, who was taken by the girl and asked Lü Buwei to give her to him. Zhao Ji lived with Prince Zichu in Zhao for several years and bore him a son, Ying Zheng, the future Qin Shihuangdi. For a time this child, born in Zhao, was known as Zhao Zheng (the ancestral name of the Qin kings was Ying). *Historical Records* even goes so far as to say that Zhao Ji was already pregnant with Lü Buwei's son when she was given to Prince Zichu. Modern scholars, however, and especially Western scholars, suspect this story to have been fabricated to discredit Ying Zheng's legitimacy because during his lifetime he was much hated for conquering the other six of the Warring States. However, this suspicion remains that: merely a suspicion.

With Qin making repeated incursions into Zhao, the Zhao court planned to kill their hostage Prince Zichu, but as promised Lü Buwei helped him escape and return to his home state of Qin. Prince Zichu eventually became heir apparent, whereupon the Zhao court released Zhao Ji and her son, presumably as a show of good will toward Qin, so that they could rejoin Prince Zichu. *Historical Records* states that the reason Zhao Ji and her son were not killed was because she came from a powerful family, but this does not sit well with the fact that she had once been a dancing girl.

Prince Zichu succeeded his father as ruler of Qin in 249, rewarding Lü Buwei with a large fief and appointing him chief minister entrusted with affairs of state; but the prince died three years later. His son Ying Zheng ascended the throne in 246, whereupon Zhao Ji became queen dowager (*taihou*). Since her son was still a minor—he was in his thirteenth year—Zhao Ji held the reins of power in conjunction with Lü Buwei, who retained his position as chief minister. The young monarch addressed Lü Buwei respectfully as Uncle (*zhong fu,* literally "second father" or "younger father"), and *Historical Records* maintains that Lü Buwei continued his affair with Queen Dowager Zhao Ji. However, as the king grew older Lü Buwei apparently had qualms, later proven to be well founded, about his relationship with the young man's mother. He installed a man named Lao Ai in his place as Zhao Ji's lover; she became obsessed with him but while he is said to have exercised excessive power, he lacked Lü Buwei's intelligence.

When the scandal of Zhao Ji's relationship with Lao Ai broke, as it was bound to, Ying Zheng killed his mother's lover and sent her to an old palace in Yong (present-day Fengxiang District in Shaanxi Province). She was later recalled, however, and welcomed back to Ganquan Palace in Xianyang after a visitor from the state of Qi

THE ZHENG SISTERS 253

argued that exiling the ruler's mother might reflect badly on him at a time when Qin was attempting to unify the nation. Zhao Ji was thus allowed to live out her life in comfort and security; she died of illness in 228.

Lü Buwei was also implicated in the scandal of Zhao Ji's affair with Lao Ai but was spared because of the contribution he had made in helping Ying Zheng's father gain the throne; a further reason may have been the large number of retainers he had at his disposal. However, suspecting that he would eventually be eliminated, Lü Buwei killed himself, in 239 B.C.E.

Lily Xiao Hong LEE

Liu Shisheng. *Zhongguo gudai funüshi.* Qingdao: Qingdao chubanshe, 1991, 77–80.
Shi ji. Beijing: Zhonghua shuju, 1959, 6.223–27, 6.230, n. 23; 85.2505–14.
Sima Guang. "Xinjiao." *Zizhi tongjian.* Taipei: Shijie shuju, 1977, vol. 1, 6.213–14.

Zheng Ce: *see* **Zheng Sisters**

Zheng Er: *see* **Zheng Sisters**

The Zheng Sisters
The Zheng Sisters Zheng Ce and Zheng Er (Zheng Ce Zheng Er Zimei), d. 43, were born during Eastern Han in Jiaozhi, northeast of present-day Hanoi in Vietnam. They are regarded as heroines of the Han dynasty, although in recent times Vietnamese historians have come to look upon them as pioneers of early Vietnamese nationalism.

The Zheng Sisters were from a wealthy aristocratic Vietnamese family. Their father had been a Luo general in Fenling District, and Zheng Ce's husband, Shi Suo, was also the son of a Luo general. The people in the Jiaozhi region had been known as Luo tribes before they were incorporated into the Chinese empire under Qin and Han rule. Each territory had its own army with a military chief similar to the Han system, and the gallantry of Zheng Ce may have had its source in the martial training she received from her military chieftain father.

The Zheng Sisters led a revolt in the year 40, during the reign of Han Emperor Guangwu (r. 25–57). The *History of the Later Han Dynasty* (Hou Han shu) records that Zheng Ce launched the rebellion to avenge the killing of her dissident husband, Shi Suo, by Su Ding, the Chinese governor of Jiaozhi. This revolt, in which Zheng Er joined, was echoed by insurrections elsewhere in other southern border commanderies, including Jiaozhi, Jiuzhen, Rinan, and Hepu. So widespread was resistance against Chinese rule that the whole Red River delta area was affected. Having successfully taken the surrounding sixty-five towns, Zheng Ce proclaimed herself queen, with her capital in her native place. The regional inspector of Jiaozhi and the Chinese governors in other commanderies were barely able to defend themselves against the local forces.

The following year, Emperor Guangwu mobilized over 10,000 troops and dispatched General Pacifying the Waves (*fubo jiangjun*) Ma Yuan and Towered Warships Gen-

254   THE ZHENG SISTERS

eral (*louchuan jiangjun*) Duan Zhi on a punitive campaign against the Zheng Sisters. General Duan, who was in charge of the naval fleet, fell ill and died soon after the first Chinese troops arrived in Hepu. Now in sole control of land and sea forces, General Ma began to advance along the coast. By 42, he had covered thousands of miles before engaging with and defeating the sisters at Langpo. More than 1,000 of the women's supporters were executed, some by decapitation, and over 10,000 were taken prisoner, but the Zheng Sisters managed to pull back to Jinxi. In the rugged valleys of this area military maneuvers were seriously hampered by toxic vapors (*zhangqi*). However, increasingly isolated and cut off from supplies, the two women were unable to sustain their defense and in 43 they were captured and executed. Their heads were taken back to the Chinese capital, Luoyang.

The Zheng Sisters' revolt marked a brilliant epoch for women in ancient southern China and reflected the importance of women in early Vietnamese society. *Nanyue zhi* tells of another Vietnamese woman, named Zhao Yu (or possibly Trieu Au), who led rebels during the campaigns of General Ma Yuan. The Zheng Sisters were also seen as pioneers of Vietnamese nationalism. During the reign of Emperor Guangwu, the farmlands of Vietnam came under the control of autocratic regional inspectors and governors who abused their privilege and practiced favoritism. The indigenous population was subjected to a program of assimilation, and Chinese studies, language, customs, clothing, farming methods, and marriage systems were introduced. The Vietnamese people had long resisted this cultural imperialism that accompanied China's increasing colonization and relentless Sinicization of that region, however, and it is believed that it was cultural conflicts rather than economic factors that spurred the Zheng Sisters to rebellion.

The significance of the Zheng Sisters' rebellion was not their exposing the suffering of their people at the hands of oppressive Han Chinese officials, nor should it be seen as an example of a peasant uprising. Its real significance was that the social status of women throughout the Jiaozhi region was very high and they wielded great influence, in sharp contrast to the sociocultural environment of China proper at that time.

LAI Mingchiu
(Translated by WONG Tse-sheung)

Chen Yulong. "Zhongguo he Yuenan, Jianpuzhai, Laozhua wenhua jiaoliu." In *Zhongwai wenhua jiaoliu,* ed. Zhou Yiliang. Zhengzhou: Henan renmin chubanshe, 1987, 670–742.
Duiker, W.J. *The Rise of Nationalism in Vietnam, 1900–1941.* Ithaca, NY: Cornell University Press, 1976.
Hou Han shu. Beijing: Zhonghua shuju, 1965, vol. 2, 24.838–40.
Liu Shisheng. *Zhongguo gudai funü shi.* Qingdao: Qingdao chubanshe, 1991, 131–34.
Mai Yinghao. "Xi Han Nanyue wangmu sui zang yiwu di zhu wenhua yinsu." In *Lingnan gu Yuezu wenhua lunwen ji,* ed. Zou Xinghua. Hong Kong: Hong Kong Urban Council, 1993, 124–39.
Népote, J. *Vietnam,* trans. E.B. Booz and S. Jessup. Hong Kong: Odyssey, 1992.
Nguyen, K.K. *An Introduction to Vietnamese Culture.* Tokyo: Centre for East Asian Studies, 1967.
Taylor, K.W. *The Birth of Vietnam.* Berkeley: University of California Press, 1983.
Tong Enzheng. "Shilun zaoqi tinggu." In *Zhongguo Xinan minzu kaogu lunwenji.* Beijing: Wenwu chubanshe, 1990, 186–99.

ZHOU QING 255

———. "Zailun zaoqi tinggu." In *Zhongguo Xinan minzu kaogu lunwenji.* Beijing: Wenwu chubanshe, 1990, 163–85.

Wu Shilian and Chen Jinghe, eds. *Da Yue shiji quanshu.* Tokyo: University of Tokyo, 1984.

Zhongshan, Empress Dowager of: *see* Feng, Concubine of Emperor Yuan

Zhou Qing, the Filial Woman of Donghai

Zhou Qing, c. 86–c. 104 B.C.E., from Donghai Commandery (in the region of the present-day provinces of Jiangsu and Shandong), is known as the Filial Woman of Donghai (Donghai Xiaofu). She was executed after being falsely accused of unfilial behavior and her story was immortalized in Guan Hanqing's Yuan dynasty play *Dou'e Wrongly Accused* (Dou'e yuan).

Soon after Zhou Qing married, her husband died, leaving her a widow and childless. She remained in her husband's home and devoted herself to caring for her elderly mother-in-law. Although her mother-in-law repeatedly tried to persuade Zhou Qing to remarry rather than spend the rest of her life as a lonely widow, the young woman refused to heed her advice. Believing herself a burden to the younger woman, the mother-in-law eventually hanged herself in the hope that this would free Zhou Qing from her filial obligations. Unaccountably, a younger sister of Zhou Qing's deceased husband accused Zhou Qing of killing her mother-in-law. Despite her innocence, Zhou Qing was unable to withstand the pressure of cross-examination and the torture associated with it and she pleaded guilty to the crime. A gentleman by the name of Yu, who was handling the case in the commandery, spoke up for her, saying that he could not believe she had killed the old woman she had looked after for ten years and that everybody knew she was a filial daughter-in-law, not a murderess. The governor ignored what Yu had to say, however, and sentenced Zhou Qing to death. As she went to her execution, Zhou Qing pointed to the bamboo pole beside her and said: "If I have been wronged, my blood will gush up from this bamboo." It was said that, indeed, as she died "her blood, a yellowish green, gushed up to the top of the bamboo."

After Zhou Qing died, the commandery experienced a severe drought; for three years it did not rain. A new governor was installed and when he came to take up his post he had a divination performed to learn what was causing the drought. The gentleman Yu told him that the filial woman Zhou Qing should not have been executed, so the governor had a cow killed as a sacrifice and had a tomb built for Zhou Qing. The drought broke immediately after this and the people finally had a good harvest that year. Zhou Qing's innocence was in this way confirmed and her filial behavior vindicated.

XIA Chunhao

Gan Bao. *Sou shen ji.* Beijing: Zhonghua shuju, 1985, vol. 3, 11.76–77.

Guan Hanqing. "Dou'e yuan." In *Yuanqu xuan,* ed. Zang Jinshu [Zang Maoxun]. Beijing: Wenxue guji kanxingshe, 1955, vol. 4, 1499–1517.

Han shu. Beijing: Zhonghua shuju, 1983, vol. 10, 71.3041–42.

256 ZHU MAICHEN QI

Zhu Maichen Qi: *see* **Zhu Maichen's Wife**

Zhu Maichen's Wife
Zhu Maichen's Wife (Zhu Maichen Qi), fl. c. 130 B.C.E., was married to Zhu Maichen
(d. 115 B.C.E.), of Wu (the present-day city of Suzhou, Jiangsu Province); her name
and her place of origin are not recorded. Zhu Maichen was from a poor family and
was content to make a living from cutting and selling firewood, never attempting to
become wealthy. Somehow, despite his poverty, he became literate and was extremely
fond of reading; he would recite and read as he went on his rounds selling firewood.
His wife often accompanied him, following behind with firewood strapped to her
back. She was deeply unhappy that he paid more attention to reading than to selling
firewood and repeatedly tried to get him to stop, which only made him recite all the
louder. So ashamed was she at his behavior that she asked for a divorce. He replied
that although he was already in his forties he was convinced he would become a
person of distinction and wealth by the time he was fifty, and then he would repay
her for her hard work and loyalty. Angered by his insouciance, she retorted: "A man
like you is doomed to starve and die in the gutter. You don't really expect to become
wealthy and noble, do you?" So Zhu Maichen's Wife left him and married a farmer.
Zhu Maichen continued cutting and selling firewood, and reading and reciting as he
went about his business. One day he passed a cemetery, where he came upon his ex-
wife and her new husband serving out their corvee labor time. Zhu Maichen was cold
and hungry at the time and his ex-wife took pity on him, asking her new husband to
give him some food.

Eventually, Zhu Maichen was called to court by Emperor Wu (r. 140–87 B.C.E.)
on the recommendation of a palace attendant (*shizhong*) named Yan Zhu, who also
came from Wu. The emperor requested Zhu Maichen to speak on the *Spring and
Autumn Annals* (Chunqiu) and the *Songs of the South* (Chu ci) and then appointed
him to the post of grand master of palace (*zhongdaifu*). Some time later, he promoted
him to senior subaltern of the counselor-in-chief (*chengxiang changshi*) and governor
of Guiji (*Guiji taishou*) in recognition of the strategy he had proposed to quell the
revolt in Dongyue. Guiji is the present-day city of Shaoxing in Zhejiang Province,
and when Zhu Maichen went to take up his post there he also visited his native place
of Wu. As he approached, the district magistrate cleared the roads of people and sent
over 100 carriages to welcome him. As Zhu Maichen crossed the border into Wu
he recognized his ex-wife and her husband among the laborers repairing the road.
He told his attendants to call them and bring them with him in one of the carriages.
He then had them served fine food and drink in the governor's residence, but after a
month of this his ex-wife could no longer stand the shame of her earlier behavior and
she hanged herself. Zhu Maichen gave her husband a considerable sum of money so
that he could bury her.

In later times, the story of Zhu Maichen's Wife divorcing him was made into a
drama entitled *Lanke Mountain* (Lanke shan), which in turn became the basis for the
folk stories *Zhu Maichen Divorces His Wife* (Zhu Maichen xiu qi) and *Sloshing Water
in Front of the Horse* (Maqian poshui). In these tales, when Zhu Maichen's Wife asks

him to take her back he throws a bucket of water on the ground in front of his horse. He then asks her to take the water back, and when she replies that she cannot, he tells her that that is how it is with them as well. The moral of the story of Zhu Maichen's Wife as it has been handed down over the generations is, of course, that a wife should remain loyal to her husband no matter what befalls him. Although it is recognized that she showed him kindness when he was cold and hungry, Zhu Maichen's Wife has traditionally been criticized both for leaving her husband and for remarrying. An interesting point in this story, however, is the clear evidence it provides for the apparent ease with which a woman could legitimately divorce her husband in Han China.

YANG Haiming

Han shu. Beijing: Zhonghua shuju, 1983, vol. 9, 64*shang.*2791–94.
Liu Shisheng. *Zhongguo gudai funü shi.* Qingdao: Qingdao chubanshe, 1991, 112–14.

Zhuo Wenjun

Zhuo Wenjun, c. 179–after 117 B.C.E., of Linqiong in Shu (Qionglai city, in the present-day city of Chengdu, Sichuan Province), was the wife of Sima Xiangru (*zi* Zhangqing, ?179–117 B.C.E.), a famous writer of *fu* (rhapsody: classical Chinese descriptive prose interspersed with verse). The earliest record of Zhuo Wenjun is found in "Sima Xiangru liezhuan," the biography of her husband written by the historian Sima Qian (145–?86 B.C.E.) and reproduced in the *History of the Han Dynasty* (Han shu, written in the first century C.E.). The romantic story, outlined below, of Zhuo Wenjun's boldness and passion has been widely adopted in fiction and opera over the centuries.

Zhuo Wenjun had been married but when her husband died she returned to the home of her wealthy father, Zhuo Wangsun, in the western commandery of Shu. At the same time, Sima Xiangru, a member of the literati who had just lost his patron, returned to Shu, where he had nothing but an empty house. Unable to earn a living, he was dependent on his old friend Wang Ji, the magistrate of Linqiong. Hearing of Wang Ji's distinguished guest, Zhuo Wangsun hosted a banquet at which Sima Xiangru agreed to play the *qin* (a seven-stringed instrument that is plucked, similar to a zither). Sima Xiangru had apparently heard how beautiful and talented Zhuo Wenjun was and used his friendship with Wang Ji to gain entrée to the Zhuo household. Zhuo Wenjun was quickly seduced by the sound of the *qin* and, secretly watching from her room, fell in love with Sima Xiangru. Events moved quickly that night. Sima Xiangru bribed a servant to declare on his behalf his love for Zhuo Wenjun, who responded by running off with him to his empty house in Chengdu (also in the present-day city of Chengdu). Infuriated, her father swore to cut her off.

Despite this romantic start to their relationship, after some time of living in poverty Zhuo Wenjun became unhappy and suggested that they return to Linqiong to borrow some money from her brothers and cousins. Sima Xiangru agreed, but instead of borrowing money, they sold their horse and carriage and bought a wine shop in Linqiong, with Zhuo Wenjun selling the wine and Sima Xiangru the shopkeeper, "in short trousers to the knees, washing containers with hired hands in the marketplace."

258   ZHUO WENJUN

Despite later scholars attributing fine motives to Zhuo Wenjun, it is quite possible that, as a daughter of a wealthy family, she was simply unable to stand being poor. It is also possible that the couple returned to Linqiong because they could not make a living anywhere else, or that Zhuo Wenjun could not endure Sima Xiangru's frustration at his talents going to waste. Whatever their motivation, Zhuo Wenjun's father was deeply shamed and shut himself up in his house, refusing to go out. Eventually, however, he gave in to the family's entreaties and gave his daughter 100 servants and one million cash, as well as clothes, blankets, and other goods when she married her lover. The couple then returned to Chengdu, bought land and houses, and lived to the full extent of their means. One could be forgiven for suggesting that Zhuo Wenjun understood her father extremely well.

Several centuries later, the southern Daoist scholar Ge Hong (283–343) added to the above tale details, unlikely to be authentic, of Zhuo Wenjun's beauty, appearance, personality, and even of the couple's sex life. "Wenjun was beautiful. Her eyebrows were like looking at faraway mountains. Her face was the color of a lotus, her skin as smooth as silk. Widowed at seventeen, she was unbridled in character, which explains why she ignored the social mores of her time and ran away with Xiangru, whom she adored. Xiangru suffered from diabetes, and after returning to Chengdu and indulging his lust for Wenjun his illness was aggravated. He therefore composed *Rhapsody on Beautiful Women* [Meiren fu] to warn himself of the dangers of indulgence, but to no avail. In the end he died of diabetes. Wenjun wrote an elegy for him, which has come down to us." Ge Hong also informs us that when Sima Xiangru became wealthy he wanted to take a concubine, prompting Zhuo Wenjun to compose the ballad *A Song of White Hair* (Baitou yin) to reproach him and let him know she would leave him. Sima Xiangru was touched by this and abandoned his plan.

The ballad *A Song of White Hair* was first published in the *History of the Song Dynasty* (Song shu; early sixth century) as "a ballad widely sung in the streets in the Han dynasty." It was said to be an ancient text, with no author given, sung to the melody *Zhaoge*. The ballad also appeared in the mid-sixth-century collection *Yutai xinyong* under the title *White as the Snow on the Mountain* (Ai ru shanshang xue), again with no author. In *Yuefu shiji* two ballads with the title *A Song of White Hair* are reproduced as "ancient text" with no author. Although in the centuries after Zhuo Wenjun's death she was not generally regarded as its author, the ballad has nevertheless long been used in traditional operas and stories about Sima Xiangru in the episode about his parting with Zhuo Wenjun. The following is a translation (by Anne Birrell, as *White as Mountaintop Snow*) of the text published in *Yutai xinyong*:

> White as mountaintop snow,
> Pale as the moon between clouds.
> I hear you have two loves,
> That's why you broke up with me.
> Today a keg of wine at a party,
> Tomorrow dawn the top of the canal.
> I trudge and trail along the royal canal,
> Canal water east then westward flows.

How bleak, bleak it is, it's so bleak, bleak.
A bride at her wedding must not weep.
I long to get a man of one heart,
Till our white-hair years he would not leave me.
Fishing rod so supple, supple!
Fishtail so glossy, glossy!
When a man prizes the spirit of love,
Who needs dagger-coins?

Two letters reproaching Sima Xiangru for inconstancy in love were also said to have been written by Zhuo Wenjun, but they are not now generally considered to be her work. The elegy that Ge Hong claims she wrote for Sima Xiangru was first published in the Ming dynasty as *Eulogy for Sima Xiangru* (Sima Xiangru lei). The source of this long text is unknown and the Qing dynasty scholar Yan Kejun believed it to have been written, under Zhuo Wenjun's name, by someone of a later age.

Kang-i Sun CHANG and YIM Chi-hung

Birrell, Anne. *Chinese Love Poetry: New Songs from a Jade Terrace: A Medieval Anthology.* London: Penguin, 1995, 44–45.
Ge Hong. *Xijing zaji.* Taipei: Taiwan shangwu yinshuguan, 1985, 2 & 3, 5–11.
Guo Maoqian, ed. *Yuefu shi ji.* Beijing: Zhonghua shuju, 1979, vol. 2, 41.599–613.
Han shu. Beijing: Zhonghua shuju, 1983, vol. 8, 57.2530–31.
Jiang Minfan and Wang Ruifang. *Zhongguo lidai cainü xiaozhuan.* Hangzhou: Zhejiang wenxue chubanshe, 1984, 1–7.
Liu Shisheng. *Zhongguo gudai funüshi.* Qingdao: Qingdao chubanshe, 1991, 110–12.
Shi ji. Beijing: Zhonghua shuju, 1989, vol. 9, 117.3000–3001.
Song shu. Beijing: Zhonghua shuju, 1974, vol. 1, 19.565–624.
Xu Ling. *Yutai xinyong jian zhu.* Beijing: Zhonghua shuju, 1985, vol. 1, 1.14–15.

Zhuya Er Yi: *see* **Two Honorable Women from Zhuya**

Three Kingdoms Through Sui

Three Kingdoms (220–280)
Wei (220–266), Shu (221–263), Wu (222–280)

Western Jin (266–316)

Eastern Jin (317–420)

The Sixteen Kingdoms (300–430)

Southern and Northern Dynasties (420–589)
Liu Song (420–479), Qi (479–502), Liang (502–557), Chen (557–589)
Northern Wei (386–534), Eastern Wei (534–550)
Northern Qi (550–577)
Western Wei (535–556), Northern Zhou (557–581)
Sui (518–618)

A

An Lingshou

An Lingshou, fl. first half of the fourth century, of Dongguan, or Donghuan, in present-day Shandong Province, was a nun in the lineage of a Parthian monk. Her secular surname was Xu, but her given name has not been recorded. She is known for the persuasive argument she put to her father when he objected to her desire to become a nun.

An Lingshou's father, Xu Chong, was an official of the Later Zhao dynasty, a regime in North China during the period of division, founded by the non-Han warlord Shi Le (274–333, r. 319–333). Shi Le was of Jie nationality and was a patron of the Buddhist religion; he donated money and materials to Buddhist establishments and built monasteries. His trusted adviser was the famous Buddhist monk Fotudeng, who was known for performing miracles, or magic. It is not surprising, therefore, that the environment in which An Lingshou grew up had a strong Buddhist influence.

An Lingshou was said to have been intelligent and, from a young age, to have loved learning, which could have included both Confucian and Buddhist learning. She was quiet by nature and not fond of worldly things, instead occupying herself with the study of Buddhist truths. She did not warm to the idea of her parents arranging a marriage for her. The debate between her and her father contained in her biography in *Lives of the Nuns* (Biqiuni zhuan) may be seen as representative of the ongoing debate between Confucians and Buddhists around that time, when women were starting to leave their homes to pursue a religious life in the monasteries. To her father's accusation that she would err against ritual if she were not to marry, she answered that since her mind was focused on spiritual matters she was above being judged by worldly criteria. She refuted the necessity of obeying the "three followings": before marriage a woman must follow her father, after marriage she must follow her husband, and after the death of her husband she must follow her son. This rule defined the physical space a woman should occupy in society and in the eyes of her contemporaries denied her any right to leave that space to live and work elsewhere. By asking, "Why must I obey the three followings before being considered a woman of propriety?" she was questioning the basic Confucian tenets of womanhood. Her father then appealed to her emotions, saying that she was disregarding her parents and caring only for herself. In line with the belief that Buddhism offers the only release from the suffering endured by all sentient beings, An Lingshou answered that her motive in seeking the truth in Buddhism was to liberate all living beings and that therefore her Buddhist faith would help her parents find salvation.

Perhaps almost convinced, Xu Chong then consulted Fotudeng, who miraculously allowed him to see in a vision that in her previous life An Lingshou had been a nun. Fotudeng predicted that if allowed to follow her desire An Lingshou would bring her family honor and glory and would guide her family to salvation. Xu Chong therefore relented. His daughter became a disciple of Fotudeng and Zhu Jingjian (*q.v.*) and established the Jinshu Monastery. Fotudeng also passed on to her some imperial treasures he had received from Shi Le.

As a nun, An Lingshou was known for her wisdom and the depth of her understanding of things abstract and spiritual. She is said to have been able to recite a text by heart after having read it only once. She became a leader in the Buddhist community and converted over 200 individuals. Through her diligence and hard work she was responsible for building five monasteries and a retreat. The Later Zhao ruler Shi Hu (*zi* Jilong, 295–349, r. 334–349) esteemed her highly and promoted her father to the position of gentleman attendant at the palace gate and governor of Qinghe (present-day Qinghe District, Hebei Province). This information, contained in the final paragraph of her biography, was presumably included to bear out Fotudeng's prediction that, if she were allowed to become a nun, An Lingshou would bring glory to her family.

When An Lingshou became a nun, the idea of a woman leaving domesticity ran counter to the traditional, mainly Confucian, prevailing social order whereby women were expected to marry, live with their husband's family, and produce children to carry on their husband's family line. This entire family-oriented society would therefore be under threat if women were to remain unmarried, something not permissible in such a patriarchal society. By fighting for her right to pursue a religious life of her choice, An Lingshou established with her argument the rationale of choosing Buddhism over family life: to bring glory and salvation to her family, an aim entirely within traditional expectations. Her story made it easier for countless other women to follow her footsteps into the monastery. Her declaration that a woman did not have to follow the traditional model in order to be considered proper was nothing less than a declaration of independence for women. In monastic life, women did not have to rely on male relatives and could pursue many worthwhile occupations other than housework and raising children. Such occupations included studying, teaching, preaching, administration, managing finances, and constructing and maintaining buildings and images in monasteries. This opened a wide vista for women who chose not to conform to the traditional model.

An Lingshou's fight for the right to become a nun was echoed by a woman in southern China. Seng Ji, fl. mid-fourth century, entered monastic life in the south although, as far as we can tell, she was a native of Jinan, in the present-day northern province of Shandong. In her case, the parent who tried to stop her becoming a nun was her mother, who secretly had her betrothed and went ahead with wedding preparations. However, when the bridegroom saw how determined his prospective bride was to enter a convent, he wisely persuaded her mother to let her choose her own destiny. When Seng Ji was ordained, her relatives and even the leading officials of her native region and commandery joined in the celebrations, signaling how the times and attitudes toward women choosing to pursue a religious life had changed in China.

Lily Xiao Hong LEE

Baochang [Pao-ch'ang]. "An Lingshou zhuan." *Piqiuni zhuan, 2.* In *Taishō shinshū Daizōkyō,* ed. Takakusu Junjirō, Watanabe Kaigyoku, and Ono Genmyō. Tokyo: Taishō Issaikyō Kankōkai, 1924–1929, vol. 50, 935.

Baochang [Shih Pao-ch'ang]. *Lives of the Nuns: Biographies of Chinese Buddhist Nuns from the Fourth to Sixth Centuries: A Translation of the Pi-ch'iu-ni chuan,* trans. Kathryn Ann Tsai. Honolulu: University of Hawaii Press, 1994, 20–21.

Hong Pimou. *Zhongguo ming ni.* Shanghai: Shanghai renmin chubanshe, 1995, 5–7.

Tsai, Kathryn Ann. "The Chinese Buddhist Monastic Order for Women: The First Two Centuries." In *Women in China: Current Directions in Historical Scholarship*, ed. Richard W. Guisso and Stanley Johannesen. Youngstown, NY: Philo Press, 1981, 1–20.

Wright, Arthur. "Biography of the Nun An Ling-shou." *Harvard Journal of Asiatic Studies* 15 (1952): 193–96.

B

Bao Linghui

Bao Linghui, after 414–before 466, was a poet who, together with her brother Bao Zhao (c. 414–466), was known for her ballad (*yuefu*) style poetry.

Bao Linghui and her brother are said to have come from a family of low status. In an age when family status was highly valued, this put them at a great disadvantage. It is perhaps due to this circumstance that very little is known about them. Bao Zhao is mentioned in the biography of his mentor and employer, Liu Yiqing, the Prince of Linchuan (403–444), where he is described as a talented man who resented his low social position since it afforded him no means of advancing in his career. Biographical information on Bao Linghui cannot be found in any history books and it is only through the comments of some literary critics and the words of her brother that we learn anything about her. We have no record of the dates of her birth or death, but since she was Bao Zhao's younger sister she must have been born after her brother. We also know that she died before her brother, who, in a letter asking for leave, said he was not able to bid his sister farewell when she died and was not present at her burial.

The Bao family came from Shandan (present-day Shaanxi Province) but subsequently moved to Donghai (between the present-day provinces of Shandong and Jiangsu). Although sources emphasize the lowliness of the family's social position, Bao Linghui and her brother both seem to have had a reasonably good education, especially in literature and music. A considerable number of their works are deliberate imitations of Han dynasty poems, indicating that they were eminently familiar with the form and content of those poems. Their concentration on the ballad style, which originated from songs of the Music Bureau of the Han dynasty, suggests that their family may somehow have been connected to the entertainment world, either as musicians or as lyric writers. From her brother's writings we learn that there were no other siblings.

It is not known if Bao Linghui ever married. In her poetry, she refers to someone as *jun,* a pronoun usually used by a woman to refer to her husband or lover, so we may assume there was a man in her life. Even that is refutable, however, as *jun* could have been simply a literary device she used in her love poems. There is a record of a collection of her poems entitled *Rhapsody of the Fragrant Tea* (Xiangming fu ji) but it is no longer extant. At least some of her poems are found in a collection of mainly love poems called *New Songs from a Jade Terrace* (Yutai xinyong) compiled by Xu Ling (507–583). These were also attached at the end of an edition of her brother's works edited by Qian Zhonglian.

Thematically, Bao Linghui's poems tend to be about the feelings—loneliness, lovesickness, and melancholy—of a woman left behind when her lover goes away on business or military service. These emotions are conveyed indirectly through imagery and allusions, such as the coming and going of the wild swan, the blooming and withering of flowers and trees, the stillness and emptiness of the boudoir, the changing of the seasons, and other evocative events. An example from her work may illustrate the point better. The following two poems, translated by Winnie Lau, are from *Written on Behalf of Ge Shangren's Wife, Guo Xiaoyu:*

I
The bright moon, how it shines!
Through the hanging curtain to shine on my silk cushion.
If I were together with you at night
I know we would both resent the coming of dawn.
In youth one does not take pride in one's beauty,
Pitiless is the frost and wind.
You did not go away in search of high position.
Traveling with the wind to serve a ruler.
I wait with a lifetime of tears,
Passing autumn and then another spring.

II
About to go far away on service
You left behind a pair of brocade scarves for me to wear on my head.
When it was time for you to leave,
You left behind a pillow of longing.
The scarves, so that you're always on my mind;
The pillow, as a reminder of our time together.
Every day you travel further from me,
My longing for you deepens a little more.

Bao Linghui's style is direct and sentimental, like many of the old songs she claimed to imitate; however, unlike those songs, she uses numerous parallel lines, a later literary device. Use of these parallel lines changes the outlook of the simple songs into something more complex and aesthetically satisfying. Hence her "imitations" are not simply that, but are a development of the ancient songs.

Bao Linghui is sometimes described as an erotic poet. The critic Zhong Rong summed up her poetry thus: "Linghui's poetry often excels and is pure, fine, and skilful, especially in imitating old poems. However, her *One Hundred Wishes* [Baiyuan] is excessive in desires." This poem is now lost, so there is no way of telling whether Zhong Rong's criticism is justified. There is certainly nothing overtly sexual in her extant poems, but they are love poems and there is sensuality in her diction and images. If there is an erotic undertone, it is subtle and in good taste. Also, we must remember that the extant poems must be only a fraction of her total output.

This biography is mainly based on a thesis written under my supervision by Winnie Yuen Kwan Lau.

Lily Xiao Hong LEE

Birrell, Anne, trans. *New Songs from a Jade Terrace: An Anthology of Early Chinese Love Poetry.* London: Allen & Unwin, 1982, 122–24, 269.
He Qingshan. "Bao Linghui—Ni qing qing he bian cao." In *Han Wei Liuchao shi jianshang cidian,* ed. Wu Xiaoru et al. Shanghai: Shanghai cishu chubanshe, 1992, 795–97.
Jiang Minfan and Wang Ruifang. *Zhongguo lidai cainü xiaozhuan.* Hangzhou: Zhejiang wenyi chubanshe, 1984, 71–75.
Lau, Winnie Yuen Kwan. "Links in an Unbroken Chain: The Poetry of Zuo Fen and Bao Linghui of the Six Dynasties." Bachelor of Arts (Honors) thesis, University of Sydney, 1996.
Qian Zhonglian. *Bao Canjun jizhu.* Shanghai: Shanghai guji chubanshe, 1980, 419–26.
Tan Zhengbi. *Zhongguo nüxing wenxueshi.* Tianjin: Baihua wenyi chubanshe, 1984, 96–97.
Wang Yanti, ed. *Zhongguo gudai nüzuojia ji.* Jinan: Shandong daxue chubanshe, 1999, 104–5.
Xu Ling, comp. *Yutai xinyong.* Sibubeiyao ed., 4.9b–10b, 10.3b.

Baoxian

The Buddhist nun Baoxian, 401–477, was surnamed Chen; her secular given name is not known. Her family was originally from Chen Commandery in the Huai River valley (in present-day Henan Province). She lived during the Southern Dynasties period and filled an important office that regulated the assembly of nuns in the capital city of Jiankang (the present-day city of Nanjing) in close association with the nun Fajing (*q.v.*).

Because of the incursions of non-Chinese armies that led to the fall of northern China to these invaders in 317, many wealthy and powerful families fled to southern China in the early fourth century. In the south during the Eastern Jin dynasty, Buddhism received popular and widespread support, and during the Southern Dynasties it enjoyed a remarkable florescence in the lower regions of the Yangzi River valley, clustering in several centers including the capital Jiankang.

After completing the three-year mourning period for her mother, Baoxian became a nun in 420 at the age of nineteen and lived in the Jian'an Convent in the capital, where she mastered both meditation and the observance of the monastic rules. Over a decade later, in 433, for the first time in China the Buddhist assembly of nuns in the capital received from both the assembly of monks and the assembly of nuns the obligations to observe the monastic rules (*vide* Huiguo). Previously in China there had not been a quorum of ten nuns with sufficient seniority, and who had themselves received the obligations from both assemblies, to bestow the obligations and thus ensure that the Chinese nuns were ordained in strict accordance with the *vinaya* (the books of monastic discipline). It is possible that both Baoxian and Fajing participated in this ceremony of the re-administering of the obligations, both women being known for their observance of the monastic rules.

Baoxian's spotless reputation attracted imperial attention. Emperor Wen (Liu Yilong, 407–453; r. 424–453) of the Liu Song dynasty treated Baoxian with great courtesy, presenting her with gifts of clothing and food, while his son Emperor Xiaowu (Liu Jun, 430–464; r. 454–464) also treated her with great respect, giving her large donations of money every month. Another of his sons, Emperor Ming (Liu Yu, 439–472; r. 465–472), appointed Baoxian as head of Puxian Convent in the capital in 465 and assigned Fajing to live there as well. The following year, 466, by imperial decree the emperor named Baoxian as the rector-general (*duyi sengzheng*) of the assembly of

268 BAOXIAN

nuns in the capital and named Fajing as the precentor-general of the capital (*jingyi du weina*). The office of rector-general had first been established in north China during the Yao Qin dynasty (384–417) for the purpose of keeping the monastics and the assemblies in general free from irregularities and faults.

What was unusual about Emperor Ming's appointments is that this was the first time women had filled these offices over a larger jurisdiction. During the Southern Dynasties the assembly of nuns reached a high point of independence, influence, and esteem. Individual nuns achieved renown for their intellectual contributions, writings, teaching and preaching, and mastery of the discipline of monastic life and of the practice of meditation. They moved in the highest circles of society.

Faying (416–482), a well-known master of monastic rules who originally came from Dunhuang at the eastern end of the Silk Road, arrived in the Liu Song capital in 453. As a specialist in the *vinaya* texts of the Sarvāstivāda School, he gave lectures and also translated *The Nuns' Rule Book of the Sarvāstivāda School* (Sarvāstivāda bhikṣuṇīprātimokṣasūtra). In 474, Faying gave a lecture in Jinxing Monastery on the *Sarvāstivāda Monastic Rules in Ten Recitations* (Shi song lü), and a group of nuns who attended his lecture consequently wished to receive for a second time the obligations to observe the monastic rules. Baoxian disapproved, however, and under the authority of her office of rector-general of the assembly of the capital she sent orders forbidding the nuns to receive the obligations a second time. Her objection appears to have been concerned with either the age of candidates who wished to enter the assembly or the length of time novices had to train in the rules before being admitted as fully-fledged nuns. Baoxian stipulated that the nuns who wanted to receive the monastic rules a second time had to be examined. If they had not met the requirements for age or length of time in training as set forth in the *vinaya*, they had to make a public confession of that breach of the rules. The instructors then had to report the results of their confession to the office of the assembly and if the office approved of what they had reported it would then ask someone to investigate the nuns further to determine if they were suitable candidates in all other respects. Only then could the nuns receive the obligations a second time, thereby confirming their legitimate membership in the assembly of nuns. Any nun who opposed Baoxian's plan was to be expelled from the assembly.

Baoxian's firm leadership thus purged the assembly of nuns of the unorthodox practices that had crept in during the forty years after the initial ceremony of 433 when the Buddhist assembly of nuns had first received the obligations from both the assembly of monks and the assembly of nuns. No further incidents are recorded during her tenure in office and she died in 477 at the age of seventy-seven.

Kathryn A. TSAI

Baochang [Pao-ch'ang]. "Baoxian zhuan." *Piqiuni zhuan, 2.* In *Taishō shinshū Daizōkyō,* ed. Takakusu Junjirō, Watanabe Kaigyoku, and Ono Genmyō. Tokyo: Taishō Issaikyō Kankōkai, 1924–1929, vol. 50, 941.

Baochang [Shih Pao-ch'ang]. *Lives of the Nuns: Biographies of Chinese Buddhist Nuns from*

BIAN, WIFE OF CAO CAO   269

the Fourth to Sixth Centuries: A Translation of the Pi-ch'iu-ni chuan, trans. Kathryn Ann Tsai. Honolulu: University of Hawaii Press, 1994, 62–64.

Canning [Ts'an-ning], *Da song seng shi lüe,* 2, 242c–243a. In *Taishō shinshū Daizōkyō,* ed. Takakusu Junjirō, Watanabe Kaigyoku, and Ono Genmyō. Tokyo: Taishō Issaikyō Kankōkai, 1924–1929, vol. 54.

Faying, trans. *Bhikṣuṇīprātimokṣasūtra,* 485a–b. In *Taishō shinshū Daizōkyō,* ed. Takakusu Junjirō, Watanabe Kaigyoku, and Ono Genmyō. Tokyo: Taishō Issaikyō Kankōkai, 1924–1929, vol. 23.

Huijiao. "Faying zhuan." *Gaoseng zhuan,* 11. In *Taishō shinshū Daizōkyō,* ed. Takakusu Junjirō, Watanabe Kaigyoku, and Ono Genmyō. Tokyo: Taishō Issaikyō Kankōkai, 1924–1929, vol. 50.

Li Yuzhen. *Tangdai de biqiuni.* Taipei: Taiwan xuesheng shuju, 1989, 126–37.

Takakusu Junjirō, Watanabe Kaigyoku, and Ono Genmyō, eds. *Taishō shinshū Daizōkyō.* Tokyo: Taishō Issaikyō Kankōkai, 1924–1929.

Tsai, Kathryn Ann. "The Chinese Buddhist Monastic Order for Women: The First Two Centuries." In *Women in China: Current Directions in Historical Scholarship,* ed. Richard W. Guisso and Stanley Johannesen. Youngstown, NY: Philo Press, 1981, 1–20.

Bian, Wife of Cao Cao, King of Wei

Empress Dowager Bian (Bian Taihou), 160–230, of Kaiyang in Langye (north of present-day Linyi in Shandong Province), was the second wife of Cao Cao (155–220), King of Wei, and the mother of Emperor Wen of Wei (Cao Pi, 187–226; r. 220–226).

The future Lady Bian lived in the chaotic years that saw the collapse of the Eastern Han dynasty and the formation of the three powerful rival states that led to the following period being known as the Three Kingdoms: Wei in the north, Shu Han in the west, and Wu in the south and east. Of lowly origin, she earned her living as a prostitute in Jiao Commandery (present-day Bo County, Anhui Province). She was twenty years old when Cao Cao took her as a concubine upon his return home to Qiao after being dismissed from his post in the Han government in 178. Lady Bian frequently accompanied Cao Cao as he moved about the countryside on his military adventures and she is said to have always shown great concern for the elderly. She was living in Luoyang when General-in-Chief (*da jiangjun*) Dong Zhuo (d. 192) rose in rebellion against Han in 189. Dong Zhuo overthrew Emperor Shao (Liu Bian, 171–190; r. 189), installing the eight-year-old Liu Xie (Emperor Xian, 181–234; r. 189–220) in his place and moving the capital to Chang'an (the present-day city of Xi'an). Disguised as a commoner, Cao Cao fled to the east intending to raise an army, but when rumors of his death spread his entourage prepared to return to their native place, having accepted defeat. Lady Bian stopped them, however, saying: "We do not know for certain that Cao Cao is dead. How could you face him if you left and he returned tomorrow? And even if calamity should befall us, would it not be better to die together?" Her words carried the day, nobody left, and when Cao Cao finally returned to Luoyang in 196 he was full of praise for her loyalty.

After Cao Cao persuaded Emperor Xian to again move the capital, this time to the city of Xuchang (in present-day Henan Province), in 196, he became increasingly powerful, until the emperor was his virtual puppet. Appointed Minister of State in

270 BIAN, WIFE OF CAO CAO

208, Cao Cao assumed the title of Duke (*gong*) in 213. The following year he deposed Han Empress Fu (*q.v.* Fu Shou, Empress of Emperor Xian), which allowed him to proclaim one of his daughters empress in 215. Finally, in 216, he took the title King of Wei, breaking the unwritten code that precluded anyone not of imperial blood from holding the title of King.

After his grieving first wife, Lady Ding (*q.v.* Ding, Consort of Cao Cao, King of Wei), returned to her native village in 196 to mourn the death of the son she had raised, Cao Cao made Lady Bian his principal wife. Lady Bian gave birth to four sons: Cao Pi, Cao Zhang, her favorite Cao Zhi (192–232), Prince of Dong'e, and Cao Xiong (who died young). After the departure of Lady Ding, however, she assumed responsibility for raising all of Cao Cao's sons; he had sired twenty-five sons by thirteen different women. Lady Bian is described as a far-sighted woman, careful and reasonable as well as very thrifty. For example, when Cao Cao assumed the title Duke of Wei and appointed their son Cao Pi as his heir, her entourage congratulated her, encouraging her to offer them gifts. Instead, she simply said: "The Duke made Cao Pi heir because he is his eldest son. I am just fortunate that this exonerates me from the charge of not having educated him properly. Why should I shower you with gifts?" This response pleased Cao Cao, who remarked: "She does not waste her energy in anger and does not lose her propriety in happiness. This is a rare virtue!" Accordingly, in 219 Cao Cao appointed Lady Bian queen (*wanghou*), saying: "Lady (*furen*) Bian has behaved as a virtuous mother in bringing up all our sons, for which I grant her the title of Queen."

Lady Bian was very fond of her brother Bian Bing (d. c. 230), a major of a regiment (*biebu sima*). Not entirely above seeking favors, she asked Cao Cao to promote her brother and reward him with money and silk. Cao Cao refused, but he did build him a mansion to which Lady Bian invited her relatives for a meal. The meal was not extravagant: "The empress dowager and her attendants had vegetable food and millet; there was neither fish nor meat." She told her natal family she had served Cao Cao in this way for over forty years and did not intend to change her frugal ways. She also told them they should be temperate and frugal and not expect anything from her; indeed, if any of them should commit a crime, she said, she would urge that their punishment be increased by one degree.

Upon the death of Cao Cao in 220, Cao Pi proclaimed himself King of Wei; when Han Emperor Xian abdicated the same year Cao Pi announced the establishment of the Wei dynasty and assumed the title of Emperor. He appointed his mother empress dowager and moved her to Yongshou Palace. Throughout her life, Empress Dowager Bian had led a simple life. She did not wear dresses of silk and all her utensils were made of black (clay). Once, when Cao Cao showed her some jewelry and asked her to choose a piece for herself, she chose an item of medium value, explaining: "It is greedy to choose the best, hypocritical to take the worst. So I have chosen one in the middle." Her attitude did not change when she became empress dowager. When the national treasury did not have sufficient funds, she offered to cut her food budget and set aside the gold and silver utensils.

While it is said that she did not compromise her integrity, she clearly exerted her influence over Emperor Wen to her own advantage. For example, when her son Cao Zhi was about to be sentenced for being drunk and disorderly, she sent this message to Emperor Wen: "I did not expect my son to do this. The emperor must not break the law by showing leniency for my sake." It was perhaps to be expected that, on receiving the message, Emperor Wen did reduce his brother's sentence. Another example concerned Cao Cao's younger cousin Cao Hong, who had saved Cao Cao's life in 190. Emperor Wen bore a grudge against Cao Hong, who had once refused to lend him 100 pieces of silk, and eventually had him sentenced to death because of a subordinate's misdemeanor. Empress Dowager Bian forced Emperor Wen to overturn the death sentence, however, threatening to depose his empress, Empress Guo (*q.v.* Guo, Empress of Emperor Wen of Wei), if he did not do so. Cao Hong was eventually removed from office and deprived of his fief, but his confiscated property was later returned, again thanks to the intervention of Empress Dowager Bian. It is also said that when Emperor Wen asked for an interpretation of a dream in which he was trying to rub off the design on a coin with the design only becoming clearer, he was told it indicated that his mother did not agree with his fiscal policy.

Emperor Wen was succeeded by his son Cao Rui (Emperor Ming, 205–239; r. 226–239), who appointed Empress Dowager Bian to the position of Grand Empress Dowager. She died in 230 at the age of seventy-one and was buried alongside Cao Cao in Gaoling at Linzhang (in present-day Hebei Province) with the posthumous title Empress Wuxuan (Wuxuan Huanghou). A former prostitute, she was perhaps fortunate to have lived in tumultuous times that paid little heed to Confucian notions of chastity in women, imperial or commoner.

SU Zhecong and Priscilla CHING-CHUNG

An Zuozhang, ed. *Hou fei zhuan.* Zhengzhou: Henan renmin chubanshe, 1990, vol. 1, 180–88.
Chen Quanli and Hou Xinyi, eds. *Hou fei cidian.* Xi'an: Shaanxi renmin jiaoyu chubanshe, 1991, 30.
Chen Shou. *Empresses and Consorts: Selections from Chen Shou's "Records of the Three States" with Pei Songzhi's Commentary,* trans. Robert J. Cutter and William Gordon Crowell. Honolulu: University of Hawaii Press, 1999, 90–95; 139; 178; 193–97, 211.
Liu Shisheng. *Zhongguo gudai funü shi.* Qingdao: Qingdao chubanshe, 1991, 148–49.
Sanguo zhi. Beijing: Zhonghua shuju, 1975, vol. 1, 5.156–59; vol. 1, 9.278; vol. 2, 19.561.
Sima Guang. *The Chronicle of the Three Kingdoms (220–265), Chapters 69–78 from the Tzu chih t'ung chien of Ssu-ma Kuang,* trans. Achilles Fang, ed. Glen W. Baxter. Cambridge, MA: Harvard University Press, 1965, vol. 1, 106, 124–25, 200–201, 210–11.

Bu, Consort of Sun Quan

Lady Bu (Bu Furen), c. 190–238, of Huaiyin in Linhuai Commandery (in the north of present-day Jiangsu Province), was the beloved consort of Sun Quan (Great Emperor, 182–252; r. 222–252), founding emperor of the Three Kingdoms state of Wu. She bore him two daughters, Sun Luban (*q.v.*) and Sun Luyu (*vide* Sun Luban), who became notorious for their ruthless politicking.

Born in the chaotic last decades of the Eastern Han dynasty, as a child Lady Bu

272 BU, CONSORT OF SUN QUAN

migrated with her mother to Lujiang (in the north of present-day Anhui Province). They were then among the many inhabitants who moved south across the Yangzi River after Lujiang was subdued in 194 by Sun Quan's older brother, Sun Ce (175–200). Nothing further is known of her early years except that she was of the same clan as Chancellor (*chengxiang*) Bu Zhi (d. 247) and it is presumably through him that at some stage she came to the attention of Sun Quan.

Besotted with her beauty, Sun Quan took her as a concubine to the virtual exclusion of his other women. However, Lady Bu was widely held in warm regard. Not of a jealous nature, she was able to retain Sun Quan's affection for a long time by recommending many other women for his sexual pleasure. Sun Quan wished to appoint her as his queen when he assumed the title of King of Wu in 221, but his officials objected on the grounds that his formal consort should be Lady Xu (d. c. 229) of Wujun (in present-day Zhejiang Province), who had raised the current heir apparent Sun Deng (209–241) almost from birth. Unwilling to bring back Lady Xu, who was already a widow when he took her to wife and whom he had deserted in Wujun ten years before because of her extreme jealousy, Sun Quan was also apparently unwilling to completely disregard the advice of his officials. He therefore made no formal decision about his consort for over ten years. In the meantime, Lady Bu became his de facto empress, unofficially addressed in everyday life as Empress Bu by all. It is said that "when her relatives sent up memorials, they referred to her as the Middle Palace (*zhong gong*)." When she died in 238, Sun Quan conferred upon her the posthumous title of empress. She was buried in Jiangling.

In his investiture of her as empress, Sun Quan expressed his grief at her premature passing and spoke of her with great affection: "Tolerant and magnanimous, benevolent and mild, she possessed the virtue of womanly obedience. The people and the officials all respected her, far and near submitting to her." He regretted that he had not conferred the title of empress on her earlier, thinking that she would enjoy a long life "and share Heaven-sent prosperity with me always; I did not dream of her sudden decease" (Sima Guang, trans. Fang, 602).

Priscilla CHING-CHUNG

Chen Shou. *Empresses and Consorts: Selections from Chen Shou's "Records of the Three States" with Pei Songzhi's Commentary,* trans. Robert J. Cutter and William Gordon Crowell. Honolulu: University of Hawaii Press, 1999, 53, 56, 126–27, 218–19.

Crespigny, Rafe de. *Generals of the South: The Foundation and Early History of the Three Kingdoms State of Wu.* Canberra: Australian National University, 1990, 511.

Sanguo zhi: Weishu. Beijing: Zhonghua shuju, 1959, vol. 1, 5.156–59.

Sima Guang. *The Chronicle of the Three Kingdoms (220–265), Chapters 69–78 from the Tzu chih t'ung chien of Ssu-ma Kuang,* trans. Achilles Fang, ed. Glen W. Baxter. Cambridge, MA: Harvard University Press, 1965, vol. 1, 576, 600–2, 690.

C

Cao Cao's Wife: *see* **Bian, Wife of Cao Cao, King of Wei**

D

Daoqiong

Daoqiong, fl. 376–438, surnamed Jiang, was from Danyang (near the southern capital Jiankang, the present-day city of Nanjing); her secular given name is not known. She was a Chinese Buddhist nun who supported the development of Chinese Buddhist art through her sponsorship of sculpture placed in convents and monasteries.

Buddhism had made its way to China in the early years of the Eastern Han dynasty but it did not gain widespread and popular support until the Eastern Jin dynasty. This foreign religion flourished during the Northern and Southern Dynasties, at which time the status of the assembly of Buddhist nuns was very high, with several convents established in and around Jiankang.

Because Daoqiong had already received a good education in the Confucian classics and history by the time she entered the assembly of nuns, it is highly likely that she came from a wealthy and aristocratic family. After becoming a nun she pursued Buddhist learning, and during the reign of Emperor Xiaowu of Jin (Sima Yao, 362–396; r. 373–396) her exalted conduct and ascetic practice attracted the attention of Empress Wang Fahui (360–380) so that many other women sought to associate with her.

In the year 431 Daoqiong sponsored, among other unspecified figures, two gold images of the Buddha complete with a curtained dais and all the accessories; a reclining Buddha (at the Final Nirvana) and a hall in which to house it; a processional image of the future Buddha Maitreya; and a processional image of the bodhisattva Puxian (Samantabhadra). In 435, Emperor Wen (Liu Yilong, 407–453; r. 424–453) of the Liu Song dynasty ordered a curb on the construction of Buddhist buildings and the making of images; yet three years later, in 438, Daoqiong also commissioned a gold Amitayus (Infinite Life) Buddha.

These images, created for religious reasons and purposes, contributed to the growth of Chinese Buddhist art, which in the early fifth century was still in the first stages of development from Indian and Central Asian models. Maitreya, Puxian, and Amitabha became popular subjects for sculpture at the same time as scriptures such as *Lotus of the True Law*, the Pure Land, and the Samantabhadra scriptures became increasingly popular. Unfortunately, too few examples remain of freestanding sculpture from this period.

Kathryn A. TSAI

Baochang [Pao-ch'ang]. "Daoqiong zhuan." *Piqiuni zhuan, 2.* In *Taishō shinshū Daizōkyō,* ed. Takakusu Junjirō, Watanabe Kaigyoku, and Ono Genmyō. Tokyo: Taishō Issaikyō Kankōkai, 1924–1929, vol. 50, 938.

Baochang [Shih Pao-ch'ang]. *Lives of the Nuns: Biographies of Chinese Buddhist Nuns from the Fourth to Sixth Centuries: A Translation of the Pi-ch'iu-ni chuan,* trans. Kathryn Ann Tsai. Honolulu: University of Hawaii Press, 1994, 40–41.

Takakusu Junjirō, Watanabe Kaigyoku, and Ono Genmyō, eds. *Taishō shinshū Daizōkyō.* Tokyo: Taishō Issaikyō Kankōkai, 1924–1929.

Tsai, Kathryn Ann. "The Chinese Buddhist Monastic Order for Women: The First Two Centuries." In *Women in China: Current Directions in Historical Scholarship,* ed. Richard W. Guisso and Stanley Johannesen. Youngstown, NY: Philo Press, 1981, 1–20.

274 DAORONG

Daorong: *see* **Zhi Miaoyin**

Dayi, Princess: *see* **Yuwen, Princess Qianjin of Northern Zhou**

Ding, Consort of Cao Cao, King of Wei

Lady Ding (Ding Furen), c. 160–219/220, was the principal wife and consort of Cao Cao (155–220), King of Wei and founder of the Three Kingdoms state of Wei. In the final decades of the Eastern Han dynasty, Cao Cao, an adopted son of the chief palace eunuch under Emperor Ling (Liu Hong, 156–189; r. 168–189), distinguished himself in a campaign to put down the Yellow Turban peasant rebellion in 184. As the dynasty grew weaker, he gained increasing political and military control as he moved about the countryside with his armies. By 196, Emperor Xian (Liu Xie, 181–234; r. 189–220) had become Cao Cao's puppet. In 215, Cao Cao proclaimed his own daughter empress, and in 216 he assumed the title King of Wei, breaking the unwritten code precluding anyone not of imperial blood from holding the title of king.

It is not known when or where Cao Cao took Lady Ding as his principal wife and nothing is known of her origins. She had no children of her own but she raised two of Cao Cao's offspring after the death of their mother, Lady Liu, who was one of Cao Cao's secondary consorts. These children—Cao Ang, also known as Zixiu, and his sister Princess Qinghe—were as dear to Lady Ding as if she had borne them herself, and when Zixiu was killed in battle she was inconsolable. She accused Cao Cao of heartlessness: "Having taken my son and killed him, you don't think of him any more." Unable to tolerate this behavior, Cao Cao sent her back to her family in the hope that time would heal her grief. When he visited her some time later, he found her kneeling at her loom, refusing to acknowledge him. He stroked her back and said, "Turn around and look at me and let us ride back together." Still she would not face him or speak. Standing by the door he asked one last time if she would go with him but again she would not reply, so he broke with her and told her family to marry her to someone else. The story goes that they did not dare marry her off, but she must have been in her forties by this time and it would have been difficult to find a suitable match after her years as principal wife of the powerful Cao Cao.

During her time as principal wife, Lady Ding had not respected Cao Cao's second wife Lady Bian (*q.v.* Bian, Wife of Cao Cao, King of Wei) or her children. However, after Lady Bian was given the title Queen in 219, she courted Lady Ding, sending her presents appropriate to the season, meeting with her privately, greeting her in person when she arrived, ceding the seat of honor to her, and seeing her off when she departed. Moved by this courtesy to a "cast-off," as she termed herself, Lady Ding apologized to Lady Bian for her previous behavior. Then, when Lady Ding died, Lady Bian asked Cao Cao to hold a funeral for her. It is said that during his last illness Cao Cao expressed regret for having cast Lady Ding aside: "In all my thoughts and deeds, there has never been anything I have been ashamed of in my heart. But if there is a soul after death, and should [my son] Zixiu ask, 'Where is my mother?'—how shall I reply?"

In an age in which power had the last word, Lady Ding dared to defy Cao Cao, apparently indifferent to his absolute power. Perhaps she lacked fear because her heart was broken and nothing further could intimidate her. It nevertheless took a brave woman to do what she did.

Priscilla CHING-CHUNG

The Cambridge History of China, ed. Denis Twitchett and John K. Fairbank. Cambridge, UK: Cambridge University Press, 1986, vol. 1, 343–52.

Chen Shou. *Empresses and Consorts: Selections from Chen Shou's "Records of the Three States" with Pei Songzhi's Commentary,* trans. Robert J. Cutter and William Gordon Crowell. Honolulu: University of Hawaii Press, 1999, 47–48, 91–92, 145–47.

Giles, Herbert A. *A Chinese Biographical Dictionary.* Taipei: Chengwen Publishing, 1971, 761–63.

Sanguo zhi. Beijing: Zhonghua shuju, 1975, vol. 1, 5.156–57.

Sima Guang. *The Chronicle of the Three Kingdoms (220–265), Chapters 69–78 from the Tzu chih t'ung chien of Ssu-ma Kuang,* trans. Achilles Fang, ed. Glen W. Baxter. Cambridge, MA: Harvard University Press, 1965, vol. 1, 77.

Ding Furen: *see* **Ding, Consort of Cao Cao, King of Wei**

Dou Tao Qi: *see* **Su Hui**

Du Xue: *see* **Yan Xian**

Du Youdao Qi: *see* **Yan Xian**

Du Zhi Mu: *see* **Yan Xian**

Dugu, Empress of Emperor Wen of Sui

Lady Dugu, 552–602, was the wife of Yang Jian (Emperor Wen, 541–604; r. 581–604), founder of the Sui dynasty; her posthumous title was Empress Wenxian. A native of Luoyang, in present-day Henan Province, she was of Xianbei (Xianbi) nationality, her family originally from Yunzhong (near present-day Datong in Shanxi Province). The Dugu were a high-ranking non-Chinese clan with a vast network of connections that enabled them to remain influential from the fourth to the eighth centuries. Her grandfather had been a chieftain, while her father, Dugu Xin (d. 557), had served Northern Wei and Western Wei, rising from being a military man to hold the post of minister of war (*da sima*) and Duke of Henei during the Northern Zhou dynasty. She was the seventh daughter of Dugu Xin; her Han-Chinese mother belonged to the prestigious Cui clan of northern China.

When she was fourteen, her father arranged a marriage for her with Yang Jian. Hers was a happy marriage, her husband being a man of unusual appearance and possessing extraordinary abilities; when they married he swore to her that he would never have children with any other woman. Yang Jian's family also occupied an elevated position in northern Chinese society: his father, Yang Zhong (d. 568), had served Northern Wei, Western Wei, and Northern Zhou, reaching the position of grand minister of works (*da sikong*) and being granted the title of Duke of Sui, a fief that Yang Jian inherited.

276 DUGU, EMPRESS OF EMPEROR WEN OF SUI

From the first, the future empress was gentle, obedient, respectful, and filial to her in-laws. Even when her family had reached the pinnacle of their influence among the noble families during Northern Zhou, with her sister (Lady Dugu, d. 558) empress to Emperor Ming (r. 557–560) and her daughter (*q.v.* Yang Lihua, Empress of Emperor Xuan of Northern Zhou) also an empress, she remained modest and respectful, confirming her reputation as a virtuous woman. On one occasion she and her husband attended a banquet held by their son-in-law, Emperor Xuan. A toast was, of course, proposed to the emperor and empress, but when someone proposed a toast to Lady Dugu and her husband she politely declined. When the banquet was over, the road was thronged with carriages returning home but Lady Dugu told her grooms to follow the carriages before them patiently, just like everyone else.

Yang Jian was a capable military and civilian leader and his power soon began to eclipse that of his son-in-law. When the latter died in 580, his young son—Yang Jian's grandson—was declared emperor (Emperor Jing; r. 579–581). As counselor-in-chief, Yang Jian was in complete control of the court and the following year, with the support and consent of some ministers and his wife, he accepted the throne yielded to him by his eight-year-old grandson and renamed the dynasty Sui; history knows him by his posthumous title of Emperor Wen. Lady Dugu was named empress.

The founding of the new dynasty created many matters that had to be dealt with. The Empress Dugu would often keep her husband company while he worked late into the night and would accompany him to court in the imperial carriage every day. She would send trusted eunuchs into the cabinet to watch him, so that if anything was handled improperly she could admonish him and have it rectified. She would wait outside until all court matters were finalized and return to the palace with him so that they could eat together and rest. They often discussed political issues and problems, and it is said that whenever their eyes met, they would smile. Her biography in the official *History of the Sui Dynasty* (Sui shu) says: "Whenever the empress discussed politics with the emperor, their ideas frequently coincided. People in the palace nicknamed them 'the two emperors.'" The emperor was very fond of her, but he was also a little afraid of her.

The Empress Dugu set herself up as an example of one who complies with the law of the land. She often admonished her daughters, who became princesses after Yang Jian became emperor, not to follow the example of the Northern Zhou princesses who failed to treat their in-laws with propriety and consequently tore their families apart. One of her cousins had put seven young women to death within a month and according to Sui law he should have been immediately beheaded for these crimes. But the emperor wished to exempt him from the death sentence because he was a relative of the empress. When she learned of this, the empress said: "This is a state matter; you cannot allow personal considerations to intrude." As a consequence, the death sentence was carried out, as decreed by law. On another occasion, her half brother Dugu Tuo performed witchcraft, casting a curse on her. This crime carried the penalty of execution, but the empress begged for her brother's life, saying, "If Tuo had interfered with governance and harmed the people, I would not have dared say a word. However, since his crime was the intent to harm me, may I be so bold as to beg for his life?" His sentence was therefore reduced by one degree and his life was spared.

Both Emperor Wen and the Empress Dugu were known for their thrift, diligence, and simple lifestyle. They had a positive influence on the economic recovery and development that marked the beginning of the Sui dynasty, when the economy was booming and there were so many bumper harvests that grain supplies were said to have been sufficient to last for over fifty years. On one occasion, when it was suggested that she should buy a basket of pearls from Tujue (a Turkic people then occupying China's northwest) worth eight million cash, the Empress Dugu said: "I don't need these. At present we are continually being disturbed by insurgents, and the officers and men of our army are war weary. It would be better to award the meritorious with this money." Everyone was impressed by what she said and admired her for being wise and generous. In general, she encouraged frugality and cutting down expenses. She wore plain clothes and forbade the palace women to wear luxurious clothes; under her influence, the emperor also started to economize in daily life. She also taught her eldest son, Yang Yong, then the heir apparent, to set a good example by being thrifty.

However, the Empress Dugu was not without faults. Traditional historians criticized her on two main grounds. One was that she was very jealous. At a time when commoner males could have three or four wives and concubines and emperors could have a harem of 3,000, the Empress Dugu held her husband to his word, demanding that he remain faithful to her alone. Throughout their marriage, she was firm in restricting other women's access to Yang Jian, even after he became emperor. Her biography tells this story about them. At one time, Emperor Wen favored a palace woman by having sexual relations with her. The empress waited until he had gone to court, then had the palace woman secretly killed. The emperor was so furious when he found out about this that he rode blindly out of the palace, not keeping to the roads, and was in a valley more than twenty miles away before two of his ministers—Gao Ying and Yang Su—managed to catch up with him. They held his horse and tried to persuade him to turn around. The emperor sighed and said: "I am in the exalted position of emperor, yet I am not free to do what I want!" Gao Ying replied: "How could Your Majesty neglect the country on account of a mere woman?" These words lessened the emperor's feelings of resentment and he turned back. When they got back to the palace, the empress wept and apologized to her husband, while Gao Ying and Yang Su tried to make peace between them; the imperial couple was reconciled.

Historians also blame the Empress Dugu for instigating the change of heir apparent from their eldest son, Yang Yong, to their second son, Yang Guang (Emperor Yang, 569–618; r. 605–617). Yang Guang turned out to be a dissipated tyrant whose reign brought the Sui dynasty to an end. The reason given in her biography for her change of mind in relation to the heir apparent is that not only was she opposed to the emperor having concubines, she also opposed all the other court officials and the princes having concubines, and especially having children with concubines. Gao Ying was an old friend of the Dugu family with whom she had initially been close and on friendly terms, but when she heard that he had referred to her as a "mere woman" she developed a grudge against him. Then, after Gao Ying's wife died and his concubine bore him a son, she became even more unfriendly and often slandered him to the emperor. Emperor Wen heeded her words and had Gao Ying removed from his position. In similar vein, the Empress Dugu disliked her son Yang Yong because he had many concubines. When Yang Yong's consort died suddenly the empress suspected she had been killed by his concubine née Yun. This is said to have been the reason she suggested bypassing Yang Yong and appointing Yang Guang as heir apparent, a suggestion that Emperor Wen accepted.

Yang Guang was an invidious character. Being the second son, he knew he had no hope of inheriting the throne unless he displayed qualities his parents valued. He therefore feigned filiality and frugality and played on his mother's hatred of men fathering children with concubines. He secretly arranged to have the babies born to his concubines killed so that he would appear to be faithful to his consort. As a result, he gained his mother's favor. In addition, he pretended that his life was in danger because Yang Yong was jealous of him. But not surprisingly, it was not as simple as that. A deep-seated conflict existed between Yang Yong and his father, who suspected that Yang Yong wished to eclipse him; Emperor Wen is said at one point to have even feared for his life. There was therefore a great deal more to Yang Yong's being deposed than simply that the empress suggested it. Historians may not have been entirely fair to the Empress Dugu in blaming the change of the heir apparent on her alone.

In 602, at age fifty, the Empress Dugu died in the palace. After her death, Emperor Wen favored two palace women, becoming so obsessed with them that he became ill. He apparently told his attendants, when he was critically ill, that if the empress were still alive it would not have come to that. Yang Guang revealed his real character at his father's deathbed: he raped his father's favorite concubines when ostensibly he was going there to care for his father. There are even suggestions that he killed his father in order to gain the throne.

The Empress Dugu was a modest and frugal woman who was eager to learn. She worked hard alongside her husband and supported him in governing the country well. She also helped him start a trend of noncorruption in Sui politics and together they contributed to the recovery of the economy. However, in the process she won the dubious honor of being described as an extremely jealous woman. While some may say it is every woman's wish to have a faithful husband, in ancient China only an empress could demand such a thing. Yet Yang Jian swore eternal faithfulness on their wedding day; is the Empress Dugu then to blame for expecting him to honor his promise? From the empress's expectation that courtiers and princes should follow the same rule it would appear that she was an advocate of monogamy more than a millennium before such an idea became commonplace in China.

Laura LONG

Guan Siping. *Houfei de mingyun.* Jinan: Shandong wenyi chubanshe, 1991, 2–7.
Li Xianshen. *Zhongguo houfei yiwen.* Shenyang: Shenyang chubanshe, 1992, 187–91.
Liu Shisheng. *Zhongguo gudai funü shi.* Qingdao: Qingdao chubanshe, 1991, 188–92.
S*ui shu.* Beijing: Zhonghua shuju, 1973, vol. 1, 4.94; vol. 4, 36.1108–9; vol. 4, 45.1229–38.
Xiao Li. *Yingxiang Zhongguo lishi de yi bai ge nüren.* Guangzhou: Guangdong renmin chubanshe, 1992, 121–24.
Zhou shu. Beijing: Zhonghua shuju, 1971, vol. 1, 16.267.

F

Fa Mulan: *see* **Mulan**

Fajing

The Buddhist nun Fajing, 409–473, fled civil unrest north of the Yangzi River together with her father and settled in Moling (near the city of Jiankang, the present-day city of Nanjing); neither her family name nor her given name is known. She filled an important office that regulated the assembly of nuns in Jiankang, the capital city of the Southern Dynasties.

Fajing's was one of the many families that had fled south because of the incursions of non-Chinese armies and the fall of the north to these invaders in 317. The Southern Dynasties saw a remarkable florescence of Buddhism in the lower regions of the Yangzi valley, clustering in several centers including Jiankang. Fajing entered Yongfu Convent in 428 when she was twenty years old, probably shortly after reaching the south.

In 433, for the first time in China, the Buddhist assembly of nuns in the capital received from both the assembly of monks and the assembly of nuns the obligation to observe the monastic rules (*vide* Huiguo). Until then there had not been in China a quorum of ten nuns with the required seniority to bestow the obligations on Chinese nuns. It is possible that Fajing and the nun Baoxian (*q.v.*) participated in that ceremony of the readministering of the obligations in 433.

In time, Fajing's spotless reputation for the observance of the monastic rules (*vinaya*) equaled that of Baoxian and attracted imperial attention. Upon ascending the throne in 465, Liu Yu (Emperor Ming, 439–472; r. 465–472) of the Liu Song dynasty appointed Baoxian as head of the Puxian Convent in Jiankang and assigned Fajing to live there as well. The following year, 466, by imperial decree Emperor Ming named Baoxian rector-general (*duyi sengzheng*) of the assembly of nuns in the capital and named Fajing precentor-general (*jingyi du weina*) of the capital. The precentor of an individual convent oversaw its everyday operation, establishing the routines of daily activities, especially the routines of the meditation hall. The precentor-general oversaw all of the convents within her jurisdiction.

What was unusual about Emperor Ming's appointments is that this was the first time women had filled these offices over a larger jurisdiction. During the Southern Dynasties the assembly of nuns reached a high point of independence, influence, and esteem. Individual nuns achieved renown for their intellectual contributions, writings, teaching and preaching, and mastery of the discipline of monastic life and of the practice of meditation. They moved in the highest circles of society.

In her work, Fajing was impartial and just, and her moral influence spread widely, causing many women to want to establish a connection with her. She had over 700 students of meditation. She died in 473 at the age of sixty-five.

Kathryn A. TSAI

280　FAJING

Baochang [Pao-ch'ang]. "Fajing zhuan." *Piqiuni zhuan, 2.* In *Taishō shinshū Daizōkyō,* ed. Takakusu Junjirō, Watanabe Kaigyoku, and Ono Genmyō. Tokyo: Taishō Issaikyō Kankōkai, 1924–1929, vol. 50, 941.

Baochang [Shih Pao-ch'ang]. *Lives of the Nuns: Biographies of Chinese Buddhist Nuns from the Fourth to Sixth Centuries: A Translation of the Pi-ch'iu-ni chuan,* trans. Kathryn Ann Tsai. Honolulu: University of Hawaii Press, 1994, 62–64.

Canning [Ts'an-ning]. *Da song seng shi lüe, 2,* 242c–243a. In *Taishō shinshū Daizōkyō,* ed. Takakusu Junjirō, Watanabe Kaigyoku, and Ono Genmyō. Tokyo: Taishō Issaikyō Kankōkai, 1924–1929, vol. 54.

Li Yuzhen. *Tangdai de biqiuni.* Taipei: Taiwan xuesheng shuju, 1989, 126–37.

Takakusu Junjirō, Watanabe Kaigyoku, and Ono Genmyō, eds. *Taishō shinshū Daizōkyō.* Tokyo: Taishō Issaikyō Kankōkai, 1924–1929.

Tsai, Kathryn Ann. "The Chinese Buddhist Monastic Order for Women: The First Two Centuries." In *Women in China: Current Directions in Historical Scholarship,* ed. Richard W. Guisso and Stanley Johannesen. Youngstown, NY: Philo Press, 1981, 1–20.

Fei Huanghou Feng Shi: *see* **Feng, Empress of Emperor Xiaowen of Northern Wei**

Feng, Deposed Empress née Feng: *see* **Feng, Empress of Emperor Xiaowen of Northern Wei**

Feng, Empress of Emperor Wencheng of Northern Wei

Lady Feng (Wenming Feng Huanghou), 442–490, was principal consort and empress of Emperor Wencheng (Tuoba Jun, ?440–465; r. 452–465) of the Northern Wei dynasty. She is more commonly known as Empress Dowager Wenming.

The Northern Wei dynasty was founded by the Tuoba clan, a branch of the nomadic Xianbei (also romanized as Xianbi) people of the steppe region north of China and therefore sometimes known as the Tuoba Wei. The Tuoba were not Han Chinese, but during the first century C.E. they had forged an alliance with the Eastern Han dynasty against their previous overlords, the Xiongnu (the Huns), and in the mid-fourth century they established the Dai kingdom in present-day Inner Mongolia. They declared sovereignty over north China in 386, establishing their Northern Wei dynasty with its capital at Pingcheng (present-day Taiyuan in Shanxi Province), and gradually adopted Chinese customs; by the Tang dynasty (618–907) they had merged completely with the Chinese population.

The Tuoba line of succession had traditionally been fraternal, authority being passed from brother to brother, although in the fifth century the Tuoba Wei began to adopt the Han system of succession from father to son. Concerned that their dynasty not fall prey to the machinations of maternal relatives, as had happened during the Han dynasty, the founder of Tuoba Wei drew up a law requiring the mother of the heir apparent to commit suicide. The Tuoba Wei also preferred to install as empress a woman from a recently conquered non-Chinese state who had no powerful relatives at court; this woman would frequently be appointed foster mother of the heir apparent.

Lady Feng was of Xianbei origin, a granddaughter of Emperor Wentong of the short-lived Northern Yan dynasty, which had been located in the region of present-day Chaoyang in Liaoning Province in the early fifth century. Although she was born in

FENG, EMPRESS OF EMPEROR WENCHENG OF NORTHERN WEI 281

Chang'an (the present-day city of Xi'an), she was a native of Xindu (near the present-day city of Chengdu in Sichuan Province) and her mother was from the Wang clan of Lelang. Presumably because of their association with the defeated Northern Yan ruling family, her family had been scattered. Her father, Feng Lang, had been executed sometime between 442 and 452; it is not known what became of her mother. Her paternal uncle Feng Mo had sought refuge with the Rouran nomads of present-day Outer Mongolia; these people, who bore the surname Yujiulü, were enemies of the Northern Wei and had suffered defeat at their hands. Her only brother, Feng Xi (d. 495), had fled to the nomadic Qiang tribes to the west, in present-day Shaanxi Province. Lady Feng herself was brought into the Northern Wei palace as a servant when she was very young but was fortunate to be taken under the wing of her paternal aunt, a concubine of Emperor Taiwu (Tuoba Tao, 408–453; r. 423–451), and be educated in the Han tradition.

When she was thirteen, in 455, Lady Feng was selected by a concubine of Emperor Taiwu as the legal consort and empress of Emperor Wencheng. This concubine, a Lady Chang (d. 460), had also originally come from Northern Yan. She had been appointed foster mother to the young emperor, son of Lady Yujiulü of the Rouran tribe, when he became ruler in 452. Empress Feng was thus only twenty-three years old when her equally young husband, Emperor Wencheng, died in 465; she is said to have been so overwhelmed during the funeral that she threw herself into a fire and lost consciousness. Tuoba Hong (Emperor Xianwen (454–476; r. 465–471) was then placed on the throne. He was eleven years old and was the son of Emperor Wencheng and a Han Chinese woman named Li, who had been forced to commit suicide in 456 when her son was appointed heir apparent. At this point Empress Feng was appointed empress dowager and it is generally by the title Empress Dowager Wenming that she has been known throughout history.

Empress Dowager Wenming attempted to seize power by becoming the sole regent for the young emperor, but her bid was unsuccessful. Instead, there ensued a three-way struggle for the regency between her, the Tuoba elite, and a faction headed by Counselor-in-Chief Yi Hun, who had fought and murdered his way to his position and dominated court politics, having gained significant control over the palace guard. Empress Dowager Wenming moved quickly to remove Yi Hun; in 466 she had him seized and executed and had his followers removed from key court positions. It is possible that she had the support of the Tuoba elite in this coup, for she was able to dominate court policy for almost a year after that. However, with the birth to the twelve-year-old emperor of his first son, Tuoba/Yuan Hong (Emperor Xiaowen, 467–499; r. 471–499), Empress Dowager Wenming retired from court politics and assumed responsibility for raising the infant, who was given to her at birth. This child was named heir apparent two years later, in 469; his mother, another Lady Li (d. 469), died the same year but nothing is known of how or why she died. According to Tuoba law, she was expected to commit suicide. However, it appears that this law was not always stricly enforced. In any case, since there is no indication in history that she did so, the glossing over might suggest that she was murdered. In 476, after he became emperor, Tuoba/Yuan Hong bestowed on this Lady Li the posthumous title of Empress Yuan.

During the period of Empress Dowager Wenming's withdrawal from court politics, Emperor Xianwen began to dismantle her power base. In 470, he eliminated her supporters, especially her Han Chinese allies, from the civil administration and executed her lover, Li Yi, and his brothers. The following year he undertook an imperial tour and upon his return to the capital announced his intention to abdicate in favor of his eldest surviving uncle, Tuoba Zitui. The reason he gave for this decision was that he was ill and, weary of worldly affairs, wished to pursue his interest in Buddhism and Daoism by going into religious retreat. The uncle he had chosen as heir apparent was only four years old and when Emperor Xianwen convened a palace conference all of his high-ranking officials opposed his plan. He therefore agreed to install the existing heir apparent (his son) as emperor but to remain active in affairs of state. He assumed the title of Emperor Emeritus (*taishang huang*) and moved to a separate palace compound, where he formally received his son, the young emperor, once a month. It is possible that he had not really intended to retire in favor of his infant uncle and that this had been simply a ploy to ensure the succession of his son, since Emperor Xianwen took a much greater personal interest in state affairs and the promotion of political reforms after his official retirement.

When Emperor Xianwen died suddenly in 475, Empress Dowager Wenming was suspected of poisoning him, acting in collusion with his paternal uncles and the Tuoba elite, whom he was beginning to strip of their powers. After his death, Empress Dowager Wenming was named Grand Empress Dowager Wenming and appointed sole regent for her eleven-year-old grandson, now Emperor Xiaowen. Grand Empress Dowager Wenming had been foster mother to her husband's grandson since his birth and exerted a great deal of control over him. She had tutored him and had administered physical punishment to him throughout his life; it is said that even when he was an adult she sometimes punished him physically. During her regency, Grand Empress Dowager Wenming was de facto ruler of Northern Wei; Emperor Xiaowen was but a titular ruler. Her regency is recorded as having lasted until her death in 490, although historical records seem to indicate that Emperor Xiaowen had started to participate in affairs of state before 486 and that he ruled independently from the time he was nineteen, in 486.

During her regency, Grand Empress Dowager Wenming maintained her power through various means. She promoted well-respected and capable officials who were not related to her. Also, by virtue of having only one brother (Feng Xi) she avoided the problem of granting excessive power to her own family: when delegating the positions traditionally assigned to distaff relatives at court, she shared these between her brother (whom she had recalled from his self-imposed exile in 455) and the family of her patron, the former concubine and later Empress Dowager Chang (d. 460). Finally, by filling key positions in the harem with her nieces (*vide* Feng, Empress of Emperor Xiaowen of Northern Wei) and bringing her nephews into the palace as companions for her grandson, Grand Empress Dowager Wenming ensured that power did not fall into the hands of Emperor Xiaowen's maternal relatives. Then, when her nephews grew to adulthood, she married them to Tuoba princesses. She also forced Emperor Xiaowen to implement the law requiring the mother of his eldest son, Tuoba Xun (b.

FENG, EMPRESS OF EMPEROR WENCHENG OF NORTHERN WEI 283

483), to commit suicide, even though Tuoba Xun was not appointed heir apparent for another ten years and never became emperor. The boy's mother, Lady Lin (d. 483), was from a Xiongnu family, and after her death Grand Empress Dowager Wenming assumed control of his upbringing.

Grand Empress Dowager Wenming was named regent twice: when Emperor Xianwen was a minor (466) and as sole regent for her grandson Emperor Xiaowen (478–490). She also fostered two imperial sons: Emperor Xiaowen and his eldest son, Tuoba/Yuan Xun. During her second regency, Grand Empress Dowager Wenming patronized the Sinicized and mixed ethnic groups at court, a policy that was not popular with the Chinese elite as it threatened to open the way for greater Xianbei and Tuoba participation in civil affairs. Her attempts at land distribution and tax reforms in 483 also met with little success because they attacked the privileged position of the Chinese elite.

Emperor Xiaowen is said to have been filial and obedient to his foster grandmother, in word if not always in deed. During a visit to Mount Fang, Grand Empress Dowager Wenming expressed a wish to be buried there and asked the emperor to build two tombs side by side, one for herself and one for him. The tombs were built and she was buried there after her death in 490 at the age of forty-eight, but Emperor Xiaowen took pains to ensure he was not to be buried in the adjoining tomb. He Sinicized his surname, changing it from Tuoba to Yuan, moved his capital south to Luoyang in 493, and never returned to the north. He was unable to escape her influence entirely, however, as it reached far beyond the grave. She had appointed her nieces as his consorts; she had chosen his ministers; and she had fostered his eldest son. Perhaps as a last defiant gesture, on his deathbed he ordered his consort Empress Feng, a niece of Grand Empress Dowager Wenming, to commit suicide.

Empress Dowager Wenming has been vilified in the official histories. As Chauncey Goodrich writes: "Less notorious, perhaps, but also formidable was [Empress Dowager Ling, née Hu's] predecessor by a few decades, the Empress Dowager Wen-ming. As in the case of the Empress Dowager Ling, illicit sexual relations and regicide disfigure the record." There is no question she was a remarkable woman: taken into the palace as a slave servant as a child, she managed to gain control of a boy emperor and ruled as regent for more than a decade over a dynasty that had once destroyed her home state.

LAU Lai Ming and Priscilla CHING-CHUNG

Bei shi. Beijing: Zhonghua shuju, 1974, vol. 2, 13.495–97.
Bei Wei shi. Taiyuan: Shanxi gaojiao lianhe chubanshe, 1992, 215–25.
Eisenberg, Andrew. "Retired Emperorship and the Politics of Succession in the Northern Dynasties of China, 386–581." Ph.D. dissertation, University of Washington, 1991.
Goodrich, Chauncey S. "Two Chapters in the Life of an Empress of the Later Han." *Harvard Journal of Asiatic Studies* 25 (1964/65): 169.
Holmgren, Jennifer. "The Harem in Northern Wei Politics." In her *Marriage, Kinship, and Power in Northern China.* Brookfield, VT: Variorum, 1995, vol. 4, 1–96.
———. "The Harem in Northern Wei Politics—398–498 A.D." *Journal of the Economic and Social History of the Orient* 26, part 1 (1983): 71–96.
Hou Xinyi and Chen Quanli, eds. *Houfei cidian.* Xi'an: Shaanxi renmin chubanshe, 1991, 71–72.

284 FENG, EMPRESS OF EMPEROR WENCHENG OF NORTHERN WEI

Sima Guang. *Zizhi tongjian*. Shanghai: Shanghai guji chubanshe, 1987, *juan* 126–136 passim.
Wei shu. Beijing: Zhonghua shuju, 1974, vol. 2, 13.328–31.
Zhang Jinlong. *Bei Wei zhengzhishi yanjiu*. Langzhou: Gansu jiaoyu chubanshe, 1996, 87–156.

Feng, Empress of Emperor Xiaowen of Northern Wei

Empress You née Feng, d. 499, was a consort of Emperor Xiaowen (Tuoba/Yuan Hong, 467–499; r. 471–499) of the Northern Wei dynasty. The Northern Wei, with its capital at Pingcheng (present-day Datong in Shanxi Province), was a non-Han dynasty that had been established by the Tuoba clan, a branch of the nomadic Xianbei (also Romanized as Xianbi) people of the steppe region north of China. They gradually adopted Chinese customs—Emperor Xiaowen, for example, changed his surname from Tuoba to the Han-Chinese name Yuan in 493—and by the Tang dynasty (618–907) the Tuoba had merged completely with the Chinese population. The Tuoba line of succession had traditionally been fraternal, authority being passed from brother to brother, although in the fifth century the Tuoba Wei began to adopt the Han system of primogeniture. Concerned that their dynasty not fall prey to the machinations of maternal relatives, as had happened during the Han dynasty, the founder of Tuoba Wei had drawn up a law requiring the mother of the heir apparent to commit suicide. The Tuoba Wei also preferred to install as empress a woman from a recently conquered non-Chinese state who had no powerful relatives at court; this woman would frequently be appointed foster mother of the heir apparent.

Empress Feng was a descendant of Emperor Wentong of the early fifth-century Northern Yan dynasty, which had been located in the region of present-day Chaoyang in Liaoning Province. In the aftermath of the defeat of Northern Yan, her grandfather, Feng Lang, had been executed sometime between 442 and 452 and her father, Feng Xi (d. 495), had fled to the nomadic Qiang tribes to the west, in present-day Shaanxi Province. Her mother, a woman named Chang, was a slave in Feng Xi's household; she bore him another daughter besides the future empress, but little is known of this girl except that she died young. Her sole paternal aunt, Feng Xi's sister, had been taken into the Northern Wei palace as a servant but in 455 had been appointed consort to Emperor Wencheng (Tuoba Jun, ?440–465; r. 452–465) and after his death had become de facto ruler as Empress Dowager Wenming (*q.v.* Feng, Empress of Emperor Wencheng of Northern Wei). Empress Dowager Wenming had recalled her brother from his self-imposed exile with the Qiang and given him a Princess Boning in marriage. Princess Boning bore Feng Xi a daughter, Feng Qing, but died soon after giving birth. Feng Xi then married his mistress, his former slave Lady Chang.

During her regency, Empress Dowager Wenming brought her brother's two older daughters into the palace as concubines for her foster grandson, Emperor Xiaowen. The unnamed girl fell ill and died but the future Empress Feng was favored by the young emperor. However, she fell ill, too, and after her aunt sent her home she entered a nunnery. The empress dowager then brought her youngest niece, Feng Qing, into the palace.

After the required three years of mourning for Empress Dowager Wenming, who died in 490, Emperor Xiaowen attempted to establish his own independence. He changed his surname from Tuoba to the Han-Chinese name Yuan and he moved the capital to Luoyang. Also, in response to the encouragement of his officials, he named Feng Qing as his empress. This first empress née Feng is said to have managed the inner palaces well and to have asked the emperor to treat his consorts fairly, visiting them in sequence rather than favoring a few. She is also said to have been very supportive of the emperor's policies and to have led the harem's move to the new capital of Luoyang.

However, once the new capital had been established, Emperor Xiaowen recalled the empress's older half-sister from her nunnery and had her brought to court. He favored her over the incumbent empress, who soon fell foul of her half-sister's arrogance and slander. The emperor deposed Feng Qing, who in her turn entered a nunnery—she is known to history as the Deposed Empress née Feng (Feihuanghou Feng shi)—and appointed her half-sister empress in 497.

Empress Feng did not produce any sons. The son of a secondary consort, Lady Gao (d. 497), was therefore named heir apparent. Soon after this youngster, Yuan Ke (Emperor Xuanwu, 483–515; r. 499–515), was named heir, his mother died suddenly. Historians imply there were rumors that Empress Feng had poisoned Lady Gao (later to be given the posthumous title Empress Dowager Wenzhao), but this can never be known. She was, however, appointed foster mother to the fourteen-year-old heir apparent, who visited her every three days to pay his respects. However, Empress Feng was unable to replicate the close and controlling relationship her aunt had built up over many years with Yuan Ke's father, Emperor Xiaowen.

The family of Feng Xi had gained great honor from having two daughters appointed empress, and his funeral in 495 was therefore something of a grand event, attended by Emperor Xiaowen; the Deposed Empress née Feng (Feng Qing) was also ordered to attend the mourning ceremonies. Wishing to increase her family's status, Empress Feng proposed a marriage between her brother, the Duke of Beiping, and Emperor Xiaowen's sister, Princess Pengcheng. The Princess did not wish to be party to this marriage so she told the emperor that the empress was sexually involved with several other men. The emperor apparently ignored these accusations. He also ignored evidence that Empress Feng and her mother, Lady Chang, had practiced witchcraft in order to bring about his early death. On his deathbed, however, Emperor Xiaowen is believed to have ordered his brothers to ensure that the empress committed suicide. It is clear that the emperor's brothers had little love for Empress Feng, for during her funeral one of them remarked: "If it hadn't been for the emperor's last command, we brothers would have been forced to get rid of her ourselves."

History has not been kind to Empress Feng. Jennifer Holmgren has this to say of the Chinese historians' appraisal of the empresses Feng: "[Empress You née Feng] is given the blackest portrait possible. All the standard vices of suspicion, jealousy, immorality, deceit, ruthlessness, and ambition are laid at her door. The younger niece [Feng Qing], however, is portrayed as a model of saintly virtue—unobtrusive, and compliant."

TAI Po Ying and Priscilla CHING-CHUNG

Bei shi. Beijing: Zhonghua shuju, 1974, vol. 2, 13.495–501.

Holmgren, Jennifer. "The Harem in Northern Wei Politics—398–498 A.D." *Journal of the Economic and Social History of the Orient* 26, part 1 (1983): 71–96.

———. *Marriage, Kinship, and Power in Northern China.* Brookfield, VT: Variorum, 1995, 72–96.

Hou Xinyi and Chen Quanli, eds. *Houfei cidian.* Xi'an: Shaanxi renmin chubanshe, 1991, 73.

Wei shu. Beijing: Zhonghua shuju, 1974, vol. 1, 7*shang*.135–190; vol. 2, 13.328–31, 332–36; vol. 5, 83*shang*.1818–23.

Feng Qing: *see* **Feng, Empress of Emperor Xiaowen of Northern Wei**

Feng Wenming: *see* **Feng, Empress of Emperor Wencheng of Northern Wei**

Feng You: *see* **Feng, Empress of Emperor Xiaowen of Northern Wei**

Fu Jian Qie Zhang Shi: *see* **Zhang, Concubine of Fu Jian**

Fu Sheng's Daughter: *see* **Song, Lady Xuanwen**

Fu Xi'e: *see* **Song, Lady Xuanwen**

G

Gan, Consort of Liu Bei: *see* **Gan, Empress of the Former Sovereign of Shu**

Gan, Empress of the Former Sovereign of Shu

Empress Gan (Xianzhu Gan Huanghou), c. 180–221, was a native of Pei (in the northern part of present-day Jiangsu Province). She was a secondary consort of the founder of the kingdom of Shu Han, Liu Bei (Emperor Zhaolie, also known as the Former Sovereign [*xianzhu*] of Shu, 161–223; r. 221–223) and the mother of Liu Shan (known as the Later Sovereign [*houzhu*] of Shu, 207–271; r. 223–263).

The future empress was born toward the end of the Eastern Han dynasty, a chaotic time that spawned massive peasant rebellions and saw the emergence of the three powerful rival states of the Three Kingdoms (*sanguo*) period: Wei in the north, Shu Han in the west, and Wu in the south and east. A physiognomist predicted that although she was of lowly origins and from a small village she was destined to one day "occupy a high place in the side apartments of the ultimate palace." It is said that by the time she was eighteen she was seductive and bewitching, with a beautiful body and skin. The warrior hero Liu Bei took her as a concubine in 194, by which time he had gained control over Yuzhou (present-day Henan Province). During his military campaigns in eastern China in this period, Liu Bei had abandoned his women three times and his various wives and children had been captured. The wives and children captured in 196 and 198 were returned to him, but whether those captured in 200 were later returned is not known. Nor is it known just how many women and children were involved in these transactions. In 196, when he entered Jingzhou (in the region of the present-day provinces of Hubei, Hunan, and southwestern Henan Provinces), he had at least one principal wife, Lady Mi, a sister of his supporter Mi Zhu. Lady Sun, a younger sister of Sun Quan (182–252; r. 222–252), later to become emperor of the kingdom of Wu, also became a principal wife of Liu Bei, possibly in 209 (*vide* Wu, Empress of the Former Sovereign of Shu).

Liu Bei had a three-foot-tall jade figurine that he kept in Lady Gan's apartment. He is reputed to have spent his days planning military strategy, retreating to the apartment at night: it is said that Lady Gan's body was as white and sleek as the jade figurine and that it was difficult to tell them apart. Realizing that Liu Bei's other concubines were extremely jealous of her and the jade figurine, Lady Gan wisely admonished Liu Bei for cherishing such a bewitching trifle, telling him that infatuation gives rise to suspicion. He heeded her warning and disposed of the jade figurine.

Whenever Liu Bei had lost his principal consorts, captured by the enemy during his many campaigns, Lady Gan had assumed the role of principal consort and become responsible for his household. In 200 she accompanied him to Jingzhou, where in 207 she gave birth to Liu Shan. When his rival pretender to the Han throne Cao Cao (155–220), founder of the kingdom of Wei, attacked Liu Bei in Danyang (present-day Anhui Province) in 208, Liu Bei abandoned Lady Gan and their son, as he had abandoned his previous consorts. They were able to escape unharmed, however, with the help of Liu's loyal follower Zhao Yun.

Lady Gan died in 221 and she was buried in Nan Commandery (in present-day Henan Province). Her body was later taken to the west, where Liu Bei had established himself as King of Shu, and when he proclaimed himself emperor in 222 he gave Lady Gan the posthumous title Lady of Imperial Regret (Huangsi Furen), intending to re-inter her in Shu. He died before her body arrived, however, and since his park and burial site had already been completed, their son Liu Shan decided they should be buried together. Liu Bei was given the posthumous title Emperor of Illustrious Achievements (Zhaolie di) and, as the mother of his successor, Lady Gan was named Empress of Illustrious Achievements (Zhaolie Huanghou).

Priscilla CHING-CHUNG

Chen Shou. *Empresses and Consorts: Selections from Chen Shou's "Records of the Three States" with Pei Songzhi's Commentary,* trans. Robert J. Cutter and William Gordon Crowell. Honolulu: University of Hawaii Press, 1999, 49–50, 115–16, 207–9.

Crespigny, Rafe de. *Generals of the South: The Foundation and Early History of the Three Kingdoms State of Wu.* Canberra: Australian National University, 1990, 294–95.

Sanguo zhi. Beijing: Zhonghua shuju, 1959, vol. 4, 34.905–6.

Sima Guang. *The Chronicle of the Three Kingdoms (220–265), Chapters 69–78 from the Tzu chih t'ung chien of Ssu-ma Kuang,* trans. Achilles Fang, ed. Glen W. Baxter. Cambridge, MA: Harvard University Press, 1965, vol. 1, 67, 685, 696.

288 GAO HUAN'S WIFE

Gao Huan's Wife: *see* **Lou Zhaojun, Empress of Emperor Shenwu of Northern Qi**

Gao Wei's Nurse: *see* **Lu Lingxuan**

Guangcheng Jun: *see* **Guo Huai**

Guo, Empress of Emperor Ming of Wei

Empress Yuan née Guo (Mingyuan Guo Huanghou), c. 210–264, from Xiping (in present-day Xining District in Gansu Province) was the second and last empress of Emperor Ming (Cao Rui, 205–239; r. 226–239) of the northern Three Kingdoms state of Wei. She came from a great clan in the northwest but was taken into the palace after her home commandery rebelled in the early 220s. She was promoted to the rank of Lady (*furen*) at the age of sixteen when Cao Rui assumed the throne and he became very fond of her, granting official positions to her father, uncle, and brother. He named her empress a few days after he fell ill in 239; he died shortly afterward.

Emperor Ming had no sons and only on the day he died did he name his successor: eight-year-old Cao Fang (Prince of Qi, 231–274; r. 239–254). As he did not have long to live, Emperor Ming may have been advised to secretly adopt Cao Fang, who was possibly a son of his first cousin Cao Kai. After Emperor Ming's death, Empress Guo was elevated to the position of empress dowager and she played an important but purely ceremonial role over the following twenty-five years, the regents formally reporting their decisions to her before implementing them.

The two men named as regents for Cao Fang—Defender-in-Chief (*taiwei*) Sima Yi (178–251) and General-in-Chief (*da jiangjun*) Cao Shuang (d. 249)—were locked in a bitter struggle for power. Cao Shuang is said to have been "arrogant and extravagant without limit" while the elderly Sima Yi was described in 248 as "no more than the surviving emanations of a corpse; his mind is deserting his body and he is incapable of causing [Cao Shuang] anxiety." Reassured by this assessment, Cao Shuang took no precautions against Sima Yi. Within a few months, however, Sima Yi had Cao Shuang's residence surrounded by troops and brought charges against him. Cao Shuang and his supporters were all eventually executed.

When Sima Yi died two years later, his de facto rulership of Wei passed to two of his sons: General-in-Chief of the Pacification Army (*fujun da jiangjun*) and Overseer of the Imperial Secretarial Affairs (*lu shangshu shi*) Sima Shi (208–255) and General Pacifying the East (*andong jiangjun*) Sima Zhao (211–265). Within another three years (254), Sima Shi had deposed Cao Fang in the name of the empress dowager, accusing him of "conducting himself with unbounded license and with indecent intimacy toward singing-girls." Displeased as she was at Cao Fang's dismissal, with troops posted outside the palace Empress Dowager Guo had no option but to approve it. She did insist, however, on handing the imperial seal in person to the next puppet emperor, thirteen-year-old Cao Mao (Duke of Gaoguixiang, 241–260; r. 254–260), a grandson of Emperor Wen. When this young man died six years later (260) leading an unsuccessful coup against the Sima family, Empress Dowager Guo was obliged to welcome a third young puppet emperor, Cao Huan (Prince of Chen, 245–302; r. 260–265), a grandson of Cao Cao (155–220), the founding father of Wei.

As matriarch of a series of short-lived or ill-fated monarchs, Empress Dowager Guo was required to preside over the last years of a crumbling dynasty. She died in February 264 and two years later, in February 266, Cao Huan abdicated in favor of Sima Zhao's son Sima Yan (Emperor Wu, 236–290; r. 265–290), who immediately declared the Western Jin dynasty with its capital the city of Luoyang. Empress Dowager Guo was buried in Gaopingling in April 264.

Priscilla CHING-CHUNG

Chen Shou. *Empresses and Consorts: Selections from Chen Shou's "Records of the Three States" with Pei Songzhi's Commentary,* trans. Robert J. Cutter and William Gordon Crowell. Honolulu: University of Hawaii Press, 1999, 53–55; 72, 112–207.

Giles, Herbert A. *A Chinese Biographical Dictionary.* Taipei: Chengwen Publishing, 1971, 669, 674–75, 760–61.

Sanguo zhi. Beijing: Zhonghua shuju, 1975, vol. 1, 4.128–32, 143–47; vol. 1, 5.168–69.

Sima Guang, *The Chronicle of the Three Kingdoms (220–265), Chapters 69–78 from the Tzu chih t'ung chien of Ssu-ma Kuang,* trans. Achilles Fang, ed. Glen W. Baxter. Cambridge, MA: Harvard University Press, 1965, vol. 1, 518, 549–50, 580, 606, 617–18; vol. 2, 19, 31–33, 165–68, 183–86, 335–38, 415, 450, 460, 505.

Guo, Empress of Emperor Wen of Wei

Empress De née Guo (Wende Guo Huanghou), 184–235, from Guangzong, in Anping (in present-day Shandong Province), was the second empress of Emperor Wen (Cao Pi, 187–226; r. 220–226) of Wei.

Members of her family had once served as provincial officials, but her parents died when she was young and she was set adrift in the chaotic final decades of the Eastern Han dynasty. Her father, Guo Yong, had thought her to be extraordinary when she was young and said that she had been the queen (*nüzhong wang*) of their household. She initially found a place serving in the household of the Marquis of Tongdi (a prefecture in present-day Shanxi Province) but was recruited as a palace woman for Cao Pi some time between 213 and 216. At that stage, Cao Pi's father, Cao Cao (155–220), was still Duke of Wei and was building the power base upon which his Three Kingdoms state of Wei was eventually founded in 220.

Lady Guo is said to have been a shrewd strategist who periodically offered advice to Cao Pi and helped him become emperor. She was made a lady (*furen*) once he became Duke of Wei and was subsequently promoted to honored concubine (*guipin*). After Cao Pi assumed the title of emperor, he appointed Lady Zhen (*q.v.* Zhen, Empress of Emperor Wen of Wei) as his empress, as she had already borne him a son and heir, Cao Rui (Emperor Ming, 205–239; r. 226–239). Almost immediately, however, Emperor Wen announced that he wished to install Lady Guo as empress in place of Lady Zhen. He was advised against this as it would set a historical precedent: because the status of an empress, who was required to govern the imperial concubines, was second only to that of the emperor, a virtuous woman should be selected as empress. He was told that the inferior would prosper and the superior would decline if a woman of low birth was suddenly promoted simply because the emperor loved her. Emperor Wen ignored this advice but he did issue an edict ordering that, to prevent disorder, women were not to participate in government, no official was to report state affairs to the empress dowager, and no members of the clans of imperial consorts were to be appointed regent or enfeoffed without due merit. In 121, he dismissed Empress Zhen, at the same time instructing her to commit suicide, and named Lady Guo empress.

Cao Pi had shown his willingness to interfere with the law a few years earlier, when one of Lady Guo's younger brothers had been charged with having stolen fabric belonging to the government and had been sentenced to death. Cao Pi had interceded on behalf of Lady Guo's brother but the magistrate, Bao Xun, not daring to take the responsibility of acquitting the culprit, reported the case in detail to Cao Cao. Thereafter, Cao Pi bore a grudge against Bao Xun, whom he eventually managed to have put to death just twenty days before his own death.

According to the *Record of the Wei Dynasty* (Wei shu), Empress Guo was known for her filial piety toward Empress Dowager Bian (*q.v.* Bian, Wife of Cao Cao, King of Wei), the mother of Emperor Wen. She is also said to have acted as a mentor to the other ladies favored by the emperor and to have covered for palace women when they made mistakes. Whenever they were reprimanded, she would explain to the emperor how the particular incident had come about, and would beg for leniency for any woman who angered him. She was frugal and economical by nature and did not like music, claiming as her model Han Empress Ma (*q.v.* Ma, Empress of Emperor Ming) who, in 77, had issued a long edict virtually outlawing extravagance.

Empress Guo advised her relatives that they should make matches with families in their own hometowns and not use their position to force marriages with people from other places. She prevented her elder sister's son from taking a concubine, saying that the few women available should be left to become wives of the officers and the men. She warned her family that if they were not careful they would be punished. She forbade her cousin to dam a river to harvest fish, saying that the river was for transporting supplies and that because there was a scarcity of timber and servants he should not use them for making dams or for fishing.

Empress Guo did not produce any sons and Emperor Wen asked her to adopt his son Cao Rui, whose mother, Lady Zhen, had been ordered to commit suicide in 221. When Cao Rui (Emperor Ming) ascended the throne, he promoted Empress Guo to empress dowager and ennobled and promoted members of her family. The commentary in the *Record of the Wei Dynasty* says that Emperor Ming had long been troubled by his mother's death and that Empress Dowager Guo died unexpectedly, "from anxiety," in 235. Empress Dowager Guo had always tried to distance herself from blame by telling the young emperor that his father had killed his mother, but Emperor Ming is said to have been angry with her and to have hounded her to death. He is said to have insisted that she be buried in the same disrespectful manner in which his mother had been buried: "Her hair was left unbound and her face was covered and her mouth was stuffed with grain husks." Nevertheless, despite resenting Empress Dowager Guo, Emperor Ming favored members of her family and bestowed posthumous honors on her parents.

Priscilla CHING-CHUNG

Chen Shou. *Empresses and Consorts: Selections from Chen Shou's "Records of the Three States" with Pei Songzhi's Commentary,* trans. Robert J. Cutter and William Gordon Crowell. Honolulu: University of Hawaii Press, 1999, 54, 106–10; 204–6.

Sima Guang. *The Chronicle of the Three Kingdoms (220–265), Chapters 69–78 from the Tzu chih t'ung chien of Ssu-ma Kuang,* trans. Achilles Fang, ed. Glen W. Baxter/ Cambridge, MA: Harvard University Press, 1965, vol. 1, 105–7, 125–26, 199–200, 208–9, 211–12.

Guo Huai

Guo Huai, fl. 282–300, *zi* Yuhuang, was an ambitious and ruthless noblewoman who lived during the Western Jin dynasty; she is said to have thoroughly abused her power, which she had gained through dishonest means. She is also known by the titles Lady of Yicheng (Yicheng Jun) and Lady of Guangcheng (Guangcheng Jun). The story of her life gives a rare glimpse into family conflicts in ancient China.

Guo Huai was the daughter of Guo Pei, governor of Yangcheng (in the region of present-day Henan Province), and the wife of Jia Chong (*zi* Gonglü, 217–282), a man who enjoyed a particularly close relationship with Sima Yan (Emperor Wu, 236–290; r. 265–290), the first emperor of Western Jin. Jia Chong had been a supporter of the Sima family during the Wei dynasty when it wielded great power acting in the capacity of regents. He had supported Sima Yan in his rise to power and had remained loyal when Sima Yan overthrew Wei and established himself as emperor of the Jin dynasty with its capital at Luoyang, in present-day Henan Province. Jia Chong was also esteemed as the man mainly responsible for establishing a new legal code for the Jin dynasty.

Guo Huai bore Jia Chong two daughters (Jia Nanfeng and Jia Wu) and two sons. Her two sons were said to have died in infancy, pining for their wet nurses after Guo Huai killed the women out of insane jealousy. Whether this is true or whether people attached this atrocity to Guo Huai because she was such a hated figure cannot be known for certain. It is clear that Guo Huai was intensely ambitious and she realized her ambitions largely through her elder daughter, Jia Nanfeng (*q.v.* Jia Nanfeng, Empress of Emperor Hui of Jin). This girl is described as having been dark and unattractive yet, despite a general court preference for another girl, Guo Huai managed to bribe the former Empress Yang (*q.v.* Yang Yan, Empress of Emperor Wu of Jin) to persuade Emperor Wu to choose Jia Nanfeng as a wife for the heir apparent, Sima Zhong (Emperor Hui, 259–306; r. 290–306).

Guo Huai was Jia Chong's second wife, something that was not normally a matter of any consequence in ancient China. In this case, however, Jia Chong's first marriage led to later complications. Jia Chong's first wife, Li Wan, was the daughter of an official who, unlike Jia Chong, had been loyal to the imperial family of the Wei dynasty and had been killed during the last days of Wei as the Sima faction finally seized power. Li Wan herself had also been incriminated and had been banished to Lelang (present-day Korea) when the dynasty fell. Because Jia Chong was a loyal member of the Sima faction, his marriage with Li Wan was therefore annulled; he then married Guo Huai. Chinese tradition allowed men to have as many concubines as they could afford but they were allowed to have only one official wife at a time, unless granted special permission. Li Wan was eventually pardoned and when she returned to China Emperor Wu decreed that in the circumstances Jia Chong would be allowed to have two official wives. However, angered by this decision, Guo Huai would not be party to it. Indeed, she was so infuriated that Jia Chong did not dare accept the emperor's generous offer, citing modesty as his reason. He nevertheless secretly installed Li Wan in a separate residence but, unlike men who divided their time between their former and their present wives, he did not visit her for fear of incurring Guo Huai's further jealousy and wrath. Jia Chong and Li Wan had several daughters who beseeched their father time and again to meet with their mother, but Jia Chong never relented. When Li Wan eventually died, a sad and lonely woman, Guo Huai rejected the daughters' request that their mother be buried with Jia Chong. Li Wan's collected works and a work on women's education, *Nü xun,* were in circulation after her death but are no longer extant.

A story about a meeting that took place between these two women is recorded in Jia Chong's biography in the *History of the Jin Dynasty* (Jin shu), but this story is viewed with suspicion by the commentator of an earlier source, *Shishuo xinyu.* The story goes that after her daughter became empress, Guo Huai decided she wanted to meet Li Wan. Jia Chong advised her against it, saying, "She has an indomitable spirit and the aura of a talented woman. It would be better that you didn't go." Disregarding his advice, Guo Huai set off in full regalia and with a host of attendants to see Li Wan. Li Wan stood up to welcome Guo Huai when she came in and, without realizing what she was doing, Guo Huai went down on her knees and kowtowed twice to Li Wan. When she got home, Guo Huai told Jia Chong what had happened and he simply said, "What did I tell you?" The story continues that whenever Jia Chong went out after that, Guo Huai would send someone to look for him, fearing he had gone to visit Li Wan.

Guo Huai and her family wielded immense power once Jia Nanfeng became empress. Since Emperor Hui was a simpleton, Empress Jia was able to monopolize court affairs and rule as a virtual dictator. Guo Huai's prestige increased to an incredible level: it is said that courtiers would bow almost before her carriage came into view.

Guo Huai's other daughter, Jia Wu, was also unusual in that she won the agreement of her parents to marry her lover, Han Shou, with whom she had been conducting an illicit affair. When Jia Chong died without a male heir, Guo Huai decided that his title and position should be passed on to their grandson, Han Mi, that is, to the son of Jia Wu and Han Shou. This confounded usual practice, which would have been to adopt a male relative of the Jia clan in the absence of a direct male heir. However, Guo Huai's elevated position as mother of the empress ensured that her request was granted. Han Mi changed his name to Jia Mi and cooperated closely with his maternal aunt Empress Jia in appointing people of their own clique to court positions, thereby gaining tighter control over court affairs. Jia Wu, Guo Huai, and other members of the Jia and Guo families belonged to this privileged clique, which quickly grew in power and wealth.

When she died in 300 Guo Huai was enfeoffed as Lady of Yicheng, and her empress daughter buried her according to ritual that far exceeded her position. The people were contemptuous of this indiscretion but no one dared make any critical comment. Guo Huai's had been, for her, a fortunate life and she remained fortunate in dying a peaceful death. However, the year she died, a successful coup toppled Empress Jia, who was forced to take poison; Jia Wu was beaten to death with a wooden rod; and Jia Mi was executed.

Lily Xiao Hong LEE

Jin shu. Beijing: Zhonghua shuju, 1974, vol. 4, 31.952, 965; vol. 4, 40.1170–75.
Lin Shimin and Li Hongfa. *Lidai ming houfei mizhuan.* Jinan: Shandong wenyi chubanshe, 1991, 60–69.
Liu I-ch'ing [Yiqing]. *Shih-shuo Hsin-yü: A New Account of Tales of the World,* trans. Richard B. Mather. Minneapolis: University of Minnesota Press, 1976, 348–49; 486–88.
Liu Yiqing. *Shishuo xinyu jian shu,* ed. Yu Jiaxi. Beijing: Zhonghua shuju, 1983, 19.682–86; 35.918–22.

Guo of Western Jin

Guo was the surname of a woman, d. c. 300, who lived in northern China during the Western Jin dynasty. She amassed a large personal fortune through her relationship with her cousin Empress Jia (*q.v.* Jia Nanfeng, Empress of Emperor Hui of Jin) by selling her influence at court and has traditionally been viewed negatively, as an example of how women ought not to behave.

History has not preserved Guo's personal name, but we know that her father, Guo Yu, was a native of Taiyuan (in present-day Shanxi Province) and that he was related to Empress Jia's mother, Guo Huai (*q.v.*). Guo Huai had been instrumental in ensuring that her daughter married into the imperial family: she had bribed Empress Yang (*q.v.* Yang Yan, Empress of Emperor Wu of Jin) to speak on behalf of her daughter, who was consequently selected as the consort of the heir apparent, Sima Zhong (Emperor Hui, 259–306; r. 290–306). Emperor Hui is said to have been slow-witted, which gave Empress Jia the opportunity to monopolize court affairs. She consolidated her personal power base by promoting her relatives, paternal and maternal, to important positions. Her mother became powerful, while her wet nurse, her sister Jia Wu, and her cousin Guo also became involved in court politics to the extent that they were able to sell their influence.

In addition to her powerful family connections at court, Guo also married into the influential Wang family. Her husband, Wang Yan (256–311), was a well-known scholar of Daoist philosophy who, because of the prestige of his family, had been drafted into official service. He had an illustrious official career, while nevertheless continuing to retain his Daoist stance. Their daughter, whose name has not been recorded, was appointed consort to the heir apparent, Sima Yu (d. 300), which for a time increased Guo's already considerable influence. However, Empress Jia had long harbored a deep antipathy toward Sima Yu and engineered an incident that ensured his disgrace. It is not clear whether Wang Yan was acting at the instigation of Guo or on his own initiative when he requested that their daughter be divorced from the disgraced heir apparent, who later committed suicide.

However, given Guo's close relationship with Empress Jia, it is hard not to believe she had a hand in distancing herself and her family from the heir apparent.

Despite the considerable reputation of the Wang clan and the personal prestige of her husband, Guo did not play the role of the submissive wife. On the contrary, she defied the advice of her husband and brother-in-law not to become involved in business deals, doing precisely as she pleased. A variety of sources allude to her political and economic activities in a negative tone, some saying she used her family's slaves to collect human feces to sell, probably as fertilizer, others accusing her of accepting huge bribes from people who wished her to use her influence on their behalf. Once, when her brother-in-law Wang Cheng, then a teenager, came home to remonstrate with her, ashamed at having seen their family's slaves picking up feces in the street, she retorted that on her deathbed her mother-in-law had asked her, Guo, to take care of Wang Cheng, not the other way around. She grabbed his clothes, intending to give him a beating, but the young man pulled himself free and ran away. Another anecdote tells of her husband's disgust at the way she had accumulated her great wealth. As a Daoist philosopher, Wang Yan was disposed to scorn money and position and he admonished her many times for her actions but was unable to stop her. Eventually he resorted to frightening her into curtailing her illicit activities by invoking the name of the famous knight-errant Li Yang, as one would frighten a child with threats of a bogyman. Another story about Guo relates to her fondness for addressing her husband using *qing,* a form of address usually only used between equals. Wang Yan remonstrated with her many times, but gave up in the end and let her continue to do as she pleased.

These anecdotes, which highlight Guo's strong will and independence of mind, may be seen as her challenge to male supremacy, while the collecting and selling of human waste for recycling may be viewed as what would now be seen as a green activity. However, some of her activities could never be seen in a positive light, even by modern standards. There can be no justification, for example, for her interfering in court politics for personal financial gain. Guo was therefore a complex person who was neither in the mold of the model woman of traditional virtues nor a model for the modern Chinese woman who devotes herself selflessly to fighting for her country and her people. It can be said, however, that she was very capable of fighting for her own rights in a male-dominated society.

Nothing is known of the manner in which Guo's life ended but, knowing something of what happened to those around her, it is not difficult to surmise. Her cousin Empress Jia was killed during an armed coup in 300, as were all the members of the Jia family and the Guo family who were in power. Her marital connection to the Wang family may have saved her from a terrible end at the hands of her political rivals, but worse could have been in store. With the virtual collapse of the Western Jin dynasty in 311, her husband Wang Yan was killed by invading Xiongnu armies, while her son Wang Xuan died soon afterward, killed by bandits as he traveled to join soldiers fighting the Xiongnu. Even if Guo survived her husband and her son, the rest of her life could not have been very pleasant.

Lily Xiao Hong LEE

Jin shu. Beijing: Zhonghua shuju, 1974, vol. 4, 43.1237–39; vol. 5, 53.1459.

Lee, Lily Xiao Hong. "Jindai canyu zhuliu shehui huodong de funü." In her *Yin zhi de: Zhongguo funü yanjiu lunwenji.* Beijing: Xinshijie chubanshe, 1999, 71–102.

Liu I-ch'ing [Yiqing]. *Shih-shuo Hsin-yü: A New Account of Tales of the World,* trans. Richard B. Mather. Minneapolis: University of Minnesota Press, 1976, 281–82.

Liu Yiqing. *Shishuo xinyu jian shu,* ed. Yu Jiaxi. Beijing: Zhonghua shuju, 1983, 10.556–60; 35.922–23.

H

Han Lanying

Han Lanying, fl. 454–493, a native of Wu Commandery (present-day Suzhou in Jiangsu Province), was a scholar and writer. During the reign of Emperor Xiaowu (Liu Jun, 430–464; r. 454–464) of the Liu Song dynasty, she presented her *Rhapsody on the Restoration* (Zhongxing fu) to the emperor, who admired her work and invited her to enter the palace, though sources do not indicate in what capacity. She was appointed to a position in the palace in the reign of Emperor Ming (Liu Yu, 439–472; r. 465–472), one source describing her position as mistress of ceremony (*siyi*).

She remained in the palace after the change of dynasties in 479, when Southern Qi replaced Liu Song. Emperor Wu (Xiao Ze; r. 483–493) was a fine administrator during whose reign the state enjoyed comparative prosperity and stability and, although he is not known to have personally encouraged literature, his reign is distinguished by the fact that two of his sons actively promoted literature and literary talent. The emperor must have been of similar mind as he gave Han Lanying the title Erudite (*boshi*) and asked her to teach his palace women. Because of her advanced age and the breadth of her knowledge, she was known as Lord Han (Han Gong), a form of address normally reserved for venerable males.

Special mention is made of Han Lanying in the *History of the Southern Qi Dynasty* (Nan Qi shu), at the end of the biography of Empress Mu of Emperor Wu, making her one of a few women of commoner background to warrant such an honor in an official history outside the chapters on palace women and virtuous women. In addition, the historian went to the trouble of recording her full name. However, we know very little about her life and have no details of her academic activities. Her *Rhapsody on the Restoration* has not survived, nor have any of her other works.

Lily Xiao Hong LEE

Jiang Minfan and Wang Ruifang. *Zhongguo lidai cainü xiaozhuan.* Hangzhou: Zhejiang wenyi chubanshe, 1984, 68–70.

Nan Qi shu. Beijing: Zhonghua shuju, 1972, vol. 2, 20.392.

Tan Zhengbi. *Zhongguo nüxing wenxueshi.* Tianjin: Baihua wenyi chubanshe, 1984, 97.

Xie Wuliang. *Zhongguo funü wenxueshi.* Shanghai: Zhonghua shuju, 1916; Zhengzhou: Zhongzhou guji chubanshe, 1992, reprint, Section IIB, 81.

Han of Eastern Jin

Lady Han, fl. 373, lived during the Eastern Jin dynasty; neither her given name nor her native place is known. She was married to Zhu Tao, a native of Yiyang (south of present-day Xinyang in Henan Province), a capable army officer who rose to the position of regional inspector of Yizhou (present-day Chengdu in Sichuan Province). Their son Zhu Xu was a famous general and it is in his biography in the *History of the Jin Dynasty* (Jin shu) that her story is recorded.

Zhu Xu was stationed in Xiangyang (in present-day Hubei Province), where he held the post of regional inspector of Liangzhou. In 373, General Fu Pi of the neighboring state of Former Qin, which was ruled by the Di, a non-Han ethnic group, attacked Xiangyang. Zhu Xu held fast, but when Lady Han ascended the city wall and walked around it she realized that the northwestern corner would be the first to fall. She therefore directed more than 100 maidservants and women of the city to build a diagonal wall that was said to be more than twenty *zhang* high (one *zhang* is equivalent to 3.8 yards), at that corner. Eventually, when the provisions of the attacking forces began to run out, General Fu Pi made a final thrust in his attempt to conquer the city. He attacked the northwestern corner and, as Lady Han had predicted, it fell. Zhu Xu's soldiers managed to reinforce the wall the women had built, however, and General Fu Pi was forced to give up and retreat. The grateful people of Xiangyang therefore named the wall The Lady's Wall.

Nowhere is there any mention of Lady Han having had any military training; perhaps it was simply common sense that led her to detect the weakness in the city's defenses. Nevertheless, Lady Han was one of many women who, faced with an emergency, rose to the occasion. While she was not given a biography of her own, the historical importance of her contribution is confirmed by its being included in her son's biography in the official history of the dynasty.

Lily Xiao Hong LEE

Jin shu. Beijing: Zhonghua shuju, 1974, vol. 7, 81.2132–33.
Liu Shisheng. *Zhongguo gudai funüshi.* Qingdao: Qingdao chubanshe, 1991, 168–69.
Xu Tianxiao. *Shenzhou nüzi xinshi [zheng xu bian].* Shanghai: Shenzhou tushuju, 1913; Taipei: Daoxiang chubanshe, 1993, rpt, 62–63.

Hu, Consort of Emperor Xuanwu of Northern Wei

Lady Hu, c. 490–528, was a secondary consort of Emperor Xuanwu (Yuan Ke, 483–515; r. 499–515) of the Northern Wei dynasty. Although never appointed empress during her lifetime, she is known in many sources as Empress Dowager Ling née Hu, the title granted her posthumously by the last emperor of Northern Wei. One of the most powerful women in late Northern Wei, she ruled as regent for her son, Emperor Xiaoming (Yuan Xu, 510–528; r. 515–528), from 515 to 520 and again from 525 to 528.

The Northern Wei dynasty was founded by the non-Chinese Tuoba clan, a branch of the nomadic Xianbei (also romanized as Xianbi) people of the steppe region north of China, and is therefore sometimes known as the Tuoba Wei. The dynasty gradually adopted Chinese customs and in 493 Emperor Xiaowen (Tuoba/Yuan Hong, 467–499; r. 471–499) Sinicized his surname to Yuan and moved his capital to Luoyang. In an effort to prevent the relatives of empresses wielding undue influence at court, in 409 the Tuoba Wei had instituted a law requiring the mother of the heir apparent to commit suicide. However, by the late fifth century this law was no longer being enforced, although it was not unusual for women who gave birth to imperial sons to meet an untimely end.

Lady Hu was ethnically Han Chinese. She was from Anding (in present-day Gansu Province); her father, Hu Guozhen (d. 518), had been a minister of education (*situ*) and her mother came from the Huangfu clan. Her paternal aunt, a Buddhist nun, preached in the imperial palaces and managed to convince the appropriate authorities that her niece, a girl of some beauty and good upbringing, should be recruited into the palace as a consort (*shi fu*).

Emperor Xuanwu's consorts were unwilling to risk giving birth to a son, fearing that this would incur the enmity of the official consort, Empress Gao (d. 518). Empress Gao was suspected of having poisoned her predecessor, Empress Yu (d. 507 or 509), who had died in mysterious circumstances after giving birth to the emperor's first son; the child had also died. Empress Gao was from a very powerful Koguryo (i.e., Korean) family from Bohai (in the present-day province of Hebei). Her aunt (posthumously titled Empress Dowager Gao, d. 497) was the mother of Emperor Xuanwu and she, too, had died unexpectedly the year her son was appointed heir apparent.

Despite the obvious dangers of bearing the emperor's child, Consort Hu is nevertheless said to have prayed for a son, believing an heir to be necessary and claiming that no woman should fear for her life when the imperial line was under threat. Her prayers were answered and in 510, to the delight of the emperor, she gave birth to a son, Yuan Xu (later known as Emperor Xiaoming). The emperor ensured the child's survival by sending him to a separate palace, where he was placed in the care of trusted nursing mothers from good families. When the child was two years old he was named heir apparent.

When Emperor Xuanwu died suddenly in 515, his five-year-old son Yuan Xu was enthroned. This triggered a lethal power struggle. General of Imperial Armies (*jinjun*) Yu Zhong (d. 518) was named regent and Empress Gao was appointed empress dowager. The day after the child emperor was enthroned, however, Empress Dowager Gao's uncle was murdered by a conspiracy of princes, relatives of the deceased Empress Yu, and eunuchs who feared he might become powerful now that his niece had been appointed empress dowager. Shortly afterward, Consort Hu was given the title Imperial Mother (*huang taifei*). Fearing she would be demoted, Empress Dowager Gao attempted to kill Consort Hu, who was quickly placed in protective custody for five months by the group that had murdered Empress Gao's uncle. Empress Dowager Gao was indeed eventually deposed: she was sent to a nunnery and died a suspicious death soon thereafter. Later that year (515) Consort Hu received the title Empress Dowager and was made regent. In accordance with tradition, her father was appointed a Duke.

Empress Dowager Hu had inherited serious economic and social problems. Despite the efforts of Empress Dowager Wenming (*q.v.* Feng, Empress of Emperor Wencheng

298 HU, CONSORT OF EMPEROR XUANWU OF NORTHERN WEI

of Northern Wei) to institute land reforms in 483, most of the best land in the north and northwest had become imperial pasturelands and gentry families in the northeast were abusing their economic privileges. Cultural and racial tensions also existed between the Han Chinese and the non-Han nomadic leaders in the provinces as well as in the government. Initially, Empress Dowager Hu had support from the group that had protected her from the Gao family. Her first task was to neutralize the regent Yu Zhong, who was in opposition to her support group and had gained considerable military power. He was recalled to court once certain problems surrounding the regency had been settled and Empress Dowager Hu then became the de facto ruler. As regent, she carried out imperial sacrifices in place of her son, issued edicts, competed in archery contests with her officials, traveled the countryside to receive petitions, interviewed new candidates for office, and took frequent pleasure trips to sacred and scenic spots.

It is said that Emperor Xiaoming began participating in policy discussions in 518, when he was eight years old, and by the time he was nearly ten (in 520) there was widespread dissatisfaction with Dowager Empress Hu. She was criticized for her softhearted handling of Yu Zhong and for the way she dealt with those who had helped her in the past and with her family members. As they frequently did when documenting the lives of female rulers, the historians offered details of Empress Dowager Hu's personal life, including her sex life. She is said to have had a number of lovers, including a brother-in-law, and several of her lovers, such as Zheng Yan and Li Shengui, wielded enormous power. She had an affair with Counselor-in-Chief Tuoba Yi, who was then murdered by her brother-in-law. In speaking of this period, her official biography began to cast her in the role of the "Last Bad Ruler" of Northern Wei, emphasizing her immorality, lack of personal restraint, neglect of government affairs, and her jealousy.

In the wake of this dissatisfaction, Empress Dowager Hu's brother-in-law, Tuoba Cha (d. 525), and the eunuch Liu Teng conspired to remove her from power. They placed her under house arrest in 520 and forced her to retire from her regency. All those who had benefited during her regency were removed from their posts and she was forbidden to have any contact with her son, Emperor Xiaoming.

However, Tuoba Cha had little interest in government, and the dissatisfaction that officials and the imperial princes had felt under Empress Dowager Hu's regency resurfaced, now directed at him. The officials and princes turned to Empress Dowager Hu when appeals to Emperor Xiaoming to remove Tuoba Cha were disregarded. Under the pretext of obtaining the emperor's permission to enter a nunnery, she was allowed to meet with her son. Thus reconciled, mother and son plotted to remove Tuoba Cha, slowly stripping him of his power. Finally, convinced that Tuoba Cha was threatening his favorite concubine, Emperor Xiaoming ordered him to commit suicide.

Instead of handing authority to her fifteen-year-old son, Empress Dowager Hu resumed her regency in 525. Her second regency, characterized by corruption and lawlessness, has been described as the beginning of the end of Northern Wei. The whole of north China was in open rebellion by then and the capable officials who had assisted her in her first regency had either died of old age or been murdered. She appointed some Han-Chinese officials whose policies turned out to be irresponsible and whose Han ethnicity alienated her Tuoba subjects. As he matured, Emperor Xiaoming grew desperate about his mother's unwillingness to allow him to rule in his own right and in 528 he sought the help of Erzhu Rong (d. 530), a chieftain of the Jie people (possibly a branch of the Xiongnu) in Xiurong (in present-day Shanxi Province), in his attempt to break free of his mother's Chinese advisers. This was a disastrous move. The Chinese advisers had Emperor Xiaoming murdered and, angered at there being no direct male heir, Jie and Xianbei military leaders stormed the capital. Empress Dowager Hu placed Emperor Xiaoming's infant daughter on the throne but this was unacceptable to the Xiongnu and Xianbei, so she placed Emperor Xiaoming's two-year-old brother on the throne instead.

Erzhu Rong had other ideas, however. He proclaimed his own protégé—Tuoba Ziyou, a grandson of Emperor Xianwen (Tuoba Hong, 454–476; r. 465–471)—emperor in 528 and married him to his daughter, whom he gave the title Empress of Northern Wei. The gates of the capital were opened from the inside the following day by relatives of Empress Dowager Hu's own favorites and two days after that she was drowned, while Erzhu Rong's soldiers killed thousands of Han Chinese and pro-Chinese officials and their families. Empress Dowager Hu's sister collected her remains and placed them in Shuangling Buddhist Temple.

In the long and uneven career of Empress Dowager Hu as ruler of Northern Wei, we see a pattern apparent in many capable rulers, be they male or female. Their careers flourish through hard work and wise administration, but when they become well established they dissipate their energies in the pleasures and vices of autocratic rule. Empress Dowager Hu was no better and no worse than male rulers of her class, despite the historians' emphasis on what Chauncey Goodrich refers to as the "autocratic actions, extravagances, sexual promiscuity, and cruelty" of Empress Dowager Ling née Hu.

It must be mentioned that Empress Dowager Hu was also a poet. Her biography quotes two lines from poems she composed when writing poetry with her ministers. Also, a *yuefu* song entitled *Yang Baihua* has been attributed to her. This love poem expresses a woman's longing for a man whose name means the willow's white flower (*yang baihua*). The story goes that Empress Dowager Hu was in love with a general named Yang Baihua but, fearing incrimination, he fled south. Empress Dowager Hu composed this poem (here translated by Lily Xiao Hong Lee) and had her palace women sing it again and again:

> In the second and third months of Spring,
> The willows flower all at once.
> One night the Spring breeze came into my boudoir,
> But the willow flower flew to the South.
> Lovesick, supported by feeble legs I came out
> And picked a willow flower; tears wet my blouse.
> Autumn is gone and Spring is here, I wish the pair of swallows
> Would take a willow bloom into their love nest.

With the exception of the paragraph on Empress Dowager Hu's literary activities, this article has in large part been abstracted, with permission, from Jennifer Holmgren's paper, cited below.

LAU Lai Ming and Priscilla CHING-CHUNG

300 HU, CONSORT OF EMPEROR XUANWU OF NORTHERN WEI

Bei shi. Beijing: Zhonghua shuju, 1974, vol. 2, 13.503–5.
Bei Wei shi. Taiyuan: Shanxi gaojiao lianhe chubanshe, 1992, 362–92.
Goodrich, Chauncey S. "Two Chapters in the Life of an Empress of the Later Han." *Harvard Journal of Asiatic Studies* 25 (1964/65): 169.
Holmgren, Jennifer. "Empress-Dowager Ling of the Northern Wei and the T'o-pa Sinicization Question." *Papers on Far Eastern History* 18 (1978): 123–70.
Sima Guang. *Zizhi tongjian.* Shanghai: Zhonghua shuju, 1936.
Wei shu. Beijing: Zhonghua shuju, 1974, vol. 2, 13.337–40.
Zhang Jinlong. *Bei Wei zhengzishi yanjiu.* Lanzhou: Gansu jiaoyu chubanshe, 1996, 255–313.

Hua Mulan: *see* **Mulan**

Hui Jia Huanghou: *see* **Jia Nanfeng, Empress of Emperor Hui of Jin**

Huiguo

Huiguo, c. 364–433, was the Buddhist name of one of the earliest known Chinese Buddhist nuns (*bhikṣunī*). Her surname was Pan but her given secular name is not known, and she was from Huainan (in present-day Anhui Province). It was she whose efforts led to the regularization of the Buddhist assembly of nuns in China.

Buddhism made its way to China in the early years of the Eastern Han dynasty, and by the late second century the ranks of foreign Buddhist monks had been augmented by fully ordained Chinese monks. Buddhism did not gain widespread and popular support, however, until the Eastern Jin dynasty, and it was not until 433, during the Northern and Southern Dynasties, that the first Chinese women were fully ordained as Buddhist nuns in strict accordance with the *vinaya* (the books of monastic discipline).

The *vinaya* rules require ten monks with at least ten years' seniority as fully ordained monks to bestow on males the monastic obligations signifying full ordination. For females, however, the rules require not only ten such monks but also ten nuns with at least ten years' seniority as fully ordained nuns. While there were in the late second century Buddhist monasteries and convents in the northern city of Luoyang, capital of the Eastern Han dynasty, at no time did any of the convents contain ten fully ordained nuns. The first Chinese woman identified as a Buddhist nun—Zhu Jingjian (*q.v.*)—received the precepts of a novice in Luoyang in 317 from a foreign instructor, but she did not receive the complete obligation until 357, and only then from the assembly of monks, not the combined assembly of monks and nuns.

The northern heartland of China was lost to non-Chinese invaders in 317, causing a large southward migration of Chinese, especially of the nobility and aristocracy, to the Yangzi River valley where the capital of the dynasties in the south was established at Jiankang (the present-day city of Nanking).

During the Southern Dynasties the assembly of Buddhist nuns attained perhaps its highest degree of social influence and esteem, making it a favorable time for Huiguo to take the action that she did. The translation of scriptures (*sūtra*), or Buddha word, and their commentaries had begun almost as soon as Buddhism first entered China, but the translation of the *vinaya* texts had lagged behind. Huiguo sought to establish the assembly of nuns in China in complete accordance with the *vinaya* texts that were at that time becoming fully available to Chinese Buddhists in the Chinese language.

Monastics and laity alike admired Huiguo for her disciplined life and adherence to the monastic rules. During the Liu Song dynasty, the governor of Qingzhou (present-day Shandong Province) appointed her to serve as abbess of Jingfu Convent, which he had built for her in the capital. The community of nuns flourished under her monastic and spiritual authority.

In 429 a group of nuns from what is now Sri Lanka arrived at Jiankang and lodged in Huiguo's Jingfu Convent. They learned Chinese and gave serious consideration to the problem of whether or not the Chinese nuns had properly received the obligations of monastic life. In the year 431 the missionary monk Guṇavarman (367–431), a Central Asian from the kingdom of Kashmir, reached Jiankang and took up residence in Jetavana Monastery at the command of Emperor Wen (Liu Yilong, 407–453; r. 424–453). There Guṇavarman translated Buddhist texts, particularly the *vinaya* and bodhisattva precepts, into Chinese.

Prompted by the nuns from Sri Lanka and the newly translated *vinaya* texts, Huiguo and other Chinese nuns investigated the discrepancies between the stated requirements of the *vinaya* and what they themselves knew about the history of the transmission of the lineage of the nuns in China. Guṇavarman argued that the established lineage of nuns in China was adequate and in conformity with the following two precedents. The first precedent was the Buddha's stepmother, Mahāprajāpatī, who had received the obligations from the Buddha alone. The second precedent was the nuns who came after her, who had received the obligations from only the assembly of monks because at that time there were no nuns of ten years' standing. Guṇavarman stressed that the important thing to observe was the two-year training period for novices. In other words, being properly trained in the obligations was more important than the number of monks or nuns who helped bestow them.

When Huiguo persisted in her quest for a second reception of the obligations in full conformity with the *vinaya,* Guṇavarman acknowledged that ten members of the assembly were required but that in some circumstances, such as in a frontier country like China, only five were required. This being the case, the number of Sri Lankan nuns in the capital at that time would have been enough. Huiguo, however, did not accept Guṇavarman's assurances that, given the circumstances, the lineage of the Chinese assembly of nuns had been properly established. In the end, Guṇavarman acquiesced to her request for a second bestowal of the obligations in full accord with the *vinaya,* saying "The Buddhist threefold action of morality, meditation, and wisdom progresses from the slight to the obvious. Therefore, receiving the monastic obligations a second time is of greater benefit than receiving them only once."

Nevertheless, the nuns from Sri Lanka who were to comprise the assembly of nuns bestowing the obligation upon the Chinese women numbered fewer than ten, and of those not all had the required seniority. Guṇavarman therefore prevailed upon some laymen from the western regions to ask more foreign nuns to come to China to complete the quorum required for the supplementary bestowal of the monastic rules upon the Chinese nuns. Guṇavarman, however, died that same year, 431, before these plans could be carried out.

302 HUIGUO

In the year 433, the Indian monk Saṃghavarman arrived in Jiankang; he remained there until 442. The nun Tessara and ten others from Sri Lanka also arrived in China in 433, possibly as a result of Guṇavarman's earlier request to send more foreign nuns to China. With a quorum of ten nuns of ten years' seniority now present, Saṃghavarman readministered the monastic obligations to some 300 women, including Huiguo, Sengguo, Jingyin, Huiyi, and Huikai.

Huiguo's persistence, coupled with the availability of complete *vinaya* texts and the presence of the nuns from Sri Lanka, set the assembly of nuns in China on a firm foundation as regards lineage and authority. No longer could China be described as a Buddhist frontier. Huiguo was over seventy years old when she died in 433, the year she had received the monastic obligations for the second time.

Huiguo's determination has given the assembly of nuns in the Chinese lineage and in the lineages that derive from China the distinction of being fully legitimate. All other traditions of Buddhist monastic life for women restrict them to remaining novices for their entire monastic life. Nuns of the Chinese traditions therefore operate with the full authority allowed them according to the *vinaya*, which gives them an advantage the other lineages do not have in their dealings with monks and with the outside world.

Kathryn A. TSAI

Baochang [Pao-ch'ang]. "Huiguo zhuan." *Piqiuni zhuan, 2,* and "Zhu Jingjian zhuan," *Piqiuni zhuan, 1.* In *Taishō shinshū Daizōkyō,* ed. Takakusu Junjirō, Watanabe Kaigyoku, and Ono Genmyō. Tokyo: Taishō Issaikyō Kankōkai, 1924–1929, vol. 50, 937.

Baochang [Shih Pao-ch'ang]. *Lives of the Nuns: Biographies of Chinese Buddhist Nuns from the Fourth to Sixth Centuries: A Translation of the Pi-ch'iu-ni chuan,* trans. Kathryn Ann Tsai. Honolulu: University of Hawaii Press, 1994, 36–38.

Huijiao. "Qiunabamo (Guṇavarman) zhuan." *Gaoseng zhuan, 3,* and "Sengjiabamo (Saṃghavarman) zhuan," *Gaoseng zhuan, 3.* In *Taishō shinshū Daizōkyō,* ed. Takakusu Junjirō, Watanabe Kaigyoku, and Ono Genmyō. Tokyo: Taishō Issaikyō Kankōkai, 1924–1929, vol. 50.

Li Yuzhen. *Tangdai de biqiuni.* Taipei: Taiwan xuesheng shuju, 1989, 126–37.

Sengyou. "Sengjiabamo (Saṃghavarman) zhuan." *Chu sanzang ji ji, 14.* In *Taishō shinshū Daizōkyō,* ed. Takakusu Junjirō, Watanabe Kaigyoku, and Ono Genmyō. Tokyo: Taishō Issaikyō Kankōkai, 1924–1929, vol. 55.

Takakusu Junjirō, Watanabe Kaigyoku, and Ono Genmyō, eds. *Taishō shinshū Daizōkyō.* Tokyo: Taishō Issaikyō Kankōkai, 1924–1929.

Tsai, Kathryn Ann. "The Chinese Buddhist Monastic Order for Women: The First Two Centuries." in *Women in China: Current Directions in Historical Scholarship,* ed. Richard W. Guisso and Stanley Johannesen. Youngstown, NY: Philo Press, 1981, 1–20.

J

Jia Nanfeng, Empress of Emperor Hui of Jin

Jia Nanfeng, *zi* Shi, 256–300, was empress to Emperor Hui (Sima Zhong, 259–306; r. 290–306) of the Western Jin dynasty. Empress Jia of Emperor Hui (Hui Jia Huanghou) was her posthumous title. It is difficult to gain a clear picture of Jia Nanfeng from her biography in the official *History of the Jin Dynasty* (Jin shu), which presents a strongly biased view of her. It uses extremely pejorative language, describing her as "jealous and power hungry," a "butcher," and a "tyrant," and seems to have been designed to accentuate Jia Nanfeng's faults, presenting abbreviated anecdotes and often omitting significant information contained elsewhere in the *History* or in other historical accounts. In short, the *History of the Jin Dynasty* presents Jia Nanfeng as the stereotypical "tyrannical usurping empress," following the model of the *Historical Records* (Shi ji) account of Han Empress Lü (*q.v.* Lü Zhi, Empress of Emperor Gaozu) and portraying her as violent, cruel, and licentious. Many of the details of Jia Nanfeng's life presented here may therefore have been colored by the exaggerated and prejudiced nature of the original sources, especially, but not limited to, the *History of the Jin Dynasty.*

Jia Nanfeng was a native of Xiangling District, Pingyang Commandery (southeast of present-day Linfen in Shaanxi Province). Her grandfather and her father had both served the Wei dynasty in a variety of official posts. Her father, Jia Chong (*zi* Gonglü, 217–282) had been an early supporter of the powerful Sima clan, which had dominated the Wei court, and upon the establishment of the Jin dynasty by Sima Yan (Emperor Wu, 236–290; r. 265–290), he was instrumental in establishing a new legal code for the new state. He had considerable political clout under the Jin and was widely feared by court officials and members of the imperial family. Jia Nanfeng's mother, Guo Huai (*q.v.*), was Jia Chong's second wife. She is reported to have been extremely jealous and violent: suspecting her husband to be sexually involved with the wet nurses of two of her sons, she killed both women. Her infant sons refused to suck from another breast and they both died. Lady Guo had no other sons. She gave birth to at least one other daughter, Jia Wu, who was three years younger than Jia Nanfeng. A politically savvy woman, Lady Guo frequently offered advice to her older daughter after her rise to prominence.

Jia Nanfeng was selected as the consort-wife of Sima Zhong, the simple-minded thirteen-year-old heir to the throne, in 272, when she was fifteen. Her selection was not without controversy, however. The boy's mother, Empress Yang Yan (*q.v.* Yang Yan, Empress of Emperor Wu of Jin), was in favor of Jia Nanfeng, whose mother had offered the empress a bribe on behalf of her daughter, while his father, Emperor Wu, preferred a daughter of the high-ranking officer Wei Guan. Emperor Wu argued the relative merits of the two prospective brides thus: "The daughter of Master Wei has five qualities; the daughter of Master Jia has five faults. Miss Wei carries the seeds of sagacity and many sons, and is beautiful, tall, and fair. Miss Jia carries the seeds of jealousy and few sons, and is ugly, short, and dark." These remarks on Jia Nanfeng's appearance ensured that scores of later commentators described her as "incomparably ugly." Empress Yang countered by recruiting several high-ranking officials to praise Jia Nanfeng's virtues and character. She prevailed and Jia Nanfeng was named consort to the heir apparent. Consort Jia gave birth to four daughters: the Imperial Princess Aixian (a posthumous title meaning "Lamentfully Sacrificed," implying an early death), and the Princesses of Hedong, Linhai, and Shiping. In retrospect, Emperor Wu's assessment of his prospective daughter-in-law was correct, for Jia Nanfeng produced no sons.

Consort Jia immediately exercised her power at court, standing as an advocate for her husband. Emperor Wu had long doubted his son's mental competence and his ability to govern, while the boy's mother had argued that the establishment of an heir should be based on his position as first-born, not on sagacity. The emperor therefore ordered his court officials to administer an examination to the heir, posing a question that required a written response from Sima Zhong. "Fearing for her own position" were her husband not to become emperor, Consort Jia hastily arranged for a scholar to draft a written response. His answer was well crafted, employing lofty language and allusions to the canon that were clearly beyond Sima Zhong's intellectual capacity. Consort Jia ordered that a simpler reply be drafted, which Sima Zhong then copied and submitted to the emperor, who was pleased. The heir's former tutor, Wei Guan, remained suspicious, however, and regularly urged the emperor to select another successor to the throne. Jia Chong warned his daughter of Wei Guan's doubts and the threat he posed to her position.

Consort Jia was reportedly both jealous of and violent toward her female rivals in the heir's palace. She is said to have strangled several women with her bare hands and to have thrown halberds at pregnant rivals, "causing their sons to fall to the floor along with the blades." Hearing these gruesome reports, Emperor Wu sought to remove her from her position and imprison her in the Metal-Walled Compound (*Jinyong cheng*), a maximum-security detention facility outside the capital of Luoyang. Several important officials rushed to her aid, however, convincing the emperor to stay his hand. One argued, "Consort Jia is young, and a wife's nature is to be jealous. When she grows up, she will get over it." Consort Jia would have been in her early twenties at the time. Another, arguing on more pragmatic grounds, reminded the emperor: "Don't forget about Jia Gonglü [Chong]." The first Empress Yang (Yang Yan) had died in 274, to be succeeded in 276 by a second Empress Yang (*q.v.* Yang Zhi, Empress of Emperor Wu of Jin). The second Empress Yang made similar pleas on Consort Jia's behalf, warning of the political fallout from offending the powerful Jia Chong, who was finally removed from the equation when he died in 282.

Empress Yang frequently admonished Consort Jia, hoping she would modify her behavior. Unaware that the empress had her best interests at heart, however, Consort Jia took the criticisms personally and developed a deep hatred for this second Empress Yang.

With the death of Emperor Wu in 290, Sima Zhong assumed the throne and Consort Jia Nanfeng was officially named empress. For the decade prior to his death, Emperor Wu had been uninterested in government, preferring to indulge in wine and women and cede political power to his father-in-law, Yang Jun (d. 291), and Yang's two brothers. As the emperor approached death, Yang Jun and his clique took measures to retain control after the accession of the heir. With the apparent aid of his daughter, the second Empress Yang, Yang Jun orchestrated a deathbed edict granting him regency over Sima Zhong. After Emperor Wu died, Yang Jun took up residence in the Basilica of the Supreme Ultimate, the palace in which imperial duties were discharged; this was tantamount to proclaiming himself emperor. The *History of the Jin Dynasty* notes that the only thing Yang Jun feared was Jia Nanfeng, now Empress Jia.

As empress, Jia Nanfeng set about consolidating her own power to combat Yang Jun and his daughter Yang Zhi, now Empress Dowager Yang, gathering about her members of the Jia and Guo clans, as well as various members of her husband's family and a group of loyal civil officials. In mid-291, citing reports of a planned coup by Yang Jun, Empress Jia ordered the arrest of Yang Jun. Yang Jun refused to surrender, his residence was set ablaze, and he was killed trying to escape the inferno. Empress Jia ensured that his daughter, Empress Dowager Yang, was also implicated in the conspiracy and had her arrested. After stripping the empress dowager of her rank and titles, Empress Jia ordered that she be imprisoned in the Metal-Walled Compound and had her starved to death. Shortly afterward, the empress invited her husband's kinsman Sima Liang to return to the capital to take up a government post, summoning Wei Guan to court under a similar pretext. Then, conspiring with Sima Wei, another imperial kinsman, she had Sima Liang and Wei Guan arrested and executed. The top civil official Zhang Hua then advised Empress Jia to arrest and execute her former ally Sima Wei, which she did. By 292, Empress Jia was in full control of the court, with her allies Zhang Hua and Pei Wei in charge of the civil government.

Jia Nanfeng's sexual conduct came in for comment in the *History of the Jin Dynasty*, her Tang biographers apparently determined to link the political power she wielded to what they regarded as negative aspects of her character. Her "public affairs" outside the palace with the imperial physician Cheng Qu and others are noted, as is a rather strange story that would be more at home in a novel than in an official history. A petty official (*xiao li*) found in possession of clothes and other objects clearly beyond his means was suspected of theft or robbery. He confessed that he had been taken to an opulent place where he had slept and feasted with a short, dark woman for several days before being given good clothes and other gifts and allowed to go. Those who heard his confession realized that the woman had been Empress Jia. The official was considered the lucky one who got away because the empress really liked him; others who had had a similar experience had been killed. Not long after this incident, one of Empress Jia's daughters became ill. Perhaps to deflect possible repercussions from the spirit world because of these killings, and to win a cure for her daughter, Empress Jia declared a general amnesty. This episode was presumably included in her biography to characterize her as greedy, lustful, and superstitious.

The miscarriage of a son led Empress Jia to adopt a young nephew, intending to have him named heir to the throne. Before he married Jia Nanfeng, Sima Zhong had sired a son born to one of his father's concubines who had been on loan to teach him the arts of the bedchamber. This boy, Sima Yu, had been raised outside the palace for fear he would attract the wrath of Jia Nanfeng, and he had eventually been named heir apparent. Jia Nanfeng's mother had advised her daughter to befriend the young heir and treat him as a son. The empress ignored this advice, however, and grew increasingly contemptuous of the heir. Early in the year 300, she invited Sima Yu to court, got him intoxicated, and had him sign a treasonous letter. Once he had sobered up and realized that he had signed a document implicating himself in a plot to overthrow his father the emperor, Sima Yu committed suicide. At this point, even the empress's most loyal supporters Zhang Hua, Pei Wei, and her own kinsmen Jia Mi and Jia Mo became

306   JIA NANFENG

disturbed at her arrogance. They discussed her removal from the throne and replacing her with another palace lady. Although these plans were abandoned, the fact that her closest allies debated this issue indicates that while it was acceptable for an empress to manipulate and to murder challengers to her husband's position, any efforts to void the emperor's wishes with regard to imperial succession could not be tolerated.

As word of Empress Jia's efforts to manipulate the succession spread, members of the Sima clan again plotted against her and against the throne itself. Sima Lun, a half-brother to Emperor Hui, and their cousin Sima Jiong entered the capital in early 300 and presented orders to the empress demanding her arrest. Challenging the orders, the empress said, "If there is such an edict, it must have come from me!" Then, confronting her husband (the *History of the Jin Dynasty* implies that the order originated with Sima Zhong, or at least that it had his seal of approval), Empress Jia said, "Your Majesty has a wife. If these subjects remove her, then you have just removed yourself!" The empress was arrested and executed, and a few days later most of her supporters, including Zhang Hua and Pei Wei, were also killed. Less than a year later, Emperor Hui was forced to abdicate in favor of his half-brother Sima Lun, thus fulfilling Empress Jia's prediction. The decade and a half of internecine warfare that ensued as various members of the Sima clan battled for control is known as "The Rebellion of the Eight Princes." These internal conflicts weakened the state, leading to conquest by nomadic warriors and the exile of the Jin court to the region south of the Yangzi in 317.

The *History of the Jin Dynasty* portrays Jia Nanfeng in a negative light as jealous, cruel, licentious, and a usurper of imperial authority, choosing to ignore her achievement in managing to hold the Jin empire together during the rule of an incapable emperor. She protected her husband's position on the throne from the families of the late Emperor Wu's empresses, from various imperial relatives, and from plotting officials. Without question, Jia Nanfeng was also protecting her own position and power, but her actions may also be viewed from the perspective of the filial daughter-in-law honoring the wishes of her husband's deceased father, particularly with regard to succession to the throne. Moreover, as empress she employed able and loyal officials to oversee the administration. That the dynasty fell apart immediately following her death speaks to her political talent. However, the notion of a female ruler ran against the sensibilities of traditional historians, so that the compilers of the *History of the Jin Dynasty* went to great lengths to emphasize the immorality of Jia Nanfeng. They spoke of her in pejorative terms and emphasized her sexual affairs in order to focus on the scandalous nature of her life, rather than the benefits to the state afforded by her rule. This was not unique to the *History of the Jin Dynasty,* a number of early texts, many of them sources for the later *History* account, adopting a similar approach. Early appraisals of Jia Nanfeng were colorful and overwhelmingly negative.

One of the most pervasive evaluations of Jia Nanfeng originates in a misreading of Zhang Hua's *Admonitions of the Female Scribe* (Nüshi zhen). The traditional interpretation of this work claims it was written around 292 to criticize Empress Jia for manipulating imperial relatives and killing political rivals. This reading is illogical, however, as Zhang Hua was himself a co-conspirator in many of these events. Moreover, for Zhang Hua to criticize the empress, even obliquely, would have undoubtedly brought about his own execution. It is more likely that the piece was a criticism of the efforts of Empress Dowager Yang Zhi and her father to manipulate the regency immediately before the death of Emperor Wu in 290. Nevertheless, Zhang's admonition is widely regarded as a "loyal critique" of Empress Jia, a view furthered by the visual representation of the essay by the noted Jin painter Gu Kaizhi (a Tang reproduction survives in collections in Beijing and London), and many commentaries on the painting attempting to link the images with the historical tale of Jia Nanfeng.

While she was clearly a strong woman, protective, and capable of holding her own in the male-dominated world of imperial politics, Jia Nanfeng is doomed to be remembered as a jealous, cruel, blood-thirsty, usurping tyrannical empress. This historiographic fact speaks more to the misogynistic power of historical memory than to any real evaluation of the woman herself.

J. Michael FARMER

Farmer, J. Michael. "On the Composition of Zhang Hua's 'Nüshi zhen.'" *Early Medieval China* 10/11.1 (2004): 151–75.
Jin shu. Beijing: Zhonghua shuju, 1974, 31.963–66.
Liu I-ch'ing [Yiqing]. *Shih-shuo Hsin-yü: A New Account of Tales of the World*, trans. Richard B. Mather. Minneapolis: University of Minnesota Press, 1976, 281, 486.
Liu Shisheng. *Zhongguo gudai funüshi*. Qingdao: Qingdao chubanshe, 1991, 155–58.
Liu Yiqing, comp. *Shishuo xinyu*. Shanghai: Shanghai guji, 1993, fascicles 10 and 35.
Sima Guang. *Zizhi tongjian*, 79–80. Taipei: Shijie shuju, 1977, 2612–40.
Zhao Mengxiang, ed. *Zhongguo huanghou quanzhuan*. Beijing: Zhongguo shehuikexue chubanshe, 2004, vol. 1, 218–32.

Jia Wu: *see* **Guo Huai**

Jingjian: *see* **Zhu Jingjian**

L

Li Luoxiu
Li Luoxiu, fl. early fourth century, was a native of Runan (present-day Runan in Henan Province), where her family had probably enjoyed a certain status. However, Li Luoxiu lived in a period of great tumult, at the juncture of Western Jin and Eastern Jin, when a great number of wealthy families gave up their land and political position in the north to seek peace and security in the south, across the Yangzi River. As a result of their displacement these families lost the exalted social standing they had enjoyed in their native place. In the case of the Li family, this decline in family fortune occurred when Li Luoxiu was young.

Li Luoxiu was the only member of her family at home one day when an important visitor appeared on their doorstep. Zhou Jun, General Pacifying the East (*andong*

308   LI LUOXIU

jiangjun) and Regional Inspector (*cishi*) of Yangzhou, had gone out hunting and, caught in the rain, he and his large entourage sought shelter at the Li residence. The Li family was well enough off to offer them hospitality but, as a young woman alone, Li Luoxiu did not show herself to her visitors. As soon as she realized an important person had arrived, she and a maidservant directed the butchering of a pig and a lamb and prepared a meal for several dozen people. They made not a sound as the food was prepared yet everything was well organized. Curious as to what was going on, General Zhou Jun peeked inside and saw a young woman of distinguished appearance. In due course, he approached the family, asking for this young woman as his concubine. Li Luoxiu's father and brothers would not consent, but she said to them, "The family's standing is not what it once was; why are you unhappy to part with one daughter? It may be of great benefit to us to contract a marriage with a noble family." Persuaded by her logic and her willingness to be married to Zhou Jun, her family agreed.

Li Luoxiu went to General Zhou Jun as his concubine (one source says she became his official wife, not a concubine) and bore him three sons—Zhou Yi, Zhou Song, and Zhou Mo—all of whom went on to take up important posts in the government. She used to lecture her sons about treating her natal family with respect, saying, "The only reason I accepted a lower position to become a concubine in your family was for the sake of my family. If you do not treat my family as your own, I do not wish to go on living." Her sons eventually heeded her words and began to treat the Li family in public as an equal of the Zhou family.

Li Luoxiu was a woman who had the welfare of her natal family firmly in mind at a time when women were supposed to put their husband's family first. It appears from her unusual behavior that she valued herself and her own aspirations more highly than society thought necessary. If she did indeed lower herself to become a concubine to Zhou Jun, such a sacrifice on her part highlights her determination to raise the status of her natal family.

Lily Xiao Hong LEE

Jin shu. Beijing: Zhonghua shuju, 1974, vol. 8, 96.2514–15.
Liu I-ch'ing [Yiqing]. *Shih-shuo Hsin-yü: A New Account of Tales of the World,* trans. Richard B. Mather. Minneapolis: University of Minnesota Press, 1976, 202–3, 350.
Liu Yiqing. *Shishuo xinyu jian shu,* ed. Yu Jiaxi. Beijing: Zhonghua shuju, 1983, 7.397; 19.688–90.

Li Wan: *see* **Guo Huai**

Liang Lüzhu: *see* **Lüzhu**

Linchuan Zhang Gongzhu: *see* **Liu Yingyuan**

Ling née Hu, Empress Dowager: *see* **Hu, Consort of Emperor Xuanwu of Northern Wei**

Lingzong

Lingzong, fl. 372–396, whose secular surname was Man, was a nun; she was known for her work with the poor. She was a native of Jinxiang in Gaoping Commandery (in present-day Shandong Province) and gained a reputation among members of her clan and her village for her purity and faith.

During her youth there was a disturbance in her area and she was captured and carried off to the north by bandits. Placing her faith in the Buddha, she recited the "Universal Gate" (Pumen pin) chapter of *Flower of the Law Sutra* (Fahua jing), a direct appeal to Guanyin, the Goddess of Mercy. However, Lingzong was also practical: she plucked her eyebrows, pretending she suffered from a nasty disease, and begged on that account to be released. Her ploy succeeded and upon her release she headed south, retracing the way they had come. When she reached Jizhou (in the region of the present-day provinces of Hebei, Shandong, and Henan), however, bandits set upon her again. This time she escaped, climbing a dead tree, where she prayed fervently and silently. Her pursuers searched the road, never thinking to look up, and, failing to find her, finally left. Lingzong continued her journey into the night. She was afraid to beg for food for fear of exposing her whereabouts, yet she was not hungry. That night she reached the ford across the Yellow River at Mengjin, in present-day Henan Province, but there was no boat to ferry her across. Afraid and anxious, again she prayed, and it is said that she was saved by a miracle: she saw a white deer and followed it across the river without getting wet. A white deer often appears in Buddhist mythology to rescue the saintly or the faithful.

When Lingzong returned home, she entered the religious life and her reputation both in religious faith and as a learned Buddhist scholar reached Eastern Jin in the south. Emperor Xiaowu (Sima Yao, 362–396; r. 372–396) communicated with her by letter.

Lingzong lived at a time when north China was ravaged by war. It was a time of upheaval during which leaders of ethnic minorities struggled for supremacy after the collapse of the Han-Chinese Western Jin dynasty. Hundreds of thousands of people were uprooted and lost their livelihoods, many becoming sick and poor. Lingzong did her utmost to provide for them, and when her own resources were exhausted she would travel to distant places begging for food or money, which she then distributed to those in genuine need of charity. A great many people owed their lives to her. She often went hungry herself and worked so hard that she grew haggard and weary. She died in her seventy-fifth year while discussing with her disciples and colleagues a fabulous dream she had had.

While it was usual for Buddhists to give to the poor, it was especially so for Buddhist nuns; Zhu Jingjian (*q.v.*), for example, is said to have distributed to the poor and needy gifts she had received from the rich and powerful. Lingzong, however, appears to have been the only Buddhist nun to devote herself entirely to this cause. Although not elaborated upon in her biography, it is known that she also worked among the sick. Much about Lingzong is reminiscent of the twentieth-century Roman Catholic nun Mother Teresa: she, too, resorted to begging to help the poor and grew haggard working so hard for those she sought to help.

Lily Xiao Hong LEE

310 LINGZONG

Baochang [Pao-ch'ang]. "Lingzong zhuan." *Piqiuni zhuan, 2.* In *Taishō shinshū Daizōkyō,* ed. Takakusu Junjirō, Watanabe Kaigyoku, and Ono Genmyō. Tokyo: Taishō Issaikyō Kankōkai, 1924–1929, vol. 50, 936.

Baochang [Shih Pao-ch'ang]. *Lives of the Nuns: Biographies of Chinese Buddhist Nuns from the Fourth to Sixth Centuries: A Translation of the Pi-ch'iu-ni chuan,* trans. Kathryn Ann Tsai. Honolulu: University of Hawaii Press, 1994, 31–33.

Hong Pimou. *Zhongguo ming ni.* Shanghai: Shanghai renmin chubanshe, 1995, 14–15.

Tsai, Kathryn Ann. "The Chinese Buddhist Monastic Order for Women: The First Two Centuries." In *Women in China: Current Directions in Historical Scholarship,* ed. Richard W. Guisso and Stanley Johannesen. Youngstown, NY: Philo Press, 1981, 1–20.

Liu Lingxian

Liu Lingxian, fl. early to mid-sixth century, from Langye (present-day Shandong Province), wrote prose and poetry and was the youngest of three famous literary sisters. The biography in *History of the Liang Dynasty* (Liang shu) of her brother Liu Xiaozhuo states that the family was originally from Pengcheng (in the region of the present-day provinces of northwest Jiangsu and southern Shandong). Her father, Liu Hui, had been an official with the Southern Qi dynasty and more than seventy of her brothers, cousins, and nephews were talented writers, a phenomenon their contemporaries during the Liang dynasty regarded as unprecedented. Liu Xiaozhuo in particular had been well known for his literary ability from childhood and gained patronage from Emperor Wu (Xiao Yan, 464–549; r. 502–549) and from the heir apparent Crown Prince Zhaoming (Xiao Tong, 501–531), who is known for compiling and editing the monumental literary anthology *Wen xuan.*

While all three of the Liu sisters are said to have been talented writers, we know the personal name of only the youngest, and probably the best known, of them. The eldest sister was married to Wang Shuying; two of her poems are extant. The middle sister was married to Zhang Cheng; unfortunately, none of her works is extant. Liu Lingxian, popularly known as The Third Miss Liu (Liu Sanniang), was married to Xu Fei, Governor of Jin'an Commandery (present-day Minhou District, Fujian Province). Xu Fei died in office and when his cortège returned to the capital Jiankang (present-day Nanjing), Liu Lingxian wrote an elegiac oratory (*jiwen*) expressing her anguish. Her father-in-law had intended to write an elegy, but gave up the idea when he read hers.

Ten of Liu Lingxian's poems and her most famous work, the elegiac oratory for her husband, have survived and are gathered in Xie Wuliang's book on the history of the literature of Chinese women cited below. Most of them are on the theme of women waiting for their loved ones and how they spend their empty days, as shown in Anne Birrell's translation (178) of one of her two poems entitled *Reply to My Husband*:

> Flowery garden lovely with rays slanting,
> Through orchid window soft breezes cross.
> The sun sinks. She freshens her cosmetics,
> Opens the blinds onto spring trees.
> Warbling orioles in foliage echo,
> Playful butterflies amid flowers flurry.
> She strums her lute in joy's own pursuit,

Her heart from sadness will not be diverted.
Their happy hour together not remote,
Yet her betrothed now she will not meet.
Would you know how much she grieves in secret?
Her spring boudoir is withdrawn and shaded.

Occasionally, Liu Lingxian ventured outside her boudoir, as evidenced by the poem below, originally entitled *Guangzhai Temple* but translated by Anne Birrell (280) as *Cloistered:*

Delightful to send my gaze down verandahs,
Pleasant to enjoy views of spacious halls.
But when will I live in cloistered rooms
Dark and gloomy, far from human noise?

Her delight at getting out of her boudoir is obvious, as is her desire for privacy in a society where it was in short supply. Only in the isolation of a Buddhist temple could she hope to enjoy such solitude.

Her poem in response to a woman named Tang Niang, or Miss Tang, who seems to have been a courtesan, is somewhat unusual. According to Birrell, Tang Niang was the mistress of Liu Lingxian's late husband and instead of the original title—*In Response to Tang Niang on the Needle She Threaded on the Eve of the Double Seven*—she gives it the title *To My Late Husband's Mistress* in her translation (180):

Singers attend to the Han River girl,
Her painted face enjoys the moon's glory.
Chain-stitch images twin stems,
Lacework forms opening buds.
But widowed rooms dismiss fine silks.
To take your gift would touch a painful wound.
Though I admit not knowing you,
I've heard it said you are well-born.
In the past Huo Kuang halted his coach here,
Liu Hsia-hui used to call in his carriage.
There is no way that we can talk together.
I'm watching sunrise through dawn mist for ever.

It is clear from this poem that Tang Niang was a courtesan and while there was no specific prohibition in early pre-modern China against respectable women befriending courtesans, such conduct was rare. This may be the earliest example of just such a cross-societal relationship. Sharing a love for the same man might have prompted Liu Lingxian to take this unusual action.

The elegiac oratory for her husband contains the following moving lines:

Although our paths are separate, one of the living, one of the dead,
Our love remains the same.
May I prepare ginger and orange for you,

312   *LIU LINGXIAN*

With the taste you favored when you were alive?
The sacrificial wine bottle was emptied in vain,
Cups overflowed for no one.
It was different when I first married you.
You left for a time to follow the army, but
Your thoughts were with the one who stayed home.
This time, like the flying tumbleweed,
You will never return from your journey.
Now that I have to bid you farewell forever,
My anguish is without end.
How long is one hundred years?
I shall meet you again only when I go to my grave.

Liu Lingxian was probably still young when her husband died and would have lived as a widow for a number of years after his death.

The poems written by Liu Lingxian's eldest sister, the wife of Wang Shuying, are sometimes attributed to Liu Lingxian. Two poems on the subject of female figures in history seem to be by the same hand, yet one—*Response to [Ban] Jieyu's Regrets*—is attributed to Liu Lingxian while the other—*Response to Wang Zhaojun's Regret*—is attributed to her eldest sister. Both poems display a deep understanding of these historic figures and empathy for their unfortunate fate. The following poem, translated by Anne Birrell (228) as *Lady Pan's Regret,* refers to the story of Ban Jieyu (*q.v.* Ban Jieyu, Concubine of Emperor Cheng) and Empress Zhao Feiyan (*q.v.* Zhao Feiyan, Empress of Emperor Cheng), praising Ban Jieyu's moral rectitude and her ability to remain aloof from palace intrigues:

Sunset closes Ying Gate,
Despairing love breeds a hundred cares.
All the more since Chaoyang Palace is close,
And winds carry songs and piping sounds.
Fickle favor she does not hate,
But her rival's heartless slander so malicious.
She just says she has loftier ideals,
Never envies that light dancer's waist.

Lily Xiao Hong LEE

Birrell, Anne, trans. *New Songs from a Jade Terrace: An Anthology of Early Chinese Love Poetry.* London: Allen & Unwin, 1982, 178, 180, 228, 280.
Jiang Minfan and Wang Ruifang. *Zhongguo lidai cainü xiaozhuan.* Hangzhou: Zhejiang wenyi chubanshe, 1984, 767–80.
Tan Zhengbi. *Zhongguo nüxing wenxueshi.* Tianjin: Baihua wenyi chubanshe, 1984, 98.
Wang Yanti. *Zhongguo gudai nüzuojia ji.* Jinan: Shandong daxue chubanshe, 1999, 111, 112–13.
Xie Wuliang. *Zhongguo funü wenxueshi.* Shanghai: Zhonghua shuju, 1916; Zhengzhou: Zhongzhou guji chubanshe, 1992, rpt, Section IIC, 82–84.
Xu Ling. *Yutai xinyong.* Sibubeiyao ed., 6.13b–16b, 8.15a–b, 9.25a, 10.11b.

Liu Sanniang: *see* **Liu Lingxian**

Liu Yingyuan

Liu Yingyuan, Grand Princess of Linchuan (Linchuan Zhang Gongzhu), b. c. 430, was the sixth daughter of Emperor Wen (Liu Yilong, 407–453; r. 424–453) of the Liu Song dynasty. After missing two chances at happiness she finally saved herself by admitting her own guilt and trying to make amends for wrongs she had committed.

Born a princess, Liu Yingyuan enjoyed all the privileges and opportunities of the nobility, including a luxurious lifestyle, a surfeit of fineries, and a good education. Coddled by nurses and maids from childhood, she probably never had to lift a finger. Princesses like her raised in such a milieu grew spoiled and reckless, used to having their own way. After marriage, however, it was for her a different matter.

Liu Yingyuan married Wang Zao, a second cousin who came from a distinguished family. He had a homosexual relationship with a favorite male companion and this made Liu Yingyuan insanely jealous. During the brief reign of her nephew Liu Ziye (known to history as the Former Deposed Emperor [Qianfeidi]; r. 464–465), she made false and malicious statements about her husband, who was imprisoned and died. Liu Yingyuan disowned her husband's family, leaving her young son with them.

When, soon afterward, Liu Yingyuan's brother Liu Yu (Emperor Ming, 439–472; r. 465–472) ascended the throne, he arranged for her to marry another man, but this man died before the marriage took place. Emperor Ming had himself narrowly escaped execution at the hands of his nephew, the Former Deposed Emperor, and this had deeply traumatized him, making him very sympathetic to men who were chosen to marry princesses. It appears that Emperor Ming's niece (the Princess of Shanyin) had been a trusted ally of her ruthless brother, the Former Deposed Emperor, and had been just as ruthless and lawless. A feisty young woman, she had accompanied her imperial brother on his rounds and demanded—and got—a male harem of her own, which she saw as her equal right. This horrible memory must have remained with Emperor Ming for he even appointed someone to write a memorial on behalf of a Jiang Xiao, who was about to marry a princess, declining the honor. This memorial enumerated all the disadvantages and risks inherent in marrying a princess and included a reference to Wang Zao, who had lost his life on account of what the emperor called a jest. Emperor Ming showed this memorial to all the princesses and when Liu Yingyuan read it she must have felt remorse for causing Wang Zao's death, for she then expressed a desire to be reunited with her son. She memorialized her willingness to return to the Wang family, a request granted by Emperor Ming. This poignant memorial, which is preserved in the *History of the [Liu] Song Dynasty* (Song shu), reads in part:

> My fate is extremely unfortunate, because I broke off relations with the Wang family. My arrogance and violent temper in the privacy of our home led to this estrangement. . . . Alone and sick, I am now so lonely. I may stop breathing any day but my only concern is my son. Our separation has caused me so much suffering; I also feel very sorry for him. Whether I flourish or wither, in good fortune or bad, my life is bound to his. I am truly willing to let go of my grudge against his family and resume with him the relationship of mother and son.

314 LIU YINGYUAN

For an arrogant princess like Liu Yingyuan it must have been difficult to admit that she had been at fault and humble herself to the point of asking to return to the family she had rejected. But for the sake of her son and whatever happiness she might still enjoy, she was willing to take this step. Her memorial is an example of writing with true feeling that touches people's hearts across the ages.

Lily Xiao Hong LEE

Jiang Fan. "Shishuo xinyu zhong fuma yu gongzhu de hunyin beiju." *Wenshi zhishi*, 2004,1, 67–73; 2004, 2, 50–56.
Song shu. Beijing: Zhonghua shuju, 1974, vol. 4, 41.1290–92.
Wang Yanti, ed. *Zhongguo gudai nüzuojia ji.* Jinan: Shandong daxue chubanshe, 1999, 104–5.

Lou Zhaojun, Empress of Emperor Shenwu of Northern Qi

Lou Zhaojun, 501–562, was the principal wife of Gao Huan, 496–547; their son Emperor Wenxuan (Gao Yang, 529–559; r. 550–559) was the founding emperor of Northern Qi. While neither was appointed emperor or empress during their lifetime, as the de facto founder of the Northern Qi dynasty Gao Huan was posthumously titled Emperor Shenwu of Northern Qi and Lou Zhaojun was posthumously titled Empress Ming of Northern Qi. Lou Zhaojun's life was inextricably bound up in the complex and violent events surrounding the breakup of the non-Han Northern Wei dynasty (386–534) and the consequent establishment of Eastern Wei (534–550), which preceded Northern Qi.

The Northern Wei dynasty had been founded by the non-Chinese Tuoba clan, a branch of the nomadic Xianbei (Xianbi) people of the steppe region north of China. The dynasty gradually adopted Chinese customs and in 493 Emperor Xiaowen Sinicized his surname to Yuan and moved his capital to Luoyang (*vide* Feng, Empress of Emperor Wencheng of Northern Wei *and* Feng, Empress of Emperor Xiaowen of Northern Wei). Lou Zhaojun was from a wealthy Xianbei family that had served as officials under the Former Yan dynasty (located in the area of present-day Chaoyang in Liaoning Province). Her clan had Sinicized its name to Lou toward the end of the fifth century.

Gao Huan, on the other hand, was from a Han-Chinese family from Bohai (present-day Hebei Province); they had lived for several generations in the area that is now Inner Mongolia and had consequently adopted a largely Xianbei way of life.

Despite Gao Huan's lack of means and low social status, Lou Zhaojun is said to have set her heart on him almost from the moment she saw him. She dispatched a maid to tell him of her interest and to give him some money; then she married him, against the wishes of her parents. The money she had given Gao Huan enabled him to set himself up with a horse, a military post, and a small group of followers, and their marriage gave him access to a wider circle of Xianbei and Xiongnu officials in the northern garrisons. It also secured him the personal support of men who had some connection with the great military houses of Northern Wei. Gao Huan became a virtual mercenary, hiring himself and his followers out to small chieftains and rebels until, around 528, as Northern Wei began to crumble, he became a general for Erzhu Rong (493–530) of Xiurong (in present-day Shanxi Province). Erzhu Rong belonged to the Jie people, possibly a branch of the Xiongnu, who came from the western regions, perhaps as far away as ancient Persia. As allies of the Northern Wei Tuoba, the Erzhu clan had been given a large fief that enabled them to control the major private source of supply of animals and fodder for the Northern Wei armies. By the end of the fifth century they had become extremely wealthy, while the rapid disintegration of Tuoba power and the outbreak of rebellion along the northern borders in 524 further extended their influence. By the late 520s, they had become the most effective military force in the empire.

Erzhu Rong's armies joined forces with Xianbei troops to storm the Northern Wei capital (Luoyang) in 528 after Han-Chinese officials murdered the young Emperor Xiaoming (Yuan Xu, 510–528; r. 515–528). Then, in a lethal series of moves and countermoves, Gao Huan outwitted Erzhu Rong in their struggle for control of the Northern Wei throne (*vide* Hu, Consort of Emperor Xuanwu of Northern Wei). Erzhu Rong's puppet emperor (Yuan Ziyou, r. 528–530) murdered him in 530; then Gao Huan had Yuan Ziyou murdered before he installed his own puppet emperor (Yuan Ye, r. 530). Finally, when the last emperor of Northern Wei (Yuan Xiu, r. 532–534) fled to Chang'an in the west and the territory that had once belonged to Northern Wei split in two, Gao Huan installed Yuan Shanbei as titular emperor of Eastern Wei (Emperor Xiaojing, r. 534–550) and assumed de facto rule of the new dynasty. The capital was moved south from Pingcheng (the present-day city of Taiyuan) to Ye (between present-day Anyang in Henan Province and Cixian in Hebei Province).

As Gao Huan's power grew, he took more wives. Lou Zhaojun encouraged him in this, understanding the importance of consolidating his already considerable influence through marriage alliances with powerful families. She herself bore six of Gao Huan's fifteen sons and she harbored ambitions for all of them; three of her sons were named emperor before she died and she helped stage a coup that deposed one of her grandsons from the Northern Qi throne.

Lou Zhaojun's eldest son, Gao Cheng (d. 550), assumed the regency of Eastern Wei upon the death of Gao Huan in 547 and retained the loyalty of the leaders within its borders while expanding its domain. However, within three years he had been assassinated and it seems likely that his assassination was arranged by his brother Gao Yang, Lou Zhaojun's second son.

Rather than assume the role of regent, Gao Yang forced the Eastern Wei emperor to abdicate in 550 and formally declared himself emperor of the new Northern Qi dynasty. The traditional Xianbei line of succession had been from brother to brother and serious political problems immediately arose, with brothers and half-brothers contending violently for the throne. Gao Yang had two of the more influential of his half-brothers executed, but his brothers, their sons, and the sons of Gao Cheng continued to jostle for supremacy. Upon the death of Gao Yang, however, his fourteen-year-old son Gao Yin (d. 560?) was placed on the throne. It was at this time that Lou Zhaojun was named Grand Empress Dowager.

The young emperor was unable to strip his uncles of their power, and Lou Zhaojun regarded the position of emperor as belonging rightfully to one of her sons rather than

316 LOU ZHAOJUN

her grandson. She therefore helped engineer a coup. Together with two of her four remaining sons she had Gao Yin's advisers seized and executed before deposing the boy; Gao Yin is thus known in history as the Deposed Emperor (Feidi, r. 559–560).

Gao Yan (Emperor Xiaozhao, r. 560–561) was the next of Lou Zhaojun's sons to become emperor. He had been party to the overthrow of his nephew, whom he arranged to have strangled to ensure he did not attempt to regain the throne. Gao Yan's brief reign came to an abrupt end when he was critically injured in a fall from a horse.

Gao Zhan (Emperor Wucheng, 537–568; r. 561–565), Lou Zhaojun's fifth son and the last to become emperor, had also been involved in her plot to overthrow the young Gao Yin. After a short reign, he retired in favor of his nine-year-old son Gao Wei (known in history as The Last Ruler [Houzhu], 556–578; r. 565–577) (*vide* Lu Lingxuan).

This series of aborted primogenital successions and successful fraternal successions in Northern Qi may have been due in part to Lou Zhaojun's desire to see all of her sons become emperor, but it also reflected the traditional Xianbei system of fraternal succession, which had been gradually replaced during the fifth century by the Han-Chinese system. It was not until after Lou Zhaojun died in 562 that the succession from father to son, in the Chinese tradition, was reinstated.

Lou Zhaojun is said to have been a resolute and intelligent woman and the record confirms this. She remained impartial, never asking her husband to appoint her relatives to high-ranking positions but instead expecting them to earn any such privilege. Such was her ambition for her husband that she encouraged him to enter into several marriage alliances and treated these consorts as her own sisters. She even stepped down from her position as principal consort, ceding it to a Rouran princess in order to ensure her people's cooperation (the Rouran were a nomadic group located in present-day Outer Mongolia; they controlled the eastern section of the area now known as the Silk Road). She managed the inner palaces for her husband and is said to have regarded all of Gao Huan's sons as her own. She wove the material from which a long gown and a pair of trousers were made for each of his sons; in order to set an example, she had clothes made for warriors who were loyal to Gao Huan. Things did not always go smoothly between Lou Zhaojun and Gao Huan, however, and he banished her in 538 after discovering that their eldest son, Gao Cheng, had had an affair with one of his concubines. Lou Zhaojun and her son each received 100 strokes in punishment and Lou Zhaojun remained in disfavor until Gao Huan's companion Sima Ziru (488–551) reminded him of the contribution Lou Zhaojun had made.

Priscilla CHING-CHUNG and TAI Po Ying

Bei Qi shu. Beijing: Zhonghua shuju, 1972, vol. 1, 9.123–24.

Eisenberg, Andrew. "Retired Emperorship and the Politics of Succession in the Northern Dynasties of China, 386–581." Ph.D. dissertation, University of Washington, 1991, 129–66.

Holmgren, Jennifer. "Family, Marriage and Political Power in Sixth Century China: A Study of the Kao Family of the Northern Ch'i." In her *Marriage, Kinship, and Power in Northern China.* Brookfield, VT: Variorum, 1995, 12–14, 28–29.

Hou Xinyi and Chen Quanli, eds. *Houfei cidian.* Xi'an: Shaanxi renmin jiaoyu chubanshe, 1991, 82.

Lu Lingxuan

Lu Lingxuan, c. 510–578, was the nurse of Gao Wei (Houzhu [The Last Ruler], 556–578; r. 565–577), the fifth and last ruler of Northern Qi. Her lifetime spanned four dynasties established by the previously nomadic Xianbei people—the end of Northern Wei, Western Wei, Eastern Wei, and Northern Qi—and she was pivotal in the political survival of the young Gao Wei from the time his father died until the fall of the dynasty almost ten years later. Little is known of her background except that she grew up under Northern Wei. It is not known if she was of Xianbei or Han-Chinese origin, but her father had served under Gao Huan (496–547), a Han-Chinese general who gained control of Northern Wei in its last five years and put a puppet emperor on the throne to establish the Eastern Wei dynasty, the predecessor of Northern Qi. Lu Lingxuan's husband, however, had taken up the cause of Western Wei and fought against Gao Huan; he was executed, probably in 534.

Lu Lingxuan was in her twenties and had a son of her own (Luo Tibo) when she was taken into the household of Gao Huan as a slave around 534. Nothing is known of her duties until 556, when she was about forty-six years old and was appointed nurse to Gao Wei, one of Gao Huan's many grandsons. Far removed from the throne at birth, Gao Wei was soon to become emperor through a series of violent reversals of fortune.

Gao Huan had several wives and fifteen sons. The traditional line of succession among the Xianbei people had been from brother to brother, although the Han-Chinese system of primogeniture was gradually being adopted in the fifth century, and most of Gao Huan's sons and grandsons were involved to some extent in a struggle for supremacy. Gao Yang (529–559), Gao Huan's second son, had very probably arranged the murder of his brother Gao Cheng (d. 550) before forcing the Eastern Wei emperor to abdicate and establishing the Northern Qi dynasty. Gao Yang declared himself emperor—he is known in history as Emperor Wenxuan (r. 550–559)—and immediately appointed his son Gao Yin (d. 560?) heir apparent. After Gao Yin was deposed by two of his uncles and his grandmother within a year of ascending the throne, and was then strangled, the throne passed in turn to those two uncles, Gao Yan (d. 561?) and Gao Zhan (Emperor Wucheng, 537–568; r. 561–565).

Gao Zhan was Gao Wei's father. He was the ninth son of Gao Huan and the fifth son of Gao Huan's principal wife, Lou Zhaojun (*q.v.* Lou Zhaojun, Empress of Emperor Shenwu of Northern Qi). He had been enfeoffed as Prince of Changguang in 550 and four years later, at the age of seventeen, he had been married to Lady Hu, a daughter of Hu Yanzhi of Anding Commandery (in present-day Gansu Province). Their son Gao Wei was born two years later and Lady Hu was officially named Gao Zhan's principal wife. Once Gao Zhan seized the throne and became emperor, Lady Hu was named Empress Hu and their son Gao Wei was named heir apparent.

As Gao Wei's nurse, Lu Lingxuan was able to maintain a good relationship with the boy's mother, Empress Hu, and she forged relationships with other important personages at court. In a significant move, she adopted two of Gao Zhan's advisers, He Shikai and Gao A-na-hui. As time went on and Gao Zhan became increasingly dependent on alcohol, he also came to depend more and more on his friend and adviser

318 LU LINGXUAN

He Shikai, encouraging him to live in the palace and spend time with Empress Hu. It was to Lu Lingxuan's advantage to have He Shikai live in the palace, and when he and Empress Hu eventually became lovers this strengthened Lu Lingxuan's relationships with both the empress and the heir. By this time, Lu Lingxuan had been named a Lady of a Commandery (*junfuren*) and her family connections with different groups of elites—Xianbei, non-Chinese, and Chinese—of the fifth and sixth centuries made her valuable to the court. She was in the empress's favor and acted with her authority in matters concerning the inner apartments.

Empress Hu had given birth to a second son, Gao Yan, in 558. She became fonder of him than of Gao Wei and by the time Gao Yan was six she felt he was the more capable and intelligent of her sons. Emperor Wucheng was also very fond of his younger son but became concerned when Empress Hu began talking of making Gao Yan the heir because the emperor had played a role in the bloodshed involved in deposing previous heirs and was aware of the political implications of demoting Gao Wei. Therefore, on the advice of a Han-Chinese official named Zu Ting, Emperor Wucheng retired in 565 and took the title of Emperor Emeritus (*taishang huangdi*). The purpose of this move was to ensure a smooth succession to his nine-year-old son. As Emperor Emeritus, Gao Zhan maintained control of the army and important affairs of state, and Gao Wei was installed as the ruler while his principal wife, a daughter of the powerful Hulü family, became Empress Hulü.

Zu Ting was promoted for his apparently sound advice, but when it was revealed that he had set his sights on the post of grand councilor (*zaixiang*) and was attempting to get rid of those close to Gao Zhan, especially He Shikai, he was beaten and sent to prison, where he went, or was made, blind. Clearly an extremely determined political player, Zu Ting managed to win a pardon and, after being sent to the provinces, made his way back into the court through the intervention of Lu Lingxuan, who persuaded the young emperor to allow Zu Ting to return.

Lu Lingxuan had consolidated her influence over the emperor, whom she had cared for almost from birth, by bringing her own son, Luo Tibo, into the palace to wait day and night upon him. Luo Tibo was probably twelve or thirteen at the time and he and the nine-year-old emperor became very close. Lu Lingxuan was promoted to the post of Lady in Palace Attendance (*nü shizhong*), a grade equivalent to a second-class official in the outer bureaucracy.

The emperor was only twelve when his father died in 569. His paternal uncles, fearing the influence his mother (now Empress Dowager Hu) and those close to her had on him, attempted to oust He Shikai and the empress dowager's brother-in-law Feng Zicong. They managed to remove Feng Zicong from the capital temporarily to take up a distant post, but were outmaneuvered when they attempted to dislodge He Shikai from his position of trust; accused of disloyalty, their ringleader (Gao Rui) was seized and dragged away by soldiers, who strangled him. The biography of Empress Dowager Hu gives credit for this coup to Lu Lingxuan and He Shikai. However, while Lu Lingxuan may have suggested and supported the decision to murder the ringleader, it would not have been possible without the full knowledge and consent of both the empress dowager and her son.

As the young emperor became increasingly dependent on Lu Lingxuan, she shored up her position. She encouraged his intimacy with a concubine whose given name was Sheli. Sheli's mother had been a slave in the family of a Han-Chinese official killed in the coup of 560 and the girl had therefore been sent into the palace. She was in the service of the emperor's principal consort, Empress Hulü, and Lu Lingxuan had adopted her. She gave birth to the first son of the fourteen-year-old emperor in 570 and this infant was named heir apparent. To protect Sheli, Lu Lingxuan advised the emperor to appoint Empress Hulü as the infant's foster mother so that her powerful family would guard him. She also asked him to bestow on Sheli the aristocratic surname of Mu. As Sheli's adoptive mother, Lu Lingxuan therefore gained the title of Great Consort (*taifei*); her son also changed his surname from Luo to Mu, thus emphasizing his ties with the emperor's son.

In keeping with his new status as maternal uncle to the heir, Lu Lingxuan's son was given a high-ranking post in the military. Lu Lingxuan's nephew by marriage was also appointed to a high-ranking civil post. With greater access to the emperor because of their relationship to Lu Lingxuan, her nephew and her son wielded greater influence than most of their superiors of the Gao and Hulü families. The emperor's confidence in Lu Lingxuan was almost absolute and she was careful not to damage this relationship by antagonizing the empress dowager. The empress dowager was afraid of her son, who was in turn frightened that his mother might try to poison him. Lu Lingxuan tried to heal the breach between them by bringing the empress dowager's niece—Lady Hu—into the palace as a concubine.

While Lu Lingxuan remained in such a powerful position, her life was in danger from the emperor's male relatives, who considered the throne a prize that could be fought for and won. The emperor had gradually stripped his thirteen-year-old younger brother, Gao Yan, of most of the official positions that gave him some degree of political influence at court and had sent him to live away from the main palace. However, the boy missed his mother, whom he could no longer see as often as he wished, blaming his mother's lover, He Shikai, for this. His mother's brother-in-law Feng Zicong therefore hatched a plot to kill both He Shikai and Lu Lingxuan and install Gao Yan as emperor. A memorial listing the crimes of He Shikai and asking for his imprisonment pending investigation was slipped into a stack of documents awaiting the emperor's seal. The emperor signed it without looking at it and when He Shikai tried to enter the palace he was seized and killed. The attempt on Lu Lingxuan's life failed, however, when the plan to lure her out of the palace was thwarted. The emperor faced down the attempted coup of Gao Yan, who claimed he had been led into it by Feng Zicong, and Feng Zicong was strangled with a bowstring on the orders of the empress dowager. Lu Lingxuan realized that Gao Yan posed the main threat to herself and the emperor and, with the help of the blind Han-Chinese official Zu Ting, she persuaded the emperor to have Gao Yan murdered.

The next betrayal and murder at court was instigated by Zu Ting. Lu Lingxuan had eased Zu Ting's path up the official ladder, which gave him greater personal access to the emperor. She also fell in with Zu Ting's plan to get rid of Grand Councilor Hulü Guang, the emperor's father-in-law and a man who had always tried to remain above politics.

320 LU LINGXUAN

Lu Lingxuan obliged by slandering Hulü Guang and accepted the pretense that he was plotting rebellion. The emperor also accepted this lie and had Hulü Guang ambushed and strangled and all his male relatives, except his youngest son, killed. Two days after his death, his daughter, Empress Hulü, was demoted to the status of commoner.

Lu Lingxuan then moved to install the empress of her choice: her adopted daughter Mu Sheli. First, she recommended to the emperor that he name his new favorite—his maternal cousin, Lady Hu—Empress of the Left and appoint the mother of his heir—Mu Sheli—to the junior position of Empress of the Right. Then she created dissent between the empress dowager and her niece, the new empress of the left, such that Empress Hu was demoted to commoner status, leaving Mu Sheli to be promoted to sole empress. As adoptive mother of the empress, Lu Lingxuan was honored with the title Lady of Supreme Deportment, Grade 1 (*taiyi*), which gave her formal authority over all princesses of the blood and made her the most powerful woman in the palace.

Meanwhile, frustrated in his campaign to become grand councilor, Zu Ting moved to alienate Lu Lingxuan from her nephew and to unseat her son. Lu Lingxuan responded by spreading anonymous rumors and innuendo to damage Zu Ting. Finally, when these stories began to have an effect on the emperor and he asked Lu Lingxuan for her opinion, since it was she who had advised him to reinstate Zu Ting, Lu Lingxuan knelt before him and said that she deserved to die for having recommended such an evil man to the throne. She had done so, she said, on the advice of He Shikai. After an investigation revealed the extent of Zu Ting's illegal orders and corruption, he was sent to take up a governorship in southeastern Shandong and was never recalled to court.

Lu Lingxuan died by her own hand after she heard that her son had defected to Northern Zhou on the eve of the defeat of Northern Qi. The emperor and Empress Mu were both executed by Northern Zhou in 578. Empress Dowager Hu was captured and survived into the Sui era.

It was not Lu Lingxuan's skill alone that had kept Gao Wei on the throne. However, while others played an important role in the emperor's survival at various stages of their careers, Lu Lingxuan remained his only constant. Her success was due to her close maternal relationship with the emperor, her wide-ranging and nonpartisan contacts within almost every sector of Northern Qi society, and her menial and dependent position in the harem, which necessitated a good working relationship with the emperor's mother, members of the imperial family, and the bureaucratic elite in the capital.

From her humble beginnings as a slave, Lu Lingxuan rose to influence the politics of Northern Qi for more than twenty years. She could make or break the careers of officials and she decided the fate of imperial consorts. The fact that she is mentioned in the biographies of several top-ranking courtiers and officials is testament to the extent of her power, which arose from her clever manipulation of relationships within an undisciplined and unprincipled ruling class. That she, too, should die by violence in such an environment was inevitable.

This article has in large part been abstracted, with permission, from Jennifer Holmgren's paper, cited below.

Priscilla CHING-CHUNG

Bei Qi shu. Beijing: Zhonghua shuju, 1972, vol. 1, 8.112–13; vol. 1, 9.126–28; vol. 1, 12.162–63; vol. 2, 39.518–21; vol. 2, 50.689–90.

Holmgren, Jennifer. "Politics of the Inner Court of Houzhu Of Northern Qi." In *State and Society in Early Medieval China,* ed. Albert E. Dien. Hong Kong: Hong Kong University Press, 1990.

Hucker, Charles O. *A Dictionary of Official Titles in Imperial China.* Stanford, CA: Stanford University Press, 1985.

Lüzhu

Lüzhu, d. 300, was a renowned musician, dancer, and music educator who lived during the Western Jin dynasty. One source gives her surname as Liang and her native place as Baizhou (present-day Bobai County in Guangxi Province). Shi Chong (249–300), investigation commissioner (*caifangshi*) of Jiaozhi (an area including part of present-day Guangdong, Guangxi, and Vietnam), bought her for three bushels of pearls. It is not recorded from whom he bought her.

Shi Chong enjoyed special treatment from Emperor Wu (Sima Yan, 236–290; r. 265–290), the first emperor of Jin, because of the support Shi Chong's father had lent him in securing the throne. Shi Chong took advantage of his position to amass a sizable fortune, part of which he used to construct a famous garden named Golden Valley Garden (Jingu yuan). In this garden, set among rolling hills and babbling brooks, with fish ponds and water mills, grew a great variety of trees and flowers, fruit, herbs, and bamboos that kept him supplied with an abundance of fresh food. He and his guests feasted and composed poetry to the accompaniment of music played by orchestras and soloists. One of these was the beautiful Lüzhu, who had become one of Shi Chong's favorites: not only was she a talented flute player, she could also set poetry to music. One of the works attributed to her is the *Aonao qu* in the style of a folk song. Some sources say Shi Chong composed this work. Perhaps Lüzhu wrote it; perhaps it was a joint effort; perhaps Shi Chong was credited with writing it because he was the literatus; or perhaps he wrote it and Lüzhu's singing made it famous. It is known that Shi Chong taught her the ballad *Mingjun qu,* which he wrote based on the story of Wang Zhaojun (*q.v.*), and Lüzhu was famous for performing a dance going by the same title.

Living a life of great extravagance in the good graces of Emperor Wu, Shi Chong inevitably incurred the jealousy and hatred of many people. When Emperor Wu died, Shi Chong's position became less secure, and when his political anchor, Empress Jia (*q.v.* Jia Nanfeng, Empress of Emperor Hui of Jin), was overthrown in a coup, Shi Chong lost his official position. Not long after this, Sun Xiu, a trusted follower of the man who had orchestrated the coup, sent an emissary to Shi Chong to ask for Lüzhu. Shi Chong had once insulted Sun Xiu, who appears to have thus been seeking revenge. Not wishing to part with Lüzhu, especially under these circumstances, Shi Chong paraded his entertainers and concubines, all wearing perfume and silks, before the emissary, asking him to choose from them. The emissary insisted on taking Lüzhu, however, and Shi Chong angrily refused to part with her. Sun Xiu was incensed and urged his superior to have Shi Chong killed. When the soldiers came for him, Shi Chong said to Lüzhu, "It is because of you that I am now incriminated." Lüzhu wept and said, "I will die before you!" She then jumped to her death from an upper floor

322 LÜZHU

of the building, an unfortunate pawn in this power struggle between the two men. Shi Chong did not believe his crime warranted the death penalty, but realized he was to be killed when his carriage approached the marketplace where executions were usually carried out. In a moment of dreadful clarity, he said, "It is only because they covet my wealth."

Lüzhu's name has traditionally been synonymous with women faithful to their husbands or a symbol of romantic love. A further and more unusual aspect is that few musicians, especially female musicians, have been recorded by name in the historical records of any country, but Lüzhu was famous in her time as a flautist. She also taught others to play. One of her pupils was the beautiful Song Wei, an expert flute player who was taken into the palace of Emperor Ming (Sima Shao; r. 323–325) of Eastern Jin. Lüzhu was also known for performing dances based on stories: it appears that dance drama was already an art form in third-century China.

The story of Lüzhu has fascinated literati and many poems have been written about her. The opera *Lüzhu Falls from the Tower* (Lüzhu zhuilou), by the famous Yuan-dynasty dramatist Guan Hanqing, was the first in a long series of dramas and fiction devoted to this subject. Even today, operas based on her story can be found in the repertoire of Peking and Sichuan opera.

Lily Xiao Hong LEE

Jin shu. Beijing: Zhonghua shuju, 1974, vol. 4, 33.1008.
Liu I-ch'ing [Yiqing]. *Shih-shuo Hsin-yü: A New Account of Tales of the World,* trans. Richard B. Mather. Minneapolis: University of Minnesota Press, 1976, 264–65, 489–90.
Liu Yiqing. *Shishuo xinyu jian shu,* ed. Yu Jiaxi. Beijing: Zhonghua shuju, 1983, 9.530–32; 36.924.
Qu Dajun. *Guangdong xinyu.* Hong Kong: Zhonghua shuju, 1974, 157–58.
Tan Daxian [Tam Tat-sin]. *Zhongguo de jieshixing chuanshuo.* Beijing: Shangwu yinshuguan, 2002, 137–38.
Wang Yanti, ed. *Zhongguo gudai nüzuojia ji.* Jinan: Shandong daxue chubanshe, 1999, 46.
Xu Tianxiao. *Shenzhou nüzi xinshi.* Shanghai: Shenzhou tushuju, 1913; Taipei: Daoxiang chubanshe, 1993, rpt. 58.
Yin Wei. *Zhonghua wuqian nian yiyuan cainü.* Taipei: Guanya wenhua, 1991, 52–55.

M

Mao, Empress of Emperor Ming of Wei

Empress Dao née Mao (Mingdao Mao Huanghou), c. 210–237, from Henei, in present-day Shanxi Province, north of the Yellow River, was the first empress of Emperor Ming (Cao Rui, 205–239; r. 226–239) of the northern Three Kingdoms state of Wei. She was recruited into Cao Rui's palace in the early 220s when he was still heir apparent and Prince of Pingyuan. She quickly won his favor and frequently traveled with him in his carriage, effectively usurping the place of his principal consort, Lady Yu. She was made an honored concubine (*guipin*) when Cao Rui ascended the throne and a year later, in late 227, she was named empress.

MING NÉE LOU, EMPRESS OF EMPEROR SHENWU OF NORTHERN QI 323

Lady Yu, who came from the same region as Empress Mao, was inconsolable at having been passed over. When Empress Dowager Bian (*q.v.* Bian, Wife of Cao Cao, King of Wei) tried to comfort her she said: "The [Caos] are fond of making regular consorts out of women of lowly status; there never has been one who was made empress because it was her due. Yet an empress takes charge of affairs within, while the sovereign listens to governmental matters outside; in this manner they complement each other. One who does not begin correctly and justly will never have a happy ending. Because of this, [the house of Cao] will probably lose the state and lack posterity to continue the ancestral sacrifice." Clearly, Lady Yu must not have realized the implications of what she was saying—Empress Dowager Bian had herself once been a lowly prostitute—and she was thus immediately sent back in disgrace to the palace in Ye (south of the present-day city of Cixian in Hebei Province).

Upon Empress Mao's investiture, males throughout the empire were promoted two degrees in rank and all those who were unable to support themselves were given grain. Her father, Mao Jia, was soon appointed Chief Commandant of the Cavalry (*jiduyu*) and her younger brother, Mao Ceng, was made a Gentleman of the Palace (*langzhong*). They received further promotions, but her father, who had been a humble runner in the Department of Public Works, remained stupid and foolish despite his sudden wealth and status. He took to referring to himself as "the Lordly Person" (*houshen*), and became a general laughingstock.

It was not long before Emperor Ming's attentions wandered and he became enamored of his Lady Guo (*q.v.* Guo, Empress of Emperor Ming of Wei). One autumn day in 237, the emperor was touring his rear garden and summoned the palace women of the rank of lady of talents (*cairen*) and above to a private feast. Lady Guo suggested that Empress Mao be invited as well but the emperor did not give his consent. Further, he prohibited anyone from informing her about it. Empress Mao nevertheless learned of it and the following day said to him, "Was yesterday's party in the northern garden pleasant?" Thinking that his attendants had divulged this information to her, he had more than ten of them put to death. He then commanded Empress Mao to commit suicide. She was buried in Minling. Emperor Ming bestowed upon her the posthumous name Dao, meaning Lamented, and promoted her brother Mao Ceng.

Priscilla CHING-CHUNG

Chen Shou. *Empresses and Consorts: Selections from Chen Shou's "Records of the Three States" with Pei Songzhi's Commentary,* trans. Robert J. Cutter and William Gordon Crowell. Honolulu: University of Hawaii Press, 1999, 111–13; 206–7.
Sanguo zhi. Wei shu. Beijing: Zhonghua shuju, 1959, vol. 1, 5.167–68.
Sima Guang. *The Chronicle of the Three Kingdoms (220–265), Chapters 69–78 from the Tzu chih t'ung chien of Ssu-ma Kuang,* trans. Achilles Fang, ed. Glen W. Baxter. Cambridge, MA: Harvard University Press, 1965, vol. 1, 201–2, 212–14, 229, 240–41, 518, 624.

Ming née Lou, Empress of Emperor Shenwu of Northern Qi: *see* **Lou Zhaojun, Empress of Emperor Shenwu of Northern Qi**

324 MINGDAO MAO HUANGHOU

Mingdao Mao Huanghou: *see* **Mao, Empress of Emperor Ming of Wei**

Mingdi Wang Huanghou: *see* **Wang Zhenfeng, Empress of Emperor Ming of Liu Song**

Minggong Wang Huanghou: *see* **Wang Zhenfeng, Empress of Emperor Ming of Liu Song**

Mingyuan Guo Huanghou: *see* **Guo, Empress of Emperor Ming of Wei**

Mulan

Mulan, also known as Hua Mulan and Fa Mulan, is China's most famous and revered woman warrior. By the late twentieth century she had also achieved international recognition through a highly successful animated film rendition of her story. She is known for her courage in replacing her father in army service for twelve years—a feat that she achieved by disguising herself as a man.

Despite her fame and the extensive exegesis on her person and the numerous texts relating to her, historical evidence on her life is sparse and inconclusive. This has led many scholars to consider her no more than a literary figure. Yucheng County in Henan Province currently claims her as a native and she is a major feature of the tourist attractions for this area. Yet there are competing arguments that she is a native of Songzhou and Yan'an, among other locations. Even her surname is disputed, being variously presented as Wei, Mu, Zhu, Hua, and Fa (a variant pronunciation of Hua). While many think that Mulan was ethnically Han, some say she was a member of the Xianbei minority. Nor is there conclusive evidence confirming her dates of birth and death. The 500 years before the Tang dynasty have all been considered as possibilities.

Despite this uncertainty around factual detail, the symbolic Mulan, rather than the historical figure, has played an important ideological function in Chinese society for over 1,500 years: for the most part she has represented filial loyalty, patriotism, and selflessness. She also provided a vision of womanhood that extended women's roles beyond the domestic sphere. Through stories of Mulan, millions of women imagined themselves in daring and adventurous escapades and achieving public recognition for their remarkable deeds. This significant function was mobilized explicitly for political goals for a brief period during the twentieth century. Mulan was also invoked within the feminist movement as a model feminist who challenged traditional values stipulating women's noninterference in public political matters.

The first historical references to Mulan appeared during the Tang dynasty (618–907), providing evidence that, if she really existed, she lived before or in the early years of Tang. Li Kang's Tang text "Du yi zhi" notes, "In ancient times there was a girl called Mulan." In the Song dynasty (960–1279), the *Taiping huanyu ji* mentions the location of a Mulan temple. As the fashion to seek evidence of remarkably virtuous women (*lienü*) gathered tempo during the Qing dynasty (1644–1911) so, too, did references to Mulan in local gazetteers. A Henan Province gazetteer produced during the Yong-zheng era (1723–1735), for example, relates how the palace awarded Mulan with the title Filial and Heroic General (*xiaolie jiangjun*) and says that the local people built a temple in her honor. However, the many Qing references to Mulan as an historical figure appear to be based upon "common knowledge" constructed through repeated mentions of her in earlier texts rather than verifiable fact.

It appears through these myriad semi-historical references to Mulan that regardless of the dearth of evidence about her life, her story had captured the imagination of both ordinary people and the literati classes. For the common people in the Henan area, Mulan became a goddess worthy of worship. Her deification probably began during the Tang dynasty when it is said that people in Yucheng constructed a temple in her honor. Every year on the eighth day of the fourth lunar month, people gathered to pay tribute to her heroism. In 1993, Yucheng declared this day Mulan Culture Holiday (*Mulan wenhua jie*) to draw broader attention to this celebration. Income generation through tourism has become a central part of Mulan's deification and reification.

The most important, and indeed the earliest, reference to Mulan is in the "Ballad of Mulan" (Mulan shi, or Mulan ci). An anonymous ballad of 62 lines and 332 characters, it provides the basis for all later renditions of her life, including the historical references, and is the major focus of scholarship on Mulan to the present day. According to *Appreciation Dictionary of the Poetry of the Han, Wei, and Six Dynasties Period* (Han Wei Liu chao shi jianshang cidian), it first appeared in 568, in an anthology of poetry: *Records of Ancient and Modern Verse* (Gujin yuelu), edited by Chen Shi Zhijiang.

The poem tells of a young woman who takes the place of her father in the imperial army conscripted to fight invaders from the north. Because her father is too old to fulfill the family's conscription quota, in an act of filial piety Mulan assumes her father's task. In order to be able to serve in his place Mulan disguises herself as a man. For over twelve years Mulan fights alongside men, with none apparently aware of her true sex. At the conclusion of the war, in acknowledgement of outstanding service, the emperor offers Mulan a prestigious position as a minister but Mulan declines and simply asks to borrow a camel in order to be able to return to his/her family. Accordingly, she returns home and is reunited with her family, resuming her life as a woman.

There is one common variation to the conclusion of the story presented in later versions. This variation presents a tension between Mulan's loyalty to the emperor and loyalty to her family. Once the emperor hears that Mulan is actually a woman he summons her back to court with the intention of taking her as a concubine. Mulan refuses and commits suicide to signal her rectitude and her devotion to her father. The empire then posthumously bestows upon her the title Filial and Heroic General. The Qing dynasty *Henan Local Gazetteer* (Henan tongzhi) and *Guide Prefectural Gazetteer* (Guide fuzhi) both ascribe her suicide to resistance to the emperor's demands. There are myriad other endings to her story, including some that have her living a quiet life in her native village well into her eighties.

Building on the popularity of the ballad, artists, writers, poets, and dramatists have all provided variations on the story that have helped sustain its currency over several centuries. Famous poets from as early as the Tang wrote on the Mulan theme, bestowing on her further status and significance. For example, Du Mu (803–852) wrote an

326 MULAN

evocative piece titled *On the Temple of Mulan* (Ti Mulan miao) in which he contrasts the strength of her archery with memories of delicately painting her eyebrows. A generation earlier, Bai Juyi (772–846) wrote two poems—*Playfully on the Magnolia Flower* (Xiti mulan hua) and *Ode to Magnolia* (Yong mulan hua)—invoking the full floral meaning of Mulan as the magnolia flower. All three poems make heavy use of the metaphors of women's cosmetics to emphasize Mulan's temporary transformation into a man.

The earliest and most influential dramatic rendition of her story was that of the Ming writer Xu Wei (1521–1593) titled *The Female Mulan* (Ci Mulan). In this version of her life, Xu Wei describes her painfully unbinding her feet as part of the adoption of male attire. Foot binding did not exist in the period when the original ballad was written, so this anachronistic addition is designed to address a key aspect of the gendered sartorial regimes of the Ming. Where Bai Juyi and Du Mu invoked cosmetics as key signifiers of femininity, Xu Wei invokes the bound foot. References to her feet continue throughout the play. With her feet newly liberated, Mulan comments after a while that she can walk with stability. Later, Mulan's mother describes her unbound feet as "big" and "strange." The play concludes with Mulan's joyous return to her family and the suggestion that she will marry a relative named Wang. Its last lines include a comic note that "A local saying runs 'you can't tell the female from the male by relying on your eyes.'"

From as early as 1878 novellas of her story were being written, usually anonymously. The 1878 *The Story of a Loyal, Filial, Brave, and Heroic Outstanding Woman* (Zhongxiaoyong lie qi nü zhuan) appears to have been reprinted several times through to 1910. Dramatic renditions including plays, and various forms of opera abounded during the first half of the twentieth century. Probably the best loved of these is the Yuju opera (a form of traditional opera originating from Henan) that first appeared in 1954 and by 1956 had been made into a film (discussed below). In the 1930s and 1940s there was another burst of writing about Mulan, probably in response to the Japanese invasion of China. She routinely features in children's books and comics—no doubt a popular theme in this early childhood education area for the plot's emphasis on a child's devotion to and sacrifice for a parent.

Almost every possible new form of media embraced Mulan's story during the twentieth century. With the advent of cinema, Mulan was the focus of a range of different films. Li Pingqian directed the first in 1927: the silent film *Mulan Joins the Army* (Mulan congjun). In 1956, Liu Guoquan filmed the Yuju opera mentioned above. The most popular song from this version of her story is "Who Said Women Are Not as Good as Men?" (Shei shuo nüzi buru nan?), sung by Yuju opera star Chang Xiangyu (1923–2004). This song is featured on the 1995 karaoke disc version of the opera produced in Xiamen, indicating its continuing popularity. The song's title draws on a Qing poem by Dong Yanjin where he commences with the line "Who says that having a daughter isn't as good as having a son?" (*Shei shuo sheng nü buru nan?*)

In 1964, Griffith Yueh Feng directed a Hong Kong film titled *Lady General Mulan*. This was a Huang Mei opera version presented in Mandarin, and it concluded with Mulan and her close comrade in arms, General Li, in love with each other but it stopped short of their marriage, with the general going off to fight another battle. Mulan waves him farewell and remains as a woman with her natal family, awaiting his return. A 1999 Taiwanese television series directed by Yang Pei-pei in forty-eight parts elaborated on the story, creating comic romance, drama, and subplots that extended the story's appeal to a contemporary television audience with expectations of episodic-yet-continuing narratives over several weeks of lounge-room viewing. The Hong Kong Ballet commissioned a ballet of Mulan in 2000 with the music composed by Joshua Kam-biu Chan. First performed in 2001, the ballet comprised three acts and twenty-eight scenes. More recently, a highly successful contemporary musical (incorporating popular Western musical conventions) has been produced in Beijing. Director Wang Xiaoying presented the musical in 2004 with overwhelming support from the Ministry of Culture as a key cultural event for the year.

Not surprisingly, Mulan has also been incorporated into a computer game, produced by MobyGames in 2003. In the genre of the Action, Adventure, Role Playing Game (RPG) MobyGames' *Hua Mulan* enables players to assume the role of the heroine, undergo numerous trials, and accrue weapons and merit as they battle a continual stream of enemies. Beyond the virtual world, Mulan has featured in the real world of martial arts. In recent times, Shanghai and Henan martial arts fans have embraced a new form, called *Mulan quan,* which incorporates the toughness and discipline of martial arts with a graceful dance-like motion.

Internationally, Mulan featured in the immensely popular 1976 novel *Woman Warrior,* by Maxine Hong Kingston (*q.v. Biographical Dictionary of Chinese Women: The Twentieth Century, 1912–2000*). This novel explores the hardships women experienced in wartime China and their immigrant experiences in the United States. In 1998, Disney produced a movie-length animated version of Mulan's story with pop songs and a comic narrative. The Disney plot enhanced the romantic aspects of the story, with Mulan falling in love with her commanding officer, in order to appeal to the Disney movie-cartoon audience expectations of stories with romantic tension that resolves in marriage after much trial and tribulation. In the Disney version, Mulan is exposed as a woman before the close of the war and is dismissed from her post. She redeems herself by rescuing the emperor from the invaders and is feted as a heroine before returning home. Her commanding officer visits her and their mutual love, newly recognized as heterosexual on the part of the commanding officer, is revealed. The movie concludes with prospects of a happy marriage, true to the form of other Disney cartoon movies of classic tales such as *Beauty and the Beast* and *The Little Mermaid.* In 2005, the Shanghai Song and Dance Ensemble and the Sydney Dance Company jointly produced the dance drama *Mulan,* which premiered in Shanghai on 18 October 2005. This was a first in international cooperation between China and another nation on a Mulan project.

The early feminist movement in China made ready use of the invocations of Mulan's story. Throughout the first decades of the twentieth century the story of Mulan was used to inspire women to join the anti-Qing movement, and famous women warriors of this period were routinely likened to Hua Mulan. Indeed, women revolutionaries such as Qiu Jin (*q.v. Biographical Dictionary of Chinese*

328 MULAN

Women: The Qing Period, 1644–1911), who sought to improve the status of women through her anti-Qing militarism, were hailed as modern-day Mulans for their daring military escapades and loyalty to the nation. No doubt young women in China have for centuries enjoyed Mulan's story precisely because she presented a model of alternative life paths for women. However, the complexity of the Mulan image ensured that she was not simply understood as a symbol of women's liberation even during the twentieth century when the feminist movement was strong. Women warriors in China have long been co-opted into a patriarchal narrative—self-sacrificing women rise to serve in times of crisis, but always resume their domestic duties once the crisis is averted. Significantly, Qiu Jin was not seeking a return to domestic duties once the revolution against the Qing was over and indeed became a martyr to her cause when she was executed by Qing authorities before the establishment of the Republic.

The complexity of her "feminist" credentials is clear in later invocations of Mulan. Filial piety, patriotism, and self-sacrifice became the features most emphasized in Mulan's story in subsequent wars. During the Sino-Japanese War (1937–1945) women who performed outstanding deeds on behalf of the nation were again often identified as modern-day Mulans. What was emphasized was their selflessness on behalf of the nation—implicitly recognizing that women do not normally join the fight—and therefore the modern-day Mulans' contribution stands as a reaffirmation of the irregularity of this "martial woman" role. The Mulans of the Sino-Japanese War period were not invoked as forerunners for women's rights but as loyal patriots who stepped out of their domestic roles because of the desperate situation faced by their nation and their families. For example, in 1943 a woman called Wang Zhongxiu dressed as a man and replaced her brother in the conscripted armies against Japan for two years. She fought in her brother's place because he, as the only son, was vital to continuing the family line.

Hua Mulan remains an important, multivalent symbol in China. She represents two significant orthodox virtues: loyalty and filiality. Yet she also presents three challenges to this orthodoxy by simultaneously falsifying notions of women's deficiency relative to men and the necessity for women to remain in the domestic sphere, and by reinstating the importance of love for one's family over duty to the nation. The rich mixture of ideology within the narrative of this one individual figure ensures that she will continue to be invoked for many years to come.

Louise EDWARDS

Ancient Poems: Yuefu Songs with Regular Five-Syllable Lines [bilingual text], trans. Lin Xi (Chinese); Yang Xianyi and Gladys Yang (English). Beijing: Foreign Languages Press, 2001.

Frankel, Hans H. *The Flowering Plum and the Palace Lady: Interpretations of Chinese Poetry.* New Haven, CT: Yale University Press, 1976.

Huang Canzhang and Li Shaoyi, eds. *Hua Mulan kao* [Research on Hua Mulan]. Beijing: Zhongguo guangbo dianshi chubanshe, 1992.

Ma Junhua and Su Lixiang, eds. *Mulan wenxian daguan* [Overview of documents on Mulan]. Zhengzhou: Henan renmin chubanshe, 1993.

N

Nanyue Furen: *see* **Wei Huacun**

P

Pan, Consort of Sun Quan

Lady Pan (Pan Furen), before 220–252, of Juzhang in Guiji (present-day Zhejiang Province) was a consort of Sun Quan (Great Emperor, 182–252; r. 222–252) of Wu and mother of his seventh and youngest son, Sun Liang (King of Guiji, 243–260; r. 252–258). The year before she died she was appointed empress to Sun Quan, ruler of the kingdom of Wu (221–280), which was the last of the three states to be established during the Three Kingdoms period. The official *Record of the Three Kingdoms* (Sanguo zhi) did not call her empress, however, because its author recognized the northern state of Wei as the legitimate successor to the Han dynasty and therefore the sole legitimate claimant to the titles emperor and empress.

Lady Pan's father had been a clerk but he was convicted of some crime and put to death. She and her elder sister were then sent to work in the palace weaving rooms, which provided woven materials for various purposes, including the imperial ancestral temple. It is said that the future Lady Pan was so beautiful that she was generally referred to in the weaving rooms as a goddess. This was reported to Sun Quan, who asked that a portrait be made of her. So pleased was he when he saw this portrait that he rubbed his scepter until it broke and ordered a carriage to take him to the weaving rooms; he then took her back to his harem. The version of their beginning given in the official history, which describes her as "of alluring appearance," is that Sun Quan caught sight of her and had her sent to his harem.

Sun Quan was besotted with Lady Pan, who soon became pregnant: she told him she had dreamt that she was presented with a dragon's head—a symbol of imperial rule—and that she received it with an apron. Sun Quan was in his sixties when she gave birth to Sun Liang and he doted on this youngest of his sons. After an extremely nasty political struggle during which the heir apparent Sun He (c. 226–253) was banished and his younger brother Sun Ba (c. 230–250) was ordered to commit suicide, seven-year-old Sun Liang was appointed heir apparent in 250. At that time, Lady Pan asked Sun Quan to release her elder sister from her work in the weaving rooms and arrange a marriage for her. The following year Lady Pan was enthroned as empress and an amnesty was granted throughout the empire.

Lady Pan is said to have been jealous of the other women in the harem and to have slandered many of them; one such was a Lady Yuan, whom she "maligned and brought to destruction." The official history describes Lady Pan as "by nature obstinate and evil-tempered" and as "insidious and jealous." During Sun Quan's last illness, in 252, Lady Pan tended him and apparently saw an opportunity for

330 PAN, CONSORT OF SUN QUAN

gaining ultimate control of the court, for she sought information on how Han Empress Lü (*q.v.* Lü Zhi, Empress of Emperor Gaozu), who is generally considered an exemplar of cruelty and ambition, had ruled as a regent. Her attendants clearly became alarmed at this turn of events. "Unable to bear her cruelty," they waited until she left Sun Quan's bedside and fell into a deep exhausted sleep, then they strangled her. Her death was initially attributed to "a sudden ailment," but the truth came out and six or seven people were charged with her murder and put to death. When Sun Quan died shortly afterward Lady Pan was buried alongside him at Jiangling.

After her son Sun Liang ascended the throne, he appointed Tan Shao, the husband of Lady Pan's elder sister, to a military command. However, when Sun Liang was dethroned in 258, Tan Shao and his family were sent back to his native prefecture of Luling.

Priscilla CHING-CHUNG

Chen Shou. *Empresses and Consorts: Selections from Chen Shou's "Records of the Three States" with Pei Songzhi's Commentary,* trans. Robert J. Cutter and William Gordon Crowell. Honolulu: University of Hawaii Press, 1999, 52, 56, 128–29; 220–22.
Sanguo zhi. Beijing: Zhonghua shuju, 1975, vol. 5, 50.1199.
Sima Guang, *The Chronicle of the Three Kingdoms (220–265). Chapters 69–78 from the Tzu chih t'ung chien of Ssu-ma Kuang,* trans. Achilles Fang, ed. Glen W. Baxter. Cambridge, MA: Harvard University Press, 1965, vol. 2, 70, 74, 104, 114.

Pan, Empress of Sun Quan: *see* **Pan, Consort of Sun Quan**

Q

Qianjin Gongzhu: *see* **Yuwen, Princess Qianjin of Northern Zhou**

Qiaoguo Furen: *see* **Xian, Lady of Qiao State**

Quan, Princess: *see* **Sun Luban**

Quan Bu Furen: *see* **Bu, Consort of Sun Quan**

Quan Cong's Wife: *see* **Sun Luban**

Quan Gongzhu: *see* **Sun Luban**

Quan Pan Furen: *see* **Pan, Consort of Sun Quan**

Quan Zhu: *see* **Sun Luban**

S

Seng Ji: *see* **An Lingshou**

Sengjing

Sengjing, 402–486, surnamed Li, was from Moling, in the vicinity of Jiankang (the present-day city of Nanjing); her secular given name is not known. She is remembered as a Buddhist nun who spent thirty years in the remote southern region of China serving as an example and teacher of Buddhism. Her biography in *Lives of the Nuns* (Biqiuni zhuan) says, "Her manner gradually changed the hearts of the barbarian peoples of the south."

Buddhism flourished during the Southern Dynasties in the valley of the Yangzi River and districts surrounding the capital city of Jiankang; the strong missionary impulse that has always characterized Buddhism also carried it to districts far from the capital. Sengjing's family had dedicated her to the monastic life before she was born, and at her birth gave her as a disciple to a nun at Jian'an Convent in the capital. By age six she was well established in her education, being able to repeat several scriptures from memory.

During the reign of Emperor Wen (Liu Yilong, 407–453; r. 424–453) of the Liu Song dynasty, Sengjing accompanied an official to Guangzhou (present-day Guangdong Province) in south China as part of his retinue. There, in 433, she happened to meet up with the group of nuns led by the nun Tessara who had come by ship from what is now Sri Lanka and were on their way to the capital. The most likely place for this meeting to have taken place was Panyu, the site of the modern city of Guangzhou, which had long been a port of call along Southeast Asian sea-lanes. The easiest route between Sri Lanka and China for Buddhist travelers at that time was by sea.

With the help of these nuns from Sri Lanka, Sengjing went through the ceremony of receiving the monastic obligations from both the assembly of monks and the assembly of nuns, thus becoming a fully ordained nun (*vide* Huiguo).

Pilgrimages to India were popular in the fifth century, and Sengjing wished to take a ship "to seek out the holy traces of the Buddha's life on earth." The people among whom she lived, however, persuaded her not to leave them. They joined together to buy land and build a convent for her, and she remained with them for more than thirty years. Eventually her good reputation reached the ears of Emperor Ming (Liu Yu, 439–472; r. 465–472), who summoned her back to the capital. This probably took place in 465, the year of his accession to the throne and the year he placed other nuns in favored convents by imperial decree (*q.v.* Baoxian; Fajing).

Sengjing served as a model and teacher for both monastics and laity during the Liu Song dynasty, and was later equally revered by members of the royal family of the Qi dynasty. At her death in 486, the well-known official and poet Shen Yue (441–513) composed the eulogy that was inscribed upon her memorial stone.

Kathryn A. TSAI

332 *SENGJING*

Baochang [Shih Pao-ch'ang]. *Lives of the Nuns: Biographies of Chinese Buddhist Nuns from the Fourth to Sixth Centuries: A Translation of the Pi-ch'iu-ni chuan,* trans. Kathryn Ann Tsai. Honolulu: University of Hawaii Press, 1994, 69–70.

Baochang [Pao-ch'ang]. "Sengjing zhuan." *Piqiuni zhuan, 3.* In *Taishō shinshū Daizōkyō,* ed. Takakusu Junjirō, Watanabe Kaigyoku, and Ono Genmyō. Tokyo: Taishō Issaikyō Kankōkai, 1924–1929, vol. 50, 942.

Chen Menglei. *Gu jin tushu jicheng kaozheng.* Shanghai: Zhonghua shuju, 1934, vol. 506.

Takakusu Junjirō, Watanabe Kaigyoku, and Ono Genmyō, eds. *Taishō shinshū Daizōkyō.* Tokyo: Taishō Issaikyō Kankōkai, 1924–1929.

Tsai, Kathryn Ann. "The Chinese Buddhist Monastic Order for Women: The First Two Centuries." In *Women in China: Current Directions in Historical Scholarship,* ed. Richard W. Guisso and Stanley Johannesen. Youngstown, NY: Philo Press, 1981, 1–20.

Shanyin, Princess: *see* **Liu Yingyuan**

Shenwu Ming, Empress: *see* **Lou Zhaojun, Empress of Emperor Shenwu of Northern Qi**

Song, Lady Xuanwen

Lady Song, also known as Lady Xuanwen (Xuanwen Jun), 283–after 362, was a scholar specializing in the Confucian classic *Zhou li,* also known as *Zhou guan.* Her given name is not known, nor is her native place, but she may have been from one of the northern provinces, as her biography in the *History of the Jin Dynasty* (Jin shu) notes that her homeland was occupied by Shi Hu (*zi* Jilong, 295–349; r. 334–349), a warlord of Jie nationality who ruled the Later Zhao dynasty almost to its close.

Lady Song was quite young when her mother died, and she was raised by her father, who appears not to have remarried. Her family had for generations been Confucian scholars, so when she was older her father taught her the pronunciations and meanings of the text *Zhou guan.* This work is a comprehensive collection of documents relating to the administration of the state, and to the various officials and their respective responsibilities. According to her father, it had been formulated by the sagely Duke of Zhou (Zhou Gong), who was the brother of the founder of the Zhou dynasty and whom Confucius greatly admired. Lady Song's father also told her that knowledge of *Zhou guan* was a family specialty that was passed from generation to generation. He is quoted as saying: "Now I do not have a son to pass it on to, you can receive it. Do not let it be lost to the world." There were great disturbances in the north at that time as the Western Jin dynasty collapsed under the onslaught of non-Han invaders, but in spite of this instability Lady Song continued to recite the classic ceaselessly, so that it would not be forgotten.

When Shi Jilong occupied her homeland, Lady Song and her husband fled to the area east of Mount Taishan in present-day Shandong Province. They traveled by foot, he pushing a small cart and she carrying on her back the books her father had handed down to her. After reaching Jizhou (present-day Hebei Province) they lived under the protection of Cheng Anshou, a wealthy man who was kind enough to support them and give them protection.

Lady Song's son Wei Cheng was still a child at that time. She would cut firewood in the daytime and teach Wei Cheng at night, yet she never stopped spinning and weaving. Cheng Anshou would sigh in admiration, saying, "It is said that a scholar's house produces many officials. Can this be what the saying refers to?" Wei Cheng completed his studies and became well known, eventually becoming an official in the government of Fu Jian (338–385; r. 357–385), third ruler of the Former Qin dynasty. Former Qin, in the north of China, was one of the many states into which China was divided during this period, now known as the Sixteen Kingdoms. Fu Jian, a non-Han of Di nationality, nevertheless admired Chinese culture, and especially the teachings of Confucius, and did much to promote it in his domain. Once he visited the National University (*taixue*) and conversed with the erudites (*boshi*) regarding the classics, saying he was saddened by the disappearance and loss of the rites and music. The erudite Lu Kun said:

> Learning has long been neglected and the texts of many classics and commentaries were lost for a time, but after years of piecing them together the texts of the authentic classics are all here as best we know them. The commentary on rites in Zhou guan is the only one for which we lack a teacher. I know that Lady Song, mother of Chamberlain of Ceremonials (taichang) Wei Cheng, is from a learned family. Her father passed on to her knowledge of the pronunciations and meanings of the text of *Zhou guan*. She is eighty years old but her eyesight and her hearing are fine. She is the only one who could teach younger scholars.

Fu Jian therefore ordered that a lecture hall be established in Lady Song's home and 120 students were assigned to study under her. She sat within a red gauze curtain when she taught and was given the title Lady Xuanwen; she was also given ten maidservants to wait on her. Lu Kun wrote: "The study of *Zhou guan* was again undertaken in the age." To her contemporaries, she was Mother Song of the Wei Family.

In primers for women in traditional China, Lady Song was held up as a role model of both a wise mother and a learned woman. Her prestige derived mainly from her learning, with little mention of her morality, especially chastity, a virtue so much admired in later centuries. This is a refreshing departure from tradition.

Lady Song was one of two women credited with passing on the Confucian classics. The other was the daughter of Fu Sheng, who lived during the reign of Han Emperor Wen (Liu Heng, 202–157 B.C.E.; r. 179–157 B.C.E.). Fu Sheng was the only surviving scholar of *Book of Documents* (Shu jing) at that time, but he was so old that his speech was not clear. His pupil Chao Cuo was a native of Yingchuan (present-day Henan Province) and, because the dialects of the two places were quite different, he was able to understand only 70 or 80 percent of what Fu Sheng said. One source says it was Fu Sheng's daughter Xi'e, a native of Zouping (or Jinan, according to another source; both places were in present-day Shandong Province), who relayed her father's words to his pupil Chao Cuo. Whereas Fu Xi'e was a mere mouthpiece for her father, Lady Song was actually a link in the chain of learned scholarship, and thus was by far the more significant of the two women. In later ages, scholars of women's learning have often compared Lady Song with the Eastern Han scholar Ban Zhao (*q.v.*). However, the Qing dynasty female scholar Li Wanfang considered Lady Song superior to Ban Zhao, saying, "Of all women, from earliest antiquity, she was the most outstanding. We should worship her and never forget her."

334   SONG, LADY XUANWEN

It must be remembered that Lady Song was allowed to pass on her father's learning only because he did not have a son. That is a large part of the reason why, from early antiquity, she was the only woman in a position to achieve what she did.

Lily Xiao Hong LEE

Gujin tushu jicheng 420. Beijing: Zhonghua shuju, 1934, reprint, 333.27b.
Han shu. Beijing: Zhonghua shuju, 1962, vol. 11, 88.3603, n. 2.
Jin shu. Beijing: Zhonghua shuju, 1974, vol. 8, 96.2521–22.
Liu Yongcong [Clara Wing Chung Ho]. "Qian Qin nüjingxuejia Xuanwen jun: jianlun houshi nüjiao zuopin zhong Xuanwen Jun xianxiang zhi jianli." In *Zhongguo funü shi lunji liuji,* ed. Pao Chia-lin [Bao Jialin]. Taipei: Daoxiang Press, 2004, 109–27.

South Marchmount, Lady of: *see* Wei Huacun

Su Boyu Qi: *see* Su Boyu's Wife

Su Boyu's Wife

Su Boyu's Wife (Su Boyu Qi), fl. 220–280, was a poet of the Jin dynasty; her native place is unknown. One anthology places her in the Eastern Han dynasty, but most other anthologies, as well as the authoritative *Siku quanshu tiyao,* place her in Jin.

Su Boyu was sent to Shu (present-day Sichuan Province) as a junior official. His wife remained in Chang'an and during their long separation she wrote *Poem on a Tray* (Panzhong shi). She wrote it on a tray in the normal fashion of rows of characters forming a square, but the poem was a palindrome and has thus been described as a spiral poem. In this poem she told how much she missed her husband. Su Boyu had already formed a liaison with another woman at his distant post but was so moved by his wife's poem that he returned home to her. This is Anne Birrell's translation of the poem, whose title she translates as *Palindrome:*

> In a hillock tree a bird sings of sorrow.
> In spring water deep carps are sleek.
> Swallows in empty barns always feel pangs of hunger.
> An officer's wife rarely meets her husband.
> She leaves the gate to watch, sees a white robe,
> Says, "That must be him!" But then it isn't,
> She goes back indoors sad at heart,
> Up the north hall, along the west stairs.
> Swift her loom winds silk, the shuttle sounds urgent.
> She sighs long sighs, who will she speak to?
> "I remember your going away.
> There was a day of departure, no promise of return.
> You tied my inside belt, saying, 'I'll always love you.'
> If you forgot me only Heaven would know,
> If I forgot you punishment is sure to follow.
> You ought to know I am being virtuous."

What's yellow is gold, what's white is jade,
What's tall is a mountain, what's low is a vale.
"Your name is Su, courtesy name Po-yü.
As a man you're gifted, quite intelligent.
Your family lives in Ch'angan, your body is in Shu.
How I regret your horse's hooves come home so seldom!
One thousand pounds of mutton, one hundred vats of wine.
You make your horse fat on wheat and millet.
Men today are not wise enough,
Give them a letter—they can't read it!
Start mine from the middle then out to the four corners."

This poem is a mixture of forms. It has forty-eight lines with twenty-seven rhymes and consists mainly of lines of three characters, but with some lines of seven characters. It starts with the *xing* literary device used in folk songs expressing a wife's desperate longing for a husband who has been away a long time. However, the poem also reflects the unequal relationship between husband and wife in traditional Chinese society whereby the husband could take a lover or remarry while the wife could not: "If you forgot me only Heaven would know, If I forgot you punishment is sure to follow." The language of the poem is simple and fluent, almost colloquial, and the feelings expressed are sincere and unaffected, straight from the heart.

Much has been made of how to read this very special poem, whose last line suggests it should be read from the center out to the four corners. This indicates that the tray on which Su Boyu's wife wrote the poem was rectangular, but someone of a later age tried to recreate her poem, writing it on a circular tray. The critic Hu Yinglin writes of the poem: "Su Boyu's Wife's *Poem on a Tray* is said to have been written on a tray in a circular manner and thus should be categorized as *huiwen* (palindrome). This poem is unequalled. 'Swallows in empty barns always feel pangs of hunger. An officer's wife rarely meets her husband.' 'What's yellow is gold, what's white is jade.' 'Your name is Su, courtesy name Po-yü.' 'Your family lives in Ch'angan, your body is in Shu.' All of these are a mixture of three-character or seven-character lines. The shape of the tray on which the poem was written remains unknown. There must be other ways of reading it but this cannot now be known."

Literati of different periods have shown overwhelming admiration for Su Boyu's Wife's poem. These are some of their comments: "*Poem on a Tray* is a wonderful poem with wonderful content from a wonderful idea. The marvelous artistry in this superb writing has never been matched." "This poem is like a folksong or a ballad (*yuefu*). It is written in mixed form yet the thoughts it conveys are sincere and candid. It is an incomparable masterpiece." "*Poem on a Tray* is an excellent piece of writing based on an excellent idea. It is the very peak of poetic perfection. This intelligent, sensitive woman perhaps had the original idea [of a spiral poem]. However, in terms of literary value, the elegant, straightforward diction, the frequent transitions and brilliant inspiration are not found in the work of any literati of any age."

Others have not thought so highly of the poem, considering it a kind of word game. "In the transition period between Han and Wei, intellectuals were fond of witty and

336 *SU BOYU'S WIFE*

cryptic writing, as, for example, Cai Yong's *Inscription for Cao E* and Cao Cao's *Chicken Ribs*. This trend lasted into the Jin dynasty. A natural development of the play on word combinations was the play on word position, as in *Poem on a Tray*. It was also natural that the word games further developed into writings with a complicated way of reading them, such as Su Ruolan's *Huiwen Poem*."

Mao Zedong liked *Poem on a Tray* very much, marking the whole piece for special attention in his copy of *Gushi yuan*. He even marked the editor's annotations: "The touching force that saddened Su Boyu came entirely from tenderness rather than from grievance. This is deep love. Learn it well."

SU Zhecong
(Translated by CHE Wai-lam William)

Birrell, Anne, trans. *New Songs from a Jade Terrace: An Anthology of Early Chinese Love Poetry*. London: Allen & Unwin, 1982, 242.
Ding Fubao. *Quan Han Sanguo Jin Nanbeichao shi*. Taipei: Shijie shuju, 1978, 7.509–10.
Feng Weina. *Gushi ji*. Taipei: Taiwan Commercial Press, 1985, 14.112–13.
Hu Yinglin. *Shisou*. Shanghai: Shanghai guji chubanshe, 1979, vol. 4, 195–96.
Lu Chang. *Lichao Ming Yuan shici*. Shanghai: Saoye shanfang, n.d., 1.9a–10a.
Shen Deqian. *Gushi yuan*. Beijing: Zhonghua shuju, 1973, 62.
Xu Ling. *Yutai xinyong*. Beijing: Zhonghua shuju, 1985, vol. 2, 406–7.
Zheng Songsheng. *Mao Zedong yu meixue*. Fuzhou: Fujian jiaoyu chubanshe, 1992, 232.
Zheng Zhenduo. *Chatuben Zhongguo wenxue shi*. Beijing: Wenxue gujishe, 1959, vol. 1, 157–58.
Zhong Xing. *Mingyuan shigui*. Shanghai: Youzheng shuju, 1918, 23a–24a.

Su Hui

Su Hui, b. c. 360, *zi* Ruolan, was the third daughter of Su Gong, magistrate of Chenliu (present-day Chenliu District, Henan Province), and the wife of Dou Tao, regional inspector of Qinzhou (present-day Gansu Province). A poet, she perfected the skill of writing palindromes (*huiwenshi*) and wove her work on a piece of brocade in successive squares, one inside the other, so that no matter where one started to read and whether one read clockwise, counter-clockwise, or diagonally, it read as a poem.

Su Hui is said to have been an elegant beauty of clear and sharp perception. Modest and quiet, she did not seek to stand out among her peers. When she was in her sixteenth year, she married Dou Tao. He was from an old family and is said to have been tall, handsome, and high-spirited, excelling not only in the classics but also in martial arts. His contemporaries held him in high esteem. Dou Tao regarded his young wife highly even though, despite her modest and quiet nature, she is said to have been quick-tempered and jealous. He kept his favorite concubine, Zhao Yangtai, a skilled singer and dancer, in a separate residence but Su Hui eventually found out about Zhao Yangtai; she grabbed her and beat her, greatly humiliating her. Not surprisingly, this displeased Dou Tao, and Zhao Yangtai made things worse by exaggerating Su Hui's weaknesses, making Dou Tao even angrier with his wife.

The ruler of Former Qin, Fu Jian (338–385; r. 357–385), looked upon Dou Tao as a trusted assistant, appointing him to a series of important positions in which he served with distinction. In 379, Fu Jian took the city of Xiangyang (present-day Xiangyang District, Hubei Province) in preparation for his plan to invade Eastern Jin, south of the Yangzi River. Worried that the area was not entirely secure, he appointed Dou Tao as General Pacifying the South, to be stationed at Xiangyang. Dou Tao asked Su Hui to go with him to his new post but, still smarting from the Zhao Yangtai incident, she refused. Dou Tao therefore took his concubine Zhao Yangtai with him to Xiangyang and stopped communicating with Su Hui.

Su Hui was twenty-one when her husband left her; she greatly regretted her decision and was filled with remorse. She wove a brilliant brocade palindrome; it was of five colors and beautiful to look at. When someone complained at being unable to read it, she said, "Only my beloved can understand it." She then sent it with a servant to Xiangyang. Dou Tao was impressed by Su Hui's ingenuity when he saw the brocade, but was even more taken with the feelings expressed in the poems. He let Zhao Yangtai go and prepared a carriage with many servants to have Su Hui brought to him. It is said that when they were reunited they loved each other even more than before.

The piece of brocade is eight *cun* square (about 26 cm, or 10.5 inches, square) and woven on it are 841 characters from which poems can be made. No matter which way it is read, a poem can be formed. It is so fine that every dot and stroke of every character is clearly visible. Su Hui called it *Xuanji tu,* which can tentatively be translated as *Picture of the North Star.* To Empress Wu Zetian (r. 684–704, *q.v. Biographical Dictionary of Chinese Women: Tang to Ming*), this name later suggested it could be read like the heavenly bodies revolving in the sky. The poet Zhu Shuzhen (c. 1135/38–c. 1180, *q.v. Biographical Dictionary of Chinese Women: Tang to Ming*) also wrote an exposition of this work. Through the ages it has been regarded as an ingenious masterpiece, both of literature and of handicraft, and is admired by both men and women.

Su Hui is said to have written more than 5,000 words of prose and poetry but all her works were lost during the upheavals of the Sui dynasty; only *Xuanji tu* survived. Empress Wu Zetian considered her poems the earliest examples of the "boudoir resentment" (*guiyuan*) genre.

Because of the challenges inherent in Su Hui's palindrome, many attempts have been made over the centuries to decode it. Empress Wu Zetian was the first to tell the story of Su Hui and she found more than 200 poems in the brocade. Eight centuries later, the lyric poet Zhu Shuzhen surpassed this, further refining the technique of decoding it, and was able to find poems of three- and four- as well as five- and seven-character (syllable) lines. Finally, the contemporary literary historian Xie Wuliang crowned all earlier efforts by finding over 3,800 poems of different lengths; he has reproduced the *Xuanji tu* and examples of his readings in his *History of Chinese Women's Literature* (Zhongguo funü wenxueshi).

Su Hui might have been inspired by Su Boyu's Wife (*q.v.*), an earlier poet who wrote palindromes on a rectangular tray; her work is known as *Poems on a Tray* (Pan zhong shi). Modern literary taste may not value such word games, but from the point of view of handicraft design and execution, Su Hui's *Xuanji tu* is undeniably a unique masterpiece.

Lily Xiao Hong LEE

338 SU HUI

Jiang Minfan and Wang Ruifang. *Zhongguo lidai cainü xiaozhuan.* Hangzhou: Zhejiang wenyi chubanshe, 1984, 57–59.

Xie Wuliang. *Zhongguo funü wenxueshi.* Shanghai: Zhonghua shuju, 1916; Zhengzhou: Zhongzhou guji chubanshe, 1992, reprint, Section II, 25–68.

Zheng Zhenduo. *Chatuben Zhongguo wenxueshi.* Beijing: Zuojia chubanshe, 1957, 177.

Su Ruolan: *see* **Su Hui**

Sun Ce Mu Wu Furen: see Wu, Wife of Caitiff-Smashing-General Sun

Sun Luban

Sun Luban, c. 215–c. 258, *zi* Dahu (Big Tiger), was the eldest daughter of Lady Bu (*q.v.* Bu, Consort of Sun Quan) and of Sun Quan (Great Emperor, 182–252; r. 222–252), founding emperor of the Three Kingdoms state of Wu. She had been betrothed to Zhou Xun, a son of Sun Quan's old friend Zhou Yu (175–210), but when he died she was married, possibly in the late 220s, to General (*weijiangjun*) and Grand Administrator (*taishou*) Quan Cong (d. 247 or 249), hence her title Princess Quan (Quan Gongzhu or Quan Zhu). Quan Cong was governor of Xuzhou (present-day Jiangsu Province) and, like his father before him, was one of Sun Quan's closest allies and brightest commanders.

Sun Luban and her younger sister Sun Luyu (d. 255) became deeply involved in court politics, supporting opposing sides in the lethal struggle to secure a successor to their aging father from among their half-brothers. Their mother, Lady Bu, had been their father's most loved consort but she had not given him a son and heir. Sun Quan initially appointed his eldest son, Sun Deng (209–241), as heir apparent, but after the latter's death he appointed his next surviving son, Sun He (c. 226–253). This young man was the son of Lady Wang, Sun Quan's second-favorite consort and the woman he intended to install as empress. Sun Luban was apprehensive about these appointments because she had earlier slandered her half-brother Sun He and his mother, Lady Wang, and feared retribution; her husband had also at some stage made an enemy of Lady Wang. A struggle ensued between Sun Luban's faction, which was attempting to have her younger half-brother Sun Ba (c. 232–250) installed as heir apparent, and Sun Luyu's faction, which was attempting to retain Sun He as heir apparent. Exasperated by these machinations, which had already led to the death "from grief," of Lady Wang, Sun Quan finally banished Sun He in 250 and ordered Sun Ba to commit suicide.

Sun Luban immediately transferred her support for heir apparent to her seven-year-old half-brother Sun Liang (243–260), the youngest son of Sun Quan, and arranged a marriage for the boy with a daughter of her husband's nephew. This girl therefore became empress when Sun Liang assumed the throne in 252. The regent appointed for the boy emperor, Chief Minister (*chengxiang*) Sun Jun (d. 256), was a second cousin of Sun Quan and he became extremely powerful, though never widely liked; at least two attempts on his life are recorded in *Record of the Three Kingdoms* (Sanguo zhi). However, determined not to stray far from the center of power, the now-widowed Sun Luban took her clansman Sun Jun for her lover. He is presented in a most unattractive light in the *Record* (as translated by Achilles Fang): "Sun Jun never enjoyed high reputation. He was arrogant and haughty, insidious and malicious. He had a large number of men sentenced to death, and the people were in a commotion. He furthermore had illicit relations with the palace ladies, and committed adultery with Princess Luban. In [254] . . . Sun Ying planned to assassinate Sun Jun. The thing leaked out, and Sun Ying died." The following year there was another unsuccessful attempt on Sun Jun's life and when this unraveled as well, Sun Luban incriminated her sister Sun Luyu. Sun Jun then killed Sun Luyu.

Sun Jun died the following year and his cousin Sun Lin (232–259) took up the reins of power as regent. However, as the young emperor began to take more interest in affairs of state, Sun Lin feared his excesses would be revealed and he attempted to avoid attending court. The emperor conspired with his half-sister Sun Luban to unseat Sun Lin but was himself dethroned, in 258. Sun Luban protested that she knew nothing of the plot against Sun Lin, shifting the blame onto her sister Sun Luyu's two stepsons, who were duly executed. Sun Luban appears to have been banished.

Sun Luban had at least one son, Quan Wu, who was the youngest son of her husband. Quan Cong had died before the deadly intrigues at the Wu court came to a head. His sons by another daughter of Sun Quan later transferred their allegiance by surrendering en masse to the northern state of Wei.

Sun Luyu, the younger sister of Sun Luban, bore the echoing *zi* Xiaohu (Little Tiger). Her first marriage, in 229, was to Cavalry General (*piaoji jiangjun*) Zhu Ju (174–250), whom her father had appointed to office because he possessed both literary and military talent, so she was known as Princess Zhu (Zhu Zhu). In 250, at the height of the heir-apparent debacle described above, Zhu Ju was flogged and demoted before being ordered to commit suicide. Sun Luyu then married Liu Zuan. This was a second marriage for both of them, Liu Zuan having been married to Sun Quan's (unnamed) second daughter, who had died. Sun Luyu had at least one child, a daughter who became empress to her own maternal uncle Sun Xiu (Emperor Jing, 236–264; r. 258–264).

Sun Luyu's body, which was placed in an unmarked grave after she was murdered in 255, was later re-interred. The last ruler of Wu, Sun Hao (Marquis of Wucheng; r. 264–280), sought the help of two shamans to find her grave, apparently in acknowledgment of the assistance she had earlier extended to his father, the heir apparent Sun He.

It is worth noting that neither Sun Luban nor Sun Luyu was chaste in the Confucian sense, both having more than one sexual partner, and that this was not considered unusual in the Three Kingdoms period, even (or perhaps especially) for women of the imperial family. Sun Luban and Sun Luyu are remembered, however, for the active roles they played in politics. Sun Luban appears to have been more influential and more ruthless, perhaps because she outlived her sister and engineered her sister's murder. However, in those rugged times there may have been no other way to survive than to assume the role of the aggressor; few people died a peaceful death from old age.

Priscilla CHING-CHUNG

Chen Shou. *Empresses and Consorts: Selections from Chen Shou's "Records of the Three States" with Pei Songzhi's Commentary,* trans. Robert J. Cutter and William Gordon Crowell. Honolulu: University of Hawaii Press, 1999, 47, 50–51, 55–56, 122–24; 163, 212–16.

340 SUN LUBAN

Crespigny, Rafe de. *Generals of the South: The Foundation and Early History of the Three Kingdoms State of Wu.* Canberra: Australian National University, 1990, 483–84, 511, 522.

Sanguo zhi. Beijing: Zhonghua shuju, 1959, vol. 5, 48.1151; vol. 5, 50.1200–1; vol. 5, 59.1369–70; vol. 5, 60.1383, n. 1; vol. 5, 64.1448.

Sima Guang. *The Chronicle of the Three Kingdoms (220–265), Chapters 69–78 from the Tzu chih t'ung chien of Ssu-ma Kuang,* trans. Achilles Fang, ed. Glen W. Baxter. Cambridge, MA: Harvard University Press, 1965, vol. 1, 683–84, 690; vol. 2, 15, 70–71, 86, 141, 160, 165, 181, 199, 228, 285, 295, 302, 313, 327, 377, 384.

Sun Luyu: *see* **Sun Luban**

Sun Polu Wu Furen: *see* **Wu, Wife of Caitiff-Smashing-General Sun**

Sun Quan Mu: *see* **Wu, Wife of Caitiff-Smashing-General Sun**

Sun Quan's Mother, Lady Wu: *see* **Wu, Wife of Caitiff-Smashing-General Sun**

T

Tanbei: *see* **Tanluo**

Tanluo

Tanluo, fl. late fourth century, was a Buddhist nun. She was responsible for the construction of many Buddhist buildings during the Eastern Jin dynasty but little else is known about her, not even her native place.

Tanluo was a disciple of the nun Tanbei (d. 396), who gained the support of Emperor Mu (Sima Dan, r. 344–361) of Eastern Jin and his empress née He. Emperor Mu is said to have suggested that Tanbei was probably the most distinguished nun in the capital, Jiankang, and in 354 Empress He sponsored the building of the Yong'an Monastery for her. Tanbei's fame grew after that, yet she is said to have remained modest, entirely lacking in arrogance.

Nothing is known of Tanluo's background, but she is said to have been widely read in Buddhist sutras and the monastic rules (*vinaya*). She was richly blessed with wit and talent, while her thinking was precise and thorough. On the death of Tanbei, Emperor Xiaowu (Sima Yao, 362–396; r. 372–396) ordered Tanluo to assume her teacher's responsibilities as abbess. She added to the monastery a four-story pagoda as well as lecture halls and living quarters; she also had an image of the reclining Buddha and a hall with a shrine of seven Buddhas built.

To construct these buildings and images, Tanluo would have required planning skills as well as the ability to manage the finances for such large projects. She may also have needed some knowledge of building and construction as well as image making. We know of no other examples of women in control of such large projects at that time, but the example she set may have helped other nuns or even secular women enjoy similar opportunities. Tanluo was therefore a woman who not only had a say in her own life but whose life and work touched many others.

Lily Xiao Hong LEE

Baochang [Shih Pao-ch'ang]. *Lives of the Nuns: Biographies of Chinese Buddhist Nuns from the Fourth to Sixth Centuries: A Translation of the Pi-ch'iu-ni chuan,* trans. Kathryn Ann Tsai. Honolulu: University of Hawaii Press, 1994, 26.
Baochang [Pao-ch'ang]. "Tanbei zhuan." *Piqiuni zhuan,* 2. In *Taishō shinshū Daizōkyō,* ed. Takakusu Junjirō, Watanabe Kaigyoku, and Ono Genmyō. Tokyo: Taishō Issaikyō Kankōkai, 1924–1929, vol. 50, 935–36.
Hong Pimou. *Zhongguo ming ni.* Shanghai: Shanghai renmin chubanshe, 1995, 10–11.
Tsai, Kathryn Ann. "The Chinese Buddhist Monastic Order for Women: The First Two Centuries." In *Women in China: Current Directions in Historical Scholarship,* ed. Richard W. Guisso and Stanley Johannesen. Youngstown, NY: Philo Press, 1981, 1–20.

Tao Kan Mu: *see* **Zhan, Tao Kan's Mother**

W

Wang Shuying's Wife: *see* **Liu Lingxian**

Wang Yan Qi: *see* **Guo of Western Jin**

Wang Zhenfeng, Empress of Emperor Ming of Liu Song
Empress Wang (Mingdi Wang Huanghou), 436–479, whose name was Wang Zhenfeng, was the principal consort of Emperor Ming (Liu Yu, 439–472; r. 465–472), sixth emperor of the southern Liu Song dynasty. She was born into the elite Wang family of Linyi, in present-day Shandong Province; her great-great-grandfather Wang Dao had helped found the Eastern Jin dynasty and had served its three first emperors as grand chancellor. Her great-grandfather Wang Shao had also served Eastern Jin, as imperial secretary (*shangshu*), as did her grandfather Wang Mu, as prefect of Linhai. Her father, Wang Senglang, was posthumously honored as one of the Three Dignitaries (*sansi*) for his services to the Liu Song dynasty. Her brother, Wang Jingwen (d. 472), had held the powerful position of prefect of Yangzhou until his death; he was ordered by Emperor Ming to commit suicide lest the emperor's young son and heir was no match should Wang Jingwen attempt to seize power after Emperor Ming's death.

Wang Zhenfeng was twelve years old in 448 when she married Liu Yu, who, as the eleventh son of Emperor Wen (Liu Yilong, 407–453; r. 424–453), was not in the direct line of succession to the throne. Liu Yu was installed as King of Xiangdong, with Wang Zhenfeng his consort, and she gave birth to two daughters, Princess Lingchang and Princess Ling'an. In 465, however, a palace coup removed Liu Yu's nephew (Liu Ziye, known to history as the Former Deposed Emperor [Qianfeidi]; r. 464–465) from the throne and Liu Yu's foster mother, Lady Lu (412–466), formally installed him on the throne. Wang Zhenfeng thus became Empress Wang. Historians appear to have held

Empress Wang in higher esteem than they did her husband. We are told that Emperor Ming enjoyed looking at naked women; he would order palace women to strip naked as his consorts looked on, deeming this entertainment. Empress Wang, however, is said to have refused to look, covering her eyes with a fan. This enraged Emperor Ming, who claimed that she should not refuse to be entertained now that they were finally in a position to enjoy themselves. Clearly, he believed that humiliation of other women, which he found entertaining, should also entertain her.

Emperor Ming's eldest son succeeded him and is known to history as the Later Deposed Emperor (Houfeidi, 463–476; r. 472–477). This emperor was the son of a secondary consort, Lady Chen, but upon his ascension to the throne Empress Wang was given the title Empress Dowager Wang and she assumed responsibility for his moral education. The young emperor refused to be led in the ways of righteousness and instead plotted to poison her. Apparently aware of his destructive nature, Empress Dowager Wang secretly lent her support to the many princes who were scheming to be rid of him. Their plot succeeded and after this emperor was killed in a coup, Emperor Ming's third son, the eleven-year-old Liu Zhun, was installed as emperor (Emperor Shun, r. 477–479). The appointment of this boy emperor presaged the demise of the Liu Song dynasty, for the man appointed his regent—Xiao Daocheng—overthrew the dynasty in 479, establishing the Qi dynasty and declaring himself emperor (Emperor Gao, r. 479–482).

With the collapse of Liu Song, Empress Dowager Wang was demoted to Consort of Ruyin; she died the same year, at the age of forty-four, and was posthumously honored as Empress Gong. The judgment history has passed on Empress Wang is that though she was a good empress she was powerless to save a dynasty that was already in decline.

Priscilla CHING-CHUNG

Chen Quanli and Hou Xinyi, eds. *Hou fei cidian.* Xi'an: Shaanxi renmin chubanshe, 1991, 61.

Hucker, Charles O. *A Dictionary of Official Titles in Imperial China.* Stanford, CA: Stanford University Press, 1985.

Nan shi. Beijing: Zhonghua shuju, 1975; 1983, vol. 1, 3.77; vol. 2, 11.324–25.

Shang Xizhi. *Tales of Empresses and Imperial Consorts in China,* trans. Sun Haichen. Hong Kong: Haifeng Publishing, 1998, 91–92, 177.

Song shu. Beijing: Zhonghua shuju, 1974; 1983, vol. 1, 8.151, 171; vol. 1, 10.193; vol. 4, 41.1295–96.

Zhu Lei and Chen Feng, eds. *Waiqi zhuan.* Zhengzhou: Henan renmin chubanshe, 1992, 397–408.

Wei Furen: *see* **Wei Shuo**

Wei Huacun

Wei Huacun, 251 or 252–334, of Rencheng (in present-day Shandong Province), is revered in the Highest Clarity (*shangqing*) sect of Daoism under various titles, including Lady Wei of the Southern Peak (Nanyue Wei Furen), Lady of South Marchmount (Nanyue Furen), and Primal Mistress of Purple Barrens (Zixu Yuanjun). She is described as the "Shangqing preceptress" for her role in revealing thirty-one scrolls of Highest Clarity scriptures to the medium Yang Xi (b. 330) between 364 and 370. While there is some doubt that she was a historical figure, it is possible that she was modeled on a practicing Daoist, as she is said to have held the rank of libationer (*jijiu*), or wise elder, in Zhang Daoling's Way of the Celestial Masters (*vide* Zhang Lu's Mother). Members of this Daoist sect spread throughout north China in the early third century and with the collapse of the Western Jin dynasty in 316 many migrated to the south, where an indigenous shamanistic religion flourished. In what some historians see as an attempt by the southern gentry to combat the religious and political dominance of these northern émigrés, a new form of Daoism emerged that incorporated both shamanistic elements and aspects of the Way of the Celestial Masters.

In 364, the southern medium Yang Xi received the first of a series of visitations from perfected beings (*zhenren*) who descended to him from the Heaven of Highest Clarity. As instructed, he recorded the dictations of these deities, and it is in Yang Xi's written record that Lady Wei is first mentioned, as a director of destinies (*siming*) and as Yang Xi's teacher. A purely spirit figure, she spoke of and quoted scriptures, most of which were concerned with practical matters such as cleanliness, hygiene, and rituals. She offered advice to Yang Xi's gentry employers on spiritual and medical matters and was the divinity whose aid it was necessary to enlist, by means of written petitions, for curing serious illnesses (*vide* Xu Baoguang).

More than a century after Yang Xi recorded these visitations, the scholar-official and Daoist Tao Hongjing (452–536) retired to Maoshan (near present-day Nanjing) and collated them into a text he named *Declarations of the Perfected* (Zhengao), adding his own commentary. To Yang Xi's portrait of Lady Wei, his commentary added a partly revealed biography that had been compiled by the perfected. In this biography were intimations of prior mortality in the form of a name (Wei Huacun), two sons, an implied husband surnamed Liu, skill in a technique of long life (eating peach skins), and earthly status as a libationer. Her given name, Huacun, literally means "Blossom Visualization," an inescapable reference to the alchemical drugs favored by Tao Hongjing on Maoshan and the Highest Clarity meditation practice of visualizing divinities within one's body. Tao Hongjing also noted that Lady Wei had transmitted sacred scriptures to Yang Xi and that one of her sons had given Yang Xi a sacred text.

As Edward Schafer has noted in his article "The Restoration of the Shrine of Wei Hua-ts'un," the rulers of the Tang dynasty (618–907) sponsored Daoist priests and priestesses, erecting friaries on mountains and in major cities throughout China. Shrines were established on the sacred mountains and Highest Clarity Daoism enjoyed increasing status. At the end of the seventh century, the Daoist priestess (*nüdaoshi*) Huang Lingwei (c. 640–721; she is also known as Huagu, or Miss Flower) discovered an overgrown shrine dedicated to Lady Wei Huacun at Linchuan, in the northeast of present-day Jiangxi Province. Her restoration and subsequent tending of the shrine, which according to tradition Lady Wei herself had erected, prompted the scholar-official Yan Zhenqing (709–784) to compose a eulogy to which he prefaced a biography of the Lady. In this biography Lady Wei gained a fully documented mortal life, complete with a birthplace, year of birth, and names and dates of father, husband, and sons, the moral and spiritual rectitude of which

344 *WEI HUACUN*

accounted for her deification. Described as possessing the marks of transcendence—"a woman of crystal lit from within, her vital organs shining like luminescent gems"—she did not die but escaped her mortal form through "sword release" (*jianjie*). After sixteen years of posthumous study on a holy mountain, she was visited by Queen Mother of the West (*q.v.*), who accompanied Lady Wei to her permanent dwelling on Great Huo Mountain (in present-day Zhejiang Province; some sources place Mount Huo in Fujian Province, others have her on Mount Heng in Hunan Province). This became the standard hagiography of Lady Wei, Wei Huacun.

Wei Huacun is very possibly a case of reverse euhemerization, whereby a purely imaginary figure gradually acquires the trappings of a previous human existence until it is generally accepted that she was a mortal who achieved divine status. It is equally possible that she had genuine earthly origins in the female libationers of the Way of the Celestial Masters. All that can be said with any certainty is that while she was revered initially as a master healer, in the Way of the Celestial Masters tradition, by Tang she had become a divine beauty—"she was luminous and pure, fresh and pellucid" (Schafer)—who had dominion over the sacred southern mountain.

Sue WILES

Bokenkamp, Stephen. "Declarations of the Perfected." In *Religions of China in Practice,* ed. Donald S. Lopez, Jr. Princeton, NJ: Princeton University Press, 1996, 166–79.
———. *Early Daoist Scriptures.* Berkeley: University of California Press, 1997, 251, 252, 262, 298.
Robson, James. "Virtual Images/Real Shadows: The Transposition of the Myths and Cults of Lady Wei." Paper presented at the Association for Asian Studies 2003 Annual Meeting, March 27–30, 2003, New York. Available at http://scbs.stanford.edu/resources/Daoism_panel/index.html.
Schafer, Edward H. "The Restoration of the Shrine of Wei Hua-ts'un at Lin-ch'uan in the Eighth Century." *Journal of Oriental Studies* 15 (1977): 124–37.
———. "Three Divine Women of South China." *Chinese Literature: Essays, Articles, Review* 1 (1979): 31–42.
Wiles, Sue. "Gone with the Yin: The Position of Women in Early Superior Clarity (Shangqing) Daoism." Ph.D. dissertation, University of Sydney, 1986, 1988, 129–30, 136–74.

Wei, Lady: *see* **Wei Huacun; Wei Shuo**

Wei of the Southern Peak, Lady: *see* **Wei Huacun**

Wei Shuo
Wei Shuo, 272–349, *zi* Maoyi, more popularly known simply as Lady Wei (Wei Furen), was China's earliest known female calligrapher; she also taught the famous male calligrapher Wang Xizhi (309–c. 365).

Wei Shuo was born during the Western Jin dynasty into a family of distinguished officials and scholars native to Anyi County in Hedong (present-day Xia County in Shanxi Province). Her ancestors had been known for their Confucian scholarship since the Han dynasty. Although her relationship with him has not been established absolutely, there is strong circumstantial evidence that she was the granddaughter of Wei Yi, imperial secretary (*shangshu puye*) of the Wei dynasty and the first member of the Wei family to be known for calligraphy. He is said to have loved various styles of writing and to have been skilled in all of them. Wei Shuo's brother Wei Zhan was chamberlain for law enforcement (*tingwei*) during Western Jin and his contribution to the legal practices of Jin have been noted in the histories. Her uncle Wei Guan (220–291) was a close and important adviser of Emperor Wu (Sima Yan, 236–290; r. 265–290), the founder of Western Jin, and held a number of important positions at both the Wei and the Jin courts. His expertise in the cursive (*cao*) style of calligraphy was overshadowed only by his political importance. Wei Shuo's cousin Wei Heng (a son of Wei Guan) was skilled in the cursive style and the clerical (*li*) style and wrote a treatise on calligraphy entitled *The Trend Towards Four Styles of Calligraphy* (Si ti shu shi). This is included in his biography in the official *History of the Jin Dynasty* (Jin shu) and became a classic in its field. While Wei Shuo married into an important family, her husband's family was not as prestigious as her own. Her husband, Li Ju, rose to the position of regional inspector (*cishi*) of Jiangzhou (the area covered by present-day Jiangxi Province) and their son Li Chong was also known for his calligraphy. We know that Li Chong held the position of magistrate (*ling*) of Shan District and editorial director of the Palace Library (*da zhuzuo*) and he is credited with creating the Four Bureaux (*sibu*) system of classifying books, which was used from the Liu Song dynasty until early modern times.

There is no biography of Wei Shuo in the official history of Jin and the little we know about her life has been pieced together from various sources, including the biographies of her male relatives and works on calligraphy. From the biography of her son, Li Chong, we know that he lost his father early in life and the family was in extremely straitened circumstances. Li Chong worked as an aide and a secretary for important officials of the central government, which probably did not bring him much financial reward, until he eventually begged one of his employers to give him a better-paid post as a local official. Not long after this, however, he met with bereavement when his mother died. This suggests that Wei Shuo raised her son under difficult financial circumstances and that she was unable to enjoy this improvement in the family's finances. Her son's biography also states that he was skilled at the regular (*kai*) style of calligraphy, one of the styles his mother was famous for, and that his skill matched that of Zhong You and Suo Jing, both famous calligraphers of the Han-Wei period. His biography makes no mention of his mother having influenced his calligraphy, yet says that his contemporaries lauded him as a calligrapher.

While her name is not found in the official history of Jin, despite the fact that her teaching and influence should have been evident from the fame her son achieved for his calligraphy, Wei Shuo is frequently mentioned in early works on calligraphy dating from the Tang dynasty (618–907). It is through these works that she is known, even though the information provided is brief and often contains mistakes. She is said to have inherited the style of Zhong You (d. 230); given that he died almost fifty years before she was born, it is clear that she could not have learned from him personally. However, her grandfather Wei Yi served in the same court as Zhong You and it is pos-

346   *WEI SHUO*

sible that the two families were friendly, so that Wei Shuo could have learned from younger members of Zhong You's family, possibly a woman. In any case, Zhong You was such a renowned calligrapher that many people would have seen and collected his works. As lovers and practitioners of calligraphy themselves, the Wei family would certainly have possessed copies and rubbings of his works. Calligraphers traditionally began their studies by copying famous works, and Wei Shuo could have copied Zhong You's works extensively, thus becoming an unofficial heir of his style.

There are no extant examples of Wei Shuo's calligraphy. One piece attributed to her was forged by Li Huailin in the Tang dynasty. However, because critics compared her with Zhong You and characterized her style as "lean," we may deduce that she had a forceful and "bony" style, perhaps not conforming to the typically feminine style, which is soft and graceful. It is said that she was very attentive to natural phenomena and applied her observations to her work: she would strive to capture in certain strokes the fall of a stone from a cliff, or the curve of clumps of old rattan resting against a tree. The styles she was known for were the clerical, the regular, and the running (*xing*) styles.

Two things stand out in Wei Shuo's career as a calligrapher. One is that she authored the treatise *Illustrated Formation of the Writing Brush* (Bi zhen tu). This treatise is only about 1,000 words long, and while the title suggests it originally included illustrations only the text survives. In this text, Wei Shuo criticizes her contemporaries for wishing to become great calligraphers overnight. She offers practical advice about the choice of brush, ink stone, ink stick, and paper, and then proceeds to describe the correct posture for doing calligraphy. She continues with an exposition of the basic strokes and the method and principle of executing them. Her treatise does not use flowery language and vague expressions, as some other works on calligraphy do; everything she says is precise and practical, helpful especially to beginners. This work influenced many later works on the use of the brush.

The second thing for which Wei Shuo is well known is that she was the teacher of Wang Xizhi, arguably the greatest calligrapher of China and East Asia. Wei Shuo was a cousin of Wang Xizhi's father, Wang Kuang. This familial relationship, in addition to the more than thirty-year age difference between them, made their female teacher/male student relationship more plausible at a time when there was a fairly strict segregation of the sexes. One source, written much later, has Wang Kuang obtaining Cai Yong's calligraphic method from Wei Shuo and teaching it to his son, Wang Xizhi. Also, in a work traditionally considered as Wang Xizhi's own, he admitted being Wei Shuo's pupil, but virtually said that learning from her was a waste of time. This particular work is not found in Wang Xizhi's collected works; it is in a collection on calligraphy compiled later, in the Tang dynasty, by Zhang Yanyuan and recent scholarship has questioned its reliability. Another Tang work on calligraphy tells the unlikely story that Wang Kuang gave calligraphers' treatises on the use of the brush to the twelve-year-old Wang Xizhi to study. Lady Wei noticed a sudden improvement in the boy's calligraphy and suspected that he had read old treatises. She burst into tears and said, "You will certainly eclipse my fame one day!" This sounds as if it were fabricated after Wang Xizhi's reputation had far exceeded that of his teacher.

Wei Shuo taught at least two more students besides Wang Xizhi. One was her son

Li Chong and the other was her husband's nephew Li Shi. The former was adept in the regular style and the latter in the clerical style, both of which were considered to have been Wei Shuo's special skills. Her other specialty, the running style, was also one of Wang Xizhi's specialties.

Whatever Wang Xizhi thought of his old teacher, it is undeniable that he once studied under Wei Shuo. Being a woman in pre-modern China, Wei Shuo did not have the opportunities Wang Xizhi had and was possibly therefore not able to develop her potential to the full. Wang Xizhi became a cult figure during the Tang dynasty and continues to be popular today, while Wei Shuo is mentioned less and less frequently in works on calligraphy after Tang. Today, we should acknowledge Wei Shuo as at least a bridge between Zhong You and Wang Xizhi, two great calligraphers of early China.

Lily Xiao Hong LEE

Jin shu. Beijing: Zhonghua shuju, 1974, vol. 4, 36.1055–68.
Lee, Lily Xiao Hong [Xiao Hong]. "Jindai canyu zhuliu shehui huodong de funü." In her *Yin zhi de: Zhongguo funü yanjiu lunwenji.* Beijing: Xinshijie chubanshe, 1999, 82–95.
Sanguo zhi. Wei shu. Beijing: Zhonghua shuju, 1959, vol. 3, 21.610–13.
Wang Sengqian. "Song Yang Xin cai gulai nengshu renming." In *Fashu yaolu,* ed. Zhang Yanyuan, bound in *Tangren shuxue lunzhu.* Taipei: Shijie shuju, 1975, 5.
Wang Xizhi. "Ti Wei furen bizhen tu hou." In *Fashu yaolu,* ed. Zhang Yanyuan, bound in *Tangren shuxue lunzhu.* Taipei: Shijie shuju, 1975, 4.
Women of China. "An Ancient Calligrapher." From *Departed But Not Forgotten.* www.womenofchina.com.cn, accessed August 21, 2005.
Xie Wuliang. *Zhongguo funü wenxue shi.* Zhengzhou: Zhongzhou guji chubanshe, 1992, vol. IIB, 6–8.
Yin Wei. *Zhonghua wuqian nian yiyuan cainü.* Taipei: Guanya wenhua, 1991, 56–59.
Zhang Huaiguan. "Shu duan." In *Fashu yaolu,* ed. Zhang Yanyuan, bound in *Tangren shuxue lunzhu.* Taipei: Shijie shuju, 1975, 128, 137.

Wei Taizu, Consort of: *see* **Ding, Consort of Cao Cao, King of Wei**

Wencheng Wenming Huanghou: *see* **Feng, Empress of Emperor Wencheng of Northern Wei**

Wende Guo Huanghou: *see* **Guo, Empress of Emperor Wen of Wei**

Wendi Yuan Huanghou: *see* **Yuan Qigui, Empress of Emperor Wen of Liu Song**

Wenming née Feng, Empress Dowager: *see* **Feng, Empress of Emperor Wencheng of Northern Wei**

Wenxian Dugu Huanghou: *see* **Dugu, Empress of Emperor Wen of Sui**

Wenzhao, Empress: *see* **Zhen, Empress of Emperor Wen of Wei**

348 WENZHAO ZHEN HUANGHOU

Wenzhao Zhen Huanghou: *see* **Zhen, Empress of Emperor Wen of Wei**

Wu, Consort of Liu Bei: *see* **Wu, Empress of the Former Sovereign of Shu**

Wu, Empress of the Former Sovereign of Shu

Empress Mu née Wu (Xianzhu Mu Huanghou), c. 190–245, was a native of Chenliu (near the present-day city of Luoyang in northern Henan Province). In 219 she became the formal wife of Liu Bei (Emperor Zhaolie, also known as the Former Sovereign [*xianzhu*] of Shu, 161–223; r. 221–223), founder of the Three Kingdoms state of Shu Han.

Their mother died when the future Empress Mu and her elder brother Wu Yi were young, and they accompanied their father when he joined his colleague Liu Yan in Shu, in the region of present-day Sichuan Province. Liu Yan was an imperial clansman of the Han dynasty and he harbored imperial ambitions, wishing to usurp the throne of Emperor Xian (Liu Xie, 181–234; r. 189–220). Therefore, when he heard that a skillful physiognomist had predicted great honor for the young daughter of his friend, Liu Yan married her to his son, Liu Mao, whose older brother Liu Zhang (d. 219) was governor of Yizhou (in present-day Sichuan Province).

This was a chaotic time marked by peasant uprisings that heralded the final collapse of the Eastern Han dynasty and saw the formation of the three powerful rival states of the Three Kingdoms (*sanguo*) period: Wei in the north, Shu Han in the west, and Wu in the south and east. The warrior hero Liu Bei, who claimed kinship to the Han royal house, had gained control of Yizhou by the early years of the third century. He had also joined forced with Sun Quan (182–252; r. 222–252) of the southeastern state of Wu and in 209 had married Sun Quan's younger sister, Lady Sun. Lady Sun is described as a formidable young woman, as courageous as her four famous brothers and with over 100 female attendants capable of bearing arms. Tradition has it that every time Liu Bei, then almost fifty, laid eyes on her his heart turned cold, even though she was barely in her twenties. Believing her capable of starting an uprising in support of her brother, Liu Bei's chief strategist advised him to return her to her home state of Wu. Then, when Sun Quan learned that Liu Bei was preparing a western campaign in 211, he sent a boat to bring his sister back to Wu. Before she left in 212, Lady Sun attempted, unsuccessfully, to kidnap the heir apparent, Liu Shan (known to history as the Later Sovereign [*houzhu*] of Shu, 207–271; r. 223–263), over whom she had exercised guardianship.

It was at this point that the future Empress Mu became part of Liu Bei's life. Liu Bei was advised to take her, now a widow, as his wife. Initially he hesitated, thinking he might be of the same lineage as her deceased husband, Liu Mao, since both men traced their ancestry to Emperor Jing (Liu Qi, 188–141 B.C.E.; r. 156–141 B.C.E.) of Western Han, which would have made her almost his sister-in-law. Such a marriage would have been unacceptable according to a strict interpretation of Chinese propriety. However, one of his advisers argued that it was permissible for him to marry her, citing a precedent of the Spring and Autumn period, so Liu Bei took her as his consort and appointed her to the rank of Lady (*furen*). In 219, he bestowed on her the title Queen of Hanzhong as he had already assumed the title King of Hanzhong. The following year the Han emperor, Emperor Xian (181–234; r. 189–220), abdicated in favor of Cao Pi (187–226), who immediately declared himself emperor (Emperor Wen, r. 220–226) of the Wei dynasty. Not prepared to swear fealty to Cao Pi's Wei dynasty, Liu Bei claimed that Emperor Xian had been murdered and, basing the legitimacy of his own claim to the heavenly mandate on his imperial bloodline, he established the kingdom of Shu Han in early 221. He declared himself emperor (*xianzhu*) and named the childless Lady Wu as his empress, to serve the ancestral temple and be mother over his empire.

Liu Bei reigned for only two years before he died, in 223, and was succeeded by his son, Liu Shan, whose mother, Lady Gan (*q.v.* Gan, Empress of the Former Sovereign of Shu), had died two years earlier. As the principal consort and empress of the young emperor's father, Lady Wu was named Empress Dowager Mu. Her brother Wu Yi was promoted to general of chariots and cavalry (*cheji jiangjun*) and appointed a Prefectural Marquis (*xianhou*). Empress Dowager Mu lived on into middle age and died in 245. She was buried in Huiling (in present-day Chengdu) alongside Liu Bei and his secondary consort Lady Gan.

Empress Mu appears to have been an unremarkable and unobtrusive woman who, because of the prediction of a physiognomist that she would one day enjoy great honor, was sought after by two men who aspired to be emperor. The culture of her time did not prevent the remarriage of widows, but this was to change in later centuries, when widows who remarried were severely discriminated against.

Priscilla CHING-CHUNG

Chen Shou. *Empresses and Consorts: Selections from Chen Shou's "Records of the Three States" with Pei Songzhi's Commentary,* trans. Robert J. Cutter and William Gordon Crowell. Honolulu: University of Hawaii Press, 1999, 49, 116–18, 209–10.

Crespigny, Rafe de. *Generals of the South: The Foundation and Early History of the Three Kingdoms State of Wu.* Canberra: Australian National University, 1990, 204, n. 8.

Sanguo zhi. Beijing: Zhonghua shuju, 1959, vol. 4, 34.906.

Sima Guang. *The Chronicle of the Three Kingdoms (220–265), Chapters 69–78 from the Tzu chih t'ung chien of Ssu-ma Kuang,* trans. Achilles Fang, ed. Glen W. Baxter. Cambridge, MA: Harvard University Press, 1965, vol. 1, 44, 48, 65–67, 588–89, 696.

Wu, Wife of Caitiff-Smashing-General Sun

Lady Wu (Sun Polu Wu Furen), c. 158–202, whose given names are not recorded, of Qiantang (near the present-day city of Hangzhou in Zhejiang Province) married into the Sun family that eventually founded the Three Kingdoms state of Wu. Twenty-six years after her death she was honored with the posthumous title Empress Dowager Wulie when her second son, Sun Quan (182–252; r. 222–252), proclaimed himself Great Emperor (*dadi*) of Wu.

With the gradual disintegration of the Eastern Han dynasty from the mid-second century onward, the three rival states emerged that gave their name to the subsequent

Three Kingdoms period. The northern state of Wei established a power base in the 190s as Cao Cao (155–220) gained increasing control over the puppet Han Emperor Xian (Liu Xie, 181–234; r. 189–220). The Shu Han to the west claimed the heavenly mandate of Han through the kinship of the warrior hero Liu Bei (161–223; r. 221–223) with Emperor Jing (Liu Qi, 188–141 B.C.E.; r. 156–141 B.C.E.). The southeastern state of Wu, however, was founded on the military accomplishments of the Sun family, which claimed descent from Sun Wu, author of the sixth-century B.C.E. military classic *The Art of War* (Sunzi bingfa).

The family of Lady Wu had migrated sometime earlier from the city of Wu (near present-day Suzhou) to Qiantang, where she lived in an extended family with her younger brother Wu Jing (d. 204) after their parents died. While her family, "the Wu of Qiantang," was not one of the four great clans of the south—those being the Zhu, the Gu, the Lu, and the Zhang—it had considerable social status. Members of her family therefore objected when the nineteen-year-old military man Sun Jian (155–192), then stationed at Yandu (near present-day Yancheng in Jiangsu Province), asked for her hand in marriage in 174, considering him "an idle, coarse fellow." They finally gave their consent, however, after Lady Wu persuaded them she would take full responsibility if the marriage turned out to be a disaster. It appears to have been a harmonious union and Lady Wu is often cited as a model ruler's wife. Her husband eventually rose to become Caitiff-Smashing-General Sun (Sun Polu).

Lady Wu gave birth to four sons—Sun Ce (175–200), Sun Quan, Sun Yi (184–203), and Sun Kuang (b. 190?)—as well as a daughter (Lady Sun, b. c. 189), while her husband fathered several children by other women. When pregnant with her first son, Lady Wu dreamt that the moon entered her bosom, and when pregnant with her second son she dreamt that the sun entered her bosom. Her husband responded by saying that because the sun and moon are the most important elements of *yin* and *yang,* her dreams signified that his descendants would be noble and would flourish. This interpretation is supposed to have foretold the historic roles her first two sons would play; however, it may well have been invented in hindsight to justify their claims to authority.

Sun Jian generally took his family with him as he pursued his military career, remaining always loyal to the Han dynasty. In 184, they were in Shouchun (present-day Shouxin in Anhui Province), where he assumed a high military command in the major campaigns to put down the Yellow Turban peasant rebellion. Two years later, Sun Jian was appointed to court as a gentleman-consultant (*yilang*) and his family joined him at the northern capital of Luoyang. Lady Wu and her children then moved to Changsha Commandery, one of the key areas of the Han empire, when he was appointed grand administrator (*taishou*), a high-ranking position outside the capital. In 190, however, Sun Jian led his army against the frontier general Dong Zhuo (d. 192), who was attempting to usurp the authority of Han, and Lady Wu and her children were sent to live in Shu county (west of present-day Lujiang in Anhui Province). There, the prominent local Zhou family put them up in a large house and Lady Wu's oldest son, Sun Ce, began his lifelong friendship with the future general Zhou Yu (175–209); both boys were then fifteen. Meanwhile, Sun Jian joined forces with Yuan Shu (d. 199), a gentry commander loyal to Han, and in 191 captured Luoyang. He was killed in a night battle toward the end of that year but his body was eventually returned to his family and he was buried at Qu'e in Danyang Commandery (present-day Danyang District, Jiangsu Province). Lady Wu and her children—the oldest was just sixteen at the time—then moved to Jiangdu County in Guangling on the northern bank of the Yangzi, south of the present-day city of Yangzhou (Jiangsu Province).

Two years later, at the age of eighteen, Sun Ce assumed command of the loyal core of his father's troops and crossed the Yangzi River to join his maternal uncle Wu Jing, Grand Administrator of Danyang Commandery. Like Lady Wu, her younger brother Wu Jing contributed substantially to consolidating the power of the Sun family. He had remained an important adviser and ally to Sun Jian, who appointed him his chief commandant of cavalry (*jiduwei*), and after Sun Jian's death he supported Sun Ce, helping him capture Liyang (in present-day Anhui Province) and eventually Jiangdong. (Jiangdong [lit. east of the (Yangzi) River] is the region where the present-day provinces of Jiangsu, Anhui, and Zhejiang intersect. The Yangzi River flows south-southwest to north-northeast between Wuhu and Nanjing, and the area on its south bank there was known as Jiangdong because it is in fact east of the river. In the Three Kingdoms period, Jiangdong indicated the area controlled by the state of Wu.) In 196, Sun Ce had his mother and his younger siblings brought to Jiangdong and appointed his fourteen-year-old brother Sun Quan to a nominal title, apparently for reasons of status rather than administration, enjoining his trusted follower Zhang Zhao to help the inexperienced boy.

Lady Wu was an important ingredient in the success of her two eldest sons. She was aware of the shortcomings of Sun Ce, an irascible young man with a tendency toward making rash decisions when he was angry, and frequently offered him sound advice. Two famous incidents will serve to illustrate her wisdom and wit as much as her compassion. In 196, Sun Ce captured an older man named Wang Sheng, the grand administrator of Hepu Commandery in the south, and was about to have him executed. However, Lady Wu spoke up for Wang Sheng: "Wang Sheng was courting me at the same time as your father. Now all of his sons and brothers are dead and this old man alone remains. Why should you be afraid of him?" Sun Ce heeded her words and spared Wang Sheng. The other incident concerned a man on the brink of execution because he had contradicted Sun Ce. All appeals to save this man—Wei Teng—had fallen on deaf ears, "but then Lady Wu stood by the side of a deep well and said to him, 'You are building a position at the south of the Yangzi, and the work is not yet done. This is the very time you should treat your worthy men well and be courteous to your officers, passing over their faults and thinking only of their good work. Officer Wei was simply doing his duty. If you kill him today, everyone will turn from you tomorrow. Rather than see such a disaster come upon us, I would first jump into this well.'" Alarmed and impressed, Sun Ce let Wei Teng go free.

After the death of Sun Ce in 200 at the age of twenty-five, Lady Wu continued to assist her eighteen-year-old son Sun Quan in the same way until her death two years later. She is credited with offering Sun Quan sound advice when she told him not to accede to the request of the powerful northern warlord Cao Cao to send hostages to his court. Even as she approached death, from an undisclosed cause, Lady Wu remained involved in affairs of state, consulting with Zhang Zhao and others to the very end. She was buried at Gaoling alongside her husband, who was given the posthumous title of Emperor Wulie in 229; her son Sun Ce was posthumously named Prince Huan of Changsha at the same time.

Lady Wu was clearly a strong and capable woman, a worthy role model for her daughter, Lady Sun, who was sent to the western state of Shu Han as a marriage partner for Liu Bei, probably in 209. Lady Sun had with her an entourage of 100 female attendants capable of bearing arms and was described as being as courageous as her brothers. It is impossible to know anything of this marriage between the fifty-year-old Liu Bei, who is said to have quaked at the very sight of his young wife, and the twenty-year-old Lady Sun, but Lady Sun was sent home when relations between Liu Bei and the Sun family began to deteriorate. Shu considered her a very risky proposition because she was capable of staging a coup. This was clearly an accurate assessment because before leaving Liu Bei in 211 or 212 she attempted, albeit unsuccessfully, to kidnap his young son and heir apparent, Liu Shan. Although not of Lady Wu's blood, one of Sun Jian's unnamed younger sisters was also familiar with military matters. She is recorded as having advised her son Xu Kun, with whom she was traveling, to cut rushes and reeds as rafts to supplement his ships to ferry troops across the Yangzi River. Her son passed this advice on to Sun Ce, who moved his army and established a new beachhead against his enemy.

Two of Lady Wu's granddaughters—Sun Luban (*q.v.*) and Sun Luyu (*vide* Sun Luban)—were politically ambitious. However, since they were not in a position to influence court affairs directly, as Lady Wu had been, they manipulated affairs through their support for contending heirs apparent, with disastrous results.

Perhaps best described as a frontier matriarch, Lady Wu appears to have set the tone for a generation of memorable women. On the other hand, she may have simply been typical of the courageous and politically active women of the Wu and Sun families, who were able to exercise their talents more fully than the vast majority of their sisters solely by virtue of where and when they were born. Finding themselves at the top of the social heap in a newly established state during a relatively chaotic age, these women grasped the opportunity to exert their influence and attain some measure of power.

Priscilla CHING-CHUNG

Chen Shou. *Empresses and Consorts: Selections from Chen Shou's "Records of the Three States" with Pei Songzhi's Commentary,* trans. Robert J. Cutter and William Gordon Crowell. Honolulu: University of Hawaii Press, 1999, 47, 50–51, 55–56, 122–24, 163, 212–16.
Crespigny, Rafe de. *Generals of the South: The Foundation and Early History of the Three Kingdoms State of Wu.* Canberra: Australian National University, 1990, 85–86, 128–29, 134–36, 147–48, 152–53, 163, 165–67, 207 n. 91, 223–24, 294 n. 8, 511, 522.
Sanguo zhi. Wushu. Beijing: Zhonghua shuju, 1975, vol. 5, 46.1093–113; vol. 5, 50.1195–96.
Sima Guang. *The Chronicle of the Three Kingdoms (220–265), Chapters 69–78 from the Tzu*

chih t'ung chien of Ssu-ma Kuang, trans. Achilles Fang, ed. Glen W. Baxter. Cambridge, MA: Harvard University Press, 1965, vol. 1, 302.

Yang Chen. *Sanguo huiyao.* Taipei: Shijie shuju, 1975, vol. 1, 9.

Wudao Yang Huanghou: *see* **Yang Zhi, Empress of Emperor Wu of Jin**

Wuxuan Bian Huanghou: *see* **Bian, Wife of Cao Cao, King of Wei**

Wuyuan Yang Huanghou: *see* **Yang Yan, Empress of Emperor Wu of Jin**

X

Xian Furen: *see* **Xian, Lady of Qiao State**

Xian, Lady of Qiao State

Lady Xian (Xian Furen), 522–602, of Gaoliang (to the north of present-day Yangjiang District, Guangdong Province), was a political and military leader in the area that is now essentially Guangdong. She belonged to the non-Han nationality of southern China known variously as the Yue, Nan Yue, or Li. The culture of these people was different from that of Han Chinese; they were still in the tribal stage and said to have been guerrillas by nature. Lady Xian's family had been leaders of the Yue people for generations, controlling tribes of over 100,000 families. She therefore received training early in life as a leader and a fighter. She is said to have gained the trust and love of her soldiers and to have been so skilled in the art of war that she was known to all the Yue tribes. Her older brother, regional inspector of Southern Liang during the Liang dynasty, grew arrogant because of his power and wealth. He made frequent incursions into neighboring regions, causing instability in the area, but eventually curbed his erratic behavior after Lady Xian repeatedly remonstrated with him. Complaints about him ceased from then on and as a result the people of Hainan Island, off the southern coast of Guangdong, came under the leadership of the Xian family.

In 535, Lady Xian married into the Feng family, which was descended from the imperial family of the early-fifth-century Northern Yan kingdom. After their nation was vanquished, a small branch of the Feng family had traveled south by ship and settled in present-day Guangdong. Because of their illustrious background, the Southern Dynasties accorded them extremely courteous treatment, appointing them to local administrative positions. However, because they were unfamiliar with local conditions they found the local population difficult to govern, consisting as it did of many minority nationalities. Feng Rong, regional inspector of Luozhou (to the northeast of present-day Huaxian District, Guangdong Province), heard of Lady Xian and asked for her hand in marriage for his son Feng Bao, who was governor of her native Gaoliang. After their marriage, Lady Xian assisted her husband in his duties. She restrained her people and directed them toward observing ritual and law. She also listened to cases together with her husband and made sure that even chieftains were not above the law. In time, order was established in the region.

354 XIAN, LADY OF QIAO STATE

When the rebel general Hou Jing besieged the Liang capital Jiankang in 548, many warlords in the remote south tried to exploit the crisis to their own advantage. Feng Bao's superior officer, Li Shiqian, called upon him to join him in a military operation to rescue the throne, but Lady Xian advised her husband against this, arguing that if Li Shiqian had been sincere about rescuing the throne, he would have called on Feng Bao when he first moved out instead of stationing himself halfway and then calling on Feng Bao. Lady Xian suspected that Li Shiqian intended to rebel against the central government and therefore she counseled her husband to wait. Within a few days, Li Shiqian did indeed announce his rebellious intention, as she had predicted. Further, Lady Xian realized that, since his army had set out to take another city, Li Shiqian's own city would be only lightly defended. She therefore suggested that Feng Bao send a letter to Li Shiqian apologizing for not responding earlier to his call; Feng Bao wrote that he had been afraid to leave his post, but was sending his wife with gifts to redeem himself. Li Shiqian happily admitted Lady Xian with her entourage of about 1,000 men, who were apparently carrying a great many gifts, and once inside Lady Xian attacked, driving Li Shiqian out of the city. She then moved out to join Liang General Chen Baxian in his rescue operation, making the acquaintance of this important personage for the first time.

The next ten years, from 548 to 557, were a chaotic period during which the Liang dynasty deteriorated rapidly. The Chen dynasty that Chen Baxian (Emperor Wu, 503–559; r. 557–559) eventually founded did not come into being until 557 and during this vacuum the Guangdong area was in a state of constant unrest. By then Lady Xian's husband had died, so she shouldered the responsibility of keeping the area safe and secure. When Chen Baxian replaced the Liang dynasty with his Chen dynasty, Lady Xian sent her son Feng Pu to the capital accompanied by the leaders of the Yue people to pledge their allegiance to the new Han ruler. Feng Pu was only a child some eight years old at the time but he was nevertheless made governor of Yangchun (in present-day Zhaoqing, Guangdong Province). This, of course, was a way of rewarding Lady Xian for her efforts in bringing the people of Guangdong into the Chen fold. Not long afterward, the inspector of Guangzhou rebelled against the Chen throne. He kidnapped Feng Pu and forced him to join him. Lady Xian refused to be blackmailed, however, and set out at the head of the chieftains of the Yue people to attack Guangzhou, defeating the rebels. For her meritorious work, her son was given the title Leader of Court Gentlemen (*zhonglang jiang*) and appointed governor of Shilong (to the northeast of present-day Huaxian District, Guangdong Province). Lady Xian herself was given the title Leader of Court Gentlemen and Lady Dowager of Shilong and materially rewarded with many ceremonial accoutrements such as a carriage with embroidered curtains, a marching band, and ceremonial flags.

Feng Pu died during the late 580s, by which time the Chen dynasty had almost run its course, and the people of Guangdong did not know where to place their allegiance. Several commanderies hailed Lady Xian as their leader and called her the Holy Mother. For her part, she kept the land safe and the people protected during those turbulent years.

In 581, the Northern Zhou minister Yang Jian (541–604) brought that dynasty to an end when he accepted the throne yielded to him by his grandson, renamed the dynasty Sui, and declared himself emperor (Emperor Wen; r. 581–604). Already in control of North China, he turned his attention to conquering Chen in the south. He sent his army to take the Guangdong area but Lady Xian in the far south did not know that Chen had fallen and therefore remained loyal to it. Facing strong local resistance, the Sui army hesitated and reported the situation to the throne. The emperor's son requested that the vanquished Chen emperor write to Lady Xian confirming the demise of Chen and advising her to give up the fight. A staff made of rhinoceros horn, which she had presented to the Chen emperor, and a military seal of the Chen dynasty were sent with the letter as credentials. Upon receiving the letter, Lady Xian gathered together more than 1,000 local leaders and wept for an entire day. She saw the futility of resisting the new regime, however, and eventually sent her grandson Feng Hun to welcome the Sui army. Thus, because of her clear-sightedness, the Sui army gained the whole of Guangdong without a fight, sparing the people the agony of war.

Soon afterward, a local man named Wang Zhongxuan rose against Sui. Lady Xian sent another of her grandsons, Feng Xuan, to aid the government troops but he hesitated to advance because he was friendly with one of the rebels. Incensed, Lady Xian had him thrown into jail, sending in his place another grandson, Feng Ang, who defeated the rebels. Riding in full armor, she accompanied an emissary from the Sui emperor on a tour of the commanderies. The leaders of present-day Guangdong and Guangxi all came forward to pay their respects, confirming her position as undisputed leader of the whole area.

Emperor Wen was amazed at Lady Xian's leadership. He appointed her two grandsons Feng Xuan (despite his previous negligence) and Feng Ang as regional inspectors and elevated her husband posthumously to the rank of Duke of Qiao State so that he might enfeoff Lady Xian. She was then given the title Lady of Qiao State (Qiaoguo Furen) and the staff of a dukedom. In addition, the seal to control the armies of the six regions with permission to act should crises present themselves was bestowed upon her.

Lady Xian took her duties seriously. She memorialized the emperor about an official who had proved corrupt and cruel to the people and had caused many members of minority nationalities to run away or rebel. The emperor investigated the incident and the culprit was charged in accordance with the law. Asked to pacify those who had run away or rebelled, Lady Xian carried the edict with her as she traveled to over ten regions to make the emperor's wishes known. All of the rebels surrendered, which so pleased the emperor that he rewarded her with an additional "bath fief" of 1,500 households. When she died in 602, the emperor gave 1,000 pieces of material toward her funeral and bestowed on her the posthumous title Loyal and Respectful Lady (Chengjing Furen).

As a member of a minority nationality, Lady Xian had the freedom to command armies and take on office, privileges that her peers of the Han nationality did not enjoy at that time. She achieved these privileges through her natural leadership abilities and because she was gifted in military affairs, but of no less importance was her readiness to take risks and deal with difficult problems. Most importantly, she had a strong sense of right and wrong

356 XIAN, LADY OF QIAO STATE

and the courage to right wrongs. It was probably because of these qualities that she won the trust and support of the people, especially non-Han people like herself. This enabled her to improve relations between Han and non-Han and bring peace to all.

Historians in the past have emphasized Lady Xian's loyalty to the reigning emperor, prompting contemporary scholars to criticize her for a narrow sense of loyalty. Modern scholars may even question the rectitude of helping the Han colonizers to rule over her people. It may be argued, however, that she saw a unified peace under a Han government as an advance on the constant fighting of the Yue people. From whichever viewpoint one approaches Lady Xian, she was undeniably an outstanding woman.

Lily Xiao Hong LEE

Liu Shisheng. *Zhongguo gudai funüshi.* Qingdao: Qingdao chubanshe, 1991, 177–79.
Ou Jianzhi. *Zhongguo lidai nüzhengzhijia.* Hong Kong: Shanghai shuju, 1978, 51–64.
Sui shu. Beijing: Zhonghua shuju, 1973, vol. 6, 80.1800–3.

Xianzhu Gan Huanghou: *see* **Gan, Empress of the Former Sovereign of Shu**

Xianzhu Mu Huanghou: *see* **Wu, Empress of the Former Sovereign of Shu**

Xiao, Empress of Emperor Yang of Sui

Empress Xiao (Yangdi Xiao Huanghou), c. 570–after 630, was empress to Emperor Yang (Yang Guang, 569–618; r. 605–617), the second emperor of the Sui dynasty. Her personal name is not recorded in the histories.

The Xiao family was from Nanlanling (northwest of present-day Changzhou in Jiangsu Province) and is known for the literary achievements of many of its members. Her great-great-grandfather Xiao Yan founded the southern Liang dynasty in the early sixth century; he reigned for forty-seven years and is known as Emperor Wu. His eldest son, Xiao Tong (501–531), compiled the famous anthology of literature *Wen xuan.* When the Liang dynasty was vanquished by the Chen, the future empress's branch of the family defected to Northern Zhou. Her father, Xiao Kui, served as an official of the Northern Zhou dynasty and was rewarded with the title of Prince of the State of Liang, which was a dependency of Northern Zhou and, later, of Sui. Her grandfather and father both left behind many scholarly and literary works and, despite their status as vassals, Emperor Wen of Sui held both men in great esteem.

While the year of her birth was not recorded, the future empress is said to have been born in the second month of the lunar year. According to local custom, girls born in that month were unlucky and were either given away or killed. Accordingly, Xiao Kui gave his daughter away to his childless cousin Xiao Ji, who raised her as his own daughter, but he and his wife died of illness when the child was eight years old, at which point she was adopted by her mother's brother, Zhang Ke, a man living in poverty who required her to do all his housework.

Emperor Wen (Yang Jian, 541–604; r. 581–604) and the Empress née Dugu (*q.v.* Dugu, Empress of Emperor Wen of Sui) decided to choose a wife for their second son, Yang Guang, in 583, when he was still a prince. They set their sights on the vassal state of Liang because the area south of the Yangzi River was known for its beautiful women. The envoy sent to Liang to select candidates found none he considered auspicious, until Xiao Kui brought forward his daughter, then still living in Zhang Ke's house. The envoy made a divination about her and received an auspicious sign, whereupon the girl was sent to court to marry Yang Guang and become his consort.

Consort Xiao is described as gentle, obliging, and sensible, a young woman who loved learning and was skilled at literary composition. The emperor and the empress were both happy about the match and her new husband was also fond of her. This rosy picture was not to last, however. The *History of the Sui Dynasty* (Sui shu) implies that when Emperor Wen lay mortally ill in 604, Yang Guang sent his guard to kill his father. Upon his father's death, Yang Guang ascended the throne, his consort becoming Empress Xiao. It was not long before Yang Guang became the notorious Emperor Yang of Sui who led a dissipated and extravagant life. He imposed many large-scale projects on the populace, including construction of the Grand Canal, which reached from the north to the south of the country, and extorted excessive taxes and levies from the people to pay for them.

The emperor enjoyed taking his empress and his palace women on pleasure trips throughout his empire, sparing no expense. He made three trips along the Grand Canal to Jiangdu (present-day Yangzhou in Jiangsu Province) and for these trips had gigantic and luxurious ships built that were several stories high and towed by tens of thousands of men clothed in silk. His entourage consisted of more than 1,000 ships of various sizes. He also made more than one trip to the far northwest, to the territory of the Tujue (the Turkic people) in present-day Gansu Province. It was on one of these trips that Empress Xiao met Princess Yicheng, a daughter of the Sui imperial clan who had been given as a wife to the Qimin Qagkan; this friendship was later to benefit the empress.

Empress Xiao tried on several occasions to admonish the emperor for his many wrongdoings, but to no avail. Eventually, afraid of annoying him to the point of causing trouble for herself, she wrote him a long rhapsody (*fu*) entitled *On My Aspirations* (Shu zhi fu) in which she expressed her views and laid down the principles by which she lived. Her words reveal how worried she was about the political situation in late Sui: "When one is in a high position the situation is surely fraught with danger; when the water is too full, one has to prevent it from overflowing." Fourteen years into Emperor Yang's reign the country was at cinder point, with peasant uprisings and soldiers' revolts breaking out everywhere, yet still he would not pay any attention to affairs of state, continuing instead his life of indulgence and dissipation. When a palace woman reported to Empress Xiao that the people were talking of rebellion, the empress told her to report this directly to the emperor. The poor palace woman did as she was told, only to be put to death for her trouble by a furious emperor. When someone else reported later that the imperial guards were talking of rebellion, Empress Xiao simply sighed and said: "The whole country has come to such a pass that nothing can be done. There is no need to tell the emperor; it would only increase his worries." From then on, everyone in the palace remained silent.

In 616, with the political situation critical, Emperor Yang ignored the safety of his throne and set off on another trip to Jiangdu with Empress Xiao, his other consorts, and his courtiers. When grain provisions ran out in Jiangdu, he decided to move further south, but his soldiers, most of whom were from the north, were homesick and quickly joined a mutiny fomented by Yuwen Huaji. Emperor Yang had little hope, beset by outside forces and sabotaged by collaborators from within. After he was killed, Empress Xiao told her attendants to wrap his body in a mat from the bed and bury him so. One source says they made a small coffin for him from bed boards.

Most of the emperor's offspring were killed in the uprising, but Empress Xiao was spared. Yuwen Huaji seized her and took her north with him but was himself killed not long afterward, and ex-Empress Xiao then passed into the hands of his killer, the warlord Dou Jiande. By this time, Qimin Qagkan of the Tujue had died and his son Shibi Qagkan had inherited both his position and his wives. Princess Yicheng had thus become a wife of the new leader, Shibi Qagkan, and she interceded on behalf of the ex-empress, requesting that Dou Jiande be asked to release her. An emissary was sent to welcome the ex-empress to Tujue and she traveled north of the Great Wall, where she was to live for some fourteen years.

Empress Xiao had two sons. Her first-born, the heir apparent Yang Yuande, died before the end of Sui and it was his son that the future Tang emperor (Li Yuan) briefly established as a puppet before assuming the throne in his place. Her other son, the Prince of Qi, was killed by Yuwen Huaji; his posthumous son Yang Zhengdao accompanied her into exile to Tujue. There they enjoyed favorable treatment from the Qagkan, who allowed them to settle in Dingxiang City (in present-day Shanxi Province) and preside over the refugees from Sui who were there. The last great change in her life came after Tang Emperor Taizong (Li Shimin, 599–649; r. 627–649) defeated Tujue in 630. In deference to her former status as empress, he ordered that she and her grandson Yang Zhengdao be brought back from Tujue and treated with respect and kindness. Ex-Empress Xiao lived out her life in the Tang palace in Chang'an, where she died peacefully.

Empress Xiao was a tragic figure who had a sad and unsettled life. Once she had a husband and a family, a comfortable and grand life, but almost overnight all this was taken from her. She was intelligent enough to see what her husband's wrongdoings would lead to, but was powerless to change him or save the situation. She witnessed the murder of her husband and children. She was seized by rebels and forced to leave her home, drifting from place to place, passed from one hand to another. All of this happened because she was married to Emperor Yang of Sui, a fate over which she had no control.

Laura LONG

Guan Siping. *Houfei de mingyun.* Jinan: Shandong wenyi chubanshe, 1991, 154–58.
Jiu Tang shu, Beijing: Zhonghua shuju, 1975, 67. 2479.

Li Xianshen. *Zhongguo houfei yiwen.* Shenyang: Shenyang chubanshe, 1992, 195–201.

Lin Shimin and Li Hongfa. *Lidai ming houfei mizhuan.* Jinan: Shandong wenyi chubanshe, 1991, 97–105.

Liu Shisheng. *Zhongguo gudai funüshi,* Qingdao: Qingdao chubanshe, 1991, 192–97.

Sima Guang. *Xin jiao Zizhi tongjian.* Taipei: Shijie shuju, 1977, vol. 10, 180.5621, 180.5630, 180.5634, 181.5647, 185.5775–82, 193.6073.

Sui shu. Beijing: Zhonghua shuju, 1973, vol. 1, 4.93; vol. 4, 36.1111–13.

Zhou shu. Beijing: Zhonghua shuju, 1971, vol. 3, 48.863–65.

Xiaowen You Huanghou Feng Shi: *see* Feng, Empress of Emperor Xiaowen of Northern Wei

Xie Daoyun

Xie Daoyun, before 340–after 399, was a poet, writer of prose, scholar, calligrapher, and accomplished conversationalist and debater of the Eastern Jin dynasty. In Chinese literature, she has long been seen as a role model for literary creativity, but above all she was admired by her contemporaries and by posterity for her outspokenness and courage as well as for her moral strength.

Xie Daoyun belonged to the Xie clan of Yangxia in the state of Chen (present-day Henan Province). The Xie were one of the two most famous clans of their time and for successive centuries, the other being the Wang clan of Langye into which she married. Xie Daoyun's great-uncle Xie Kun (280–322) was a scholar and the first member of the clan to win a reputation, distinguishing himself when the usurper Wang Dun (266–324) was intent on raising an army against the Eastern Jin court by being the only adviser to speak against the plan. After the downfall of Wang Dun, the court heaped honors and rewards on Xie Kun and his family in recognition of his integrity. Xie Daoyun seems to have inherited his moral courage, as events in her later life reveal.

Xie Kun's son Xie Shang, 308–357, inherited his position and went on to attain both power and prestige as he advanced his career. However, when he died without an heir, his positions and his title were transferred to males in Xie Daoyun's branch of the family: his position went to her father, Xie Yi (d. 358), while his title went to her brother Xie Kang, who was appointed his posthumous heir. Xie Yi was not known as an outstanding scholar or official, but his younger brother Xie An (320–385) scaled great political and cultural heights. He was a recluse who scorned wealth and position until his brothers had either died or been disgraced, at which time he stepped forward and returned to society to uphold the reputation of the Xie clan, quickly rising to a position equivalent to that of prime minister. He was masterful when Eastern Jin's northern neighbors, the Former Qin dynasty, established by the Di ethnic minority people, invaded Jin and threw the entire population of the capital, Jiankang (the present-day city of Nanjing), into panic. Xie An managed to restore calm and dispatched his younger brother Xie Tie and his nephew Xie Xuan (343–388)—this was one of Xie Daoyun's brothers—to defend the northern borders. They succeeded in driving the invaders off during the famous Battle of Fei River (*Feishui zhi zhan:* this took place near present-day Huainan in Anhui Province) of 383 and securing the border for the dynasty.

360 XIE DAOYUN

Culturally, Xie An was well versed in debate and philosophical conversation and had an enormous influence on public opinion.

We know nothing about Xie Daoyun's mother except that she gave birth to seven children. We know the names of her four sons—Xie Quan, Xie Kang, Xie Jing, and Xie Xuan—but of her three daughters we know only Xie Daoyun. Xie Xuan, hero of the Battle of the Fei River, was by far the best known of the four sons.

Xie Daoyun was Xie An's favorite niece and she was possibly closer to him than to her own father since, as a recluse living at home, Xie An spent a great deal of time in the company of his family, especially his sisters-in-law and nieces and nephews, while the other men of the family were away, involved in political and military activities. Xie An enjoyed gatherings of young people with whom he could talk about literature and philosophy and he often asked them questions as a kind of test to see which of them were outstanding. Xie Daoyun would excel in answering these questions. The best known of several anecdotes about these sessions took place one snowy day when Xie An asked his young relatives what the flurries of snowflakes resembled. After her male cousins' mediocre attempts, Xie Daoyun came up with the best, and most memorable, answer. They were like "willow catkins borne on the wind," she said, to her uncle's delight. This story has become a classic example of a talented young girl. In centuries to come, her name and the word *xu* (catkin) became linked with female literary talent and achievement.

About 360, Xie Daoyun married Wang Ningzhi, a young man from the extremely prestigious Wang clan. However, the marriage fell short of her expectations and she complained bitterly about her husband when she returned to her natal home for a visit. Concerned, her uncle Xie An tried to console her, pointing out that Wang Ning- zhi was the son of the famous calligrapher Wang Xizhi (309–c. 365) and the young man himself was not at all bad. Xie Daoyun replied that, having grown up around young men like her brothers and cousins, she could not have imagined there could be someone like Young Wang. While Xie Daoyun found her young husband miserably lacking, the historical record shows that Wang Ningzhi did well in his political career and the surviving fragments of his literary works and correspondence reveal that he wrote fluently, with a good style. Moreover, he was known as a good calligrapher, as were his famous father and his brothers. He seems to have been a fervent believer in the Daoist-influenced Five Bushels of Rice sect, a belief that had run in his family for generations.

Despite her scorn for Wang Ningzhi, she stayed in the marriage and bore him several sons and at least one daughter. Her husband does not appear to have placed any constraints on her and she continued to enjoy a life of comparative freedom. She joined in debates, one well-known example being the time she offered to rescue her brother-in-law Wang Xianzhi from defeat at the hands of his guests. Seated behind a green silk screen, she extended Wang Xianzhi's argument and none of his guests, all famous scholars, was able to defeat her. To volunteer to participate in what was a male-dominated intellectual activity—and then to win—required both courage and talent. Xie Daoyun appears to have totally disregarded the teachings of humility and submissiveness for women.

Xie Daoyun and her children accompanied Wang Ningzhi when he was sent to Jiangzhou (present-day Jiangxi Province) to become regional inspector (*cishi*). This must have been fairly late in her life as she was already a grandmother by then. In 399, the extreme unrest in eastern China, led by the religious leader Sun En, spread to Jiangzhou. Instead of making preparations to defend the area, as the regional inspector would have been expected to do, Wang Ningzhi retreated to his meditation room as the rebels approached. He made supplications to the Great Dao and emerged to tell his generals and lieutenants that he had been promised spirit soldiers would fly to his aid. Not surprisingly, the rebels quickly overran the place and killed Wang Ningzhi and his sons. Hearing the dreadful news, Xie Daoyun sallied forth, borne aloft in a sedan chair by her brave maids, with sword drawn. She is said to have killed several insurgents before being taken prisoner. When the rebels threatened to kill her young grandson Liu Tao, who was living with her, Xie Daoyun protested angrily, "This is a matter concerning the Wang family, what has it to do with another clan? If you do it, you will have to kill me first!" It is said that Sun En, cruel and ruthless though he was, was moved by Xie Daoyun's courage and spared the child. No longer a young woman, Xie Daoyun demonstrated great courage in confronting the men who had killed her husband and sons and in convincing a rampaging pirate to change his mind and not harm her grandson. So stark is the contrast between her behavior and that of her fanatic of a husband that we can perhaps understand why she so despised him.

After her husband's death, Xie Daoyun lived a widow's life in the Wang ancestral home in Kuaiji (present-day Shaoxing in Zhejiang Province), managing her household with strict discipline. Yet she did not retire from society entirely. When Liu Liu, the Prefect of Kuaiji, asked if he might discuss philosophical matters with her she agreed to talk with him. She did her hair up in a bun and sat behind curtains on a white cushion while Liu Liu, dressed neatly in formal attire, sat on a chair. Her biography describes her performance thus:

> Daoyun's words were pure and elegant, delivered in a lofty style. She started by talking about her family. Overwhelmed by emotion, she wept bitterly. Gradually, she proceeded to answer his queries relating to philosophy, never hesitating or appearing to be short of words or arguments. When Liu had taken his leave, he sighed and said, "She really is a lady like no other I have ever known! Having heard her words and observed her style, one cannot help but admire her, body and soul."

It was unusual by any standards for a widow to conduct a conversation such as this with a man she did not know without any family members present, yet Xie Daoyun was unabashed. As far as we can discover, none of her contemporaries seem to have criticized her for it.

There is a record of Xie Daoyun holding another conversation with a man. This time it was Huan Xuan (369–404), who eventually usurped the Jin dynasty. Huan Xuan was from a military family and had gained power by force. He aspired to be held in the same high esteem as Xie An and became jealous when he was unable to achieve this. Whenever possible he would put Xie An down, one of his favorite barbs being to ridicule him for his inability to remain a recluse and seeking an official career later

362 XIE DAOYUN

in his life. When Huan Xuan asked Xie Daoyun for an explanation for her uncle's behavior, the gist of her retort was that, to a lofty person, to be active or nonactive are two sides of the same coin, neither side being superior to the other. In this way she robbed Huan Xuan's portrayal of her uncle of any negative connotations.

There is a biography of Xie Daoyun in the *History of the Jin Dynasty* (Jin shu). That it is the longest in the chapter devoted to women (*juan* 96) can be seen as a reflection of her importance both during her own time and in the eyes of the Tang dynasty historians who compiled the official history of Jin between 646 and 648. Most of the anecdotes mentioned above are found in this official biography, which indicates that the historians must have approved of her unusual behavior. Her biography also states that her poems, rhapsodies, eulogies, and odes circulated among her contemporaries. The bibliographic chapter of the *History of the Sui Dynasty* (Sui shu), which was completed in 656, records her personal collection in two *juan* but none of her works are extant. Only fragments culled from a variety of sources are available and it is difficult to evaluate the quality of her writing from these. However, they do indicate that she dealt with a wide range of genres and subject matter, including poems of the "Philosophical School" (*xuanyan shi*) and those on the quest for immortality, which was popular during that time, as well as treatises on Confucian subjects, which is probably a reflection of her heritage from her earlier Confucian ancestors.

There were strong Daoist tendencies in Xie Daoyun's personality and her thought. She has been called a female "famous scholar," a term having specific connotations when used to refer to people of the Wei and Jin periods. It was usually applied to scholars of distinguished families who had also earned fame in conversation and debate on philosophical topics. On one occasion a nun who had free access to women of good families was asked to compare two of the most famous women of their period: Xie Daoyun and Zhang Xuan's sister, whose personal name we do not know. The nun gave the following elegant oral evaluation:

> Lady Wang's [Xie Daoyun] expression is relaxed and open, therefore she has the style of the Seven Worthies of the Bamboo Grove, while Gu's wife [Zhang Xuan's sister] has a pure heart like a piece of gleaming jade, and quite naturally is an outstanding example among women.

This evaluation of Xie Daoyun gives us a succinct view of her style: relaxed and open. This is by no means a feminine portrayal; at most it can be seen as neutral, perhaps even a little masculine in the context of ancient China. Associating her with the Seven Worthies of the Bamboo Grove, a group of male scholars well known for their significantly Daoist ideas as well as their nonconformist behavior, reveals her Daoist links.

In literature, Xie Daoyun symbolizes female talent. In later dynasties, hers was an iconic image: many women poets of late pre-modern China used the character *yun* from her name Dao*yun* as well as the character *xu,* willow catkin, as part of their names or in the titles of their poetry collections. Her name was also included as one of the women calligraphers mentioned in works on calligraphy compiled in the Tang dynasty. The extent of Xie Daoyun's fame can be gauged by the fact that her story is incorporated in *The Three-Character Classic* (Sanzi jing), the ubiquitous children's primer used for many centuries in China. A Ming dynasty (1368–1644) musical composition for the Chinese *qin,* "Evening Talk by a Snowy Window" (Xuechuang yehua), is based on the gathering of Xie Daoyun with her uncle Xie An and her cousins described above.

Lily Xiao Hong LEE

Chen Bangyan, ed. *Shi da cainü.* Shanghai: Shanghai guji chubanshe, 1991, 38–54.
Jin shu. Beijing: Zhonghua shuju, 1974, vol. 7, 79.2069–80; vol. 7, 80.2093–104; vol. 8, 96.2516–17.
Lee, Lily Xiao Hong. "Xie Daoyun: The Style of a Woman Mingshi." In her *Virtue of Yin: Studies on Chinese Women.* Sydney: Wild Peony, 1994, 25–46.
Liu I-ch'ing [Yiqing]. *Shih-shuo Hsin-yü: A New Account of Tales of the World,* trans. Richard B. Mather. Minneapolis: University of Minnesota Press, 1976, 64, 354–55.
Liu Yiqing. *Shishuo xinyu jian shu,* ed. Yu Jiaxi. Beijing: Zhonghua shuju, 1983, 2.131–32, 19.697–99.
Thompson, John. "Evening Talk by a Snowy Window." In *John Thompson on the Guqin Silk String Zither.* www.silkqin.com/02qnpu/16xltq/x1042xcyh.htm, accessed 30 April 2006.
Xie Wuliang. *Zhongguo funü wenxue shi.* Zhengzhou: Zhongzhou guji chubanshe, 1992, vol. IIB, 8–10.

Xu Baoguang

Xu Baoguang, b. 470, from Qiantang (in the region of the present-day city of Hangzhou in Zhejiang Province), was a Daoist practitioner in the tradition of the Way of the Celestial Masters (*tianshidao*). She lived in southern China at a time of great religious and social change. Celestial Master Daoism had been brought to the south in the mid-fourth century by Chinese émigrés from the north who supplanted the old southern aristocracy and attempted to suppress the indigenous shamanistic, or ecstatic, religion. Southern Daoists responded by crafting what Stephen Bokenkamp terms "a 'new' Daoism, claiming access to yet higher heavens and more exalted deities than those known to the Celestial Masters, while at the same time incorporating much Celestial Master belief." In a further attempt to lay claim to greater legitimacy, this Highest Clarity (*shangqing*) Daoism also adopted theories on spiritual cultivation from the comparatively new but highly regarded foreign religion of Buddhism.

Xu Baoguang was born into the Zhang family and thus originally had the same surname as Zhang Daoling (fl. 140), the first Celestial Master and legendary founder of religious Daoism (*vide* Zhang Lu's Mother). Her father died when she was three years old and her mother moved back to Yongjia, almost 200 miles to the south. There, her mother remarried; her second husband belonged to the Xu family so the child came to be known as Xu Baoguang. The Xu family had been closely associated with Celestial Master Daoism for several generations and when Xu Baoguang was ten years old she left her family (*chu jia*) in order to prepare for a religious career under the supervision of a Daoist master. She traveled back north to Yuyao, near Qiantang, and eventually set up her own meditation hall as a center for Celestial Master type ritual activity. Seemingly acting as the family head, in 498 she took charge of the upbringing of her one-year-old

364   XU BAOGUANG

nephew Zhou Ziliang (497–516), who was the son of her younger half-sister, Xu Jing-guang, and whose father (Zhou Yaozong, d. 503) she had converted to Daoism.

During her many years of religious training, Xu Baoguang studied the major texts of southern Daoism, including *The [Scripture of the] Yellow Court* (Huangting), regarded as one of the most important texts of religious Daoism. She learned how to write petitions to divinities seeking such favors as healing illness and postponing a summons to official position in the occult bureaucracy, which in real-world terms was a notification of a practitioner's imminent death. She also learned how to draw amulets used for protection against illness and evil spirits. As his teacher, she passed these skills on to her nephew Zhou Ziliang. Described as "by nature extremely upright," she claimed never since childhood to have harmed even an insect nor unnecessarily picked plants or flowers and to have eaten but one meal a day. She also admitted to being of a stern disposition and to being a strict disciplinarian.

After twenty-four years, however, her simple religious life came to an abrupt end in 504 when she was forced to reenter lay life and marry in response to an anti-Daoist edict published by Emperor Wu (r. 502–549) of the Liang dynasty soon after his conversion to Buddhism. Despite the pro-forma objectives of her union with a man of the Zhu family of Shangyu, she had sexual relations with him, a lapse from her life of devout chastity that caused her continuing shame and regret, which in turn caused her to develop a stomach illness, described as "a knot of qi" or a tumor in her abdomen. In 505 or 508, when she was in her late thirties, Xu Baoguang gave birth to a son (Zhu Shansheng) and left her husband, taking her son and Zhou Ziliang back to Yongjia.

Maoshan, some thirty miles from the capital, Jiankang (present-day Nanjing), was a center of religious activity where individual male and female adepts and hermits followed various practices and small groups established abbeys and temples. The great Daoist master Tao Hongjing (456–536) had retired to Maoshan in 492 to carry out editorial work on a series of manuscripts recording ecstatic visions (*vide* Wei Huacun) and his personal influence over the recently converted Emperor Wu guaranteed the continuation of Daoist activities in the Maoshan region after the suppression of 504. In 508, Tao Hongjing traveled to the south and quite early on in his four-year tour came upon Zhou Ziliang, who was then a Celestial Masters novitiate. He took Zhou Ziliang with him when he returned to Maoshan in 512 and a year later Xu Baoguang, her son, her sister, a brother, and a nephew were all permitted to settle on Maoshan in the outbuildings of a temple. Xu Baoguang intensified her religious practice and became an important member of Tao Hongjing's religious community. She kept scriptures in a separate room in her cottage and her relationship with her nephew remained that of a teacher, even though Tao Hongjing had adopted the youth as his disciple. From mid-515, Zhou Ziliang began to have visions in which divinities appeared and spoke to him. These divinities said that his aunt Xu Baoguang had committed no major sins and that in a later incarnation she might become a transcendent (*xian*), that is, a Daoist immortal. In other words, she was "transcendent material" but it could take her two or three more lifetimes to attain that state. Her forced marriage had upset her spiritual balance, which is why she suffered from ill health. The divinities claimed her illness would not kill her but would be difficult to heal.

Besides being at this spiritual disadvantage, the traditional Celestial Masters rituals Xu Baoguang propagated clashed with the new rituals practiced among Tao Hongjing's followers, who engaged in intensive and often drug-supported meditation, during which they went on spiritual journeys and met with fanciful immortal figures. In Xu Baoguang's eyes these figures were evil ghosts and the practices through which they were contacted remained suspect. On the other hand, Tao Hongjing and her nephew Zhou Ziliang viewed her more pedestrian religious beliefs and activities, which centered on the control of malignant and in particular illness-causing ghosts, as inferior and even as hostile. Zhou Ziliang accused her of attempting to ruin his spiritual career, arguing that by demanding his support in the writing and application of talismans she forced him into contact with minor spirits and thus obstructed his communication with deities of "supreme purity." Tao Hongjing reinforced these accusations when he proposed that the conflict with Xu Baoguang was one of the reasons for the young man's suicide, by means of a lethal drug, in 516.

The story of Xu Baoguang and her spiritual practices is told in the commentary, probably by Tao Hongjing, to Zhou Ziliang's written record of the visions he experienced in the year before his death. Through these footnoted comments we discover a woman determined from childhood to follow a spiritual path and not to marry, a woman who was literate and devout, and a woman who experienced the uncertainties of a period during which local indigenous religion, various strands of religious Daoism, and Buddhism were contending for supremacy in southern China.

Barbara HENDRISCHKE and Sue WILES

Bokenkamp, Stephen. "Answering a Summons." In *Religions of China in Practice,* ed. Donald S. Lopez. Princeton, NJ: Princeton University Press, 1996, 188–202.

———. "Declarations of the Perfected." In *Religions of China in Practice,* ed. Donald S. Lopez. Princeton, NJ: Princeton University Press, 1996, 166–71.

Russell, Terrence C. "Revelation and Narrative in the *Zhoushi Mingtongji*." *Early Medieval China* 1 (1994): 34–59.

Stein, Rolf A. "Religious Taoism and Popular Religion from the Second to Seventh Centuries." In *Facets of Taoism: Essays in Chinese Religion,* ed. Holmes Welch and Anna Seidel. New Haven, CT: Yale University Press, 1979, 53–60.

Strickmann, Michel. "On the Alchemy of T'ao Hung-ching." In *Facets of Taoism: Essays in Chinese Religion,* ed. Holmes Welch and Anna Seidel. New Haven, CT: Yale University Press, 1979, 150–51, 158–61, 190.

———. "A Taoist Confirmation of Liang Wu Ti's Suppression of Taoism." *Journal of the American Oriental Society* 98, no. 4 (1978): 467–75.

"Taoist Culture & Information Centre." www.eng.taoism.org.hk.

Zhoushi mingtong ji (Master Zhou's records of his communications with the unseen). In *Daozang* TT.152 [= HY.302]. Shanghai: Shangwu chubanshe, 1924–1926.

Xuanwen Jun: *see* **Song, Lady Xuanwen**

Xuanwu Ling Huanghou: *see* **Hu, Consort of Emperor Xuanwu of Northern Wei**

Xun Guan

Xun Guan, b. c. 303, lived during the turbulent times that saw the collapse of the Western Jin dynasty and the establishment of Eastern Jin. Her father, Xun Song, was an official during Western Jin. He had been appointed governor of Xiangcheng (present-day Kaifeng, Henan Province) and was later appointed commander-in-chief of military affairs of Jingzhou and areas north of the Yangzi River (*du du Jingzhou jiangbei zhu junshi*); in this latter post he was stationed at Yuan (present-day Nanyang in Henan Province). Her father and grandfather were not military men but, according to her father's biography, were scholar-officials who immersed themselves in Confucian studies. Members of her family appear to have been loyal courtiers for generations. One of her ancestors, a man named Xun Yu, had distinguished himself as a close adviser of Cao Cao (155–220), de facto ruler at the end of the Eastern Han dynasty. However, when it became clear that Cao Cao was planning to usurp the Han throne, Xun Yu openly opposed him and was forced to commit suicide.

Xun Guan was with her father in Yuan (some sources suggest the city under attack was Xiangyang or Xiangcheng) in about 316 when a force of 2,000 men under the command of the insurgent Du Zeng attacked the city. Du Zeng was known for his martial prowess, yet after defeating several other local officials he surrendered to Xun Song, who, because his own army was very small, wanted Du Zeng as an ally. It soon became clear, however, that Du Zeng had feigned his surrender and he surrounded the city. Xun Song found himself in a perilous situation, with a weak army defending a city that was almost completely out of food. There seemed to be no way he could seek help and reinforcements from his former subordinate General Pacifying the South (*pingnan jiangjun*) Shi Lan, who was also governor of Xiangcheng.

Xun Guan volunteered to go for help. She was only thirteen at the time but she took command of a group of brave men, climbed the city wall at night, and broke out of the city. Enemy soldiers pursued the group but she urged her men forward, fighting as they went, until they managed to escape to Luyang Mountain, leaving their pursuers behind. Xun Guan made her way alone to Shi Lan and begged him for troops to rescue her father. She also wrote a letter on her father's behalf to Leader of Court Gentlemen of the South (*nan zhonglangjiang*) Zhou Fang, pleading for reinforcements and asking him to become her father's blood brother. Zhou Fang responded to her plea by sending his son Zhou Fu with 3,000 men. Together with Shi Lan they went to rescue Xun Song, but Du Zeng had got wind of this and his forces had already disbanded by the time the reinforcements arrived.

Xun Guan's biography in the official *History of the Jin Dynasty* (Jin shu) is very brief and does not mention any form of military training she may have had. Yet it would appear that she must have had some training, as well as the courage to undertake such a challenge. Perhaps she inherited this courage from her upright ancestor Xun Yu. Also, there would have been many men, not least the army officers under her father, in the besieged city who would or should have been willing to break out and go for help. It would not have been left to a thirteen-year-old girl to lead the party unless she had had some training that would enable her to fight on the run.

Her story is also told in her father's biography in the *History of the Jin Dynasty,* in which the details vary slightly. It has been passed down through the ages as an example of a woman's heroism in extreme circumstances. This kind of story recurs again and again in Chinese history, the best known such tale being that of the soldier Mulan (*q.v.*). The fact that a society such as ancient China's, in which a woman's place was firmly in the home, should still find it possible to salute a heroine like Xun Guan is quite contrary to our expectations.

Lily Xiao Hong LEE

Jin shu. Beijing: Zhonghua shuju, 1974, vol. 7, 75.1976; vol. 8, 96.2515; vol. 8, 100.2620.
Liu Shisheng. *Zhongguo gudai funü shi.* Qingdao: Qingdao chubanshe, 1991, 160–61.

Xun Song's Daughter: *see* **Xun Guan**

Y

Yan Xian
Yan Xian, fl. third century, was a native of Jingzhao (the present-day city of Xi'an in Shaanxi Province). She lived through the late Wei and early Western Jin dynasties. Historians describe her as a woman of foresight.

Yan Xian was married to Du Youdao in her thirteenth year but had become a widow by the age of eighteen. She had a son named Du Zhi and a daughter named Du Xue, both of whom she brought up and educated with propriety. Du Zhi became quite well known and was appointed governor of Nan'an (present-day Shaanxi Province), while Du Xue was also known for her virtue.

The prime example of Yan Xian's ability to understand power relationships was in relation to a suitor for her daughter's hand in marriage. Two factions were fighting for supremacy in the last years of the Wei dynasty: one belonged to Cao Shuang, uncle of the emperor, and the other to Grand Mentor (*taifu*) Sima Yi, who was in control of the army but who was attempting to lull his rivals into a false sense of security by feigning illness and not attending court. A supporter of Sima Yi, a man named Fu Xuan, had asked for Du Xue's hand in marriage; she was to be his second wife, his first wife having died. Yan Xian's family urged her not to accept his offer, however, pointing out that no one else was willing to let their daughter marry Fu Xuan because he had become a political target for two of Cao Shuang's extremely powerful supporters, He Yan and Deng Yang. The family claimed that He Yan and Deng Yang were so much more powerful than Fu Xuan that the unequal contest between them was like "crumbling mountains pressing on an egg or pouring boiling water on snow." Yan Xian saw things differently, however. "You only know one thing," she told her relatives. "The arrogance and extravagance of people like He Yan will always lead to their own downfall. Grand Mentor Sima is only hibernating. I'm afraid you will find that when the egg is broken and the snow is melted, he will still be there." Without further hesitation, she went ahead with her daughter's marriage to Fu Xuan.

It came about, much as she had anticipated, that He Yan and Deng Yang were killed

368 YAN XIAN

in a coup led by the sons of Sima Yi. Further, Fu Xuan rose to a high position during the Western Jin dynasty established by the Sima family upon the collapse of Wei. Fu Xian, the six-year-old son of Fu Xuan by his first wife, once visited Yan Xian with his stepmother Du Xue. Yan Xian foresaw a fine future for the boy, and eventually arranged for him to marry one of her nieces. Again, her foresight was remarkable: Fu Xian, her daughter's stepson, became a nationally famous writer.

Another incident recorded about Yan Xian related to her husband's nephew Du Yu (222–284), who was being wronged by his superior officer. Yan Xian wrote to him as follows: "There is a saying: 'Those who can take humiliation will attain the post of the Three Dignitaries [*san gong,* the highest possible official position].' You can now be said to have been truly humiliated. The Three Dignitaries chair will therefore be yours." Du Yu was later instrumental in the Jin dynasty's victory over the state of Wu, which led to the unification of China under Emperor Wu (Sima Yan, 236–290; r. 265–290), and he was given the title Unequalled in Honor (*yi tong sansi*), much as Yan Xian had predicted.

Perception and foresight were qualities that were highly valued in men at the time Yan Xian lived, but it seems that women possessing these qualities were also held in high esteem, which is why Yan Xian's biography appears in the *History of the Jin Dynasty* (Jin shu).

Lily Xiao Hong LEE

Jin shu. Beijing: Zhonghua shuju, 1974, vol. 8, 96.2509.

Yang Lihua, Empress of Emperor Xuan of Northern Zhou

Yang Lihua, d. 609, was principal consort and empress of Emperor Xuan (Yuwen Yun, 558–580; r. 578–579) of the Northern Zhou dynasty. The Yuwen clan belonged to the eastern branch of the Xianbei (Xianbi), originally a nomadic non-Han Chinese people from the steppes of north China, which had been located in Liaodong, the region adjoining present-day Korea. Both of Yang Lihua's parents were from families that had helped the Yuwen clan establish Northern Zhou with its capital at Chang'an (the present-day city of Xi'an).

Her paternal Yang family was Han Chinese and came from present-day Shaanxi Province. Members of this family had been officials under the non-Han dynasties of the north and had maintained their position through intermarriage with powerful families. Her grandfather Yang Zhong (d. 568) served Northern Wei and after the division into Eastern Wei and Western Wei he chose to remain with the Yuwen clan in Western Wei. He continued to serve the Yuwen family after the dynastic name change from Western Wei to Northern Zhou and was rewarded with the title Duke of Sui. Yang Lihua's father, Yang Jian (541–604), had begun his career at the age of thirteen when he was appointed to a minor post in the final years of Western Wei; he had been promoted annually until he was made Duke of Daxing.

Yang Lihua's mother (*q.v.* Dugu, Empress of Emperor Wen of Sui), whose name is not recorded in the histories, was the seventh daughter of Dugu Xin and his

Chinese wife from the prestigious Cui clan of northern China. The Dugu were a high-ranking non-Han clan with a vast network of connections that enabled them to remain influential from the fourth to the eighth centuries. Like the Yang family, Dugu Xin had served Northern Wei, Western Wei, and Northern Zhou before his forced suicide in 557.

Emperor Wu (Yuwen Yong, 543–578; r. 561–578) of Northern Zhou chose Yang Lihua to enter the Eastern Palace as the wife of the heir apparent Yuwen Yun. Emperor Wu was extremely strict with his son and heir and had subjected him to intense training in practical government affairs. He had placed him under rigorous surveillance and appointed two guardians to provide corrective instruction. The relationship between father and son can be gauged from the following episode. When the guardians reported the misconduct of the eighteen-year-old Yuwen Yun in 576, Emperor Wu had him whipped and his entire personal staff dismissed. When Yuwen Yun ascended the throne two years later, he reappointed the same personal staff his father had dismissed and they became his inner cabinet.

Emperor Wu died suddenly in 578 and Yuwen Yun ascended the throne. Yang Lihua, his principal consort, was named empress. Emperor Wu's relatively long reign had been due to his ability to make political compromises without jeopardizing the authority of the throne; he did this by consulting his courtiers as well as his closest paternal relatives. Emperor Xuan, however, rejected his father's style of government and instead appears to have tried to make his reign an autocratic one in which he made all decisions in consultation with his closest advisers. His main concern was to eliminate the political clout of his paternal uncles and the close advisers of his deceased father; the tactics he adopted to do this were murder and "divide and rule."

Emperor Xuan replaced his father's policy of co-opting his rivals with his own style of confrontational politics. He had his influential uncle Yuwen Xian killed in the month following his enthronement; the following year he sent his five surviving uncles to positions scattered throughout his empire; he executed all the members of Emperor Wu's innermost clique.

Emperor Xuan named five women as empresses, ranked in order of seniority, with his principal consort Yang Lihua the most senior empress. The next three in line were all from families that had little or no influence in Northern Zhou politics. However, although Yang Lihua was the senior empress, the emperor did not favor her. Indeed, he appears to have disliked her intensely. Once, when he attempted to humiliate her with groundless accusations, Yang Lihua responded with quiet resistance. Infuriated, the emperor, whom historians describe as confused and violent, ordered her to commit suicide. Her mother, the powerful Lady Dugu, learned of this and went down on her knees to the emperor to beg for her daughter's life. Lady Dugu admitted to any and all wrongdoings of the Yang family and kowtowed until her forehead bled. Emperor Xuan rescinded the order for Yang Lihua to commit suicide but said that instead he might exterminate her entire family.

Emperor Xuan announced his retirement in 579 in favor of his young son Yuwen Chan (Emperor Jing, b. 573; r. 579–581), who was then about six; Emperor Xuan died the following year at the age of twenty-two. As his senior widow, Yang Lihua was named empress dowager. Her father, Yang Jian, was named regent and he controlled the young emperor, eventually deposing him to found the Sui dynasty. Yang Jian assumed the title of emperor and is known to history as Emperor Wen (r. 581–604).

As emperor of the new Sui dynasty, Yang Jian changed his daughter's title from Empress Dowager to Princess of Leping and granted her a large fiefdom. Since she was still very young—twenty years old—her mother urged her to remarry but she refused to do so. Yang Lihua already had a daughter, whose name was Eying, and after an elaborate selection process a Li Min was chosen to be Eying's husband. Eying and her husband had at least one child, a daughter named Li Jingxun who died in 608 at the age of eight. This child was given an extravagant burial befitting her royal background and among the objects unearthed in her elaborately decorated sarcophagus was a gold necklace inlaid with pearls, lapis lazuli, and bloodstone gems. This necklace was probably brought along the Silk Road from Iran or west central Asia.

Yang Lihua died in Hexi in 609 while she was accompanying her younger brother Yang Guang (Emperor Yang, 569–618; r. 605–617) on a tour of present-day Gansu Province. According to the histories, she was forty-eight years old when she died, but this may not be accurate; given that her mother was born in 552, Yang Lihua could not have been more than forty-three or forty-four when she died in 609. Her body was returned to the capital, Chang'an, where she was buried in Dingling alongside her husband, Emperor Xuan. Before her death she had asked her younger brother to take care of her daughter Eying and her son-in-law Li Min. Some years later, however, Emperor Yang had Li Min killed on suspicion of treason; a few months later Eying was poisoned.

Yang Lihua suffered from marriage to a violent and unpredictable husband and was further endangered by her father's increasing power and her husband's growing suspicion. When her father usurped the throne, she was placed in the awkward position of having been empress dowager in one dynasty and being a mere princess in the next. Her parents tried in many ways to humor her, most conspicuously by instituting an unprecedented selection process for her son-in-law. Yang Lihua also attempted to ensure her daughter's happiness by having her son-in-law appointed to high official position and by beseeching her brother, the emperor, to take care of the young couple after she died. But all her precautions were in vain and ultimately she was unable to protect them from the vicious political climate of the time, making her tragic life even more tragic in death.

Priscilla CHING-CHUNG

Eisenberg, Andrew. "Retired Emperorship and the Politics of Succession in the Northern Dynasties of China, 386–581." Ph.D. dissertation, University of Washington, 1991, 224–32.
Chen Quanli and Hou Xinyi, eds. *Hou fei cidian.* Xi'an: Shaanxi renmin jiaoyu chubanshe, 81, 82, 83–84.
Sui shu. Beijing: Zhonghua shuju, 1973, vol. 4, 37.1124–25.
Wright, Arthur E. *The Sui Dynasty.* New York: Alfred A. Knopf, 1979, 54–56.
Xiong, Victor Cunrui. "China: Dawn of a Golden Age." *AJA Online Publications* (January 2005), 8–9. www.ajaonline.org/pdfs/museum_reviews/AJAonline_China_Dawn_of_a_Golden_Age. pdf, accessed 8 June 2005.
Zhou shu. Beijing: Zhonghua shuju, 1971, 1983, vol. 1, 9.143, 145–46; vol. 1, 16.263–68.

Yang of Emperor Xuan, Empress: *see* **Yang Lihua, Empress of Emperor Xuan of Northern Zhou**

Yang Yan, Empress of Emperor Wu of Jin

Yang Yan, *zi* Qiongzhi, 237–274, was the first wife and empress of Emperor Wu (Sima Yan, 236–290; r. 265–290), founder of the Western Jin dynasty, and the mother of Emperor Hui (Sima Zhong, 259–306; r. 290–306). Prime Empress Yang of Emperor Wu (Wuyuan Yang Huanghou) was her posthumous title.

Yang Yan was a native of Huayin District, Hongnong Commandery (present-day Huayin in Shaanxi Province), and her father's family had served in the upper echelons of the imperial government of the Eastern Han dynasty for four generations, some attaining the highest-ranking civil office of the Three Dignitaries (*san gong*). After the fall of the Han dynasty her father, Yang Wenzong, served the Wei dynasty, holding the post of vice director of the secretariat (*tongshi lang*), and was given benefice as the Neighborhood Marquis of Mao (*Mao tinghou*). Yang Yan's mother, a woman of the Zhao clan of Tianshui Commandery (present-day Gangu in Gansu Province), died young, leaving her infant daughter to be raised by relatives. The child went first to her maternal uncle's family, where her aunt nursed her, employing someone else to breastfeed her own son. After her father remarried, Yang Yan was supported by her stepmother's family, surnamed Duan. Her biography in the official *History of the Jin Dynasty* (Jin shu) describes the young Yang Yan as "intelligent and good with books," "beautiful in appearance," and "spending her time on womanly crafts."

While still a young unmarried woman, Yang Yan was examined by a fortune-teller, who predicted that she would become "a supremely exalted" woman. Hearing this report, the powerful Wei official Sima Zhao (211–265, posthumously given the title Emperor Wen of Jin), quickly arranged for her to marry his son Sima Yan. Sima Yan was quite fond of his bride, who gave birth to six children: Sima Gui (Prince Dao of Piling), Sima Zhong (the future Emperor Hui), Sima Jian (Prince of Qinxian), and the Princesses of Pingyang, Xinfeng, and Yangping. When Sima Yan deposed the last Wei emperor and established the Jin dynasty in 266, he named Yang Yan as his empress, thus fulfilling the earlier prediction that she would achieve high status.

Empress Yang sought to use her position to benefit herself and her kinsfolk. She objected when her husband failed to bestow upon her and her son (the heir) the benefices of a bathing fief of forty prefectures as prescribed by Han law. Despite her protest, the emperor withheld these income-generating properties. She was more successful in her efforts to repay the kindness of her kinsfolk who had nurtured her after the death of her mother, gaining a government position for a maternal uncle and admission into the imperial palace for two of her female relatives.

As empress, she advised her husband on a number of family matters with significant political implications. The weightiest of these was the selection of an heir to the throne. Her firstborn son, Sima Gui, died at the age of two, leaving her second son, Sima Zhong, in line to inherit the throne. This would not normally have been cause for concern, but serious questions were raised at court regarding Sima Zhong's ability to rule. The historical accounts indicate that Sima Zhong was naive and a bit slow of

372 *YANG YAN*

thought, but offer little evidence of mental illness. His condition was nevertheless serious enough to warrant discussion between the emperor and his top officials regarding the line of imperial succession and the prospects of removing the simple-minded prince from that line. Several high-ranking officials argued for the promotion of Emperor Wu's younger brother, the Prince of Qi, to the position of heir apparent but when Emperor Wu raised this matter with Empress Yang she chastised him, saying, "The establishment of an heir is based on his position as first born [of each generation], not on sagacity! How could you do this?" Her remark, while showing clear self-interest, appears to have hit the mark, for in 267 Sima Zhong was named heir apparent to the Jin throne. Yang Yan thus secured her place in the palace hierarchy as both empress and mother of the future emperor.

Empress Yang also asserted herself in the selection of a consort-wife for her son, the heir. The *History of the Jin Dynasty* notes that, before Sima Zhong had been formally declared heir, Lady Guo (*q.v.* Guo Huai), wife of the powerful courtier Jia Chong (*zi* Gonglü, 217–282), sent a bribe to Empress Yang asking that their daughter be chosen as Sima Zhong's consort. Empress Yang was happy to accept this daughter of Jia Chong and Lady Guo, but Emperor Wu preferred a daughter of the high-ranking official Wei Guan, arguing, "The daughter of Master Wei has five qualities; the daughter of Master Jia has five faults. Miss Wei carries the seeds of sagacity and many sons, and is beautiful, tall, and fair. Miss Jia carries the seeds of jealousy and few sons, and is ugly, short, and dark." Empress Yang countered by enlisting several trusted ministers to extol the virtues of her choice—Jia Nanfeng (*q.v.* Jia Nanfeng, Empress of Emperor Hui of Jin)—and the emperor finally conceded and approved the marriage in 272.

A final anecdote illustrates Empress Yang's ability to influence even her husband's choice of women for the inner palace. Desiring to increase the number of women in the palace, Emperor Wu issued an edict in 274 prohibiting marriage throughout the empire. He then sent eunuchs and officials to inspect the daughters of aristocratic families, ordering that those found to be of suitable beauty and/or talent were to be conveyed to the palace for further inspection. While there was no tradition of empresses playing a role in the selection of additional consorts, Empress Yang personally oversaw the process at the palace, selecting only morally upright and mature women for the inner palace and sending back the most beautiful young girls. The *History of the Jin Dynasty* attributes these actions to the "jealous nature" of the empress. Reportedly infatuated with a beautiful young daughter of Bian Fan, the emperor mentioned her to Empress Yang, who noted that since the Bian clan had had three generations of empresses it would do this young woman an injustice to bring her into the palace at a position lower than empress. She declared this should not be done and the emperor ceased his pursuit of Bian Fan's daughter forthwith. The empress's careful selection of women saw the inner palaces filled with the daughters and kinswomen of many prominent officials, the historical records noting that many of these women were better known for moral and literary talents than for their appearance. Zuo Fen (*q.v.*), for example, was described as homely but gifted in literary ability.

YANG YAN 373

Shortly after the selection of these additional palace women, Empress Yang became seriously ill. Nearing death, she feared that her husband would promote a new favorite, Lady Hu (daughter of an important general), as empress and the lady's son as heir apparent. To circumvent this eventuality, she laid her head on the emperor's lap and requested that instead he promote her cousin Yang Zhi (*q.v.* Yang Zhi, Empress of Emperor Wu of Jin) as empress. The emperor tearfully consented. Empress Yang Yan died on 22 August 274 at the age of thirty-seven. According to popular accounts, she died in the emperor's arms immediately after extracting his promise to advance her kinswoman. Following her death, the emperor issued an edict ordering nationwide mourning, the relocation of the graves of her ancestors to a site near the capital, and the issuing of posthumous titles to the clans of her mother and stepmother. She was buried at Junyang tumulus (north of Luoyang in Henan Province), where Emperor Wu, who died sixteen years later, was later laid to rest.

Two contemporary funerary laments survive. The first, by an anonymous author, is a generic lament with no personal details on Yang Yan. The second, composed by palace lady Zuo Fen and recorded in the *History of the Jin Dynasty,* comments on various aspects of the empress's life and activities, including her education, adherence to ritual protocol, service in the ancestral temple, counsel to the emperor, and comparison with sagely women of antiquity who benefited their ruler-husbands.

A recent biography of Yang Yan in *Complete Biographies of Chinese Empresses* (Zhongguo huanghou quanzhuan) offers a somewhat negative evaluation of her life. Noting that she is said to have possessed both talent and beauty, it claims that she committed two major errors that "brought great sorrow to her family and the nation": the establishment of the "retarded" Sima Zhong as heir, and the selection of the "secretive wolf" Jia Nanfeng as his consort.

Traditional accounts of Yang Yan's life illustrate the extent of the personal influence women could have over men, especially their husbands, in imperial China. In both the establishment of an heir to the throne and the selection of a consort to the heir, Yang Yan was able to override her husband's wishes and secure the outcome she desired. While traditional, and some contemporary, historians view Yang Yan's influence over her husband in a negative light, her power within the family and state is in marked contrast to the common stereotype of palace women as powerless playthings of an imperial patriarch. Yang Yan enjoyed the power to select even her own rivals for her husband's attention and affection, choosing women on the basis of character and talent, and dismissing those whose physical charms surpassed her own. Her final political act, the selection of her cousin as her successor empress, sealed the fate of her son, securing his place as the next emperor, and ensured Yang Yan's place in history as the mother of an emperor.

J. Michael FARMER

Jin shu. Beijing: Zhonghua shuju, 1974, vol. 4, 31.952–54, 958–61.
Sima Guang. *Zizhi tongjian,* 79–80. Taipei: Shijie shuju, 1977, 2532–33, 2535.
Zhao Mengxiang, ed. *Zhongguo huanghou quanzhuan.* Beijing: Zhongguo shehuikexue chubanshe, 2004, vol. 1, 206–10.

Yang Zhi, Empress of Emperor Wu of Jin

Yang Zhi, *zi* Jilan, *ming* Nanying, 257–291, was the second empress of Emperor Wu (Sima Yan, 236–290; r. 265–290), founder of the Western Jin dynasty. Grievous Empress Yang of Emperor Wu (Wu Dao Yang Huanghou) was her posthumous title.

Yang Zhi was a native of Huayin District, Hongnong Commandery (present-day Huayin in Shaanxi Province). Her father, Yang Jun (*zi* Wenchang, d. 291), had served in several low-ranking government offices, including manager of Gaoling Tumulus and garrison general of the Imperial Guards, but was regarded as incapable of holding higher office. No information is available about Yang Zhi's mother. An elder cousin, Yang Yan (*q.v.* Yang Yan, Empress of Emperor Wu of Jin), had been the first wife of Sima Yan and had been promoted to empress following the establishment of the Jin dynasty in 264. Yang Zhi's biography in the official *History of the Jin Dynasty* (Jin shu) provides no information on her early life or talents.

Yang Zhi's rise to prominence was intimately linked to the influence of her cousin Yang Yan, the first Empress Yang, who on her deathbed had begged Emperor Wu to name Yang Zhi as her successor, praising her as "possessing virtue and beauty." It is unclear whether Yang Zhi had already entered the imperial palace at that time or had become a palace lady by then.

After the two-year mourning period for Empress Yang Yan had been completed, Yang Zhi was duly promoted to the office of empress, in 276. Although she was "deeply favored" by the emperor, who clearly had a preference, previously thwarted, for younger women, she did not bear any children for six years. In 282 she finally gave birth to her only child, a son, Sima Hui. This infant died two years later and was given the posthumous title Tragic Prince of Bohai (Bohai shang wang).

Empress Yang Zhi's biography in the *History of the Jin Dynasty* notes her participation in the revival of ancient court rites. In 288, she led a group of palace women to the Western Suburb to pick mulberry leaves, afterward presenting each participant with a bolt of silk. This ritual served as the female counterpart to the rite of imperial plowing, evoking good fortune in both agriculture and sericulture, and had not previously been performed by the emperor and empress in the quarter-century of Jin rule.

Empress Yang Zhi is best defined by her relationship with Jia Nanfeng (*q.v.* Jia Nanfeng, Empress of Emperor Hui of Jin), consort of the heir apparent Sima Zhong (Emperor Hui, 259–306; r. 290–306). Consort Jia was known for her jealous nature and violent temper. When word reached Emperor Wu that his daughter-in-law had strangled several of her pregnant palace rivals to death with her bare hands, he immediately sought to have her removed as consort to the heir (a position he had opposed from the beginning). Speaking in support of Consort Jia, Empress Yang reminded Emperor Wu of the powerful support offered to the state by the consort's father, Jia Chong (*zi* Gonglü, 217–282), and warned of the consequences of offending him. The wisdom of her advice was not lost on the emperor, who dropped the matter. Knowing the precarious position Consort Jia was in, Empress Yang frequently chastised her, hoping to inspire in her a change of behavior. However, unaware of the goodwill behind the empress's chastisement, Consort Jia took the criticism as a personal attack and developed a deep hatred for her.

Yang Zhi's promotion to empress brought increased status and power to her kinsmen. Her father, the previously low-ranking Yang Jun, was promoted and from 280 on found himself the most powerful individual at the Jin court. His power was compounded by the emperor's lack of interest in government affairs in his later years, which gave Yang Jun and his two brothers free rein in virtually all aspects of the Jin court. In early 290, as Emperor Wu was nearing death, he sought to finalize the succession of his son Sima Zhong. Concerned over the limited mental capacity of the thirty-two-year-old heir, he drafted an edict naming as co-regents Yang Jun and an imperial uncle, Sima Liang. Before the document could be distributed, however, Yang Jun intercepted it and hid it. Emperor Wu's condition continued to deteriorate and when, two days later, Empress Yang asked him if Yang Jun should be appointed regent the emperor merely nodded. The *History of the Jin Dynasty* says of this incident, "Thus the Secretariat Supervisor and Director Hua Yi and He Shao were called in and [Empress Yang Zhi] orally proclaimed the emperor's wish and made them write the emperor's will." This suggests that Emperor Wu may have merely nodded because he was too ill to contradict his empress or to add a joint regent. While Empress Yang might not have known that her father, Yang Jun, had hidden the original will in which Sima Liang was named as co-regent, she undeniably played a role in suggesting Yang Jun as sole regent.

When Emperor Wu died on 16 May 290, Yang Jun became sole regent and his daughter was promoted to empress dowager. Although the emperor was an adult, Yang Jun positioned himself as the de facto ruler, taking up residence in the Basilica of the Supreme Ultimate (the hall in which the emperor discharged official business), an act tantamount to proclaiming himself emperor. Again, Yang Zhi's role as empress dowager in her father's efforts to retain power is unclear.

However, the power of the Yang clan at the court of Emperor Hui was soon challenged by his empress, Jia Nanfeng. Acting on reports of a military coup orchestrated by Yang Jun, Empress Jia summoned to the capital soldiers of her husband's kinsman Sima Wei. Yang Jun's residence was set ablaze and he was killed trying to escape the inferno. Empress Jia immediately issued a communiqué accusing Empress Dowager Yang Zhi of involvement in a plot to overthrow the dynasty. A number of court officials and members of the Sima clan issued statements, some supporting and some opposing the empress dowager and her purported role in the plot. Some suggested that she be executed, others that she be demoted to commoner status, others that she simply be stripped of the titles of empress and empress dowager. The final outcome was that Yang Zhi was initially stripped of both titles and demoted to commoner status; then she was arrested and imprisoned in the Metal-Walled Compound (*Jinyong cheng*), a detention facility outside the capital, Luoyang. Her food supply was cut off by order of Empress Jia and she starved to death in prison. Fearing that the spirit of Yang Zhi would offer a negative report on her to the spirit of her deceased father-in-law Emperor Wu, the superstitious Empress Jia placed several talismans in Yang Zhi's coffin as a preventive measure. At the time of her death, Yang Zhi was thirty-four years old and had been in the imperial palace for fifteen years.

Yang Zhi's role in her father's activities continued to be debated by officials and rulers throughout the Jin dynasty. In 301, her imperial titles of empress and empress

376 YANG ZHI

dowager were restored following the removal of Empress Jia from power. A separate shrine was also established for her spirit to receive offerings. However, her spirit tablet was not placed alongside that of her husband, Emperor Wu. Later, in 341, court officials argued that she had rightfully succeeded her cousin as empress, and it was her father's rebellion that had brought her trouble, not any of her own actions. After she had been thus exonerated, her spirit tablet was moved next to that of Emperor Wu and her spirit was "authorized" to receive the offerings due an empress.

Yang Zhi is generally regarded as a tragic victim of imperial politics. Her posthumous title of "Dao" (Grievous) emphasizes this. Her Tang biographers, who compiled the *History of the Jin Dynasty,* present her as being without malice, a woman whose well-intentioned support of Consort Jia returned to haunt her. In particular, the biography shows the consort's misunderstanding of the empress's criticisms leading to hatred and to murder. The official biography is oddly silent, however, about Yang Zhi's role in her father's efforts to retain power after the death of Emperor Wu.

While the compilers of the *History of the Jin Dynasty* may have refrained from comment on her role in the manipulation of the regency of Emperor Hui, contemporary sources did weigh in on the matter. Yang Zhi's meddling may have prompted Zhang Hua's famous didactic poem *Admonitions of the Female Scribe* (Nüshi zhen), which warns of the imminent fall of the mighty and urges palace women to cultivate inner virtue over outer beauty. Most critics have identified the target of the admonition as Empress Jia, but textual and contextual evidence indicates that this is incorrect. Moreover, another Jin historian, Cao Jiazhi, specifically identifies Yang Zhi and her kinsmen as the objects of Zhang Hua's warning, implying that her role in her father's plot may have been much greater than presented in her *History* biography. It appears, therefore, that the compilers of the *History* preferred to portray Yang Zhi as tragic victim in order to illustrate the jealousy and cruelty of Jia Nanfeng, rather than as an active player in imperial politics herself. Her political role is made a little clearer in her father's biography, however, revealing an inconsistent approach on the part of the historians who compiled the *History of the Jin Dynasty.* In the final analysis, Yang Zhi was clearly a more complicated personality than her own official biography would have us believe, though one whose true role in the affairs of the Jin court may never be fully revealed.

J. Michael FARMER

Farmer, J. Michael. "On the Composition of Zhang Hua's 'Nüshi zhen.'" *Early Medieval China* 10/11.1 (2004): 151–75.
Jin shu. Beijing: Zhonghua shuju, 1974, vol. 4, 31.954–57; vol. 4, 40.1177–80.
Sima Guang. *Zizhi tongjian,* 79–80. Taipei: Shijie shuju, 1977, 2599–607.
Zhao Mengxiang, ed. *Zhongguo huanghou quanzhuan.* Beijing: Zhongguo shehuikexue chubanshe, 2004, vol. 1, 210–15.

Yangdi Xiao Huanghou: *see* **Xiao, Empress of Emperor Yang of Sui**

Yicheng, Princess: *see* **Xiao, Empress of Emperor Yang of Sui**

Yicheng Jun: *see* **Guo Huai**

You née Feng, Empress: *see* **Feng, Empress of Emperor Xiaowen of Northern Wei**

Yuan Qigui, Empress of Emperor Wen of Liu Song

Empress Yuan (Wendi Yuan Huanghou), 405–440, whose name was Yuan Qigui, was the principal consort of Emperor Wen (Liu Yilong, 407–453; r. 424–453), third emperor of the southern Liu Song dynasty. The founder of Liu Song, Liu Yu (Emperor Wu, 363–422; r. 420–422), had been a military commander under the Eastern Jin dynasty but he overthrew the Jin regents in 420, dethroned the last ruler, and declared himself emperor of his own Song dynasty.

Yuan Qigui was born into a prominent family from Yangxia, in present-day Henan Province. Her grandfather had served the Eastern Jin dynasty as prefect of Liyang and her father, Yuan Zhan, had served the same dynasty as grand master for splendid happiness of the left (*zuo guanglu dafu*). However, despite the prominence of her family Yuan Qigui had grown up in poverty, as her mother had been only a maid in the Yuan household. Her paternal connections nevertheless ensured that she did not remain in obscure poverty and, recruited for her beauty, she was given in marriage to Liu Yilong, the third son of Emperor Wu. As principal consort of Liu Yilong, who as a younger son was not in the direct line of succession for the throne, she was given the title Consort of a Prince (*wang fei*). She gave birth to Liu Shao (426–454), the eldest of Liu Yilong's nineteen sons, and a daughter named Ying'e, later to become Princess Dongyang. Yuan Qigui became empress when Liu Yilong was installed as emperor after court officials removed his older brother Liu Yifu (Emperor Shao; r. 422–424) from the throne. Their son Liu Shao was named heir apparent at the age of six.

Empress Yuan is said to have frequently asked Emperor Wen for money for her family, which had not benefited from her rise to eminence and remained very poor. The emperor was very frugal in his giving, offering only 30,000 to 50,000 cash and thirty to fifty bolts of silk in response to her requests. Yet, at the same time, he was quick to lavish money on another of his palace women, Lady Pan (d. 453), who was then his favorite: when she asked for thirty million cash for her family, he granted her request in full after reflecting on it for only a day. This enraged Empress Yuan, who feigned illness and refused to see Emperor Wen. In 440, she became seriously ill and the historical record tells us that when Emperor Wen visited her on her sickbed he held her hand and cried. She gazed at him for a while without saying a word, then covered her face with her bed cover; she died soon after, at the age of thirty-six. Emperor Wen is said to have been so grieved at her death that he ordered the famous scholar and literary man Yan Yanzhi to write a eulogy for her.

More than ten years after her death, Empress Yuan's son, Liu Shao, and her daughter were said to have practiced witchcraft and allowed the witch Yan Daoyu to live in their house. Liu Shao's half-brother, the emperor's third son, Liu Jun (Emperor Xiaowu, 430–464; r. 454–464) was also implicated. This angered Emperor Wen. When Lady Pan, who had been foster mother to Liu Jun, learned of the emperor's intention to either

378 YUAN QIGUI

kill or demote his two sons for their involvement in witchcraft she warned her foster son who, in turn, warned his half-brother Liu Shao. Liu Shao murdered his father and Lady Pan, whom he had always hated, blaming her for his mother's death. He then assumed the Liu Song throne, but Liu Jun raised an army against him, defeating him and wiping out his entire family. Liu Jun (Emperor Xiaowu) was then enthroned.

After her death, Empress Yuan is said to have worked little miracles. One such was when Emperor Wen ordered his concubine Lady Shen (414–453) to commit suicide. Lady Shen went to the palace in which Empress Yuan had resided and begged for her help, saying that she had not committed any crime and should not be sentenced to death. At this, there was a loud noise and the windows of the temple flew open. Hearing of this small miracle, Emperor Wen relented and allowed Lady Shen to live. The palace women quite possibly sympathized with Empress Yuan over Emperor Wen's unfair treatment of her and consequently claimed her spirit had the power to bless other innocent women. This may have been one way in which the populace was able to voice its opinion.

CHAN Hui Ying Sarah, AU YEUNG Ka Yi, and Priscilla CHING-CHUNG

Chen Quanli and Hou Xinyi, eds. *Hou fei cidian.* Xi'an: Shaanxi renmin jiaoyu chubanshe, 1991, 58–59.
Giles, Herbert A. *A Chinese Biographical Dictionary.* Taipei: Chengwen Publishing, 1971, 499, 507, 520.
Nan shi. Beijing: Zhonghua shuju, 1975; 1983, vol. 2, 11.320–21; vol. 2, 14.386–95.
Song shu. Beijing: Zhonghua shuju, 1974; 1983, vol. 4, 41.1283–46; vol. 5, 52.1497.
Zhu Mingpan. *Nan chao Song huiyao.* In *Xu xiu siku quanshu.* Shanghai: Shanghai guji chubanshe, [1995]–2002, 767, 483, 532.

Yuan Wang Fei: *see* **Yuan Qigui, Empress of Emperor Wen of Liu Song**

Yuwen, Princess Qianjin of Northern Zhou
Princess Qianjin née Yuwen, d. 593, was addressed as Princess Dayi after 584. Her personal name is not known but she was related to the ruling family of the Northern Zhou dynasty. Her father, the Prince of Zhao, was a brother of two Northern Zhou emperors and she was a first cousin of the reigning Northern Zhou emperor when her marriage to Eastern Turk's Taspar Qaghan was finalized in 579. Northern Zhou had exchanged her for the return of its enemy, the Northern Qi prince, who was then seeking refuge with the Eastern Turks. Shortly after journeying from Chang'an to the Eastern Turk court (near present-day Qaraqorum, Mongolia), she learned that her father, three brothers, and two uncles had been executed in Chang'an by the Sui dynasty, which supplanted Northern Zhou in 581.

As wife to the Eastern Turk Qaghan, Princess Qianjin had a certain degree of military influence and tried to turn him against the Sui—a strategy she continued to pursue from 581 to 583 with her second husband, Ishbara Qaghan. In 584, however, due to the weakened position of the Eastern Turks, she negotiated a peace treaty with Sui by which Sui adopted her under the new identity of Princess Dayi and the Sui dynasty replaced the Northern Zhou in her marriage alliance with the Eastern Turks.

After Ishbara died, she married his son (her stepson), Dulan Qaghan, in 587, all the time secretly nursing a hatred for the Sui imperial house that had wiped out her dynasty and her family. Two years later, when the Sui emperor sent her a room panel belonging to the imperial family of the short-lived Chen dynasty that the Sui had just crushed, Princess Qianjin wrote on it a poem lamenting its collapse and comparing it to her own fate as a princess of the defunct Northern Zhou dynasty:

Rise and decline—like dawn and evening
the course of the world floats like duckweed.
Honor and splendor are truly hard to retain;
ponds and terraces are leveled in the end.
Now, where are wealth and dignity?
Void of feelings, I sketch out a painting.
Cupfuls of wine bring no lasting pleasure;
how can music and song create resonance?
I was after all born of the imperial family
who drifted into the caitiffs' camp;
Going through success and defeat—
my heart subjected to sudden ups and downs.
Since ancient times things have been thus
I am not alone in registering my name—
But only the tune of Wang Zhaojun
truly evokes the trauma of marrying far away.

The Sui emperor was much displeased when he heard about the poem, and when rumors surfaced that Princess Qianjin had assisted a Sui turncoat and plotted with the Western Turks against the Sui, he bribed her husband's cousin to have her killed. In 593, Princess Qianjin died by the hand of her husband, Dulan Qaghan, as a condition of peace and another marriage with a Sui princess.

Despite her political activism and after serving as wife to three Qaghans in the fourteen years spent in the court of the Eastern Turks, Princess Qianjin remained powerless in her life. Her first marriage was a hostage exchange arranged by the Northern Zhou dynasty, and her death was contracted by the same Sui dynasty that had massacred her family. We have no information on whether any descendant survived her, or whether she ever gave birth to any children. What she bequeathed to history is the poignancy of her tragic life as a princess bride (*vide* Wang Zhaojun), as preserved in her poem.

Jennifer W. JAY

Jagchid, Sechin, and Van Jay Symons. *Peace, War, and Trade Along the Great Wall. Nomadic-Chinese Interaction Through Two Millennia.* Bloomington: Indiana University Press, 1989, 147–50.

Lin Enxian. *Tujue yanjiu.* Taipei: Taiwan shangwu yinshuguan, 1988, 190–91.

Lin Enxian and Cui Mingde. "Lun Zhongguo gudai heqin di gongneng ji yingxiang." *Renmin xuebao* 3, no. 20 (1996): 1–37.

Pan, Yihong. "Marriage Alliances and Chinese Princesses in International Politics from Han through T'ang." *Asia Major* 10, no. 1–2 (1997): 95–131.

380 YUWEN, PRINCESS QIANJIN OF NORTHERN ZHOU

————. *Son of Heaven and Heavenly Qaghan: Sui-Tang China and Its Neighbors.* Bellingham: Center for East Asian Studies, Western Washington University, 1997.

Sima Guang. *Zizhi tongjian.* Beijing: Zhonghua shuju, 1956, vol. 12, 175.5449; vol. 12, 178.5542–43.

Sui shu. Beijing: Zhonghua shuju, 1973, vol. 1, 1.3; vol. 6, 84.1864–72.

Zhou shu. Beijing: Zhonghua shuju, 1971, vol. 1, 13.202–3; vol. 3, 50.912.

Z

Zhan, Tao Kan's Mother

Zhan was the surname of a woman, fl. third century, who was a native of Xingan (present-day Xingan in Jiangxi Province) and who lived during the period spanning late Western Jin and early Eastern Jin. Only her surname is known; her given name is not found in the historical records. She is remembered as a mother for whom no sacrifice was too great in order to help her son become an official, but also as one who reprimanded him for rewarding her with ill-gotten gains.

Zhan was a concubine of General Tao Dan and she bore him a son named Tao Kan (259–334), who later became a well-known minister at the Eastern Jin court. The family became very poor after Tao Dan died and Zhan supported herself and her dependents through her weaving. She was determined, however, that through her son her family would escape their poverty and become a scholar-official family. The story goes that one cold and snowy day, Fan Kui, a scholar who was recommended as a "filial and incorrupt" (*xiaolian*) and was therefore eligible for official appointment, was traveling to the capital, Luoyang, and stopped at the Tao home. There was nothing in the house to offer their guest and his entourage of men and horses. However, unwilling to let slip this opportunity for her son to consolidate his friendship with a rising literatus, Zhan told him to ask Fan Kui to stay for dinner. She then set to work. She cut off her long hair and sold it as two wigs, using the proceeds to buy several bushels of rice; she cut into the pillars (presumably of an outside shed) and split them for firewood; she shredded the straw mats as feed for the guests' horses. That night, she presented a fine feast for Fan Kui and provided plenty to eat for the servants as well. Fan Kui had been impressed with Tao Kan's talent and debating skills, but he was even more touched by his great hospitality. The next morning, as Tao Kan accompanied Fan Kui a little way on his journey, Fan said, "Please go home now. When I reach Luoyang, I will praise you to everyone there." Fan Kui kept his promise and Tao Kan came to be known to members of the elite at the capital, one of whom recommended him as a junior rectifier (*xiao zhongzheng*) and started him on his official career.

To a modern reader, the behavior of this mother and son might seem excessive, even incredible. Indeed, the story may have become exaggerated and embellished over time, but it does show the extent to which some people would go to better their station in life in a highly stratified society such as the Jin dynasty.

Although Zhan tried to better her family's status, she does not seem to have coveted the perks an official life could offer. Another anecdote tells of the time Tao

Kan was in charge of fish weirs. He sent his mother some salted fish but she returned the fish untouched along with a letter criticizing her son for giving her government property. This story, incidentally, has also been told as having happened to Meng Zong, an official of an earlier time, and his mother.

Zhan was also credited with inculcating in her son an awareness of the harm excessive drinking can cause. When later in life Tao Kan drank with friends and subordinates, he always exercised control. If anyone urged him to drink more, he would say that he once did something wrong when intoxicated and his parents made him promise never to get drunk again. Since his father died when Tao Kan was very young, it must have been his mother who had kept him to this promise.

Tao Kan is known in history as an upright minister who was diligent and incorrupt. Historians often credit this to the fine education and moral principles he received from his mother. One interesting point about Zhan is that she may have been a member of one of China's minority peoples. A treatise discussing Tao Kan's ethnic origins suggests that he was a member of the Xi ethnic group, which flourished in what is now Jiangxi Province in the early centuries of the Common Era. If that is the case, it is more than likely that his mother, who was a native of Jiangxi, was Xi since Tao Kan's father's family came from Yunyang in present-day Hubei Province.

Lily Xiao Hong LEE

Chen Yinke. "Wei shu Sima Rui zhuan jiangdong minzu." *Chen Yinke xiansheng lunwenji, Zhongyang yanjiuyuan lishi yuyan yanjiusuo tekan* 3 (1971): 408–9.
Jin shu. Beijing: Zhonghua shuju, 1974, vol. 8, 96.2512.
Liu I-ch'ing [Yiqing]. *Shih-shuo Hsin-yü: A New Account of Tales of the World,* trans. Richard B. Mather. Minneapolis: University of Minnesota Press, 1976, 350–52.
Liu Shisheng. *Zhongguo gudai funü shi.* Qingdao: Qingdao chubanshe, 1991, 164–65.
Liu Yiqing. *Shishuo xinyu jian shu,* ed. Yu Jiaxi. Beijing: Zhonghua shuju, 1983, 19, 20.690–93.

Zhang Baoguang: *see* **Xu Baoguang**

Zhang, Concubine of Fu Jian
Zhang was the surname of a concubine of Fu Jian (Fu Jian Qie Zhang Shi). She died in 383. We do not know her given name, where she was from, or indeed whether she was of Han or non-Han nationality. She is remembered for her perception and judgment in state affairs.

Fu Jian (338–385; r. 357–385), who usurped the throne of King Li (Fu Sheng; r. 355–357) of Former Qin and titled himself Heavenly King of Great Qin (Da Qin tianwang), was a warlord of the Di nationality and third ruler of the Former Qin dynasty in North China. He strengthened his regime's rule over North China, but when he became ambitious to conquer the Eastern Jin dynasty south of the Yangzi River many of his ministers advised against it. However, Fu Jian was determined to pursue his dreams of empire. Zhang's biography in the *History of the Jin Dynasty* (Jin shu)

382 ZHANG, CONCUBINE OF FU JIAN

contains a passage quoting her counsel to Fu Jian. It is in a similar vein to that of his ministers and, while it is not clear whether this quotation is of something she said or from a memorial she wrote, from the style it appears more likely to have been a written document. It says in part:

> Now all the ministers at court have said it should not be done; what then does Your Majesty base your action on? It is said in *Book of Documents* (Shu jing), "Heaven hears and sees what the people hear and see." If even Heaven is like this, how much more so should a ruler be? I have heard that a ruler who intends to conquer another country should observe the signs in the sky and collect auspicious manifestations on earth. The way of Heaven is high and far away, not something I understand but, judging from the affairs of men, I see nothing positive about it.

Fu Jian is quoted as saying: "Women should not participate in military decisions." He invaded Eastern Jin and Zhang asked to go with him. As she had warned, he suffered a devastating defeat, in the famous Battle of Fei River (*Feishui zhi zhan*) at Shouchun (in present-day Anhui Province). Zhang killed herself after the battle, the reason for her suicide not clearly stated in her biography. We can only surmise it was because she was extremely angry with Fu Jian for not heeding her advice.

In fairness it must be pointed out that this biography was written from the standpoint of Fu Jian's enemy and vanquisher, the Eastern Jin dynasty, and, by highlighting Zhang's ultimately correct judgment, it may have been intended to show Fu Jian in a poor light.

Lily Xiao Hong LEE

Jin shu. Beijing: Zhonghua shuju, 1974, vol. 8, 96.2522–23.
Xie Wuliang. *Zhongguo funü wenxueshi.* Shanghai: Zhonghua shuju, 1916; Zhengzhou: Zhongzhou guji chubanshe, 1992, reprint, Section IIB, 77.
Xu Tianxiao. *Shenzhou nüzi xinshi.* Shanghai: Shenzhou tushuju, 1913; Taipei: Daoxiang chubanshe, 1993, reprint, 68.

Zhen, Empress of Emperor Wen of Wei

Empress Zhao née Zhen (Wenzhao Zhen Huanghou), 182–221, was from Wuji in Zhongshan (present-day Dingyuan District, Hebei Province). Her personal name is not recorded in the histories. Empress to Emperor Wen (Cao Pi, 187–226; r. 220–226) of the Wei dynasty, she was the mother of Emperor Ming (Cao Rui, 205–239; r. 226–239).

Men from Empress Zhen's family had been provincial officials of the Han government for several generations: she was a descendant of Grand Guardian (*taibao*) Zhen Han and a daughter of Zhen Yi (d. 185), the Marquis of Shangcai. She was the youngest girl in a family of four sons and five daughters and her father's death when she was only three caused her great distress. It is said that every time she went to sleep, her family saw a figure bringing a jade garment to cover her. Summoned to examine all nine children, the physiognomist Liu Liang pointed her out as someone who would become great. The *Record of the Wei Dynasty* (Wei shu) in *Record of the*

Three Kingdoms (Sanguo zhi) describes her as disliking frivolity but enjoying writing from the age of nine, by which time she could recognize words. She used her elder brothers' brushes and ink stones, telling them she needed to understand writing in order to learn history because all of the worthy women of antiquity had studied history in order to better themselves. One of her brothers died when she was fourteen and she served his widow with humility and respect, caring for their child and asking her mother not to be harsh with the young widow. She lived with the young widow and they grew to love one another.

Born during the chaotic final years of the Eastern Han dynasty, the future Empress Zhen witnessed the emergence of the three powerful rival states of the Three Kingdoms (*sanguo*) period: Wei in the north, Shu Han in the west, and Wu in the south and east. As the Han dynasty disintegrated, famine spread throughout the land and many people sold their precious objects and jewelry for food. With its large stores of grain, the Zhen family was able to profit by buying up these precious objects. It is said that in her teens she advised her family they should not do this as it might later be seen as criminal behavior and she suggested instead that they give away their grain to relieve their kinsmen and neighboring villages and thus earn their gratitude. The family agreed and opened their storehouse to those most in need.

As the intensity of the fighting increased in the last decade of the second century, the young woman was taken to wife by Yuan Xi, governor of Youzhou (in the region of present-day northern Hebei Province and Liaoning Province) and son of the warlord Yuan Shao (d. 202). She remained behind with her mother-in-law in Jizhou, which Yuan Shao's rival militarist Cao Cao (155–220) occupied in 204. When Cao Cao's oldest son, Cao Pi, came upon her in a state of terror as he entered the house of the Yuan family he was struck by her beauty and immediately appropriated her as his wife. He grew extremely fond of her and she bore him a son (Cao Rui) and a daughter (Princess of Dongxiang). It should be noted that she was still the wife of Yuan Xi when Cao Pi took her as a concubine, so that her relationship with Cao Pi was bigamous. The *Record of the Three Kingdoms* also casts some doubt on the paternity of her son, Cao Rui, the future Emperor Ming, saying that he may have been born in 204 while Cao Pi may not have taken her as a concubine until early 205.

In 220, Cao Pi left his concubine Zhen behind in Ye Commandery (in the southwest of present-day Lingzhang District, Henan Province) when he undertook a campaign in the south against the nascent state of Wu. The same year he signaled the end of the impotent Han dynasty when he dethroned Emperor Xian (Liu Xie, 181–234; r. 189–220) and established the Wei dynasty. He immediately declared himself emperor and appointed his concubine Zhen as his empress. There are contradictory accounts of Empress Zhen's consequent behavior toward Cao Pi's many other consorts. She is said to have advised and encouraged those in the inner palace who were favored, and consoled those who were not. She is also said to have encouraged her husband to take many wives so that he could have many sons. For example, at one point, her husband was about to banish Lady Ren, describing her as rash by nature, neither pleasant nor agreeable, and prone to angering him. Empress Zhen argued against him, however: "Ren is from a well-known clan of your hometown and her virtue and beauty are more than someone such as I can match. Why banish her?" Her husband relented when Empress Zhen revealed her concern that it would make things difficult for her if Lady Ren were banished because people would think that she had been responsible. Empress Zhen's behavior changed, however, when her husband began to lose interest in her: he became enamored of ex-Emperor Xian's two daughters, who had been sent to him as concubines, and he also favored three other concubines (their family names were Guo, Li, and Yin) over Empress Zhen. When it became known that he intended to make Lady Guo (*q.v.* Guo, Empress of Emperor Wen of Wei) his empress, Empress Zhen became increasingly difficult. However, her bitter complaints served only to enrage Emperor Wen, who sent word that she was to commit suicide; at the age of forty, in 221, Empress Zhen committed suicide as instructed. She was buried in Ye Commandery. "Her hair was left unbound and her face was covered and her mouth was stuffed with grain husks." Six years later, her son Cao Rui (Emperor Ming) succeeded to the throne. Disturbed by his mother's death, he asked how it had happened. Empress Dowager Guo told him she was innocent of any wrongdoing and that the late emperor had killed his mother. According to historical accounts, Emperor Ming had Empress Dowager Guo killed or frightened to death and only then was he told the manner of his mother's burial. He ordered that Empress Dowager Guo be buried the same way and in 231 had his mother re-interred in a more lavish tomb. He bestowed honors upon his mother, granted her the posthumous title Empress Wenzhao, granted posthumous titles and territory to her father and her brother's family, and personally presented the tablet of lament and performed the sacrifice to initiate the funeral.

A contradictory, and less generally accepted, account of Empress Zhen's death has it that when Emperor Wen was to name an empress he sent her a letter bearing his seal inviting her to accept the position. She declined on the grounds that she was not worthy, suggesting he promote a worthy and good woman to the position instead and adding that she was sick and therefore unable to fill such an exalted position. It is said that she died shortly after having declined the invitation three times and that Emperor Wen grieved for her, issuing a proclamation to bestow on her the seal and ribbon of empress. However, given the extraordinary lengths to which Emperor Ming went to redress the injustice he felt his mother had suffered, it is generally accepted that Empress Zhen did indeed commit suicide, as instructed by her husband.

Empress Zhen had been fond of literature since childhood and during the period she was out of favor she composed ballads (*yuefu*). The ballad *The Pond* (Tangshang xing), which is attributed to her in the early work *Ye zhong gushi* and in the poetry collection *Wen xuan,* compares her life to flourishing cattails and tells of her grief at her sudden fall from the emperor's favor, being ignored and finally cast aside. The sadness it conveys has so struck readers over the centuries that it is often alluded to when referring to a deserted wife. Anne Birrell, whose translation of this poem appears below, has titled it *Empress Chen* and attributes it to Ts'ao P'ei (i.e., her husband, Cao Pi):

Rushes grow in my pool
Their leaves so thick and lush.
A perfect, dutiful marriage
None knows so well as your wife.
Common gossip that melts yellow gold
Has forced you to live apart.

I remember when you left me,
Alone I grieve, ever keen my sorrow.
I imagine I see your face,
Feelings tangle, bruise my heart.
I remember you, ever keen my sorrow,
Night after night unable to sleep.

Don't through glory and renown
Reject one you loved before.
Don't because fish and meat are cheap
Reject the leek and shallot.
Don't because hemp and jute are cheap
Reject straw and rushes.

Outdoors I feel a deeper grief,
Indoors I feel a keener grief.
Many the sad border winds,
Trees how they rush and roar.
May army life though lonely make you happy!
May your years last one thousand autumns!

A final point about Empress Zhen is the romantic story involving her brother-in-law, the talented poet Cao Zhi, who is said to have been in love with her. However, because of the hopelessness of his love, he composed *Rhapsody of the Luo River Goddess* (Luoshen fu) in which he compared her with an elusive goddess. Though this story has little substance, it is a romantic love story that has been kept alive by generations of literati.

Priscilla CHING-CHUNG and SHEN Lidong

Birrell, Anne, trans. *New Songs from a Jade Terrace: An Anthology of Early Chinese Love Poetry.* Boston: Allen & Unwin, 1982, 64–65.
Chen Shou. *Empresses and Consorts: Selections from Chen Shou's "Records of the Three States" with Pei Songzhi's Commentary,* trans. Robert J. Cutter and William Gordon Crowell. Honolulu: University of Hawaii Press, 1999, 72–76; 95–105; 199–201.
Guo Maoqian. *Yuefu shiji.* Beijing: Zhonghua shuju, 1979, vol. 2, 521–22.
Liu Shisheng. *Zhongguo gudai funü shi.* Qingdao: Qingdao chubanshe, 1990, 149–51.
Sanguo zhi: Wei shu. Beijing: Zhonghua shuju, 1975, vol. 1, 5.159–64, 166–67.
Shen Lidong. *Lidai houfei shici jizhu.* Beijing: Zhongguo funü chubanshe, 1990, 90–93.
Sima Guang. *The Chronicle of the Three Kingdoms (220–265), Chapters 69–78 from the Tzu chih t'ung chien of Ssu-ma Kuang,* trans. Achilles Fang, ed. Glen W. Baxter. Cambridge, MA: Harvard University Press, 1965, vol. 1, 37–38, 40, 48, 68–71, 373, 483.
Xu Ling. *Yutai xinyong.* Sibubeiyao ed., 2.2b–3a.

Zhi Miaoyin

Zhi Miaoyin, fl. 372–396, was a nun in the lineage of Kashmir or Indo-Scythian missionaries. Neither her secular name nor her native place is known. However, since she lived in the southern capital Jiankang (the present-day city of Nanjing) during the latter part of the Eastern Jin dynasty and had close connections with the court it is reasonable to assume that she may have been from a southern province, or perhaps even from the capital itself. She was admired by Emperor Xiaowu (Sima Yao, 362–396; r. 372–396) and the Eastern Jin nobility and as a result wielded considerable political power.

Zhi Miaoyin is described in her biography in *Lives of the Nuns* (Biqiuni zhuan) as an intelligent woman widely read in both Buddhist and non-Buddhist fields who was also skilled at literary composition. Both Emperor Xiaowu and his younger brother Sima Daozi (364–403), the Prince of Guiji and Grand Mentor, to whom the emperor had delegated all governing authority, had great respect for her. She frequently conversed with them and wrote compositions with them as well as with their courtiers, enjoying a reputation as a fine and talented writer.

Sima Daozi established the Jianjing Monastery for her in the year 385 and invited her to become the abbess, with more than 100 nuns and novices under her care. Her association with the powerful and influential Sima Daozi caused a great many people to fawn on her in an attempt to gain his ear. Donations flowed into her monastery in a seemingly endless stream and she became one of the wealthiest people in the capital. People from all walks of life sought her out as a teacher and master; it is said that every day more than 100 carriages stopped at her door.

The extent of her political influence is clear from the following episode. When Wang Chen, the regional inspector of Jingzhou, died, Emperor Xiaowu is said to have chosen a man from the same clan to fill the vacant position. This man, Wang Gong, was known as a disciplinarian and the prospect of his becoming regional inspector did not please a governor under the jurisdiction of Jingzhou, a warlord by the name of Huan Xuan who had suffered badly under Wang Chen. Huan Xuan therefore sent his man to Zhi Miaoyin to try to obtain the position of regional inspector for his preferred candidate, Yin Zhongkan, who was a much weaker man. In due course, the emperor asked Zhi Miaoyin who the people were saying should be appointed to the post and, after initially feigning reluctance to meddle in political affairs, Zhi Miaoyin told him that public opinion favored Yin Zhongkan. When the emperor then appointed Yin Zhongkan to the position, everybody saw it as confirmation of Zhi Miaoyin's overwhelming influence over the court and they all stood in awe of her.

Zhi Miaoyin's political activity is corroborated in the biography of Sima Daozi in the official *History of the Jin Dynasty* (Jin shu) where a memorial to Emperor Xiaowu is cited criticizing Sima Daozi for encouraging "hoards of monks and nuns" who hid behind their religious garb but did not practice the basic religious rules. It also cites another memorial attacking Sima Daozi's protégé Wang Guobao, who was so frightened by this that, through a friend, he asked Zhi Miaoyin to write to the mother of the heir apparent testifying to his loyalty.

Zhi Miaoyin was not, of course, the first nun to possess, and wield, political influence. During the reign of Emperor Ming (Sima Shao; r. 323–325) the nun

Daorong had gained imperial trust and respect, and when Sima Yu (Emperor Jianwen, r. 371–372) ascended the throne many years later, Daorong persuaded him to transfer his faith from Daoism to Buddhism. She did this through what can only be described as a truly miraculous event. Daorong's biography in *Lives of the Nuns* claims that it was because of her that Buddhism subsequently became popular in southern China. While it is difficult to verify this claim, it is clear that Daorong was honored by three emperors—Emperor Ming, Emperor Jianwen, and his son Emperor Xiaowu—and that her influence was felt during three reigns in Eastern Jin.

Lily Xiao Hong LEE

Baochang [Shih Pao-ch'ang]. *Lives of the Nuns: Biographies of Chinese Buddhist Nuns from the Fourth to Sixth Centuries: A Translation of the Pi-ch'iu-ni chuan,* trans. Kathryn Ann Tsai. Honolulu: University of Hawaii Press, 1994, 33–34.
Baochang [Pao-ch'ang]. "Zhi Miaoyin zhuan." *Piqiuni zhuan, 2.* In *Taishō shinshū Daizōkyō,* ed. Takakusu Junjirō, Watanabe Kaigyoku, and Ono Genmyō. Tokyo: Taishō Issaikyō Kankōkai, 1924–1929, vol. 50, 936.
Hong Pimou. *Zhongguo ming ni.* Shanghai: Shanghai renmin chubanshe, 1995, 16.
Jin shu. Beijing: Zhonghua shuju, 1974, vol. 6, 64.1734; vol. 7, 75.1971.
Tsai, Kathryn Ann. "The Chinese Buddhist Monastic Order for Women: The First Two Centuries." In *Women in China: Current Directions in Historical Scholarship,* ed. Richard W. Guisso and Stanley Johannesen. Youngstown, NY: Philo Press, 1981, 1–20.

Zhisheng

Zhisheng, 427–492, whose secular surname was Xu, was a Buddhist nun of the Liu Song and Southern Qi dynasties. Her family was originally from the northern city of Chang'an but had lived in Guiji in the south for three generations. She is credited with having written commentaries to Buddhist scriptures.

When she was six years old her grandmother took her to visit Waguan Monastery in Jiankang (present-day Nanjing), the capital of what was then the Liu Song dynasty. The magnificence of the monastery, filled with beautiful decorations and adornment, including Gu Kaizhi's painting of Vimalakīrti, attracted the young girl and she wanted to leave household life right then and there, but her grandmother refused, saying she was too young. Zhisheng was twenty before she could become a nun. Hardships and upheavals wrought by the political and social instability of the time had kept her from carrying out her wishes, but clearly she attained a certain amount of education that was to be of great importance in her monastic life.

Having taken up residence in Jianfu Convent in the capital city, Zhisheng gradually impressed those around her with her intelligence, memory, morality, sanctity, generosity, and reserve. She resisted lechers, observed the monastic precepts diligently, attracted supernatural responses to her worship, gave both of herself and her possessions to help others and to build monuments to Buddhism and to the imperial rulers, and did not gad about visiting, as other nuns did, but remained in the convent for thirty years observing the obligations of the monastic life. Because of these qualities an empress dowager ordered her to be the abbess of Jianfu Convent.

388   ZHISHENG

Zhisheng is recorded as having learned *The Great Final Nirvana Scripture* (Da ban-niepan jing, Mahāparinirvāṇasūtra) as well as the books of monastic discipline (*vinaya*). She was invited by the Southern Qi heir apparent Wenhui (458–493), the eldest son of Emperor Wu (r. 483–493), to lecture on various Buddhist scriptures, and she also wrote several dozen scrolls of commentaries to Buddhist scriptures that are described as both well written and of subtle and penetrating content. Sadly, none survives.

Auspicious omens occurred frequently during her lifetime and at the time of her death. Zhisheng died on the Buddha's birthday (the eighth day of the fourth lunar month) in the year 492 at the age of sixty-six.

Kathryn A. TSAI

Baochang [Shih Pao-ch'ang]. *Lives of the Nuns: Biographies of Chinese Buddhist Nuns from the Fourth to Sixth Centuries: A Translation of the Pi-ch'iu-ni chuan,* trans. Kathryn Ann Tsai. Honolulu: University of Hawaii Press, 1994, 73–76.
Baochang [Pao-ch'ang]. "Zhisheng zhuan." *Piqiuni zhuan, 3.* In *Taishō shinshū Daizōkyō,* ed. Takakusu Junjirō, Watanabe Kaigyoku, and Ono Genmyō. Tokyo: Taishō Issaikyō Kankōkai, 1924–1929, vol. 50.
Soper, Alexander Coburn. *Literary Evidence for Early Buddhist Art in China.* Ascona, Switzerland: Artibus Asiae, 1959, 35–36, 63.
Takakusu Junjirō, Watanabe Kaigyoku, and Ono Genmyō, eds. *Taishō shinshū Daizōkyō.* Tokyo: Taishō Issaikyō Kankōkai, 1924–1929.
Tsai, Kathryn Ann. "The Chinese Buddhist Monastic Order for Women: The First Two Centuries." In *Women in China: Current Directions in Historical Scholarship,* ed. Richard W. Guisso and Stanley Johannesen. Youngstown, NY: Philo Press, 1981, 1–20.

Zhixian

Zhixian, fl. 541–574, was a Buddhist nun. A daughter of the Liu family from Pufan (in present-day Shaanxi Province), she left household life as a young girl, beginning her practice of meditation at the age of seven. Thus, her insight developed and she often predicted the future with startlingly correct results. She assumed responsibility for raising the future Emperor Wen (Yang Jian, 541–604; r. 581–604) of the Sui dynasty, who became a fervid supporter of Buddhism.

When Yang Jian was born at Pingyi in Tongzhou (present-day Shaanxi Province) in 541, Zhixian unexpectedly appeared and said to the child's father, "Your son is blessed by Heaven and by the Buddha. Be not anxious for him." She called the boy Nārāyaṇa, meaning that he was like an indestructible diamond, and further said, "Because this child's origins are extraordinary he cannot be brought up in an ordinary household. I shall rear him for you." The family then converted part of their private house into the Prajñā Convent where the child lived with her until his thirteenth year.

Once, when his mother, née Lü, came to nurse him, she suddenly saw him turn into a dragon with scales all over his body and a horn growing from his head. In her surprise she dropped him on the floor, an event that Zhixian interpreted as predicting that the child would become emperor. When the boy was seven years old she told him that Buddhism would be destroyed but that he would restore it.

Issued by a woman not given to unnecessary words, this and other predictions she made

ZHU, PRINCESS 389

all came true. From 574, when Emperor Wu (r. 561–578) of the Northern Zhou dynasty persecuted both Buddhists and Daoists, Zhixian took refuge in Yang Jian's household. Since the Yang family was closely related to the Northern Zhou imperial house, this served as a safe haven for her and she was able to continue to practice the monastic life in secret.

After Yang Jian (Emperor Wen) assumed the throne, he would at times talk with his officials about his childhood in the convent under Zhixian's care. He supported Buddhism with great fervor but also careful control, causing monasteries and shrines to be built throughout the country to restore what Emperor Wu of Zhou had destroyed and to enhance his own reign. Later, in 601, 602, and 604, when he thrice ordered Buddhist relics to be distributed throughout the country, he ordered a portrait of the nun Zhixian to be painted in the pagodas built to hold the relics.

Zhixian is recorded as having stayed within Prajñā Convent for over thirty years, until the proscription of Buddhism and Daoism in 574, and it is likely that she died sometime after the persecution began and before Yang Jian claimed the throne in 581. Emperor Wen commanded his own court historiographer Wang Shao to write Zhixian's biography.

Kathryn A. TSAI

Bei shi. Beijing: Zhonghua shuju, 1974, vol. 2, 11.399, 424.
Daoshi. *Fayuan zhulin, 40.* In *Taishō shinshū Daizōkyō,* ed. Takakusu Junjirō, Watanabe Kaigyoku, and Ono Genmyō. Tokyo: Taishō Issaikyō Kankōkai, 1924–1929, vol. 53, 601 ff.
Daoxuan. *Guang hongming ji, 17.* In *Taishō shinshū Daizōkyō,* ed. Takakusu Junjirō, Watanabe Kaigyoku, and Ono Genmyō. Tokyo: Taishō Issaikyō Kankōkai, 1924–1929, vol. 52.
———. *Ji gujin fodao lunheng, 2.* In *Taishō shinshū Daizōkyō,* ed. Takakusu Junjirō, Watanabe Kaigyoku, and Ono Genmyō. Tokyo: Taishō Issaikyō Kankōkai, 1924–1929, vol. 52, 379a.
———. *Xu gaoseng zhuan, 26.* In *Taishō shinshū Daizōkyō,* ed. Takakusu Junjirō, Watanabe Kaigyoku, and Ono Genmyō. Tokyo: Taishō Issaikyō Kankōkai, 1924–1929, vol. 50, 611c, 667b–c.
Sui shu. Beijing: Zhonghua shuju, 1973, vol. 1, 2.69.
Takakusu Junjirō, Watanabe Kaigyoku, and Ono Genmyō, eds. *Taishō shinshū Daizōkyō.* Tokyo: Taishō Issaikyō Kankōkai, 1924–1929.
Wright, Arthur F. "The Formation of Sui Ideology, 581–604." In *Chinese Thought and Institutions,* ed. John K. Fairbank. Chicago: University of Chicago Press, 1957, 71–104.
Zhenhua. *Xu biqiuni zhuan.* In *Gaoseng zhuan heji,* ed. Huijiao et al. Shanghai: Shanghai guji chubanshe, 1991, Supplement 2.
Zhipan. *Fozu tongji, 39.* In *Taishō shinshū Daizōkyō,* ed. Takakusu Junjirō, Watanabe Kaigyoku, and Ono Genmyō. Tokyo: Taishō Issaikyō Kankōkai, 1924–1929, vol. 49, 359b.

Zhong Lingyi: *see* **Zhu Jingjian**

Zhou Yi Mu: *see* **Li Luoxiu**

Zhou Yi's Mother: *see* **Li Luoxiu**

Zhou Ziliang's Aunt: *see* **Xu Baoguang**

Zhu, Princess: *see* **Sun Luban**

Zhu Daoxin

Zhu Daoxin, fl. second half of the fourth century, from Taishan (in present-day Shandong Province), was a nun in the lineage of an Indian monk and the first nun to expound Buddhist sutras. Her secular surname was Yang but her given name has not been recorded.

Zhu Daoxin was meticulous by nature and possessed great powers of concentration. She caused offense to no one and therefore got along well with everybody. As a novice, she ran errands for the other nuns and would frequently recite sutras as she went about her work so that by the time she was twenty she was able to recite the complete *Flower of the Law Sutra* (Fahua jing) and *Vimalakriti* (Weimojie jing) from memory. After receiving full ordination, she observed the monastic rules closely and sought the truth meticulously, her ascetic practices becoming more stringent as she grew older.

She lived in the Eastern Monastery of the northern city of Luoyang, where the mainly southern vogue of "pure talk" (*qingtan*) had presumably also taken hold. This was a popular intellectual activity that began in the third century as literati embraced the Daoist philosophy of Laozi and Zhuangzi along with some elements of the Legalist School (*fajia*) and the School of Logicians (*mingjia*). As Buddhism gained popularity, the Chinese literati added discussions of Buddhist philosophical concepts to the practice of "pure talk." In the Eastern Jin period in the south, monks and, to a lesser extent, nuns joined the literati in these gatherings. Although she lived in the north, Zhu Daoxin was skilled at "pure talk" and she gained increased status through her special expertise in *The Smaller Perfection of Wisdom* (Ashrasāhashrikā-prajñā-pāramitā-sûtra). It is said that what she valued in "pure talk" was the logic of the argument; she did not use flowery language. Buddhist scholars throughout the region esteemed her as a master. In her "pure talk," she elucidated *The Smaller Perfection of Wisdom,* and perhaps other sutras as well, thus becoming the first nun to expound Buddhist sutras.

A woman named Yang Lingbian, who was a firm believer in the Daoist philosophy of the Yellow Emperor and Laozi (Huang–Lao) and practiced Daoist breathing exercises, had gained many pupils in Luoyang. Between about 366 and 371, however, her teachings were falling out of favor. This coincided with the time when Zhu Daoxin's teachings were becoming popular and, under the pretext that they shared the same secular surname (Yang), Yang Lingbian tried to get close to Zhu Daoxin. Secretly, she was so jealous of Zhu Daoxin that she wished to bring her harm and she bided her time until an opportunity arose. Yang Lingbian and Zhu Daoxin visited one another several times and on one occasion Yang Lingbian poisoned Zhu Daoxin's food. Zhu Daoxin fell ill and although she tried many cures nothing seemed to work. As a prominent nun, Zhu Daoxin was often invited to the homes of the faithful, so her disciples asked her whose home she had visited before she got sick. Zhu Daoxin replied, "I know who it is. It is all due to bad karma. I would not tell you even if, by telling you, something could be done; since nothing can be done, that is all the more reason I shall not tell you." She is said to have eventually died with her secret, which implies that the author of her biography must have discovered from another source what had happened.

The intellectual distinction Zhu Daoxin achieved was reflected on Buddhist nuns in the eyes of the general public in China. Many nuns of later ages followed this scholarly tradition, which is still alive in the twenty-first century.

Lily Xiao Hong LEE

Baochang [Shih Pao-ch'ang]. *Lives of the Nuns: Biographies of Chinese Buddhist Nuns from the Fourth to Sixth Centuries: A Translation of the Pi-ch'iu-ni chuan,* trans. Kathryn Ann Tsai. Honolulu: University of Hawaii Press, 1994, 29–30.
Baochang [Pao-ch'ang]. "Zhu Daoxin zhuan." *Piqiuni zhuan, 2.* In *Taishō shinshū Daizōkyō,* ed. Takakusu Junjirō, Watanabe Kaigyoku, and Ono Genmyō. Tokyo: Taishō Issaikyō Kankōkai, 1924–1929, vol. 50, 936.
Hong Pimou. *Zhongguo ming ni.* Shanghai: Shanghai renmin chubanshe, 1995, 12–13.
Tsai, Kathryn Ann. "The Chinese Buddhist Monastic Order for Women: The First Two Centuries." In *Women in China: Current Directions in Historical Scholarship,* ed. Richard W. Guisso and Stanley Johannesen. Youngstown, NY: Philo Press, 1981, 1–20.

Zhu Jingjian

Zhu Jingjian, c. 292–c. 361, a nun in the lineage of an Indian monk, is generally recognized as the first Buddhist nun in China. Her secular name was Zhong Lingyi. Her family came from Pengcheng (in the region of the present-day provinces of northwest Jiangsu and southern Shandong) but her father, Zhong Dan, was governor of Wuwei (present-day Wuwei District in Gansu Province), a district far from their native place. It is not known whether Zhu Jingjian went to live in Wuwei when her father was stationed there, but both Pengcheng and Wuwei were on the Silk Road, through which Buddhist influence entered China. This was particularly so in the case of Wuwei because of its proximity to Central Asia, whence came many Buddhist monks to preach in China. Thus it is conceivable that Zhu Jingjian initially came into contact with Buddhism while she was living in one of these cities. However, in later life she moved to Luoyang, the eastern capital of the Jin dynasty, where her convent life was mainly spent.

Her biography says that from childhood she was fond of learning. Coming from a scholar-official family, it is not unusual that she acquired the basic skills of the literati: playing the lute and chess, calligraphy, and painting. Later she would have to fall back on those skills to earn a living. She married young and was widowed early. We do not know her husband's name or what he did, but it is reasonable to suggest he may have been an official serving in the capital: his death left the family in straitened circumstances, forcing Zhu Jingjian to teach the children of noble families in Luoyang.

It was probably also in Luoyang that Zhu Jingjian first pursued Buddhist teachings in earnest. Though these teachings gave her great joy, she could find no one from whom to learn more. Eventually the monk Fashi, who was thoroughly versed in the sutras and practices, established a temple at the West Gate of Luoyang during the Jianxing reign period (313–317) and Zhu Jingjian visited him. She gained great insight into Buddhist truths after listening to Fashi expound the law. Her faith grew stronger and she was motivated to seek further the benefit of the law. She borrowed sutras from Fashi to study at home and from these she gained the central principle of Buddhist truth.

392 ZHU JINGJIAN

She asked Fashi what the terms *bhikṣu* and *bhikṣunī* meant in the sutras. Fashi replied that in India there were two monastic assemblies—the male and the female—and the female assembly was known as *bhikṣunī,* or nuns. In China, however, there were at that time no books of rules for nuns. Fashi further explained that the books of rules for nuns were different from those for monks and since he did not have the appropriate text he was not able to teach nuns. He said that a woman could receive the basic ten rules from a monk, but that without a female monastic instructor she would have no one to rely on in her training as a nun. Zhu Jingjian immediately shaved her head to receive the ten basic rules. With twenty-four other women who shared the same aspiration she established the Zhulin Monastery at the West Gate of Luoyang. Since they did not have a female monastic teacher, they consulted Zhu Jingjian, whose instruction was said to have been superior even to that of venerable monks. Zhu Jingjian fostered her disciples with purity and distinction and whenever she preached, her impact on the audience was described as "like wind moving grass."

During the Xiankang reign period (335–342), the monk Sengjian obtained a copy of a nun's ritual and rule book of the Mahāsānghika sect and by 357 this book had been translated into Chinese in Luoyang. A foreign monk (whose origin is not specified) then built a dais for the purpose of bestowing the precepts on nuns. However, the Chinese monk Daochang objected to this on the basis that, according to the monastic rules, an assembly of nuns was required to be present at the ordination of nuns and therefore, since there were no nuns in China at that time, the ordination could not take place. His objection was not acknowledged but, according to one interpretation of Zhu Jingjian's biography in *Lives of the Nuns* (Biqiuni zhuan), she and four other women received the precepts according to the newly translated rule book on a boat on the Si River, possibly because of the objection. Zhu Jingjian is therefore honored as the first Chinese Buddhist nun.

Zhu Jingjian followed the precepts closely and was diligent in learning Buddhist teachings. She received a great many donations from the faithful but distributed them as soon as she received them, always satisfying the needs of others before her own. She died at the end of the Shengping reign period (357–361) in her seventieth year.

Being the first Buddhist nun in China is not the only distinction Zhu Jingjian held; she is also admired for her initiative and persistence in achieving a goal. She made possible something others thought impossible. It was her inquisitiveness that led her to first discover the concept of women leaving their homes to pursue a religious life and it was due to her persistence that, step by step, she overcame the obstacles to pursuing such a life. Although technically her ordination was not quite legitimate, it was many years before a group of women could fulfill all the requirements and become "real nuns" (*vide* Huiguo). However, to most people, Zhu Jingjian remains the first Buddhist nun in China.

Lily Xiao Hong LEE

Baochang [Shih Pao-ch'ang]. *Lives of the Nuns: Biographies of Chinese Buddhist Nuns from the Fourth to Sixth Centuries: A Translation of the Pi-ch'iu-ni chuan,* trans. Kathryn Ann Tsai. Honolulu: University of Hawaii Press, 1994, 17–19.

ZUO FEN 393

Baochang [Pao-ch'ang]. "Zhu Jingjian zhuan." *Piqiuni zhuan, 2.* In *Taishō shinshū Daizōkyō,* ed. Takakusu Junjirō, Watanabe Kaigyoku, and Ono Genmyō. Tokyo: Taishō Issaikyō Kankōkai, 1924–1929, vol. 50, 934–35.

Hong Pimou. *Zhongguo ming ni.* Shanghai: Shanghai renmin chubanshe, 1995, 3–5.

Li Yuzhen. *Tangdai di biqiuni.* Taipei: Taiwan xuesheng shuju, 1989, 126–37.

Tsai, Kathryn Ann. "The Chinese Buddhist Monastic Order for Women: The First Two Centuries." In *Women in China: Current Directions in Historical Scholarship,* ed. Richard W. Guisso and Stanley Johannesen. Youngstown, NY: Philo Press, 1981, 1–20.

Zhu Xu Mu: *see* **Han of Eastern Jin**

Zixu Yuanjun: *see* **Wei Huacun**

Zuo Fen

Zuo Fen, c. 252–300, also sometimes known as Zuo Jiu Pin, was a native of Linzi in the state of Qi (present-day Linzi in Shangdong Province); she lived during the Western Jin dynasty. Hers was a family of Confucian scholars of fairly low status. However, her father, Zuo Yong, rose from the minor post of clerk to imperial censor (*dianzhong shi yushi*). Her mother died young, leaving Zuo Fen and an elder brother, Zuo Si (d. 306), in the care of their father. Zuo Yong educated both children well so that, although she was a girl, Zuo Fen received excellent training in history and literature.

Zuo Fen was known among her contemporaries for her talent and learning. In 272, she was selected to become a minor consort for Emperor Wu (Sima Yan, 236–290; r. 265–290), the founding emperor of Western Jin. The emperor already had an empress, Empress Yang (*q.v.* Yang Yan, Empress to Emperor Wu of Jin), to whom he was very devoted, but he enjoyed a peaceful and flourishing reign and his thoughts often turned to the pleasures of life. He ordered that a search for beauties from good families be made throughout the nation and decreed that no marriages or engagements were to take place until he had made his selection from these beauties. Empress Yang was entrusted with the task of selecting the finalists and it is said that she chose the less attractive women, as she did not want any competition for the emperor's affections. Zuo Fen was selected during this general search, not for her beauty, but, according to her official biography, because Emperor Wu heard that she was learned and skilled at composing literary works. She was appointed Lady of Cultivated Deportment (*xiuyi*) and later promoted to Honored Concubine (*guipin*). Because of her homely appearance, the emperor did not favor her sexually. However, she was treated with respect because of her talent and was allowed to reside in a separate part of the palace because of her weak constitution. She was given an apartment in the section where the silkworms were kept, which was much warmer than the rest of the palace and more comfortable for a sickly person. Every time the emperor visited his imperial Hualin Park he made a detour to visit Zuo Fen and would discuss literature and philosophy with her. Her words were said to have been elegant and beautiful and all who were in attendance praised her for them.

As the emperor's writer-in-residence, from time to time she was asked to write compositions on assigned themes or topics. When she first arrived in the palace, the emperor asked her to write a rhapsody (*fu*) on a sad subject. Recently separated from her family as she was, she wrote about her own feelings in *Rhapsody on Separation* (Li si fu). It is evident from some of her other works that whenever the emperor received anything strange or foreign, he called upon her to write something to commemorate the occasion. Thus she composed rhapsodies on the peacock and on the tulip. She was also assigned to compose the eulogies for ancient Chinese women included in *Biographies of Eminent Women* (Lienü zhuan). More important than these, however, were the two elegies she wrote on the deaths of Empress Yang and Princess Wannian, both of whom had been very dear to the emperor. Naturally, it was imperative that these elegies be well written and that the feelings she expressed not be her own but those of the emperor. Her skill is evident in that she was able to express poignantly the emotions of another and to have them ring true.

It is possible for readers to have a glimpse into her feelings through her more personal works, such as *Rhapsody on Separation* mentioned above. Not long after Zuo Fen entered the palace, her brother Zuo Si advanced through the civil service and was appointed to the fairly prestigious position of assistant in the Palace Library (*mishu lang*). He moved to the capital, Luoyang, where his sister lived, but so strict were the regulations of the palace that he was unable to see her face to face. The profound sadness this caused Zuo Fen is reflected in her *Rhapsody on Separation*. She also wrote two poems in reply to her brother's *Two Poems of Mournful Separation to My Sister*. Her poems, entitled *In Reply to My Brother's Poems of Separation* (Da xiong gan li shi), reveal her loneliness, her yearning for her brother, and her fervent wish to see him again. For some, to be chosen as an imperial concubine meant glory and honor, but for Zuo Fen and her family it brought only sadness. It is possible that her father had died by then, making the pain of being the only surviving members of their family even more palpable for Zuo Fen and her brother.

Zuo Fen died in 300, probably in the extended upheaval known as the War of the Eight Princes. Her grave stele was unearthed in 1930 in Luoyang, showing the year of her death.

Zuo Fen was versatile in her choice of genres. She wrote rhapsodies, elegies (*lei*), eulogies (*song*), and four- and five-syllable *shi* poems. Since most of her compositions were written at the command of the emperor, the language used is formal and sometimes even archaic. Yet her brilliance shows through. The real emotions of her personal pieces are moving and have endured the passage of time. Even some of her shorter compositions seem to have some philosophical significance. For example, her *Ode to the Tulip* (Yujin song) alludes to the lonely beauties of the palace who, like the tulip, bloomed for no one. Her poem *The Woodpecker* (Zhuomu shi) is a metaphor for the literati of her time who, because of the dominance of the great families in government positions and the dangers of a volatile political environment, became hermits and "had nothing to do with others." At the end of the poem, she issues a subtle warning to those who were not "pure" like the woodpecker: "the corrupt will be disgraced."

Zuo Fen is traditionally categorized as skilled in the "palace style" (*gongti*) of literature, a thematic designation for verses centered on the life of the imperial palace. It may include such things as court functions and festivals, palace objects and architecture, and, later on, the women and their lives. However, she broke out of that mold to write about real feelings, composing works with more than one level of meaning. Her literary achievement should not be belittled because of her circumstances.

Zuo Fen probably has the doubtful honor of being one of the few women selected into the imperial palace not because of her beauty but because of her talent and learning. This is proof that, in her time, there was no discrimination against being talented.

This biography is mainly based on a thesis written under my supervision by Winnie Yuen Kwan Lau.

Lily Xiao Hong LEE

Jiang Minfan and Wang Ruifang. *Zhongguo lidai cainü xiaozhuan*. Hangzhou: Zhejiang wenyi chubanshe, 1984, 48–52.
Jin shu. Beijing: Zhonghua shuju, 1974, vol. 4, 31.957–62.
Lau, Winnie Yuen Kwan. "Links in an Unbroken Chain: The Poetry of Zuo Fen and Bao Linghui of the Six Dynasties." Bachelor of Arts (Honors) thesis, University of Sydney, 1996.
Xie Wuliang. *Zhongguo funü wenxueshi*. Shanghai: Zhonghua shuju, 1916; Zhengzhou: Zhengzhou guji chubanshe, 1992, reprint, Section IIB, 10–19.
Xu Chuanwu. "Zuo Fen zai gudai funü wenxueshi shang de diwei." *Wen shi zhe* 6 (1966): 71–74.

Zuo Jiu Pin: *see* **Zuo Fen**

Glossary of Chinese Names

Abiding Wet Nurse of Wei	魏節乳母	Antiquity–Zhou
Ai Jiang, Wife of Duke Zhuang of Lu	魯莊哀姜	Antiquity–Zhou
An Lingshou	安令首	3K–Sui
Ban Jieyu, Concubine of Emperor Cheng	班婕妤, 漢成帝妾	Qin–Han
Ban Zhao	班昭	Qin–Han
Bao Linghui	鮑令暉	3K–Sui
Bao Si, Wife of King You of Zhou	周幽褒姒	Antiquity–Zhou
Baoxian	寶賢	3K–Sui
Bian, Wife of Cao Cao, King of Wei	卞氏, 魏王曹操夫人	3K–Sui
Bo, Concubine of Emperor Gaozu	薄姬, 漢高祖妾	Qin–Han
Bo, Empress of Emperor Jing	薄氏, 漢景帝皇后	Qin–Han
Bo Ji, Wife of Duke Gong of Song	伯姬, 宋恭公夫人	Antiquity–Zhou
Bo Ying, Wife of King Ping of Chu	伯嬴, 楚平王夫人	Antiquity–Zhou
Bow Artisan of Jin's Wife	晉弓工妻	Antiquity–Zhou
Bu, Consort of Sun Quan	步氏, 孫權夫人	3K–Sui
Cai Yan	蔡琰	Qin–Han
Cao Jie, Empress of Emperor Xian	曹節, 漢獻帝皇后	Qin–Han
Chen Jiao, Empress of Emperor Wu	陳嬌, 漢武帝皇后	Qin–Han
Chen Siqian	陳思謙	Qin–Han
Chen Ying's Mother	陳嬰母	Qin–Han
Chunyu Tiying	淳于緹縈	Qin–Han
Crone of Quwo of Wei	魏曲沃婦	Antiquity–Zhou
Daoqiong	道瓊	3K–Sui
Dazi of Tao's Wife	陶荅子妻	Antiquity–Zhou
Deng Mengnü, Empress of Emperor Huan	鄧孟女, 漢桓帝皇后	Qin–Han

Note: The section in which each woman's biography is to be found is shown after the Chinese characters for her name, as follows:

Antiquity–Zhou = Antiquity Through Zhou
Qin–Han = Qin Through Han
3K–Sui = Three Kingdoms Through Sui

398 GLOSSARY OF CHINESE NAMES

Deng Sui, Empress of Emperor He	鄧綏, 漢和帝皇后	Qin–Han
Diao Chan	刁嬋	Qin–Han
Ding, Consort of Cao Cao, King of Wei	丁氏, 魏王曹操夫人	3K–Sui
Ding Jiang, Wife of Duke Ding of Wei	定姜, 衛定公夫人	Antiquity–Zhou
Discerning Woman of the Chu Wilds	楚野辯女	Antiquity–Zhou
Dou, Empress of Emperor Zhang	竇皇后, 漢章帝	Qin–Han
Dou Miao, Empress of Emperor Huan	竇妙, 漢桓帝皇后	Qin–Han
Dou Yifang, Empress of Emperor Wen	竇猗房, 漢文帝皇后	Qin–Han
Dugu, Empress of Emperor Wen of Sui	獨孤皇后, 隋文帝	3K–Sui
Duke Mu of Xu's Wife	許穆公夫人	Antiquity–Zhou
Duke Zhuang of Li's Wife	黎莊公夫人	Antiquity–Zhou
Ehuang and Nüying	娥皇、女英	Antiquity–Zhou
Fajing	法敬	3K–Sui
Fan Ji, Wife of King Zhuang of Chu	樊姬, 楚莊王夫人	Antiquity–Zhou
Feng, Concubine of Emperor Yuan	馮昭儀, 漢元帝	Qin–Han
Feng, Empress of Emperor Wencheng of Northern Wei	馮皇后, 北魏文成帝	3K–Sui
Feng, Empress of Emperor Xiaowen of Northern Wei	馮皇后, 北魏孝文帝	3K–Sui
Feng Liao	馮嫽	Qin–Han
Filial Widow from Chen	陳寡孝婦	Qin–Han
Foxi of Zhao's Mother	趙佛肹母	Antiquity–Zhou
Fu, Concubine of Emperor Yuan	傅昭儀, 漢元帝	Qin–Han
Fu Shou, Empress of Emperor Xian	伏壽, 漢獻帝皇后	Qin–Han
Fu Xi'e	伏羲娥	Qin–Han
Fu Zi, the Shang Woman Warrior	婦好	Antiquity–Zhou
Gan, Empress of the Former Sovereign of Shu	甘夫人, 蜀先主	3K–Sui
Gao Xing, a Widow in Liang	梁寡高行	Antiquity–Zhou
General of Gai's Wife	蓋將妻	Antiquity–Zhou
General Zhao Gua's Mother	趙括將軍母	Antiquity–Zhou
Goiter Girl of Qi, Wife of King Min	宿瘤女	Antiquity–Zhou

GLOSSARY OF CHINESE NAMES 399

Gongcheng of Lu's Elder Sister	魯公乘姊	Antiquity–Zhou
Gongsun Shu's Wife	公孫述妻	Qin–Han
Guo, Empress of Emperor Ming of Wei	郭皇后, 魏明帝	3K–Sui
Guo, Empress of Emperor Wen of Wei	郭皇后, 魏文帝	3K–Sui
Guo Huai	郭槐	3K–Sui
Guo of Western Jin	郭氏, 西晉	3K–Sui
Guo Shengtong, Empress of Emperor Guangwu	郭聖通, 漢光武帝皇后	Qin–Han
Han Lanying	韓蘭英	3K–Sui
Han of Eastern Jin	韓氏, 東晉	3K–Sui
Han'e	韓娥	Antiquity–Zhou
Hu, Consort of Emperor Xuanwu of Northern Wei	胡氏, 北魏宣武帝宮人 (胡太后)	3K–Sui
Hua Rong, Consort of Prince of Yanla	華容夫人, 漢燕剌王	Qin–Han
Huan, Liu Changqing's Wife	桓氏, 劉長卿妻	Qin–Han
Huangfu Gui's Wife	皇甫規妻	Qin–Han
Huiguo	慧果	3K–Sui
Huo Chengjun, Empress of Emperor Xuan	霍成君, 漢宣帝皇后	Qin–Han
Instructress for the Daughter of Qi	齊女傅母	Antiquity–Zhou
Jia Nanfeng, Empress of Emperor Hui of Jin	賈南風, 晉惠帝皇后	3K–Sui
Jiandi	簡狄	Antiquity–Zhou
Jiang, Queen of King Xuan of Zhou	姜后, 周宣王	Antiquity–Zhou
Jiang Yi of Chu's Mother	江乙母	Antiquity–Zhou
Jiang-Clan Woman of Qi, Wife of Duke Wen of Jin	齊姜, 晉文公夫人	Antiquity–Zhou
Ji-Clan Woman, Wife of Duke Mu of Qin	穆姬, 秦穆公夫人	Antiquity–Zhou
Jieyu's Wife	接輿妻	Antiquity–Zhou
Jing, Concubine of Minister Guan Zhong of Qi	管仲妾婧	Antiquity–Zhou
Jing, Daughter of Shanghuai Yan of Qi	傷槐衍女婧	Antiquity–Zhou
Jing Jiang	敬姜	Antiquity–Zhou
Juan, Daughter of an Official of the Ford of Zhao	趙津吏女娟	Antiquity–Zhou
Kind Mother of the Mang Family of Wei	魏芒慈母	Antiquity–Zhou

400 GLOSSARY OF CHINESE NAMES

Kong Bo Ji	孔伯姬	Antiquity–Zhou
Lao Laizi's Wife	老萊子妻	Antiquity–Zhou
Li, Concubine of Emperor Wu	李夫人, 漢武帝	Qin–Han
Li Ji, Wife of Duke Xian of Jin	驪姬, 晉獻公夫人	Antiquity–Zhou
Li Luoxiu	李絡秀	3K–Sui
Li Mujiang	李穆姜	Qin–Han
Liang Na, Empress of Emperor Shun	梁妠, 漢順帝皇后	Qin–Han
Liang Nüying, Empress of Emperor Huan	梁女英, 漢桓帝皇后	Qin–Han
Lingzong	令宗	3K–Sui
Liu Jieyou	劉解憂（解憂公主）	Qin–Han
Liu Lanzhi	劉蘭芝	Qin–Han
Liu Lingxian	劉令嫻	3K–Sui
Liu Piao, the Grand Princess	劉嫖, 長公主	Qin–Han
Liu Xijun	劉細君（江都公主）	Qin–Han
Liu Yingyuan	劉英媛（臨川長公主）	3K–Sui
Liu Yuan	劉元	Qin–Han
Liuxia Hui's Wife	柳下惠妻	Antiquity–Zhou
Liyu	麗玉	Qin–Han
Lou Zhaojun, Empress of Emperor Shenwu of Northern Qi	婁昭君, 北齊神武帝皇后	3K–Sui
Loyal Maid of Zhu of Zhou	周主忠妾	Antiquity–Zhou
Lu Lingxuan	陸令萱	3K–Sui
Lü Xu	呂嬃	Qin–Han
Lü Zhi, Empress of Emperor Gaozu	呂雉, 漢高祖皇后	Qin–Han
Lü's Mother	呂母	Qin–Han
Lüzhu	綠珠	3K–Sui
Ma, Empress of Emperor Ming	馬皇后, 漢明帝	Qin–Han
Man of Cai's Wife	蔡人之妻	Antiquity–Zhou
Man-Clan Woman of Deng, Wife of King Wu of Chu	鄧曼, 楚武公夫人	Antiquity–Zhou
Mao, Empress of Emperor Ming of Wei	毛皇后, 魏明帝	3K–Sui

GLOSSARY OF CHINESE NAMES 401

Meixi	妹喜	Antiquity–Zhou
Mencius's Mother	孟軻母	Antiquity–Zhou
Meng Guang	孟光	Qin–Han
Meng Ji, Wife of Duke Xiao of Qi	孟姬, 齊孝公夫人	Antiquity–Zhou
Meng Jiangnü	孟姜女	Antiquity–Zhou
Mother Piao	漂母	Qin–Han
Mother Teacher of Lu	魯之母師	Antiquity–Zhou
Mu Jiang, Wife of Duke Xuan of Lu	穆姜, 魯宣公夫人	Antiquity–Zhou
Mulan	木蘭	3K–Sui
Nanzi, Wife of Duke Ling of Wei	南子, 衛靈公夫人	Antiquity–Zhou
Nü Wa	女媧	Antiquity–Zhou
Nüzong, the Wife of Baosu of Song	女宗, 鮑蘇妻	Antiquity–Zhou
Official from Zhounan's Wife	周南大夫妻	Antiquity–Zhou
Pan, Consort of Sun Quan	潘氏, 孫權夫人	3K–Sui
Pure Jiang, Wife of King Zhao of Chu	貞姜, 楚昭王夫人	Antiquity–Zhou
Qi, Concubine of Emperor Gaozu	戚夫人, 漢高祖	Qin–Han
Qian Lou of Lu's Wife	黔婁妻	Antiquity–Zhou
Qing, the Widow from Bashu	巴蜀寡婦清	Qin–Han
Qishi Woman of Lu	漆室女	Antiquity–Zhou
Qiu Hu's Wife, the Pure Woman	秋胡妻	Antiquity–Zhou
Queen Mother of the West	西王母	Antiquity–Zhou
Righteous Nurse of Duke Xiao of Lu	魯孝義保	Antiquity–Zhou
Righteous Respected Female Elder of Lu	魯義姑姊	Antiquity–Zhou
Righteous Stepmother of Qi	齊義繼母	Antiquity–Zhou
Ruji	如姬	Antiquity–Zhou
Sengjing	僧敬	3K–Sui
Shangguan, Empress of Emperor Zhao	上官皇后, 漢昭帝	Qin–Han
Shaonan Woman of Shen	召南申女	Antiquity–Zhou
Shen, Concubine of Emperor Wen	慎夫人, 漢文帝妾	Qin–Han
Shu Ji	叔姬	Antiquity–Zhou

402 GLOSSARY OF CHINESE NAMES

Sima, Yang Chang's Wife	司馬氏, 楊敞妻	Qin–Han
Song, Lady Xuanwen	宋氏, 宣文君	3K–Sui
Su Boyu's Wife	蘇伯玉妻	3K–Sui
Su Hui	蘇蕙	3K–Sui
Sun Luban	孫魯班	3K–Sui
Sun Luyu	孫魯育	3K–Sui
Sun Shou	孫壽	Qin–Han
Sunshu Ao's Mother	孫叔敖母	Antiquity–Zhou
Tai Jiang	大姜	Antiquity–Zhou
Tai Ren	大任	Antiquity–Zhou
Tai Si, Wife of King Wen of Zhou	大姒, 周文王妻	Antiquity–Zhou
Tanbei	曇備	3K–Sui
Tang, Consort of Prince Hongnong	唐姬, 漢弘農王	Qin–Han
Tangshan, Concubine of Emperor Gaozu	唐山夫人, 漢高祖	Qin–Han
Tanluo	曇羅	3K–Sui
Tao Ying, a Widow in Lu	陶嬰	Antiquity–Zhou
Tian Ji of Qi's Mother	田稷母	Antiquity–Zhou
Tushan Woman	塗山女	Antiquity–Zhou
Two Honorable Women from Zhuya	珠崖二義	Qin–Han
Two Obedient Women of the Wei Ancestral Temple	衛宗二順	Qin–Han
Virgin of Egu	阿谷處女	Antiquity–Zhou
Wang Ba's Wife	王霸妻	Qin–Han
Wang, Empress of Emperor Ping	王皇后, 漢平帝	Qin–Han
Wang, Empress of Emperor Xuan	王皇后, 漢宣帝	Qin–Han
Wang, Empress of Wang Mang of Xin	王皇后, 新莽	Qin–Han
Wang Ling's Mother	王陵母	Qin–Han
Wang Wengxu	王翁須	Qin–Han
Wang Zhang's Wife	王章妻	Qin–Han
Wang Zhaojun	王昭君	Qin–Han

GLOSSARY OF CHINESE NAMES 403

Wang Zhenfeng, Empress of Emperor Ming of Liu Song	王貞風, 劉宋明帝皇后	3K–Sui
Wang Zhengjun, Empress of Emperor Yuan	王政君, 漢元帝皇后	Qin–Han
Wang Zhi, Empress of Emperor Jing	王娡, 漢景帝皇后	Qin–Han
Wei Huacun	魏華存	3K–Sui
Wei Ji, Wife of Duke Huan of Qi	衛姬, 齊桓公夫人	Antiquity–Zhou
Wei Shuo	衛鑠	3K–Sui
Wei Zifu, Empress of Emperor Wu	衛子夫, 漢武帝皇后	Qin–Han
Wen Jiang, Wife of Duke Huan of Lu	文姜, 魯桓公夫人	Antiquity–Zhou
Wen Jijiang	文季姜	Qin–Han
Widow of Wei	衛寡夫人	Antiquity–Zhou
Wife of the Chariot Driver for Yanzi, Minister of Qi	晏子僕御妻	Antiquity–Zhou
Woman of Integrity from the Capital	京師節女	Qin–Han
Wu, Empress of the Former Sovereign of Shu	吳夫人, 蜀先主	3K–Sui
Wu, Wife of Caitiff-Smashing-General Sun	吳夫人, 孫破虜將軍	3K–Sui
Xi Clan Head's Wife	曹僖氏妻	Antiquity–Zhou
Xi Shi	西施	Antiquity–Zhou
Xian, Lady of Qiao State	冼氏, 譙國夫人	3K–Sui
Xiao, Empress of Emperor Yang of Sui	蕭皇后, 隋煬帝	3K–Sui
Xie Daoyun	謝道韞	3K–Sui
Xu Baoguang	徐寶光	3K–Sui
Xu Deng	徐登	Qin–Han
Xu, Empress of Emperor Cheng	許皇后, 漢成帝	Qin–Han
Xu Pingjun, Empress of Emperor Xuan	許平君, 漢宣帝皇后	Qin–Han
Xu Shu	徐淑	Qin–Han
Xu Wu of Qi	徐吾	Antiquity–Zhou
Xuan Jiang, Wife of Duke Xuan of Wei	宣姜, 衛宣公夫人	Antiquity–Zhou
Xun Guan	荀灌	3K–Sui
Yan Ming	嚴明	Qin–Han
Yan Xian	嚴憲	3K–Sui

404 GLOSSARY OF CHINESE NAMES

Yan Yannian's Mother	嚴延年母	Qin–Han
Yang Lihua, Empress of Emperor Xuan of Northern Zhou	楊麗花, 北周宣帝皇后	3K–Sui
Yang Yan, Empress of Emperor Wu of Jin	楊艷, 晉武帝皇后	3K–Sui
Yang Zhi, Empress of Emperor Wu of Jin	楊芷, 晉武帝皇后	3K–Sui
Yin Lihua, Empress of Emperor Guangwu	陰麗華, 漢光武帝皇后	Qin–Han
Ying, Wife of Duke Huai of Jin	嬴氏, 晉懷公夫人	Antiquity–Zhou
Youdi	友娣	Qin–Han
Yu, Consort of the Hegemon-King of Chu	虞姬, 西楚霸王妃	Qin–Han
Yu Ji, Wife of King Wei of Qi	虞姬, 齊威王夫人	Antiquity–Zhou
Yuan Qigui, Empress of Emperor Wen of Liu Song	袁齊媯, 劉宋文帝皇后	3K–Sui
Yue Ji, Wife of King Zhao of Chu	越姬, 楚昭王夫人	Antiquity–Zhou
Yue Woman	越女	Antiquity–Zhou
Yue Yangzi's Wife	樂羊子妻	Qin–Han
Yuwen, Princess Qianjin of Northern Zhou	宇文氏, 北周千金公主	3K–Sui
Zang Sun of Lu's Mother	臧孫母	Antiquity–Zhou
Zhan, Tao Kan's Mother	湛氏, 陶侃母	3K–Sui
Zhang, Concubine of Fu Jian	張氏, 符堅妾	3K–Sui
Zhang Lu's Mother	張魯母	Qin–Han
Zhang Tang's Mother	張湯母	Qin–Han
Zhang Yan, Empress of Emperor Hui	張嫣, 漢惠帝皇后	Qin–Han
Zhao E	趙娥	Qin–Han
Zhao Feiyan, Empress of Emperor Cheng	趙飛燕, 漢成帝皇后	Qin–Han
Zhao Gouyi, Concubine of Emperor Wu	趙鉤弋婕好, 漢武帝妾	Qin–Han
Zhao Hede, Concubine of Emperor Cheng	趙合德, 漢成帝妾	Qin–Han
Zhao Ji	趙姬	Qin–Han
Zhao, Wife of the King of Dai	趙夫人, 代王	Antiquity–Zhou
Zhen, Empress of Emperor Wen of Wei	甄皇后, 魏文帝	3K–Sui
Zheng Mao, Wife of King Cheng of Chu	鄭瞀, 楚成王夫人	Antiquity–Zhou
Zheng Sisters	徵側、徵貳姊妹	Qin–Han

GLOSSARY OF CHINESE NAMES 405

Zhi Miaoyin	支妙音	3K–Sui
Zhisheng	智勝	3K–Sui
Zhixian	智賢	3K–Sui
Zhong Zi, Wife of Duke Ling of Qi	仲子, 齊靈公夫人	Antiquity–Zhou
Zhongli Chun of Qi, Wife of King Xuan of Qi	鍾離春, 齊宣王夫人	Antiquity–Zhou
Zhou Qing, the Filial Woman of Donghai	東海孝婦周青	Qin–Han
Zhu Daoxin	竺道馨	3K–Sui
Zhu Jingjian	竺淨檢	3K–Sui
Zhu Maichen's Wife	朱買臣妻	Qin–Han
Zhuang Zhi, Wife of King Qingxiang of Chu	莊姪, 楚頃襄王夫人	Antiquity–Zhou
Zhuo Wenjun	卓文君	Qin–Han
Zuo Fen	左芬	3K–Sui

About the Editors

Lily Xiao Hong Lee was born in Jiangxi, China, and after 1949 lived in Hong Kong, British Malaya, Singapore, and the United States before moving to Australia in 1971. After a career in librarianship she completed a Ph.D., and taught at the School of Asian Studies (now the School of Languages and Cultures) of The University of Sydney until she retired in 2003. She is an honorary associate of that School and continues to research and publish. She has produced two books and contributed to several edited volumes, in addition to writing numerous papers and journal articles on Chinese women and the literature of the Wei–Jin period. She has recently added Silk-Road studies to her research interests.

A. D. Stefanowska was senior lecturer at the University of Sydney where she taught Classical Chinese for thirty years. She is currently honorary research associate at that university. Since 1988 she has been co-editor of the University of Sydney East Asian Series. Her current research interest is the literature of the Sung dynasty.

Sue Wiles is a translator, researcher, and editor with academic ties to both The University of Sydney and the University of Western Sydney. Her area of research interest is Daoist women of the Wei–Jin period. Her published translations include the books *T'ai Chi* and *Witnessing History*, and short stories and essays by Taiwan writers published in the University of California, Santa Barbara's *Taiwan Literature: English Translation Series, Folk Stories from Taiwan*, and *Children's Stories from Taiwan*.

Elizabeth Childs-Johnson is Associate Research Professor in the College of Arts and Letters and Adjunct Associate Professor in the Departments of Art History and Asian Studies at Old Dominion University. She is a Sinologist specializing in Chinese art and archaeology of the Neolithic through Zhou eras, as reflected in her monographs and articles on Shang religion and art, and on China's Jade Age. Her most recent and upcoming publications include *The Chinese Jade Age: Early Chinese Jades in American Museums* [Chinese and English] and *The Meaning of the Graph Yi and Its Implications for Shang Belief and Art* (*East Asia Journal Monograph*). She has also documented archaeology in film, as represented by the PBS documentary film *Great Wall Across the Yangtze* that aired in 2000.

Constance A. Cook is Professor, Chinese Language and Literature, and Director, Asia Studies, at Lehigh University, Bethlehem, Pennsylvania. Professor Cook specializes in ancient Chinese excavated manuscripts and has recently published the book *Death in Ancient China: The Tale of One Man's Journey*. She edited with John Major and contributed to the book *Defining Chu: Image and Reality in Ancient China* and has also written a number of articles on ancient inscriptions, peoples, food, medicine, and ritual.

Yin Lee Wong is a Professor in the History Department of Hong Kong Baptist University. Professor Wong was born in Guangdong, but grew up in Hong Kong, where her family moved when she was very young. She received her Ph.D. in 1992 from the University of Hong Kong, her area of research being the history of Chinese thought and Chinese cultural history. She has taught at Hong Kong Baptist University since 1980 and has taken up visiting positions with both Yale University and Peking University. Her major publications in Chinese include *A Study of Chu Shu-chen, A Study of Five Han Women Writers*, and *Four Major Lyric Writers of the Qing Dynasty*.

CPSIA information can be obtained
at www.ICGtesting.com
Printed in the USA
JSHW021513221219
3113JS00001BA/28